D0081053

DISCARDED

BESIEGED

An Encyclopedia of Great Sieges From Ancient Times to the Present

PAUL K. DAVIS

ABC-CLIO

Santa Barbara, California
Denver, Colorado
Oxford, England

Library of Congress Cataloging-in-Publication Data

Davis, Paul K., 1952–
  Besieged : an encyclopedia of great sieges from ancient times to the present / Paul K. Davis.
    p. cm.
  Includes bibliographical references and index.
  ISBN 1-57607-195-2 (hardcover : alk. paper); 1-57607-544-3 (e-book)
  1. Sieges—Encyclopedias. 2. Military history—Encyclopedias.
  I. Title.
  D25.5.D32 2001
  355.4'4'03—dc21   2001004934

06 05 04 03 02 01   10 9 8 7 6 5 4 3 2 1

This book is also available on the World Wide Web as an e-book. Visit abc-clio.com for details.

ABC-CLIO, Inc.
130 Cremona Drive, P.O. Box 1911
Santa Barbara, California 93116–1911

This book is printed on acid-free paper.
Manufactured in the United States of America

For Jerri
and
my parents,
whose love and support have sustained me for an awfully long time

CONTENTS

100 GREAT SIEGES (Listed Alphabetically)

Acre (1189–91)
Alamo (1836)
Alesia (52 BC)
Antwerp (1584–85)
Aquileia (452)
Arcot (1751)
Athens (Acropolis) (1825)
Badajoz (1812)
Baghdad (1258)
Basra (1982–87)
Beirut (1982)
Bilbao (1937)
Boston (1775–76)
Boulogne (1544)
Calais (1346–47)
Cartagena (1815)
Carthage (149–146 BC)
Chitor Garh (1567–68)
Chitral (1895)
Constantinople (717–18)
Constantinople (1453)
Cuautla (1812)
Delhi (1857)
Dien Bien Phu (1953–54)
Famagusta (1571)
Fort Fisher (1864–65)
Fort Niagara (1759)
Fort Stanwix (1777)
Gaeta (1860–61)
Genoa (1800)
Gibraltar (1779–83)
Granada (1491)
Grozny (1994–95)
Havana (1762)

Hsiang-yang (1268–73)
Humaita (1866–68)
Imphal (1944)
Jericho (1405 BC)
Jerusalem (1099)
Jerusalem (70)
Khartoum (1884–85)
Khe Sanh (1968)
Kinsale (1601–02)
Kut-al-Amara (1915–16)
La Rochelle (1627–28)
Leningrad (1941–44)
Liege (1914)
Lille (1708)
Londonderry (1689)
Louisbourg (1745)
Maastricht (1673)
Madrid (1936–39)
Mafeking (1899–1900)
Magdeburg (1631)
Malta (1565)
Malta (1940–42)
Manila (1898)
Masada (73–74)
Monte Cassino (1944)
Montsegur (1243–44)
Nicopolis (1396)
Numantia (134–133 BC)
Orleans (1428–29)
Osaka (1614–15)
Paris (885–86)
Paris (1870–71)
Pavia (773–74)
Pavia (1524–25)

Peking (1900)
Pensacola (1781)
Petersburg (1864–65)
Plataea (429–427 BC)
Plevna (1877)
Port Arthur (1904–05)
Puebla (1863)
Quebec (1759)
Quebec (1775–76)
Quemoy (Kinmen) (1958–59)
Rhodes (1522)
Rome (1849)
Rome (537–38)
St. Augustine (1702)
Sarajevo (1991–95)
Sevastopol (1854–55)
Sevastopol (1941–42)
Singapore (1942)
Stalingrad (1942–43)
Syracuse (415–413 BC)
Syracuse (213–212 BC)
Tenochtitlan (1521)
Tobruk (1941)
Toulon (1793)
Troy (1250 BC)
Turin (1706)
Tyre (332 BC),
Veii (404–396 BC)
Vicksburg (1863)
Vienna (1529)
Vienna (1683)
Yorktown (1781)

PREFACE

siege *n.*: **1.** The surrounding of a town or fortified place in an effort to seize it.
2. A steady attempt to win something.

Civilization began with the creation of cities, the congregation of people for mutual support. By their very decision to assemble and collect resources, cities became targets for raiding populations that found taking someone else's possessions easier than producing their own. The need for defense meant that the towns soon built walls around their perimeters to keep the raiders at bay. The desire to overcome those defenses to acquire what was inside resulted in siege warfare.

As the above definition states, a siege is not necessarily a complete encirclement of a target; indeed, many if not most sieges are of positions not completely cut off from outside contact. Thus, protracted warfare with steady pressure on a target position or city falls under the definition. Because the nature of dealing with fortifications is so different from dealing with an opposing army in the field, siege warfare has been both a proving ground and a source of inspiration for engineers throughout history. Building defenses and overcoming those seem-ingly impregnable has been a major segment of warfare since earliest times and has no less importance today.

This work discusses both types of siege throughout history, from the first recorded siege in 1405/1406 B.C. to the most recent in 1996. We have attempted to include topics from across the span of time, as well as from as many places around the world as possible. Thus, many sieges covered here will be completely unknown to most readers, but with effects nonetheless for local and area populations. As it seems most of the world's wars have been ethnic, religious, and political struggles in and around Europe, sieges from this region necessarily dominate. Every effort has been made to keep this focus from being exclusive.

I would like to thank the historians who have contributed to this work: Tom Davis, freelance historian, Brandy Durham of St. Mary's University, Major Michael A. McClain, USA (Ret.), and Allen Lee Hamilton of St. Philip's College, all in San Antonio,

BESIEGED

An Encyclopedia of Great Sieges From Ancient Times to the Present

JERICHO

DATE: 1405/1406(?) B.C.
LOCATION: just west of the Jordan River in modern eastern Israel.

FORCES ENGAGED:
Hebrew: unknown. Commander: Joshua.
Canaanite: unknown. Commander: unknown.

IMPORTANCE:
The Hebrew destruction of Jericho cleared the first major hurdle for settlement in the Promised Land.

Historical Setting

Like the siege of Troy, the siege of Jericho is the subject of much speculation over the recorded source (which was written after a significant amount of time had elapsed) and the archaeological evidence. Although the details of the biblical account of the fall of Jericho are much sketchier than the extended story of Troy told by Homer, modern evidence unearthed at Tel es-Sultan (the modern site of ancient Jericho) gives a greater substantiation to the Hebrew-Canaanite battle.

According to the Holy Bible, the Hebrews left Egypt in a massive exodus, probably around 1446/1445 B.C. (The exodus, too, is a matter of great debate, but not precisely relevant to the events at Jericho.) After a forty-year tour of the Arabian desert to weed out those deemed unfit for entrance into Canaan (the Hebrews' Holy Land), the people of the twelve tribes of Israel approached their target. Their first battle was with the Amorite kings Sihon and Og, whose forces they obliterated. That victory gave them clear access to the Jordan River north of the Dead Sea for their crossing. They easily crossed the Jordan owing to an earthquake that blocked the riverbed upstream. (Similar blockages have been recorded in later accounts, as in 1267 during Sultan Baybars' campaign against the crusaders and in 1927 when archaeologist John Garstang

was excavating in the region.) The timing of the earthquake certainly must have had a positive psychological effect on the invading Hebrews.

With his people across the river, the Hebrew leader Joshua sent spies into Jericho. As it is no more than 5 miles from the river, it seems highly unlikely that the town's inhabitants were unaware of the Hebrew presence, yet they did nothing to oppose the river crossing. The two spies found themselves in the company of Rahab, whose dwelling was on the city walls. Jericho is thus far the oldest walled city located by modern archaeology, and investigations have shown that houses were built in such a way that the city wall was the back wall of the dwelling. Rahab has always had the epithet "the Harlot" attached to her name, and it is indeed possible that she was engaged in the world's oldest profession although some scholars find the original Hebrew language suggests innkeeper. Certainly an inn would be a logical place to go to catch up on the local news and gossip. Here they learned from Rahab that Jericho's population was terrified of the approaching Hebrews: "your terror is fallen upon us, and that all the inhabitants of the land faint because of you. For we have heard how the Lord dried up the water of the Red Sea for you, when ye came out of Egypt; and what ye did to the two kings of the Amorites, that were on the other side of Jordan, Sihon and Og, whom ye utterly destroyed" (Joshua 2:9b–10). When the king of Jericho learned that two probable spies were staying at Rahab's, he sent soldiers to capture them. Rahab hid the Hebrews, then aided in their escape. For this she was promised safety during the upcoming battle.

The Siege

Jericho around 1400 B.C. was already a well-established town built around the spring of Ain es-Sultan. It was in the Plain of Jericho, a lush agricultural area in the midst of surrounding barren land. As a stopping place for travelers and merchants it had to have been wealthy, and possession of it would give the Hebrews a fertile base from which to operate as well as a key access point for trade. Twentieth-century excavations have shown that the level of Jericho at the end of the fifteenth century had a retaining wall 12 to 15 feet high topped by a mud-brick wall an additional 20 to 26 feet in height and 6 feet thick. Outside the retaining wall was a second wall of mud bricks. Rahab lived between the walls in what has been regarded as the poorer quarters of the city, which numbered perhaps 1,200 within the 6 acres enclosed by the interior walls. An earlier level of excavation shows the city had been destroyed by Egyptians perhaps 150 years earlier, and it is probable the walls of Joshua's time were built using the earlier walls as a foundation. The spring gave the city a ready water supply and food was plentiful. Supplies were not a problem, but the condition of the walls might have been.

Joshua's orders to his soldiers were to do nothing more than walk to the city, then around the walls, then back to the river. This was to be done for six days, with no sound to come from the marchers. By marching and not attacking, or even threatening the city, this probably lulled the defenders. "For six days the entire Israelite host solemnly filed around the walls of Jericho in full array. And for six days the good burghers of Jericho sprang to their weapons and manned the ramparts, at first in uneasy expectancy, afraid both of the marching columns and the possible magic involved in this procession headed by the priests and the Ark of the Covenant. But after the first terror and anxiety had subsided, the people of Jericho grew accustomed to the strange performance and relaxed" (Herzog and Gichon, *Battles of the Bible*, p. 48).

A change in pattern on the seventh day, however, should have alerted the defenders. The silent marchers appeared as before, but this time marched around the city seven times. This completed, they turned toward the walls and the priests leading the column each blew a

ram's horn and the multitude shouted. At this, the walls fell (another well-timed earthquake?). According to the King James Version of the Bible, the "walls fell flat." In his 1990 work on Jericho, Bryant Wood remarked that the better translation from the Hebrew would be "fell beneath itself," in other words, collapsed. Such an occurrence would have given an easy slope up the earthen embankment between the inner and outer city walls, allowing the Hebrews to proceed "up into the city, every man straight before him" (Joshua 6:20). No description is given of resistance, only of results. "And they utterly destroyed all that was in the city, both man and woman, young and old, and ox, and sheep, and ass, with the edge of the sword" (Joshua 6:21).

Results

After looting the city of its gold, silver, and brass, the Hebrews burned it. Joshua pronounced a curse on the site, predicting the death of the firstborn of whoever would rebuild a city there. The fulfillment of that prophecy came in the time of Israel's King Ahab, more than 500 years later, when reconstruction took place under the direction of Hiel of nearby Bethel. Only Rahab and her family survived the onslaught, as previously promised. Excavations carried out by an Italian team in 1996 found that a section of the north wall did not fall as did the rest of the city walls; perhaps that was where Rahab lived.

With Jericho in hand, the Hebrews were positioned to fan out into the remainder of Canaan. Although the biblical account describes a long series of battles and victories, most scholars seem to think that the remainder of the occupation was probably more in the nature of a migration than a conquest. That view seems to be supported when later accounts of the experiences of the Hebrews describe their falling in with local customs and religions rather than conquering and slaughtering the population as the biblical book of

Joshua describes. Joshua divided the lands among the twelve tribes of Israel and for a time they remained a united people. After the reigns of David and Solomon, however, they divided into two nations, Israel and Judah. That division laid the groundwork for future conquests by other powers, including Assyria, Babylon, and Rome. The conquest of Jericho, however, gave the Hebrew practitioners of the Jewish faith a homeland that they claim to this day, although the fighting for the land continues.

References: John Garstang, "Jericho and the Biblical Story," in *Wonders of the Past*, ed. J. A. Hammerton (New York: Wise, 1937); Chaim Herzog, and Mordechai Gichon, *Battles of the Bible* (London: Greenhill, 1997); Kathleen Kenyon, *Digging up Jericho* (London: Ernest Benn, 1957); Bryant Wood, "Did the Israelites Conquer Jericho? A New Look at the Archaeological Evidence," *Biblical Archaeology Review* 16, no. 2, March–April 1990, pp. 44–58.

Crater depicting the conquest of Troy, from Falerii Veteres. (Scala/Art Resource, NY)

TROY

Date: ca. 1250 B.C.
Location: on the Aegean coast of Asia Minor at the mouth of the Dardanelles, possibly modern Hisarlik.

FORCES ENGAGED:

Greek: unknown. Commander: King Agamemnon of Argos.
Trojan: unknown. Commander: King Priam.

IMPORTANCE:

The sack of Troy, if it did indeed take place, broke the city as a local power, allowing the Greeks to begin colonization of Ionia, as they called the east coast of Asia Minor.

Historical Setting

This siege is one of the most difficult to write about, for so much of the action lies deep in Greek mythology. Indeed, the entire war between the Greeks and Trojans is possibly nothing more than a literary exercise rather than an historical event. Still, the excavations begun in the late nineteenth century by Heinrich Schliemann give some basis for a real siege at a town on Asia Minor's Aegean coast sometime in the fourteenth to twelfth century B.C. The main source for the action at Troy comes from Homer's epic work *The Iliad*, so-called because the Greek word for the object of their attack was not Troy, but Ilion. It is possible the Trojans were inhabitants of a region rather than merely a city. As Homer is believed to have recorded oral tradition handed down over some four centuries, exact details of the actions of the siege can only be taken on faith. Other works, such as the *Kypria* and the *Aeneid*, offer details not included in Homer's account, making the facts even more elusive.

According to Homer's account, the background to the Greek attack on the Trojans is incredibly complex. Briefly, the goddesses Hera (Zeus' wife) and Artemis and Athena (Zeus' daughters) vied for a golden apple provided by

Eris (or Discord) that was inscribed "For the Fairest." Unwilling to alienate his wife or daughters, Zeus sent the three to Paris, son of the Trojan King Priam. In return for his rewarding the golden apple to Athena, she granted him with his heart's desire: Helen, the wife of King Menelaus in Mycenae. Paris traveled to Greece and was given hospitality by Menelaus and Helen. When Menelaus left for Crete to attend a funeral, Paris convinced Helen to run away with him. Upon returning to find his wife gone, Menelaus appealed to the Trojans for her return. When they refused, he gathered a coalition of Greek kings, many of whom had courted Helen and been obliged (by her father) to swear to defend her.

The cream of Greek warrior society responded, including the heroes Ajax, the demi-god Achilles, and Odysseus. Agamemnon (Menelaus' brother-in-law), as commander of the largest contingent, was named commander-in-chief. Homer explains that from the outset the struggle between Greeks and Trojans was almost a plaything of the gods, with many of them choosing to aid or harm one side or the other. The expedition got off to a bad start when a seer, Calchas, interpreted a sign as indicating a siege lasting nine years with the Greeks being successful in the tenth. Further, contrary winds (thanks to the goddess Artemis) forced Agamemnon to sacrifice his daughter Iphegeneia in order to get out of the harbor. The thousand ships then sailed for Asia Minor, with a stop at the island of Tenedos to offer a sacrifice. There one of the warriors, Philoctetes, was abandoned after suffering a snakebite. From Tenedos envoys were sent to the Trojans again requesting Helen's return, but they were rejected and even threatened with death.

Thence (according to the *Kypria*), the Greeks' first landing was at Teuthrania in Mysia, south of Ilion, which the Greeks mistakenly took for their real target. Some scholars believe this was the Trojans' home city. The *Kyprion* states that the Greek fleet departed and was scattered by a storm before reaching their goal. Homer's account of the expedition does not mention Teuthrania, but describes the Greeks landing on the beaches before Ilion. There the Trojans fought them. After initial success, they withdrew into the city, after which the Greeks settled in for a siege.

The Siege

Apparently the Greeks were in sufficient strength to keep the Trojans penned up long enough for the invaders to build a fortified position around their anchorage. The accounts of the siege claim that it lasted ten years, but the first nine are without much record. Xenophon wrote that it was unlikely that the entire Greek force was on site for the nine years, as supply problems would have been great. Also, a complete investment would have starved out the defenders well before ten years had passed. Apparently Achilles and other Greeks also pillaged several towns around the region as well as the isle of Lesbos. Occasional sallies by the Trojans and the fairly even outcomes of those combats imply that the invaders were not always at full strength. Although relative strengths are unknown, the citizens of one city could hardly have matched the warrior population of Greece in numbers.

The Iliad begins its coverage of the siege in the tenth year. Once again the gods are intervening. Agamemnon had captured and enslaved the daughter of Chryses, a Trojan prophet of Apollo. Apollo punished the Greeks with nine days of plague, upon which an assembly called by Achilles demanded the girl be returned to her father. In compensation, Agamemnon demanded and took Briseis, Achilles' slave girl/lover. Enraged, Achilles withdrew from the battle and took his followers, the Myrmidons, with him. The Trojans learned of this and attacked, hoping to take advantage of the absence of the greatest of the Greek warriors. The Trojans broke through the Greek defenses and burned a number of their ships. In the battle Hector, King Priam's second son and the Trojan champion, killed Achilles' best friend Patroclus. Mad for revenge, Achilles returned to the fray and, after killing a number of Trojans, cornered Hector. Hector fought the invulnerable Achilles and was killed; Achilles desecrated his body by dragging it behind his chariot around the city walls. After funeral ceremonies for Patroclus, Achilles granted King Priam's request for his son's body for proper burial.

Although Hector's death was certainly a serious blow to their morale, the Trojans did not surrender. Indeed, allies arrived including the Amazons under Queen Penthesilea and Ethiopians under King Memnon. Achilles slew both in battle, but died himself when Paris (with Apollo's aid) shot an arrow into Achilles' heel, his one vulnerable spot. At his funeral ceremonies, the Greeks sacrificed King Priam's daughter Polyxena. At this point Odysseus becomes a major character when he is awarded Achilles' armor, forged by the god Hephaestus. Calling on the seer Calchis, the Greeks learned that a necessary condition for taking Ilion was possession of Achilles' bow and arrows, which he had left with Philoctetes on the island of Tenedos. Odysseus and Neoptolemus (Achilles' son by Deidamia, daughter of King Lycomedes of Scyros) sailed to the island and brought back both man and weapons. Philoctetes then proceeded to kill Paris with an arrow shot from Achilles' bow. The Greeks captured another of Priam's sons, Helenus, a prophet, who was forced to reveal the city's weaknesses. Helenus set out the conditions. The Greeks needed to possess the Bone of Pelops, for whom the Peloponnesian peninsula was named. It was fetched from Pisa. They also needed the aid of Neoptolemus, which Odysseus obtained. Finally, they needed possession of the Palladium, a statue of the goddess Pallas sculpted by Athena. Disguised as a beggar, Odysseus slipped into Ilion to steal it. Helen, who by this time had no desire to stay in the city, discovered him and helped him spirit the statue away.

Still unable to win by force of arms in spite of the fact they had met all of the prophet's conditions, Odysseus convinced the Greeks to resort to trickery. They would build a giant horse (an icon sacred to Athena) and leave it outside the city gates as an offering for a safe voyage home. The army would then load up their ships and sail. Once out of sight, the fleet would hide in the lee of Tenedos. Odysseus and a band of picked men (some sources say 30, others 300) would hide inside the horse and wait for it to be taken inside the city. Once there, they would sneak out, open the gates, and the returning Greeks could storm in.

Upon discovering the horse, the citizens of Ilion debated the wisdom of accepting it. The strongest voice in opposition was Laocoon, whose protests were literally drowned out when the sea god Poseidon sent a serpent to drag him and his sons into the sea. Hotter heads prevailed and the horse was dragged toward the city. However, in order to get it through the gates, part of the walls and the gate's lintel had to be removed. This too was a necessity (according to prophecy) for the city to be captured. After moving the horse inside and celebrating far into the night, the sleeping Trojans failed to see Odysseus and his men accomplish their task. The Greeks destroyed the city. Neoptolemos killed Priam. Priam's wife and daughter were taken captive, as was Hector's wife Andromache.

Results

Since the Greeks not only destroyed the city but also desecrated the temples in the process, the gods visited revenge upon them. The Greek kings, if they survived the voyage home, found sedition and rebellion everywhere. Menelaus' voyage home took seven years; that of Odysseus ten. Agamemnon went home to be killed by his wife, who also killed his concubine Cassandra, one of Priam's daughters.

As stated at the outset, virtually none of the details of the siege can be proven. However, there is evidence of a major burning and destruction of the city of Hisarlik (at the mouth of the Dardanelles) at about the right time. Amateur archaeologist Heinrich Schliemann began digging there in the late nineteenth century, using Homer's text as his guide. A number of cities were built atop one another at that site, and level VI-h or VII-a has been dated to the general time period of the thirteenth century B.C. These levels show evidence of destruction by fire. Was that the site of the siege? Was the destruction caused by Mycenean-era invaders from Greece? The truth will almost certainly never be known.

If the war did take place, was Helen's abduction the cause? Many believe that the Trojan War as described by Homer and others was merely a grand elaboration on a major raid conducted against the Turkish coast, whether for loot or colonization. Control of Ilion/Troy/Hisarlik could have given the Greeks the base necessary to control the Dardanelles, for they later planted colonies both on the Black Sea shores and on the eastern Asia Minor coast. All of this might seem a slender reed on which to build a case for the Greco-Trojan conflict, but as it remains one of the world's best known sieges, it finds inclusion here.

References: Homer, *The Iliad*, trans. Robert Fitzgerald (Garden City, NY: Anchor, 1974); Thucydides, *History of the Peloponnesian War*, trans. Rex Warner (London: Heinemann, 1969–1977); Michael Wood, *In Search of the Trojan War* (London: BBC, 1985).

PLATAEA

DATE: May 429–summer 427 B.C.
LOCATION: province of Boeotia, some 50 miles northeast of Athens, Greece.

FORCES ENGAGED:
Spartan: unknown, possibly 30,000 troops. Commander: Archidamos II.
Plataean: 400 Plataeans and 80 Athenians. Commander: a command council.

IMPORTANCE:
Plataea marked the introduction of siege machinery and tactics to Greek warfare and began the social and psychological decline of Hellenic society.

Historical Setting

The town of Plataea was unfortunately situated—in the ancient Greek province of Boeotia at the opening of two passes from southern Greece, one of which led toward the Peloponnese (home of Sparta) and one toward Attica (home of Athens). While this was an excellent location for trade, it was a crossroads for war as well, and any neighboring aggressor had to control Plataea to expand or defend its territory. Two powerful neighbors to the south was bad enough, but the occasional expansionary desires of Thebes, 9 miles to the north, also was a consideration. Thebes was also the most regular aggressor, and Plataea was often obliged to seek aid from one of her powerful southern neighbors.

In 519 B.C. that aid came from Athens when Thebes attempted to force the creation of a Boeotian League, with itself as the leader. Thirty years later Plataeans fought alongside Athenians against the Persian army at Marathon. A decade later, Plataea was the site of the final Persian army defeat in Greece. In the 460s–450s B.C., Plataea also aided Sparta in suppressing a peasant revolt.

In the 450s, Plataea aided Athens in establishing control over Boeotia; when Boeotia successfully revolted in 447, Plataea remained an Athenian ally. Thus, when Athens and Sparta fell out in 432/431 B.C., Plataea had friendly relations with both sides and no real desire to fight either of them.

Within Plataea the issue was hotly debated. The bulk of the population favored close relations with Athens, while the upper classes preferred to join the resurgent Boeotian League. The aristocrats secretly plotted with Thebes, allowing a small force of 300 into the city one night in the spring of 431. Rather than seize any pro-Athenian leaders, the Thebans instead tried to reason with them. The population rose up and killed or captured the Theban soldiers. The 180 prisoners were held hostage to force the withdrawal of an advancing Theban army, then they were murdered. Although Athenian leaders realized the stupidity of that act, they still evacuated non-essential personnel from Plataea and added 80 soldiers to the 400-man garrison left behind. That obliged them to remain on Athens' side when war with Sparta broke out. After a couple of failed invasions of Attica, Spartan troops and their Theban allies marched against Plataea in 429.

With thousands of men encamped around the city, the Plataeans sent emissaries to the Spartan King Archidamos II. They reminded him that after the Persian defeat in 479, all Greek city-states had sworn to defend Plataea. Archidamos replied that he would go along with that if Plataea would fight against the aggressive Athenians or at least stay neutral. Given that their women and children were in Athens, the Plataeans could hardly agree to that. The Spartan king then offered an unusual alternative: let Sparta possess Plataea and its surrounding countryside for the duration of the war, all the while paying rent, while the Plataeans could have safe conduct anywhere they wanted to go to avoid the fighting. At war's end they could return home and Sparta would leave. That seemed reasonable to the garrison, but Athens overrode the deal. When informed of that decision, the Spartans began their siege.

The Siege

Archidamos began by plundering the countryside of supplies, then having as many trees as possible cut down. He ordered a surrounding palisade built to keep any defenders from escaping. He then used his large army (the size is unknown, but could possibly have numbered 30,000) to move earth against the city walls, which were only accessible from the south and southeast. Building a ramp would

allow his men to enter the city without having to scale the walls or batter down gates. With the vast superiority in numbers, it is difficult to understand why Archidamos did not order the walls stormed. Perhaps a failed attempt at forcing the town of Oenoe two years earlier discouraged him. Further, Plataea's stone walls were reportedly 30 feet high, making the use of scaling ladders difficult. At a reported 10 feet thick, the walls would also have been an insurmountable challenge given the siege machinery of the day.

For weeks the besiegers moved dirt. The Plataeans responded both by building up their own walls facing the growing mound and by burrowing through their own walls and removing dirt the Spartans had placed next to the wall. This kept the mound from reaching the wall until the Spartans responded by dropping in pieces of clay wrapped in reeds that were too large to remove through the burrows. (This Plataean tactic suggests that the Spartans should have tried undermining, but inexplicably they did not.) The Plataeans then built a second semicircular wall within the city (a lunette). This would present the attackers with another barrier to breach once their mound reached the top of the original wall. The curvature would make the attackers easier targets as well.

As the Spartan mound grew, Archidamos finally brought in battering rams. They had little success against clever Plataean countermeasures. They would drop nooses over the ends of the rams and then hoist them up over the walls. They also suspended heavy logs atop their walls to drop on top of the rams, breaking them. Frustrated at this, Archidamos ordered the use of fire. Brush was piled alongside the wall, covered with sulfur, pitch, and (some sources say) arsenic, making it the first recorded use of chemical warfare. They also threw as much brush as they could inside the city walls to spread the fire, for the counterwall the Plataeans built had used up most of the building material provided by nearby houses. Unfortunately for the Spartans, the wind did not cooperate and there was possibly a well-timed thunderstorm as well.

Archidamos finally sent many of his troops home to attend to the harvest, while having the remainder build a stronger encircling wall as well as a wall of circumvallation, 16 feet outside the first wall, facing outward to defend against any relief force. Some 2,000 Spartan and Beotian troops remained on guard duty through the winter.

The small garrison and wise stockpiling of food meant that the defenders were in no immediate danger of starvation. However, since no Athenian aid seemed in the offing the soothsayer Theaenetus, along with Eupompidas (son of General Daimachus) offered a breakout plan sometime in the winter of 429–428. On a stormy, moonless night the garrison would sneak out of the city. The defenders were observed taking shelter in towers along the encircling wall during bad weather, so scaling it should prove easy. Pull up the ladders, cross to the outer wall and scale it, then be off into the night. When the appropriately rainy night arrived, only 220 decided the attempt was worth the risk. They succeeded in scaling the first wall, but loose bricks falling alerted the defenders. The Plataeans quickly seized the two towers flanking their breakout and with archers were able to keep the Spartans and Thebans at bay. The second wall was scaled during the fighting, but on the opposite side lay a ditch filled with freezing water. This ditch had been the source of the clay for the brick walls they had just climbed. In spite of the neck-deep cold water, all but one of the escapees made the crossing; the one that did not surrendered.

The Spartan-Theban besiegers lit signal fires to alert reinforcements in Thebes, but the Plataeans countered that by building multiple fires of their own, which confused any signal being sent. The escapees in the darkness fooled the Spartans by fleeing not toward Athens but toward Thebes. When they were sure the pursuit was headed in the wrong direction, they safely took a circuitous route to Athens. The Plataeans who had stayed behind thought the escape an utter failure until they asked permission to bury the dead. Only then did they learn the wisdom of the escape plan. They had more than a year to ponder on their decision to stay behind, for the decreased garrison was able to take further stretch the city's food supply until the summer of 427. By then a Spartan force convinced the remaining defenders to surrender.

Results

After a trial, two hundred Plataeans and twenty-five Athenians were executed and the women who had remained behind to cook for the garrison were sold into slavery. Those who escaped, as well as those who fled to Athens before the siege, were awarded Athenian citizenship. They remained in Athens until war's end, then returned to their city. A later Spartan-Theban conflict found the city on the side of Sparta, but the Plataeans found them little better allies in the end than the Athenians had been. Thebes occupied the city after a surprise attack in 373 B.C. Not until the arrival of Philip's invading Macedonians did Plataeans once again control their own city, in 338.

Thucydides' account of the siege of Plataea is the first recorded description of both Greek siege machinery (primarily battering rams) and the use of walls of circumvallation. There is much debate over how the Spartans came to use these siege tactics. Some think that they learned them from the Persians or the Carthaginians (in Syracuse, Sicily). Others propose that Archidamos himself should be given credit for initiating rams, approach mound, and walls. Whatever the true answer, the results here and for the remainder of the Peloponnesian War were the same: no besieged city was taken by attack in the entire conflict. The strategy of deceit remained the primary Greek method for overcoming strong walls.

There was a psychological effect to the siege

as well. The surrendering Plataeans were offered freedom, except for those guilty of crimes. The Spartan trial consisted of one question to each defender: What good have you done for Sparta in this war? The Plataeans blamed Thebes for forcing them into an Athenian alliance; after all, the Thebans were no good since they had conspired with the Persian invasion. The Thebans responded that that was a leadership decision, not one of the citizens, and thus the citizens only followed orders. Neither of these arguments changed the ultimate Spartan query: What have you done for us, Plataea? When no one could offer a positive response, all were killed. "The significance of the Spartan action, brutal as it may have been, did not lay with the execution of the Plataeans. . . . why they acted was more important than what they did, for the reasoning brought to the surface, without apologies and for all to examine, the attitude which destabilized their own world. . . . Alliances between states, as between families, evolved over generations. . . . If Sparta, the greatest champion of conservative values of the Greek elite, could brush aside profound attachments which had been established in the memory of men still living and which solemn rituals kept alive year by year, then there was no basis for long-term loyalty to any state" (Crane, "Plataia").

References: Gregory Crane, "The Case of Plataia," perseus.tufts.edu/~gcrane/Pel. War.conf.html; Paul Bentley Kern, *Ancient Siege Warfare* (Bloomington: Indiana University Press, 1999); Thucydides, *The Peloponnesian War,* trans. Benjamin Jowett (New York: Twayne, 1963).

SYRACUSE

DATE: 415–413 B.C.
LOCATION: on the east coast of Sicily.

FORCES ENGAGED:
Syracusan: unknown, although probably roughly equal to Athenians; included 4,400 Spartans. Commander: Gylippus.
Athenian: approximately 200 galleys and 45,000–50,000 men. Commander: Nicias, then Demosthenes.

IMPORTANCE:
The Athenian defeat broke their naval dominance of the eastern Mediterranean; led to their downfall as the dominant Greek polis; and kept them from possibly establishing their authority throughout the Mediterranean world, including Carthage and Rome.

Historical Setting

After the defeat of the Persians at Salamis and Plataea in 480 and 479 B.C., Athens rose to the top in Greek politics. As the leading naval power she made herself the strongest member of the Delian League, a grouping of Greek polises (city-states) dedicated to continuing the war against Persia, offensively and defensively. Athens reached the point where she could demand virtually any dues to the League and did not have to account for the money sent to the League treasury. The Athenians spent much of that money turning their city into a cultural and architectural showplace, which did not please the polises contributing the money.

Athens entered into a shifting set of alliances, some voluntary and some forced on weaker neighbors. Between 460 and 445, Athens challenged Sparta and her allies in a number of battles, at the same time providing aid to Egyptians rebelling against Persia. With no clear winner, Sparta and Athens agreed to a truce in 445, but their political rivalry continued. It is difficult to find a more convoluted set of circumstances than the ones that set off the Peloponnesian War. Athenian domination over the northern Greek polises kept them resentful, yet more diplomatic maneuvering and alliance-making resulted in Athens being poised to establish a Greek Empire. The

An undated engraving of the destruction of the Athenian army at Syracuse. (North Wind Picture Archives)

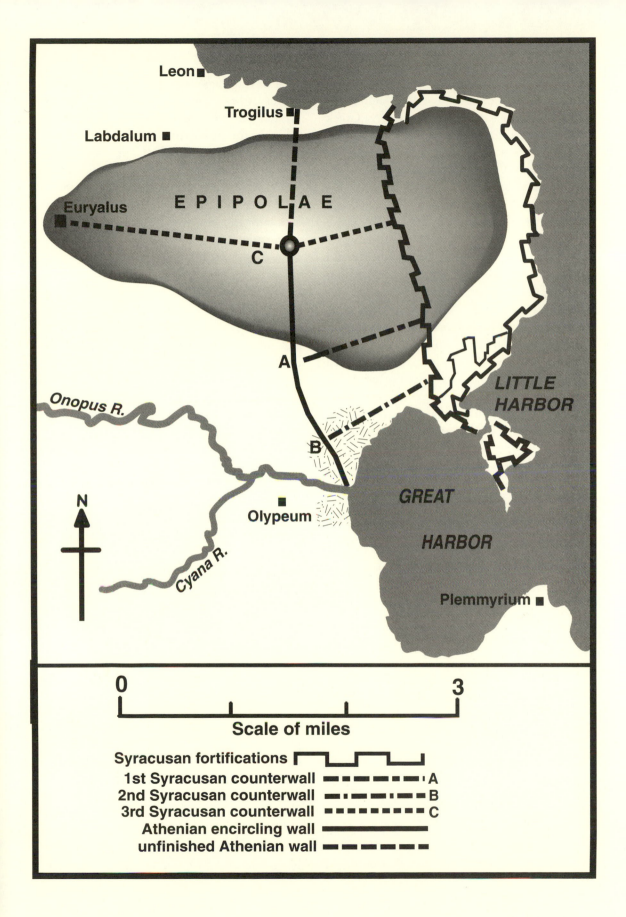

Leon ■

Trogilus ■

Labdalum ■

E P I P O L A E

Euryalus ■

C

A

Onopus R.

B

N

Olypeum ■

Cyana R.

LITTLE
HARBOR

GREAT

HARBOR

Plemmyrium ■

0   3

Scale of miles

Syracusan fortifications
1st Syracusan counterwall ━ ━ ━ ━ A
2nd Syracusan counterwall ━ ▪ ━ ▪ ━ B
3rd Syracusan counterwall ■ ■ ■ ■ C
Athenian encircling wall ──────
unfinished Athenian wall ▄ ▄ ▄ ▄

Athenian navy enforced as well as expanded the city-state's dominion over as much of the Mediterranean as possible. Finally, most Greek polises turned to Sparta for leadership. When Athens attempted to meddle in the political affairs of the Peloponnese, long Sparta's sphere of influence, fighting resumed in 431.

The war has been described as the struggle between the elephant and the whale. Sparta had the finest army of the day and Athens possessed the greatest navy, but neither could come to grips with the other. Sparta and her allies besieged Athens after capturing the surrounding countryside, but because they were unable to capture the port of Piraeus, Athens brought in a constant supply of food and other necessities. The Athenian navy also conducted raids on the Spartan coastline, liberating the helots who toiled under Spartan rule. Both powers hurt the other, but neither could finish the other off. Fighting was fairly constant for ten years, until another peace was negotiated in 421. The two main adversaries were glad of the break, but some of their allies were unhappy the peace treaty had not restored lands they had lost in the war. Sparta's and Athens' client states argued and fought among themselves and, when pressed, called on the two powers for aid. Peace was kept for six years, but much of the blame for the renewal of war between them in 414 can be laid at the feet of Alcibiades, a rabble-rousing Athenian general.

Alcibiades convinced the citizenry of Athens to go to war against Syracuse on the island of Sicily. They were providing valuable foodstuffs to Sparta, he claimed. If Athens could establish herself in Sicily (and the Syracusans were originally Greek colonists), then she would be in a commanding position. She would cut off the needed food to Sparta, weakening her to the point of subjection, and possession of Syracuse would allow Athens to dominate the western Mediterranean as well. Defeating the nascent powers of Carthage and Rome, Athens could draw on the manpower of Italy, North Africa, and Iberia (homeland of most of Carthage's mercenary army) to defeat Sparta. Athens could be ruler of the known Western world. Alcibiades' speaking ability won over the citizens to his plan, over the more cautious suggestions of his political rivals. Athens voted to attack. Better still, the Sicilian city of Segesta, currently threatened by Syracuse, offered to pay for the expedition. Alcibiades went to Sicily, with Nicias and Lamachus as co-commanders.

The Siege

The Athenian invasion force departed in June 415, numbering 134 triremes and 130 transports, the latter carrying about 5,000 hoplites (heavy infantry), 1,300 archers, various javelin throwers and slingers, and 30 horses (about 27,000 troops); 130 supply ships sailed with them as well. The Syracusans ignored rumors of a Greek invasion until the enemy arrived. The only thing that saved them was the standard Greek inability to agree on anything. Nicias wanted to go home once they learned Segesta could not pay for the mission. Lamachus wanted to launch an immediate attack on Syracuse, taking advantage of their lack of preparation and low morale. Alcibiades' oratory again won out. He argued that the Athenians should traverse the island, gathering support from the cities that disliked Syracuse. That, however, gave the Syracusans time to begin training their troops and repairing their defenses. Alcibiades' plan failed, for no Sicilian city voluntarily joined them.

Word soon arrived from Athens that Alcibiades had been convicted in his absence of blasphemy. He was taken away to face judgment but managed to escape his jailers when the ship stopped in Italy. He fled to his former enemy, Sparta, where he revealed Athens' plan for empire and the effect the loss of Syracuse would have on Sparta. At first the Spartans refused, still observing their truce with Athens, but in the end promised to send a general to command the Syracusan army and a fleet from Sparta's ally, Corinth.

Meanwhile, the Athenians began to attack Syracuse. They defeated a poorly prepared Syracusan force but failed to win a complete victory. Worse, Lamachus was killed in the fighting, leaving the indecisive Nicias in sole command. As winter approached they settled into siege warfare, building a wall parallel to the city's defensive wall, which would cut the city off from any landward help, while the superior Athenian fleet would keep the seaward side covered. Both measures failed. The Syracusans raided the Athenians just often and successfully enough to keep their wall from being finished. Still, morale in the city slipped and a town meeting was called to discuss opening surrender negotiations. The Corinthians arrived in time to stop them. The Spartan general, Gylippus, landed up the coast and raised a force of some 2,000 to fight with him against the Athenians. He marched onto the high plateau just to the west of Syracuse, so surprising Nicias that the Athenians were unable to stop them from reaching the city. Gylippus oversaw the construction of a counterwall to stop the Athenian effort, which split the plain and gave Syracuse control of the northern half and access to the rest of the island.

In the summer of 414 Nicias counseled Athens to abandon the invasion or to dispatch a second force equal to the first. Athens sent another force, but Sparta broke the truce and attacked to delay or cancel it. In Sicily the summer was spent wall-building and Gylippus got the better of it. In the spring of 413 he was ready to attack the Athenians. This he did with a two-pronged assault, starting with his navy attacking Nicias' base at Plemmyrium on the southern end of Syracuse's harbor. When the defenders left their positions in order to watch the sea battle, Gylippus attacked and captured the town. While the Athenian fleet badly hurt the attacking Corinthians, they had lost their base. They were forced to move to another mooring deeper in the harbor, which severely limited the navy's superior maneuverability. This was the beginning of the end for the Athenian military effort in Sicily.

Hearing of the dispatch of the second Athenian force, Gylippus was determined to win before they arrived. He launched another attack on the Athenians, this time using his army first to distract the Athenian sailors. Again he was successful, for when his ships entered the harbor bent on close-quarters action with the Athenians they found a disorganized navy scrambling to man its ships and engage. The engagement lasted intermittently for three days, with the combined fleet of Corinth and Syracuse gaining the upper hand. At close quarters they were able to rain arrows down on the Athenian ships, killing large numbers of sailors. It was a major but not decisive defeat. When the second force under Demosthenes arrived in July 413, Athenian hopes revived.

Demosthenes took command of the entire Athenian force from an ailing Nicias and immediately went on the offensive to regain control of the plateau overlooking the city. He sent a force secretly up the steep slope of the western end of the plateau that captured a surprised Syracusan force at the town of Euryalus. However, Gylippus ordered a counterattack and in the confusion of the night fighting the Athenians lost their momentum and the battle. Unable to reestablish a position on the plain, Demosthenes loaded his army onto ships to return home, but stopped at the last minute because of a full lunar eclipse on 27 August 413. The superstitious Nicias decided to wait a month before sailing, giving Gylippus his last chance to win. He anchored his fleet across the mouth of the harbor and chained the ships together. Again the small harbor kept the Athenians from using their superior maneuverability; they lost fifty ships to the Syracusans' twenty-six. At that point the Athenian crews refused to fight and demanded a retreat by land. On open ground Gylippus separated the Athenians into two groups and defeated each individually.

Results

Of the 45,000 to 50,000 men Athens had sent to capture Syracuse and Sicily, only 7,000 survived the final battles. They were all sold into slavery except Nicias and Demosthenes, who were killed against Gylippus' orders. The Syracusans, poorly prepared for the war and on the verge of surrender, survived thanks to the Spartan Gylippus. The city remained free and a major power in the western Mediterranean for another two centuries, until crushed in the Punic Wars of the third century B.C.

Athens' fortunes waned. The ships and crews lost in Sicily were not irreplaceable, but Athens found her naval power and prestige badly damaged. Delian League members seized the opportunity to break away, Persian forces opened an offensive to regain their lost territory in Asia Minor, and Sparta began investing in sea power, with both their own ships and others provided by Persia. That refocused Athens' attention on her eastern possessions, and when her lost ships were replaced that was where she sent them. The replacement crews, however, did not match the quality of those lost in Sicily, and Athens was destroyed as a naval power at Aegospotami in 405. There, in the Hellespont connecting the Aegean and the Black seas, a Spartan fleet commanded by Lysander attacked the last Athenian fleet, capturing intact 170 ships while their crews were ashore. Without their fleet, the city of Athens could not resist the siege that Sparta was then conducting. The city held out through the winter of 405–404, but surrendered in the spring.

Had the Athenians followed Lymachus' advice and attacked as soon as they landed, Syracuse certainly would have fallen and a major Athenian power center would have been established. Carthage and Rome were at the time mere shadows of their future selves; it would have been little problem for Athenian ships and troops to control them. With the supplies and manpower available from these acquisitions, no one would have been able to match Athenian power, and Alcibiades' empire could have come to pass. Rome may never have built their empire and Europe, at least, would never have been the same. Instead, the defeat ended Athens' reign as the dominant polis. No one successfully dominated Greece until Philip of Macedon arrived in the 340s to unite the polises under one ruler; his son Alexander built an Eastern empire instead of the Western one Athens would have built. Thus, the fate of Asia changed as well.

References: J. F. C. Fuller, *Military History of the Western World*, vol. 1 (New York: Funk and Wagnalls, 1954); Donald Kagan, *On the Origins of War* (New York: Doubleday, 1995); Thucydides, *The Peloponnesian Wars*, trans. Benjamin Jowett (New York: Twayne, 1963).

VEII

DATE: 404(?)–396(?) B.C.
LOCATION: approximately 12 miles up the Tiber River from Rome.

FORCES ENGAGED:

Roman: unknown. Commander: Appius Claudius, later Marcus Furius Camillus.
Veiian: unknown. Commander: unknown.

IMPORTANCE:

Roman victory brought an end to Rome's most threatening neighbor and began its rise to prominence in the central Italian peninsula.

Historical Setting

Near the close of the sixth century B.C., the Etruscan monarchy ended, but various city-states remained potent forces. One of the chief among them was Veii, on the western bank of the Tiber River just 12 miles upstream from Rome. The two populations were expansionary and were entirely too close to each other to be cooperative. The two were economic rivals as well, for dominance of the Tiber meant control of access to interior markets as well as the salt production from the port city of Ostia, downstream from Rome.

In the 480s a powerful Roman clan, the Fabians, built a fortress-villa roughly halfway between the two cities. The Fabii had familial connections in both cities, but the Fabian strongpoint at the junction of the Tiber and Cremora rivers was too threatening to Veiian security. The battle of Cremora in 476 ended in Veiian control of the key river junction as well as the Janiculum Hill, overlooking Rome itself. This attack broke a truce that the Romans and Etruscan city-states had been observing for nearly forty years. Rome replied to the threat with a siege of Fidenae, a colony also at the junction of the rivers. The siege lasted three years and was ended when the Romans dug under the city walls. Throughout the siege the Veiians had appealed to other Etruscan city-states for aid, but none responded. Veii had broken the truce, they could face the consequences.

The two cities observed an uneasy peace until the end of the fifth century. Then, for reasons that are unclear, Rome began besieging Veii itself. (The dates of the siege are the focus of some dispute. Roman tradition described a ten-year siege from 400 to 390, but most historians think that ten-year period was fabricated to give Rome its own *Iliad*. Some dates suggested are 405–396, 404–396, or 406–395.)

The Siege

Appius Claudius was the initial Roman commander. Rome's republican government depended on the landowning citizens to provide military service. Duty and rank depended on income and the ability to arm oneself. As the Romans were primarily an agricultural population, this meant that campaigning was restricted to the summer, after the spring planting and before the fall harvest. Veii was so strongly fortified, however, that it could not possibly be overcome in a few months. Thus, the Roman government reluctantly authorized long-service enlistments with pay and supplies to be provided by the government. This was the beginning of the professional Roman army. A Veiian sally, which destroyed months of labor on the siege works, helped to motivate the government to change the army's recruiting practices.

Three years into the siege, two Etruscan cities launched attacks on Roman camps. They did this in their own interest, thinking Roman armies might target them next. The Veiians, however, thought that all Etruria had finally responded to their call and sent out a sally themselves. The Romans held for a time against this two-pronged assault, but a personal dispute between two Roman commanders ended in forcing a Roman retreat all the way back to their home city. Roman armies returned to the siege the following year and held their positions with little trouble for two more years.

The length of the siege, coupled with a harsh winter, a hot summer, and a plague, began to wear on Roman morale. A solemn banquet was held to honor the gods and invoke their aid, but the nature of Rome's electorate held the key to the problem (or so the patricians thought). Claiming that their problems stemmed from lower-class criticism of the nobility, the tribunal elections brought two patricians to office. One of these tribunes was Marcus Furius Camillus, destined to be Veii's conqueror.

In spite of the seeming placation of the gods, one main omen caused the most anxiety. The Alban Lake, near Rome, rose to an unusual level in the summer of 398. The Romans sent an emissary to Delphi to consult the oracle. In the meantime, a Veiian citizen appeared on the city walls one day and called out in a loud voice that Veii would remain unconquered as long as the Alban Lake remained at its abnormally high level. Under the pretext of requesting a consultation with the wise old Veiian (a *haruspex*), a Roman soldier kidnapped him and took him to the Senate. There, the haruspex revealed that the gods had turned against Veii; the messenger to Delphi soon returned with an answer that corroborated the old man's prophecy. Thus, work began to dig drainage channels out of the lake's basin.

Rather than bringing about an immediate change in the situation, news from the north alarmed the Romans. The Etruscans were beginning to feel pressure from invading Gauls and had decided to aid Veii, rid themselves of the Roman threat, then put together a united front against the barbarians from the north. This problem motivated the Romans to name the tribune Camillus to the position of dictator. He appointed the able Publius Cornelius Scipio as commander of the cavalry and called for a mass levy of troops. Few failed to respond. The new army won two quick victories over Etruscan troops from Falerii and Capena and gathered immense booty from their camps. Camillus, rather than distribute it to the troops in payment for a job well done, instead sent most of the loot back to Rome, to be used to construct a temple.

With the Etruscan threat beaten back for a time, Camillus returned to Veii and began serious work. He ordered the men to keep their distance from the city walls, and instead to strengthen their trenches. He also began work on a tunnel through the rock supporting Veii's walls. As the tunnel drew nearer its destination, word spread through Rome that the attacking forces would be free to loot Veii at will. That promise motivated a huge percentage of the population to join in the siege. When all was ready, Camillus offered up a prayer to the gods and ordered a massive assault on the walls. The move surprised the defenders, who had been lulled into passivity since Camillus had taken his command and ordered his men to keep away from the walls. As the city leaders gathered in the temple of Juno to ask for direction, a handpicked force of Roman soldiers burst out from their tunnel into the temple and began the slaughter. The troops soon spread through the city, attacking the defenders from the rear and opening the city gates to the horde outside.

Results

Camillus was able to restrain his troops from slaughtering the women and children, who begged for mercy, but the pillage went on unabated. The wealth of the city was greater than anyone had imagined. Fearing the gods might think the mortals too proud of themselves, Camillus asked that a minor misfortune take place in order to show the need for humility. As he finished praying, he turned and stumbled. Picking himself up and dusting himself off, he mused on the rapidity and mildness of the immortals' answer to his plea.

The city of Veii was not only looted of everything of value, it was then completely destroyed. This action was at variance with the normal manner of Roman conquest, which was to absorb the region and population into the Roman social and political realms. Fearing Veii's long-standing power and potential for rebirth, the government deemed a complete destruction in Rome's best interest. From this point forward Etruria put forth little serious opposition to Rome. Unfortunately for the Romans, however, the threat of Gallic invasion proved all too real. In 390 the Gauls defeated a Roman army at the Allia River, then sacked the city. Camillus was reappointed as dictator and managed to drive the Gauls away, but with bribes rather than power. When they returned in 367, however, he once again assumed the position of dictator and this time succeeded in beating back the invaders. No Roman enemy entered the city in victory again for 800 years.

References: Livy, *The Early History of Rome*, trans. Aubrey de Sélincourt (Baltimore: Penguin, 1987); Vezio Melegari, *The Great Military Sieges* (New York: Crowell, 1972); "The Struggle with Veii," myron.sjsu.edu/romeweb/glossary/timeln/t15.htm.

TYRE

DATE: February–31 July 332 B.C.
LOCATION: on the eastern Mediterranean coast (modern Lebanon).

FORCES ENGAGED:

Macedonian/Greek: approximately 30,000 men. Commander: Alexander of Macedon.
Tyrian: at least 8,000 soldiers, with perhaps 40,000 civilians. Commander: King Azimilik.

IMPORTANCE:

This was Alexander's first experience with siege warfare, and it demonstrated his imagination in engineering. His harsh treatment of civilians in the wake of the leniency shown to Sidon set a precedent followed by later conquerors such as Genghis Khan.

Historical Setting

In the 350s B.C. Philip I assumed the throne of Macedon, a relatively poor province north of Greece. He developed a first-class army and, taking advantage of the temporary weakness of

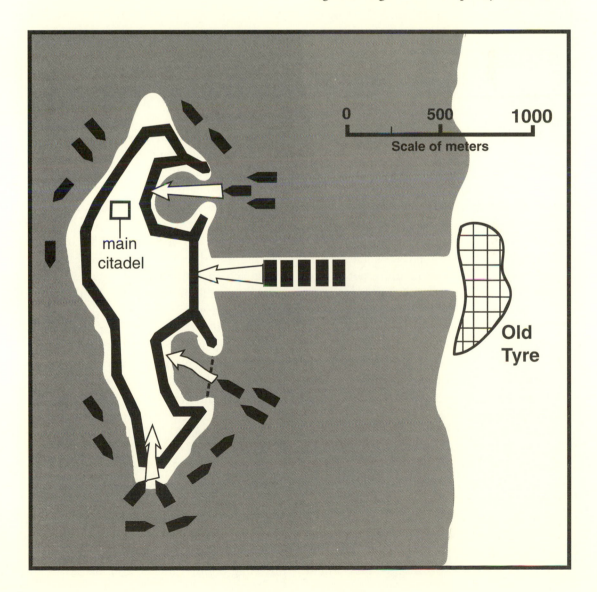

main citadel

Old Tyre

0   500   1000
Scale of meters

Athens (Greece's dominant city-state) after the Social War (358–55), began conquering Athenian-dominated provinces on the Greco-Macedonian frontier. While the Greek polises continued their almost constant squabbling, Philip extended Macedonian control over areas to Macedon's north, then he attacked Greece itself. In 338 B.C. Philip's army defeated an Athenian-Theban alliance at Leuctra, giving him mastery of the Greek peninsula. He established the Hellenic League the following year, uniting almost all the Greek polises into an alliance aimed at defeating the Persian Empire. As the forces of the Hellenic League prepared to cross the Hellespont into Asia Minor in 336, Philip was assassinated and succeeded by his son Alexander.

In spite of the fact he was only twenty years old, Alexander won the immediate loyalty of his father's Macedonian army due to tutelage at his father's side and his valor at the battle of Leuctra. The rest of the League was not as true, however. While putting down rebellions in the north, Alexander learned that Athens had bolted the League, thinking him dead. He returned to Athens very much alive and reinforced his authority; he then turned to continue his father's plan of invading Persia. Educated by Aristotle, Alexander was both a brilliant scholar and a Greek "nationalist"; he aimed not only to defeat Persia and avenge the destruction they had inflicted on Greece in the invasion of Xerxes (480–79 B.C.) but to spread Greek culture and knowledge wherever he went.

He quickly established a reputation as a courageous and innovative general. In 333 B.C. he began his invasion of Asia Minor, defeating armies sent against him by local Persian governors or by the Persian Emperor Darius III. At Issus late in the year Alexander's 30,000 soundly defeated Darius' army three times that size while losing but 450 men. Alexander's strategy was to take control of the eastern Mediterranean coastline. He had no fleet while the Persian navy could roam at will, harassing his supply lines and provoking revolts in Greece. Denying the Persians their ports would

force them to either abandon the eastern Mediterranean or defect to the Macedonian cause. His first conquest was simple. Sidon surrendered without a fight, for it had long suffered under Persian dominance. Its sister city Tyre, however, had profited from a Persian alliance and was determined to hold out against the invaders while Darius rallied another army inland.

Alexander's army marched to Tyre sometime in January 332. He spoke with the city elders, expressing a desire to worship their god Melkart, a Phoenician version of Heracles. When they suggested he worship in Old Tyre, where there was a better temple, he took it as an insult and prepared his attack.

The Siege

Tyre was well situated to withstand a siege. It was built on an island half a mile offshore, making direct assault without a fleet extremely difficult. Two harbors served the city, meaning that supplies could be brought in at will. Further, Tyre had ties to Carthage, which promised to send assistance in case of attack. Having no ships meant Alexander's forces could approach the city only one way: if they could not walk on water, they would have to build a causeway.

Although neither his staff nor army favored his idea, Alexander began dismantling the city of Old Tyre and placing the stones in the water. He scoured the countryside for timber for piling for the causeway, manpower, and supplies. This was an unbelievably massive engineering feat, for Alexander ordered that the causeway be built 200 feet wide. At first the Tyrians jeered the effort, then began to worry as the Greeks moved ever closer. The first counterstroke came with eight Tyrian ships sailing in close to the workers and pelting them with massed archery fire. In response, Alexander built towers to place his archers in a commanding position in case a similar attack was attempted. Instead, in the next foray the Tyrians launched a massive fire ship into the mole at the point where the towers were built; in the confusion smaller vessels landed commando parties that killed laborers on shore and destroyed Alexander's siege engines.

This lightning raid would have broken the spirit of a lesser man than Alexander, but he ordered the causeway widened and new towers built. He knew, however, that he needed protection from these naval attacks. Alexander reasoned that in the wake of his victory at Issus he would attract widespread support, and he was correct. Ships from Cyprus, Byblos, and Rhodes sailed to join with the Sidonian fleet and Alexander soon had almost 225 vessels. He drafted engineers from Phoenicia and Cyprus to construct siege artillery on the decks of barges and transports. As they were building, Alexander led an expedition into the hills to beat back marauders who had been harassing his timber crews and his supply lines. He returned to Sidon with his position secure and a fleet far larger than that of the isolated city. He arrived to find more good news: 4,000 mercenaries from Greece had arrived to swell his ranks. He boarded a Macedonian galley and set sail for Tyre.

The Tyrian admiral rowed out for a naval battle, but upon seeing Alexander's massive fleet he changed his mind and fled for his home port. The allied ships gave chase but the Tyrians narrowly reached port and blocked the harbor mouth with all their ships facing side by side, showing nothing but bows and rams. Alexander did not press the attack, but placed his Cypriot ships in a blockade.

Freed from any naval interference, Alexander's laborers made rapid progress with the mole. A summer storm battered his causeway, but he placed untrimmed cedars on the windward side and they acted as a breakwater. After the storm passed, Alexander soon found himself within range of the city to employ his catapults, with archers and slingers placed forward to keep the tops of the walls clear. Similarly, the siege engines that had been built on barges began pounding the walls from the seaward side. The Tyrians responded by placing skins on the walls to absorb some of the shock, then building backup walls. Their archers attempted to keep the attackers at bay with flaming arrows, but the seaward assault was showing positive effects. A planned night amphibious assault had to be canceled owing to bad weather. The landward side of the city, however, had the strongest walls and was resisting well.

Alexander had floating platforms moor right beside the walls in order to use rams against them. The Tyrians responded by dropping large blocks into the shallows so the barges could not get close enough. They began building weapons for the upcoming hand-to-hand combat that would commence when the causeway reached the city walls. Then, after having so much go their way, the Tyrians learned that the promised aid from Carthage would not be coming. Meanwhile, the hand-to-hand combat was beginning outside the walls. Alexander's ships brought up derricks to remove the blocks dropped from the city, and Tyrian divers attacked, cutting the lines and ships' anchor cables. It was a temporary setback for the Macedonians, who replaced the anchor lines with chains. Finally, after six months, Alexander's causeway reached the city.

He brought up siege towers 150 feet in height and he rolled them close enough to drop drawbridges onto the walls. The fighting was fierce, with the Tyrians pouring red-hot sand and gravel onto the attackers, forcing a retreat. After beating back a naval sally, Alexander sailed around the island city looking for the weakest point. He chose to assault the walls at the mouth of the northern harbor and brought up his barge rams and catapults to begin the barrage. It failed to break through. Undaunted, he moved his assault ships to the southeastern face, near the Egyptian harbor, and finally began to see the walls crumble. He threw in an assault team that was beaten back by a hail of arrows. Still, he knew this was the crack he had been looking for.

On 31 July he threw in his crack troops, and when their commander was killed Alexander charged in himself. He led forces along the battlements while his ships broke through into the harbor, landing more troops within the city. Rather than be caught between two forces, the soldiers withdrew into the city center and made a last stand at the shrine of Agenor.

Results

After such a long and arduous siege, Alexander did nothing to restrain his troops in their moment of victory. Pillage, loot, rape, and murder were the order of the day. The only saving grace for any of the citizens came from Alexander's allied troops from Sidon, who took pity on the inhabitants and smuggled about 15,000 of them out of the city. Tyre's King Azimilik with his advisers sought refuge in the temple of Melkart, and Alexander spared them. When the blood lust finally paled, 30,000 citizens survived only to be sold into slavery. Beforehand, however, Alexander crucified 2,000 men of fighting age. He then proceeded to sacrifice to Melkart as he had originally requested, following the service with a massive feast, games, and naval review.

The operation of 332 B.C. was the first truly amphibious assault in history, with the Macedonians having to develop the tactics that would be followed to modern times: preparatory bombardment, combat swimmers, obstacle removal, and fire support and harassing fire from offshore vessels. Even the use of ramps off the ships for unloading assault troops began here.

Alexander's capture of the city did indeed deny Persia one of its primary harbors, but the slaughter that ensued only impressed some of the other cities. When his forces reached Gaza, they again had to besiege the city, and the resulting aftermath was as bloody as that in Tyre. Possession of the city gave Alexander the ability to secure his supply lines overland from Macedon, as well as supplement them with naval transport. His forces pressed southward into Egypt, where they spent the winter of 332/331. There, Alexander established a new city that he named after himself (the first of many) and apparently received a revelation that he was directly descended from Apollo. From then on he assumed an increasingly divine demeanor, and accomplishments like the causeway at Tyre certainly did little to diminish his ego. The link between land and island over time has widened; the southern harbor has filled with silt and the island of Alexander's day is the end of peninsula with the foundation laid by Macedonian engineers more than 2,300 years ago.

References: Arrian, *The Campaigns of Alexander* (Middlesex: Penguin, 1971); Robin Lane Fox, *Alexander the Great* (London: Allen Lane, 1973); Peter Green, *Alexander of Macedon: A Historical Biography* (Berkeley: University of California Press, 1991); Carl O. Schuster, "The Siege of Tyre," *Command*, no. 25, November–December 1993.

SYRACUSE

DATE: 213–212 B.C.
LOCATION: on Sicily's southeastern coast.

FORCES ENGAGED:
Roman: naval contingent: 100 warships.
Commander: Marcus Claudius Marcellus.
Army contingent: 4 legions, 16,000 men.
Commander: Appius Claudius Pulcher.
Syracusan: unknown Commander: Hippocrates.

IMPORTANCE:
Roman victory reestablished their control over the island of Sicily, which originally had been gained in the First Punic War (264–241 B.C.).

Historical Setting

Early in the third century B.C. the reigning power in the western Mediterranean was

Carthage (near modern Tunis, Tunisia), originally a colony established by the Phoenicians. Carthage's navy dominated the sea both economically and militarily and the city had subject colonies and settlements across North Africa, into Spain, and in Sicily. The Carthaginians were never able to control all of Sicily, however, owing to the powerful city-state of Syracuse. After a long series of battles on the island, Carthage in 264 B.C. captured the key city of Messana (modern Messina) on the northeastern corner of the island within view of the tip of the Italian boot. That potential threat to Italy, along with an appeal by a stranded band of Latin mercenaries, motivated the increasingly powerful citizens of Rome to go to war. The struggle between Carthage and Rome, the First Punic War, lasted until 241, when a great Roman naval victory convinced Carthage to sue for peace. Although nominally loyal to Carthage at the outset of the war, Syracusan King Hiero II was forced to swear allegiance to Rome. He later proved to be remarkably loyal.

By 218 B.C. Carthage had recovered much of its military power and had spent the previous two decades establishing a strong presence in Spain. When a border dispute broke out between Carthaginian and Roman claims in the region, the Second Punic War began. When the Carthaginian general Hannibal crossed the Alps with his army and entered northern Italy, that became the primary theater of operations. However, Hiero in Syracuse maintained his alliance with Rome, thus denying Carthage a direct line of supply to their force in Italy. That loyalty wavered, however, upon Hiero's death in 215. He was succeeded by Hieronymos, a mere fifteen years old but already regarded as a degenerate. He entered into negotiations with Hannibal and received two of his envoys, Hippocrates and Epicydes, two brothers of mixed Carthaginian and Syracusan parentage. While in the city of Leontini (just northwest of Syracuse) trying to rouse anti-Roman support Hieronymos was assassinated. "Even the Carthaginians regarded him as untrustworthy, unreliable and expendable"

(Dorey and Dudley, *Rome against Carthage*, p. 122). In the confused situation that resulted, most of Hiero's family was killed and Hippocrates and Epicydes managed to get themselves elected to the city's Board of Generals.

Although seriously threatened by Hannibal's rampage through Italy, Rome dispatched an army to Sicily to thwart Carthage's designs. Overall command of this expedition went to Marcus Claudius Marcellus. The first Roman action was to storm and capture Leontini. Upon gaining control of the city, Marcellus beheaded some 2,000 people, claiming they were Roman deserters. Hippocrates and Epicydes, who managed to escape the city before its fall, immediately went to Syracuse and gave graphic accounts of the massive slaughter the Romans had perpetrated. This so roused the Syracusan populace that pro-Roman citizens were killed or expelled. After Leontini's experience, none that remained in Syracuse considered negotiation with the invaders. Any Roman attempt at negotiation was violently rejected.

The Siege

The initial Roman strategy was to launch an infantry attack under Appius against the northeastern wall at Hexapylum, while Marcellus led the fleet in an assault on Achradina, where the wall met the sea. Here the Romans found to their dismay that the city was defended by one of the finest scientific minds of the age, Archimedes. While Hiero had ruled, Archimedes was given permission and money to design defensive machines for the city, and he had let his imagination run wild. He built catapults and mangonels to throw rocks and darts at an attacker at both long and short range. In the most original of inventions, he had a wooden arm on a pivot reaching well past the wall. The Romans had designed an assault device they called a harp—a massive scaling ladder secured on the decks of two ships lashed together. It possessed a covered box on the end from which archers could lay down a covering fire as soldiers climbed the ladder. Archimedes' pivoting arm had a large hook on the end of a chain that caught the ship's prow; by lifting the arm with a counterweight, the ship would be stood on end, then released to crash into the water and sink. Other pivoting arms carried stones on the end that would be dropped onto the attacking "harps" and their ships. The scientist had also carved loopholes into the walls to protect archers who kept up a deadly fire on exposed sailors. On the landward side, Appius had no better luck against catapult and mangonel fire. Although the city's walls were quite long and the Romans had assumed the Syracusans would be unable to adequately man the defenses, this opening setback convinced them otherwise. Starvation instead of storm became the next strategy.

As long as the harbor remained open the Syracusans could receive aid. When the Romans tried to occupy it, the defenders responded by launching fire ships that drifted among the Roman craft and did immense damage. While the investment proceeded, the action shifted away from the city and out to the countryside. The Carthaginian government sent Admiral Himilco with 25,000 infantry, 3,000 cavalry, and 12 elephants to reinforce Carthaginian strongholds on the island. Marcellus left two-thirds of the Roman army at Syracuse and led the rest into the interior to reduce the Carthaginian influence over as many cities as he could. He caught Hippocrates with 10,000 men sallying from Syracuse to join Himilco and soundly defeated the Syracusan force, but Hippocrates and his cavalry force escaped and joined the Carthaginians. Both sides had their successes and failures. The Romans landed a strong force to swell the besiegers' ranks while Himilco was able to rouse some cities to rebel against Roman occupation. In the winter, Appius went home to assume the consulship and was replaced by Quinctius Crispinus, who assumed command of the Roman fleet. Marcellus went into winter quarters surrounding the city.

In the spring of 212 Marcellus tried to enter into a conspiracy with pro-Roman factions inside Syracuse, but the plot was discovered and the guilty were executed. The break the Romans needed came by accident. Syracuse sent an agent to King Philip in Macedon to explore the idea of an alliance against Rome. He was captured by the Romans and asked to be ransomed. Roman representatives approached the city walls and met regularly with Syracusan officials to discuss the ransom. As the negotiations proceeded, a Roman soldier noticed that the walls at this point were actually not as high as they seemed from a distance, and much shorter ladders could be used to scale them. Unfortunately, that point was heavily defended. A pro-Roman sympathizer in the city, however, got word to Marcellus that the annual festival honoring Artemis was taking place and the food shortage in the city was being ameliorated by an excess of wine. That was all Marcellus needed to know. He quickly organized an assault force of 1,000 to scale the shorter walls in the dark of night. They easily overcame the drunken sentries and were able to move along the walls to Hexapylum, where they opened the gates. The Romans were in the city before the alarm could be raised. When Epicydes learned of the breach he responded, thinking it was merely a localized incursion, but all of Marcellus' army was inside the walls by dawn.

Epicydes withdrew with as many troops as possible to the defenses at Achradina and the island at the head of the Great Harbor. Marcellus made no headway offering to negotiate, as the bulk of that force was made up of Roman deserters who remembered clearly the fate of the Leontini defenders. Marcellus proceeded to spend the rest of the year consolidating his hold on the city, occupying the Epipolae, the plateau extending west from the city. He also spent his time looting the area he controlled, but he maintained discipline among his troops and no serious abuse of the population occurred.

Carthage responded by sending Admiral Bomilcar with a hundred ships to attack the Roman base in the harbor. He landed his troops and joined with some under Hippocrates for an attack on the Roman camp, and coordinated it with a sally out of Achradina. The Romans beat back both. That ended most of the fighting, and the rest of the siege and its attendant casualties were targets of disease. The Carthaginians encamped near the Great Harbor were in a marshy area that encouraged epidemic. Many of the Sicilians supporting the Carthaginians went home for the winter. Although the defenders in Archadina held firm, Carthaginians in the countryside were almost completely wiped out.

In the spring of 211 the Sicilian citizens reorganized themselves and occupied two Roman-held towns near Syracuse. Bomilcar returned with a fleet of 130 warships and 700 transports, hoping with the local forces to besiege the Romans inside the city. Unfortunately for the Syracusans, Bomilcar's armada was kept out of the harbor by bad weather that forced him to anchor off the south coast. Fearing the Carthaginian admiral might abandon the relief effort, Epicydes sailed to join and encourage him, leaving some mercenary captains in charge. When the weather abated and the fleet sailed for Syracuse, Marcellus with a smaller fleet emerged from the harbor to do battle. Bomilcar lost his nerve and fled. Epicydes, who had sailed from Syracuse to confer with Bomilcar, found himself stranded in the town of Agrigentum.

Fearing all was lost without reinforcements, the Sicilian army encamped outside the city sent representatives to Marcellus to propose negotiations. He allowed them safe passage through his lines to speak to the leaders in Archadina. Once inside the fortress, they killed the mercenary leaders and convinced moderates among the population to join them. When they returned to meet with Marcellus, however, the Roman deserters among the garrison retook control. Unfortunately for them, the mercenary troops decided to treat with the Romans. A mercenary leader, a Spaniard named Moericus, allowed Marcellus to secretly land troops at the walls near the harbor

entrance. They launched an attack on Archadina that drew reserves from the island, and Marcellus landed an amphibious force that seized the defenses there. That broke the siege, for the Syracusans in Archadina opened the gates. Marcellus appropriated the royal treasury but allowed his soldiers to plunder the city at will, for they had waited three years for this victory. During this pillaging a Roman soldier killed Archimedes, perhaps on Marcellus' order and almost certainly with his blessing.

Results

The fall of Syracuse did not mean an end to fighting on the island of Sicily, however, for that continued another year. Carthage reinforced their garrison in Agrigentum about the time that Marcellus retired to Rome, and that force raided the countryside, striking at whatever Roman forces and towns they could. Their looting did nothing to endear them to the local population, who increasingly turned to the Romans. It was internecine struggle between the Carthaginians and their Numidian allies that spelled their doom, however, for the Numidians conspired with Marcellus' replacement M. Valerius Laevinus. He opened the gates of Agrigentum and the Romans slaughtered the garrison, although Epicydes managed to escape. That ended the Sicilian resistance, for other towns gave up rather than face capture and sacking. Laevinius then focused his energies on getting Sicilian agriculture productive again, so corn supplies would be available for Rome. The entire island of Sicily from that point was a Roman province, and the Carthaginian plan to capture the island as a way station for supplying their forces under Hannibal in the Italian peninsula came to naught. Although Hannibal continued to rampage around Italy until 205 B.C., he was effectively cut off from supplies or reinforcements from home, meaning his expedition would inevitably be a failure.

References: Brian Caven, *The Punic Wars* (London: Weidenfeld and Nicolson, 1980); T. A. Dorey, and D. R. Dudley, *Rome against Carthage* (Garden City, NY: Doubleday, 1972); Gilbert Charles Picard, *The Life and Death of Carthage* (New York: Taplinger, 1969); Plutarch, *Makers of Rome*, trans. Ian Scott-Kilvert (New York: Penguin, 1965).

CARTHAGE

DATE: 149–146 B.C.
LOCATION: near modern Tunis, Tunisia.

FORCES ENGAGED:

Roman: 80,000 infantry, 4,000 cavalry.
Commanders: Manius Manilius, later
Scipio Aemilianus.
Carthaginian: inside the city: undetermined.
Commander: Hasdrubal of Numidia.
Mobile force: 25,000–30,000 troops.
Commander: Hasdrubal.

IMPORTANCE:

The capture and destruction of the city of Carthage
ended the Third Punic War, finally destroying that
nation's power.

Historical Setting

For many years two powers slowly grew in strength and ambition, one on the southern coast of the central Mediterranean, the other directly north on the Italian peninsula. Carthage grew wealthy by the sea, her ships trading from Spain in the west to Lebanon and Egypt in the east. Her income allowed her to hire the best mercenaries in the world, primarily from colonies she established in Iberia. Rome, on the other hand, grew strong through the hardiness of her farmer citizenry, upon which rested the city's economic and military strength. They coexisted peacefully until 254 B.C., when a dispute over the island of Sicily brought about the First Punic War. After

twenty-four years of fighting the Romans prevailed, although both sides were seriously weakened. After twenty-four years of peace they began fighting again, this time in a dispute over allies in Spain. The Second Punic War lasted seventeen years, with the great Carthaginian Hannibal rampaging through Italy but unable to capture Rome itself. Rome again prevailed, when Scipio invaded Carthaginian territory and forced Hannibal to return to defend his homeland. After the Roman victory at Zama in 202 B.C. Carthage was forced to surrender her navy and pay a heavy indemnity.

Under the leadership of Hannibal, who proved to be as talented an administrator as he was a commander, the indemnity was paid well ahead of schedule and Carthage once again focused on trade. The city-state began once more to strengthen and grow wealthy, for the land she possessed, unlike today's Tunisia, was among the most productive farmland of its age. Although Hannibal was forced through political pressure to flee Carthage and die in exile, his home city scrupulously followed the terms of the peace Rome had imposed in 201. Fifty-two years of peace, however, was not a guarantee of avoiding another war with Rome.

The Numidian King Masinissa, whose country abutted Carthage to the west, indirectly provoked the Third Punic War. Through his alliance with Rome in the previous war, he was able to gain permission to reacquire lands Carthage had taken from Numidia. Since Carthage was originally established on Numidian land and with its cooperation, Masinissa could theoretically have occupied all of the territory Carthage controlled. Rather than attract too much attention from Rome, the Numidian king reclaimed small pieces of territory at a time when Rome was occupied in other parts of the Mediterranean world. In 155 B.C. Carthage complained to Rome about their ally's acquisitions, but received little satisfaction. Three years later Rome sent an embassy to investigate, the leading member of which was the senator Cato. Seeing the renewed bounty Carthage

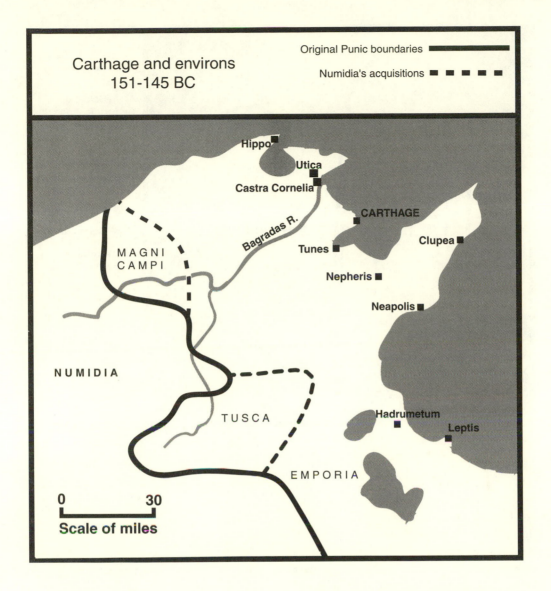

Carthage and environs
151–145 BC

Original Punic boundaries
Numidia's acquisitions

Hippo
Utica
Castra Cornelia
Bagradas R.
CARTHAGE
MAGNI CAMPI
Tunes
Clupea
Nepheris
Neapolis
NUMIDIA
TUSCA
Hadrumetum
Leptis
EMPORIA

0   30
Scale of miles

enjoyed, Cato feared they could yet again challenge Rome's position and from the day he returned home Cato argued with all his might that Carthage had to be destroyed.

Within Carthage, political factions struggled. In 151 a strong democratic party that took an aggressive stance expelled those citizens who favored cooperation and perhaps even union with Numidia from the city. Carthaginian complaints to Rome grew more strident as their rejections of Masinissa's envoys grew more insulting. Masinissa also sent appeals to Rome, pressing his claims. In 151 a Carthaginian army under their leader Has-

drubal attacked Numidia, but was defeated and after being besieged in their camp was virtually destroyed by starvation. That violation of the peace terms, as well as Cato's oratory in the Senate, convinced the Roman government military action was necessary. Hasdrubal, however, was evicted from power in Carthage and emissaries were sent to beg forgiveness on any terms to avoid war. An army had been dispatched by the time the embassy arrived, and they gave the Senate a virtual blank check to avert conflict.

The Senate demanded that their army should be allowed to do anything it wished, all

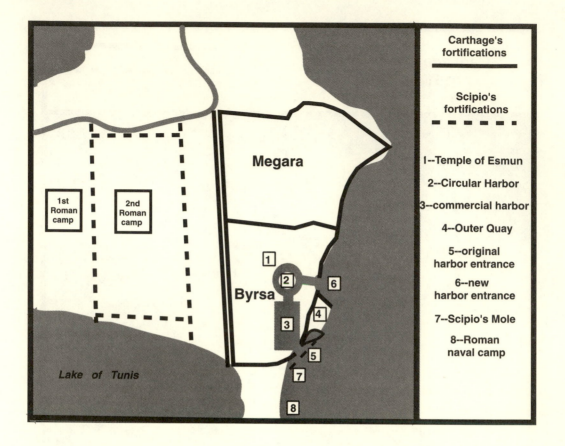

Carthage's fortifications

Scipio's fortifications

1--Temple of Esmun

2--Circular Harbor

3--commercial harbor

4--Outer Quay

5--original harbor entrance

6--new harbor entrance

7--Scipio's Mole

8--Roman naval camp

Megara

Byrsa

1st Roman camp

2nd Roman camp

Lake of Tunis

territory and possessions of Carthage to become Roman-controlled, and 300 hostages surrendered. The ambassadors agreed to this total surrender, a *deditio in fidem*. In return for their surrender, Rome guaranteed the Carthaginians freedom, their own laws, nominal control over all their territory, and possession of personal and public property. Unfortunately, the arrival of the army brought even more difficult conditions. The Roman commander Manius Manilius obliged the city to surrender all its weapons of war; they did. Reportedly armor and weapons for 200,000 men were turned over to the Romans, as well as 2,000 catapults. One final condition was unacceptable: the demand that the city of Carthage be destroyed and all the inhabitants removed inland. "Whenever you look on the sea, you remember the great fleets you once had, the spoils you captured, the harbours into which you brought them, to fill your dockyards and arsenals" (Appian, quoted in Dorey and Dudley, *Rome against Carthage*, p. 161). Carthage responded by declaring war on Rome.

The Siege

Carthage could not hope to take the war to Rome, only to force the Romans away from their capital. Carthage was the best-fortified city of its day, completely walled for its 21-mile perimeter and with access to the sea for resupply. The city was divided into northern and southern halves (Megara and Byrsa respectively). In spite of the earlier surrender of weapons, the citizens began producing new swords, spears, shields, javelins, and catapults at a prodigious rate. The women of the city cut their hair to serve as rope for the catapults. In their desperate situation, the Carthaginian government pardoned Hasdrubal and he took command of an army of 25,000 to 30,000 outside the city, based in the province of Byzacena to the south and southwest. The main city there, Nepheris, dominated the supply route to the farmland beyond.

Rome had 80,000 infantry and 4,000 cavalry on site, with the port city of Utica (which had surrendered without a fight) just to the northwest to serve as a base. They had no siege engines, however, and three direct assaults against the western walls proved disastrous. A foray across the Lake of Tunis to gather wood ran into serious Carthaginian cavalry opposition, but ultimately sufficient wood was gathered to build two rams. The Romans had some success against the southern fortifications, but the defenders rebuilt the walls, then sallied to destroy the rams. As the summer of 149 grew hotter, the Roman camp between the lagoons became too unhealthy, so they relocated to the southern end of the city. Roman ships anchored there to provision the army, but they were almost completely devastated by Carthaginian fire ships. By year's end the Romans had made little progress.

In 148 B.C. Manilius changed his strategy somewhat. He moved his camp from south of Carthage to the northern flank. Rather than press the siege he instead gathered supplies and made plans to attack Nephiris, where Hasdrubal's force was based. On Manilius' staff was the young Scipio Aemilianus, adopted grandson of the Scipio Africanus who had won glory in the Second Punic War. He advised against the Nephiris attack but was overruled. When Manilius was on the verge of defeat at the hands of the Carthaginian cavalry commander, Himilco Phameas, Scipio's timely arrival with reinforcements covered the Roman retreat. He then played a key diplomatic role. Masinissa's offer of assistance early in the conflict had been brusquely rebuffed; now the Romans needed all the help they could get. Masinissa invited Scipio to join the Roman delegation visiting him. When they arrived, they found Masinissa dead (he was in his eighties) and his three sons awaiting Scipio, who was

charged with choosing the successor. He chose all three: one to rule in the palace, one as minister of foreign affairs, one as minister of justice, each according to his talents. Scipio brought Foreign Minister Gulussa with him back to the Roman camp, along with a large cavalry force.

The arrival of Numidian reinforcements had a profound effect on Himilco Phameus, who perhaps sensed a change in the winds and defected to the Romans. That was the one high point of 148 for the Roman campaign. Manilius had decided to attack other Carthaginian cities both to keep his army busy and to allow them some booty to maintain their morale. These attacks had mixed success and Carthage even spared some manpower to aid at the siege of Hippo and some money for an uprising in Macedonia. With Roman fortunes at a low ebb, Scipio campaigned successfully in Rome for the command appointment; the people overwhelmingly backed the Scipio name, and he seemed to be in the mold of his adopted grandfather. Scipio took charge in the spring of 147.

He arrived to confront a crisis. Manilius had gained some success against the Megara section of the city, but his men had been cut off and morale was low. Scipio went to work, expelling the multitude of camp followers and focusing the army on its task: no rewards without victory. In the meanwhile, Hasdrubal was recalled to take charge of the city's defenses, leaving Diogenes (probably a Greek mercenary) in charge of the mobile force. Scipio launched an attack on Megara with early success, but withdrew under pressure. Hasdrubal responded by concentrating his force in Byrsa, then torturing Roman prisoners on the walls. This was intended to stiffen his troops' defensive resolve, but it instead motivated the Romans. Even with Megara's defenses lightened, Scipio realized that an assault on Byrsa was necessary, since the harbor was there. He spent the summer building fortifications: a series of palisaded ditches with sharpened stakes at the bottom, a wall facing the city with regularly spaced observation towers, and a four-story tower in the center. This completely isolated Carthage from landward approaches.

Scipio next began attempts to block off Carthage's seaward supplies. He began building a mole across the mouth of the harbor. The Carthaginians responded by digging a new outlet to the sea due east from their circular harbor. They also began building ships out of whatever material they could find. When both fleet and outlet were complete they sallied, but inexplicably did not attack the empty Roman ships. When they finally mounted an assault on the third day, the Romans were ready and drove them back. Unfortunately, a bottleneck in the new outlet kept many Carthaginian ships exposed, and the Roman ships dealt with them harshly. Scipio then assaulted the outer quay protecting the commercial harbor, bringing in catapults and rams. This strategy suffered a setback when a night attack from the city destroyed most of them, but Scipio patiently rebuilt them and constructed fortifications as well. He finally managed to breach the walls, then breach them again after the first repair.

Scipio maintained pressure on the city but could not insert his men through the breach. He spent the remainder of 147 capturing what towns still remained loyal to Carthage, and defeated their mobile force at Nephiris after a twenty-two-day siege. That left the city of Carthage completely alone, with no source of supply. This provoked an offer to negotiate from Hasdrubal, but he would not concede to Scipio's demand that the city be razed. In the spring of 146 Scipio invoked the Carthaginian gods to abandon the city, then he launched his final assault. It came from the weakened walls near the outer quay and this time the Romans did break through. Hasdrubal set the harbor buildings alight but it did not slow the Romans down. What did slow them was the sack of the temple of Apollo, whose golden dome proved too inviting to the soldiers. When reinforcements entered the fray, the slow work of reducing the Byrsa citadel proceeded. Tall houses along narrow lanes proved to be individual fortresses, and the fighting was house-to-house, room-to-room, hand-to-hand for six days. Scipio finally ordered the houses burned to allow easier passage, and many noncombatants died in the conflagration. That proved the final blow to Carthaginian resistance. On the seventh day they surrendered wholesale, 50,000 men, women, and children giving themselves up to slavery. Hasdrubal and his family, along with 900 Roman deserters, were all that remained in the temple of Esmun. He did not display the valor of his earlier namesakes, but crawled to Scipio begging mercy as the deserters decided to die in the flames of the temple. Seeing his dishonor, Hasdrubal's wife called out to him: "'Wretch!' she screamed, in a voice which raised itself above the universal din, 'is it thus you seek to save your own life while you sacrifice ours? I can not reach you in your own person, but I kill you hereby in the persons of your children.'" (Abbott, *History of Hannibal*, pp. 292–293). She stabbed his two sons, threw them into the flames, then dived in after them.

Results

Scipio rewarded his men with time to plunder the city at their leisure. That done, the remainder of the city was set ablaze and burned for ten days. The city-state of Carthage became the Roman province of Africa, of which a new Carthage built and settled by Romans was the capital. As the original city burned, however, Scipio wept. His tutor, the historian Polybius, spoke to him. "'Is this not a splendid sight?' He grasped his hand and said: 'A splendid sight indeed, Polybius, and yet I am in fear—I know not why—that some day the same order will be given to destroy my own country'" (Appian, quoted in Dorey and Dudley, *Rome against Carthage*, p. 174).

Control of the North African farmland provided the storehouse of grain for Rome for the next several centuries. Not until the Vandals conquered the region in the fifth century A.D.

did it cease being Rome's granary. It became so once again, however, when Belisarius captured the province for the Eastern Emperor Justinian a century later.

References: Jacob Abbott, *History of Hannibal of Carthage* (New York: Harper & Brothers, 1876); T. A. Dorey, and D. R. Dudley, *Rome against Carthage* (Garden City, NY: Doubleday, 1972); Gilbert Charles Picard, *The Life and Death of Carthage,* trans. Dominique Collon (New York: Taplinger, 1969).

NUMANTIA

DATE: 134–133 B.C.
LOCATION: on the Duero River, near present-day Soria in northeastern Spain.

FORCES ENGAGED:
Roman: 60,000 legionnaires. Commander: Scipio Aemilianus.
Celtiberian: 4,000 troops. Commander: Avarus.

IMPORTANCE:
The fall of Numantia marked the end of organized Celtic resistance to the Roman occupation of Spain.

Historical Setting

The Roman Republic first showed an interest in Iberia in the wake of the First Punic War. Iberia had long been the major source of mercenaries for the Carthaginian army, as well as a source of natural resources. For a time Carthage controlled the southern part of the peninsula and Rome the upper part near the Pyrennees. The Second Punic War began over a border dispute in Iberia, and in the wake of Rome's victory at Zama all of Iberia fell under Roman sway. Unfortunately, the inhabitants, a mixture of Celts and local populations, were fiercely independent and resisted Roman rule at every turn.

The First Celitiberian War was fought in the years 181–178 B.C. Roman forces under the leadership of Tiberius Gracchus subdued many of the tribes, and he developed a reputation for fairness in dealing with his defeated enemies. Until 155 the region remained fairly peaceful, as the Romans consolidated their hold on the coastal regions and the interior tribes recovered from the war. In 154 the Lusitani (of modern Portugal) attacked Roman territory but in 151 they were defeated by the Roman Sulipicius Galba. He offered them terms of surrender that they accepted; he then slaughtered 8,000 men who had given up their weapons. This act of treachery was unfortunately not uncommon, for most officials sent to Spain had little desire to be there and faithlessness in their dealing with the Celtiberians was a regular practice.

Along with the Lusitanian uprising, the Aravaci tribe of northeastern Iberia also made war against the Romans. They joined with the Lusitanian leader Viriathus and for a few years made life miserable for successive Roman officials, until the consul Q. Serivlius Caepio bribed two of Viriathus' officers to assassinate him in 139. The Aravaci continued their resistance after Viriathus' death. Their main city was Numantia, on the Duero River. When the Third Celtiberian War broke out in 143, the Romans attempted to reduce Numantia by siege. Because the city was located on steep bluffs overlooking the river and garrisoned by aggressive warriors, the Romans had no luck. Quintus Pompeius Metellus was the first to try in 143, and all he could achieve was an agreement to leave the city independent. He violated that agreement in 139, and the Numantines appealed to the Roman Senate for justice. They got none. Pompeius was removed and replaced by Marcus Popilius Lenatis. He made no headway against the city either, so was succeeded by Caius Hostlius Mancinus, who ordered a number of assaults on the city, all of which were repulsed. His army was ambushed and he was obliged to sign a treaty very favorable to the Numantines.

The Senate in Rome rejected that treaty and in 136 another commander tried to take the city, then another in 135. Increasingly dissatisfied with the progress in Iberia, the Senate finally gave in to public demand to reappoint Scipio Aemilianus Africanus to the consulship. He was the victor over the Carthaginians in the Third Punic War and captor of the city of Carthage itself in 146. If anyone could overcome the strong defenses of Numantia, he would be the man.

Scipio was indeed the man for the job, but he had obstacles to overcome before he confronted Numantia. The army's morale was extremely low, and getting recruits to go to Iberia was difficult. The Celtiberian guerrilla tactics frustrated most Roman soldiers, so veterans had little desire to reenlist. As the countryside had been fought over continuously for decades, and the population was tribal rather than urban, potential recruits could not be lured by the promise of plunder, for almost none existed. Scipio had to raise an army on his reputation, and he managed to amass a force of 20,000 Romans. This was expanded by a further 40,000 allies and mercenaries, mainly locally recruited but also including cavalry from Numidia in North Africa.

Scipio's first task was to whip his army into shape. He drove his new recruits and the troops he inherited upon his arrival in Iberia, making them march, dig in, and then march some more. He hardened their bodies and their spirits, and occasional skirmishes with Iberian tribes enhanced their morale while decreasing that of the locals. In the fall of 134 he was ready. He marched to Numantia and began encircling it. Knowing the Numantines' vaunted aggressiveness, he decided to neutralize their fighting spirit by not letting them fight. He would not storm the city, but lock it up and starve it out.

The Siege

Scipio established two camps immediately upon his arrival at Numantia, and over the course of the siege he set up five more. Between the camps he built a wall, ultimately with seven towers interspersed along it. The walls were 10 feet high, and from the towers Roman archers and slingers could hit targets within the city. Where the Romans could not build a wall because of a swamp, Scipio had a dam constructed to back up the water flow, which created a lake between his walls and those of Numantia. The Duero, which had protected the city, now encircled it. At the river's entry and exit points Scipio had towers constructed on both banks, between which was strung a cable. Dangling from the cable were beams with sharp blades embedded in them, hanging into the water, to block both boats and swimmers. The Numantines were well known for their ability to swim the river, but now their only points of egress were blocked. Further, Scipio had his men build walls of contravallation, to defend against any relief force.

The defenders grew increasingly hungry and frustrated with the inaction. Only once did they attempt a sally, and it was easily repulsed. One of the leading Numantine warriors, Rhetogenes, led a small party over the walls, down the river, and through the barricade. They went to their fellow tribesmen for aid, but the Aravaci were too fearful of Roman power to join the conflict. Rhetogenes then went to the Lutians, where he got a more positive response from the younger warriors of the tribe. The older citizens counseled against aid, however, and they warned Scipio of the planned relief. Scipio left a holding force at Numantia and marched to Lutia and surrounded it. He demanded and received the 400 young men who responded to Rhetogenes, then cut off their hands so they could offer no assistance. He then resumed his siege at Numantia.

Seeing his hope of aid gone, the Numantine leader Avarus sent envoys to negotiate with Scipio. Thy offered to surrender in return for their city's liberty. Scipio refused, demanding unconditional surrender. When the envoys returned to the city with Scipio's response, the population did not believe their report. Thinking the envoys had cut a separate deal, the people killed them.

Unable to sally and unwilling to surrender, the Numantines starved. Anything that could be used for food was consumed, even the bodies of their own dead. There are reports of some people killing weaker citizens for consumption, rather than waiting for them to die. Disease soon compounded the starvation process, and the few remaining citizens began considering conceding to Scipio's demands. Rather than face the shame of such an outcome, many of the survivors chose death over dishonor, killing their families and then themselves. The last survivors surrendered to Scipio, but only after setting their city ablaze.

Results

Sources differ on the length of the siege, some saying eight months and others sixteen. Late summer 133 B.C. is the generally accepted time of the surrender. Upon receiving the surrender of the remnants of the population, Scipio ordered the ruins of the city leveled. For a cost of virtually no casualties of his own, Scipio removed the Numantine threat from Roman occupation of Iberia. By the time of the Third Celtiberian War the Aravaci had been a serious local power; after Numantia's fall what resistance remained was scattered.

In 77 B.C. another Iberian rising challenged Roman power in the Numantia area, and the general who suppressed it was Pompey, one of the Triumvirate that was instrumental in Julius Caesar's rise to power. Caesar later was appointed consul in Iberia and in order to enhance his own military and political reputation, he raised a local force and conquered Galicia, the last holdout of Celtic resistance in the peninsula. It was that conquest, in 59 B.C., which finally secured Roman rule over all Iberia.

References: Richard Herm, *The Celts* (New York: St. Martin's, 1976); Christopher Mackay, "Spain—Roman Policy," www.geocities.com/Athens/Delphi/3579/numantia.html; Vezio Melegari, *The Great Military Sieges* (New York: Crowell, 1972); H. H. Scullard, *Scipio Africanus: Soldier and Politician* (Ithaca, NY: Cornell University Press, 1970).

ALESIA

DATE: July–October 52 B.C.
LOCATION: Gaul, near modern Alise-Ste.-Reine, France.

FORCES ENGAGED:

Roman: approximately 70,000 men. Commander: Julius Caesar.
Gallic: reportedly 80,000 infantry and 15,000 cavalry. Commander: Vercingetorix.
Relief force: reportedly 240,000 infantry and 8,000 cavalry. Commander: unknown.

IMPORTANCE:

Caesar's victory established Roman dominance in Gaul for the ensuing 500 years. It also enhanced his political reputation, leading to his invasion of the Italian Peninsula.

Historical Setting

In 60 B.C. Julius Caesar entered into a political alliance with the two most powerful men in Rome, Crassus and Pompey, forming the "Triumvirate." The three ruled the Roman Republic together while at the same time each tried to maneuver himself into a position of dominance. In order to do this, wealth and political influence were necessary, but military experience and army support were vital. Crassus had experience, making himself famous by crushing the Spartacus slave uprising. He then assumed the governorship of Syria so he could gain more laurels and wealth in a war against the Parthians. He died trying. Caesar took the position of governor of Cisalpine and Transalpine Gaul (northern Italy and southern France), where he hoped to gain the military and financial power he needed.

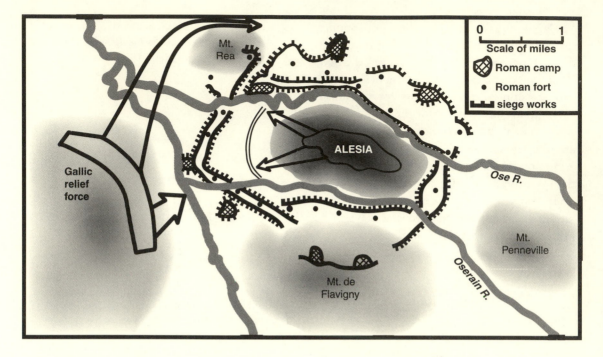

Caesar began fighting almost immediately: between 58 to 53 B.C. he campaigned against tribes of Gauls (the Roman term for the population of northwestern Europe/France; they called themselves Celts) throughout modern France and across the Rhine into Germany. His string of victories brought leadership experience while he enriched himself with untold pillage. He established a strong Roman presence in the region of modern Belgium by the spring of 53, when he defeated the Nervii and Belgae tribes. Caesar then left for northern Italy to reinforce his political contacts.

Those victories did not awe many Gauls, but they began to realize that as long as they practiced their traditional internecine warfare they would never defeat Rome's power. In 53 B.C. the tribes finally rallied around a single leader, Vercingetorix, chieftain of the Arverni. Forging a Gallic coalition was a virtually impossible feat, and it is a tribute to Vercingetorix's personality and leadership characteristics. Dozens of tribes and literally hundreds of thousands of people swore allegiance to him, including many Caesar had thought were securely loyal. Vercingetorix organized and

trained the Gallic warriors to a level they had never before attained, then launched his first offensive against Cenabum (modern Orleans) in late 53 B.C. After capturing the town, he slaughtered the entire Roman population and took control of Rome's major grain cache in Gaul. Hearing of these events, Caesar realized that the entire Roman position above the Alps was in danger. In January 52 he returned from Italy to his headquarters in Provence.

From Provence Caesar marched his troops north to Belgica (modern Belgium), joined his legions there, then countermarched to attack Cenabum on the Loire River. He recaptured the city (the source of the current rebellion), then divided his army, marching southward while sending a sizable force under Labienus to secure northern Gaul. All of this marching and fighting took place in the late winter months, a factor Vercingetorix used to his advantage. He commanded the destruction of every bit of food and forage that was available along Caesar's assumed line of march, out to a distance of a day's march. This was a brilliant strategy, and Caesar soon felt its effects. To make matters worse, Caesar's primary ally in Gaul, the

Aedui (on whom he had depended for food), began showing signs of disloyalty. Some leaders convinced the tribe that the Romans had been ravaging the countryside and killing Aedui hostages. Caesar intercepted a column of 10,000 Aedui who had been marching to reinforce the Romans before being persuaded to join Vercingetorix. When Caesar produced the hostages that had supposedly been killed, the rabble-rousers fled and the remainder of the force joined with the Romans.

Caesar next besieged the town of Avaricum (modern Bourges) in March 52, capturing the town before Vercingetorix could arrive to relieve it. With refilled Roman supply wagons, he next attacked and captured Gergovia, Vercingetorix's capital. Although he laid siege in April and May he could not live off the land, for the countryside surrounding the town had been stripped of supplies, which were now stockpiled inside the fortress. Desperate to take the town before a relief force could arrive, Caesar ordered an assault that cost him more than 700 casualties, including almost fifty centurions. The defeat and the lack of supplies forced him to retreat. Marching north he joined Labienus, who had just captured Lutetia (Paris); together they aimed toward Provence. Vercingetorix was determined that they would not reach it.

The Siege

Accurately predicting Caesar's intent, Vercingetorix withdrew his army of 80,000 infantry and 15,000 cavalry into the fortress town of Alesia (Alise-Ste.-Reine), near the source of the Seine River. He also sent a cavalry force north to harass and delay the Romans. They engaged Caesar's Germanic auxiliary cavalry at Vingeanne; the Gauls had the worst of it, losing some 3,000 men, but they bought Vercingetorix time to herd all the region's cattle into Alesia.

The town sat atop an oval mesa-like hill,

Mount Auxois. The flat top fell off on steep sides, virtually impossible to climb. The city walls were almost an extension of the mountainside. Running east to west above and below the town were the Oze and Ozerain rivers. Vercingetorix had a trench dug on either side of the hill running north-south between the rivers, making an approach to the city almost as difficult as an assault. With his 95,000 soldiers, Vercingetorix was sure Caesar could not possibly harm him.

Caesar's army consisted of 40,000 Roman legionnaires, about 5,000 Germanic cavalry, and about 15,000 auxiliary troops of one type or another. He began the siege sometime in July 52. The Romans dug a trench completely around the hill stretching 10 miles in circumference. The Roman soldier was used to digging: he had done so on every day of every campaign while he had been in the army. It was standard procedure to dig a trench and set up a palisade around camp every evening. The Alesia trenchwork was much more elaborate. It was 15 to 20 feet wide with a 12-foot-high wall and observation towers every 130 feet. To discourage sorties against their lines, the Romans dug more trenches at the foot of the mesa in which they drove sharpened stakes. Interspersed with foot-long wooden blocks with protruding iron rods, these were designed to slow attackers during the day and to disrupt any night foray.

Vercingetorix had dispatched riders just prior to the investment, ordering them to rally the tribes to his aid. If the siege went on too long, the Romans could easily find themselves fighting back Gallic relief attacks while attempting to maintain their siege. Caesar ordered the digging of a line of circumvallation—a second set of trenches and walls outside the first. These stretched for 14 miles and would be a defensive line against a relieving force. Although giving the maximum defensive strength, it had the negative aspect of potentially having his besieging army becoming besieged themselves.

In October the relief force arrived, numbering perhaps 240,000 infantry and another 8,000 cavalry. (Although ancient sources often exaggerate enemy strength, modern historians accept these numbers as fairly accurate.) Caesar gathered whatever food was within foraging distance into his lines and continued the siege. The relief force attacked twice, using ladders and sandbags against the outer trenches, while Vercingetorix led sorties out of Alesia in support. The Romans with difficulty managed to beat back all assaults. The third attack almost succeeded. The Gauls discovered what they thought to be the weakest point of the Roman position, the northwest corner of the outer line. They approached at night, screening themselves behind a hill all morning. When a diversionary attack shifted Roman attention to the south, the northern attack hit. Multiple waves of Gauls pressed the assault, gaining ground then turning the attack over to the next, fresher line of men. The Romans were pressed to the breaking point when the German cavalry struck the Gallic rear. That broke the assault and the Gauls fled. At the height of the battle Caesar led the last reserve into the fight, wearing a bright red cloak so his men knew he was with them.

Food supplies in Alesia were almost gone. Vercingetorix had expelled all civilians and the wounded, but Caesar forced them to stay at the base of the hill, starving. Vercingetorix finally admitted defeat, giving himself to his subordinates to kill him or turn him over to the Romans. The entire force surrendered.

Results

Although the garrison fell into Roman hands, most of the relief force scattered and returned to their homes. Final casualty figures are unknown, but there were enough prisoners for each Roman soldier to be awarded one as a slave; each officer received several. Vercingetorix was taken in chains to Rome, where he was a showpiece in Caesar's triumphal parade. He languished in a cell for six years before he was finally executed.

After Alesia there were no more serious uprisings against Roman rule in Gaul. Caesar in six years succeeded in establishing Roman power in the province, and Gaul proved to be one of Rome's most profitable acquisitions. It also stretched the limits of Roman civilization well past the Italian peninsula. "The siege of Alesia decided the fate of Gaul and the character of French civilization. It added to the Roman Empire a country twice the size of Italy and opened the purses and markets of 5,000,000 people to Roman trade. It saved Italy and the Mediterranean world for four centuries from barbarian invasion; and it lifted Caesar from the verge of ruin to a new height of reputation, wealth, and power" (Durant, *Caesar and Christ*, p. 177). This may overstate the Gallic threat to Italy; even organized behind Vercingetorix they probably would not have maintained a united effort had they won at Alesia. There were too many tribal feuds for that to happen. Still, it could well have placed Celtic society in northern Italy, where one had been less than a century earlier. Even a disorganized invasion could have wrought immense havoc throughout the Italian peninsula. The great Roman general Marius had built a personal army to turn back a similar invasion in 102 B.C.; perhaps another such leader would have arisen. It probably would not have been Julius Caesar, and the course of Roman history would have been radically altered.

Instead, Caesar was victorious, and his fame provoked the jealousy of the remaining member of the Triumvirate, Pompey. Illegally appointed to be the sole consul (there were normally two), Pompey demanded Caesar return to Rome without his army or be declared a traitor to the Republic. Caesar marched his legions into Italy, crossing the Rubicon River on 11 January 49 B.C. That brought an end to the Republic and laid the foundation for the empire.

References: Julius Caesar, *War Commentaries of Caesar*, trans. Rex Warner (New York: New American Library, 1960); Will Durant, *Caesar and Christ* (New York: Simon and Schuster, 1944); Christian Meier, *Caesar*, trans. David McLintock (New York: HarperCollins, 1995 [1982]); Donald O'Reilly, "Besiegers Besieged," *Military History* 9, no. 6, February 1993.

JERUSALEM

DATE: March–8 September 70.
LOCATION: central Israel.

FORCES ENGAGED:

Roman: 70,000 men. Commander: Titus.
Jewish: three factions: 15,000 men under Simon Bar-giora; 6,000 men under John of Gischala; 2,400 under Eleazar.

IMPORTANCE:

Roman capture and destruction of Israel's capital marked the beginning of the Jewish Diaspora.

Historical Setting

The Zealots were a revolutionary faction in Israel during the Roman occupation, active in the first century A.D. Although the Romans rarely did anything to hamper the Jews of Israel in the practice of their religion, the Roman worship of their own gods offended many Jews. The affront they felt to their faith, coupled with a series of harsh Roman rulers, set off a revolt that had ruinous consequences for the Jewish people.

The first mention of a popular leader resisting Roman rule is that of Judas of Galilee in A.D. 6/7. He preached resistance to the census ordered by the Romans, possibly the same one mentioned in the biblical book of Luke. He was killed in this revolt, and his death gave rise to the Zealots. They were politically active in opposing Roman rule and were fundamentalist in their interpretation of the Jewish Law. They followed the extremely conservative teachings of Shammai, a member of the Sanhedrin, the semi-governing body of interpreters of Jewish Law. Any Israelite who cooperated with Rome became a target of Zealot wrath. A small faction of the Zealots, the Sicarii (from *sica*, a dagger), became assassins, attacking not only Romans but Jews who cooperated with them. For a time the Zealots remained a religious faction preaching their conservative values, but they came to the fore in A.D. 41, when the Romans attempted to place a statue of the emperor in Jerusalem's temple. Zealots attacked a Roman patrol, and the Romans responded by violating a neighborhood synagogue. Such incidents could well have been blown out of proportion and used to inflame the population. Still, the uprisings remained limited until the appointment of Gessius Florus as procurator of Israel in A.D. 67.

Florus was unusually corrupt and made no attempt to take Jewish sensibilities into account in his actions. It is reported by Flavius Josephus (the only recorder of these incidents) that Florus provoked the Jews so he could bring in troops and use the disturbances as an excuse for plunder. Florus' high-handed activities, coupled with a division within the Jewish ranks over how to respond, led to violence. When the population of Jerusalem publicly jeered Florus, he let loose his legionnaires to ransack the city. He then provoked the people further by demanding that they welcome two arriving Roman cohorts; when the Jews did so and their actions were not fully appreciated, they again vented their vocal ire. Again the troops were set loose and fighting took place throughout the city. Angry Jewish forces occupied the temple and the Zealots began taking over the abandoned forts of Masada and Herodion, built decades earlier by King Herod, which still held sizable armories.

The leading citizens of Jerusalem saw the ultimate impossibility of defeating Rome and counseled moderation, but many of the religious

Titus destroys the Temple of Jerusalem, painting by Nicholas Poussin. (Nimitallah/Art Resource, NY)

leaders supported the rebellion. The area governor, Agrippa II, sent troops to Jerusalem, but they proved too few to recapture the city. When the rebels massacred a Roman garrison that had been granted safe passage out of the city, it was merely a matter of time before Rome exacted revenge. Throughout Israel the Zealots and their supporters seized the population centers, with only a few remaining in Roman control. The Roman legate in Syria, C. Cestius Gallus, marched to Israel with a legion and regained much of the countryside, but was not strong enough to besiege Jerusalem. He withdrew northward but was ambushed in Beth Horon pass; those Romans not killed fled, abandoning a large store of weapons. The Jews now held siege machinery and had received a major boost in confidence.

Any hope of a negotiated peace was gone, but the Zealots could not capitalize on their early success. Instead, they quarreled among themselves, to the point of combat, and did little to prepare themselves for a war against Rome. They were rebels, not soldiers, and the leadership and discipline necessary to train and prepare did not exist.

When word of the revolt reached Rome, Emperor Nero reinforced the military with troops under the command of Vespasian, a general who had proven his worth in campaigns in Britain. He reestablished Roman control over the countryside but hesitated to attack Jerusalem, not only owing to its difficulty but because of the power struggle in Rome that followed Nero's death in June 68. Finally Vespasian himself was named Caesar and returned to Rome, leaving his son Titus in command of operations against the Zealots. In the months that Vespasian waited for news from Rome, the Zealots had not used the time to improve the defenses of the city but continued to fight among themselves.

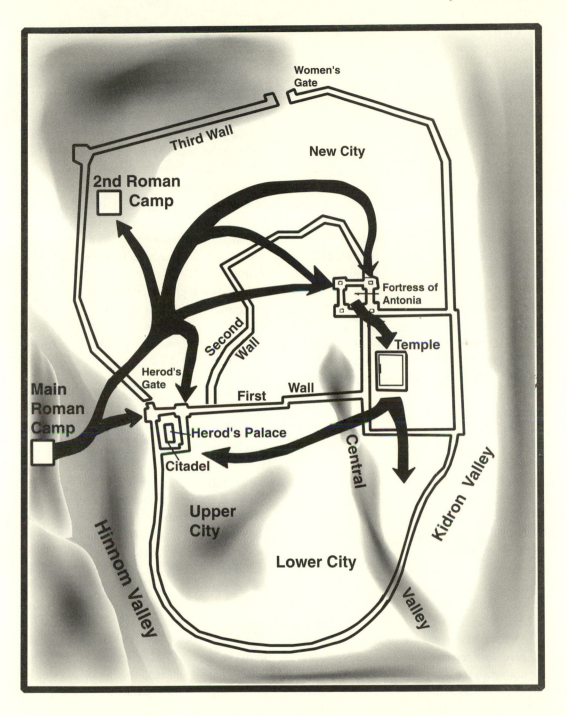

The Siege

Titus laid siege to Jerusalem in the spring of 70, with four legions and auxiliary troops on hand. He weakened the city's defense by allowing pilgrims to enter to celebrate Passover, then bottling them up inside to strain the food supply. Titus placed three of his legions on the western side of the city and the fourth opposite on the Mount of Olives. They were surprised by a sally from the city and lost heavily. Titus, rather than ordering an immediate assault, instead sent Flavius Josephus to negotiate with the defenders. Josephus had commanded the Jewish forces during the forty-seven-day siege of Jotapata in 67; after his capture he joined the Roman forces after prophesying Vespasian's accession to power. His writings are the primary contemporary source material for the Roman war in Palestine. His appeals to the defenders were in vain. A second sally, made by a number of Jews disguising themselves as turncoats, also killed a number of Romans and so boosted the defenders' morale that they began fighting among themselves again.

After a personal reconnaissance around the city walls in mid-May, Titus ordered the assault to begin with a ram pounding the city's recently completed third wall, on the northern part of the city's western face. That attack once again united the factions, but they could do little but retreat behind the second wall of the city when, after two weeks, the Roman battering ram completed its work. Titus established a new camp inside the third wall, then made plans for his next assault. The second wall, just west of the Fortress Antonia (the city's only fortress), fell after a mere four days' battering, although the Jews constantly counterattacked and harassed the Romans manning the ram. Once through the wall, the Zealots lured Roman soldiers into the narrow streets of the city and dealt them such severe punishment that Titus ordered his men out. Another pounding on the second wall created another breach several days later, after which Titus ordered the entire wall destroyed.

The Romans ceased attacking for a few days and Josephus resumed his fruitless appeals for negotiations. Titus ordered the construction of four siege towers near the Fortress Antonia, but well-executed undermining destroyed two of them and a "forlorn hope" attack set the other two afire. A council of war considered options on how to proceed against the Zealots. Although the food supply in the city was rapidly dwindling, secret passages out of Jerusalem allowed foraging parties to acquire

food and attack Roman detachments. Titus ordered a wall of circumvallation to stop this practice. The Roman soldier, who spent more time digging than probably any soldier in history, was exactly the means Titus needed to get this built quickly: it took but three days to surround Jerusalem with 4.5 miles of wall. Construction of four more siege towers also began.

The next Roman assault was aimed at Fortress Antonia. Rams on the siege towers began their pounding with minimal success, but a mine the Zealots had dug weeks earlier collapsed and created a breach in the fortress wall. A second wall, already built, greeted the Romans that attacked, and they failed in an attempt to scale it. Two nights later, however, a secret attack overpowered sleeping Zealot guards and the Romans were inside and racing for the temple, on the highest ground in the city. Fighting raged for hours around the temple, and Titus had to be content to hold Antonia.

Roman battering rams pounding on the temple walls made little progress in six days, but fighting along the walls resulted in fires that began to burn the temple itself. Titus apparently did not want to see the temple destroyed, but in the chaos of fighting the flames became unquenchable. The Romans swept past the ruined sanctuary into control of the northern half of the city, and Jewish resistance began to crumble. The lower city also was destroyed by fire, and the upper city, the southwestern corner, held out until a ramp was built that allowed the Romans access; during its construction, thousands of Jews surrendered, including some priests who surrendered many of the temple treasures to Titus. The city came completely under Roman control on 7 September 70, three weeks after the temple had been destroyed.

In the face of the Roman enemy, the defenders finally buried their differences and held fast even though conditions in the city grew progressively desperate. With their experience in siege warfare, however, the Romans made steady progress against the successive walls the

Jews defended, capturing them at the rate of one a month through the summer. In September the last of the city fell to Roman soldiers and was almost completely razed.

Results

The numbers of people killed during the siege are incredible: Josephus claimed 1.1 million, while the Roman historian Suetonius numbered casualties at 600,000. True, Jerusalem was a major city and was packed with pilgrims attending holy day services when the siege began, but many historians think the number reflects the casualties inflicted on all Jews in the entire campaign and not just in the siege. Certainly thousands were killed, sold into slavery, or kept prisoner to be sacrificed at the games for Roman sport. Jerusalem's fall certainly marked the beginning of the end of a Jewish homeland, for the Diaspora soon saw Jews spreading across the world as their political and religious capital was no more. A few Zealot holdouts kept up the fight for three more years, but Roman power was established until the forces of Islam swept through Palestine in the seventh century.

References: George C. Brauer, *Judaea Weeping* (New York: Crowell, 1970); Rupert Furneaux, *The Roman Siege of Jerusalem* (New York: David McKay, 1972); J. Alberto Soggin, *A History of Ancient Israel*, trans. John Bowden (Philadelphia: Westminster, 1984).

MASADA

DATE: 73–74.
LOCATION: southeast of Jerusalem on the shores of the Dead Sea.

FORCES ENGAGED:
Roman: X Legion. Commander: Flavius Silva.

Sicarii: 960 men, women, and children. Commander: Eleazar ben Yair.

IMPORTANCE:
Capture of the hill fortress of Masada ended final resistance against Roman occupation of Palestine.

Historical Setting

Conflict between imperial Rome and Palestine was probably inevitable, given the Jewish belief in a single God versus the polytheism of Rome. Although Roman practice was to allow fairly wide autonomy in conquered provinces, the rise of the emperor cults flew in the face of Jewish beliefs. Disbelieving in Juno, Hera, Apollo, and the rest could be allowed, but not rejection of the divinity of the emperors such as Caligula and Vespasian. The placing of idols in sacred areas of Jerusalem, along with the appointment of less-than-tolerant procurators, provoked a rebellion among the Jewish population of Palestine. This grew stronger when an ambush of Roman legions in the Beth Horon Pass northwest of Jerusalem gave the Jews an overly optimistic view of their chances against Rome's might.

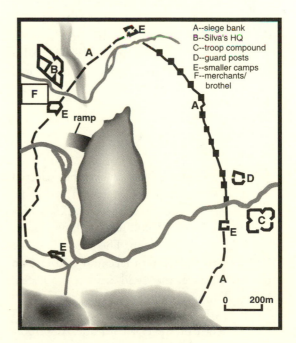

A--siege bank
B--Silva's HQ
C--troop compound
D--guard posts
E--smaller camps
F--merchants/ brothel

ramp

0   200m

The only thing that may have prevailed against the Roman army was a strongly unified Jewish leadership, but such did not exist. Only in the direst straits did any of the factions cooperate, and that led almost directly to the Roman capture of Jerusalem after an extended siege. One faction that was not present in Jerusalem was the Sicarii, an offshoot of the Zealots. The Sicarii, or "knife men," practiced assassination of anyone they deemed dangerous: Romans, Jews who aided Romans, or even Jews who did not actively fight the Romans. Soon after the conflict began in A.D. 66, the Sicarii seized the fortress atop the hill of Masada, a palace and defensive complex built a century earlier by Herod the Great. Little is known of their activities there while the rest of Palestine was being conquered. They certainly did nothing to aid their fellows during the siege of Jerusalem, like sending in extra manpower, harassing Roman lines of supply, and the like. Chief among their activities was raiding the countryside for supplies and punishing those they considered collaborators. At the village of En Geddi, over 700 women and children were killed for not living up to the Sicarii standards.

After Jerusalem fell, however, the Romans could focus all their attention on Masada, for the rest of the country was in their control. Still, it was almost a year before Flavius Silva marched his X Legion to Masada and initiated the final conquest in Palestine.

The Siege

Herod had chosen well when he selected Masada as an emergency retreat. Masada, translating as "mountain stronghold," is a mesa measuring 600 by 1,900 feet, with an area of some 23 acres on its top. The sheer sides rise 600 feet on the western face and 820 feet on the eastern face; the Dead Sea lies 1,300 feet below. The only approach to the top is up a "snake path," a narrow trail of switchbacks along the face on the Dead Sea side. A 20-foot-high wall was built around the perimeter bearing 38 towers, each 80 feet high. Two sumptuous living areas were constructed for the king, as well as barracks, storehouses, and large cisterns that allowed the garrison inside to hold out almost indefinitely.

Flavius Silva saw the impossibility of assaulting the fortress up the snake path, so began work on two projects. The first was to construct a 6-foot thick wall of contravallation that finally reached some 3 miles in length. Observation towers were built every 60 to 80 yards. Silva established his headquarters to the northwest, with camp followers settling themselves nearby. A subsidiary camp was established to the east and a smaller bivouac between Silva's camp and Masada, with others placed due east, north, and southwest of the hill. Observation posts to the east and south kept an eye out for attempted escapes from the fortress. The second major project was to begin building a ramp up the northwestern face. This was built up rather quickly, as the Sicarii had no real defensive weapons and could do little to slow the Roman progress. Although the Roman soldier was famous for his ability to handle earthmoving projects, the ramp was built by Jewish prisoners. A visitor to Masada today can still see the ramp and imagine the amount of labor involved in its construction. When the ramp was finally complete and the Romans were able to bring up their battering rams, the defenders' time was almost up.

What happened from the time of the initial assault until the final conquest of the fortress is a matter of intense speculation. The reason for this is that but one contemporary account exists, and its author is suspect. Josephus was a former general in the Jewish resistance to Rome, but after being captured at the siege of Jotapata he endeared himself to Vespasian, the Roman commander, by predicting his imminent rise to the position of Caesar. He traveled with the Roman army, advising them at the siege of Jerusalem. His account of the action, *The Jewish War*, was written over the space of some years in Rome, with the Masada tale being written perhaps seven years after the fact.

His ability to both survive and advance himself by playing to Roman vanity means that his account of the actions at Masada is more than a little suspect.

Josephus writes that when the ramp was finally complete, the Romans assaulted the fortress with rams, having previously bombarded the walls with their ballistae. The Sicarii could do little to stop the assault, but as the walls began to crumble they hastily built a wooden wall behind the breach and filled the intervening space with dirt and rubble. That delaying tactic lasted until the Romans set the back wall afire. None of this seems to be in dispute, but Josephus' account of the next several hours certainly is. With the breach virtually complete, the Romans stopped their assault, left their siege engines in place, and retreated down the ramp to spend the night; the final assault was to take place the following morning. During the night, the Sicarii leader Eleazar gave two stirring speeches to his people, announcing that the outcome of the battle was God's will, for the sinful Jews had lost His favor. Rather than be taken captive, paraded through Rome as objects of scorn, and have their women abused and their children enslaved, it would be best to rob the Romans of their victory by killing themselves. After burning their possessions, each man was to kill his own wife and children. Then, ten men chosen by lot would kill the men and one of the ten would kill the other nine. The lone survivor would then kill himself, being the only one who would suffer a horrific afterlife for committing the sin of suicide. All of this was done and when the Romans attacked the next morning they found a dead garrison.

In the 1960s, Professor Yigael Yadin undertook the first serious excavations at Masada and discovered evidence that some of Josephus' story was accurate. The ramp, of course, remained, and many of the physical features Josephus described were accurate. He even found a shard with the name Eleazar on it, possibly one of the lots cast before the mass killing. The Roman attack and Sicarii defense certainly occurred, but the details are questionable and many questions have no answer.

Why did the Romans stop their assault on the verge of victory? The breach apparently occurred late in the day, but they had experience in night fighting; the final assault at Jotapata in which Josephus was captured was conducted at night. How did Josephus know what was contained in Eleazar's oratory? He said that the Romans captured a handful of women after the battle who claimed to have listened in on the secret meeting attended only by the fighting men. How did the Roman sentries, placed on the ramp to guard against any escape or assault from the fortress, fail to see fires built for the destruction of the defenders' possessions or hear anything unusual that might have indicated a mass killing was taking place inside? Why destroy their possessions, but leave untouched Herod's armory with weaponry for 10,000 soldiers? These questions have no answers.

It is possible that the delay in the attack did not take place, that some of the Sicarii did indeed kill themselves and their families, and that some fires were deliberately set by the Jews in a last attempt to deny any loot to the Romans. Certainly parts of Josephus' story can be accepted, but on the whole there are too many gaps and inconsistencies to accept the entire tale.

Results

The fall of Masada signaled the last gasp of Jewish resistance to the Roman occupation of Palestine. Some of the Sicarii and other Zealots apparently escaped Jerusalem and Masada before the Roman capture of those two cities, for rumors of guerrilla activities in Egypt and Cyrenaica pop up shortly after the conquest, and no reports of any such action had been noted there beforehand. Those, however, were not the only Jews to leave Palestine, for the great Diaspora began in the wake of the Roman occupation and the destruction of the temple in Jerusalem.

Just as Jews around the world for centuries dreamed of "next year in Jerusalem," so did Masada take on special meaning once the State of Israel was created in 1948. It came to represent to Israelis not a symbol of suicide and futility, but of resistance at all costs to anyone who would again occupy their land. In impressive ceremonies on the mountain stronghold, members of the Israeli Defense Forces today swear to defend their homeland, to experience death before dishonor.

References: Shaye Cohen, "Masada: Literary Tradition, Archaeological Remains, and the Credibility of Josephus," *Journal of Jewish Studies* 33, Spring–Autumn 1982; Gaayla Comfeld, ed., *Josephus: The Jewish War* (Grand Rapids: Zondervan, 1982); Yigael Yadin, *Masada: Herod's Fortress and the Zealots' Last Stand* (New York: Random House, 1966); Yael Zerubavel, *Recovered Roots* (Chicago: University of Chicago Press, 1995).

AQUILEIA

DATE: 452.
LOCATION: in the modern province of Udine, northern Italy.

FORCES ENGAGED:
Hun: unknown. Commander: Attila.
Roman: unknown. Commander: unknown.

IMPORTANCE:
The Hun victory marked their final success in western Europe. The survivors of the ruined city fled to the Adriatic marshes, creating the city of Venice.

Historical Setting

The Huns were one of the myriad of tribes that rode out of central Asia, but little can be determined of their origin. Probably they were the Huing-nu, who failed in wars against the Chinese and turned (or were forced) westward.

Occasional early sources opine that they were the Nebroi mentioned by Herodotus as a semi-mythical people living on the fringes of territory controlled by the Scythians. Some of the earliest direct references come from clashes with the Goths around the area north of the Black Sea in the mid-fourth century A.D. The first Hun conquest was of the Alans, who were then used in the vanguard of Hun attacks against the Goths or emigrated into the Roman Empire. The Huns settled into Pannonia (roughly modern Slovenia) along the Adriatic coast.

By 432 the Huns were well established and a force to be reckoned with. Emperor Theodosius II paid tribute to the Hun leader Ruas and gave him a general's commission. Ruas' sons Bleda and Attila renewed the treaty and fought for Constantinople in campaigns against Persia. Attila grew tired of doing another's fighting and made war against the Eastern Romans. Between 441 and 443 he rampaged through the Balkans and defeated a Roman army outside Constantinople, but could not capture the city. He finally stopped upon receiving an increase in tribute. Attila killed his brother and, in 447, reopened his war against the Romans. Although turned back from Constantinople again, Attila did manage to gain a threefold increase in tribute and cession of the eastern bank of the Danube. Theodosius' successor stopped paying the tribute in 450, by which time the Huns were looking westward.

Attila hoped to split the attention of the Western Roman Empire between himself and the Vandals, who were making trouble in North Africa; further, he was invited to aid a Frankish chieftain in a succession struggle, so there seemed to be plenty of reason to march into Gaul. He crossed the Rhine north of modern-day Mainz with between 100,000 and 500,000 warriors, their families carrying supplies. The Huns and their auxiliaries advanced along a 100-mile-wide front, destroying everything in their path but Paris. The Roman general Aetius formed an army of Franks, Germans, and Alans, but could muster no more than half Attila's strength. In mid-June 451 the two armies fought at the site of modern-day Châlons, and Attila could not prevail. He retreated eastward, and western Europe was saved from Asian domination.

Aetius had hoped that he could cooperate with the Huns, using them against the Visigoth threat in Gaul. He therefore left the Alpine passes undefended and Attila marched his forces through them into northern Italy in 452. Attila had demanded the hand of Honoria, the Western Roman emperor's sister, along with much of the Western empire as a dowry; he was refused. The Huns appeared on the plains around Padua and laid siege to Aquileia, a city with a long history of sieges owing to its location on the road into and out of Italy into the rest of Europe.

The Siege

The city of Aquileia, owing to its location, was not only a pathway for invaders but also for trade, and it was a wealthy mercantile center in 452. Numerous sieges (all beaten back by the defenders) had given the city of Aquileia some experience in wall construction, and the Huns were not skilled in siegecraft. Like the rest of the Asian hordes that invaded Europe, they were horsemen and depended on speed and archery for their victories over enemies on open ground. Although the Huns had overcome a few cities in the past, such as Metz, many more had been bypassed on their campaigns. Attila coerced area engineers into his service, and soon possessed "a formidable train of battering rams, movable turrets, and engines, that threw stones, darts, and fire" (Gibbon, *Decline and Fall*, p. 1094).

Attila's machinery made little headway against the city's defenses, and he decided on a starvation strategy. For three months there was little action, and owing to a lack of supplies for his own army the Hun leader was on the verge of retreat when an omen changed his mind. As he was reconnoitering the walls one evening, he saw a stork fly out of the city, carrying its young. "He seized, with the ready penetration of a statesman, this trifling incident, which chance had offered to superstition; and exclaimed, in a loud and cheerful tone, that such a domestic bird, so constantly attached to human society, would never have abandoned her ancient seats, unless the towers had been devoted to impending ruin and solitude" (Gibbon, *Decline and Fall*, p. 1094).

Targeting the section of walls over which he had seen the stork fly, Attila recommitted his rams and soon breached the walls. The details of the ensuing battle are lost. The only commentary is that the Huns were so thorough in their destruction that for decades afterward the exact location of Aquileia was hard to determine.

Results

Apparently a number of the citizens of Aquileia were able to escape out the opposite side of the city walls and they fled through the marshes to the east for the islands off the coast. Fishing villages had long been established here, but the newcomers and their wealth built (according to legend) the port city of Venice, which because of its ultimate wealth and power, became a dominant economic, political, and military force throughout the Mediterranean.

Attila's forces also reduced the cities of Padua, Vicenza, Verona, Brescia, Bergamo, Pavia, and Milan. Aetius, whose army remained in Gaul, returned to face Attila, but the Huns were having problems. One of Attila's commanders had been defeated in Illyricum (northern Greece) and the Italian countryside proved to be disease-ridden and without supplies. Attila met with Pope Leo I outside Rome and, after an unrecorded discussion, turned the Huns northward and left Italy.

Attila died in 453. His sons fought for his throne while subject tribes revolted. The remnants of the Huns retreated northeast of the Danube, leaving rebelling tribes to their own devices. In the end the Huns proved to be little more than plunderers, raiding from one ripe target to the next, never settling down or building any cities. They accomplished little more than mass destruction. The Western Roman Empire, already in decline after the sack of Rome in 410, saw its hold on possessions outside the Italian peninsula weakening. The Gallic tribes paid little attention to the empire, other than to raid it, until it was reborn under Charlemagne in the eighth century.

References: Marcel Brion, *Attila: The Scourge of God* (New York: Robert McBride, 1929); J. B. Bury, *The Invasion of Europe by the Barbarians* (New York: Russell and Russell, 1963); Edward Gibbon, *The Decline and Fall of the Roman Empire* (New York: Heritage, 1946 [1776]); E. A. Thompson, *Romans and Barbarians* (Madison: University of Wisconsin Press, 1982).

ROME

DATE: 2 March 537–12 March 538.
LOCATION: on the Tiber River near Italy's central western coast.

FORCES ENGAGED:
Byzantine: 3,000 troops of various nationalities. Commander: Belisarius.
Visigoth: 50,000 troops. Commander: Vittigis.

IMPORTANCE:
Belisarius' successful defense of the city meant a Byzantine presence in Italy until the time of Charlemagne in the 800s.

Historical Setting

After a thousand years untouched by enemy hands, Rome fell to Alaric the Goth in 410. Having fallen once, it seemed that Rome could never defend itself again. Successive invaders from across the Alps pillaged the Italian penin-

sula and Rome. The Ostrogothic conquest in 455 put that population in control for the next seven decades. None of this had any real effect on the Roman Empire, however, for the Emperor Constantine had recentered it in Constantinople in 330. Even in what passed for an "empire" in Italy was controlled no longer from Rome, but from Ravenna. Thus, by the sixth century, "the glory that was Rome" had long since faded into fable.

Still, the name had power, and in Constantinople the Eastern Roman Emperor Justinian longed to reestablish single control over the old empire that had stretched from the Middle East to Spain. He possessed the necessary military power and ambition to accomplish this feat, but for some reason was determined to do it on the cheap. Luckily for Justinian, he had the services of one of the most talented generals of all time, Belisarius. Rising from the ranks, the young man had defeated successive enemies in Parthia and North Africa, and Justinian assigned him the task of reconquering Italy. Unfortunately, the emperor allowed him only 5,000 soldiers with which to accomplish this task. Units in the Byzantine military, inheriting a tradition begun by Marius in the old Roman Republic, were raised and maintained by generals rather than directly by the state. Loyalty was personal rather than national, and private armies were often the path to the throne. Although Belisarius never gave his emperor the slightest impression of ambition to rule, history made Justinian overly cautious. This can be the only reason he gave his top general so few men with which to accomplish so much.

Belisarius landed in Italy with Naples as his first target. He needed a good harbor to maintain his supply lines and Naples was the best in the neighborhood. After a month's siege he captured the city, and his men were none too restrained in their pillaging. Although Belisarius had hoped to keep damage and local hostility to a minimum, the news of Naples' fate convinced other Italian cities to surrender without a fight. In Rome, Pope Silverius invited the Byzantine army to occupy his city. Unfortunately, he did not first consult the Ostrogoths, whose army held it at the time. Still, the city fell without a fight, for the Ostrogothic King Theodatus was a weak leader too intent on personal pleasure. For his decision to flee rather than fight, Theodatus was killed by his own people and replaced by the more aggressive Vittigis.

Upon assuming the throne, Vittigis did not countermand the order, but instead consolidated his forces in the northern part of Italy around Ravenna. Before dealing with the Byzantines, he concluded a peace with the Franks (of modern France) to secure his rear. Then he aimed toward Rome. Although criticized for allowing the city to fall without a fight, Vittigis reminded his followers that Rome had never withstood a siege and Belisarius' tiny army could not possibly do so now.

The Siege

Although Vittigis arrived at Rome on 2 March 537 with perhaps 50,000 men, that was still too few to invest the city completely. He therefore built a series of six camps around the eastern perimeter, facing various gates in the city walls. Most of Rome lies on the eastern bank of the Tiber River, with the Milvian Bridge being the primary span across the river to the west. Belisarius needed to hold that bridge to keep himself from being completely surrounded and to maintain an avenue of approach for the reinforcements he begged from Justinian, for after leaving garrisons at other cities Belisarius' army was reduced to some 3,000. He built a tower there to hold the bridge, but his garrison of mercenaries occupying the tower decided to turn coat.

When Belisarius led a thousand cavalry on a reconnaissance the next day, only then did he discover the tower was no longer his. A major battle ensued in which the Byzantines killed

1,000 Ostrogoths and drove them back to their camp. Reinforced there, however, the Ostrogoths assumed the attack. Belisarius fought his way back to the city only to find the gates closed. The population, so quick to give him control of the city, now seemed equally eager to give him up in order to avoid Gothic retribution. Hard-pressed by an ever-increasing number of Gothic attackers, Belisarius could do nothing but order an attack. Stunned by this sudden turn of events and convinced the Byzantines must have assistance coming from another direction, the Ostrogoths withdrew and Belisarius got the gate opened. The Ostrogoths, however, now held the bridge and by building a seventh camp in the area of the Vatican had the city surrounded.

While Vittigis prepared to launch an assault, Belisarius strengthened the city's defenses. He drafted local workers to dig a trench at the base of the wall to slow any attackers and keep siege towers at bay. He strengthened walls of Hadrian's tomb, later to be named the Castel Sant' Angelo, which stood on the northwestern corner of the city walls. Catapults were placed on the walls as well. He also organized some of the city's population into fighting units, interspersing his own troops to stiffen morale and offer training and guidance.

The Ostrogothic attack began on 21 March. Vittigis had constructed siege towers with battering rams to be hauled by oxen up to the walls. Belisarius heartened the defense by killing key Ostrogothic officers with astounding shots from his bow. He then ordered his archers to ignore the attacking troops and target the oxen. The siege engines halted well short of their goal. Two Ostrogothic attacks ensued. The main one was directed against Hadrian's tomb and the defenders, once out of arrows, broke up statues and pelted the attackers with stone until the assault failed. Meanwhile, a small force had found a weakness at a corner of the eastern walls, an old stable where animals had been kept prior to taking them to the Coliseum. Belisarius relieved the pressure of the attacks by launching sorties from other gates that attacked the Ostrogoth army. The attackers withdrew after sustaining 30,000 dead.

In the wake of that disaster, Vittigis decided to starve the city. The monotony was interrupted by occasional Byzantine cavalry sallies that inflicted serious damage on Gothic units. Indeed, the attacks were so successful that the Roman populace became more interested in military service. They pressed Belisarius to allow them to launch a major sally, to which he reluctantly agreed. After initial success, the citizens became too interested in looting the Gothic camp than looking out for a counterattack. They found themselves chased back into the city after suffering more casualties than they inflicted. Other than those incidents, it was a matter of waiting. Vittigis had the aqueducts that served the city destroyed, hoping to halt production in the mills. Belisarius simply began using the Tiber to keep the mill wheels turning. What little supply of food that was trickling in from outside dried up when the Goths seized the port serving Rome, controlling the mouth of the Tiber. That disheartened the citizenry, and Belisarius began rotating guards so no one became too friendly with the besiegers. He intercepted a note from the pope offering to aid Vittigis and immediately deposed him and installed a replacement.

Finally, in early 538 the Goths asked to negotiate. A truce was declared as they sent representatives to Constantinople to speak with Justinian. During the truce, some long-awaited reinforcements arrived: another 3,000 infantry and 800 cavalry along with some food supplies. With extra manpower, Belisarius dispatched much of his cavalry to ride through northern Italy. They threatened Ravenna and raided areas where the Ostrogoths had violated the truce. That action, along with the dwindling amount of food available around Rome, provoked Vittigis to launch a final attempt on the city. He tried to sneak troops into the city via the aqueducts but alert guards blunted that approach. Attempts to get the guards drunk also failed. A last assault with ladders could not scale the walls.

Results

On 12 March the Ostrogoths broke camp and withdrew after a siege lasting a year and nine days. The war between Ostrogoths and Byzantines continued, however, when another army arrived from Constantinople commanded by Narses, one of Justinian's closest advisers and a man jealous of Belisarius. Successive campaigns took the Byzantines to Ravenna, where they bottled up Vittigis and his army. The Goths offered to make Belisarius emperor of a western empire. He went along with the offer until Ravenna opened its gates, then seized the city and sent Vittigis in chains to Justinian. Although the ruse proved successful, Justinian's paranoia turned Belisarius' action into a threat and the emperor ordered his general home in 541.

Narses was not the general Belisarius was. The Ostrogoths soon regained most of what they had lost. Justinian sent him back in 544, again with too few troops—4,000. The Byzantines not only took back the lost territory but Belisarius withstood another siege in Rome. Yet again Justinian could not stand his general's success. War raged across the Italian peninsula for the next few centuries, devastating the countryside so completely that some regions still have not recovered. The Byzantines maintained a presence in Italy through the ninth century, when Italy finally came under the control of the Franks under Charlemagne.

References: J. B. Bury, *History of the Later Roman Empire* (New York: Dover, 1958); J. A. S. Evans, *The Age of Justinian* (New York: Routledge, 1996); Erik Hildinger, "Belisarius' Bid for Rome," in *Military History* 16, no. 4, October 1999; Procopius, *The Wars of Justinian*, trans. H. B. Dewing (London: Heinemann, 1914.)

CONSTANTINOPLE

DATE: August 717–15 August 718.
LOCATION: on the Sea of Marmara,
modern Istanbul.

FORCES ENGAGED:
Byzantine: unknown. Commander: Emperor Leo the
Isaurian.
Muslim: 210,000. Commander: Maslama.

IMPORTANCE:
Defeat of Muslim forces in their first serious
attempt to overpower the Byzantine Empire
led to another seven centuries of Christian power
in southeastern Europe.

Historical Setting

Constantine the Great established the city of Constantinople as his capital in 323. In doing so, he occupied the former city of Byzantium, which for centuries had controlled the straits separating Asia and Europe. The Sea of Marmara is flanked northeast and southwest by the Bosphorus and the Dardanelles, two narrow straits linking the Mediterranean and the Black seas. Unless one goes completely around the Black Sea, the passage from Europe into Asia Minor is across one of those straits. Therefore, Byzantium/Constantinople/Istanbul has been an extremely strategic possession for both land and naval warfare, as well as overland and maritime trade. As Rome faded and Constantinople rose in power, it became the seat of the Eastern Roman, or Byzantine, Empire.

Muhammad the Prophet founded Islam in Arabia in the seventh century. Claiming his divinely inspired teachings, the Koran, to be the successor to the Bible and the fulfillment of God's plan for humanity, he spread his faith by both proselytization and warfare. By coincidence (or divine intervention) Muhammad arrived on the scene just as the two Middle Eastern powers, Persia and the Byzantine Empire, had fought each other to an exhausted standstill. He was therefore able to acquire massive territorial gains hand in hand with the spread of his faith. Both Persians and Byzantines suffered major losses of real estate as well as major losses of converts to Islam, who found it less oppressive than the ultraconservative Orthodox Church.

Muhammad the Prophet had a public career of ten years (622–632), then died without publicly naming a successor. His close associate Abu Bakr was elected to succeed him but ruled only two years; upon his death Omar reigned as caliph ("deputy"), the religious and political head of Islam. For ten years Omar oversaw Islam's expansion into Byzantine territory, Persia, Syria, modern Iraq, and Egypt. It spread further still under the caliphate of Othman (644–656), ultimately stretching west to the Atlantic shore of North Africa as well as east to Armenia and Afghanistan. After he was assassinated Islam split into two major factions: the followers of Muhammad's nephew Ali became the Shi'ites, while the supporters of the Syrian governor Muawiya started the Sunni faction. Muawiya established the Umayyad dynasty, which ruled from Damascus between 661 and 750.

Muawiya's goal was the downfall of the Christian Byzantine Empire, for reportedly whoever was involved in capture of the capital city of Constantinople would have all his sins forgiven. Intermittently between 674 and 678 Muslim forces attempted to capture the city, by both land and sea, but the double walls protecting it proved too formidable. Muawiya settled for a peace treaty with the Byzantine emperor, which provided for an annual tribute from Damascus to Constantinople. For the next thirty years Muslim armies carried the faith as far as Spain and India, but the lure of Constantinople, the key to Europe, always beckoned. Caliph Walid (705–715) organized the forces necessary to seize the city, but died before the project began. Thus, his successor

Suleiman sent men and ships to the Byzantine capital in 717.

The Byzantine Empire had suffered through a series of mediocre emperors since the last assault. Anastasius was now emperor. He came to the throne in 713 and was in the market for able soldiers to defend his realm. In his army served a general named Conon, better known as Leo the Isaurian. (He was probably from Syria rather than the Anatolian province of Isauria [modern Konia], however.) He had been a soldier since 705 and in 716 took command of the *theme* (district) of Anatolia. He harried the approaching Muslim army as it marched out of Syria toward Constantinople, then took the throne from Anastasius in March 717. Crowned Leo III, he immediately set about laying in as many provisions as he could for the siege he knew was coming, a daunting task for a city of perhaps half a million people. He also oversaw the repair and strengthening of the city's two walls and the placement of weaponry to repel attacks from land or sea.

The Siege

Caliph Suleiman named Muslama as commander of his army, reportedly 80,000 men marching through Anatolia toward Constantinople. His plan was to invest the city from the western, landward side while a huge fleet blocked any supplies from reaching the city. That fleet numbered some 1,800 ships carrying a further 80,000 men under the command of a general named Suleiman, not to be confused with the caliph. The Muslim fleet was divided into two divisions: one to blockade the Dardanelles (or Hellespont) and keep any relief from coming to Constantinople from the Mediterranean, and one to hold the Bosphorus to the north, keeping out any relief from Black Sea ports. Muslama crossed the Hellespont in July 717, then divided his forces. He took command of the main body that began the siege,

while sending a detachment to Adrianople to keep an eye on the Bulgars, who had been pillaging through southeastern Europe and had attacked Constantinople in 712.

Immediately upon his arrival Muslama threw an attack against the walls, but it was easily beaten back. That convinced him against undertaking a frontal assault, so he began digging trenches to prevent any breakout from the city. Most of the fighting, therefore, took place on the water. Admiral Suleiman left part of his navy at the Dardanelles, as ordered, but led the remainder northward to take up station on the Hellespont. As they approached Constantinople, however, the leading ships were caught in a swift and unfamiliar current that began to tangle them. Seizing his opportunity, Leo quickly lowered the chain that protected the Golden Horn (the upper harbor of the city) and dashed out into the Muslim fleet before they could form into line of battle. Using Greek fire, his ships quickly destroyed or captured a large number of vessels while the rest retreated. Suleiman feared sailing past the city now, for another such battle could destroy the rest of his fleet. Thus, the northern avenue for aid for a time was kept open.

The Muslim effort was off to a poor start, and soon bad news came from Damascus. Caliph Suleiman had died of a stomach ailment (probably from overeating) and Omar II, not known for his military acumen, had replaced him. For the next several months little happened except for bad luck. The winter of 717–718 was much colder than usual and snow lay on the ground for more than three months. For an army born and raised in Arabia and Egypt this was disconcerting at best, deadly at worst. Delays in the delivery of supplies from Egypt, coupled with the bad weather, meant the deaths of thousands of besieging soldiers.

The Muslims hoped to take the initiative in the spring of 718 with the arrival of a new fleet from Egypt bringing 50,000 reinforcements. The 400 ships of the fleet from Egypt slipped past the Byzantine fleet in the Golden Horn at night, thus avoiding a naval battle, and anchored at the Hellespont. That cut off the flow of supplies and would eventually have spelled the city's doom, but Leo's navy again saved the day. He was aided by the desertion of large numbers of crew members from the new Egyptian fleet, sailors who were Coptic Christians and had been pressed into Muslim service. Learning of the enemy fleet's disposition, Leo launched a surprise attack in June that caught them completely unawares. The Greek fire (an unknown mixture of materials with many of the characteristics of napalm) once again caused both destruction and terror; the Christian crews deserted wholesale to the welcoming Byzantine forces. The northern blockading fleet was destroyed and Leo followed up his victory with an attack on Muslim forces on the Asian side of the Sea of Marmara, opposite the capital. That attack was so unexpected that Muslim soldiers and sailors were slaughtered by the thousands.

Leo at this point proved himself to be a diplomat as well as a general. He sent envoys to the Bulgars, who persuaded their King Tervel to attack the Muslim army from the west. In July Tervel's soldiers drove back the Muslim holding force at Adrianople and attacked Muslama's forces in the rear, defeating them and inflicting some 22,000 casualties. This new threat was reinforced by the rumor that a Frankish army was marching across Europe to assist their fellow Christians. The Muslims had not yet fought the Franks, but had heard tales of formidable military power. Caliph Omar decided it was time to bring the siege to a close. On 15 August 718 Muslama led the army away from Constantinople.

Results

The defeat at Constantinople was the first disastrous loss the armies of Islam had suffered. There had been occasional defeats, but never a catastrophe such as this. Of the 210,000 Muslim soldiers and sailors who took part, it is reported that only 30,000 actually saw their homeland again. Of the more than 2,000 ships reported to have been involved, only five supposedly made it home.

Had Muslama's armies captured the city, the route into eastern Europe would have been virtually unguarded. Little organized resistance could have been mounted against hordes of Muslim troops until they reached central Europe. Constantinople, the seat of political, religious, and economic power in the Christian East, probably would have become Islam's capital as it did in the wake of the Muslim capture of the city in 1453. The Eastern Orthodox Church may have disappeared, with untold consequences in eastern Europe and Russia, although such did not happen in 1453. Sea power would have been completely in Muslim hands, for no European population at the time owned a significant navy. None would until the Vikings a century later. Even with the Frankish victory at Tours in France fifteen years afterward, Islam could well have become the dominant European, and therefore world, religion.

The Byzantine victory insulated Europe from Islam, but also from other outside influences. Hellenistic knowledge and culture survived and in many ways flourished in the Middle East and Africa, while Europe entered the Dark Ages. Militarily Europe was strong, but cultural progress was at a crawl. Not until the Crusades and the resulting revival of trade with the East was the old knowledge rediscovered, and the Renaissance was the result. It is interesting to speculate what Europe may have been like had Constantinople fallen seven centuries before it did.

References: J. F. C. Fuller, *Military History of the Western World*, vol. 1 (New York: Funk and Wagnalls, 1954); Edward Gibbon, *The History of the Decline and Fall of the Roman Empire*, vol. 6 (London: Methuen, 1898); Warren T. Treadgold, *Byzantium and its Army, 284–1081* (Stanford: Stanford University Press, 1991).

PAVIA

DATE: September 773–June 774.
LOCATION: northern Italy, southwest of Milan.

FORCES ENGAGED:
Frankish: unknown. Commander: Charlemagne.
Lombard: unknown. Commander: Desiderius.

IMPORTANCE:
The defeat of the Lombards rid Rome of a consistent threat to papal security and laid the foundation of the Holy Roman Empire.

Historical Setting

The relationship between the pope and the kingdom of the Franks started in 756. Pepin III, known variously as "the Short" and "the Great," responded to a call from Pope Stephen II to save Rome from depredations by the Lombards, the population that dominated the northern Italian peninsula. The amity on which this response was based rested on Stephen's support and blessing of Pepin's deposition of the last king of the Merovingian dynasty, Childeric III, in 751. That initiated close ties between politics and religion in the Frankish lands, for Pepin and his heirs were to hold the title of *patricius Romanus* and protect the Catholic Church from spiritual and temporal threats. Thus, in 755 Pepin marched his army into Italy to capture the city of Pavia and stop the aggressive actions of the Lombard King Aistulf. As soon as he returned to France, however, Aistulf again threatened Rome. Pepin returned in 756, defeated Aistulf again, and is reported to have promised the pope possession of a large portion of the Italian peninsula. When Aistulf died shortly thereafter, he was replaced by Desiderius, who promised to respect papal authority and possessions. That he did not do.

Upon Pepin's death in 768, his realm was divided between his two sons, Carloman II and Charles. The two apparently got along well with each other. Although the Lombards con-tinued to harass successive popes, for a time the Franks and Lombards enjoyed friendly rela-tions. At the urging of his mother, Charles in 770 put away his wife in order to marry Desiderata, daughter of the Lombard king. Charles returned her to her father a year later for unknown reasons; possibly she was pre-sumed barren. That did nothing to endear Charles to Desiderius. In 771 Carloman died, leaving Charles as sole king of the Franks. Carloman's wife left for Lombardy, however, seeking sanctuary in the king's court, and Desiderius began backing Carloman's son as the rightful Frankish monarch.

Meanwhile, Charles' relations with Rome had been strained, for Pope Stephen III criti-cized him for his marriage to Desiderata. When Charles ignored the criticism, Stephen grew closer to Desiderius, allowing Lombard appointees to hold important places in the Roman government and to persecute any opposition. Stephen died in 772 and his suc-cessor, Hadrian I, quickly cleaned house of these aggressive Lombards. That provoked a violent response. Desiderius, while sending messages requesting an audience with the pope, sent his troops into ever deeper invasions of papal territory, until the town of Otriculum, a mere day's march away from Rome, fell. Hadrian called out what troops he could and sent them to Charles for assistance.

Hadrian's emissary traveled by sea to Mar-seilles, for Desiderius had troops blocking all overland routes into France. The emissary finally reached Charles (who was holding court in Thionville on the Moselle just north of Metz) and delivered this message: "They would attack us by land and water, conquer the city of Rome and lead ourselves into captiv-ity. . . . Therefore we implore you by the living God and the Prince of Apostles to hasten to our aid immediately, lest we be destroyed" (Win-ston, *Charlemagne*, p. 107). The note con-tained a list of all the people supposedly allied to Desiderius, many of whom threatened Charles' authority in one way or another. Charles sent envoys to Rome and Lombardy to offer a diplomatic solution, but at the same time he readied his army. When he received confirmation of Desiderius' aggression, as well as the Lombard king's refusal of a large monetary payment for the return of the cities he had taken from the pope, Charles led his Frankish troops on the march in the early summer of 773.

The size of Charles' army is unknown. Not only in this campaign but in virtually all his military actions this is the case. Although some sources claim he could only muster several thousand knights, others propose an ability to field a force of 100,000 cavalry and infantry. Whatever the army's size, he divided it in half for the passage through the Alps into Italy. His uncle Bernard led half the army through the St. Bernard Pass, while Charles led his contingent through the Dora Susa by Mount Cenis farther west. They passed easily over the highest point and began winding their way down the valley toward open land, when they ran into a fortification blocking their way manned by Desiderius' army. An assault failed to break through, so Charles entered into fruitless negotiations while his men grumbled. He finally gave permission for a small force to scout a possible alternate route. One was found, possibly by luck or (according to tradition) via the efforts of a Lombard minstrel who defected and was handsomely paid for turning coat. Whatever the method, when a band of cavalry appeared on the Lombard flank the defenders panicked and fled for the walled city of Pavia, southwest of Milan. It is also possible that they learned of the approach of Bernard from the east and that motivated their flight. Charles' previously unhappy men gorged themselves on the riches of the abandoned Lombard camp and soon marched to Pavia, where the siege began in September 773.

The Siege

The fact that Charles had sufficient men to surround the city for ten months implies a rather large force, especially since he was able to march away from the siege in order to spend Easter in Rome. Although they had no siege engines to batter the walls, they had the resources of the fields surrounding the city at harvest time. Unprepared for a siege, the defenders had not stocked the city well. Not only was Desiderius locked up inside, but his son Adelchis had fled to hide behind the stronger city walls of Verona, there to watch over Carloman's wife and children. Charles left the bulk of his force at Pavia and led a small contingent to Verona, which surrendered without a fight. Adelchis fled to Constantinople, while Charles' sister-in-law entered into his keeping and vanished from history. Through the latter months of 773 and into the first months of the following year, Charles rode around the environs of Pavia establishing his authority, while none of Desiderius' subordinates in other cities made any attempt to relieve him. Apparently, he made no attempt to break out.

"It was now the tenth month of the siege: disease and probably famine were pressing the defenders hard: and Desiderius, who had never been a popular sovereign, heard on every side of the defection of his countrymen. At length on a certain Tuesday in June [774] the city opened the gates to her conqueror" (Hodgkin, *Charles the Great*, p. 101). Charles accepted the homage of the Lombard aristocracy, and named himself king of the Franks and the Lombards. Desiderius was sent with his family to northeastern France, where he was invited to enter a monastery; by most accounts he took well to religious life.

Results

With Desiderius removed from the Lombard throne, there was a major power shift in Italy. Hadrian and Charles were well-matched to share an unusual arrangement: Hadrian wanted political power in Italy, which he could not wield without Charles' army; Charles was a Christian knight who wanted to do God's work, as long as there was little real oversight. These aims seem at first to be at cross-purposes but, apparently, the two men reached an understanding of where their respective authorities lay. During Charles' Easter 774 visit to Rome the two men treated each other as equals, but Hadrian was able to wring from Charles confirmation of the pope's possession of large amounts of land in Italy (most of the peninsula, actually) which Pepin had granted to Pope Stephen II. As king of the Lombards much of that land was now in Charles' hands, but most of it was still occupied by forces of independent nobles or the Byzantine Empire, leftovers from Belisarius' conquests during Justinian's reign. Thus, it was not all Charles' land to grant, and whether Hadrian expected him to conquer the remainder of it for Rome is a question that has never been answered. As Charles spent most of his reign north of the Alps in campaigns against his enemies there, he apparently never had any serious intention of being on hand to act as Hadrian's enforcer. Still, he had the pope's blessing and fought to spread both Christianity and the borders of his realm with equal diligence.

Pope Hadrian died in 795 and was succeeded by Leo III. He was unpopular with the citizens of Rome, who accused him of a variety of crimes. Following a failed assassination attempt in 799, Leo fled Italy for Aachen, where Charles had established his capital. He demanded that Charles restore him to the papal throne. Charles sent him back to Rome with an armed escort, then followed along himself, arriving in December 800. He obliged Leo to publicly swear he had done nothing wrong and he was reconfirmed as pope. Leo's response changed Europe for centuries. On Christmas Day Charles went to St. Peter's to celebrate Mass. He knelt before the altar to pray and, as he raised his head Leo placed a crown on it with the words, repeated three times: "Hail to Charles the Augustus, crowned by God the great and peace-bringing emperor of the Romans."

There has been widespread speculation over the motivations of both Charles and Leo in this coronation. Charles seems to have been eager to hold a position equal to that of the ancient caesars, but his contemporary biographer, Einhard, claims that had Charles known what Leo was to do he would not have gone to church that day. One can only suppose that while he wanted to be emperor of a latter-day Roman Empire, he wanted it on his own terms. Leo, by initiating the ceremony, placed himself in the equation. While he paid homage to Charles, now Charles the Great (Charlemagne in French, Karl der Grosse in German), the coronation was performed by the head of the Catholic Church. Thus, who was the superior? The emperor, or the man who made him emperor? Leo, possibly humiliated by the public oath Charles had made him swear, could have been saying that only the pope could make an emperor, no matter how much the pope depended on that emperor's temporal power. In their lifetimes both men benefited: "The coronation had results for a thousand years. It strengthened the papacy and the bishops by making civil authority derive from ecclesiastical conferment. . . . It strengthened Charlemagne against baronial and other disaffection by making him a very vicar of God; it vastly advanced the theory of the divine right of kings" (Durant, *The Age of Faith*, p. 469).

Charlemagne's victory at Pavia, by making him the major military power in Italy and placing him in a partnership with the pope, put him in a position to establish a dynasty whose role was defender of the faith: "the coronation established the Holy Roman Empire in fact, though not in theory" (Durant, *The Age of Faith*, p. 469). That political entity came into official being under Otto I in 962, after the end of the Carolingian dynasty.

References: Will Durant, *The Age of Faith* (New York: Simon and Schuster, 1950); Einhard and Notker the Stammerer, *Two Lives of Charlemagne*, trans. Lewis Thorpe (New York: Penguin, 1969); Thomas Hodgkin, *Charles the*

Great (Port Washington, NY: Kennikat, 1970 [1897]); Pierre Riché, *The Carolingians*, trans. Michael Idomir Allen (Philadelphia: University of Pennsylvania Press, 1993).

PARIS

Date: 25 November 885–October 886.
Location: on the Seine River in northeastern France.

Forces Engaged:

Parisian: 200 men-at-arms. Commander: Count Odo.
Norse: perhaps 30,000 men. Commanders: Sigfred and Rollon.

Importance:

The siege proved the strategic value of Paris to the remainder of France, and the negotiations to lift the siege brought about the downfall of King Charles the Fat, ending the Carolingian dynasty.

Historical Setting

While Charlemagne ruled western Europe the Vikings of Scandinavia made little headway in the region. They spent their time instead attacking the British Isles, awaiting a more opportune time to try France. After Charlemagne's death, his son Lothar reigned. Upon Lothar's death, however, the Salic law followed in the kingdom dictated a division of land among his three sons. None had their forebear's strength of arm or will, and internecine bickering meant that there could be no united front against any outside threat. The Vikings took advantage.

The Danes sailed up the Seine River and threatened Paris in 845; in the 860s there were three attacks that achieved limited results for the invaders, who did little more than pillage on a large scale. The acquisition of either loot or bribes led to their withdrawal each time, but no serious military opposition arose to face them. Thus, they returned to France regularly for loot and bribes. A quick succession of Frankish rulers did nothing to enhance the region's security. Charles the Bald died in 877, his son Louis the Stammerer a year and a half later, Louis' two successors died by 884. In the wake of these short-term reigns, the three provinces into which Charlemagne's kingdom had been divided once again saw a single king: Charles the Fat. Charles had shown no talent for leading men in battle, but he was of the proper bloodline. Neustria, as the westernmost province was called, was ruled by Charles' appointed subordinates. The Duchy of France, the region that lay between the Seine and Loire rivers, came under the rule of Count Odo, whose brother Robert was grandfather of Hugh Capet, who initiated the French Capetian dynasty. Odo's father, Robert the Strong, had driven back Viking raiders and begun to fortify Paris, so Odo inherited a fairly strong position. It was soon tested.

The Siege

The Danes under Sigfred had often raided northeastern France to their profit. In 885 they entered again, hoping to receive a bribe from King Charles. He refused, and the Vikings decided to take by force what they could not acquire by demand. Seven hundred ships sailed up the Seine toward Paris, carrying perhaps 30,000 men. The town of Paris in 885 was nothing more than an island in the Seine, but it could bar passage to any ships. Two bridges, one of stone and one of wood, granted foot access to the island but were too low to allow the shallow-draft Viking ships to pass. Both bridges were protected by defensive towers built on either end. To man the defenses Odo could draw on no more than 200 men-at-arms, including his brother, two counts, and a marquis from the neighboring aristocracy. He also had the valiant aid of the abbot of St. Germain, Joscelin.

The Vikings arrived at Paris on 25 November 885. Sigfred opened contact by negotiation rather than combat, but his request for monetary tribute was rejected. He wasted little time in employing the military option. The next day the Danish mangonels were launching arrows into the city while catapults threw large stones. The opening attack was launched against the northernmost tower, but was driven back from the walls when the defenders poured boiling oil on the Vikings. Repeated assaults were turned back. On the 27th the Vikings awoke to find the tower had been built up another story during the night. They attacked again with catapults, battering rams, fire, and mining, but all proved futile. The abbot Joscelin was in the thick of the fighting: "not content with merely exhorting the people, [he] appeared before them casque on head, and, armed with bow and an axe, planted a cross on the outer defenses, while his nephew, Ebles, a man of enormous physical strength, fought beside him" (Lansdale, *Paris*, p. 102).

For the next two months the Vikings dug trenches and scoured the countryside for provisions. In late January they tried a new tactic. After launching several feints, they assaulted the bridge directly by trying to fill the shallows with brush, tree trunks, and the bodies of animals and executed prisoners, hoping to bypass the tower with their infantry. Two days of such attempts brought them no success. On the third day, they set three of their ships on fire and floated them downstream toward the wooden bridge. Unfortunately for the Danes, the ships burned and sank before their fire could set the bridge alight.

The fire attack may have weakened the bridge somewhat, however, for when heavy rains began to fall on 6 February the debris-clogged river soon overflowed its banks and the bridge supports gave way. That meant that the tower on the far bank now stood alone, held by a mere dozen men. They refused a call for surrender and eleven died; the sole prisoner soon broke free and killed many of his captors before he was overcome.

Now free to bypass Paris, the Vikings left a holding force to watch the city as the bulk of the army sailed farther upriver to pillage as far as Chartres and Le Mans. Odo slipped messengers through the encirclement to beg Charles (then in Italy) to march to the town's aid. News that Henry of Saxony was marching to help them, coupled with a sally that brought in supplies and reinforcements, raised the defenders' morale while lowering that of the besiegers. Sigfred tired of the inaction and offered to leave for a mere 60 pounds of silver. He and his men left the battle in mid-April, but the remaining Danes under Rollon were still hopeful of ultimate victory and greater spoils. The morale pendulum swung the other way when, in mid-May, Joscelin died of a sickness that was becoming rampant within Paris.

In desperation, Odo himself finally stole through the Viking lines to carry his plea to Charles. He acquired a few more followers while on his mission and fought his way back into Paris with news that Charles was marching from the south and his brother Henry of Saxony was approaching from the east. Unfortunately for the defenders, Henry was killed on the way and Charles dallied. Hoping to seize victory before the relief arrived, the Vikings launched another major assault in mid-summer. This too was beaten back by defenders confident in their ultimate delivery. By October Charles' army approached, driving back the scattered Vikings that had been out looting. Soon, the Danish camp was surrounded as Charles encamped his army at the foot of Montmarte.

Unfortunately for France, the man in charge was King Charles the Fat. When the Viking force did not flee at the sight of his army, he apparently had second thoughts about a full-scale battle. Instead, he contacted the Danes and opened negotiations. He granted them everything that the defenders had been fighting to withhold: free passage of the Seine and a ransom of 700 pounds of silver, to be delivered on the Vikings' withdrawal the following spring.

Results

The people of Paris, not unnaturally, felt betrayed. Odo swore not to pay the ransom and to continue the battle. He refused to let the Vikings past his island, so they instead dragged their boats overland to the Marne River, from which they sailed off toward Burgundy. That, indeed, had apparently been Charles' intention, for the Burgundians were then in revolt and they would have their hands full with the Vikings. What seemed good politics to Charles seemed cowardice to his people. "They had been prepared to die themselves in order to hold the rest of the kingdom safe. This safety Charles, with breathtaking ingratitude, with an almost criminal heedlessness, had bargained away" (Brent, *Viking Saga,* p. 58). The following year, 888, Charles was deposed and his kingdom divided among more worthy rulers. Odo became king of Neustria, the western Frankish kingdom; in two generations the crumbling dynasty established by Charlemagne was replaced by the house of Capet.

The defense of Paris illustrated better than any other argument how valuable was its location. Neither Charlemagne nor Charles had used it for a capital, but its situation covering the convergence of rivers that spread throughout France proved that whoever controlled it controlled north-central France.

Odo did indeed pay the promised ransom to the Vikings as they sailed away in 889, and true to their word they never attacked so far inland again. Their settling in the coastal lands that became the province of Normandy meant that the Norsemen (Normans) finally came to stay rather than hit and run.

References: Peter Brent, *The Viking Saga,* (New York: Putnam's 1975); Gwyn Jones, *A History of the Vikings* (London: Oxford University Press, 1968); Maria Hornor Lansdale, *Paris: Its Sites, Monuments and History* (Philadelphia: Henry Coates, 1898).

JERUSALEM

DATE: 9 June–18 July 1099.
LOCATION: central Israel.

FORCES ENGAGED:

Crusader: 1,250 knights and 10,000 infantry. Commander: Duke Godfrey de Bouillon. Muslim: approximately 20,000 men. Commander: Emir Iftikhar.

IMPORTANCE:

The crusader victory at Jerusalem established their kingdom in the Holy Land, which lasted on and off for another three centuries.

Historical Setting

Late in the eleventh century two major struggles arose, one dealing with the Catholic Church in Europe and one with the Byzantine Empire. In Europe, the pope was trying to stave off a challenge by the Holy Roman Emperor as to who would reign supreme in both European politics and religion. Although officially protector of the Church, the Holy Roman Emperor at times assumed the role of dictator, attempting to name the pope as well as lower-ranking officials in the Church hierarchy. Thus, the pope was looking for something with which to increase his prestige in the eyes of European nobility. In the Byzantine Empire the Seljuk Turks, who had been gradually consolidating their power throughout the Middle East, scored a major victory over the weakening Byzantines at the battle of Manzikert in 1071. That battle placed the bulk of Asia Minor in Turkish hands, with the capital at Constantinople destined to become a target.

Godfrey of Bouillon gives thanks to God in the presence of Peter the Hermit after the taking of Jerusalem by Crusaders, 15 July 1099, painting by Emile Signol. (Réunion des Musées Nationaux/Art Resource, NY)

These two problems dovetailed nicely for both pope and emperor. The Byzantine Emperor Alexius Comnenus brilliantly played off his opponents while restocking the treasury. That allowed him to pay for European troops if they would come to his aid. He appealed to Pope Urban II, claiming that the Muslims were barring Christians from holy sites in Palestine. Indeed the routes were closed, but more because of squabbling among Muslim factions than through anything intentional. Still, it was a religious focal point on which Urban hoped to rally his European flock. That would increase his status, spread Christianity, make the Eastern Orthodox Church indebted to Rome, and take feuding nobles out of Europe to focus their warlike natures on infidels rather than each other. Earlier popes had granted religious sanctions for campaigns against Muslims in Spain, so the concept of Holy War was familiar in the West.

The massive response surprised both Urban and Alexius. All across Europe people flocked to the cause, and for a variety of reasons. Some had a true desire to spread the faith; some wanted to receive the forgiveness of sins the Church promised. Others merely went for the adventure or the potential fortune in loot or land. Younger sons who stood to inherit nothing on their fathers' deaths saw this as an opportunity for advancement they might never achieve at home. Unfortunately, no one had any real conception of the difficulty involved. Tens of thousands of poor people joined the People's Crusade behind the religious zealot Peter the Hermit. They foraged their way through eastern Europe and into Asia Minor, but with no military training and precious little weaponry the Turks slaughtered them. A worse fate befell the German Crusade, for after killing any Jew they found at home they marched for Constantinople via Hungary. They never made it through that country, but were dispersed by Hungarian troops. Neither Crusade did anything to inspire Byzantine confidence, but they had more to fear when the warriors actually got organized and began their march. Concerned they might find his capital city too rich to pass without looting, Alexius forced each passing crusader army to swear fealty to him before they could obtain passage across the Bosporus and supplies for the expedition. After some violence he was able to save his city from the more rambunctious crusaders and they finally crossed over into Asia Minor.

Before reaching the Holy Land itself the crusaders had to capture Turk strongholds at Nicea and Antioch. Nicea fell 19 June 1097 after a month-long siege. Battles at Doryleum (modern Eskisehir), Incomium (Konia), and Heraclea (Eregli) took the crusaders to the northeastern corner of the Mediterranean at the Turk stronghold of Antioch by October. Not until early June 1098 did the city fall after two relief armies were beaten back. The crusaders almost immediately found themselves besieged, but a bold sally in late June drove off the attacking Muslim army. The victors then squabbled among themselves for six months over what to do next. One of the main generals, Duke Bohemund of Taranto, stayed in Antioch to establish his own principality. The remainder marched onward for Jerusalem in January 1099. A fleet from Pisa sailed alongside the force, carrying their supplies, until they reached the town of Arsuf. At that point the crusaders turned and marched inland to Jerusalem.

Some 12,000 soldiers remained by this point, with Duke Godfrey de Bouillon of Lorraine in command, assisted by Count Raymond of Toulouse and Tancred, king of Sicily. The force defending the city numbered probably 20,000, under the leadership of Emir Iftikhar. Jerusalem lay outside the territory controlled by the Seljuk Turks and in a region under the jurisdiction of the caliph of Cairo. The Muslims there were of the Fatimid sect, followers of the Prophet's daughter as the true ruling lineage down from Muhammad. They were therefore more Arab in their ethnicity than Turkish. It mattered little to the crusaders: one infidel seemed much like another.

The Siege

The siege began on 9 June 1099. There were too few crusaders to fully encircle the city, so the only way to take the city was by storm rather than starvation. Indeed, the besiegers suffered a more severe water shortage than did the defenders. The Muslims had poisoned the cisterns and wells outside the city before the crusaders' arrival, and the summer sun beat upon them unmercifully. On the 12th they launched their first assault; it proved disastrous. New machines were necessary to reduce or overcome these walls, yet little wood was available. On the 17th, however, the necessary materiel arrived aboard six ships that had docked in the recently acquired port of Jaffa. Genoese engineers assisted the crusaders in the construction of mangonels or trebuchets (a mangonel consists of a long arm with a sling on one end and a massive counterweight on the other). Along with siege towers and scaling ladders, the besiegers hoped to destroy or climb the walls.

On the night of 13–14 July a second assault took place. It had little success, but on the 15th a siege tower was finally placed against the city wall. The gangplank fell, creating a bridge into the city. The Muslim defense crumbled almost immediately. Some retreated to the El Aqsa mosque, but they were hotly pursued by the Sicilian, Tancred. He promised mercy, but little was extended once the crusaders had the city in their control. Although he tried to protect those in the El Aqsa mosque, a killing rage consumed the vast majority of the invaders and almost the entire population of the city was put to the sword. One chronicle claimed that within the mosque the blood was knee deep. Raymond of Agiles reported that "wonderful things were to be seen. Numbers of the Saracens were beheaded . . . others were shot with arrows, or forced to jump from the towers; others were tortured for several days and then burned in flames. In the streets were seen piles of heads and hands and feet. One rode about everywhere amid the corpses of men and horses" (Durant, *The Age of Faith*, p. 592).

The Jewish citizens fared no better. European Christians had long blamed the Jews for killing Christ, so there seemed to be no reason to spare them either. Most were burned to death inside the city's main synagogue. Afterward, the "victors flocked to the church of the Holy Sepulcher, whose grotto, they believed, had once held the crucified Christ. There, embracing one another, they wept with joy and release, and thanked the God of Mercies for their victory" (Durant, *The Age of Faith*, p. 592).

Results

Once the frenzy had passed, Godfrey de Bouillon was named Guardian of Jerusalem and Defender of the Holy Sepulcher; he refused to be named king of Jerusalem. The crusaders had little time to enjoy their victory, for a 50,000-man relief force was on its way from Egypt. Although he could muster only 10,000 knights and infantry to face them, the crusaders won a fairly easy victory at Askelon on 12 August 1099. Unlike the Turks, whose steppe heritage taught them to harry an enemy with archers mounted on horseback, the Egyptians fought in the more traditional Muslim fashion. They depended on speed and fanaticism to overwhelm their enemy in one mad rush. Against the discipline of the European infantry and the heavy cavalry of the knights the Muslims were like a wave breaking on a rock; the crusader countercharge that overran the Muslim camp pushed much of that army into the sea.

After Askelon the First Crusade was over. Most of the participants returned to Europe, but those that had staked out claims after victorious sieges stayed behind. Crusader principalities were established at Antioch under Bohemund, Edessa (about 100 miles northeast of Antioch) under Baldwin de Bouillon, Tripoli under Raymond of Toulouse; all were supposedly under the authority of Jerusalem. When Godfrey died just a year after Jerusalem's fall, his brother Baldwin succeeded him and assumed the title of king. He ruled only with the consent of his subordinates, who acted virtually independently within their "counties."

Baldwin also ceded control of most of the ports to the Genoese and Pisans in return for a steady flow of supplies from Europe. A European-style feudal system was imposed that made most of the locals, including Christians, long for the return of Muslim rule.

These isolated fiefs survived for almost fifty years only because the Muslims themselves were too disorganized to mount an effective offensive against them. Still, the Europeans did prove difficult enemies even when an effective Muslim campaign was mounted. In the first half of the twelfth century came the establishment of military orders of monks, dedicated to serving the Church and protecting pilgrims visiting holy shrines. In 1119 eight knights following Hugh de Payens established an order based in the area around Solomon's temple in Jerusalem, and these came to be known as the Knights Templar. The following year the staff of a hospital in Jerusalem that had operated since 1048 organized themselves as the Knights of the Hospital of St. John, or the Knights Hospitalers. Although these two orders despised each other, they both carried out the same tasks of protection of pilgrims; later they made war on the Muslims.

All of this, the feudalism, the attacks, the persecution, motivated the Muslims (finally) into a response. In 1144 the prince of Mosul, Zangi, counterattacked and recaptured the city of Edessa. After his assassination, the more aggressive Nur-ed-Din continued the war against the European Christians. That provoked the Second Crusade; many more followed as the ancient crossroads of history saw innumerable armies and battles over the following two centuries.

References: Karen Armstrong, *Holy War: The Crusades and their Impact on Today's World* (New York: Doubleday, 1991); Malcolm Billings, *The Cross and the Crescent* (New York: Sterling, 1990 [1987]); Will Durant, *The Age of Faith* (New York: Simon and Schuster, 1950); Jonathan Riley-Smith, *The First Crusade and the Idea of Crusading* (Philadelphia:

University of Pennsylvania Press, 1986); Sir Steven Runciman, *The First Crusade* (New York: Cambridge University Press, 1992 [1980]).

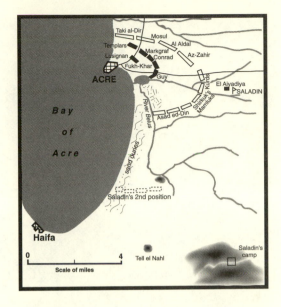

ACRE

DATE: August 1189–12 July 1191.
LOCATION: eastern Mediterranean Sea coast, in modern Israel.

FORCES ENGAGED:

Crusader: unknown. Commander: King Richard I of England.
Arab: unknown. Commander: Salah al-Din (Saladin), sultan of Egypt.

IMPORTANCE:

Crusader victory kept a European presence in the Holy Land for another century, until finally expelled in 1291.

Historical Setting

Acre is the best natural harbor on the coast of Palestine. As such it is of vital concern to anyone wishing to control trade and travel into and out of Palestine. European forces during the First Crusade initially captured it in 1104 and the city eventually became of more importance to the Latin kingdom the crusaders established than Jerusalem itself. It remained under European control throughout the crusading period, except for the years from 1187 to 1191. In 1187 the crusaders suffered a crushing defeat at the hands of Saladin at the Horns of Hattin. After this battle, almost all major crusader-held cities rapidly fell to Saladin's army, including Acre and Jerusalem. Saladin visited Acre several times over the next two years, strengthening the walls and fortifications and stationing his best troops there.

The only major Christian city to withstand the Muslim onslaught was Tyre, which provided a refuge for crusaders fleeing the Arab army. It was from here, in August 1189, that Guy de Lusignan led a small force to recapture Acre. Although they could easily have been destroyed, they were virtually ignored by the Muslim forces that were currently occupied with their siege of Beaufort. It was not until they had become entrenched in front of the city that Saladin took notice and moved his headquarters to the Plain of Acre.

The Christian forces controlled access to the harbor and continued to fortify their position on the landward side of the city with ditches and timber palisades, eventually besieging the city. The crusaders themselves were threatened by the Islamic force encamped to the east of the city. However, due to a continuing stream of reinforcements from Tyre and Europe, they were strong enough to defend themselves against attacks from the city and the encampment. They were not strong enough, however, to both capture the city and drive off Saladin.

In Europe, the defeat of the Christian army at Hattin and the loss of Jerusalem had rekindled the crusading spirit and preparations were made for what would become known as the Third Crusade. Armies under three of the mightiest

The siege of Acre, from a fourteenth-century manuscript. (Archive Photos)

European kings, Richard I (the Lionhearted) of England, Philip II of France, and Frederick I (Barbarossa) of Germany, set out in 1189.

The news of this impending threat, especially that of Frederick I, almost paralyzed Saladin and much of the Arab world. His treasury was empty and the cost of paying troops during the winter was high. In addition, there was a general fear in the Arab world that the vengeance of the new invaders would lead to a general bloodbath and the loss of Jerusalem, Syria, and Egypt.

These three armies would easily have turned the tide at Acre and been a serious threat to Muslim control of Palestine if they had arrived with their original strength. However, many did not complete the journey (including Frederick, who drowned). Those who made the trek did not arrive until 1191, leaving Guy de Lusignan and his army to hold out as best they could. Fortunately for the Christian army, Saladin was unable to reinforce his army in the meantime.

The Siege

Although the crusaders controlled access to the harbor, occasionally some Muslim ships were able to break through and provide much needed supplies and reinforcements. By the middle of September 1189, the siege was taking its toll on the city's inhabitants. At this time Saladin's army broke through to the city and opened the road to Tyre, allowing reinforcements and provisions into the city. Saladin himself came to Acre to inspect the defensive arrangements.

The crusaders counterattacked in October 1189, forcing the retirement of the Muslim right wing and provoking an attack by a portion of their main force. The crusaders attacked the center, but did not press home the attack and were themselves surrounded. Saladin's army inflicted heavy losses on the Christian army, but he failed to follow up his gains. Both sides retired to their initial positions and settled down for the winter. During this time Saladin visited Acre and strengthened its fortifications.

Fighting resumed in the spring of 1190. The crusaders attacked the city while trying to keep Saladin's field army at bay. They bombarded the city and mined the walls. In April 1190 they reached the walls of the city, but an attack from the east forced them to withdraw. An Egyptian fleet entered the harbor and supplied the city.

Fighting settled into a series of skirmishes through the following summer and autumn. Although the crusaders were periodically strengthened by fresh units, there were never enough to allow them to drive off Saladin's army and capture the city. Both sides again settled into winter camps with little or no fighting taking place. The spring of 1191 would see the tide turn in favor of the Christian army.

The French fleet arrived in April 1191, but King Philip did not want to mount any new assaults until Richard arrived. Richard's forces began arriving in June, with Richard in the first group. Philip wanted to mount an attack quickly on the city, but Richard was sick and wanted to postpone any attacks until the rest of his forces arrived along with their equipment for building siege engines. Philip carried out the assault anyway, but the inhabitants of Acre signaled Saladin, who brought his forces up and attacked the Christian rear. The defenders under Guy de Lusignan held off the Muslim attack, but the Christian army was unable to breach the city walls and hold off Saladin's army simultaneously. The assault on the city failed, Philip was forced to retreat, and the defenders of Acre destroyed the Christian siege equipment with Greek fire.

Richard's health improved to the point where he could begin directing assaults on the city. He focused his efforts on one tower, which his men mined and battered until it collapsed. He then offered a bounty to any man who would remove stones from the wall, doing so while the city's defenders bombarded them from the walls. Richard's continued attack on the city walls made it evident to the inhabitants that despite their best efforts and Saladin's attempts at relieving the pressure their days were numbered. Saladin reassured the garrison that reinforcements were coming, but when they failed to arrive as promised, he allowed the defenders make peace on the best terms they could.

Initially they offered to give up the city free and clear, the Holy Cross, 200 of their Christian captives, and fifty of their own men. These terms were unacceptable to the two European kings. The terms finally agreed on required the Muslims to totally abandon the city, taking nothing with them but clothing, pay a ransom of 200,000 Saracen talents, free 2,000 noble Christian and 500 lesser captives, and return the Holy Cross by the end of the month. The most noble and important of the inhabitants were to be left behind until all the other terms had been fulfilled.

On 12 July the Muslim inhabitants of the city left. The Christian army entered and divided its spoils and captives between the two kings. Saladin moved his army to a mountain farther away.

Results

Unfortunately, the Muslim leaders in Acre had made promises in the name of Saladin without his knowledge or his ability to comply. Saladin either could not, or would not, return the Holy Cross or release the captives as had been promised. And no one, not even Saladin, had the ransom money. Richard gave Saladin the benefit of the doubt and let the time limit come and go without action.

However, Richard could not continue with the Crusade and take care of 2,700 prisoners. On 21 August the hostages were led out of Acre and executed in full view of the Muslim army who, despite a pitched battle, could not stop the slaughter. Christians of the time viewed this as retribution for past injustices. Muslims considered the slain as martyrs for the faith and Saladin continued to treat Richard with respect and admiration.

Richard continued to crusade in Palestine and tried to recapture Jerusalem, but without success. Intrigues at home drew his attention away from the Holy Land and he could no longer afford to continue the quest. On 2 September, 1192, Richard signed a treaty with Saladin that left Jerusalem in Muslim hands, but allowed Christian pilgrims to visit it. All the cities of the Palestinian coast, except Ascalon, would remain in Christian hands.

Acre remained the capital of the inappropriately named Kingdom of Jerusalem. It was the main port of entry for crusaders, pilgrims, and merchants until it fell to the Muslims and the crusading era ended in 1291.—Tom Davis

References: Meron Benvenisti, *The Crusaders in the Holy Land* (New York: Macmillan, 1970); *Itinerarium Peregrinorum et Gest Regis Ricardi*, ed. William Stubbs, trans. James Brundage, Rolls Series, vol. 3 (London: Longman, 1864); Robert Payne, *The Dream and the Tomb: A History of the Crusades* (New York: Dorset, 1990); Amin Maalouf, *The Crusades through Arab Eyes*, trans. John Rothschild (New York: Schoken, 1983).

MONTSEGUR

DATE: November 1243–14 March 1244.
LOCATION: southern France, in the province of Languedoc.

FORCES ENGAGED:

Inquisition: 1,500 soldiers at first, as many as 10,000 at its height. Commander: Hugues de Arcis.
Cathar: 11 knights, 150 soldiers. Commanders: Raymond de Pereille and Pierre-Roger de Mirepoix.

IMPORTANCE:

The fall of Montsegur effectively destroyed the Cathar religious sect, deemed a heresy by the Catholic Church.

Historical Setting

Although Martin Luther is credited with beginning the Reformation, he was not the first to openly point out the worldliness of the Catholic Church. Almost since Constantine's legal acceptance of Christianity in the fourth century, various sects challenged the belief system the Catholic Church expounded. These doctrinal challenges were deemed by the head of the Church in Rome to be heresies—incorrect practices that not only challenged Catholic doctrine but also the will of God. Thus, to keep the ignorant from following the wrong Path, the heresies needed to be stamped out.

In France, one of the main challenges to Rome's authority came from the Cathars. (As the southern French town of Albi was a major center of the faith, they were also called Albi-

This reproduction of a medieval manuscript illumination depicts the capture of Monteségur castle, a Cathar stronghold, during the thirteenth-century Albigensian Crusade ordered by Pope Innocent II. (The Art Archive/Bibliothéque de Carcassonne/Dagli Orti)

gensians.) Starting sometime in the tenth century, the Cathars preached a form of Christianity closely akin to the Eastern religion of Manichaeism. Like the followers of Mani in Persia, the Cathars believed in an everlasting

struggle between two forces, good and evil. The world was under the control of the Devil, and since the God of the Old Testament had created the world he was to blame for the world's evil. The forces of good came into existence with the advent of Jesus Christ, who showed a way to escape the world's sin. Thus, the Cathars believed in a life devoted to good works in order to overcome the world. The leaders of the movement were called parfaits, or perfecti, those who had reached a state of purity. Indeed, the word *Cathar* is believed to have its root in the Greek *katharos*, purity.

As the Catholic Church became more and more powerful politically and economically as well as religiously, the Cathars preached that it had come under the influence of the world and was therefore evil as well. By performing charitable works when the Church's priests did little and the hierarchy displayed unseemly wealth, many common people began to look with favor on the Cathar movement. Some of the nobility also supported them as well, the most notable being Count Raymond VI of Toulouse. The nobles also resented the increasing power of the Church and saw in Catharism a possible way to strengthen their own authority. Further, Frenchmen in the south feared northerners using the power of the Catholic Church to extend their own authority southward.

In 1165 an ecclesiastic council condemned the Cathars as heretics. It was little more than a formality until Innocent III became pope. He attempted to convince the Cathars to change their ways and return to the Church, but his legates accomplished nothing. When one of them was killed, the Cathars were blamed for the murder and a Crusade was declared in January 1208. French troops under the command of Simon de Montfort crushed Cathar strongholds without mercy. On 22 July 1209 the inhabitants of Béziers were ordered to surrender the Cathars in their city. Their refusal brought an attack that quickly overwhelmed the city's defenses. All the 15,000 to 20,000 inhabitants were killed, even though probably no more than 200 Cathars were in the town. When asked why all were being killed indiscriminately, the Church's representative is said to have replied, "Kill them all! God will recognize his own."

Some cities surrendered without a fight in the wake of this slaughter. Others resisted and received similar treatment. The city of Toulouse fell and Count Raymond was banished. For a time the Crusade was over and some Cathars emerged to continue practicing their faith. In 1233, however, Pope Gregory IX instituted the Inquisition in an attempt to wipe out all heresies. Their high-handed tactics provoked resistance, and Raymond VII of Toulouse took up his father's cause in support of the Cathars. He led an insurrection in 1242 that was quickly suppressed by French King Louis IX. With the main supporter of Catharism neutralized, the Church aimed at the final stronghold of the sect: Montsegur.

The Siege

Montsegur Castle sits atop a mesa-like hill 400 feet above the surrounding wooded plain. It has a smaller outer fortification, a barbican, just to the west outside the main walls. The population had long regarded Montsegur as the headquarters of the Cathar movement, and it was certainly one of the last strongpoints. The lord of the castle, Raymond de Pereille, had long been a Cathar supporter, and the Cathars used the site as a temple, performing the rite of *consolamentum*, the initiation ceremony upon reaching the level of perfecti. The Cathars lived in homes outside the walls on the hilltop, as the castle itself was too small to house everyone. When the French troops marched on the castle, a force of eleven knights and 150 soldiers and their families brought the number in the defenses to about 500. The fighting men were under the command of Pereille's son-in-law, Pierre-Roger de Mirepoix.

The invading force of 1,500 under command of Hugues de Arcis arrived in May 1243. He hoped to starve the defenders into submission, but the size of his force and the wooded terrain meant that he was never able to completely invest the position. Local supporters easily and regularly passed through the besiegers in the night, taking supplies to the fort. The height of the fort was such that no catapults available to Arcis could reach the top. Over the next several months, Arcis received reinforcements until his force finally reached almost 10,000. Still, the locals were able to sneak supplies through the lines.

Circumstances changed in November, when Arcis was able to position a force on a level piece of ground near the top of the hill. Once in possession of that point, Arcis' forces spent the next two months slowly hauling siege equipment up the rugged slope. In December they got some catapults constructed and in operation, raining stones down on the barbican. Local Cathars smuggled an engineer into the fort who oversaw the building of a catapult of their own, which returned fire from the barbican. The besiegers were forced to expose themselves both to severe winter weather and heavy return fire. Just after Christmas, the French (probably with the aid of a local turncoat) took a circuitous path along the edge of the mesa to the base of the barbican, which they took in a rush. That placed them some 60 yards from the fort, but the only access to it was across a 6-foot-wide pathway that fell off precipitously on both sides. Still, they had two catapults now and both were turned against the fort.

All accounts of the battle record that after the fall of the barbican, two Cathars stole from the fort with a large amount of gold, silver, and treasure, and got through the enemy lines. To this day no one knows where the treasure was taken. But the fact that it was removed indicates the garrison was assuming the worst was soon to happen. The only hope came from a few crossbowmen who sneaked into the fort with a message from Count Roger: could they hold on until Easter? Roger was raising a relief force, the defenders were told. Also, an agent approached a Spanish mercenary about bringing in fifty men-at-arms to stiffen the defense. They could not get through the French lines. The garrison attempted a sortie at the end of February to retake the barbican or at least destroy the catapults, but it failed. A follow-up assault on the fort was thrown back as well. On 1 March, Raymond de Pereille and Pierre-Roger de Mirepoix appeared on the ramparts, calling out that they wanted to negotiate.

The talks were brief and the terms fairly lenient. The knights and soldiers could leave with their possessions, if they would go to the Inquisition and confess their sin at fighting in the Cathar cause. The Cathars had fifteen days' peace to consider their position. If they would abandon the Cathar faith, they could go free with light penance. No criminal charges would be pressed. The fort would become the possession of the French Crown. Hostages were surrendered, and after a few days the soldiers left. On the evening of 15 March, the Cathars celebrated Easter, and any who desired it received the consolamentum. None of them abjured their faith.

Results

On the morning of 16 March 1244, French soldiers escorted the Cathars out of the fort and took them to their camp below. As heretics who would not recant, they were all to burn. Rather than be given a stake each, they were gathered into a corral stacked with firewood. After rejecting a last call to return to the Catholic Church, the Cathars watched the pyre set alight. All of them, as many as 225 (the number varies by account), walked up ladders and threw themselves into the flames. Those too old or infirm to climb the ladders were unceremoniously tossed into the fire.

The immolation of the Cathars at Montsegur marked the official end of the sect, although a few hardy souls continued to practice the faith surreptitiously. In 1255 a number of Cathars were discovered at Queribus; they were overcome by an attack ordered by King Louis IX, later St. Louis. The province of Languedoc remained semi-independent until 1271, when the last remaining heirs to the position of count of Toulouse died without issue. From that point it became royal property. In spite of that, the region never lost its independent spirit, especially where religion was concerned. When Louis XIII made war against the Protestant Huguenots in the early 1600s, Languedoc was a major center of Protestantism.

The Inquisition, launched as a response to Catharism, was a major force in western Europe until the final triumph of Christendom over Islam in Spain in 1492. "But the repressive terrorism which the Inquisition for several centuries imposed, as a policy, on the nations of the West—this was to undermine the Church's edifice from the inside, and to bring a terrible lowering of Christian morality and Catholic civilization. . . . The victory was bought at too great a price. . . . she only did so at the cost of a moral capitulation the consequences of which she is still suffering today" (Oldenburg, *Massacre at Montsegur*, pp. 366–367).

References: Hoffman Nickerson, *The Inquisition: A Political and Military Study of its Establishment* (Port Washington, NY: Kennikat, 1968 [1932]); Zoe Oldenburg, *Massacre at Montsegur*, trans. Peter Green (New York: Pantheon, 1961 [1959]); Jonathan Sumption, *The Albigensian Crusade* (London: Faber & Faber, 1978).

BAGHDAD

DATE: 22 January–10 February 1258.
LOCATION: on the Tigris River, approximately 500 miles upriver from the Persian Gulf.

FORCES ENGAGED:

Mongol: possibly 200,000. Commander: Hulagu. Arab: unknown, reportedly 100,000 citizens in the city. Commander: Caliph Mustasim.

IMPORTANCE:

Mongol destruction of Baghdad made it a minor city until modern times.

Historical Setting

In the wake of Genghis Khan's death in 1227, the Mongols continued conquering, with their horsemen reaching eastern Europe and threatening the Middle East. In the 1230s, the Mongols pastured in the region of modern Georgia and Azerbaijan, while in the Middle East rival populations fought among themselves rather than face the Asian conquerors: crusaders and Muslims struggled in the Holy Land, Byzantines and Seljuk Turks fought over Anatolia, while in Egypt the Mamluke dynasty was beginning its rise to power.

In the 1250s the great khan was Mangu. His brother, Hulagu, commanded the Mongols of the southwestern sphere and he began extending Mongol power into Persia. There, the primary obstacle was the cult of the Assassins, who had terrorized the area since 1090. When he was informed that the Assassins were targeting him, Mangu ordered Hulagu to remove them. Hulagu led his troops into the mountains of northern Persia, where the Assassins held a hundred fortresses protecting their main headquarters at Alamut. He reduced a number of them before reaching Alamut, which held out for three years before Grand Master Rukn ad-Din sued for peace. He surrendered on 19 November 1256, but none of his followers were spared. Men, women, and children were all slaughtered; the historian Juvaini who was traveling with Hulagu wrote that "the world was cleansed" of them. Hulagu's men proceeded to destroy the remaining castles and kill all the inhabitants until no Assassins were left. Only Rukn ad-Din was spared, to be presented to Mangu, but the great khan refused to meet with him. The grand master was killed afterward, probably by his guards.

With the Assassins gone, Hulagu directed his army westward toward Baghdad, seat of Caliph Mustasim, spiritual leader of all Islam. As the Mongols practiced a strict tolerance for all religions, a faith that was aggressive in spreading its own word was too much of a threat to the Pax Mongolica. Further, Mangu's chief wife was a Nestorian Christian who harbored no love for Islam. Hulagu's army was reinforced by other Mongols fresh from battles against the Seljuk Turks and with a contingent of Christian soldiers from Georgia. Hulagu sent messengers to the caliph, asking why he had not provided aid in the campaign against the Assassins; such an oversight could only be corrected by tearing down Baghdad's walls and swearing fealty to Mangu.

Mustasim was no match for the Mongols, but he had the experience of history on his side. He reminded Hulagu, in a haughty response, that many armies had tried and failed to take Baghdad. Unfortunately, Mustasim could not back up history with contemporary strength. The city walls had long been in disrepair and the caliph's grand vizier Ibn al-Alkami was a self-serving sycophant who exercised entirely too much influence over Mustasim. The vizier assured the caliph that all of Islam would rise up to protect the center of the faith, although Mustasim's generals argued for an immediate call-up of troops and repairs to the walls. Comfortable in his conceit, Mustasim continued his profligate ways and ignored any warnings. He had 50,000 soldiers on hand, but although "the caliph still had the authority to summon soldiers from all the Moslem empires, there were only two of them left, and while his taunting opposition had lost him the loyalty of the Mamluks, the princes of Syria, whom he had supported, were already busy preparing their own defences" (Chambers, *The Devil's Horsemen*, p. 144).

Several more exchanges of messages, arriving from increasingly nearer Mongol forces, finally convinced Mustasim to offer tribute, but not loyalty. That provoked Hulagu to order his men into four columns to strike Baghdad. Finally Mustasim ordered work done on the walls and the arming of the citizenry, but Ibn al-Alkami continued to subvert the defense. He allegedly was in secret contact with Hulagu and was hoping that he could trade his treason to Mustasim for the caliph's throne under the Mongols. Further, as a Shi'ite, the vizier had

often persecuted the region's Sunni Muslims, so they decided they had little interest in answering the caliph's call for troops.

As word of the Mongols' approach reached Mustasim, he finally ordered 20,000 cavalry out of the city to confront them on 11 January 1258. It was a futile gesture. The Mongols broke the Tigris River dikes and flooded the Muslim camp; when the troops engaged, most of the Muslims had either drowned or fled. Few returned to Baghdad. By the 18th the Mongols stood before the city.

The Siege

Baghdad, although the center of religion in the Islamic world, had long been a fading flower intellectually and commercially. By the time of the siege the business district was almost deserted and was therefore easily occupied. Mongols also soon took over the city suburbs, dug a ditch around the city's eastern walls, and brought up their catapults. With little stone in the area, ammunition had to be brought from the mountains. Until that time the Mongols used tree trunks, and stone pillaged from the houses, to bombard the city. They also shot arrows into the city with messages promising safety to any who would surrender. Mustasim finally sent messengers offering to swear fealty, but it was too late. Hulagu by this point would accept only unconditional surrender.

After round-the-clock bombardment, the Mongols launched their assault on 6 February. They were soon in possession of the eastern wall. Once in possession, Hulagu stopped the attack and sent in messengers calling on the defending soldiers to surrender, implying that they would be allowed safe passage to Syria. They were not. Instead, as they marched out of the city unarmed, Hulagu had them executed. Mustasim offered up himself, his three sons, and 3,000 courtiers, all of whom were taken prisoner. That encouraged the population to emerge, but they too found themselves slaughtered as had the soldiers. Only those who sought refuge in the Christian churches were spared as the sack began on 13 February.

Results

Mustasim watched his citizens being slaughtered, then he lost his own life on the 15th. Hulagu had feasted with Mustasim as the city was being sacked, taunting him: why did you not use your immense wealth to pay your soldiers? After revealing the location of his hidden treasure, Mustasim and his sons were sewn up in carpets and trampled by Mongol horses. The number of Muslim citizens killed is open to question, but the estimates range from 80,000 to a million. The Mongols were finally obliged to remove their camp to avoid the smell of rotting corpses.

Two wagon trains of treasure left Baghdad for Karakorum, the Mongol capital and Mangu's home. Baghdad was looted for a month, until few citizens or buildings remained standing. Ibn al-Alkami survived to be named ruler of the city's remains, but he lived only three months, dying it is said of a broken heart.

The fall of Baghdad motivated most of the Muslim fortress cities to surrender. Only Aleppo fell in combat, to a combined force of Mongols and crusaders, who saw the steppe horsemen as allies of convenience in their war against Islam. Mustasim's death, along with that of his sons, brought to an end the Abbassid caliphate, established 500 years before by Muhammad's uncle Abbas. All of Islam could have been in peril, but both timing and Mongol tradition saved them. As Genghis Khan's death had stopped the invasion of Europe, so did Mangu's death halt the sweep into the Middle East. Hulagu returned to Karakorum to take part in the election of the new great khan. He left behind a smaller army under his subordinate Kit-boga, who was defeated by Mamluk forces at Ain Jalut on 3 September 1260. That ended the threat of Mongol domination of the Middle East while making the Egyptian Mamluk dynasty the reigning power in the region.

References: James Chambers, *The Devil's Horsemen* (New York: Atheneum, 1979); Stuart Legg, *The Heartland* (New York: Farrar, Straus, & Giroux, 1970); Vezio Melegari, *The Great Military Sieges* (New York: Crowell, 1972).

HSIANG-YANG

DATE: 1268–1273.
LOCATION: on the Han River in central China.

FORCES ENGAGED:
Mongol: 60,000, plus auxiliaries. Commander: Liu Cheng.
Sung: unknown. Commander: Lü Wen-huan.

IMPORTANCE:
Mongol victory broke the main line of resistance protecting the collapsing Sung dynasty.

Historical Setting

The Sung dynasty in China succeeded the T'ang dynasty in 960. They came to control territory stretching from modern Manchuria to the northern borders of Vietnam and westward a thousand miles from the China Sea. In 1127 the Jurchen Mongols conquered the northern lands, so the Sung dynasty concentrated their authority in richer southern China, building a new capital city at Hangchow, at the mouth of the Yangtze River. The southern Sung dynasty was something of a golden age in China, as expanding trade routes brought immense wealth. They reintroduced Confucianism, which had been losing popularity to Buddhism and Taoism. That led to a new form of bureaucracy, with examinations on Confucian principles being the basis of gaining a position in the civil service, a practice maintained until the twentieth century.

Unfortunately, the Sung dynasty was not blessed with a sufficiently strong military to be as aggressive as earlier dynasties, or even strong enough defensively to beat back the Jurchens in the early twelfth century or the Mongols under Genghis Khan a century later. Genghis was recognized as ruler in the north when his army captured Peking (Beijing) in 1215. Upon his father's death in 1227, Genghis' son Ogadai continued the conquest of rebellious northern territories. While subduing the Jurchens, Ogadai's nephew Tului gained safe passage through Sung lands to complete a wide encircling movement that led to the Jurchens' ultimate demise. For that cooperation, the Sung asked for a return of some of their lost northern territory. When the Mongols refused, the Sung forcibly annexed the province of Honan, setting off a war with the Mongols that lasted thirty-five years.

Ogadai's nephews Mangu and Kubilai directed most of the fighting against the Sung, but an invasion was postponed owing to internal political problems. Mangu succeeded Ogadai as the great khan, but his death in 1260 provoked a civil war between Kubilai, named great khan by one Mongol faction, and his brother, supported by a second group. The two fought for four years before finally Kubilai took the throne. With his position secure, Kubilai returned to his war against the southern Sung. He hoped to conquer them quickly and easily, but some Sung strongholds and generals made that hope a vain one.

Kubilai put a Sung defector, Liu Cheng, in charge of the invasion. He possessed an intimate knowledge of the primary target cities the Mongols would have to capture and experience in naval warfare. That was an aspect of fighting with which the Mongols had no knowledge but was one of the main strengths of the Sung military. Naval power coupled with the manpower of the Mongol land forces proved a potent combination. The key fortress on which Kubilai focused was Hsiang-yang, on the Han River. This city, with the almost equally strong Fan-cheng directly across the river, controlled access to the Yangtze River Valley, which the Mongols needed to reach the Sung capital at Hangchow. It proved to be one of the most difficult fortresses the Mongols ever had to attack.

The Siege

During Kubilai's accession struggle, the Sung had begun preparations for the invasion. The primary figure in this was the prime minister, Chia Ssu-tao. His actions are the subject of some dispute, for the official Chinese chronicles paint him as self-centered, grasping, and corrupt, misleading his emperor as to the potency of the Mongol threat while enriching himself. Less biased observers describe him in a more favorable light, believing that his unpopularity resulted from increased taxes for military operations. Whatever the truth of the matter, Hsiang-yang was prepared when the Mongols arrived. The city's commander, Lü Wen-huan, held a strong position as well as supplies for years of isolation, plus contact via a series of bridges with the city of Fan-cheng across the Han.

Kubilai sent 60,000 veterans under Liu Cheng, which began their investment of the city in March 1268. The Mongols had built their Asian Empire on massive cavalry forces. Since the days of Genghis, however, they had been quick to adopt the technology of whatever population they conquered, so they had besieged cities before. They quickly built 10 miles of fortified lines surrounding the city, plus a fleet to stop any aid from reaching the city by river. The Mongols fortified the towns of Po-ho-k'ou and Lu-men Shan, downriver from Hsiang-yang, to harass any relief fleet sailing up the Han from the Yangtze. The city continued to receive aid from Fan-cheng, however, so in October Kubilai ordered a force under A-chu to surround that city. That created a panic in Hsiang-yang, and the Sung forces attempted a sally against them on 6 December. It was such a disaster the defenders never again left the city.

Even with Fan-cheng surrounded, the siege was irregular in its effectiveness. The perimeter was so vast a complete investment was impossible, so the Mongols shifted troops regularly. Time dragged on with neither side willing to concede defeat. In February 1269 Kubilai sent an emissary to the siege to report on its progress and make recommendations for improvement. That resulted in an extra 20,000 men to strengthen the downstream fortifications. A Sung attempt at resupply came in August 1269, with 3,000 boats, but it was easily thrown back. In April 1270 Liu Cheng and A-chu received a further 70,000 men and 5,000 ships just as Chia Ssu-tao launched another major resupply effort in October 1270; it too failed to break through.

The only success the Sung relieving forces gained was in September 1272. Two forces, one of supply ships and one of warships, made their way down a Han tributary. While the warships pinned down the Mongol fleet, a number of the supply ships along with 3,000 men reached Hsiang-yang. They brought some necessary supplies, including salt, then tried to cut their way back out of the encirclement. Apparently one of their number defected to the Mongols and the 3,000 sailed into a trap that annihilated them. The lines around the city tightened somewhat after this incident.

Increasingly frustrated with the lack of progress, Kubilai sent word to his nephew Abakha, ruling the Mongol domain in Persia. In late 1272 two Persian engineers arrived, skilled in the construction and employment of siege machinery. After surveying the situation, they oversaw the construction of a mangonel and a catapult. These were deployed in March 1273 against Fan-cheng; within a few days sufficient damage had been done to allow a successful assault against the city. "The battle raged from street to street, from house to house; and, when there was no longer any possibility of continuing the contest, the officers, sooner than surrender, slew themselves, in which they were imitated by their men. The Mongols had indeed captured Fanching [sic], but their triumph was only over a city of ruins and ashes" (Boulger, *The History of China*, vol. 1, p. 338). When it fell, Lü Wen-huan realized his city could not survive a similar attack. After some preliminary bombardment the Mongols offered generous terms. Lü Wen-huan accepted them, as well as an offer to serve in Kubilai's army.

Results

The fall of Hsiang-yang turned the tide of the Mongol war against the Sung. Previously the Sung emperor and his court, confident in their defenses, had rejected Mongol emissaries. With the Han River now open to the Yangtze, the Mongols had a clear path to Hangchow. Prime Minister Chia Ssu-tao took direct command of the Sung armies in a desperate attempt to save his reputation, position, and emperor. Instead of mounting a major expedition earlier against the besieging Mongols, during which he could have cooperated with a coordinated sally from the city, he now had to face a large army under a new commander. Responding to the advice of one of his primary Chinese advisers, Kubilai placed all of his southern army under a single general, Bayan, grandson of Genghis' most gifted subordinate, Subotai. Bayan apparently inherited his forebear's military talent and he had campaigned with the Mongols in Persia and the Middle East.

Bayan moved downstream with a growing army, offering traditional Mongol terms to every town he encountered: surrender to leniency or fight to the death. Most Sung commanders chose the former alternative. The Sung emperor Tu-tsung died in August 1274 and power was in the hands of the dowager Empress Hsieh, but she was little equipped to exercise that power. Bayan defeated Chia Ssu-tao's 130,000-man army in mid-March 1275, and the final bar to Hangchow was removed. The empress tried negotiations, but after so many earlier rejections and with momentum on his side, Bayan would accept nothing less than unconditional surrender. With the Mongol army at Hangchow's gates, she finally conceded in late January 1276.

Kubilai Khan announced the end of the Sung dynasty in the midst of the siege of

Hsiang-yang; in 1271 he declared the beginning of the Yuan dynasty. Although it proved relatively short-lived, Kubilai's government was not without positive accomplishments. Realizing the superiority of Chinese administration over that of the traditional Mongol state, he adapted his government to that of the conquered. The efficient civil service remained in place and the trade routes that they had used were reopened. Kubilai's dynasty permitted the uninterrupted flow of Chinese culture and bureaucracy, and gave to it a unified empire larger than it had ever encompassed. Kubilai's successors ruled badly and quarreled among themselves. A rebellion in 1368 chased the Mongols westward past the Great Wall and founded the Ming dynasty. The enlarged territory that Kubilai left to China remained for the most part the China that exists to this day.

References: Demetrius Charles Boulger, *The History of China*, vol. 1 (Freeport, NY: Books for Libraries Press, 1972 [1898]); Ch'i-ch'ing Hsiao, *The Military Establishment of the Yuan Dynasty* (Cambridge, MA: Harvard University Press, 1978); Kwanten Luc, *Imperial Nomads* (Philadelphia: University of Pennsylvania Press, 1979); Morris Rossabi, *Khubilai Khan: His Life and Times* (Berkeley: University of California Press, 1988).

CALAIS

DATE: 4 September 1346–3 August 1347.
LOCATION: on France's northern coast, directly opposite Dover, England.

FORCES ENGAGED:
English: 30,000 men. Commander: King Edward III.
French: 7,000–8,000 population. Commander: Jean de Fosseux.

IMPORTANCE:
Capture of the port gave the English a foothold in France for the next two centuries.

Historical Setting

The Anglo-French conflict that came to be called the Hundred Years War was based on rival claims to land and leadership. The death of Charles VI of France in 1328 left a void in the French monarchy. The Capetian dynasty had ruled most of France since 987, but there was now no direct male heir. The best legal claim came from Edward III of England, grandson of Philip the Fair (1285–1314), but the French nobility could not conceive of a foreigner as king. Instead, they chose Philip VI Valois, ending the Capetian dynasty. Edward resisted this choice, not only because he wanted the throne for himself, but also because he was technically a vassal of the French king. Since he controlled some territory in France, he might be called on to obey his liege lord with actions detrimental to England. Further, the French had supported the Bruces of Scotland in their struggle for independence from the English. Finally, England coveted Flanders, nominally under French control but tied to England via the wool trade. Add to all this the traditional dislike the French and English have always harbored for each other, and war seemed inevitable.

Although possessed of a larger and wealthier population, France did not have a strong central administration to direct military operations or collect the taxes necessary to pay for a war. England was better organized, had more consistent military leadership, and had superior weaponry in the form of the longbow. The war was fought in three phases over the space of 116 years. First, Edward provoked trouble in Flanders by instituting an embargo on English wool, placing the merchants and trade guilds in economic jeopardy. The cities of Flanders were obliged to recognize Edward as king of France in order to reopen trade. They signed a treaty of alliance with England, but proved to be less than faithful to it. With this foothold on the Continent, Edward organized an invasion force. He drew first blood with a naval victory over the French at the battle of Sluys in January 1340, a battle that gave him control of the

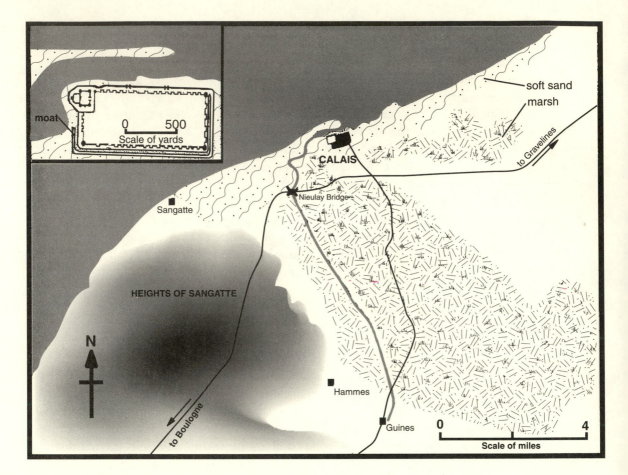

English Channel. He was unable to follow this up because of a lack of Flemish support, so he was forced to conclude a truce with France.

Edward ended the peace in 1346 when English forces invaded Normandy and won a series of victories culminating in their triumph at Crecy. He did not want to fight the French at the time but, since his ships had left Calais to evacuate the wounded and booty, he could not escape. While marching for Flanders he met French forces at Crecy and had to stand and fight. Edward's army of knights and longbowmen faced a French army much superior in numbers of mounted knights and foot soldiers. He won by defense and poor French leadership. Philip attacked late in the afternoon of 26 August, and by midnight the French army was in tatters. In the wake of this victory, Edward retreated to Calais with an exhausted army.

The Siege

Calais is located near the border with Flanders and had major fortifications constructed in the thirteenth century. The English Channel and Calais harbor lie on the northern side, while a double moat and strong walls surrounded the remainder of the town. In the northwest corner of the city was a citadel with its own walls and moat. Making the position even stronger was the natural defenses of marshy terrain, across which siege engines could not be moved. Just before the English arrived, Lieutenant Governor of Artois Jean de Fosseux brought in last-minute reinforcements and took command of the defense.

When Edward's troops approached the city on 4 September 1346, they immediately saw the futility of a direct assault. They therefore began digging trenchworks for a prolonged siege. Luckily for them, this campaign proved sufficiently popular among the population and aristocrats of England that a steady stream of supplies arrived from across the Channel, through Gravelines, and across causeways to the troops. It was an amazing administrative feat for its time. Only a mid-September raid by Genoese ships allied to Philip interrupted the convoys sailing regularly from southeastern England. In spite of a commanding sea presence, the English failed through the fall of 1346 to keep French ships from revictualling and reinforcing Calais. On land, however, the French king seemed paralyzed. He sent a few troops to keep an eye on the English from a distance as well as to watch the border with Flanders, but did nothing to interfere with the English supply lines.

Increasingly frustrated by the French defense, Edward tried to assault the city. In mid-November fifty fishing vessels carrying long ladders arrived. Other boats brought stone-throwing catapults and several cannon. With these the English tried to scale and batter the walls, but without success. The last recorded assault took place on 27 February, after which Edward decided to let hunger do its work. Although his army remained well supplied, the damp, cold winter coupled with the marshy ground produced a huge number of sick. Others despaired of the situation and deserted.

In the spring of 1347 the French launched a major resupply fleet out of Normandy, which delivered perhaps 1,000 tons of supplies in early April. The English did almost nothing to stop this convoy, but it proved to be the last to aid the garrison. Later attempts were turned back by serious English naval power. Meanwhile, there continued to be no pressure at all from the landward side.

By June the defenders were reduced to eating what animals they could find in the city, and fresh water also became scarce. When a resupply convoy failed to break through on 25 June, second-in-command Jean de Vienne

wrote King Philip that soon the only meat available would be that of the dead people in the city. Edward intercepted the letter, but having read it he added his royal seal and forwarded it on to Philip. In mid-July the king sent an eight-barge convoy filled with supplies but the English captured all of them. In the wake of that failure, the French commanders expelled 500 children and old people. The English would not let them approach, so those turned out of the city starved beneath its walls.

The arrival of spring had brought reinforcements to Edward's army, which reached some 32,000 strong: 5,300 knights, 6,600 infantry, and 20,000 archers. By summer, the Flemings had a further 20,000 men, which they put under his command. King Philip finally gathered his own troops for a relief attempt. With a force of perhaps 20,000 he slowly moved north until he finally reached the Sangatte heights, overlooking the Calais marshes some 6 miles to the south. The marshes, intended to protect the city, now protected the besiegers. Philip realized he could not possibly advance on the English and bring his superior cavalry to bear. Negotiation proved fruitless, as did a challenge to come out and fight on ground suitable to both sides.

On the night of 1 August, signal fires in Calais warned King Philip of the town's imminent surrender. He responded by destroying their camp rather than leave it for the English or be caught on open ground trying to transport it away. Seeing this, the French inside asked for terms. Edward, furious at the length of the siege, offered none. His advisers prevailed upon him to soften his position against a future time when the situations might be reversed. He would spare the population's lives but would possess the town and all within it. He demanded six prominent citizens abase themselves before him with the keys to the city. When they arrived Edward ordered his executioner to work. Only the pleadings of his closest advisers, and then his queen, forced him to relent.

Results

Edward took the highest-ranking noblemen hostage, then fed the rest of the citizens and sent them packing. His men received an equal share of everything in the town. As Calais was a center for piracy over the previous decades, the division of spoils made his troops quite happy. The displaced citizens received a royal pension for almost twenty years. The city they left behind became an English colony, populated for the next 200 years by English merchants.

Philip assumed that Edward would be happy with his capture and go home, leaving a garrison behind. Edward indeed began to send his troops across the Channel, but only until he knew Philip had dispersed the French army. Edward then reorganized his army and began raiding all across northern France. Philip was finally able to negotiate an armistice that proved longer lasting than anyone had believed—not because of honor, but because the Black Death arrived in France and ravaged the countryside for seven years. The war resumed in 1355 and went on intermittently until 1453, after which Calais remained the only English possession in France. Not until January 1558 did it return to French control.

References: Christopher Allmand, *The 100 Years War* (New York: Cambridge University Press, 1988); Desmond Seward, *The Hundred Years War* (New York: Atheneum, 1978); Jonathan Sumption, *Trial by Battle* (London: Faber & Faber, 1990).

NICOPOLIS

Date: 12–24 September 1396.
Location: on the Danube River, roughly 200 miles west of the Black Sea, at modern Nikopol, Bulgaria.

Forces Engaged:

Ottoman: in Nicopolis, unknown. Commander: Dogan Beg.

Relief force: 16,000–20,000 Janissaries and cavalry. Commander: Sultan Bayazid I. Crusader: possibly as many as 6,000 French and 10,000 Hungarian troops. Commander: King Sigismund of Hungary.

Importance:

Ottoman victory marked the end of Catholic Church-sponsored crusading against Islam.

Historical Setting

Just as Islam exploded into power in the eighth century in conjunction with the timely weakness of both the Parthians and the Byzantines, so too did Sultan Bayazid I arrive in the Balkans at precisely the right time. Through much of the fourteenth century the region was enjoying a virtual renaissance, primarily under the leadership of Serbian King Stephan Dushan (r. 1331–1355). He was the strongest of the Serbian medieval monarchs, and his many victories brought Albania, Bosnia, Macedonia, Thessaly, and other, smaller provinces under his thumb. He codified the laws of his dominions and patronized the arts. His campaign to conquer Constantinople, however, saw his death from disease and the resulting death of his kingdom.

Without a man of power and vision in control, the provinces turned to their own devices, following political or religious goals at odds with those of their neighbors. Squabbling princes and minor kings oversaw a constant shifting of alliances and influence, none of which could bring unity. They remained safe enough as long as the Ottomans were focused on capturing Constantinople, but when the Byzantine King John V Paleologus was obliged to swear fealty to Sultan Murad in the early 1370s, Muslim forces turned northwestward. Muslim soldiers occupied the Gallipoli peninsula below Constantinople in 1355 and by 1361 took the city of Adrianople, which became their capital. Pope Urban V called for a Crusade to expel them, but it came to grief in 1371 at the River Maritsa.

Muslim armies conquered northern Greece but were checked by Serbian troops under

Lazar I at Plochnik in 1388. It was only temporary; the following year the Serbs and their allies were crushed in Kosovo and the new King Stephen Lazarevic became a Muslim vassal. Bayazid I became sultan upon his father's death in battle in 1389, and he continued to spread Islam's power. In 1392 Wallachia became his vassal and the following year he made great strides into Bulgaria.

In the face of this threat King Sigismund of Hungary rose to the fore. Son of the German Emperor Charles VI, he married into the ruling Hungarian dynasty. With his connections in western Europe, he was able to draw on both military and religious support. Responding to Sigismund's call for aid, both Pope Boniface X in Rome and the Avignon Pope Benedict XIII urged their knights to fight the infidel. Count Jean of Nevers led the main French and Burgundian contingent of perhaps 10,000 knights plus their support troops. The Knights Hospitalers sent ships and men from their new base in Rhodes. Venice supported the cause with a fleet to carry supplies. All of this was possible because Bayazid temporarily returned to besiege Constantinople when the new Emperor Manuel renounced his predecessor's vassalage.

The Siege

The French force easily made its way to the Danube, then downstream with its supplies transported by ship. At Budapest they joined with Sigismund's army of about 10,000 men, which included a contingent from Wallachia under King Mercia. The combined force crossed to the south side of the river at Orsova, then proceeded farther downstream rather than marching on Adrianople. They knew that by capturing successive towns along the river they would attract Bayazid's attention and draw his army toward them. In early September 1396 the crusaders captured Vidin without a fight, then Rashowa after a mere five-day siege. The next target was Nicopolis, whose Turkish garrison under Dogan Beg was both

strong and motivated. Although Count Jean had left France with probably 10,000 knights, casualties, desertions, and the establishment of garrisons had weakened his army to perhaps 6,000 by this time.

Nicopolis was the key to dominating the Danube Valley, for it lay near the junction of rivers leading north into Wallachia and south into Bulgaria. The Danube at Nicopolis is about a mile wide, with marshes and small islands. Italian and Hospitaler supply ships arrived from the Black Sea on 10 September and anchored just out of arrow-shot. The Franco-Burgundian force in the army's vanguard arrived on the 12th and encamped opposite the citadel. Sigismund and the Hungarians came up the next day and surrounded the city. On two sides the city sat atop steep bluffs, but on the third the walls faced more level ground, although it was scarred by ravines. Scaling ladders were built and mines begun, but neither proved successful against the city's defenses. For all their sea power, the crusaders had failed to bring siege engines of any type, so the Turkish force could only be defeated by starvation. Perhaps the besiegers did not plan on actually capturing the city, but were only trying to attract Bayazid's army. If such was the case, it was successful, for Bayazid lost no time in answering their challenge.

Inexplicably, the crusaders posted few if any lookouts. Bayazid was therefore able to move his army rapidly from Constantinople to Edirne to Tarnovo, where they combined on 21 or 22 September with Bosnian troops led by Stephan Lazarevic. By the 24th they encamped within sight of the crusader army. Some Ottoman sources claim that Bayazid personally stole through the lines to speak to Dogan Beg.

With the crusaders now caught between two forces, a dual attack by the Muslim forces seemed likely. Instead, Bayazid dug in. If he had any knowledge of the French knighthood, he would certainly have known that they would come to him. Bayazid placed a force of his Janissary archers behind embankments on a gentle slope facing the crusaders. They were screened by light cavalry. The remainder of his army he placed on the reverse of the hill in hiding. On 24 September Sigismund sent Enguerrand de Coucy on a reconnaissance that engaged the light cavalry but did not discover the bulk of the Muslim army. That night Sigismund and Nevers argued over strategy. The Hungarian and Wallachian force was predominantly light cavalry archers, the French army heavy cavalry knights. A general engagement with Sigismund's larger force might have drawn Bayazid out of hiding, after which a killing blow by the French knights could have been successful. Instead, Nevers demanded and received the right to open the attack. Before the attack, hundreds of Ottoman prisoners were slaughtered: too many men would have had to be spared to watch them in case of a sortie from the city.

Apparently the hard lesson of Crecy fifty years earlier had been forgotten, and the Franco-Burgundian knights charged into battle without waiting for Sigismund's troops to arrive on the field. They easily drove the Ottoman light cavalry back, but that brought them into range of the Janissary archers, who brought down hundreds of horses. As the French regrouped and charged again, Bayazid led his cavalry from both flanks in a double envelopment that massacred most of the knights. Sigismund arrived too late to help, and the Muslims immediately followed up their opening victory with a massive pursuit of the unready Hungarians. A coincident attack from Nicopolis finished the rout.

Results

Bayazid spared two dozen knights for ransom, then executed most of his prisoners in retaliation for what the crusaders had done to their prisoners. Few of the crusader force survived, but Sigismund managed to reach the Danube and flee on the supply ships.

For almost four centuries following the Ottoman victory at Nicopolis, Bulgaria was part of their empire. With no other western European force available and the Hundred Years War still dragging on in France, little could have stopped a continued Muslim sweep toward central Europe. Instead, Bayazid turned back to Constantinople. He almost succeeded in capturing the Byzantine capital, but the timely arrival of the fearsome conqueror Timur-i-lang (Tamerlane) from the east forced him to again abandon his siege to meet another threat. This time Bayazid was not so lucky, and it took the Ottomans half a century to recover from Timur's devastation.

The disaster at Nicopolis also spelled the end of European crusading. National rivalries were rising in the West and the wars they engendered made the Ottoman threat seem less important; it was finally turned away for good when Suleiman the Magnificent was defeated at Vienna in 1683.

References: A. S. Atiya, *The Crusade of Nicopolis* (London: Methuen, 1934); Hans Delbruck, *Medieval Warfare*, trans. Walter Renfroe (Lincoln: University of Nebraska Press, 1990 [1923]); David Nicolle, *Nicopolis, 1396* (London: Osprey, 1999).

ORLEANS

DATE: 12 October 1428–7 May 1429.
LOCATION: central France.

FORCES ENGAGED:

French: garrison: 2,400 soldiers and 3,000 armed citizens. Commander: Jean Dunois, comte de Longueville.
Relieving force: 4,000 soldiers. Commanders: duke of Alençon and Jeanne d'Arc.
English: 5,000 soldiers. Commander: earl of Salisbury until his death, then the earl of Shrewsbury.

IMPORTANCE:

French victory marked the psychological turn of the tide against England in the Hundred Years War.

The French patriot and martyr St. Joan of Arc, also known as the Maid of Orleans, leads an attack out of Orleans, painting by William Etty. (Art Resource)

Historical Setting

There were a number of momentum shifts during the course of the Hundred Years War. Edward III's victories at Sluys and Crecy gave England the early advantage, but during the middle part of the fourteenth century the spread of the bubonic plague halted fighting and robbed both sides of any advantage. During the several years that the Black Death ravaged France and England, major societal changes occurred. As farmers either died from the plague or fled the countryside for the cities, feudal lords saw their incomes fall rapidly. The cities, on the other hand, began to enjoy a blossoming economy. The fear of death encouraged many citizens to pay for extravagant sundries to enjoy their last days on earth, so merchants and craftsmen grew rich. As the cities gained wealth and the manors declined, the king began courting the financial support of the townspeople for his royal projects, including warfare. Soldiers thus became paid employees rather than feudal pawns. The aristocrats' fortunes waned further.

More important from a social point of view, the unexplained epidemic meant that many people turned to the church for answers and solace. Thus, the power of the church also grew as the population became increasingly religious. Some viewed the plague as the wrath of God, while others blamed the traditional scapegoats, the Jews. In France, blame was laid on the English. Whatever the cause, people believed that if the plague came from God, so must the deliverance.

While the plague raged, the war took a back seat and English gains melted away. By default, momentum shifted to the French. When Henry V came to the throne of England in 1413, he claimed the French throne as Edward had. After his victory at Agincourt in 1415, he was able to wrest the throne away from the heir of Charles VI and for a few years reigned as king of England and France. His untimely death in 1422 reopened the succession question.

The English named Henry's infant son as rightful king, while the French supported Charles VI's son as King Charles VII. He certainly had the proper bloodline for claiming the throne, but unfortunately nothing else. While officially claiming the throne, he did nothing to actually rule, for he was an incredibly weak character. While Charles vacillated, the regent for England's Henry VI, the duke of Bedford, proceeded to reestablish English dominance in France. Aided by the powerful Duchy of Burgundy, Bedford placed all of France north of the Loire under English control. Everything seemed to be going England's way, and the decades of war, plague, and poor leadership all conspired against France. The people of France could only pray for a miracle to deliver their country.

Enter Jeanne d'Arc. Born to a well-to-do common family in the eastern province of Lorraine, Jeanne lived a normal life until her teen years. At age 13 she began hearing voices, which she was convinced came from Saints Margaret and Catherine (earlier queens of France) and the archangel Michael. When she was age 17 the voices informed her that she was chosen to assist in France's liberation and force the useless Charles VII to actually take control of France.

The Siege

Jeanne's heavenly directive coincided with Bedford's latest offensive against the French. With almost all of northern France under his control, he aimed to conquer Armagnac, the lands south of the Loire. His first target was one of the fortress cities that lined the river: Orleans. English forces commanded by the earl of Salisbury arrived at Orleans on 12 October 1428 and proceeded to surround the city as best they could, for they numbered only about 5,000. Their first objective was to seize the for-

tified bridge across the Loire. This they did on the 24th, but Salisbury was killed in the attempt. His temporary successor was the earl of Suffolk, followed in December by John Talbot, earl of Shrewsbury.

The English maintained a steady artillery barrage against the city, but the cannonballs were made of stone and hence did little harm to the thick stone walls. The size of the besieging force meant that a secure investment of the city was impossible, so the English built small forts to protect their hold on the bridge as well as their encampments. Occasional forays by the French netted some supplemental supplies during the siege, but by the spring of 1429 the condition of the besieged was getting desperate.

It was Orleans that Jeanne was supposed to relieve. Through her uncle, a soldier, she managed to gain an escort to Chinon, where she finally gained an interview with Charles after a month's grilling by church and military personnel. Why Charles should have granted a teenage girl command of an army is a question that has never been answered, but his personal vice of visiting soothsayers may have influenced his decision to deal with someone who heard voices from the beyond. She was named co-commander, along with the duke of Alençon, of a force of 4,000. As they approached Orleans, Jeanne sent a letter to the English demanding their withdrawal; not surprisingly it was ignored. Commanded by her voices to enter the city from the north, she had to overcome the wishes of the other officers, who feared challenging the English directly. She convinced them to ferry her and the army across the Loire to the north bank, between the city and the English camp at St. Loup. She marched her troops north, waited a night, then marched them back to the city on 29 April 1429 and through the gate she had been instructed to use. She had so far followed her instructions against little enemy opposition.

For a few days little happened, for the defenders within Orleans did not want to attack the English. Jeanne assured them of God's leadership and protection. When she heard of English reinforcements approaching she celebrated, ordering that she be alerted as soon as they arrived, or she would behead the Comte de Langueville, commander of the Orleans garrison. On 1 May, after a short truce, Jeanne jumped up from her slumber and announced that it was time to attack. She quickly donned her armor, mounted her white horse, and rode out of the city. She found that a French sally against the fort at St. Loup was in progress and faring badly. She dashed to the battle, rallied the French, and the fort fell. The French lost only two men, while all the English defenders were killed in the battle. She commanded the entire army to praise God and confess their sins, then proceeded to banish all prostitutes following the army. She allowed no fighting the following day, the Feast of the Ascension, but announced that the English would be gone within five days. Another demand for an English withdrawal was met with obscene shouts, so she had no choice but to prepare for battle.

On 5 May Jeanne led a sortie out of the south gate of the city, which led to the bridge whose southern end the English had captured in the first days of the siege. She bypassed the bridge and led her troops across the shallows to an island in the Loire, then used a boat bridge to reach the southern bank. The French quickly captured the fort at St. Jean le Blanc, then marched toward the larger fort at Les Augustins, near the bridge. The fight for that fort was difficult and costly for both sides, but Jeanne led a charge that swept an English sally back into the fort and ultimately into French hands. On the 6th the French assaulted Le Tournelles, the towers at the southern end of the bridge. In the midst of the fighting Jeanne was struck by an arrow and carried from the field. It turned out to be little more than a flesh wound and by late afternoon she was back in the fight. After ten minutes of prayer she led her exhausted troops in an attack that forced another English sortie back into the towers.

On 7 May a French knight took Jeanne's banner and made for Les Tournelles. She tried to stop him, but when the French soldiers saw her banner they rushed to follow it. Bringing assault ladders they scaled the walls, Jeanne in the lead. The 400 to 500 English defenders tried to flee, but died as the burning bridge that was their escape route collapsed. The next day the English abandoned the siege, and the French troops reentered Orleans after killing or capturing all the English troops left on the south side of the river. When the English destroyed their camps and marched away on the 9th, many French soldiers wanted to attack the retreating column, but Jeanne forbade it: it was Sunday and only fighting in self-defense was allowed. On Monday they struck the English and captured some artillery and supplies.

Results

When Charles heard of the relief of Orleans he took complete credit, never mentioning Jeanne in his missives. The French citizenry knew who had really won the battle, however, and the French army grew. Jeanne led attacks against English garrisons in towns throughout the region, liberating a number of them. On 18 June she led a charge against Shrewsbury's army, lately reinforced by 1,000 mercenaries. Her 6,000 troops inflicted 4,000 English casualties as the enemy was routed. The next day at the battle of Patay, the French surprised an English ambush and routed them yet again; Shrewsbury was captured. "[B]eyond the local decisions at Orleans and Patay, an answer had at last been found to that English system of war which enabled the smaller nation to bring France to the edge of national collapse. Most obviously the solution lay in the release of moral forces. *In hoc signo vinces* can be quite as useful a military weapon as a sword or a cannon" (Pratt, *Battles that Changed History*, p. 128).

Jeanne met with Charles and urged him to make his way to Reims to be crowned king of France. She led the force that escorted him, capturing the city of Troyes from a Burgundian garrison without a fight. Reims also was under

Burgundian control and the French had no siege equipment, but Jeanne was undaunted. She told her troops to "advance boldly and fear nothing" and that city also surrendered without opposition. Charles was duly crowned king on 16 July 1429.

Jeanne led an attack on Paris, also held by Burgundian forces, although she heard no voices directing her to do so. She was wounded in the leg during the fighting and Charles ordered a retreat. After the disbanding of his army, only a few hundred men of Jeanne's personal unit campaigned with her in 1430, and their numbers were too few to accomplish the heavenly directives she received. She fell prisoner to the Burgundians and Charles refused to ransom her. Sold to the English, she was tried as a witch. The trial was a sham that resulted in her execution at the stake on 30 May 1431. In spite of the stacked deck against her, the prosecution could find not one witness to speak against her.

Jeanne d'Arc is better known outside France by her English appellation Joan of Arc. Much about her short life and career, although well-documented, remains mysterious. What caused the voices she heard and the bright lights that accompanied them, which only she could hear and see? Whatever may be the actual cause, the heavenly explanation is the only one that matters. Everyone in France knew of her voices, but in a time of religious intolerance of anything uncommon, she convinced experts and lay people alike that she indeed was blessed. A population newly emerged from the horror of the Black Death and intent on following God's will saw her as a divine emissary. Clad in a white-enameled suit of armor, riding a white horse, carrying a white and blue banner emblazoned with two angels and the words "Jhesus Maria," called *La Pucelle* (the Virgin) by her troops—everything about her spoke of holiness. For a citizenry that had believed only a miracle could rescue France, she filled the bill. Nothing else explains why hardened veterans would not only follow her into combat, but also accept without com-plaint her demands that they neither curse nor whore.

Jeanne's strategy changed the fortune of this war. She began reversing the tactics practiced by the French throughout the conflict, that of frontal assault against prepared English lines. As long as she kept to that plan, French forces won. More important, it was the shift in morale that secured the English defeat as much as their loss of troops in the field. After Orleans and Patay the fortunes of the English in France began to wane. The war itself dragged on for more than twenty years, but after Orleans the fate of France seems to have been sealed. Considering the lack of leadership Charles provided, it is amazing that the French fighting spirit survived Jeanne's death. But infighting among the English and Burgundians proved as helpful to France as did the Maid of Orleans. Few in France doubt the wisdom of Jeanne's sanctification by the Catholic Church in 1920.

References: J. F. C. Fuller, *Military History of the Western World*, vol. 1 (New York: Funk and Wagnalls, 1954); Frances Gies, *Joan of Arc: The Legend and the Reality* (New York: Harper & Row, 1981); Fletcher Pratt, *The Battles that Changed History* (Garden City, NY: Doubleday, 1965); Jonathan Sumption, *The Hundred Years War: Trial by Battle* (Philadelphia: University of Pennsylvania Press, 1991); Bonnie Wheeler and Charles T. Wood, eds., *Fresh Verdicts on Joan of Arc* (New York: Garland, 1996).

CONSTANTINOPLE

DATE: February–May 1453.
LOCATION: on the Sea of Marmara, modern Istanbul.

FORCES ENGAGED:

Turkish: 80,000 men. Commander: Sultan Mohammed II.
Byzantine: less than 10,000 men. Commander: Emperor Constantine XI Paleologus.

IMPORTANCE:

The fall of Constantinople represented the final destruction of the Byzantine Empire while opening Europe to the spread of Islam; it also marked the arrival of Ottoman Turks as the dominant Muslim faction until the twentieth century.

Historical Setting

Constantine the Great established the city of Constantinople as his capital in 323. He occupied the former city of Byzantium, which for centuries controlled the straits separating Asia and Europe. It lies on the Sea of Marmara, flanked to northeast by the Bosphorus and to the southwest by the Dardanelles, two narrow passages linking the Mediterranean and the Black seas. The only direct route from Europe into Asia Minor is at Constantinople, so it has been an extremely strategic possession for land and naval warfare and trade.

Constantinople became the seat of the Eastern Roman, or Byzantine, Empire. It not only was the political capital of much of the Mediterranean and Middle East, but also the seat of the

The conquest of Constantinople, painting by Palma Giovane. (Scala/Art Resource)

Greek Orthodox Church, rival to the power of the pope in Rome for the souls of Christians everywhere. In the end it was that religious rivalry that spelled Constantinople's doom.

In the seventh century Muhammad the Prophet founded Islam. By coincidence (or divine intervention) he appeared in Arabia just as the two major Middle Eastern powers, Persia and the Byzantine Empire, had fought each other to an exhausted standstill. He therefore conquered a massive amount of land hand in hand with the spread of his faith. Both Persia and the Byzantines suffered major territorial losses as well as major losses of converts to Islam, who found it less oppressive than the ultraconservative Orthodox Church.

For seven hundred years the forces of Islam and Orthodoxy struggled, with both sides trading ascendancy. By the fifteenth century, however, the Byzantine Empire had shrunk to almost nothing: Constantinople and a handful of Aegean islands. An earlier Islamic threat to the city resulted in the Crusades in the twelfth century, but that too ended in further alienating the Catholic and Orthodox churches. When in 1452 Sultan Mohammed II, son of Murad II, decided to attack Constantinople, European responses to pleas for help were almost nonexistent. England and France were just winding down the very costly Hundred Years War; Germanic and Spanish princes and kings offered aid but sent none. Genoa and Venice, however, did not want to see Constantinople fall into the hands of Arab merchants, and Rome promised aid if the Orthodox Church would submit to papal will. Reluctantly Emperor Constantine XI Paleologus agreed to Rome's demand, but it netted him a mere 200 archers for his meager defenses as well as the hostility of his people; many claimed they preferred Turkish domination to Roman.

In the spring of 1452 Mohammed II sent 1,000 masons to the Bosphorus to build a fort to protect his army while crossing the straits.

Constantine could do little more than lodge a protest. Among his populace were a mere 5,000 native and 2,000 foreign soldiers. He had tradition on his side, however, for the triple walls that blocked the city from the landward side had survived twenty sieges, even though at this point they were not in good repair. As of January 1453, he also had the services of Italian soldier of fortune Giovanni Giustiniani, who brought 700 knights and archers. Giustiniani was well known in Europe for his talents in defending walled cities. Mohammed also had some European assistance in the form of a cannon maker named Urban from Hungary, who provided the Muslim army with seventy cannon, including the "Basilica," a 27-feet-long canon that fired stone balls weighing upwards of 600 pounds. It could only fire seven times a day, but did significant damage to anything it struck.

A single wall that ran the circumference of the city's seaward sides defended the rest of Constantinople. Mohammed sent his men across the Bosphorus north of the city, so the southern approach to the Mediterranean was open. A chain boom protected the primary harbor, the Golden Horn, across its mouth supported by twenty-six galleys. Thus, if anyone sent relief, the route was open.

The Siege

Mohammed II arrived on 6 April 1453. He led 70,000 regular troops and 20,000 irregulars called Bashi-Bazouks, whose sole pay was the loot they might gain if and when the city fell. The premier troops were the Janissaries, slave soldiers taken captive in their youth from Christian families and raised in a military atmosphere to serve the sultans. They were heavily armored and highly skilled, and at this time they were beginning to use personal firearms. Mohammed first seized the town of Pera, across the Golden Horn from Constantinople. At first this action was little more than symbolic, but it had serious ramifications later. He then deployed his forces on the city's western face and began the siege. A single wall near the imperial palace protected the northern end of the city. It was there, the Blachernae, that Constantine placed most of his men.

For twelve days the Muslim cannon pounded the city walls, and on 18 April Mohammed decided that had softened up the defenses sufficiently. The Byzantines easily defended a narrow breach in the walls, killing 200 attackers and driving off the rest without loss to themselves. On the 20th, four ships approached from the south: three Genoese transports with men and supplies from Rome and a Byzantine ship hauling corn from Sicily. After a hard fight with the Muslim fleet they broke through, cleared the boom, and entered the Golden Horn. Mohammed decided he had to control the harbor. He could not pass the chain boom, so he ordered ships dragged overland, through the town of Pera, to the harbor. It was a monumental engineering feat and on 22 April thirty Turkish ships were in the Golden Horn. An agent of the sultan betrayed the Byzantine counterattack, which managed to destroy only a single Turkish ship. In spite of this Turkish accomplishment, it had little effect on the siege.

Mohammed continued his cannonade against the walls. By 6 May it had opened a breach at the Gate of St. Romanus, where the Lycus River enters the city. Giustaniani built a new wall just behind the breach, rather than trying to repair the wall while under fire. The Turks attacked on 7 May but their 25,000 men were thrown back after three hours of fighting. On the 12th another force assaulted a breach in the wall at Blachernae; only quick reinforcement by Constantine and the Imperial Guard stemmed the tide. Mohammed then tried mining the walls. Constantine's engineer Johannes Grant managed to locate each of the mining attempts and either undermine the mines or

destroy the attackers inside with explosives, flooding, or the incendiary Greek fire. None of the fourteen mines succeeded.

Mohammed then determined to scale the walls. His men built a siege tower and rolled it into place before the Charisius Gate, the northernmost opening in the city walls. Muslim artillery fire had destroyed one of the defending towers, and the siege tower was able to provide covering fire for Turks filling in the moat. Constantine's call for volunteers to attack the siege tower produced spectacular results. The sally surprised the Turkish guards and the Byzantines broke pots of Greek fire on the wooden siege tower. Meanwhile, their compatriots spent the night rebuilding the city wall and its destroyed tower. The next morning Mohammed saw the charred remains of his assault machine smoldering before the newly rebuilt tower in the city wall.

In both camps officers debated the progress of the siege. The defenders were exhausted and running out of supplies. In Mohammed's camp, some factions wanted to end the siege before a rumored rescue fleet could arrive. The sultan favored those who counseled continuation and decided to launch one more attempt before withdrawing. As the most serious damage to the walls had been inflicted along the Lycus River entrance to the city, it was there he proposed to launch his final assault. Constantine learned of the plan from a spy, but could his dwindling force survive another battle? The Bashi-Bazouks began hurling themselves against the Byzantine defenses at 0200 on 29 May. For two hours the Byzantines slew them with arrows and firearms, but grew increasingly tired in the process. With the first attack repulsed, Mohammed threw in a second wave before the defenders could recover. Even though these were regular troops with better discipline and equipment, the narrow breach provided the defenders with less area to cover and they threw back that assault as well.

After another two hours of fighting the

Byzantine troops could barely stand. Moham-med sent in the third wave, made up of Janis-saries. Constantine's exhausted troops managed to repulse them as well. During this fighting, a small band of Turks discovered a small open gate and rushed a handful of men through before it could be closed. They occupied a tower near the Blachinae and raised the sultan's ban-ner, and the rumor quickly spread that the northern flank had been broken. At the same moment, Giovanni Giustiniani was severely wounded. Hearing of his evacuation, coupled with the report from the north quarter, the defenders began to fall back. Mohammed quickly exploited his advantage. Another assault by fresh Janissaries cleared the space between the walls and seized the Adrianople Gate. Attackers began to pour through.

Results

Constantine XI led his remaining troops into the Turkish onslaught, dying for his city and his empire. Almost all his co-defenders as well as a huge portion of the civilian population joined him, for the Turks went berserk. Mohammed II limited very little of the pillage, reserving the best buildings for himself and banning their destruction. He claimed and protected the Church of St. Sophia, and within a week the Hagia Sophia was hosting Muslim services. Thirty ships of a Venetian fleet sailing to Constantine's relief saw the Turkish flags fly-ing over the city, turned around, and sailed home.

The looting finally subsided and the bulk of the population that was not killed, possibly 50,000 people, were enslaved. The bastion of Eastern Christianity fell after more than 1,100 years as Constantine the Great's city. Mohammed II proceeded to conquer Greece and most of the Balkans during the remaining twenty-eight years of his reign.

Western Europe, which had done so little to assist Constantinople, was shocked that it fell after so many centuries of standing against everyone. In Rome, the Catholic Church was dismayed that they would now have no Eastern Christians to convert, for they were all rapidly becoming Muslim. The Eastern Orthodox Church survived, however, for Mohammed allowed a patriarch to preside over the Church. It remained a viable religion, now far from the reach of the Catholic Church's influence. As such, its survival encouraged others who resented the Catholic Church. Within sixty years Martin Luther led a major protest against the Church, starting the Reformation.

The trading centers of Genoa and Venice feared having to deal with hard-bargaining Arab merchants who now controlled all prod-ucts coming from the Far East. The major cities of eastern Europe began to fear the Turkish hordes approaching their gates, and for the next 450 years Austria and the Holy Roman Empire carried on the European/Christian struggle against the Ottoman Empire. The Ottoman Turks established themselves as the premier Middle Eastern Muslim power, con-trolling at their height almost as much as had the Byzantine Empire: the Balkans, the Middle East, much of North Africa, and the eastern Mediterranean.

The flood of refugees from southeastern Europe, especially Greece, brought thousands of scholars to Italy, further enhancing the peninsula's Renaissance. Italian merchants, shocked at the prices the Muslims charged for spices and silks from the East, began to search for other ways to get those goods. Certainly the age of European exploration came much sooner because of Constantinople's fall.

References: Michael Antonucci, "Siege Without Reprieve," *Military History* 9, no. 1, April 1992; J. F. C. Fuller, *Military History of the Western World*, vol. 1 (New York: Funk and Wagnalls, 1954); John J. Norwich, *Byzantium: The Decline and Fall* (London: Viking, 1995); Sir Steven Runciman, *The Fall of Constantino-ple—1453* (Cambridge: University of Cam-bridge Press, 1968 [1903]).

GRANADA

DATE: June–December 1491.
LOCATION: southern Spain.

FORCES ENGAGED:
Castillian: 50,000 infantry, 12,000 cavalry.
Commander: King Ferdinand.
Moorish: reportedly 200,000 inhabitants in the city.
Commander: King Muhammed XI, Abu Abdullah
(Boabdil).

IMPORTANCE:
The fall of Granada marked the end of Muslim
domination of Iberia.

Historical Setting

In A.D. 711 Muslim forces in modern Morocco crossed the Straits of Gibraltar into Spain. This was another in a series of conquests over the previous millennium: Carthaginians, Romans, Vandals, and Visigoths. The Visigothic kingdom was too weak and fragmented to stop the onslaught. Not until 732 did the Muslim forces suffer a defeat at Tours in central France, following which they stayed south of the Pyrenees. In spite of overwhelming numbers and motivation, the Muslims failed to conquer all of Spain, and isolated pockets of Christians remained to harry them.

The Christian kings and princes in northern Spain were rarely unified, but neither were the Moors, as the Muslims were known in Spain. Various Moorish factions made up the occupying population: Arabs in Andalusia and Aragon to the east; Berbers from just across the Straits in the mountainous country and high plains of central Spain, territory most like their homeland; Syrians in the south in the region that came to be called Granada. There an exiled heir of the Ummayad dynasty established a caliphate in Cordova to rival the recently established Abbasid dynasty in Baghdad. Over the succeeding centuries the two populations absorbed some of each other's cultures and mil-

itary methods, with activity waxing or waning depending on such actions as the Crusades or a jihad launched by the militant Almoravids or Almohads in North Africa.

The conflict that culminated in the siege of Granada began in 1478. By then the Christians had regained much of Spain and the declining Moors were forced to pay tribute to remain unmolested. Abu-al-Hassan, king of Granada, decided to stop paying the tribute of gold and slaves. When reminded of his obligation, he replied with threats.

The Christians were led by Ferdinand, recently crowned king of Aragon, who had united his province with Castile through marriage to Queen Isabella. He could not at first respond to Abu-al-Hassan's reply, for he was engaged in a war with Portugal. With that completed in 1481, Ferdinand turned to his unfinished Moorish business. Abu-al-Hassan attacked first, however, destroying the fortress city of Zahara just after Christmas. Ferdinand responded by sending the marquis of Cadiz to capture Alhama, near the city of Granada.

The fighting went back and forth for almost ten years, during which time Abu-al-Hassan was deposed by his son, Abu Abdullah (called Boabdil by the Christians). Both men had their supporters. Boabdil's father-in-law, Ibrahim Ali Atar, also had a following rivaling that of the other two. Ibrahim was killed in 1482 at the battle of Sierra de Rute, a battle in which Ferdinand captured Boabdil. Forcing Boabdil to swear loyalty, Ferdinand influenced the struggle within Granada itself even when he was not attacking it. Disgusted that Boabdil would work with the Christians, his uncle Muhammad ibn Sa'ad (known as al-Zagal) broke Abu-al-Hassan's power, then challenged Boabdil. Fighting between these two kept them from cooperating against the Christians.

As the Moors fought each other, Ferdinand engaged in a scorched earth strategy to deny them any supplies for their army or citizens in Granada. Between 1486 and 1489 the Christian forces ravaged the countryside, occasionally

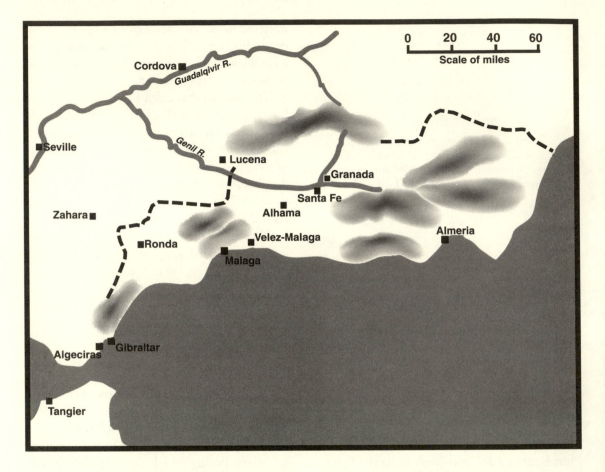

fighting the Moors or capturing one of their castles. By 1489 the Moors possessed only four major cities, with Boabdil controlling Granada. By offering generous surrender terms, Ferdinand convinced many of the garrisons to surrender. Boabdil in 1490 sent two envoys to discuss terms, but then decided to stand fast with his people and challenge Ferdinand's army. The Christian king obliged, leading an army to Granada in the early summer of 1491 to lay siege.

The Siege

In mid-July Queen Isabella, who was with her husband's army surrounding Granada, decided to get a closer view of the city. She and her retinue entered the town of Zubia, overlooking the Moorish capital. Granada is built on two

hills, with the Alhambra palace atop one and the Alcazaba fortress atop the other. The city's houses and businesses lie in the valley between. A contingent of heavy cavalry under the command of the marquis of Cadiz escorted the queen. As they deployed in the plain below Zubia, Boabdil assumed they were offering battle, so he opened the gates and marched his troops out to meet them. As Isabella had come merely to observe, she gave orders for her army not to fight. However, a Moorish challenge for single combat was offered and accepted, for Ferdinand overrode his wife's order in what was an affair of honor.

A Moorish officer named Yarfe challenged Garcilasso de la Vega, who represented his superior officer Hernando de Pulgar, who had sneaked into Granada to fasten a copy of the Ave Maria on the mosque door. Yarfe dragged that document in the dust behind his horse, thus the challenge. Pulgar was not on hand, so de la Vega stood in for him. The two combatants met in the open between the two forces. De la Vega was victorious, but that provoked a Muslim attack. Being attacked, the knightly Christians were freed from their ban on combat and charged. Combat between the Christian heavy cavalry and the Moorish heavy and light cavalry flowed back and forth until the Spanish gained the upper hand and Boabdil's men retreated back into the city, leaving behind 2,000 casualties.

That night, a candle in Isabella's tent caught a drapery on fire and the blaze soon spread throughout the camp. By the following morning nothing was left but ashes. Fearing the Moors would rally at this event, Ferdinand ordered his men to deploy before the city to show they were still ready to fight. Boabdil sent his troops out again and another battle took place on the plains before the city. It turned into a series of individual combats of which the Christian forces had the upper hand. At the end of the day the Moors once more retreated behind the city walls. For the next three months the Moors looked down on the Christian camp as it was rebuilt into a small, permanent town that came to be called Santa Fe. They watched, and starved.

In November Boabdil asked to negotiate and was presented with a list of demands, the Capitulations. They were extremely fair: there was no retribution against the inhabitants and they were guaranteed freedom of worship, locally elected magistrates, and protection of Islamic culture. Those citizens who did not wish to remain were free to emigrate to North Africa, a trip for which the new Christian government would pay. Although the settlement was reached on 25 November 1491, it was not scheduled to go into effect for another two months. When a small group opposed to the surrender began agitating for resistance, Boabdil asked for an early exchange of power. Thus, Ferdinand received the keys to the city from Boabdil's hand on 2 January 1492.

Results

With Granada occupied the *Reconquista* (reconquest) was finished after a struggle that had lasted almost 800 years. Spain entered into a new era for herself and the world. Ferdinand's consolidation of the kingdoms of Spain under one monarch began the process of forming a nation. Once this was a fact after 1492, a spirit of nationalism grew in Spain. That meant, regrettably, a spirit of intolerance, and the promises Ferdinand made to Boabdil and the Moors were soon forgotten. The aggressive Catholicism for which Spain became famous took hold, and both Moors and Jews suffered persecution, exile, and death. It is possible that such an expulsion of non-Christians solidified Spanish culture as well as its population.

Spain's nationalism was perfectly timed and placed. Located between the Atlantic and Mediterranean, Spain was positioned to take advantage of possibilities in both. Portugal had recently been looking into possible alternatives to overland trade with the Far East by exploring maritime routes around Africa. Spanish monarchs had an almost immediate opportunity to establish an alternate route themselves with the timely appearance of Christopher Columbus, requesting ships to discover a western pathway to the Far East. The potential profit involved in bypassing Muslim middlemen was the primary consideration, but so was the religious possibilities. Rumors of Far Eastern Christian realms had long flourished in Europe. If such existed they might be recruited to cooperate with European Christians; then a pincer on the Middle East could crush Islam and recover the Holy Land for Christianity. A combination of expanding both his wealth and his religion was too much for Ferdinand and his queen Isabella to forego. A divided Spain could never have engaged in such a project, but a united Spain took the chance, establishing an international empire that brought the country immense wealth and power.

That empire, although profitable for Spain,

destroyed the native cultures of the western hemisphere. The warrior class in Spain, *conquistadors*, which had fought Islam for centuries found themselves with little to do in Spain after Granada's fall. Ferdinand commissioned many of them to take their talents to the New World, and the resulting conquest enriched both warrior and king while causing the deaths of millions, primarily via European diseases. When or if a Muslim administration in Iberia would have undertaken such a venture is impossible to surmise. Instead, Christianity and European values entrenched themselves in the Americas. A Muslim Spain engaging in similar explorations would certainly have been just as aggressive in spreading their faith to the New World. The effects of such a culture in that part of the world at the time would certainly have altered the entire world.

References: J. F. C. Fuller, *Military History of the Western World*, vol. 1 (New York: Funk and Wagnalls, 1954); L. P. Harvey, *Islamic Spain, 1250–1500* (Chicago: University of Chicago Press, 1990); J. N. Hillgarth, *The Spanish Kingdoms, 1250–1516* (Oxford: Clarendon, 1976).

TENOCHTITLAN

DATE: 26 May–13 August 1521.
LOCATION: outside modern Mexico City.

FORCES ENGAGED:

Spanish/allied: 86 cavalry, 118 crossbowmen and arquebusiers, 700+ infantry, plus 50,000 Tlaxcalan allies. Commander: Hernan Cortés.
Aztec: unknown. Commander: Cuauhtemoc.

IMPORTANCE:

Capture of the capital of the Aztec empire spelled its doom, as Spain became the dominant force in Central America for the next 300 years.

Historical Setting

Until their mysterious disappearance about A.D. 1200 the Toltecs dominated much of Central America. Their fall was coincident with the arrival of nomadic tribes from the north. One of them, the Aztecs (People from Aztlan) drifted into the valley of central Mexico and became subject to whatever power achieved temporary hegemony. The Aztecs settled on the western side of Lake Texcoco, adapting themselves to the practice of building "floating gardens" of built-up silt. Here they established Tenochtitlan in the mid-fourteenth century. A second Aztec faction built a second city, Tlatelolco. The two cities placed themselves under the protection of rival powers—Tenochtitlan under Culhuacan, Tlatelolco under the Tepanecs.

In the late fourteenth century the Tepanecs dominated the valley and expanded their power across the mountains to the west to encompass an area of perhaps 20,000 square miles. This consolidation was accomplished under King Tezozomoc, but after his death in 1423 the various city-states he had dominated began rebelling. Three powers joined together into a Triple Alliance to replace the Tepanecs, one being the Aztecs of Tenochtitlan. Despite an occasional disagreement, the three worked fairly well together and dominated central Mexico for ninety years. They consolidated their hold over the former Tepanec domain, then in 1465 began to expand. The Aztecs became the dominant partner in the triumvirate, but the three tribes collectively spread the empire from the Atlantic to the Pacific and as far southward as the modern-day border between Mexico and Guatemala. Only two tribes remained recalcitrant, the Tlaxaltecs and the Tarascans. The Aztecs established garrisons along disputed borders and occasionally warred against but never subjugated them.

The Aztecs led the expansion in order to increase their trade routes while incorporating a larger tax base among the conquered peoples.

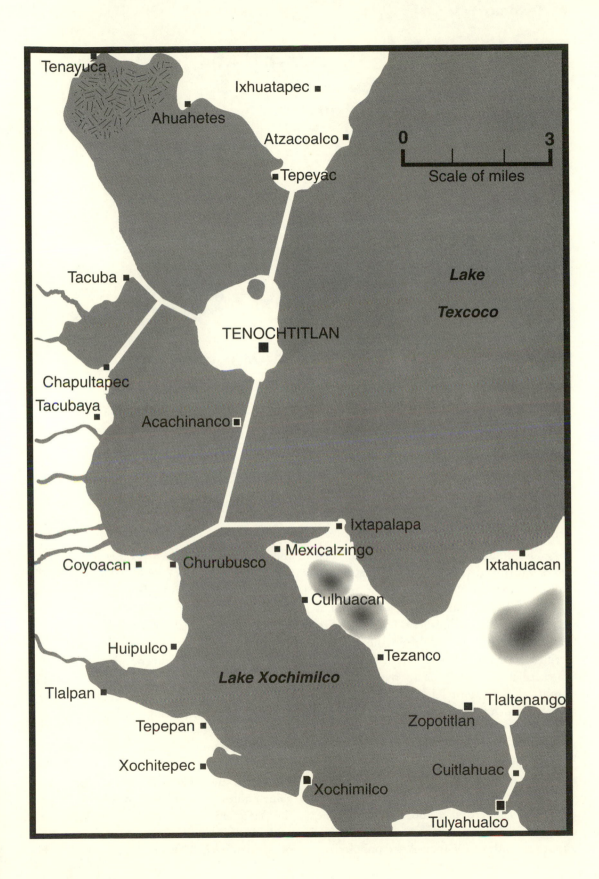

Tenayuca

Ixhuatapec

Ahuahetes

Atzacoalco

Tepeyac

0   3

Scale of miles

Lake

Texcoco

Tacuba

TENOCHTITLAN

Chapultapec

Tacubaya

Acachinanco

Ixtapalapa

Mexicalzingo

Coyoacan   Churubusco   Ixtahuacan

Culhuacan

Huipulco

Tezanco

Lake Xochimilco

Tlalpan   Tlaltenango

Tepepan   Zopotitlan

Xochitepec   Cuitlahuac

Xochimilco

Tulyahualco

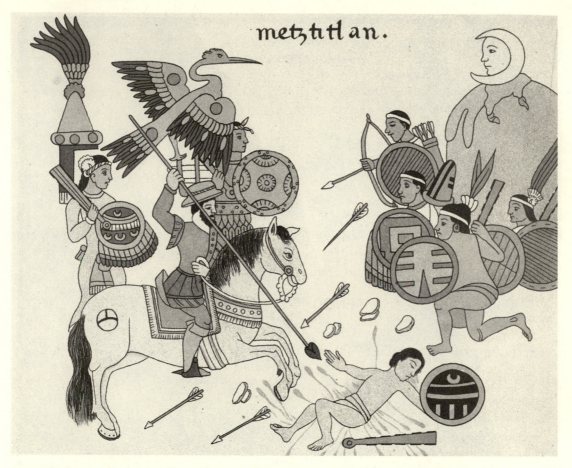

Sixteenth-century depiction of the battle for Tenochtitlan between Cortéz and the Aztecs. (The Art Archive/Antochiw Collection Mexico/Mireille Vautier)

They also fought for religious reasons. The Aztecs worshiped (among others) the god of the sun, Huitzilopochtli. The Aztec religion taught that history moved in cycles, the end of which came with the destruction of the sun. To keep the god healthy and shining he required sacrifices to eat, so the Aztecs went conquering for sacrificial offerings. The pyramids that dominated the city of Tenochtitlan were large altars on which prisoners of war were executed daily. On days of special celebration, several thousand would be sacrificed. This need for offerings drove the Aztecs to conquer, but did not create loyal subjects.

Once their empire was consolidated, Tenochtitlan was expanded and beautified. The city reached a population of perhaps 200,000, about one-fifth of the total Aztec population; the number of subject peoples might have taken the empire's population as high as 6 million. When Moctezuma II came to power in 1502, the Aztec empire was well established and he was responsible for much of the lavish architecture and decoration in the capital city. Their sister-city Tlatelolco, which they took under their control in 1475, became the commercial center containing the largest market in Central America, hosting perhaps as many as 60,000 people on market days.

The constant need for sacrificial victims created resentment among the subject peoples, and when the Spaniards arrived they easily gained allies to assist them in their attacks on the Aztec empire. In 1519 the Spanish conquistador Hernan Cortés landed on the coast of Mexico with 550 men and 16 horses. He had heard of a powerful tribe known as the Aztecs who ruled a vast, rich empire located in a land far to the west of Cuba, his Caribbean base. Landing at modern Vera Cruz, Cortés learned that the tribes subject to the Aztecs feared and resented their masters. Seeing Cortés as a possible savior, they allied with the strange newcomers.

Among the peoples of Central America was a belief in a great white god, Quetzalcoatl, who had visited the region in ages past and promised to return. Cortés played on that belief, for his horses, iron armor, and firearms were otherworldly items to the natives.

Cortés began his march into the interior in August 1519, gaining allies by reputation or by force. His major confrontation came with the Tlaxcalans, against whom he fought a number of battles throughout September. Spanish firepower and cavalry on open ground allowed Cortés to slaughter large numbers of the natives. Tlaxcala surrendered to him in the middle of the month, realizing that the Spaniards could prove vital in overthrowing the Aztecs. The Tlaxcalans warned Cortés that the route by which Moctezuma had invited him to travel, through the religious center of Cholula, was surely an ambush. When Moctezuma learned that Cortés had avoided the ambush, the emperor was convinced that only a god could have had foreknowledge of the plan. From that point Moctezuma seemed to have ceded the initiative to the Spanish. Cortés and his men entered Tenochtitlan on 8 November, where they gaped at the wealth the city contained.

The Siege

After discussions with Moctezuma, Cortés learned that an Aztec governor near the coast had attacked and killed some Spaniards near Vera Cruz. Cortés used that as an excuse to seize Moctezuma and began to rule through him. Knowing no other ruler, the Aztecs would follow none of their own people who tried to make himself emperor in the face of Moctezuma's apparent surrender. Cortés pushed his luck too far when he banned the Aztec religion in order to introduce Christianity. That decision provoked dissent. Then Cortés learned that a Spanish expedition from Cuba, sent by his rival, Governor Diego Velazquez, had arrived off Vera Cruz. For a few weeks Cortés carried on a long-distance negotiation with the expedition's commander, Pánfilo de Narváez. By carefully leaking news of the immense wealth available, Cortés subverted many of Narváez's men. In the spring of 1520 Cortés led 250 of his men to fight Narváez; Cortés won and quickly incorporated the men sent to capture him into his army.

When he left Tenochtitlan, Cortés had placed in command Pedro de Alvarado, who began fighting the Aztecs in Tenochtitlan. He soon found himself badly outnumbered and besieged in one of the palaces. Cortés returned to Tenochtitlan with a force of nearly 1,100 men. No sooner had he reestablished himself than all his work began to fall apart. Moctezuma refused to cooperate in any way and managed to secure the release of his brother, Cuitlahuac, claiming that the people would lay down their arms if Cortés displayed that act of good faith. Instead, the war chiefs of the city quickly elected Cuitlahuac as emperor in Moctezuma's place. Near the end of June, an assault was launched on Cortés' position. The massive amounts of javelins and arrows wrought havoc in the Spanish lines. Fire from cannon and arquebus slaughtered many Aztecs, but employing human wave tactics they broke through the palace walls. The nature of Tenochtitlan, a city laced with canals, made maneuver nearly impossible since the Aztecs controlled all the bridges. Cortés sallied against the attackers but was always overwhelmed and forced to retreat. "Men who had fought against the Moors declared afterwards that they had never faced such a fierce and determined enemy, and veterans of the Italian wars said that even the French king's artillery was easier to face than these Indians" (Innes,

The Conquistadors, p. 164). Soon every Spaniard not killed had been wounded. Cortés displayed Moctezuma on a rooftop to convince his people to stop fighting so the Spanish could evacuate the city. After some debate, the more warlike Aztecs prevailed and arrows and stones were soon flying. Moctezuma was struck in several places and died three days later.

Cortés had large wooden towers built, hoping to give his crossbowmen sufficient height to control the streets, but the Aztecs were too numerous. Even aided by a few thousand Tlaxcalans within the palace walls Cortés was badly outnumbered. He won a small, hard-fought victory at the pyramid temple near the palace, but his only hope of survival was to escape. For two days he fought his way through the streets to the causeway to Tacuba, then had to capture the gaps in the road where the Aztecs had destroyed eight bridges. Slowly, they captured each barricade, tore it down to fill the gap in the causeway where the bridge had been, then fought to the next barricade. Cortés thought he had bought a cease-fire when envoys promised to stop fighting if their high priest was released. Instead, Aztecs needed him to perform ceremonies to install Cuitlahuac as emperor. The attacks started again and the Spaniards were forced back to their palace. Hastily building a portable bridge, Cortés ordered a force of 150 of his soldiers and a few hundred Tlaxcalans to lay the bridge across the first gap in the causeway, then defend it while the bulk of his survivors crossed. They would then lay down fire for the second gap to be bridged. The evacuation took place on the night of 30 June–1 July, which the Spaniards called *Noche Triste*, the Night of Sorrows. They broke out of the palace with almost all of their cannon, but they carried as much gold as they could and that slowed their escape. In the end they succeeded, but they lost all their artillery and most of their gold, as well as some 600 men and two-thirds of sixty-eight horses. The Tlaxcalan allies lost around 2,000. They made a stand at Tacuba, then escaped northward the following night, harassed constantly to Tlaxcala.

Had the Aztecs continued to launch hit-and-run attacks, Cortés' force would certainly have been wiped out. Instead, Cuilahuac decided on a battle. Having fought the Spaniards only in the city, he had no idea what heavy cavalry could do in the open. He learned the hard way. At the town of Otumba on 7 July they fought. Cortés had but twenty-two horses, but with armor and lances they were still formidable. By attacking the gaudily dressed commanders, the Spanish robbed the Aztecs of their leadership; still, it was an all-day battle. There is no accurate count of Aztecs engaged, but there must have been many thousands. Spanish discipline defeated them. The day after the battle the Spaniards reached the Tlaxcalan border and the Aztecs withdrew.

Cortés sent to Vera Cruz for all the gunpowder and cannon available. He spent the next several months rebuilding his force, and with Tlaxcalan assistance pacifying the neighborhood and gaining allies. During this period Cortés was aided by an unexpected benefactor. An African slave with the Narváez expedition, afflicted with smallpox, died in the town of Zempoala. The disease spread from that one man across all of Mexico, and it severely weakened Cortés' enemies. The germs ran rampant through Tenochtitlan, killing Cuitlahuac. He was succeeded on the throne by Cuauhtemoc, one of Moctezuma's sons-in-law.

Cortés sent ships to Jamaica to buy ordnance and horses. He also began constructing thirteen small ships (brigantines) to operate on Tenochtitlan's lake. By Christmas 1520 he was ready. By April 1521 his men captured one town after another along Lake Texcoco's shores. After fighting his way completely around the lake, Cortés summoned his allies for the final assault. He now commanded 86 cavalry, 118 crossbowmen and arquebusiers, and more than 700 infantry armed with swords and pikes. A further 50,000 Tlaxcalans supplemented his army. Cortés divided his force into three columns: two were to march counter-clockwise around the lake and occupy Tacuba and Coyoacán, west of Tenochtitlan, and the third was to capture Iztapalapa to the southeast. That would put them in control of the mainland end of the causeways entering Tenochtitlan. A fourth contingent Cortés himself commanded: the thirteen brigantines he had built to operate on the lake and deal with the canoe-borne Aztec warriors.

The attack got off to a bad start when one of the Tlaxcalan chiefs defected. He was quickly executed for desertion, with the approval of the other Tlaxcalans. Then two of Cortés' commanders quarreled and refused to cooperate with each other; he used all his diplomatic skills to settle the conflict. On 26 May his first two columns were in position and destroyed the aqueduct taking water to the city. On 31 May a swarm of Aztec canoes attacked Cortés' small flotilla. In the early morning hours they rowed away from the attackers, but when the dawn brought a friendly breeze Cortés faced about and attacked. The cannon aboard his small ships did amazing damage; by day's end he was master of Lake Texcoco. The attack on the city was another matter, for gaps in the causeways were now too large to be bridged. Unfortunately for the Aztecs, one gap was sufficiently wide for the Spanish ships to sail through and set up a crossfire on the defenders, forcing their retreat. A force of crossbowmen entered the city and attacked one of the temples, but was quickly forced back by overwhelming numbers.

The battle raged for ten weeks. Each day the Spaniards saw their fellows, taken prisoner by the Aztecs, sacrificed to the god of war atop the city's central pyramid. That steeled their resolve, and the lack of fresh water inside the city took its toll. The brigantines kept Aztec canoes at bay while the Spanish advanced up the damaged causeways. Occasional Aztec ambushes slowed the Spanish. The Aztecs also threw body parts of sacrificed prisoners at the attackers in an attempt to break their spirit. The siege took place during the rainy season, dampening the Spanish spirits. A few Aztecs slipped out of the city to carry severed heads of Spaniards and their horses to neighboring towns, attempting to raise support, but a Tlaxcalan punitive expedition brought in more allies to the Spanish cause. Finally the Spanish filled the gaps in the causeways and moved closer to the city. In desperation, the Aztecs launched larger and larger attacks that the Tlaxcalans beat back with enormous losses. Fighting went on street by street as the invaders gained more and more of the city. Finally, on 13 August, Cortés launched a massive attack on the last 15,000 defenders. Most died, a handful of survivors fleeing in canoes. The Spanish and their allies occupied the Aztec capital, but it contained only rotting bodies.

Results

Although the Aztecs were in many ways more advanced than the Europeans, they lacked the necessary weaponry and resistance to foreign diseases to defeat their invaders. Even without the arrival of the Spaniards, it is questionable how much longer the tribes of Central America would have accepted their military dominance and religious practices.

Cortés and the Spaniards who followed him completely dismantled Aztec society. Disease killed an estimated 90 percent of the population. However, the Spanish were intent on altering the country rather than adapting to it. One of their first goals was to ban the Aztec religion, for human sacrifice and cannibalism were unacceptable to staunch Catholics. With the new governing power completely in Spanish hands, if any citizen of New Spain had any idea of advancing himself in the New World order, learning the Spanish language was vital. Within a generation, the Aztec religion and language had virtually ceased to exist. The Aztec culture, as reflected in their artwork (the Aztecs were reputedly expert goldsmiths), also disappeared. Almost all Aztec artwork in gold and silver was melted down into bullion for easier distribution as booty for the soldiers as well as ease of transport in the ships that took the wealth of the New World back to Spain.

The immense wealth looted from Central America, coupled with that obtained in South America, made Spain the richest and most powerful nation on earth. With that financial foundation, the intensely Catholic Spanish king Charles V proceeded to spend that money in Europe on military power to enforce the will of the Church, embroiled at the time with the new Protestant movement. For a century Spain dominated Europe, but the defeat of the Spanish Armada at the hands of the English at Calais in 1588 began their decline from international preeminence to that of also-ran by the end of the nineteenth century.

References: David Carrasco, *Moctezuma's Mexico* (Niwot: University Press of Colorado, 1992); Hammond Innes, *The Conquistadors* (New York: Knopf, 1969); Jon Manchip White, *Cortés and the Downfall of the Aztec Empire* (London: Hamish Hamilton, 1971).

RHODES

DATE: 28 July–21 December 1522.
LOCATION: island 12 miles off the southwestern coast of Asia Minor, with the capital city lying on the northeastern tip of the island.

FORCES ENGAGED:

Turkish: unknown, perhaps as many as 100,000 soldiers. Commander: Sultan Suleiman. Knights of St. John: 500 knights and sergeants, perhaps 6,000 Rhodian citizens. Commander: Philippe Villiers de l'Isle Adam.

IMPORTANCE:

Suleiman's capture of the city and island gave the Ottoman Empire total control of the eastern Mediterranean Sea.

Historical Setting

The Order of the Knights of the Hospital of St. John (also known as the Knights Hospitalers) were organized during the First Crusade and operated a hospital in Jerusalem. These were Christian knights dedicated to spreading and protecting their faith. When the forces of Islam recaptured the city, the Knights withdrew to the port city of Acre. When Muslim forces captured that city after a six-week siege in 1291, a handful of Hospitalers escaped and returned to Italy to rebuild their forces. When, in 1307, the French King Philip IV arrested all members of another military order, the Knights Templar, in an attempt to weaken the military power of the Catholic Church, the Knights Hospitalers fled to avoid the same fate.

The Knights of St. John chose the island of Rhodes as their headquarters. Since their expulsion from the Holy Land they had concentrated on enhancing their naval as well as military power and owning an island so near their hated Muslim enemy would allow them to harass Muslim shipping and trade in the eastern Mediterranean. The Knights captured the island, and Pope Clement V confirmed their possession of it in 1309. For the next two centuries the Knights were a continuous thorn in the side of Muslim merchant and naval fleets.

After Sultan Mehmet reestablished the power of the Ottoman Empire and captured Constantinople in 1453, he set about conquering territory from southeast Europe to the frontiers of Persia. He was unstoppable. Finally deciding to rid himself of the Knights, he mounted an invasion of Rhodes in 1480. The main assaults, under the command of Mesic Pasha, against the fortifications of the city of Rhodes came from the seaward side, but the stout walls the Knights had constructed proved too difficult for the Turks to overcome. When a landward assault also ended in failure, the invaders went home. A concurrent assault against the Italian peninsula was ended prematurely in the wake of the Ottoman defeat at Rhodes, and the Knights' victory probably saved western Europe from Muslim incursion and possibly control.

In Rhodes, the grand master of the Knights

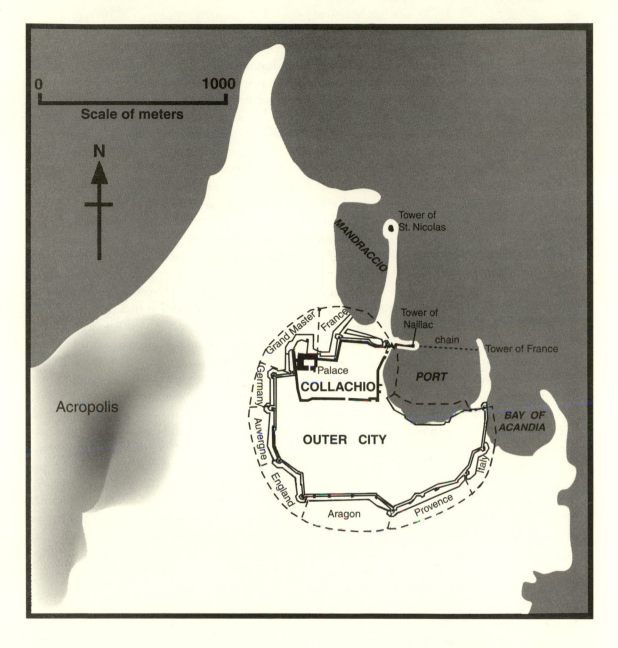

The Siege

Suleiman led the invasion, which one of his chroniclers claims consisted of 700 ships and 200,000 men, although the army probably numbered no more than half that. Unlike Mesic's strategy in 1480, Suleiman decided to concentrate on an attack from the landward side, a decision that allowed the Knights to receive reinforcements throughout the siege. The Knights had built well under del Carreto's

of St. John, Fabrizio del Carreto, oversaw the strengthening of the city's defenses over the next few decades. By the time of his death in 1521, Rhodes possessed the strongest fortifications of any Christian bastion in the world. Their naval attacks on Muslim merchants continued to nettle successive Ottoman sultans, and in 1522 the recently enthroned Sultan Suleiman ("the Magnificent") tried again to dislodge the Knights and protect his trade routes in the eastern Mediterranean.

direction. Attackers now had to cross two ditches before the walls instead of the normal single ditch, and the walls themselves had been thickened some 200 percent and heightened since the previous invasion. Each section of the walls was assigned to a different *langue* of the Knights, who were divided into national units.

Seeing the difficulty of a direct assault, Suleiman employed the thousands of miners he had brought to undermine the walls. Luckily for the Knights, just before the siege the Venetian engineer Gabriele Tadini da Martinengo slipped into the city. He developed an instrument made of tightly stretched parchment that vibrated at the slightest motion. Warned by this device where the Turkish tunnels were, he was able to have his men undermine the mines. In spite of his best effort, the Turks' numerical superiority allowed them to dig more mines than the Knights could counter. On 4 and 24 September, and again on 30 November, the Turks were able to collapse some of the walls and rush the resulting breaches. Fighting was intense at each of the three battles, but the defenders prevailed at heavy cost to all of them.

In October Chancellor André do Amaral, the chief rival to L'Isle Adam for the position of grand master, was accused of treason. One of his servants was discovered carrying a message urging the Turks to continue the siege. He was a haughty and unpopular man; many readily believed that he was capable of such an act. But the witnesses at his trial were of dubious trustworthiness and Amaral himself refused to say anything, even under torture. No contemporary Turkish sources mention contact with him, but it is possible he was working against the defenders. In 1856 a huge explosion under the Church of St. John in Rhodes destroyed the church and the nearby grand master's palace. Such a blast indicated the possibility that the long-sealed church vault contained a large amount of gunpowder, when the defenders of 1522 were in short supply. Still, no such charge was leveled against Amaral at his trial. He was convicted and executed.

By December the Knights were in dire straits, although there had supposedly been ammunition and food supplies stocked away for a year's siege. Islands the Knights held in the region had all surrendered to other Turkish attacks, as had their last mainland stronghold at Halicarnassus (Bodrum, Turkey). Unlike the 1480 siege that had ended with the approach of winter, Suleiman was violating normal strategy and maintaining pressure despite the season. After losing as many as 15,000 casualties, Suleiman offered the Knights honorable terms if they would surrender, and the citizens of Rhodes supported the idea. When L'Isle Adam's council also agreed, the grand master contacted the sultan. On 20 December the fighting stopped, on the condition that there would be no retribution against any of Rhodes' citizens and that they should be allowed to continue the free practice of Christianity. The Knights were allowed free passage away from the island, along with all the wealth they could carry.

On 1 January 1523 the Knights marched down to the docks and embarked on their galleys. L'Isle Adam's ship hoisted a flag to half staff, the banner bearing a picture of the Virgin Mary crying over her crucified Son over the motto *Afflictus to spes unica rebus* ("In all which afflicts us thou art our only hope"). Suleiman supposedly commented, "It saddens me to have to oblige this brave old man to leave his home" (Sire, *The Knights of Malta*, p. 59).

Results

Suleiman lived to regret that moment of compassion, for seven years later the Knights relocated to Malta and continued to challenge the power of Turkish navies in the Mediterranean. The final campaign of the sultan's long reign was against Malta, and it proved a failure. Still, the capture of Rhodes was significant in allowing free trade for Islam throughout the eastern Mediterranean. Had L'Isle Adam not accepted terms but continued on in defense of his city, he almost certainly would have been defeated and the Order of the Knights of the Hospital of St. John would have been exterminated. Support from European powers for a stronghold in the lion's mouth had long been waning, but the order gained a new lease on life in Malta. Their continued existence provided the bulwark of Christianity on that island and in the Mediterranean.

References: Ernle Bradford, *The Shield and the Sword* (New York: Dutton, 1973); Eric Brockman, *The Two Sieges of Rhodes* (London: J. Murray, 1969); H. J. A. Sire, *The Knights of Malta* (New Haven, CT: Yale University Press, 1994).

PAVIA

DATE: 30 October 1524–24 February 1525.
LOCATION: northern Italy, some 20 miles south of Milan.

FORCES ENGAGED:

Holy Roman Empire: 9,000 men, primarily mercenaries. Commander: Don Antonio DeLeyva. French: 25,000 men. Commander: King Francis I. Relief force: 20,000 men. Commander: the Charles DeLannoy Duke of Naples.

IMPORTANCE:

French defeat ended in King Francis' capture and the subsequent signing of the Treaty of Madrid, ceding much of France's land in northern Italy.

Historical Setting

France's King Louis XII was intent on expanding his country's borders into the Italian peninsula, but he met with only mixed success. When his son Francis I came to the throne in 1515, he followed in his father's footsteps. Although a war with England had just been concluded, Francis immediately allied himself to England's Henry VIII and the city-state of Venice, arraying themselves against Spain, Milan, Florence, Switzerland, the Papal States, and the Holy Roman Empire.

Francis' capture of Milan in September 1515 was sufficient to break the alliance against him and he ended the war in possession of most of northern Italy. Five years later he was at war with Charles I of Spain, soon to assume the position of Holy Roman Emperor Charles V as well. Francis' invasion through the Pyrenees in 1521 sparked renewed fighting in Italy as well, but Francis was defeated at Milan and marched back home in 1523. In the spring of 524 the forces of the Holy Roman Empire and its allies recaptured northern Italy, then invaded Provence in southern France. A short siege of Marseilles ended when Francis marched a new army down the Rhône River Valley, and imperial troops under Spanish General Charles de Lannoy withdrew across the Alps. French troops marched through the Argentiére Pass in October 1524. Lannoy, finding Milan in the grip of a plague, retreated farther south toward Lodi. Francis had no qualms about capturing the ailing city and left a force of 4,000 infantry and 600 men-at-arms as a garrison.

Leading elements of the French army reached Pavia on 28 October, but the bulk of the army and its siege train did not arrive until late on the 30th. Francis' army numbered some 33,000 men, but he detached almost 6,000 men under the duke of Albany to strike southward and seize Naples, in an effort to curry Pope Clement VI's support.

The Siege

The advance troops took up positions in villages around Pavia's walls, while Francis (with the main body) encamped in the Visconti Park, a kite-shaped area enclosed by a wall almost 8 miles in length. The park was bisected by the Vernavola Stream running north-south, then turning southeast to intersect the Ticino River just east of Pavia. As trenchworks were being dug around the city, a French force built a pontoon

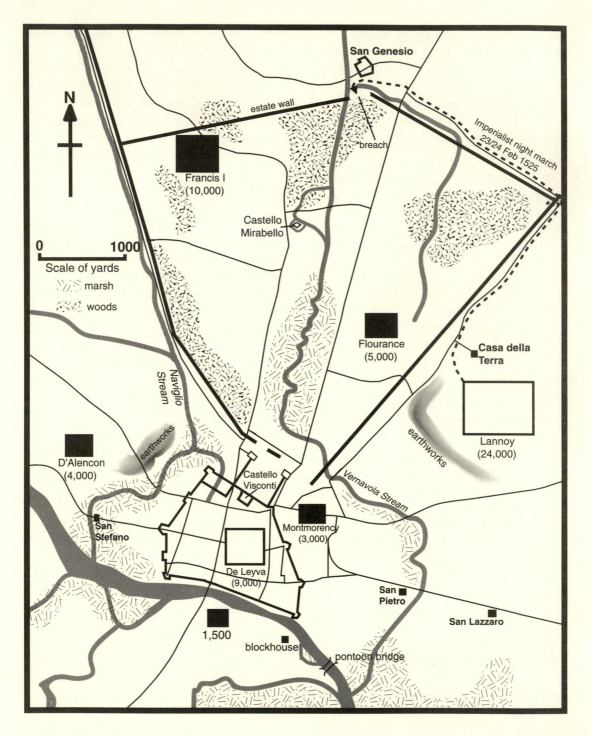

bridge across the Ticino and seized the only road entering Pavia from the south.

The two sides sparred for a few days, the French failing to exploit a breach in the northern corner of Pavia's wall but successfully turning back a sortie from the garrison. Heavy rains brought a halt to any combat from 5 to 10 November. Francis surveyed the situation and decided that the only way to coordinate attacks from both sides of the city would be by hold-

The arquebusiers of the mainly Spanish imperial army proved the decisive factor, and the battle turned into a rout that virtually annihilated the French army and resulted in the capture of French King Francis I. (Archive Photos)

ing a Spanish blockhouse covering the Ticino Bridge out of the city's southern wall. Possession of that would give view to both French forces east and west of the city, allowing for signaling and coordination. A day-long bombardment on the 10th forced the blockhouse's surrender. Francis kept up an intense bombardment of the city walls, hoping for a breach to exploit.

Don Antonio de Leyva, commanding the 9,000-man garrison, had them and the city's population build an earthen wall parallel to and inside the city walls, with a ditch dug between them. He then placed light artillery in key positions to sweep the ditch should French forces break through the wall. He also had the citizens arm themselves with pieces of marble to throw at the attackers. By 21 November the French had created a breach in the east wall and in the west, and the besiegers attacked them simultaneously. The interior embankment proved its worth and three assaults were

thrown back; the French left hundreds of casualties in the ditches.

Francis pondered his next move, which was hindered by muddy ground and cold weather. Only on the city's south face was the ground solid enough to move cannon about, but the army was fast running out of gunpowder. While it lasted, however, the artillery succeeded in creating a new breach in the southwest wall. The Ticino River blocked access for an attack, however, until Francis ordered the river dammed. It was not a complete job, but it did succeed in lowering the river's level sufficiently to allow for an attack. Before the attack could be launched, a new set of storms flooded the river and destroyed the dam works. The same flood washed away the French pontoon bridge east of the city, stranding the force on the southern bank.

Constant rain caused the artillery barrage to cease, and the French decided to starve out the defenders rather than pursue the assaults.

Throughout December Francis both depleted and expanded his force, as he sent Swiss mercenaries south to protect the duke of Albany's force from attack by the imperialist force commanded by Charles de Lannoy, duke of Naples, but received reinforcements from France and Milan. The expedition against Lannoy kept him away from Albany while inflicting some 1,000 imperial casualties. Unfortunately, Francis lost some of his Swiss mercenaries when they left to protect their homeland. Throughout the battle both sides had to deal with the shifting loyalties of mercenaries, which were the primary military forces of southern Europe at the time. It was the arrival of money from Austrian bankers, however, that meant fresh mercenary troops for Lannoy's imperialists in mid-January 1525. With an expanded force he marched southwest from Lodi toward Pavia.

While awaiting Pavia's starvation, Francis had had his men digging lines of contravallation to protect against the attack of any relieving forces. When Lannoy's army arrived on 2 February, Francis did not move his forces at all, so confident was he of his position. The stone wall surrounding the park served as an anchor for the French lines. The imperialist force of 24,000 dug in at the Casa de Levrieri, facing the southeastern wall, and began exchanging artillery barrages with French guns on the other side. For three weeks the two sides probed each other's positions without much success. Finally, on the night of 23–24 February, the imperial army made its move. Although Lannoy was in overall command, the operation was directed by Fernando D'Avolos, marquis of Pescara, one of the Holy Roman Empire's most talented commanders.

In a driving rainstorm, a small team of laborers marched to the northern point of the park walls and spent the night knocking them down. In the early morning mist, the imperial army marched northward with the French apparently believing them to be withdrawing from the battle owing to unpaid mercenaries. Instead, they entered the park through the breach and formed up on the French left flank. Francis himself led a cavalry charge to hold the imperialists while his force moved up from the west. The surprise was key to the battle, however, for the two French forces on opposite sides of the park could not coordinate their moves and bring sufficient manpower to bear. The pressure from the surprise attack, coupled with well-timed sorties from Pavia, doomed the French. In the confusion of the battle, part of the French forces fled across the Ticino and destroyed the bridge behind them, stranding their comrades. By the day's end, not only was the French army defeated, Francis was taken prisoner.

Results

The end of the battle brought 10,000 French casualties, including much of France's nobility dead and captured. The imperial army, by contrast, had lost but 500 men. With two weeks the imperial forces reoccupied Milan, although Lannoy had to deal with unpaid mercenaries by offering promissory notes backed up by his own estates. By contrast, Francis' mother, the regent Louise, made sure that all mercenaries in French service were rapidly paid, keeping her country secure from invasion. She also refused to hand over Burgundy and other annexed territories in return for her son's release. She signed a treaty with Henry VIII, convincing him of the threat of an overly strong Holy Roman Emperor. Francis negotiated in his own behalf in Madrid, however, and the following January signed the Treaty of Madrid whereby he promised to cede Burgundy. Immediately after his release, however, he gained permission from Pope Clement to ignore the pact. With threats arising from both Turkey and Germany, Emperor Charles could not spend the resources to force the issue.

Although Francis returned to Italy on later campaigns, never again did he have the opportunity to deal the Imperial cause a crushing blow as he had in the 1524–1525 Pavia campaign.

References: Angus Konstam, *Pavia, 1525: The Climax of the Italian Wars* (London: Osprey, 1996); F. L. Taylor, *The Art of War in Italy, 1494–1529* (Cambridge: Cambridge University Press, 1921); D. Waley, *The Italian City-Republics* (New York: Longman, 1988).

VIENNA

DATE: 27 September–14 October 1529.
LOCATION: central Austria.

FORCES ENGAGED:
Austrian: 16,000 troops and 72 guns. Commander: Archduke Ferdinand.
Ottoman: approximately 250,000 troops. Commander: Sultan Suleiman.

IMPORTANCE:
Turkish defeat at Vienna was the high-water mark of Ottoman expansion in Europe, signaling the beginning of a long decline in Ottoman power.

Historical Setting

Just as the weakened condition caused by Byzantine-Persian hostility had opened the door for Islam to break out of Arabia in the seventh century, Europe in the 1520s presented to a potential outside aggressor a wonderful opportunity. It was political rivalry in Europe that made the Continent susceptible. King Francis I of France and Charles V, Holy Roman Emperor, argued and fought over land that today is the Franco-German frontier, as well as control over northern Italy. France had a powerful military based on artillery and heavy cavalry. Charles, as head of the Habsburg family, controlled not only the Holy Roman Empire (which consisted of Austria and parts of whatever countries bordered it) but also Spain, whose military power was based on the *tercio,* a phalanx of pikemen supported by smaller

contingents of soldiers each armed with the *arquebus,* a matchlock musket. Against these formations cavalry made no impression, as France discovered when the two armies met at Pavia in northern Italy in 1525. Francis not only was defeated, he was taken prisoner. During and after his captivity he plotted revenge and pondered on possible allies.

Charles was enjoying his military success, but was bothered by Pope Clement VII. Although technically the Holy Roman Empire was the defender of the Catholic Church, just who was the senior partner had been a point of contention since Charlemagne took on the job in 800. Clement resented Charles controlling so much of Italy, since before his accession to the papacy Clement had been the wealthy and powerful Giulio de Medici. Thus, Clement's attitude toward Charles translated into a lack of political and religious support in dealing with the rise of the Protestant Reformation. Thus, Charles had his hands full with rivals in Rome and France, and in his own backyard.

Sultan Suleiman in Constantinople saw this. He was the ninth sultan of the Ottoman Empire, successor to a long line of able, resourceful, daring, and strongly religious rulers. He inherited an empire stretching from the Persian frontier to Morocco, as well as much of the Balkans. He also inherited a military that was as impressive as anything Charles or Francis could field. The pride of the Ottoman army lay in two arms: heavy infantry and artillery. Since the days of the second sultan, the Ottoman government had accepted tax payment in kind in the form of male children of Christian families. They became slaves, were raised as Muslims, and from their youth were trained as soldiers. They developed into a fearsome unit called the Janissaries, completely dedicated to their faith and their sultan, ready to go anywhere and fight any enemy in the service of both. The Ottoman Turks had also learned from western Europe the craft of casting artillery, and they had far outstripped their teachers. The Ottomans produced the largest

Troops of the Holy Roman Empire clash with Turkish Janissaries, trying to stem Suleiman's advance on Vienna. (Hulton Getty/Archive Photos)

guns of their day, capturing Constantinople in 1453 with them after the city had stood unconquered for more than a thousand years. Heavy siege guns were the Turks' specialty, and many cities became Ottoman possessions because of those weapons, just as many armies fell before the talent and élan of the Janissaries.

Suleiman was an open-minded and interesting political ruler whom the Europeans viewed as a man with whom they could do business, but he was also caliph of all Islam thanks to the recent acquisition of Egypt and deposition of the last spiritual leader. He was therefore bound by the tenets of his faith to spread Islam, to convert unbelievers or exact tribute from them. As such, he conducted campaigns against the Persians and wanted to extend his political and religious dominion into Europe. The vengeful King Francis contacted him, encouraging an invasion to threaten Charles' eastern front and correspondingly weaken his French frontier.

Suleiman's venture into Europe began in the summer of 1526, when he captured Buda and placed Hungary under his sway, naming the Transylvanian Governor John Zapolya as his tributary monarch. Ferdinand, archduke of Austria and king of Bohemia, contested that throne. As Suleiman was off campaigning in Persia in 1528, a rebellion broke out in Hungary with some factions claiming to fight for Ferdinand's cause. Once his Persian problems were settled—at least temporarily—Suleiman made ready to march on Vienna to add Austria and the Holy Roman Empire to his own Ottoman Empire.

The Siege

Suleiman led his army out of Constantinople on 10 April 1529. When Ferdinand learned of this he called a council in Bohemia to gather manpower. For the most part his requests went unanswered. Austria and Bohemia and the empire made lots of promises, but few troops actually arrived. Charles was busy with trouble in Italy and had to keep an eye on both Francis and Clement. In Vienna, the 250-year-old city walls, no more than 5 feet thick, were in many places badly in need of repair. They could not be mended with masonry as there was no time, so for the most part dirt and the debris of the suburbs were used, for the outlying houses were razed in order to open up a field of fire. The official in charge in Vienna was Philip, count palatine of Austria. Two talented men, Graf Nicholas zu Salm-Reifferscheidt and William von Roggendorff, assisted him. Graf Nicholas oversaw the wall repairs, gathered in as much food and ammunition as he could, and expelled from the city as many women and children as he could in order to ease the supply burden. During the siege itself he oversaw the placement of the artillery, 72 guns of varying size. When the siege began the city was defended by a garrison of 22,000 infantry and 2,000 cavalry. Including the garrisons Suleiman had absorbed along his line of march, reinforcements commanded by his lackey King John Zapolya, and innumerable camp followers, the Ottoman horde that stood before Vienna on 26 September 1529 was possibly as large as 350,000 people, of which there were probably 80,000 Turkish soldiers and another 6,000 Hungarians.

The Ottoman advance was a wonder to behold. Many of the Janissaries advanced up the Danube in boats, where they and Suleiman stopped for five days at Buda to recapture the city and massacre the defenders. News of that action, as well as the activities of some 20,000 *akinji* ("sackmen") devastating the countryside along the line of march, motivated the defenders to improve their walls as best they could. The first Turkish contingent arrived in sight on 23 September and skirmished with the Viennese cavalry. By the 27th the city was surrounded and Suleiman sent a delegation to demand its surrender. It was comprised of four captured cavalrymen, fabulously dressed in Turkish clothing. The sultan stated that an immediate surrender would end in no occupation of the city but for a few functionaries; he would have breakfast

there on the morning of the 29th. Resist, and the city would be destroyed so thoroughly no one would ever find a trace of it. Graf Nicholas, de facto commander, sent back four richly dressed Turkish prisoners that carried no answer at all, which was answer enough.

The fate of Vienna lay neither in the city walls nor the attacking army, but in the weather. The summer of 1529 was the wettest in memory, and the supply wagons vital to supporting the immense Turkish force lagged far behind. Worse still for the Ottoman cause, the massive siege artillery also could not be moved along the muddy roads. All the artillery Suleiman had with him were 300 smaller pieces that lacked the destructive power necessary to break down even those old walls.

Suleiman's only alternative was to mine the city walls. Mining involves digging a tunnel from one's own protected trenches under the walls of the enemy, then filling the tunnel with gunpowder and exploding it. The collapsing tunnel then brings down a section of wall. Such operations began immediately, but the defenders were lucky enough to learn the placement of the mines from a deserter. They counter-mined, digging their own tunnels under those being dug by the Turks in order to collapse them, or digging at the same level, which resulted in underground battles, which the defenders tended to win. Not all of the mines could be discovered, however, and some worked. The breaches, which were occasionally large enough to ride several horses through abreast, could not be exploited. Behind the walls the defenders had dug trenches and built wooden palisades from which they beat back the attackers. The breaches were held by the same stolid pikemen that had won the battles of western Europe, and the swords of the Janissaries were of little use in the cramped confines of the battle. A major battle in one breach on 12 October resulted in the Janissaries leaving behind 1,200 dead.

On the night of the 12th Suleiman held a council of war. The supply wagons had not arrived, and the countryside was not providing sufficient food to support his army. The city was proving unexpectedly tough. Winter was approaching. The defenders had won every encounter in the breaches, and the attackers' death toll was between 14,000 and 20,000, primarily Janissaries and aristocratic cavalry. For the first time in their history, the Janissaries complained that they were being sacrificed. To do just that had been their duty and indeed their entire life for nearly two centuries. Suleiman offered them a huge bonus for undertaking one more attack. On the 14th another mine blew up, but the collapsing wall fell outward, creating such a pile of rubble that it was impossible for the attackers to rush the breach. The pikemen once again stood firm in the face of the Janissary onslaught, and once again turned them away.

That night, the Ottoman army struck its tents, which had covered the plain outside Vienna for as far as the eye could see. They burned everything they could not carry, then threw their prisoners in the flames as well. The army marched away the next morning as it began to snow.

Results

A relative handful of men saved western Europe from the Ottoman Empire, although at first it seemed that little had changed. John Zapolya still ruled in Suleiman's name in Buda and Hungary was part of the Ottoman domain. Although Suleiman returned three years later to finish the job he had started, a spirited resistance at the town of Guns (modern Koszeg, Austria) and a major deployment of imperial troops under Charles V once again convinced him to return home. Another uprising in Persia diverted Suleiman's attention, so he made peace with Ferdinand and turned his armies eastward. He returned to Europe in 1541 to recapture Hungary from Ferdinand's invasion, but went no farther.

Suleiman presided over the Ottoman Empire at its zenith, in both power and territory. After him, the long line of talented sultans ended. His son Selim (called "the Sot") had none of his father's talents. From Selim's rule forward the Ottoman Empire began a long decline, until by the nineteenth century it was regarded by the world as "the sick man of Europe." Had Suleiman captured Vienna, he could have wintered there and proceeded the following season to invade Germany. Any sort of French cooperation would have placed the Holy Roman Empire in a vise. That would have served Francis' aims in the short term, but he certainly overestimated his influence on the sultan. Islam could well have triumphed against a divided enemy.

Within the Ottoman military the zenith also passed. Vienna marked the beginning of the end for the Janissaries, for their once invincible front had been shattered. They could be beaten, and not only did their enemies know it but so did they. The bribe they were offered for that final attack was proof that their élan was gone. "The Janissaries themselves degenerated from the mighty force they had been. They used their power to improve their personal lives, at the expense of the state" (McCarthy, *The Ottoman Turks*, p. 164). "The Janissaries were to turn into unruly Praetorian guards, who made and unmade sultans, and this was perhaps inevitable. But even determinism must admit that Vienna started them down the long slide" (Pratt, *Battles that Changed the World*, p. 149). The elite force that had been the instrument of Ottoman expansion became the instrument of internal instability.

The decline in quality leadership after Suleiman was compounded by the success of the previous Ottoman line. The empire by the middle of the sixteenth century was too large to be efficiently governed by the overly centralized authority in Constantinople. Although the limits of the empire were (for the most part) as far as an army could march from Constantinople in one campaign season, that was too large for imperial rule. Since their primary enemies at the time were the Holy Roman Empire and Persia, only two complete armies could maintain authority. To create them would mean an increase in cost and a corresponding decrease in quality, especially with the decline of the Janissaries. Thus, they could not expand their borders any farther, and conquest and booty had always been a major contributor to the economy. Over the following century the Turks began to experience a rise in unemployment and banditry, which the weakening government could not successfully address. Unfortunately for the Ottoman Empire, Vienna spelled a change of fortune: just when a strong and visionary ruler was vital to maintain or expand the empire, the talent pool dried up.

References: Noel Barber, *The Sultans* (New York: Simon and Schuster, 1973); Andre Clot, *Suleiman the Magnificent: The Man, His Life, His Epoch*, trans. Matthew J. Reisz (London: Saqui, 1989); Justin McCarthy, *The Ottoman Turks* (New York: Longman, 1997); V. J. Parry, *A History of the Ottoman Empire to 1730* (Cambridge: Cambridge University Press, 1976); Fletcher Pratt, *Battles that Changed History* (Garden City, NY: Doubleday, 1956).

against France. The continental gains made by previous kings had gradually slipped away until England controlled nothing more than the port city of Calais. Henry made war against France irregularly over the course of his reign, usually because the French gave support to Scottish independence movements. In 1513 Henry crushed the French at the battle of the Spurs outside Thérouanne just as his subordinate, the earl of Surrey, similarly routed a major Scottish army in northern England at Flodden Field. That double victory allowed Henry to spend some time dealing with domestic matters, but in 1522 he was back in France. Little was accomplished other than ravaging the countryside, and in 1523 a sick and demoralized army returned to England.

Henry spent the next two decades focused on his personal and religious problems, trying to find a wife with whom he could produce a male heir. That pursuit led to his break with the pope and, by extension, Spain, whose King Charles V was the champion of the Catholic Church. Henry's rejection of papal authority

BOULOGNE

DATE: 19 July–18 September 1544.
LOCATION: on the English Channel coast of France, southwest of Calais.

FORCES ENGAGED:
English: 16,000 men. Commander: duke of Suffolk, then King Henry VIII.
French: unknown, perhaps 2,000 men. Commander: unknown.

IMPORTANCE:
King Henry was unable to capitalize on the English victory and soon signed a peace treaty with France, bringing his military career to a close.

Historical Setting

Henry VIII ascended the English throne in 1509 and within two years began making war

Engraving by T. A. Dean of Henry VIII, King of England. (Library of Congress)

further alienated the Catholic Scots, so another Franco-Scottish cabal was in the offing. Only France's King Francis I and Charles V's inability to cooperate for any length of time kept them from allying against England. Henry awaited an invasion, but when none came he prepared to strike first before the continental allies could invade his country. He sent the duke of Norfolk to crush a Scottish uprising in 1543 then, with his rear secure, aimed to cross the Channel.

Charles V was in a sticky political position. Not only was he king of Spain, he was also Holy Roman Emperor, controlling much of central Europe. While he and Francis were both Catholics, they had plenty of conflicts over mutual frontiers. To threaten Charles, Francis entered into an alliance with the Ottoman Turks, always interested in expanding their influence in southeastern Europe. So for Charles, an alliance with Henry (who had rejected the authority of the pope) against a fellow Catholic was balanced by the desire to expand his own holdings against a French king allied with Muslims. Temporarily, Charles ignored his religious position and allied with Henry against King Francis. Both monarchs pledged to send 40,000 men to France in 1544 in a cooperative pincer movement against Paris. However, Henry apparently decided instead to expend his effort securing the region around Calais.

The Siege

In June 1542, 42,000 English troops debarked at Calais, supported by 4,000 auxiliaries sent from Charles and a number of mercenaries. The force divided, one section under the duke of Norfolk advancing against Montreuil on the Canche River due south of Calais, the other section under the duke of Suffolk marching on the port city of Boulogne. Norfolk's army pursued their siege only half-heartedly, while Suffolk's troops began a close investment of Boulougne on 19 July. Charles protested that Henry was dawdling when he should be advancing on Paris, but Henry replied that the two towns were vital if he was to maintain his lines of supply. The siege of Boulogne became more intense when Henry arrived to take command of the 16,000-man force on the 26th. The lower town was only lightly fortified, and Henry's troops captured it after a heavy bombardment. A Roman-era lighthouse, known as the "Old Man," also fell in the initial attack. The bombardment continued through August. On 1 September Henry launched an assault against the main fortifications protecting the upper town. It was captured, but his men were unable to approach the city's castle. The French resistance and firepower were sufficiently intense to keep the English troops at bay for a time. For another two weeks, Henry's artillerists and engineers did their work, and mines under the castle walls created sufficient damage for the defenders to lose their resolve. On 13 September, they asked for terms. King Henry accepted the surrender of the 1,630 surviving defenders when he entered the town in triumph on the 18th.

Meanwhile, the siege at Montreuil was making no progress. Rather than going there and taking command, Henry stayed in Boulogne, making plans to go home. While doing so, he learned that Charles and Francis had signed a peace treaty on 18 September, just as he was occupying Boulogne. In spite of this news, Henry returned home anyway, leaving Norfolk and Suffolk in France. Norfolk soon abandoned Montreuil, however, learning of the approach of a 30,000-man French army. He fled to Boulogne, then he and Suffolk fled again for Calais, leaving only 4,000 men to defend Boulogne. Francis and his army arrived before Henry's newly won city on 7 October to see that the breaches the English artillery had created in the city walls had yet to be repaired.

On the night of 9 October, Francis decided to launch a night attack. He directed the twenty-three companies of French and Italian infantry to wear white shirts over their armor for greater visibility in the dark, giving this operation the nickname the "camisade of

Boulogne." From some inexplicable reason the English were not paying attention to their defenses and the French easily broke into the city. Unfortunately, their operation began falling apart almost immediately. The assault commander was wounded and withdrew, just as rumors began to spread that the English had recaptured the breaches. Rather than retreat in an orderly fashion, the attackers instead abandoned all thoughts of fighting in favor of plunder. Sir Thomas Poynings, commanding the English forces in the citadel, rallied them and launched a counterattack that not only expelled the French forces, but also resulted in the loss of 800 French and Italian dead and prisoners. Francis abandoned the siege with the approach of winter, planning to return the following year.

Results

Without continental allies, Henry expected Francis to launch an invasion of England at the opening of the campaign season of 1545. He stationed three armies along the coast in preparation, but Francis launched little more than small-scale raids. Still, it was enough of a distraction to encourage the Scots to once again rise up and give Henry fits. At Boulogne, the French dug siege lines but did not commit sufficient men to the operation, while the 4,000 defenders were too few to drive the French away. Henry appointed two successive commanders to Boulogne, but neither proved successful in beating Francis' troops. Henry kept Boulogne, but it served him no useful purpose.

Finally, on 7 June 1546, Henry and Francis signed a peace treaty. Henry had assembled yet another invasion force, but in late spring changed his mind. "Perhaps the burden of war had crippled him; perhaps the desperate shortage of food which bad harvests brought in their train and his failure to raise victuals and enough munitions on the continent drove him to peace; perhaps Charles's evident intention to strike in Germany and thus ignore his erstwhile ally pulled him up; perhaps it was all of these

things which now made imperative the discretion which the [Privy] Council had urged upon him with great vigour months before and had probably continued to urge thereafter" (Scarisbrick, *Henry VIII*, pp. 462–463). Still threatening an invasion, however, Henry was able to maintain possession of Boulogne for eight years, at which time it would be returned for a huge indemnity (which Henry was positive would never be paid).

Another section of the treaty said that Henry would not go to war against the Scots unless they violated the peace. He had hoped to get the French to promise a withdrawal of all present and future aid for the Scots, but he was unable to accomplish that. In Great Britain, Henry's last overseas adventure had the effect of keeping Scottish resistance alive. Instead of focusing on Scotland and imposing his will there, Henry could count little gain in the north or in France when the fighting ended.

Henry did get Francis to sign the peace treaty giving him recognition as head of the Church of England and Ireland, so at least one domestic issue was positively addressed. It proved to be a temporary victory, however, for at Henry's death in 1547 his daughter Mary invited papal authority once again to the British Isles.

References: Paul Cornish, *Henry VIII's Army* (London: Osprey, 1987); Jasper Ridley, *Henry VIII* (New York: Viking, 1985); J. J. Scarisbrick, *Henry VIII* (Berkeley: University of California Press, 1968).

MALTA

DATE: 21 May–8 September 1565.
LOCATION: 60 miles south of Sicily.

FORCES ENGAGED:
Maltese: 700 Knights of Malta, 8,500 local men-at-arms. Commander: Grand Master Jean Parisot de la Valette.

Ottoman: Army: approximately 32,000 men, including 9,000 Spahis, 4,000 Iayalars, 6,300 Janissaries. Commander: Mustapha Pasha.
Navy: 185 ships, including 130 galleys and 30 galliots. Commander: Admiral Piali.
Reinforcements: 3,000 Algerians. Commander: King Dragut of Tripoli.

IMPORTANCE:

Victory of the Knights of Malta blunted Sultan Suleiman's dream of Ottoman control over the entire Mediterranean Sea, a dream completely crushed at Lepanto.

Historical Setting

The Knights of Malta was a religious/military order born of the Crusades in the twelfth century, when they were originally known as the Knights of the Order of St. John of Jerusalem. When the Muslims regained control of the Holy Land, the Knights relocated to Rhodes. There, they fought the Ottoman Sultan Suleiman in 1522, putting up such an impressive defense that after a protracted siege Suleiman allowed them to withdraw with honors. Once again relocated, this time to Malta thanks to Holy Roman Emperor Charles V in 1530, the Knights' navy harassed Ottoman shipping and served as the cork in the Mediterranean bottleneck that was Malta.

Sultan Suleiman, who led the Ottoman Empire long and well, regretted allowing the Knights to go free so many years earlier. Determined that Islam should control the entire Mediterranean Sea, in 1565 he sent ships and men to Malta to secure it for his empire and his

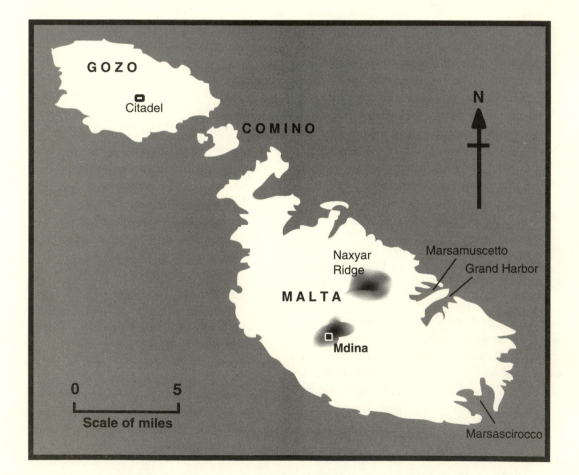

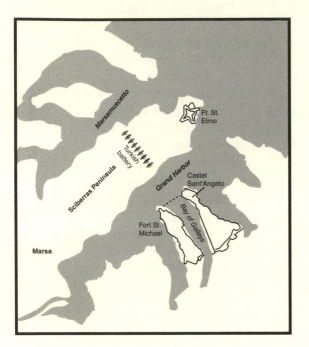

bor. There, two peninsulas entered the harbor and both possessed strong defenses. The western peninsula, called Senglea, was completed encircled by the walls of Fort St. Michael. The eastern peninsula, Birgu, had the smaller Castel Sant'Angelo on its tip while its approaches were walled off by the bastion of the Post of Castile. The fortified village of Birgu lay in between. The walls fronting both the peninsulas were not very strong, as the defense had been planned to beat back a naval attack, not one from the landward side. Across the harbor juts another peninsula, Sciberras. It is the northern boundary of Grand Harbor and the southern boundary of another, the harbor of Marsamuscetto. At its tip, protecting the entrances to both harbors, was Fort St. Elmo.

faith. He was able to amass 185 ships carrying 32,000 men and 8,000 sailors, plus innumerable galley slaves. Although prepared for battle, they were in this instance primarily a transport fleet, for capturing Malta and its sister island Gozo was a matter of bombardment and ground assault. In an unusual move, Suleiman did not command the invasion; instead, he appointed his favorite general, the seventy-year old Mustapha Pasha, to lead the army while naming his grandson by marriage, Admiral Piali, to command the fleet. The two disliked each other and in a second unusual decision, Suleiman put neither in overall command. To assist both army and navy, corsair King Dragut of Tripoli provided a further 3,000 soldiers and was to be the mediator between the two Turks.

Malta, site of many a siege in its history, was a formidable target. Jean de Valette was in command of the defense, a seventy-year-old who had fought Suleiman's forces years earlier at Rhodes. The Knights themselves, 700 strong fighting alongside 8,500 Maltese men-at-arms, tough enough opponents, were made even tougher by strong fortifications on the southern edge of Malta's main port of Grand Har-

The Siege

The Turkish fleet sailed into view on 20 May 1565, having first unsuccessfully scouted the northern shore for a suitable landing site. Vallette ordered as many civilians as possible to take refuge in the center of the island in the hill fortress of Mdina. The Turks sailed into the harbor of Marsamuscetta and debarked, then began to establish a strongpoint for their artillery. They brought (in addition to their normal complement of artillery) three specially cast cannon for the battle, one firing 200-pound stone balls, the other two firing 90-pound iron balls. Their initial target was Fort St. Elmo, and on 27 May the cannonade began. Although much less strong than the forts across the harbor, Fort St. Elmo held out for a month. Mustapha had hoped to attack the fort from both the landward side and from the harbor against the southern face, but a chain strung across the mouth of Grand Harbor made the naval bombardment impossible. The elite Turkish Janissaries attempted to scale the walls with ladders, but Knights armed with Greek fire and their own artillery repeatedly turned them back. At night boats would ferry reinforcements across Grand Harbor and remove the wounded. When the fort finally fell on 23 June only nine Knights remained alive. These prisoners Mustapha beheaded, then crucified the bodies and floated them across the harbor so the remaining Knights could ponder their own fate. Valette returned the favor by executing Turkish prisoners and firing their severed heads out of his cannon.

After losing some 8,000 men taking the weakest of the three forts, Mustapha tried to offer the Knights terms to abandon the island, as Suleiman had done at Rhodes. In return, Valette offered him the ditch at the base of his fort's walls, where he was welcome to leave the bodies of his Janissaries. Mustapha prepared for a fight to the death and ordered the bulk of his army around the harbor to attack Forts St. Michael and Sant'Angelo. He also dragged eighty galleys across the Sciberras peninsula, just as Sultan Mehmet had done to facilitate his conquest of Constantinople in 1453. This gave Mustapha the ability to bombard the forts from both landward and seaward sides. To counter this, Valette ordered another chain strung across the Bay of the Galleys. As the Turks were marching off Sciberras to take up positions below St. Michael and Sant'Angelo, reinforcements numbering 600 Spanish soldiers, 56 artillerymen, and 42 Knights landed on the north side of Malta and quickly marched overland and entered Birgu before the Turks could stop them.

The first assault on St. Michael came on 15 July, when boatloads of Turks debarked from the galleys and tried to land on the Singlea peninsula's western shore. They were held back by underwater wooden stakes driven into the floor of the harbor while a second thrust attempting to get past the chain at the mouth of the Bay of Galleys was destroyed by cannon fire from Sant'Angelo. After that the Turks held back on their attacks but maintained an almost continuous bombardment of both peninsulas. When an attack against Fort St. Michael broke

through the outer walls on 7 August, a timely attack on the Turkish rear by a cavalry force from Mdina relieved the pressure and forced a withdrawal, saving the fort.

By the first of September both sides were growing desperate. The defenders had lost some 5,000 killed, including more than 200 Knights. Only about 600 men (including walking wounded) manned the walls. The Turks, while suffering casualties from both combat and disease, still heavily outnumbered the Knights of St. John, but they were unprepared for a siege that would last through the winter. The arrival of promised reinforcements from Sicily under Garcia de Toledo brought the siege to an end. Toledo secretly debarked 8,000 troops on the island's northern Bay of Mellieha, then marched them to occupy the high ground of Naxxar, between Mdina and the harbor. Hearing of this, Mustapha began embarking his men. When, however, he learned of the size of the relief force, he ordered his men back off the ships and into combat. It was not a wise decision. Tired and dispirited Turkish troops had little success trying to beat back a mad charge by the newly arrived Knights of St. John, who lusted for revenge. A small force briefly held some high ground, but when they were overrun the remnants of the Turkish army fled for their galleys. Mustapha himself commanded a rearguard that bought his men sufficient time, but by the evening of 8 September the Ottoman ships were rowing eastward for Constantinople.

Results

Casualties suffered by the Ottoman Turks are difficult to estimate. Different sources number them from a low of 20,000 to a high of 30,000; casualties suffered by Dragut's Barbary corsairs must be added to that count, and their losses are also a matter of conjecture. The defeat was one of the few that Christian Europe dealt to Suleiman, but it broke the myth of Muslim invincibility that had been growing for thirty years. The Turks made no serious attempt to operate in the central or western Mediterranean after their defeat in 1565, and their naval defeat at Lepanto six years later destroyed any remaining dreams of making the Mediterranean an Ottoman lake.

For the Knights of St. John, the victory reaffirmed the order as the primary shield of Christianity against the forces of Islam. European monarchs contributed heavily to the rebuilding of their headquarters on Malta, built on the site of the modern city of Valetta on the Sciberras peninsula and named for the commander during the siege. A defeat and the loss of Malta would almost certainly have spelled their doom, but instead the "fame of 1565 was to make the Knights of Malta the acknowledged paragons of Christian chivalry for as long as that idea held sway in Europe" (Sire, *The Knights of Malta*, p. 72).

The timely arrival of Spanish troops from Sicily, which saved the day, reaffirmed the predominance of Spain as the champion of Catholicism in Europe. The Spanish would have been obliged to undertake the task of recapturing Malta in order to deny it to the Muslims had they taken the island, and the commitment of manpower to that enterprise would probably have weakened their concurrent efforts to battle the Protestant Netherlands and amass the Spanish Armada invasion force that attempted to take control of England in 1588. The subsequent rise of Protestantism could well have been established decades sooner than it was.

References: Francesco Balbi di Correggio, *The Siege of Malta*, trans. H. A. Balbi (Copenhagen: Gollcher and Rostock, 1961); Ernle Bradford, *The Great Siege* (London: Hodder and Stoughton, 1961); Alison Hoppen, *The Fortification of Malta by the Order of St. John, 1530–1798* (Edinburgh: Scottish Academic Press, 1979); H. J. A. Sire, *The Knights of Malta* (New Haven, CT: Yale University Press, 1994).

CHITOR GARH

DATE: 21 October 1567–23 February 1568.
LOCATION: northwestern India in the province of Rajputana.

FORCES ENGAGED:

Mogul: 4,000 troops, 5,000 engineers. Commander: Abu-al-Fath Jalal-ud-Din Muhammad Akhbar.
Rajput: 8,000 troops, 40,000 peasant auxiliaries. Commanders: Princes Jaimal and Patta.

IMPORTANCE:

Akhbar's victory ended the last serious resistance in northern India to Mogul rule.

Historical Setting

In 1192 the forces of Islam under the leadership of Muhammad of Ghor established the Mogul dynasty in the wake of their victory at the second battle of Taraori (Tarain). The Hindus had dominated India since the days of the Gupta Empire after Alexander the Great's failed invasion in the fourth century B.C., and they still maintained a strong presence on the subcontinent. The strongest, numerically and militarily, were the Rajputs, of modern Rajasthan. The were what later came to be called one of the "martial races" of India, with a strong military aspect to their entire society. Their military prowess had made them for a time the dominant group in northern India, but that came to an end after Taraori.

The strongest cities in Rajputana were at Chitor and Ranthambhor, where the most imposing fortifications were built. Chitor Garh (a fort) for centuries was considered the most impregnable fortress in India, and in the sixteenth century it was under the control of the powerful Sesodian clan. Unfortunately for the Rajputs, the Sesodians were at midcentury ruled by a weak *raja* (king), Udai Singh II.

Since Taraori, the Muslim Mogul dynasty had gradually expanded its power out from its capital city at Delhi. In the middle of the six-teenth century the Moguls were led by one of their most able kings, Akhbar. His grandfather Babur had conquered much of northern India for Islam, and Akhbar followed in the family footsteps by spreading Mogul control over the northern two-thirds of India. Even though Akhbar was known for his enlightened rule and tolerance of rival religions, the Rajputs chafed under any foreign leader. A mixture of stunning victories and magnanimity won many Rajputs over to his side, but the Sesodi-ans yearned to lead a united Rajputana back to former glory. Unfortunately, Udai Singh's dreams far exceeded his talent.

Akhbar knew that his realm would never be peaceful as long as the Sesodians ruled, so in 1567 he decided to capture Chitor and impose his will once and for all. His forces arrived at the city's outskirts on 20 October. They looked up a steep hill to see a fortress 558 feet over-head. The fortress was massive, its walls encompassing a city $\frac{3}{4}$ mile wide and $3\frac{1}{4}$ miles long. Eight thousand warriors defended it, supported by a population of 40,000 peasants. When Akhbar arrived, several other Rajput ranas were there with their entourages, but Udai Singh immediately fled the city leaving two teenage princes, Jaimal and Patta, in com-mand. They oversaw a garrison well supplied and better armed with muskets and cannon than Akhbar's force.

The Siege

Akhbar's force ascended the hill and began their siege on 21 October 1567. Akhbar posi-tioned his artillery in three batteries around the fort, commanding the main one himself oppo-site the fort's main northern gate. Against orders some Mogul troops rushed the walls and were badly mauled for their trouble; after that, Akhbar determined that encirclement and star-vation were the better tactics, with any assault coming only after intense preparations.

Mogul engineers began their digging to undermine the walls, while workers began dig-ging and building *sabats*. These are trenches with walls built up above ground level, then covered with strong wooden planks and rawhide. This was done to provide cover for the troops and to place them close to the city walls for quick assault when the mines were ready. The sabats were massive, reportedly wide enough to handle ten cavalry abreast and deep enough to allow passage of Akhbar's war ele-phants. The walls also had loopholes for firing on the defenders.

In mid-December two mines were dug under Chitor Garh's walls and gunpowder set for collapsing them. A massive explosion sig-naled a rush for the breach and the Moguls seemed to have seized the momentum. How-ever, the explosion was only in one of the mines; when the second blew up Moguls and Rajputs were fighting hand to hand just above and mixed body parts flew over a wide area. The Rajputs were the first to recover and they repaired the breach.

More mining operations began and the con-struction of sabats continued. Akhbar often went to the front to inspect the work and to take shots at the defenders. Mogul accounts record that he was a crack shot and killed a number of Rajput musketeers. At one point in the siege the Rajputs sent out a delegation swearing fealty, but Akhbar uncharacteristi-cally rejected it. He wanted Udai Singh sur-rendered to him before he would cease his attack, but because Udai Singh had hidden somewhere in the countryside the garrison could not comply.

By 22 February new mines were ready and sabats were completed. That night, in the wake of fresh explosions bringing down sections of walls, the Moguls broke into the city. A general Rajput retreat from the walls at first aroused Akhbar's suspicions. Soon, light from three large fires illuminated the darkness. This was *johar*: the Rajputs were collectively burning their families rather than have them captured and tortured. Once that was completed, they had nothing left to live for and were intent on victory or death. It was discovered later that Akhbar had shot Prince Jaimal and the loss of their leader had convinced the defenders to engage in their sacrifice.

Results

By the morning of the 23rd Akhbar was able to enter the city on the back of one of his elephants. He had brought 300 with him and they had spent the night leading elements of his force through the city streets, routing the defenders. Supposedly, one elephant seized a trampled Rajput in his trunk and delivered him to Akhbar: it was Prince Patta. At battle's end some 30,000 of the garrison and city had died. This was the only time Akhbar allowed his army to engage in widespread killing and pillage in the wake of a victory. A number of Rajput musketeers, however, managed to escape by disguising themselves as Mogul soldiers and escorting their wives out of the city as if they were prisoners. The death count among the Moguls is not reliably recorded, as the contemporary account claims but one death in the assault although many hundred had died during the abortive attacks and the construction of the sabats.

The capture of Chitor Garh was instrumental in bringing the rest of Rajputana under Mogul control. Udai Singh escaped and established a new capital city, Udaipur. After Akhbar's death in 1616 his son, Jahangir, announced that the Sesodians could return to Chitor, but they had settled in Udaipur and preferred to stay there. Jahangir would not allow the fortress to be rebuilt. Its remote location, however, has kept its remains intact and Chitor Garh is the best surviving example of Hindu fortifications.

References: S. M. Burke, *Akbar, the Greatest Mogul* (New Delhi: Munshiram Manoharlal, 1989); Virginia Fass, *The Forts of India* (London: Collins, 1986); Jeffrey Say Seck Leong, "Storming the Last Hindu Fortress," *Military History* 15, no. 6, February 1999.

FAMAGUSTA

DATE: April–1 August 1571.
LOCATION: eastern end of the island of Cyprus.

FORCES ENGAGED:
Turkish: perhaps 70,000 men. Commander: Lala Mustapha Pasha.
Cypriot: 5,000 men. Commander: Marcantonio Bragadin.

IMPORTANCE:
The fall of Famagusta gave Turks complete control over Cyprus, which they exercised for 307 years, acting as the anchor for Turkish naval dominance of the eastern Mediterranean.

Historical Setting

When the crusaders lost Acre to the Muslims in 1291, the forward port for European trade became Famagusta, on the western end of Cyprus. Between 1300 and 1370 the city prospered and became internationally known for its opulence. That changed in 1372, when Genoa captured the city in a surprise attack. They looted and pillaged the city in a style that would do credit to the worst of the barbarians, and slaughtered a huge segment of the population. Genoese control lasted until 1464, during which time the city's depths matched its previous heights. Occasional attempts by Cypriot kings to recapture the city failed.

In 1489 the Cypriot Queen Catarina Cornaro (of the Norman Lusignan family) ceded the island to Venice in return for a handsome pension. Famagusta at that point became a Venetian possession, and they attempted to restore the city's defenses if not its fabulous

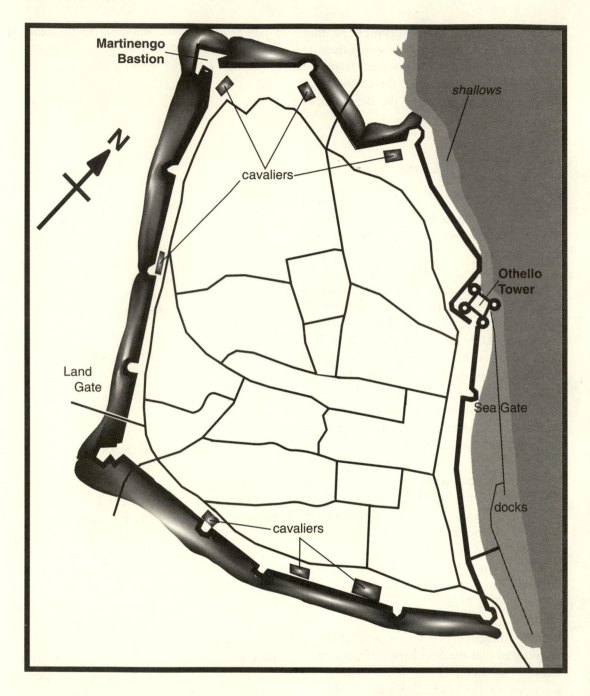

Martinengo
Bastion

shallows

N

cavaliers

Othello
Tower

Land
Gate

Sea Gate

cavaliers

docks

wealth. Cyprus became part of the front line against Muslim expansion after Constantinople fell to the Ottoman Turks in 1453. The Venetians were determined to hold their strategic and trade position as far to the east as possible. The city and its defensive reconstruction suffered from storms and earthquakes in 1546 and 1568. Further, the development of gunpowder weaponry had made the Norman masonry fortifications obsolete. The two earliest Venetian governors, Nicolo Foscarini and Nicolo Priuli, began the refortification of Famagusta. They cut a ditch around the city out of solid rock, then built an earthwork faced with masonry around the south and west sides of the city. A ravelin (large bastion) protected the main entrance on the southwest; an arsenal tower was constructed at the southeastern corner, where the wall met the ocean. They then strengthened the castle by building a new wall 20 feet outside the existing one, then filling the space with earth as a gun platform. Only the north side of the castle, facing the harbor, was unchanged. The inner harbor was drained.

In 1550 the engineer Giovanni Sammichele arrived from Venice to update the works. He had a wall built facing the sea on the eastern side of the castle reaching to the arsenal tower. Along the north side he built a new rampart that extended to a new bastion, the Martinengo (now Djamboulat), at the northwest corner of the city. As this construction was going on, other cities on the island were also receiving improvements.

All of this upset the Ottoman Sultan Suleiman the Magnificent. Cyprus had been under the suzerainty of Egypt and the Cypriot royalty had paid their annual tribute regularly. Even when Egypt became an Ottoman possession (thereby receiving Cyprus into their empire) the Venetian governors continued to pay tribute to Constantinople. As the strengthening of the island could only be for defense against Ottoman attack, Suleiman knew that his possession of the island was only a formality; in order to really control it, he would have to conquer it. When Suleiman died and his son Selim took the throne in 1566, Cyprus' priority on the Ottoman agenda rose. Crusader galleys operating from Cyprus had harassed ships taking pilgrims to Mecca, and that could not be tolerated. The growing Muslim threat worried the Venetians so much that they appealed to Pope Pius V for aid. He created a Holy League, but only Spain offered any substantial aid. Venetian control of the trade from the East had made too many enemies over the years.

Ottoman troops arrived at Cyprus on 1 July 1570, landing at the town of Larnaca. The Cypriot people, never happy with Venetian rule, did nothing to resist the Turkish landings, which consisted of 50,000 infantry, 2,500 cavalry, and 80 guns. The Venetians gathered what manpower was available into the fortresses of Nicosia and Famagusta. In total there were only about 5,000 infantry and 500 cavalry, under the overall leadership of Astore Baglione, general of the militia. When his plan to resist the landings was overruled by the political leadership of Nicosia, he took his men to Famagusta and placed himself under the command of Marcantonio Bragadin. The Turkish commander, Lala Mustapha Pasha, decided to besiege the capital at Nicosia first. It fell on 9 September 1570, and the rest of the island offered their loyalty to Lala Mustapha. Only Famagusta defied him.

The Siege

Lala Mustapha left some 4,000 men to garrison Nicosia, then marched to Famagusta. His army camped in Pomodamo, 3 miles south of the city, during the winter. He received reinforcements in April 1571 and started the siege. He began by placing his artillery 1,000 yards south of the city, the fire from which gave cover to his men as they dug their zigzag trenches toward the walls. By the end of May they were to the outer defense lines, through the counterscarp, and up to the walls. They began mining the ravelin at the city gate and the arsenal tower. The defenders countermined and succeeded in capturing large amounts of gunpowder to expand their dwindling supplies. On 21 June the Turks blew up the walls of the arsenal tower, but General Baglione led the counterattack that plugged the resulting breach after five hours of fighting. On the 29th the ravelin exploded and another assault, led by Lala Mustapha himself, charged the breach. A second attack on the arsenal breach was launched as well. A six-hour, hand-to-hand struggle repulsed both these assaults. In the wake of this battle, the defenders set explosives under the bastion, determined to destroy it if they could not hold it.

On 9 July the Turks launched an assault all along the south wall. They succeeded in capturing the ravelin, but the mine the defenders placed there exploded with such force that 1,000 Turks were killed. The tower was so completely destroyed there was nothing for either army to occupy. Through the rest of the month the Turks pounded the wall and arsenal tower with their artillery while exploding the occasional mine. Each breach was assaulted, but defenders behind a second defensive line built of sandbags held the attackers at bay. It was brave, but hopeless. The Turks received regular reinforcement and resupply while the defenders began starving. On 1 August they sent envoys to Lala Mustapha to discuss surrender terms.

Results

The Ottoman commander was surprisingly generous in his terms: complete surrender would result in free passage of the defenders out of the city and transportation to Crete with all their arms and property. The city's inhabitants could stay or go as they pleased. The settlement was negotiated and signed in a day. On 4 August forty Turkish ships entered the harbor and loaded the sick and wounded on board, followed by the remainder of the garrison. Because many of the townspeople wanted to evacuate as well, Bragadin asked for additional ships; the Turkish soldiers, he complained, were mistreating many of the civilians. Lala Mustapha promised two more ships and requested a meeting with Bragadin. They met the evening of the 4th in Lala Mustapha's pavilion outside the city. For a time the meeting was cordial, but a dispute occurred over Venetian hostages being held as insurance for the return of the Turkish ships. When Bragadin refused, saying he would not go beyond the terms previously signed, Lala Mustapha declared the terms broken and all captives to be executed. Other sources say that he ordered the mass executions when he learned of the few defenders that had kept his massive army at bay for so long. All the defenders and citizens were killed and the city pillaged. Bragadin was held prisoner for two weeks, then bound to a pillory,

and finally killed. Most sources state that he was killed by being flayed, his skin was then stuffed with straw and taken to Constantinople. His remains were later purchased by his brother (some say stolen) and buried in Venice's Church of St. Giovanni and Paolo.

Although loathe to aid the Venetians prior to the invasion of Cyprus, Pope Pius' Holy League responded rapidly to Famagusta's fall and the news of the slaughter. Ships from Spain, Venice, Genoa, and the Papal States gathered together and sailed eastward, encountering the Turkish fleet off Greece near Lepanto on 7 October. In one of the decisive battles of history, the Ottoman fleet was badly damaged and westward expansion through the Mediterranean halted.

Cyprus remained the lynchpin of Ottoman naval superiority in the eastern Mediterranean, but Famagusta fell into ruin. For the next few centuries the stones of the walls and houses were used for construction across the island and across the Ottoman world, including the construction of Port Said in Egypt with the opening of the Suez Canal.

References: Sir George Francis Hill, *A History of Cyprus*, 4 vols. (Cambridge: Cambridge University Press, 1940–1952); Frederic Chapin Lace, *Venice, a Maritime Republic* (Baltimore: Johns Hopkins University Press, 1973); "Medieval Famagusta," www.pio.gov.cy/ features/history; "The Venetian Period in Cyprus," www.cypnet.com/.ncyprus/ venedik.html.

ANTWERP

DATE: August 1584–17 August 1585.
LOCATION: at the mouth of the Scheldt River, in modern Belgium.

FORCES ENGAGED:

Spanish: 10,000 infantry and 1,700 cavalry. Commander: Alessandro Farnese, duke of Parma.

Dutch: 20,000 troops. Commander: Philippe de Marnix.

IMPORTANCE:

Spanish victory gave them control of the southern provinces of the Netherlands, modern Belgium, which they retained until 1832.

Historical Setting

In the wake of Martin Luther's revolt against the Catholic Church, Europe rapidly began to divide into Protestant and Catholic factions. These opposing sides had more than religion to keep them apart, for Rome had long dominated Europe's politics and economy. Therefore, the supporters of Luther and other Protestant leaders had political and economic independence in mind as well. Northern Europe bred the main Protestant movements, and in German and Dutch states the political revolts were against the Holy Roman Empire, led by the Spanish Habsburg King Charles V. He saw suppression of the Protestant heretics as vital to both his religion and his lands.

In the Netherlands, the northern states tended toward Calvinism while the southern states remained predominantly Catholic. In spite of their religious sentiments, however, the southern states were just as ambitious for independence since Dutch maritime power was on the rise and there were world markets to exploit, markets that the Spanish navy jealously guarded. The main Dutch leaders, particularly William of Orange, were aristocrats and members of the Habsburg court; they found themselves torn between duty to their sovereign and loyalty to their people and their business interests.

King Charles' son Philip lived in the

The siege and capture of Antwerp by Alexander Farnese, Duke of Parma, in 1585. (The Art Archive/British Library)

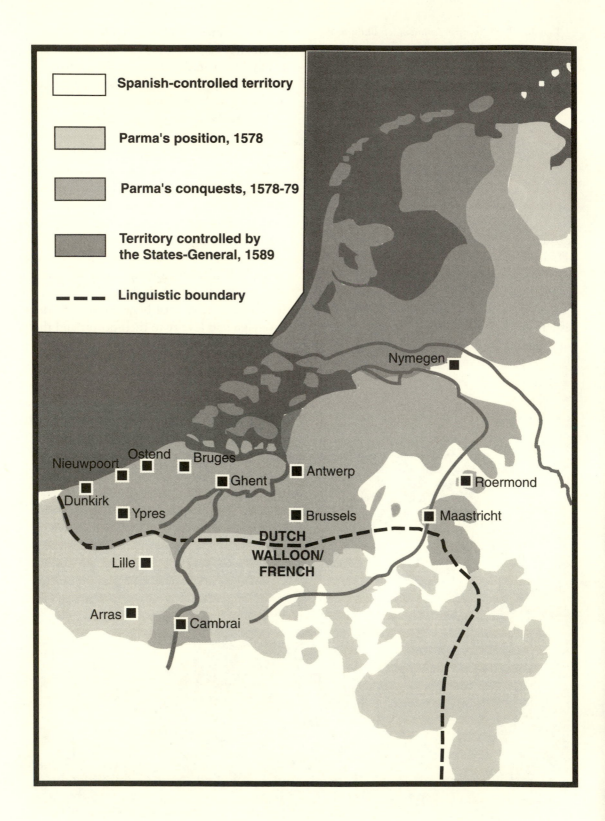

Spanish-controlled territory

Parma's position, 1578

Parma's conquests, 1578-79

Territory controlled by
the States-General, 1589

Linguistic boundary

Nymegen

Nieuwpoort   Ostend   Bruges

Ostend   Bruges   Antwerp

Ghent   Roermond

Dunkirk   Ypres

Brussels   Maastricht

DUTCH
WALLOON/
FRENCH

Lille

Arras   Cambrai

Netherlands, overseeing his father's interests and trying to maintain Spanish authority. The local aristocracy got along well with him, but when Philip became King Philip II in 1559, that amity began to wane. Philip came to believe that Protestants just could not be loyal subjects, and his increased taxes on Dutch cities certainly provoked disloyalty. Believing the Church to be the most secure avenue of wealth and popular control, Philip began distancing himself from the Dutch aristocracy while creating a stronger Church hierarchy in the Netherlands. When Dutch Protestants forced Philip's regent (his half-sister Margaret of Anjou) to ease the laws against "heresy," Philip responded by sending in the duke of Alba to restore control. Between 1567 and 1572 Alba crushed revolts and executed leaders, but could not convince the population to accept absolute Spanish authority and the resulting high taxes.

Alba raised an army of 30,000 men, but they were primarily German mercenaries, who also served as the bulk of William of Orange's army. With deeper pockets (at least for the time being), Alba waited until William's hirelings left him for want of pay. Alba then began taking a series of fortresses necessary to exercise control over the Netherlands. He continued to build his army until it reached 80,000, but that proved too expensive for Philip to maintain. When Alba's army took Antwerp in 1575, the unpaid mercenaries pillaged the city (the "Spanish Fury"), leaving some 8,000 dead in their wake.

Philip replaced Alba with his nephew Alessandro Farnese, the duke of Parma. With increased silver reserves coming in from the western hemisphere, Parma had fewer financial worries, but the Dutch proved difficult enemies. In 1584 William of Orange was assassinated, and Parma began a major offensive hoping to take advantage of the loss of that stubborn leader. He besieged Ghent, Brussels, and Mechlin, but the key to controlling the southern Dutch states was Antwerp.

The Siege

With Parma's onslaught in the second half of 1584, the Dutch looked for foreign aid. The country most logical to approach was England, whose Protestant Queen Elizabeth was always eager to thwart Philip's plans. England, however, still had a strong Catholic minority and Elizabeth was still unwilling to openly confront Spain's power, although she had been financially aiding William for some time. The Dutch therefore looked to France, whose King Henry III feared having strong Spanish forces to both his north and south. They offered Henry the Dutch throne, but strong Catholic resistance in his country convinced him to decline. Elizabeth began to make overtures and offered an expensive proposition: 4,000 infantry and 400 cavalry in return for possession of two coastal towns as security for her expenses. As the two sides dickered, the sieges went on. Ghent surrendered first in early 1585, with Brussels falling in March. Two other southern cities fell from internal subversion. The longest and most difficult siege was at Antwerp.

Parma led 10,000 infantry and 1,700 cavalry to Antwerp, beginning his siege in October 1584. The city lay on the Scheldt River just inland from the English Channel. It thus was able to maintain itself as long as shipping could be sent from the northern states. The city was defended by some 20,000 men under the command of Philippe de Marnix, whom William had assigned the task. The city's defenses were sufficiently stout to defy direct assault, so Parma decided that the only option was to block the Scheldt. He designed a floating blockade, which was built through the winter of 1584–1585 by two Italian engineers. The task was completed 25 February. Thirty-two barges chained together and anchored to the river bottom formed the center of the boat bridge, measuring 420 yards in length. The 180 yards to either shore were held in place by pilings and covered by a fort on either end. A platform was constructed crossing the entire structure, and an earthen embankment was built on both ends to protect bridge traffic from musket fire. To beat back any potential attack on the bridge from the river, each barge had a cannon mounted fore and aft. Ten guns were placed in the flanking forts, named Santa Maria and San Felice. To further protect the bridge, pontoons along the sides bristled with pointed beams. To round it off, twenty galleys cruised the river.

Antwerp had the services of an Italian engineer as well: Federico Giambelli of Mantua, later called the "Archimedes of Antwerp." A Flemish engineer named den Bosch assisted him. The two developed a number of original weapons with which to attack the bridge. Barrels filled with gunpowder and iron stakes were floated downstream without success. Large sheets of canvas were then floated in hopes of catching on the pilings and blocking the current, building up sufficient pressure to break the bridge. This strategy did not work either. A raft loaded with explosives ran aground on one of the banks before it reached the bridge, and a huge barge carrying a thousand arquebusiers also ran aground and was destroyed by Spanish cannon.

The Antwerp engineers finally had some success on 5 April with four massive shrapnel explosives. Giambelli fitted out flat-bottomed barges with a channel of gunpowder running stem to stern. "At the bottom there were bombs, millstones, marble chips, gravestones, chains, nails, and cutting blades. All this was pressed together by iron bolts and the whole mass was covered with wood treated with pitch and strewn with sulfur so that it would appear to be an ordinary incendiary device. The explosion was to be set off at the proper time by clockwork mechanisms" (Melegari, *Great Military Sieges*, p. 143). Three of the four failed to detonate, but the fourth did incredible damage: 260 feet of bridge destroyed and 800 men killed. Parma himself barely escaped. For some inexplicable reason, no sally from Antwerp appeared. Indeed, Parma's engineers not only repaired the bridge, but also included movable

sections that could be detached to let any future craft float through.

No more great efforts were expended. The siege lasted for another four and a half months, as the defenders gradually starved. They finally attempted a sortie in May, in conjunction with a small relief force. The two managed to link up and destroy the Kouwenstein dike, but the Spaniards soon retook and repaired it. In early August, Parma decided the time had come to challenge the city's defenses directly. After almost two weeks of fighting, the city citadel finally fell on 17 August.

Results

The city may have held on a few more weeks, but de Marnix had lost his spirit. For the length of the siege he had kept morale high and quashed sedition, but news of the surrender of other major cities deflated him. No major relief force arrived overland and no serious attempt to force the river appeared. French King Louis refused to intervene, and de Marnix had no faith in English promises. When the population began to speak of abandonment by the Protestant northern states, de Marnix began to believe it as well. Even though relief ships were only waiting on a favorable wind, the defenders knew nothing of it.

Parma had a habit of treating defeated cities generously, and Antwerp was no exception. The peace terms called for a return to loyalty to King Philip and the reestablishment of the Catholic faith. Protestants were allowed four years to remove themselves. No Spanish garrison was stationed there, but the citadel was destroyed, to be rebuilt upon the total conquest of the Netherlands. Antwerp's fall gave Spain control over all the southern Dutch states, which had been heavily Catholic anyway (with some exceptions, like Antwerp). This region became the basis of the modern nation of Belgium, while the northern states ultimately formed the nation of Holland. Many in the region and throughout Europe expected Parma's ultimate conquest would be completed. It did not happen. The northern states strengthened their hold on the rest of the country's rivers, and Parma could not force his way across them. Further, the Dutch navy (after the Spanish Armada's defeat at English hands in 1588) controlled the coastal waters. "The town which Parma, thanks to his indomitable spirit, his military genius, and his knowledge of human nature, had succeeded in conquering, now withered, as it were, beneath his hand" (Geyl, *The Revolt of the Netherlands*, pp. 200–201).

By the end of the four-year grace period Parma allowed the Protestants, almost all of them had left for the northern states. Primarily merchants, they left when the blockade strangled the city's trade, as well as to exercise their own religion. Antwerp's loss proved Holland's gain. "The peace and order which Parma gave to [the states of] Flanders and Brabant very much resembled the stiffening of death. On the other hand all the best vital forces of the Netherlands people drew together in the small area north of the rivers" (Geyl, *The Revolt of the Netherlands,* p. 201).

References: Pieter Geyl, *The Revolt of the Netherlands, 1555–1609* (New York: Barnes and Noble, 1958); Vezio Melegari, *The Great Military Sieges* (New York: Crowell, 1972); Geoffrey Parker, *The Dutch Revolt* (Ithaca, NY: Cornell University Press, 1977).

KINSALE

DATE: 2 October 1601–3 January 1602.
LOCATION: Ireland's southern coast.

FORCES ENGAGED:
English: 6,800 infantry and 600 cavalry. Commander: Charles Blount, Lord Mountjoy.
Spanish: 3,300–3,400 men. Commander: Don Juan de Aguila.

Irish relief force: approximately 6,000. Commander: Hugh O'Neill.

IMPORTANCE:
English victory marked the consolidation of English occupation in Ireland.

Historical Setting

The roots of Anglo-Irish rivalry go back, according to mythology, to prehistory. In historical times, it began in the twelfth century with the Norman invasion of Ireland after the heirs of William the Conqueror had established firm control over England. Ireland remained a vassal state of sorts until 1541, when Henry VIII named himself king of Ireland as well as England. Over the next five decades an English administration slowly tried to exert its control over a population that it at once despised and feared. Strict English control was limited to an area known as the Pale along the eastern coast, but "beyond the Pale" the remainder of the island was deemed savage. In the 1570s the English began to spread from the Pale into the remainder of the country and to meet resistance when the earl of Essex began pacifying Ulster with extreme brutality. Not until the 1590s, however, was any effective and organized resistance mounted.

The primary leader of the Irish was Hugh O'Neill, earl of Tyrone in the northern province of Ulster. He had been raised in England and brought up Protestant, as a member of the English army he had campaigned in Ireland. In 1585 he acceded to the earldom and maintained fairly close relations with Queen Elizabeth's government, but in 1595 began a guerrilla campaign against the English forces in Ireland and in 1598 was declared a traitor when he led Irish forces to a victory over the English at the battle of Yellow Ford. His chief ally was "Red Hugh" O'Donnell, earl of Tyrconnel on Ulster's western coast.

Although O'Neill had succeeded in organizing a fairly effective fighting force, his attempts to train them in European tactics had

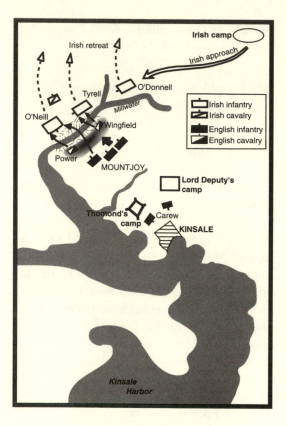

Irish camp

Irish retreat

Irish approach

Tyrell
O'Donnell
Millwater
O'Neill
Wingfield
Power
MOUNTJOY

Irish infantry
Irish cavalry
English infantry
English cavalry

Lord Deputy's camp

Thomond's camp
Carew
KINSALE

Kinsale Harbor

been less successful. Still, given the fact that the English knew little of Ireland outside the Pale, a guerrilla force was probably the best suited for the Irish needs. When, however, Queen Elizabeth I dispatched a new lord deputy, the superior financial, manpower, and manufacturing resources of England meant that the Irish rebels would need some outside assistance. Who better to approach than Spain? The Spanish monarchy was still smarting from the disastrous effort of the Spanish Armada in 1588, and aid to Ireland's rebels would both harass England and show solidarity with another Catholic population in the face of the rising influence of Protestantism. Further, by placing forces in Ireland, Spain's King Phillip III hoped to force Elizabeth to withdraw some of her military from the Netherlands, where Spain was desperately trying to put down a Protestant-led rebellion that the English were supporting.

O'Neill's representatives in Spain succeeded

in convincing Phillip to send troops, but how many to send and where they would land were points of considerable disagreement. If Spain could dispatch in excess of 6,000 (complete with siege train), then an attack on Ireland's southern province of Munster would put the English between two relatively equal forces. If fewer than that were sent, however, O'Neill was convinced it would be better to have them land in Ulster and join with his forces. Unfortunately, that strong suggestion did not reach Spain until the force had already sailed. The fleet that sailed from Lisbon carried 4,432 Spanish and Italian soldiers. Their overall commander was Don Juan del Aguila, a veteran commander. Most of his troops, however, were recruits. The fleet was commanded by Don Diego Brochero, and his orders came from the king, not from Aguila. Given Aguila's harsh command style, the two men cooperated little.

The Spanish sailed in mid-September and arrived off the southern Irish coast on 2 October. The fleet had weathered a storm that scattered the ships, however, and not all of them were able to make the rendezvous at the small port of Kinsale, just south of Cork. The force that Aguila was able to debark was reduced to 3,300 to 3,400 men. One of the ships that was unable to make its way to Kinsale carried most of the veteran troops and much of the army's powder. Although Brochero offered Aguila as many of his ships' guns as he cared to take, Aguila kept only four; as he had so little powder with which to fight, he decided to keep what he had primarily for use in his arquebusiers.

The English were quick to respond. The garrison at Kinsale was allowed to depart and they alerted the lord deputy. This position was held by Charles Blount, Lord Mountjoy, who arrived in Ireland in 1600. He had expanded the garrisons manning a string of forts around the Pale, but weakened them in order to take as many men as possible to Kinsale. He arrived in Cork on 8 October and by the 27th had mustered about 6,800 infantry and more than 600 cavalry, with assurances from London that more would be sent. That strategy encouraged O'Neill to launch numerous raids out of Ulster to harass the English and rally support, and he hoped to divert Mountjoy's force from the south. He did not. When he learned that the English had laid siege to the Spanish in Kinsale, O'Neill reluctantly left Ulster for the south with 3,000 infantry and 400 cavalry. His ally O'Donnell also marched south with 2,000 infantry and 300 cavalry.

The Siege

On 26 October Mountjoy established his camp about 5 miles from Kinsale. His force never completely encircled the town, but they did seize the high ground and subject the Spaniards to regular artillery fire. Mountjoy's cavalry rode at will through the surrounding land destroying crops and livestock so none would succor the garrison. Both commanders issued proclamations to the population, Mountjoy calling for obedience to London and resistance to foreign interference and Aguila for all Catholics to unite against the cruel English (he threatened papal action if they did not—a threat he did not have the authority to issue).

O'Neill overrode local opposition to his departure and was on the march by the end of October. It was a risky decision, for he was leaving Ulster open to attack by the garrisons along the frontier and he was taking his men, only partially trained in contemporary European tactics, across the island without any supplies except what they could carry. Once in the south, they would be forced to live in the open as winter approached and live off the land that Mountjoy was in the process of devastating. The Spanish force might or might not gain reinforcements and resupply, but Mountjoy was certain to get both. Whether the Irish and Spaniards would be able to maintain contact and coordinate action was also problematic.

In early November Mountjoy's besieging force enjoyed the most success. In an attack on

Spanish outposts, he forced their withdrawal after slaughtering what livestock Aguila had on hand. His artillery kept up a steady fire that Aguila's sallies were unable to stop. An outer fort fell to the English on the 11th. Mountjoy, hearing of O'Donnell's approach, sent his lieutenant Sir George Carew to intercept him, but O'Donnell eluded him. When Carew returned to Kinsale, he brought with him reinforcements locally recruited by the earl of Thomond: 1,000 infantry and 100 cavalry. Still, O'Donnell and O'Neill were able to sever the English line of supply back to Dublin and the resulting shortage of supplies, combined with increasingly foul weather through the month of December, began to take its toll on the besiegers. At year's end 400 Spaniards, who had landed down the coast at Castlehaven, marched to join the Irish. They urged O'Neill to break through Mountjoy's weakening position and join with Aguila. O'Neill doubted that the English were really that weak, but O'Donnell added his persuasive voice to those of the Spaniards.

It has been debated since 1602 how coordinated the Irish and Spanish forces were to be; possibly they had been unclear on just when the Irish attack was to take place so Aguila could sally out against the English rear. On the morning of 3 January 1602 (according to the newly adopted Gregorian calendar; the English used the Julian calendar and their date for the battle is Christmas Day) the Irish force divided into three columns. The vanguard was commanded by Richard Tyrell, an Englishman dissatisfied with earlier treatment by Elizabeth. He led 1,000 Irish infantry and about 200 Spaniards. The main body was O'Neill's 3,000 men, and O'Donnell led the rearguard with his 2,000. They mounted a night march of some 6 miles, but through lack of training or possibly conflict between the commanders they were not on site and in line when dawn broke.

Mountjoy, who had had his scouts combing the region since he first heard of the Ulstermen's arrival, was alerted to the march and had his men ready. He left five regiments in his own camp and four regiments of Thomond's to cover Kinsale, while he led the remainder of his force (1,500 to 2,000 infantry and 400 to 500 cavalry) toward a ridge northwest of Kinsale overlooking Millwater Ford. O'Neill's men occupied that ridge and found the English deployed. He stood fast, waiting for Aguila to sally from Kinsale. When the Spanish showed no signs of activity, he ordered his men to withdraw through the marshes around the ford onto firmer ground to the west, hoping to draw the English into the swampy land that would hamper their superior cavalry. He was awaiting the arrival of O'Donnell's men as well as the deployment of Tyrell's as he did this.

As O'Neill attempted to form his men into a "tercio" (the standard square defensive formation of the day), Mountjoy ordered his part of the cavalry under Sir Richard Wingfield to attack. They easily swept aside the few skirmishers covering the marsh and rode at O'Neill's troops, but were driven back by the Irish cavalry. Hard on Wingfield's heels, however, were two more cavalry units commanded by Mountjoy and Power, and the force of their charge was more than the ill-trained Irish cavalry could withstand. They fled through O'Neill's men, completely disrupting the developing formation. O'Neill's men, under attack by both cavalry and English infantry, broke and were pursued by English cavalry. Tyrell turned his men and attempted to dash between O'Neill and the oncoming cavalry, but found himself attacked in his own flank as he tried. O'Donnell's men refused to follow Red Hugh into the fray when they saw the debacle and marched away.

Although the sounds of battle were clearly heard in Kinsale, Aguila did not sally, thinking it to be an English ruse to draw him out. Unfortunately, the English victory volley sounded to him like approaching Irish and he then ordered his men out of the town, but quickly retreated when he spied the English banners.

Results

For a loss of no more than a dozen men, Mountjoy had inflicted a crushing defeat on the Irish. Their casualties numbered perhaps as many as 1,200 while the Spaniards with them lost about 90 men. Mountjoy resumed pounding the defenses at Kinsale, upon which he had inflicted serious damage throughout December. On 12 January, Aguila surrendered after three days of negotiations. He and his men were granted parole and provided with shipping and supplies to return to Spain. Thus ended the Spanish interest in Ireland.

O'Neill returned to Ulster with O'Donnell and spent another year in his more familiar role as guerrilla leader, but agreed to fairly lenient terms with the English government shortly after Elizabeth's death. Whatever fighting he may have done in that last year was superfluous, for the Irish rebellion was crushed at Kinsale. Lughaidh ÓClérigh, one of O'Neill's early biographers, wrote, "there was not lost in any defeat in recent times in Ireland so much as was lost there. . . . there were lost besides nobility and honour, generosity and great deeds, hospitality and kindliness, courtesy and noble birth, culture and activity, strength and courage, valour and steadfastness, the authority and sovereignty of the Gaels of Ireland to the end of time" (Foster, *Modern Ireland*, p. 38). Whether it was really that drastic is debatable, but England did solidify its administration in Ireland. Although the Catholic Church was blamed for causing the rebellion, the English engaged in remarkably little religious persecution. Protestant-Catholic tension by no means ever went away; indeed, it remained the primary Anglo-Irish point of conflict. Taxation, another motivation for rebellion, continued as before, as did the establishment of shires, the organization for government the English used at home. At times their boundaries conflicted with those of traditional clans, but the counties they designated remain to this day. From 1601 Ireland was firmly in English hands, where it remained until the passage of the Government of Ireland Act in December 1920.

References: John Barratt, "The Battle of Kinsale," *Renaissance Notes and Queries*, no. 2, 1998; R. F. Foster, *Modern Ireland, 1600–1972* (London: Penguin, 1988); G. A. Hayes-McCoy, *Irish Battles* (Harlow, Essex: Longman, 1969); John J. Silke, *Kinsale* (New York: Fordham University Press, 1970).

OSAKA

DATE: winter campaign: 8 November 1614–22 January 1615; summer campaign: May–June 1615.
LOCATION: southwestern part of Japan's main island of Honshu.

FORCES ENGAGED:
Eastern Army: 195,000 troops. Commander: Tokugawa Ieyasu.
Western Army: 90,000 troops. Commander: Toyotomi Hideyori.

IMPORTANCE:
Tokugawa's victory ended organized resistance to his establishment of his family as the dynasty holding the position of shogun for two and a half centuries.

Historical Setting

In October 1600, Tokugawa Ieyasu led his army to victory over Ishida Mitsunari at the battle of Sekigahara. Ishida had been trying to maintain the Toyotomi family in the position of shogun, military ruler of Japan. He had with him before the battle the infant heir to the position, Toyotomi Hideyori. After the battle, Tokugawa assumed the shogunate and placed Hideyori in the family castle at Osaka. Although Tokugawa commanded the largest army in Japan after Sekigahara, he was not without rivals. In 1614, the now teenage Hideyori became the center of disaffected nobles who began organizing a coalition against Tokugawa.

Tokugawa had attempted to curb the power of the nobles, called *daimyo*, by obliging them to leave their castles and spend half the year in residence at the capital city of Edo, modern Tokyo. This allowed him to keep an eye on any possible resistance movement while forcing the daimyo to spend so much money on two residences that they would be unable to afford to raise troops in revolt. The strategy was only partially successful. In 1614 young Toyotomi Hideyoshi began renovations to both his castle and to a badly damaged shrine. The Great Buddha had been partially destroyed by an earthquake in 1596, and when Hideyori completed the restoration he installed a large bell at the accompanying temple. On it were written two phrases: "May the state be peaceful and prosperous" and "In the East it greets the pale moon, and in the West bids farewell to the setting sun." In the first phrase, the ideograms for *ie* and *yasu* appear. The second phrase seems to indicate that Tokugawa's residence, in the east at Edo, was of less importance than the eastern Toyotomi residence at Osaka Castle. Tokugawa viewed both of these as insulting and tension began to grow.

The daimyo who had been on the losing side at Sekigahara began to gather forces at Osaka. Also, *ronin* (masterless samurai, or what would be called in the European feudal system "free lances") began to join the coalition against the shogun. Among these ronin were many who had converted to Christianity, a religion Tokugawa despised. By November 1614, over 113,000 men were gathered at Osaka Castle, and Tokugawa was not about to let their number expand any further. He gathered together a reported 194,000 troops and marched for Osaka.

The Siege

The campaign against the Osaka Castle began on 19 November with an amphibious assault

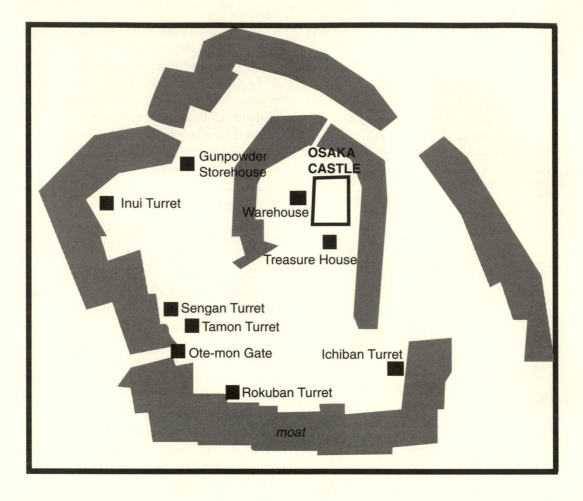

by Tokugawa's Eastern Army forces against a fort at the mouth of the Kizu River. Three thousand men in forty boats crossed the river, overcame the handful of defensive river craft, and burned the fort. A week later the battle of Imafuku, northeast of Osaka, took place. A force of 1,500 attackers seemed to have an easy victory in hand until the 600 troops defending the village were saved by a strong sally from Osaka Castle. Timely reinforcements, including a large contingent of men carrying European-supplied arquebusiers, saved the attack and Tokugawa's men secured the village to serve as a base of operations. At the same time, another larger battle was being fought across the river at Shigeno. Five thousand Eastern Army troops fought to a draw against 2,000 men sent out from Osaka.

On 29 November Tokugawa ordered another amphibious operation against one of Hideyori's forts covering the Kizu River at Kizugawa. The fort fell easily while, in a stubborn ship-to-ship fight against Hideyori's naval commander Ono Harunaga, a support force under Tokugawa's naval commander Kuki Moritaka kept any reinforcements from aiding Kizugawa. The Eastern Army made steady progress against Osaka. The strength of the castle's defense was at Sanada-maru, a barbican earthwork protruding out from the castle's walls. The barbican position was defended by Sanada Yukimura with 7,000 men. Ten thousand Eastern Army troops assaulted the position on 4 December but were thrown back. Sanada's men maintained their position for days, occasionally launching sallies against the

The siege of Osaka Castle in 1615, detail of a folding screen commissioned by Kuroda Nagamasa, Edo period. (Werner Forman/Art Resource, NY)

Eastern Army siege lines. In a night attack on 17 December, one such sally scored a victory against a section of Tokugawa's army in a battle fought by lantern light. That convinced the shogun to refrain from further attacks and let his artillery do the work. He brought up 300 cannon and began pounding the castle, as miners began digging under the walls. The siege came to a negotiated end on 22 January 1615, when Tokugawa agreed to withdraw if Toyotomi Hideyori would swear to end any thought of rebellion. He was also obliged to allow Tokugawa to fill in the castle moat.

The winter campaign thus came to an end, but Hideyori did not end his plotting. In April Tokugawa received word that Toyotomi Hideyori was not only trying to stop the filling in of his moat, but had gathered even more troops than the previous November. The summer campaign was more a series of battles than a

siege. Hideyori's Western Army began raiding isolated Eastern Army contingents, the first battle taking place at Kashii. On 29 April the Western Army force numbered 3,000 men, and attacked Wakayama Castle, on the coast south of Osaka. Many of the samurai loyal to the castle's owner, Asano Nagaakira, had left to go into siege lines near Osaka Castle when the Western Army troops attacked. The best defense being a good offense, the remaining defenders sallied out of the castle and drove the attackers away at Kashii; Hideyori's men withdrew to Osaka Castle.

By early June Tokugawa's army was approaching. Hideyori hoped to seize some key ground from which to keep the Eastern Army at bay, but in the opening confrontation at Domyoji on 6 June his advance force of 2,600 ran into 23,000 of Tokugawa's men. Hideyori's commander at this battle, Goto Mototsugu, skillfully withdrew his men to some high ground as fog developed, which hindered the arrival of reinforcements from Osaka. In the ensuing battle Goto was killed, and Hideyori lost one of his best commanders. The Eastern Army forces continued on toward the Yamato River, where they encountered 12,000 men sallying from the castle. That battle ended in a mutual withdrawal at day's end. Simultaneously, two battles were being fought to the north of Osaka. At Yao, 5,000 of Tokugawa's troops defeated 5,300 of Hideyori's. At Wakae, 4,700 troops of Hideyori's Western Army were overrun by a cavalry charge.

The summer campaign ended a few days later in a major battle at Tennoji. The plan Hideyori and his generals devised called for a hammer-and-anvil operation. An attack with 55,000 men on the Tokugawa army center would hold them in place, while a flanking movement with 16,500 men would strike the rear. A mobile reserve of 14,200 was in place behind the main body. Once the battle was engaged, Hideyori would emerge from the castle leading 3,000 men behind his father's standard to strike the finishing blow. Tokugawa's army, numbering some 155,000, were commanded by his son Hidetada. They deployed in four parallel defensive lines with flanking units. Their strong defense meant that Hideyori's army had to work perfectly for their plan to succeed. They did not. The ronin broke ranks too soon in order to attack the Eastern Army center. That obliged the main force to follow on their heels before the flanking force was positioned. Hideyori's General Sanada Yukimura, as he led his men into the charge, sent word for Hideyori to sally from the castle.

The missed timing was fateful, but an accident in Tokugawa's army almost turned the tide against the Eastern Army. Once the battle was engaged, Tokugawa's reserve force advanced without orders into the main body of the army. This gave the impression that he had turned coat and was attacking from the rear. Only quick action by Tokugawa preserved order and the situation was soon remedied. Sanada ordered up the mobile reserve and Tokugawa's men were slowly being pushed back. The failure of other reserves to attack and the death of Sanada broke the Western Army morale. Hideyori's charge out of the castle came too late. He had barely sallied forth when he ran into his retreating army being chased by Tokugawa's men. There was no time to put up a defense at the castle itself, and Eastern Army troops were quickly inside the walls as Hideyori withdrew with what men he could gather into the keep. Under artillery fire it was soon on fire, and Hideyori committed suicide.

Results

As Tokugawa entered the keep to claim the victory, he found Hideyori's eight-year-old son and had him beheaded, ending the Toyotomi line. This also ended any resistance of the daimyo to Tokugawa's family occupying the shogunate for two and a half centuries. The only other challenge to the family's authority came in 1637–1638, when a Christian faction rebelled against the anti-foreign policies of the Tokugawa regime. When that was crushed, the dynasty held firm until the mid-nineteenth century.

The long peace maintained during the Tokugawa shogunate served to bring to an end the samurai warrior way of life. With no wars to fight, they were forced to become businessmen if they wanted to maintain a reasonable income, and although the class remained the martial ability waned. Not until the arrival of Matthew Perry in 1854 and the resulting realization that Japan had slipped too far behind the rest of the world's technology did the warrior spirit begin to reemerge with the rebuilding of Japan's military might.

References: George Sansom, *A History of Japan* (Stanford: Stanford University Press, 1961); Stephen Turnbull, *The Samurai Sourcebook* (London: Arms and Armour, 1998); idem, *Samurai Warriors* (New York: Macmillan, 1977).

LA ROCHELLE

DATE: 10 September 1627–27 October 1628.
LOCATION: in the center of France's Atlantic coast, roughly halfway between Brest and Spain.

FORCES ENGAGED:

Huguenot: unknown, but included virtually the entire male population of the city. Commander: Major Jean Guiton.
British: 5,000 troops. Commander: George Villiers the duke of Buckingham.
Royalist: 30,000 troops at the height of the siege. Commanders: King Louis XIII and the duke d'Angoulême.

IMPORTANCE:

The fall of La Rochelle signaled the end of French toleration for Protestantism, forcing a mass migration overseas.

Historical Setting

The Huguenots (French Protestants) had existed in France since the 1520s, but had had an uneasy relationship with predominantly Catholic France. Between 1562 and 1597 eight religious wars were fought between the two factions, the Catholics primarily being represented by the monarchy. That changed when Henry of Navarre became King Henry IV, founder of the Bourbon dynasty. Although raised a Protestant, he accepted Catholicism in order to be more acceptable to his people; however, in 1598 he issued the Edict of Nantes, which granted religious freedom throughout the country.

All was well until Henry was assassinated and his son Louis XIII came to the throne. In the years since Henry's accession the Huguenots had been granted prominent positions in the royal court and were given greater local autonomy than were Catholic regions. Strong in their faith and in their independent attitudes, the Huguenots ultimately drew the envy and the wrath of French Catholics. Under the influence of his prime minister, Cardinal Richelieu, Louis came to the conclusion that

he could never be the absolute monarch he intended to be unless the Huguenots lost their political privileges.

The main Huguenot leaders were Duke Henri de Rohan and his younger brother Soubise. It was Soubise who first acted in defiance of King Louis's new policy. In January 1625 he raised a small force in the province of Poitou and temporarily occupied the island of Rhé, just off the Huguenot port city of La Rochelle. He then stole ten ships and captured the nearby island of Oléron, defeating the royal garrison there. His brother Henri began raising troops in the strongly Protestant southeastern province of Languedoc. Richelieu rightly feared that with many nobles supporting the Huguenots, England and possibly the Netherlands would come to their aid, if not for religious reasons then for political ones.

The Huguenots sent Louis a list of demands. His response: "I incline to peace, and I shall assure Languedoc and other provinces to you. But as for La Rochelle, my intention is different" (Burckhardt, *Richelieu and his Age*, p. 218). His conditions for peace in that city were harsh. The seemingly impregnable walls built since Henry IV's time were to be destroyed and the city restricted to its 500-year-old walls; a royal superintendent was to be the highest legal authority in the city; no warships could enter the harbor. Under those conditions, they could maintain their rights under the Edict of Nantes. La Rochelle was the most Protestant of French cities, but the factionalism among the Protestant population meant that Rohan could not bring together a united effort to resist Richelieu. To save La Rochelle, Soubise in England had to bring in foreign aid.

As usual, French politics were Byzantine. Richelieu had negotiated treaties with England and the Netherlands, so feared provoking their Protestant populations. Spain was Catholic but always on the alert for self-aggrandizement, and a Protestant uprising in France could easily be transformed into a need for implementing a counter-Reformation and inserting Spanish troops. The duke of Savoy could only be depended on to support the side that profited him most. By focusing their attention only on La Rochelle and not the entire Huguenot movement (not yet, at any rate), Richelieu believed he could keep everyone but the English out of the conflict. In England, Soubise gained the support of the population and the influential George Villiers, the duke of Buckingham, close friend to England's King Charles. Buckingham gathered an army of 5,000 and a fleet in June 1627 and sailed for La Rochelle.

The Siege

La Rochelle was well suited for defense. Covered by three islands (Rhé, Aix, and Oléron), its harbor was flanked by two watchtowers between which a chain was strung, barring all ships when it was raised. A seaborne assault being virtually impossible, the landward approach was only slightly better. The northern flank of the city was covered by marshes, narrowing the pathway any army would have to take. Fort St. Louis covered the approach, and the city walls were new and extremely stout. The adult male Huguenots of the town were all expected to be soldiers in time of need, and all their merchant ships were fitted for quick transformation to warships.

By the time Buckingham's force arrived off the city, Richelieu had placed strong royal forces back on both Rhé and Oléron, as well as a feeble garrison in Fort St. Louis, but its Royalist garrison rankled the citizens. Buckingham could easily have overcome the fort's defenses and installed himself in La Rochelle, which may have served to unite Huguenot support across the country. However, he feared the Royalists controlling sea access to the city so he attacked Rhé first.

The English soldiers landed on the beaches on the far eastern point of the island and beat back an assault by the 200 Royalist cavalry and 2,000 infantry. The Royalists retreated into Fort St. Martin and Buckingham soon had the

fort surrounded. The most formal courtesies between the nobles of both sides were conducted along with the constant bombardment of the fort, which proved too strong for assault to overcome. Representatives sent to negotiate with King Louis could not convince him to order his men to surrender. The siege dragged on through the autumn of 1627.

Unfortunately, while Buckingham received steady supplies from England and Holland, the citizens of La Rochelle were unsure of which course to take. There had been no official break of the Anglo-French treaty, so allowing the English into the city would certainly provoke a royal attack. King Louis arrived outside the city in August with 11,000 infantry, 600 cavalry, and 24 guns. His message to the inhabitants: "If the citizens are prepared to show themselves good Frenchmen, they have nothing to fear" (Burckhardt, *Richelieu*, p. 228). Moderates and radicals in the city argued while Buckingham starved St. Martin's garrison.

In the meantime, however, the townsfolk profited from selling their wares to the English and the Royalists, but depleted their own supplies in the process. They were unable to acquire any supplies from the rest of the country and were not allowed to leave the city to harvest their crops. They did, however, strengthen their fortifications, but without direct aggression on Louis' part the Protestants in the rest of the country made no move to rise up. Louis offered peace, while Buckingham offered troops and supplies as soon as Fort St. Martin fell. All hung in limbo until 10 September, when Royalist engineers began strengthening the walls of Fort St. Louis. Had the king ceded control of that fort to La Rochelle's Huguenots they would have turned against the English, but when it was reinforced instead the city leaders could no longer trust royal promises. They fired a volley at the fort, which returned fire, and the fragile peace was gone.

The situation quickly deteriorated for the Protestants. On 7 October a fleet of forty-six supply ships took advantage of a storm and landed supplies for Fort St. Martin a day before its commander had warned of surrender from starvation. The English, although at first well-supplied, were now suffering from dysentery. The weather was turning cold, and public and royal support in England was fading fast. On 7 November Buckingham threw his men into an assault against the fort, but they could take no more than the outer walls. As Buckingham planned his withdrawal, Royalist troops landed that night and on the morning of the 8th 4,000 men faced the battered English force. After a cavalry charge failed to intimidate the French, Buckingham led a fighting withdrawal toward his ships. Six hundred men from St. Martin sallied to join the 4,000 and the English were slaughtered as they retreated. Buckingham was one of the few who managed to reach the ships and flee in the night.

In January 1628 the besieging force reached 30,000, but La Rochelle remained open to resupply by sea. The French could not put forth sufficient ships to blockade all the approaches to the city, so Richelieu supported an idea proposed by the marquis de Spinola, visiting from Italy, to build a dike across the mouth of the harbor that could more effectively block any ships bringing succor. Through the early months of 1628 the dike was built of pilings which held in place small craft filled with rocks sunk to create the breakwater. The city of La Rochelle was so far inland that its guns could not reach the harbor mouth and stop the construction. An opening in the center of the dike allowed the tides to flow, but was small enough to protect from attack with floating batteries and a chain.

Richelieu learned from a deserter of a way into the city via a sewer. On the night of 12–13 March the cardinal armed himself and took command of 4,000 infantry and 1,000 cavalry, preparing to break into the city as soon as the grating that covered the sewer was blasted away. It never happened. The engineers got lost in the marshes, and by the time they reached their goal the sun had risen and they were exposed. The defenders quickly made good the potential weakness in their defenses and the siege dragged on. Although Richelieu made sure the troops were paid well and regularly, their spiritual needs tended to, and their discipline honed, the long winter was taking its effect on them as well. Only signs of weakness in the city brightened Richelieu's demeanor.

Stories from deserters told of increasing hunger behind the city walls, along with cases of scurvy. Attempts were made on the lives of city leaders. The English garrison left from the previous summer were restless and demanding more pay. The long-awaited relief Rohan had promised from Languedoc never materialized. Then, King Charles in England promised supplies by April in return for an agreement to accept him as benefactor. Unfortunately for the defenders, Parliament was exceeding slow in appropriating funds, more worried about lodging complaints about Buckingham. When Buckingham's brother Admiral Lord Denbigh finally arrived off La Rochelle with a convoy of rotting food, he refused to force the French fleet or the dike. Instead, he sent a message to the city fathers suggesting they begin surrender negotiations while his fleet stayed in sight, a seeming threat to the blockading fleet.

Although no English aid arrived, Richelieu could not prevail on his king to assault La Rochelle and finish it off. Throughout the summer the siege continued, with hundreds of deserters escaping the city while hundreds more died inside. In late September a new English fleet packed with troops and supplies arrived offshore, but French agents among the sailors made them mutinous, and no aid went ashore.

Results

On 27 October, the mayor of La Rochelle, Jean Guiton, led 4,000 of the 5,000 survivors to Richelieu. On the 29th they met with King Louis. Later that day Richelieu led the procession that occupied the city; he refused to accept

Guiton's formal surrender and banished him. King Louis entered on 1 November, then departed for Paris on the 18th.

In the wake of the siege, Richelieu ordered the city walls destroyed. More important, he celebrated Mass and Catholicism was officially reintroduced to the city. The fall of La Rochelle signaled the fall of the Huguenots as well. Because they could not agree on a strategy, they fell prey to Richelieu's single-mindedness. Although the Protestant faith was not persecuted immediately, Louis XIII had begun the French monarchy's journey to absolutism. His son Louis XIV, who revoked the Edict of Nantes in 1685 and crushed the Huguenots unmercifully, finally achieved it. A massive exodus of perhaps 800,000 fled France for Britain, Germany, Switzerland, and the North American colonies.

References: Carl J. Burckhardt, *Richelieu and his Age*, trans. Edwin and Willa Muir (New York: Harcourt, Brace, & World, 1967 [1940]); Roger Lockyer, *Buckingham* (London: Longman, 1981); O. I. A. Roche, *The Days of the Upright: The Story of the Huguenots* (New York: C. N. Potter, 1965).

MAGDEBURG

DATE: 20 March–10 May 1631.
LOCATION: on the Elbe River, west-southwest of Berlin, Germany.

FORCES ENGAGED:

Protestant: unknown. Commander: Diedrich von Falkenberg.
Holy Roman Empire: unknown. Commander: Jan Tserkales, Baron von Tilly.

IMPORTANCE:

The destruction of Magdeburg after its capture inspired many wavering northern German factions to support Sweden's Gustavus Adolphus, turning the tide of the Thirty Years War toward the Protestant cause.

Historical Setting

Ever since Martin Luther had nailed his 95 Theses to the church door in Wittenberg in 1517, violence between northern European Protestants and the champions of the Catholic Church was inevitable. Through the sixteenth century Spain's armies battled for the faith against the heretics, then late in the 1500s the Holy Roman Empire assumed the cause. The immediate causes of the Thirty Years War originated in Prague in 1618, where a struggle over succession between Catholic and Protestant pretenders focused the attention of both faiths. Rather than submit to the rule of a ten-man administration (seven of whom were Catholic), rebels led by Count Matthias von Thurn threw them out of a window of the palace in Prague. The Protestant Union raised an army to aid the new Protestant administration in the city, while the Holy Roman Empire dispatched troops to restore order. The imperial forces were defeated. After that initial setback, however, they won a series of victories, culminating in the reestablishment of Catholic rule in Bohemia in 1623. The hero of the imperial cause was Jan Tserkales, Baron von Tilly.

In 1625 the war flared again owing to the initiative of King Christian IV of Denmark, who hoped to make himself both religious and political leader of northern Europe. Baron von Tilly continued to have regular success against Protestant forces, as did Albert von Wallenstein, the duke of Friedland, who had raised an army to fight for the empire. In 1629 the Catholic Church issued the Edict of Restitution, effectively banning most Protestant worship. Failing in his goals, King Christian signed the Treaty of Lübeck and returned to Denmark. Wallenstein had made himself into a powerful commander, so much so that many Catholic princes feared his ambition and convinced the Holy Roman Emperor to dismiss him once the fighting ended.

In 1630 the third phase of the war began when King Gustavus II Adolphus of Sweden entered the fray. Gustavus had transformed his

The Catholic League German army lays siege to the north German town of Magdeburg and slaughters its inhabitants during the Swedish phase of the Thirty Years' War, after an engraving by Matthaus Merian. (Archive Photos)

relatively poor country into a major military power and he had spent the 1620s establishing Swedish dominance in the Baltic Sea region. With that task accomplished, he landed on the coast of Pomerania in July 1630 with the intent of reviving the battered Protestant cause. He also hoped to control the Germanic provinces of Pomerania and Prussia, which would make the Baltic a virtual Swedish lake. Gustavus received financial assistance in his endeavor from France's Cardinal Richelieu, who hoped to enhance his nation's position in Europe at the expense of the Holy Roman Empire. Unfortunately for Gustavus, many north German princes feared his ambition in spite of his assurance that he was motivated primarily by religious factors. Although the Swedish king quickly occupied Pomerania, he could not compel the cooperation of key German leaders, most notably Elector Georg Wilhelm of Brandenburg and Elector Johan Georg of Saxony. It was their hesitation to deal with Gustavus that spelled the doom of the city of Magdeburg.

Magdeburg's population was both Catholic and Protestant, and there had been struggles over leadership there as well as in the rest of the countryside. Former Archbishop Christian William offered to raise an army for Gustavus in return for the Swedish king's support in regaining his position. In June 1630 Christian succeeded in raising the standard of revolt in Magdeburg against the Holy Roman Empire and took control of the city. In August Gustavus promised "to interest himself for the city in all dangers, to defend it at his own cost, not to forsake it in any need, and to conclude no peace in which it was not comprised" (Fletcher, *Gustavus Adolphus*, p. 146). Christian began to raise troops and conduct operations against imperial detachments, but he should have awaited Gustavus' arrival to begin attracting attention to himself. While the Swedes were still making their way across the Brandenburg, imperial soldiers began overrunning the region around Magdeburg up to the very walls by December.

The Siege

Gustavus was in Berlin, trying to convince the elector of Brandenburg to allow Swedish troops access through his territory, when word came of the imperial drive toward Magdeburg. Gustavus sent Diedrich Falkenberg to assist Christian William in defense of the city. The city leaders named him governor for the duration of the siege. Unfortunately, the king did not send any troops with him. Magdeburg was a rich and well-fortified city, and apparently Gustavus assumed it possessed a sufficiently staunch population to persist until he could arrive. He never expected to be as long-delayed as he was.

The imperial troops that began the siege of Magdeburg were under the command of Baron von Pappenheim, a subordinate of Tilly's. Tilly at this point was the senior imperial commander, Wallenstein having been relieved of his command when Catholic princes began to fear the power of his personal army. Pappenheim had 3,000 troops with him, enough to ravage the countryside and control most access into the city, but too few to sustain a close investment. He also had little or no artillery to batter the walls. He did have, however, a strong pro-imperial faction within the city that subverted much of Falkenberg's effort at a strong and active defense. Still, the first few months of the siege were not too intense from either attacker's or defender's point of view. Gustavus, unable to make any headway with either Brandenburger or Saxon elector, continued to attack imperial garrisons at towns toward Mecklenburg. These winter operations surprised the imperial army, for such seasonal warfare was not conducted at the time. Tilly did his best to keep Gustavus busy and away from Magdeburg, and the Swedish and imperial armies sparred with and maneuvered around each other through the last months of 1630 into the first months of 1631.

In mid-March, after a costly victory over a Swedish detachment at the city of Kniphausen, Tilly withdrew toward Pappenheim and

Magdeburg. Gustavus hesitated over whether to march directly to the city's relief or to stage another attack that would draw Tilly back into the field. He decided on the latter and pointed his army toward Frankfurt an Der Oder. The Brandenburger town of Küstrin temporarily barred his way on orders from the elector, but Gustavus demanded and received passage through the town. On 12 April he arrived before Frankfurt and took the town and its garrison of 5,000 to 6,000 by storm the following day, killing 1,700 (some sources say 3,000) defenders during and after the battle in retribution for Tilly's slaughter of Swedish garrisons at Kniphausen and elsewhere. However, Gustavus' quick success was counterproductive. Tilly, upon hearing of Gustavus' approach to Frankfurt, began marching to its defense. Upon hearing of its rapid fall, however, he turned back to Magdeburg and intensified the siege rather than face the Swedes in the open as Gustavus had hoped.

Pappenheim, who had been investing the city since mid-December, tired of the boredom of the siege and tried to achieve a quick end. He offered Falkenberg a fortune to give up the defense but was flatly rejected. Pappenheim begged Tilly for more men in the opening days of 1631 so he could storm the city, but Tilly was too busy with his own campaigning to spare any troops. In early March, Falkenberg sallied against the imperial force with some success, but when Tilly arrived with the bulk of the imperial army on 5 April, the investment became complete. The force surrounding Magdeburg at this point reached some 30,000. Almost immediately they began assaulting the outer defensive works and capturing them, depriving the city of both ordnance captured and men killed.

Gustavus, however, did not march. He wrote to Falkenberg in late April to hold on another two months during which time his activities would surely draw Tilly's troops away from the city. He was wrong. "Tilly looked upon it as a point of honor that the stronghold to which the attention of all Europe was now turned, and the capture of which was the only issue that could offset the blow sustained at Frankfurt, should be overcome, and he directed his measures with energy to this end" (Fletcher, *Gustavus Adolphus,* p. 147). Indeed, Tilly brought in another 10,000 men, but this placed a great strain on the resources of the area and soon half his force was out of action with disease.

On 28 April Tilly ordered Pappenheim to assault the Toll Redoubt, protecting the bridge across the Elbe. His attack succeeded after two days and Falkenberg withdrew the redoubt's garrison into the city, burning the bridge behind them. In reality that action did the imperial army a favor, for it allowed them to leave only a holding force on the eastern bank and concentrate the bulk of the army on the city side of the river. With the increasing number of troops facing him, Falkenberg ordered the city's suburbs burned to deny the enemy any cover in an advance toward the city walls. At this, Tilly sent the city a surrender demand that Falkenberg rejected, for he knew that the Swedish army was on the march.

In a council of war on 19 May Pappenheim finally won Tilly over, and the imperial commander ordered a full-scale assault. Although Falkenberg had through sheer force of will maintained the city's defenses, many of the citizens would not join him in his zeal. If the king of Sweden was approaching, they reasoned, why get too involved in a defense that would shortly be relieved? However, as time went on and Gustavus did not appear in spite of Falkenberg's constant assurances, many on the city's ruling council began to counsel a negotiated surrender. This relaxation of attention was the imperial army's greatest ally. Pappenheim's assault was to be launched at dawn, but at the last moment Tilly canceled the operation. As the sun rose and no attack took place, the guards on the walls left for breakfast or caught a nap. Some sources say that pro-empire factions in the city signaled for an attack. When Tilly relented two hours later and the attack got under way, the defenders were unready for

Pappenheim's furious assault. Falkenberg, addressing the council, rushed to the walls and led the defense, but was soon killed in the fray. Without his inspired leadership, there was little coordination among the remaining troops and citizens. As troops left the walls to concentrate on those imperial troops which had entered the city, other gates were left unguarded and thus allowed the attackers access at multiple points.

What happened next was for decades the subject of intense debate. Although it is undeniable that the imperial troops showed no mercy to the city's inhabitants, it was the fact that the city almost completely burned to the ground that was the memory most people had of the siege. In Frederick Schiller's history of the war, he stated that Tilly ordered the city's destruction. "To augment the confusion and to divert the resistance of the inhabitants, the Imperialists had, in the commencement of the assault, fired the town in several places. The wind, rising rapidly, spread the flames till the blaze became universal" (Schiller, *History of the Thirty Years War*, p. 218). Later writers lay the blame for the fire on the citizens themselves. "When it became certain that the enemy could no longer be kept off and that Falkenberg had fallen, they executed their determination. At more than twelve points the city was at the same time set on fire, and except the cathedral and about fifty houses, sank into soot and ashes" (Gindely, *History of the Thirty Years War*, vol. 2, p. 65). Other sources say that Falkenberg had the fires set in order to deny the city as a base for the imperial army. Whoever was responsible, Tilly at the time was blamed.

Results

The pillage of the city became famous as one of the most extreme in history. The most general estimate of the deaths numbers 20,000, but some claim twice that many. The slaughter was the result of months of tedium, starvation, and disease, multiplied by the facts that this was a war of religious factions fought by mercenaries who had no pay other than plunder, and few wars exceed the horrors than those fought over religion. "Neither innocent childhood, nor helpless old age; neither youth, sex, rank, nor beauty, could disarm the fury of the conquerors. Wives were abused in the arms of their husbands, daughters at the feet of their parents; and the defenseless sex exposed to the double sacrifice of virtue and life. No situation, however obscure or however sacred, escaped the rapacity of the enemy. In a single church fifty-three women were found beheaded. The Croats amused themselves with throwing children into the flames" (Schiller, *History of the Thirty Years War*, pp. 217–218). Other accounts tell similar stories.

The loss of Magdeburg for a time hurt Gustavus' reputation, for Tilly was able to resume the offensive and all of the Swedish king's promise as the Christian champion seemed hollow. Yet he really could not get to the city without assurances from Saxony. Without that, he would have been exposing his army across Saxony while maintaining uncertain lines of supply back to the coast. However, the stories of the slaughter served to inflame the passions of Protestant Germany, although Elector Johan Georg of Saxony continued to withhold his support for Gustavus until Tilly invaded his territory. That support, such as it was, helped turn the tide in the war in favor of the Protestants. A few months later, when Wallenstein had been restored to his command, Gustavus and Johan Georg faced him and Pappenheim at Breitenfeld outside Leipzig. Although the Saxons broke at the opening of the battle, their diversion of a portion of Wallenstein's army aided Gustavus in one of the pivotal victories of history. Although the war lasted another seventeen years before it was concluded with the Peace of Westphalia, Protestant momentum that ultimately resulted in equal standing before the law in Europe dates to Magdeburg and Breitenfeld.

References: Ronald Asch, *The Thirty Years War* (New York: St. Martin's, 1997); C. R. L. Fletcher, *Gustavus Adolphus and the Thirty Years War* (New York: Capricorn, 1963); Anton Gindely, *History of the Thirty Years War*, vol. 2 (Freeport, NY: Books for Libraries Press, 1972 [1885]); Frederick Schiller, *History of the Thirty Years War*, trans. A. J. W. Morrison (New York: John B. Alden, 1883).

MAASTRICHT

DATE: 13–26 June 1673.
LOCATION: on the Meuse River, approximately 50 miles east of Brussels, Belgium.

FORCES ENGAGED:

French: 24,000 infantry and 16,000 cavalry. Commander: King Louis XIV.
Dutch: 4,500 infantry and 1,200 Spanish cavalry. Commander: unknown.

IMPORTANCE:

The French victory marked the introduction of the engineering genius of Vauban. It also led to an expansion of the Dutch War beyond King Louis' original intentions, beginning a decline in the standard of living in France.

Historical Setting

The Netherlands in the seventeenth century were a disjointed group of provinces. The northern area was known as the United Provinces and was controlled by the Dutch, whereas the southern provinces (modern Belgium) were under the control of the Spanish Habsburg monarchy, which had ruled all the Netherlands prior to the successful Dutch rebellion in the sixteenth century. It was the southern provinces that first attracted French interest when King Louis XIV decided to establish a more secure northern border at the expense of the Spanish, perennial French rivals. Louis believed that the Scheldt River should serve as a natural northern boundary for France, and in 1667 he set about to make it so.

Louis developed an extremely tenuous legal claim to that territory by way of his marriage to Princess Maria Theresa, who was the daughter of Spain's Philip IV by his first marriage. Although Charles II came to the Spanish throne, he was the son of Philip's second marriage; Louis claimed that Maria Theresa's inheritance should outrank that of the progeny of Philip's second marriage and that the Netherlands were hers. It was an incredibly weak claim, but almost no one was in a position to challenge it. Louis had created one of the largest European armies ever, numbering some 120,000 men, and he entered the Spanish Netherlands on 24 May 1667. He enjoyed early success against the unprepared Spanish. By October Louis' Marshal Henri Turenne captured a vast number of towns and forts and controlled the entire region. Having accomplished such easy victories in the north, Louis then turned eastward in 1668 to occupy the Habsburg province of Franche-Comte, on the Swiss frontier.

Although the warring parties ended the fighting with the Treaty of Aix-la-Chapelle in 1668, Louis was not about to give up so easily. He still looked to the Netherlands as a threat to his northern border, and in 1672 he decided to invade again in order to force the Dutch to cede him sufficient territory for Louis to feel secure. The Dutch were in no position to match Louis' military power with their own, so they responded the only way they could: they broke the dikes and flooded the countryside. That stopped the French advance in its tracks after minimal gains, and by 1 August Louis was back in France.

The following fighting season Louis was ready to try it again. In the meantime, the Dutch had made contact with the Habsburgs in both Spain and the Holy Roman Empire, so Louis had to look to his flanks. After asking the advice of his chief military advisers Turenne, Louis II prince of Condé, and Sébastien

Vauban, he positioned 30,000 men (under Turenne) facing the Spanish in Flanders and another 30,000 (under Condé) facing the empire's forces in Germany. With the rest of his army, numbering 48,000, he marched once again into Holland. His target was the city of Maastricht, the capture of which would protect the gains he had made the previous year. Unfortunately, an ally of Louis, Elector of Cologne Max Heinrich, had a claim to Maastricht as well. In the 1648 Treaty of Westphalia that ended the Thirty Years War, Maastricht had been ceded to the Dutch but was to be ruled by the bishop of Liege, a position in 1673 held by Heinrich. He wanted Louis to capture the city, then turn it over to him. By threatening to bypass it completely, Louis convinced the elector to allow the French to maintain control after the city's capture.

The Siege

Louis began his campaign by marching his men up the Scheldt River in a feint toward Ghent, then turning eastward to threaten Brussels. He bypassed that city and marched directly for Maastricht, camping his army before the city walls on 11 June 1673. Turenne also sent a force to approach the city from the east, barring any potential reinforcements that might try to make for the city. Under Louis' command was the master engineer of the day, Sébastien Vauban. He had risen through the ranks to become one of the French king's chief advisers, and he had done so on talent alone. Vauban was the age's master of siegecraft, from both the offensive and defensive aspects. No one could design fortifications as he could, and none could capture them as well. Maastricht was the first major city he tackled.

Vauban immediately went to work with the siege tactics he had developed, being shown publicly for the first time. These began with a trench parallel to the section of the city walls that had been chosen for assault. Once dug, artillery was placed and on 18 June twenty-six

cannon began their bombardment. As that progressed, zigzag lines of trenches moved forward to a closer position, where another parallel line was dug and the artillery brought closer. The zigzag design made it more difficult for the city's defenders to get a straight shot at men as they went to and fro between parallels.

By 24 June Vauban's parallels were completed. As it was the feast day of St. John the Baptist, King Louis expressed his desire to celebrate Mass within Maastricht's cathedral. The King's Regiment and the Company of the Gray Musketeers led the assault, under the command of Charles de Batz de Castelmore, count d'Artagnan, upon whom Alexander Dumas later modeled his fourth musketeer although he was at the time a field marshal. The fighting was intense as the French troops approached the counterscarp before the moat, went through the moat itself, and then entered one of the crescent fortifications covering the walls. Although the defending Spanish soldiers dislodged the bulk of the attacking force from the crescent, thirty men under the marquis de Villars held their ground throughout the night.

The next morning James Scott, duke of Monmouth (and son of Catholic King Charles I of England), sent his men to take the covered road, the embankment protecting the moat. After losing 300 men he withdrew. This setback was followed by another when the Spanish succeeded in exploding a mine beneath the lightly held crescent and then recapturing it. Again the duke of Monmouth sent his men in to yet another unsuccessful attack, one in which d'Artagnan was fatally wounded in the throat.

Having failed to celebrate Mass within the city, Louis ordered his artillery back into action. That did the trick. The city's governor gave in to the demands of his troops and the citizenry on 2 July, surrendering his city.

Results

The French capture of Maastricht marked the successful beginning of Louis' Netherlands campaign. He succeeded in recapturing the Franche-Comte region on France's eastern frontier, but the captured cities became diplomatic bargaining chips. In the Peace of Nijmegen, he returned Maastricht to the Dutch, plus four other cities to the Spanish Netherlands (modern Belgium). In return, Louis acquired St. Omer, Ypres, Cambrai, Mauberge, and Valenciennes. Like most of the treaties signed in Louis' reign, it provided only a temporary peace.

Most important about the siege of Maastricht is not the political gain or loss, but the work of Vauban. In him one finds an engineering genius not seen in military history since, perhaps, Archimedes. His development of tactics to reduce fortresses revolutionized siege warfare, as did his development of fortresses that his own tactics could (possibly) not overcome. His work gave France a virtually impregnable northern frontier that in the future occasionally lost a piece but was never in that age successfully breached.

References: John Lynn, *The Wars of Louis XIV* (New York: Longman, 1999); Vezio Melegari, *The Great Military Sieges* (New York: Crowell, 1972); Paul Sonnino, *Louis XIV and the Origins of the Dutch War* (New York: Cambridge University Press, 1988).

VIENNA

Date: 14 July–12 September 1683.
Location: central Austria.

Forces Engaged:
Austrian: 11,000 soldiers and 5,000 civilian volunteers. Commander: Count Ernst Rüdinger von Starhemberg.
Relief force: 75,000–80,000 mixed Polish, German, and Austrian troops. Commander: Polish King Jan Sobieski.
Ottoman: 140,000–240,000 mixed troops from across the empire. Commander: Prime Minister Kara Mustapha.

Importance:
Timely relief saved Vienna, ending the Ottoman threat to western Europe forever.

Historical Setting

Since the establishment of the Ottoman Empire, the Turks regularly attempted to extend their influence as far westward into Europe as possible. Their best chance of doing so came in 1524, when Sultan Suleiman the Magnificent tried but was turned back at Vienna. After that, a long series of ineffective sultans had ruled the empire with big dreams but little talent. In 1664, another foray into central Europe was turned back at St. Gotthard Pass in Switzerland. That campaign ended with the signing of the Treaty of Vasvar, mandating a twenty-year truce between the Turks and the Holy Roman Empire.

In 1672 the Holy Roman Empire, based in Austria, went to war with King Louis XIV of France over possession of the United Provinces of Holland. At the same time, the Turks were fighting the Poles. This seemed a propitious time for a nationalist rising in Hungary. The Magyars of the region had been most recently under the control of the Holy Roman Empire, while other parts of the region had been under occasional Turkish domination. With both overlords otherwise occupied, Emmerich Tököli in 1674 led a Magyar independence movement. For no other reason than to bother his enemy Leopold I, the Holy Roman Emperor, Louis XIV asked the Ottoman government to assist Tököli. The grand vizier, Kara Mustapha, responded that he would aid the uprising as soon as his war with Poland was over, but it was immediately followed by a war with Russia. When that ended in 1682, the Turks were able to fulfill their pledge.

Hearing of the proposed Ottoman advance, Emperor Leopold offered concessions to the Hungarians, but Tököli rejected them. He consolidated his claim to leadership by marrying into the Transylvanian royal family and

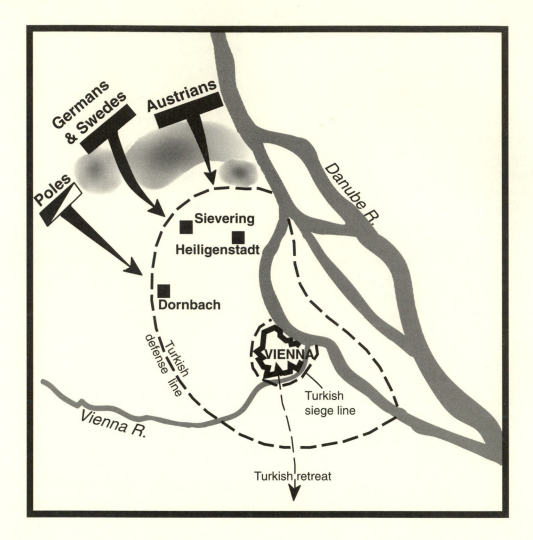

proclaiming himself prince of Hungary under Ottoman suzerainty. Ottoman Sultan Mohammed IV led an army out of Constantinople in late 1682, then ceded command to Kara Mustapha. Sources vary widely on the number of troops in the Ottoman horde, ranging between a low of 140,000 and a high of 240,000 troops from all parts of the Ottoman Empire. A leisurely advance brought the army to the Vienna Woods in mid-summer 1683.

Emperor Leopold fled Vienna, leaving command of the imperial army to Charles V of Lorraine. Charles commanded a force of 24,000 men and wisely decided not to confront the Ottoman army, which was up to ten times his army's size. Instead, he deployed 10,000 infantry, 600 cavalry, and all his artillery in Vienna under the command of Count Ernst Starhemberg. Charles took the remainder of his men away from the city to plead for aid from any nation that might be willing to provide some. Poland's King Jan III Sobieski responded positively, as did a variety of German principalities. Unfortunately, this proffered aid was from such a span of territories that the forces could not quickly gather and advance to Vienna's aid. Starhemberg would have to hold on as best he could.

In Vienna the citizens rallied to the army's support, providing volunteer troops and working feverishly to shore up the city walls. Women volunteered to dig trenches. They were all organizing themselves when the Turks began to deploy around the city on 14 July

Seventeenth-century portrait of Kara Mustafa II, commander of the Turkish army at the siege of Vienna in 1683. (The Art Archive/Museum der Stadt Wien/Dagli Orti)

1683. The bulk of the besieging army was positioned on the southwest side of the city, opposite the Danube River, where mining operations would be less bothered by water. That was also the area where the walls were strongest.

The Siege

Things started out badly for the Turks. Charles of Lorraine's mobile force attacked and defeated a Hungarian force under Tököli at the Kerms Bridge across the Danube. A Turkish attempt to recapture it was beaten back. Ottoman attempts to storm the city failed, and Kara Mustapha (when he returned to command from taking the baths at Baden) saw that his heavy artillery was making little impression on Vienna's walls and Austrian counter-battery fire from 300 cannon was effective in keeping Turkish infantry at bay. It would be necessary to take Vienna the hard way, by mining and starvation. Small breaches occasionally appeared in the walls, which the

Turkish elite Janissary troops assaulted, but they were always turned away after heavy fighting. Meanwhile, Kara Mustapha found it increasingly difficult to feed his massive force and disease soon was common.

As the siege slowly progressed, the vizier learned of the approach of Sobieski's relief force, numbering 70,000, comprised of Charles of Lorraine's 27,000, Sobieski's 20,000 Poles, and another 20,000 Bavarians, Saxons, and Swedes. Charles was the chief of staff responsible for operational planning, but Sobieski was in overall command as he was the highest-ranking nobleman present. Kara Mustapha pressed his engineers to hurry their assault on the walls, to breach them before the relief arrived. They redoubled their efforts, with some success. On the night of 9 September a courier swam the Danube to get a message from Starhemberg to Charles: "There is no more time to lose, my lord, no more time to lose."

On the 11th the relief force appeared on the Kahlemberg, a hill overlooking Vienna. Kara Mustapha found himself in a terrible position, having to face a strong relief force with a potential coordinated sally from the city. On the morning of the 12th Sobieski took comand of his Poles on his army's right flank, the Germans and Swedes occupied the center, and Charles' Austrians deployed on the left. Charles scored the opening success when his cavalry turned back a charge by elite *spahis*, the Turkish cavalry. That opened the road to Vienna. Sobieski charged into the bulk of the Turkish army, the vanguard being his winged hussars. Twenty thousand cavalry, made up of one German-Austrian and three Polish groups, charged down the Kahlemberg led by King Jan Sobieski. The cavalry broke through the Turkish lines as the garrison in the city attacked the Turkish rear. The demoralized Turks broke, and the battle turned into a rout.

Results

The Turks left 10,000 to 15,000 dead on the field and abandoned 300 cannon and a mass of other supplies, including the exotic beans that were to capture the taste buds of Europe and the world, coffee. The loot left behind took a week to gather and distribute. Emperor Leopold returned to his capital a few days later, but Sobieski was soon in pursuit of the fleeing Ottoman army. He caught and defeated them at Parkan in October and again at Szecsen in November. Soon, Hungary was cleared of all Ottoman military. Kara Mustapha fled to Belgrade, where he was executed on Christmas Day.

Contemporary sources claim that Kara Mustapha did not heavily bombard the city of Vienna because he wanted to capture it intact as his own personal city. That hesitation to fight to the fullest certainly aided the defenders. Had he taken the city and reorganized there through the winter of 1683–1684, he would have had few enemies to face to the west. Louis XIV had his tacit support and no other power in Europe existed had the Holy Roman Empire been in retreat. Kara Mustapha had bragged at the outset of the campaign that he would advance to the Rhine and the Tiber, that his cavalry horses would be stabled in St. Peter's in Rome. That was certainly an overly ambitious goal but even a temporary hold on Vienna would have strengthened Louis in France and put him in perhaps an impregnable position in western Europe. Instead, the Holy Roman Empire regained some stature and gained recruits to continue the war against the Turks intermittently for another fifteen years. Islam's conquests reached only into the Balkans, leaving western Europe under solidly Christian influence. Poland, savior of the West, had its moment in the sun, but in 1920 it saved the West from the East again when Polish forces turned back the oncoming Red Army that was hoping to spread the communist revolution out of Russia.

References: Thomas M. Barker, *Double Eagle and Crescent* (Albany: State University of New York Press, 1967); John Stoye, *The Siege of Vienna* (New York: Holt, Rinehart, and Winston, 1965).

LONDONDERRY

DATE: 21 April–31 July 1689.
LOCATION: Ireland's northern coast.

FORCES ENGAGED:

Protestant Irish: 7,361 men. Commander: Lieutenant Colonel Robert Lundy, then Major Henry Baker. Jacobin: 4,000 men. Commander: Marquis de Maumont, then General Conrad von Rosen.

IMPORTANCE:

Inability of Jacobites to capture the town indicated the general weakness of their entire effort in Ireland, and marked the spiritual beginning of Protestant domination of Ireland.

Historical Setting

After the death of Oliver Cromwell and the short, unhappy rule of his son, King Charles II assumed the English throne in 1660. The restoration of the monarchy to the house of Stuart after the English Civil War brought a Catholic back to the throne of the predominantly Protestant nation. Although his reign was relatively uneventful, the accession of his son, Charles, duke of York, to the throne as James II in 1685 was a cause of some disquiet. James was intensely Catholic and began a campaign to increase the authority of the Church throughout the nation. When James fathered a son in 1688, the prospect of a continued Catholic dynasty was more than many Protestants could face. Parliament invited King William of Orange in the Netherlands to assume the throne. When he arrived the English army put up no resistance; James fled for France.

In Ireland, the most powerful leader was the earl of Tyrconnel, named lord deputy of Ireland during James' reign. Since 1685 he had been purging the Irish military of Protestants, which resulted in their replacement by Catholics of irregular military quality. In late

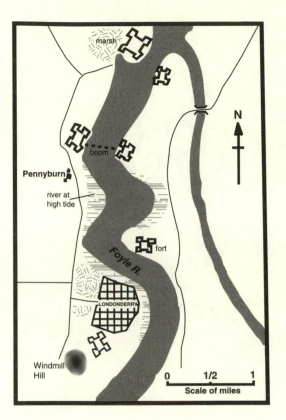

from France. All of this took place in the midst of the Nine Years War, a struggle between Louis XIV's France on one side and a coalition of the Netherlands and the Holy Roman Empire on the other. With William diverted by his new responsibilities in England, Louis decided that he could weaken the continental effort against himself by supporting Tyrconnel's Irish Catholic movement. He prodded a reluctant James into leading a force to Ireland, which landed at Kinsale on the south coast on 12 March 1689.

While awaiting French support, Tyrconnel had been consolidating his hold over all of Ireland, including most of Protestant Ulster in the north. When James arrived from France with 1,200 men, the Catholics escorted him to Dublin, where he assembled a parliament. James proclaimed religious freedom for all who remained loyal to him, then his parliament repealed the Settlement Act of 1652 whereby Englishmen had appropriated Irish lands. They also passed a Bill of Attainder declaring some 2,000 locals to be opponents of the king and thus in forfeit of their lands.

Some 30,000 Protestants fled to the port city of Londonderry, one of the key centers of Protestant English influence. Robert Lundy was still in command of the city's garrison. His exact role in the events is the subject of much debate. He slightly improved the city's defenses but he also negotiated with James' forces. When the Jacobins approached in early April, Lundy fielded an incredibly disorganized force that was quickly driven back into the city after a skirmish at Lifford. When reinforcements arrived from England, Lundy informed them that Londonderry was indefensible and they should return home. When news of that decision leaked out, the citizens decided Lundy was at best untrustworthy and at worst a traitor, so he was expelled. Command of the defense fell to Major Henry Baker and Reverend George Walker, named co-governors. Military command lay in the hands of Colonel Adam Murray, whose arrival with reinforcements prompted Lundy's removal.

1688, before James left England, Tyrconnel had sent a force of Catholic soldiers to garrison Londonderry, replacing one of the few remaining Protestant forces in Ireland, stationed there under Lord Mountjoy. The approach of the ragged Catholic troops stirred up rumors in the town of an upcoming massacre of the almost completely Protestant population. When the troops appeared, a handful of young apprentices (on their own initiative) quickly lowered the city's gates, barring the force's entry. Tyrconnel decided to leave Mountjoy in command for the time being, as news of William's arrival in England had just been received. Mountjoy was soon on his way to England, succeeded by his second in command, Lieutenant Colonel Robert Lundy.

Tyrconnel hoped to take advantage of the "Glorious Revolution" in England to strengthen Ireland's autonomy. While negotiating with the new king, he also sought aid

James II arriving at Kinsale, April 1689. In the background is the walled city of Londonderry (actually on the opposite end of Ireland from Kinsale), to which James and his army marched to lay siege. (Archive Photos)

When James arrived, believing the city awaited his presence in order to submit, he was met with cries of "No surrender!" from the garrison manning the walls.

The Siege

Londonderry is situated with the Foyle River on its eastern and northern sides and a bog on its western side through which a causeway offered access. The town was crowded with refugees, but many inexplicably were allowed to flee the city early in the engagement; about 20,000 civilians remained. A force of 7,361 men defended the city. The besieging Jacobite army numbered at first about 4,000, but owing to their open line of communications back to Dublin, reinforcements came and went and the besiegers probably fielded a force of some

12,000 at its greatest strength. They lacked the necessary artillery to reduce the city's walls, possessing only a handful of mortars that maintained a steady bombardment of the city, destroying houses and spreading terror. The defenders possessed twenty cannon, but little is mentioned of any significant damage they may have inflicted on the attackers.

On 21 April Murray sortied from the town to attack an Irish force deploying northward toward the village of Pennyburn. French reinforcements rode to stiffen the Irish, who were badly outnumbered. As Murray's force retreated toward Londonderry, the pursuing cavalry chased them down a lane along which Murray had earlier placed several hundred musketeers. Their ambush virtually wiped out the Jacobin cavalry at one blow, and General Maumont, the French officer commanding the siege, was killed. He was replaced by Colonel John Hamilton.

On the night of 5–6 May, Hamilton ordered a force to seize Windmill Hill, roughly a half-mile southwest of Londonderry. Although they took the hill from a small Protestant force rather easily, 1,000 men sallying from the town dislodged their own force of 3,000 the following day. Murray then strengthened his position by erecting a line of redoubts from the bog (which covered the town's western face) southward to the windmill thence to the Foyle. The remainder of the month passed quietly, but inside Londonderry the food and water situation grew increasingly desperate. Tensions heightened and arguments between officers became frequent. Outside the town, however, the Jacobins were doing little better. The spring had been wet and many were suffering from disease, for the Irish had with them virtually no medical service.

The besiegers, fearful of rumors that reinforcements were sailing from England, mounted two cannon on the bank of the Foyle north of the town and built a log boom to bar the river to any ships. Forts on both sides of the river protected the boom. With the northern flank covered, Hamilton on 4 June mounted another assault on Windmill Hill, now protected by entrenchments. The attack involved possibly as many as 6,000 men, mixed cavalry, infantry, and grenadiers. The attack was met by virtually the entire garrison and was beaten back, the cavalry losing many horses (there were less human casualties, as the soldiers' cuirasses were effectively bullet-proof). Unable to cross the trenches, the Jacobin army fell back. Casualties among the attackers far outnumbered that of the defenders, and Irish morale began to deteriorate.

A few days later lookouts on the town walls sighted English ships entering Lough Foyle to the northeast. It was for a time only a tantalizing vision, for the relief force's commander, Major General Percy Kirke, hesitated to challenge the boom and artillery blocking the river. Instead, he debarked his 2,000 troops upstream and set up camp. There was no way to establish communications with the garrison, although messengers were dispatched from both town and fleet. None got through, and one (who died trying) carried a message captured by the Jacobins that the city had no more than a week's rations remaining. It was not that bad; the governors had painted a bleak picture in order to motivate Kirke. Still, it was bad. The citizens had for a while eaten well off the horse-meat from the dead cavalry mounts after the second Windmill Hill battle, but by late June they were back to eating dogs, cats, rats, and anything else that could be caught and killed.

Hamilton was about to offer Londonderry rather generous terms when General Conrad de Rosen arrived with word from King James to finish the town off. Rosen rounded up a number of local Irish and herded them in front of the town walls where they would starve unless taken in; the defenders responded by displaying their own prisoners alongside a quickly built gallows in plain sight of the Irish army. Rosen backed down.

In the meantime, Kirke had reloaded his men aboard their ships and sailed around to Lough Swilly to the northwest. This placed him in a position to attack the Jacobin force from the rear. Through the efforts of a young boy messages were now being exchanged with the garrison and Kirke learned that the situation was in reality as desperate as had been described in the earlier lost dispatch. The besiegers were in only slightly better condition. While their food supply was much better, they were losing large numbers to a variety of diseases, including smallpox. James ordered Hamilton to offer terms to the garrison too good to reject, and for a time the two sides negotiated, for in spite of his strong position Kirke would not move without orders from England. In mid-July he received a directive to force the boom and break through to Londonderry. He again embarked his troops and sailed back to Lough Foyle. The merchantman *Mountjoy* ran hard against the boom, severely damaging it, but foundered in the process. Another ship, the *Phoenix*, darted past the Irish artillery and sped for the town with fresh food.

Results

The breaking of the boom meant that, with sufficient suppression gunfire from aboard, ships could run the river and relieve the garrison. The Jacobin army fired a few shots at the ships the next day, but they knew they had failed. On 1 August, after 105 days of siege, the Irish army retreated. They had suffered perhaps 8,000 casualties. The defenders had suffered severely as well. Of the 7,000 defenders more than half had died, and the percentage of civilian deaths was approximately the same, primarily from starvation.

Although the battle of the Boyne the following year marked the "official" end of James's attempt at restoration, the defeat at Londonderry was a psychological turning point. It has over the intervening three hundred years become a Protestant landmark in Ireland, and the annual Apprentice Boys parade in the city marks the occasion of the initial Protestant defiance of James' intervention and the establishment of the Protestant ascendancy. Militant Ulstermen use it as a rallying point, citing Lord Macaulay's nineteenth-century account from the *History of England*: "Five generations have since passed away . . . still the Wall of Londonderry is to the Protestants of Ulster what the trophy of Marathon was to the Greeks." Had the Jacobin force captured the city, James could possibly have both consolidated his hold on Ireland and used it as a base to strengthen the concurrent rising in Scotland. Whether he could have defeated William in open combat somewhere in England no one can say, but the challenge to the new ruling house could have been successful; it certainly had a greater chance of succeeding than did Bonnie Prince Charlie's 1745 rising.

The call of "No surrender" from the walls of Londonderry has remained an Irish Protestant battle cry ever since 1689.

References: Thomas Bartlett and Keith Jeffery, eds., *A Military History of Ireland* (Cambridge: Cambridge University Press, 1996); Ian McBride, *The Siege of Derry in Ulster Protestant Mythology* (Dublin: Four Courts, 1997); Patrick Macrory, *The Siege of Derry* (London: Hodder and Stoughton, 1980).

ST. AUGUSTINE

DATE: 10 November–29 December 1702.
LOCATION: north coast of Florida, United States.

FORCES ENGAGED:

Spanish: 230 soldiers, 180 Indians and free blacks. Commander: Governor Jose de Zuniga y Cerda. English: 500 soldiers and 300 Indians. Commander: Carolina Governor James Moore.

IMPORTANCE:

Spanish victory reaffirmed their possession of Florida as a base to protect their Atlantic trade and resist American expansion.

Historical Setting

After Christopher Columbus' voyage of 1492, Spain began establishing control over the islands of the Caribbean Sea. When their reach extended to Central and South America, the wealth of the Aztec and Inca empires began flowing across the Atlantic to Spanish coffers. As early as 1522, other European nations saw the potential of profiting from Spain's work by attacking Spanish ships laden with treasure. Spain responded by landing men on the peninsula of Florida, hoping to establish naval bases which (coupled with those of Cuba) would deter pirates from entering the Caribbean. When the French attempted to start a colony in northern Florida in 1564, Spain hurriedly began settling men at St. Augustine to both remove the French threat and begin the pacification and conversion of the local Indians to Christianity.

A series of nine wooden forts were constructed over the course of the next century to protect the settlement, all of them destroyed by attacks, weather, or termites. Stronger defenses were considered unnecessary until 1665, when English colonists farther up the Atlantic coast began to encroach on Florida. As British pirates began to raid more aggressively into the Caribbean, the Spanish began to see the need for a more formidable fortress to protect their northern flank. When an English assault destroyed the final wooden fort in 1668, that provided the motivation necessary for the Spanish monarchy to provide the financing for the construction of a stone fort.

The Castillo de San Marcos was built with local material called *coquina*, a vaguely coral-like substance that is fairly soft and damp when quarried but dries hard but not brittle. Cannon balls tend to be absorbed by it. Construction began in August 1671, but progressed quite slowly and was constantly over budget. Not until 1695 was the fortress completed and work begun on a protective sea wall. The original cost projection of 70,000 pesos ended up being slightly more than half the final cost.

During the twenty-four years of construction tensions remained high between Spanish Florida and the English colony of Carolina, with occasional military forays launched by each against the other. Although much of the conflict played out in the heavily wooded frontier, attacks toward St. Augustine by both English colonists and pirates proved the necessity of building the fort. While the walls were thick and strong, the artillery mounted on the parapets was obsolete. Florida's Governor Jose de Zuniga y Cerda sent a representative to Spain to remedy the problem with modern weaponry, but in the meantime Carolina's Governor James Moore decided to attack the fort before the updated guns could arrive.

The Siege

Moore collected a force of some 500 militia soldiers and 300 Yamasee Indians with the willing support of the Carolina legislature, who felt the need to act once word arrived in mid-summer of the outbreak of the War of the Spanish Succession in Europe. Since England and Spain were at war, so should their respective colonies be. The legislature appropriated the funding for the expedition and promised to any participant in the attack an equal share of whatever loot might be captured.

Fourteen ships departed Charleston on 16 October 1702. The plan was for Moore to attack Spanish outposts along the coast with a seaborne force while a land-based force under Colonel Robert Daniel marched on St. Augustine. Daniel's troops landed in the Spanish province of Guale (some 60 miles north of St. Augustine), on 3 November. They proceeded to kill, capture, or drive off all the Spanish and Indian inhabitants of villages, who retreated south. Moore's force had similar success attacking various villages along the coast. Fleeing Spaniards and Indians reached St. Augustine on the evening of the 4th with news of the attack.

Governor Zuniga immediately gathered the inhabitants of St. Augustine into the citadel and appropriated all available food. He also sent a frigate to Havana begging for aid, while other messengers were dispatched to the Spanish outposts at Pensacola and Mobile. He sent a small force northward to slow or stop the English colonists, but they had little success. English sails were sighted 9 miles north of the town by the evening of the 5th. The next day, three English ships sailed south past St. Augustine to the mouth of the Matanzas Inlet, the southern approach to St. Augustine harbor. The remaining ships sailed up to the harbor on the morning of 8 November, but owing to the shallow bar at the entrance the men debarked on the south side of the harbor and marched around to join Daniel's force.

On the 9th Zuniga brought the final citizens of the town into the fortress. The following morning his scouts reported the approach of Daniel's men. When the English colonists arrived in St. Augustine and took up positions, Moore then landed his men from the ships. Inside the fort Zuniga oversaw approximately 1,500 people, of whom some 600 were either soldiers (just over 200) or citizens he could use for the defense. His fourteen cannon were old, his ammunition in short supply, and his artillerymen without experience. From interrogated prisoners Zuniga learned that the English had brought supplies for a three-month siege. As he could not match that, his only hope was relief from Havana.

The English were not fully in occupation of St. Augustine until 14 November, at which point Zuniga sent out a sally to burn down all the houses in the immediate neighborhood. They were destroyed to a distance of about 75 yards from the fort, giving the muskets a clear field of fire. The English had few cannon of their own, but began digging parallels to bring them as close as possible. The Spanish cannon fire did little direct harm but did keep the English cautious and under cover. The siege trenches were dug in anticipation of heavy artillery arriving from Jamaica; Moore dispatched Daniel there to fetch weapons and reinforcements.

The siege settled into a waiting game, with Zuniga occasionally able to get messengers carrying requests for aid through the English force. On 14 December an Indian, calling himself Juan Lorenzo, and his wife approached the Castillo San Marcos gate. When admitted inside, he claimed to be a deserter from the English force. He informed Zuniga that the English morale was rapidly deteriorating and that they would soon abandon the siege. After questioning, Lorenzo and his wife went to join the other Indians in the fort. He then tried to provoke a rebellion against the Spanish. When this was reported to Zuniga, Lorenzo was taken into custody and tortured for information, which he refused to give. His wife, however, admitted that they had been sent by the English, hoping they could explode the fort's powder magazine.

By the 19th the English trenches were within 100 yards of the walls, but the English still lacked strong enough guns to create a breach. Spanish morale plummeted when two sails came into view on Christmas Eve and they

were topped by the Union Jack. The English ships did not carry heavy ordnance from Jamaica; however, they did bring more men and ammunition. Zuniga ordered a Christmas party and a bonus for the defenders in order to keep up spirits. It did not succeed, but the arrival of four Spanish ships on the 26th did raise morale. The ships did nothing until the 29th, apparently unready to engage the English ships on hand. On the 29th, however, they finally unloaded 212 soldiers just down the coast. That was sufficient to bring Moore to the decision to withdraw. The return of Spanish ships from their unloading of troops blocked an escape by sea, so he ordered his own ships burned and retreated by land. Luckily for him, he had stationed reserve ships up the coast and they were used to ferry the remaining 500 men back to Carolina.

Results

Moore ordered St. Augustine set to the torch as his men withdrew, and on 30 December Zuniga's men reoccupied the town and controlled the fires. The siege was over, but St. Augustine had to be almost completely rebuilt. The English destruction of Spanish settlements at Apalache, Timuca, and Guale left St. Augustine the only Spanish strongpoint in northern Florida, and over the next twenty years the town was rebuilt with a surrounding wall.

The retention of the Spanish hold on Florida was not completely accepted by the English colonists to the north. Although the War of the Spanish Succession ended in 1713, military action did not completely stop. In 1728 Colonel William Palmer of Carolina marched against the fort but "refrained" from capturing the town once he saw the fort. The next and last serious attack came in 1740, when the founder of the colony of Georgia, James Oglethorpe, led an expedition against Castillo de San Marcos in order to secure his southern border from expected Spanish incursion. Spanish Governor Manuel de Montiano commanded a sortie be launched against the English while their forces were divided and that paralyzed the English attack. They proceeded to bombard the fort with naval gunfire for twenty-seven days, but inflicted little damage and few casualties. With hurricane season approaching, the force finally retreated to Georgia.

The Castillo de San Marcos, when finally completed, performed its mission. It maintained Spanish authority in northern Florida by resisting every attack launched against it. Their final additions to the fort were built in 1762, at the end of the Seven Years War, but the fort saw no more action after Oglethorpe's abortive attack. Spain ceded Florida to Britain the following year as penalty for being on the losing side in the Seven Years War, but regained it in the wake of the American Revolution. The Spanish possessed Florida until 1819, when the territory was finally sold to the United States. By then Spanish power was little but a fond memory and the United States was just starting down the path to greatness.

References: Charles W. Arnade, *The Siege of St. Augustine in 1702* (Gainesville: University of Florida Press, 1959); National Park Service, *Castillo de San Marcos* (Washington, DC: U.S. Government Printing Office, n.d.).

TURIN

DATE: 14 May–7 September 1706.
LOCATION: Savoy, northern Italian peninsula.

FORCES ENGAGED:

Savoyard: 4,000 defenders. Commander: Count von Daun.
Harassing force: 6,000 cavalry. Commander: Victor Amadeus, duke of Savoy.
Relief force: 30,000 men. Commander: Prince Eugene of Savoy.
French: 40,000 troops initially, with another 20,000 by the end of the siege. Commander: General Louis François Aubusson, duke de la Feuillade.

IMPORTANCE:

French failure to capture Turin spelled the doom of Louis XIV's dream of acquiring control over the Italian peninsula.

Historical Setting

The world of European politics is rarely so confusing as when a succession struggle arises. In 1700 Charles II of Spain died without issue, and the scramble to succeed him attracted candidates from across western Europe. Charles had named as his successor Phillipe, the duke of Anjou, but nobles with equally valid claims to the throne included Holy Roman Emperor Leopold I and Victor Amadeus, duke of Savoy. Leopold and Victor, although with legitimate claims, were mainly afraid that if Phillipe assumed the throne Spain would come directly under the control of France, for France's King Louis XIV was Phillipe's uncle. Everyone in Europe had cause to fear any action that increased Louis' authority, for he was one of the most brilliant and ambitious monarchs in all of European history. Emperor Leopold organized a coalition to combat Phillipe's claim, joining Great Britain, the Netherlands, Prussia, and Hanover to his own Holy Roman Empire. Louis responded by gathering together allies of his own: Bavaria, Mantua, Piedmont, and, initially, Savoy, which had long been aligned with France.

The result of these alliances was the War of the Spanish Succession. Louis hoped not only to place his nephew on the Spanish throne, but also to acquire as much of Italy as he could. Louis sent forces to Italy in 1701, but they were consistently beaten by one of the finest military leaders of the age, Prince Eugene of Savoy, serving in Leopold's army. During 1701 and 1702, Louis saw his armies defeated and in 1703 he demanded increased aid from Victor Amadeus of Savoy (who was Eugene's cousin). Victor, however, responded by changing alliances. Victor apparently planned on having Eugene on hand to defend his homeland, but the general went to Vienna to beg for more money and supplies for his army. Thus, he was unavailable when French troops swept through Savoy in 1704 and occupied most of the country, excepting only a few fortresses and the capital city of Turin.

Emperor Leopold soon appointed Eugene his commander-in-chief and sent him off to aid the Englishman Marlborough in the Blenheim campaign, thus leaving Savoy without its savior.

Turin was a formidable target. A pentagonal wall ringed the city and was fronted by a crescent-shaped fortification facing the countryside. Sixteen bastions anchored the defenses. In order to preclude an enemy mining the walls, tunnels had been dug far past the walls to undermine enemy tunnels or destroy trenches and gun emplacements. The French engineering mastermind, Marquis de Vauban, sent directives to French forces detailed to assault the city, but they were ignored.

The Siege

The man ordered to capture Turin was General Louis François Aubusson, the duke de la Feuillade. He was a mere thirty years old and headstrong, and he first attacked the city in August 1705 by attempting to destroy its system of countermines. He had too few men to succeed before the winter, and so returned with 40,000 men in May 1706. He ignored not only Vauban's directives but also common sense by failing to capture and fortify the Mount of Capucins overlooking the city. Instead of using that position to bombard the city, he placed his guns on the plains and began a steady bombardment designed to breach the walls. He hoped to avoid a long siege with a quick assault.

While the bombardment proceeded, Victor Amadeus led 6,000 cavalry out of the city in an attempt to link up with Eugene, who he hoped would be coming to his aid. Eugene indeed intended to march on Savoy, but la Feuillade

had stationed strong forces blocking the Alpine passes. Thus, Victor began a strategy of harassing the French supply lines while la Feuillade attacked Turin. Victor had left a mere 4,000 soldiers to defend the city, but they were ably led by Count von Daun. The defenders threw back a major French assault, but found themselves short of gunpowder afterwards. Von Daun decided to concentrate his powder in mining operations rather than in an artillery duel.

Apparently disheartened by his failure to carry Turin by storm, la Feuillade began a proper siege with trench works and mining, but von Dan's strategy succeeded in defeating these attempts. Growing tired of the boring siege, la Feuillade led a large number of cavalry away from the city to chase Victor, ultimately employing about 2,050 of his force in this foray. Meanwhile, Eugene was marching far south through neutral Venice to outflank the French lines positioned to keep him away from Turin. In early July his 30,000 men crossed the Adige River and drove off the defending French holding the southern end of their line. The French commander detailed to hold the passes and keep Eugene at bay was the very able Louis Joseph, the duke de Vendôme. Unfortunately for the French ambitions in Italy, he was recalled to France in the wake of another of Marlborough's victories, along the Franco-Dutch frontier at Ramillies. King Louis's nephew Phillipe, the duke of Orléans, was an inferior replacement who could not defeat the far more talented Eugene. Eugene linked up with Victor's cavalry on 26 August 1706, just 20 miles from Turin.

The siege was pressed in greater earnest. The French finally succeeded in locating and attacking a Savoyard mineshaft and the two rival forces of engineers engaged in a bitter struggle in the smoke-filled underground passages before the French were forced to withdraw. Von Daun countered with a new mineshaft that he exploded under a newly emplaced artillery battery, destroying twelve of its fourteen guns. On 27 August, however, the French finally undermined a section of city wall and la Feuillade threw his infantry into the breach. Savoyard enfilading fire was quite effective, but still the fighting was hand-to-hand for hours before the French finally retreated.

Failure to break into the city combined with Eugene's proximity convinced some of la Feuillade's subordinates to advise abandoning the siege and turning their 60,000 men against the relief force. The French commander refused and continued his artillery bombardment. As he did so, Eugene's forces arrived and occupied the Mount of Capuchins. From there, he looked down on the flank of he French entrenchments, with their guns pointing at the city. On the morning of 7 September, Eugene ordered his Prussian cavalry to strike the weakest point of the French lines, their right flank northwest of the city. Both Eugene and Victor Amadeus fought with their troops and were instrumental in rallying them against French counterattacks. Once inside the trench lines, the Savoyards turned French artillery on their former owners, forcing them to break. On the far left flank, la Feuillade was able to withdraw his men in a more orderly fashion, until von Daun led a sally out of Turin that broke the French spirit and turned their retreat into a rout.

Results

The combined forces of la Feuillade and the duke of Orléans returned to France, leaving behind nearly 3,000 men killed and wounded and twice that many as prisoners. The bulk of the French artillery was also abandoned to Savoy. The withdrawal out of Savoy meant that Louis XIV would not achieve his ambition of controlling the rest of the Italian peninsula. Savoy continued to block his access and Louis was forced to turn his attention away from Italy and look northward, to his ongoing struggle to extend French control into the Netherlands. The War of the Spanish Succession dragged on until 1713, when it was concluded by the Treaty of Utrecht. In that treaty, Louis succeeded in placing Phillipe of Anjou on the Spanish throne as he had hoped, but was forced to swear that France and Spain would not unite. The lands he had hoped to acquire in Italy went instead to Austria, which exercised the major influence there until Italian unification in the late nineteenth century.

References: Olivier Bernier, *Louis XIV: A Royal Life* (Garden City, NY: Doubleday, 1987); Kenneth Czech, "Breaking the Siege of Turin," *Military History* 14, no. 6, February 1998; Gregory Hanlon, *The Twilight of a Military Tradition: Italian Aristocrats and European Conflicts, 1560–1800* (New York: Holmes & Meier, 1998); Nicholas Henderson, *Prince Eugene of Savoy* (New York: Praeger, 1965).

LILLE

DATE: 18 August–11 December 1708.
LOCATION: Northern France, near Belgian Border.

FORCES ENGAGED:

Allied: 40,000–50,000 Austrian and Holy Roman Empire troops. Commander: Prince Eugene of Savoy.
French: 15,000–16,000 troops. Commander: Marshal Louis François de Bouflers.

IMPORTANCE:

The capture of Lille provided a base of operations for Anglo-imperial armies to attempt an invasion of France, which ultimately proved unsuccessful.

Historical Setting

As the childless Charles II of Spain lay dying in 1700, he named as his heir his somewhat distant nephew Philip of Anjou. That decision in and of itself was not as important as to whom Philip of Anjou was related: he was the grandson of King Louis XIV of France. Over the previous few decades Louis had proven himself an extremely aggressive monarch, expanding and strengthening his borders at the expense of his neighbors, Italy, the Spanish Netherlands, and Austria, seat of Holy Roman Emperor Leopold I. Leopold, as a Habsburg (as was Charles of Spain), tried to name his second son Charles to the vacant Spanish throne. This was not only to maintain Habsburg power, but also to limit that of Louis's house of Bourbon. When Leopold made known his intentions to challenge the French for the Spanish monarchy, he had no shortage of European powers ready to help him oppose Louis.

When Louis struck first, by capturing some fortifications along his frontier with the Netherlands (controlled by Austria), a coalition of forces immediately formed consisting of Austria, the Dutch, Savoy, and England. The opening battles of the war were fought in Italy, but in 1702 English forces under the duke of Marlborough joined the fray and the focus of the war shifted to France's northern frontier. Marlborough and Eugene proved themselves masterly commanders in a series of victories at Blenheim (1704), Ramillies (1706), and Oudenarde (1708). After that last battle, Marlborough was determined to invade France and drive on to Paris, but Eugene convinced him that first it was necessary to establish a base of operations and proposed the city of Lille. Marlborough assigned the task of taking the city to Eugene, while he maintained a mobile force of some 70,000 prepared to beat back any French interference.

With 50,000 men Eugene marched on Lille. It was a city not only surrounded by walls but also possessing a citadel designed by the master of fortifications, Vauban. Defending the city was a force of some 15,000 to 16,000 French soldiers under the very able command of Marshal Louis de Bouflers. Although past eighty years old at the outset of the siege, Bouflers was remarkably active and experienced in siegecraft, having successfully commanded forces at Namur thirteen years earlier.

The Siege

Marlborough at this point commanded some 40,000 men. He sent Prince Eugene with his 50,000 troops to Lille while he followed closely behind as a screen. Marlborough had summoned a supply train and eighty siege guns from Brussels, and they arrived at Lille unmolested by any French forces. Immediately upon arriving on 12 August, Eugene had his men begin digging the siege lines. The lines of contravallation stretched around the city from due north counterclockwise to due east, while the northeastern sector was chosen for the assault lines. A line of circumvallation covered the southern half of the siege lines.

Inside Lille the French were commanded by Marshall Louis Francois, the duc de Bouflers, hero of the defense of Namur in 1695. He entered the city only slightly ahead of the allied arrival, bringing manpower to raise the garrison to 16,000, including 2,000 city militia. He seemed likely to make this defense successful as well. The besiegers would have to deal with marshy ground around the city and the attendant sickness. The city was not far from major French bases that could launch relief attacks or force supplies through. Further, the allied force was depending on Brussels as its base of supply, but this was a tenuous link at best since French units at Mons, Charleroi, and Namur could easily threaten the lines of communication. All in all, Bouflers' position seemed more tenable than Marlborough's.

By 21 August the allied lines were dug and the siege began in earnest. By the 27th eighty-eight cannon were bombarding Lille's walls as the new parallels were dug. King Louis XIV ordered his forces in the region to march to the relief. Marshall Vendome brought troops from Ghent while Marshall Berwick marched north from Mons; they rendezvoused at Lessines, some 40 miles east of Lille. The French force of 110,000 men proceeded (under Berwick's command) to Tournai, where they crossed the Scheldt River then swung southward. Marlborough shadowed them, using interior lines to keep himself at all times between the French and Lille. When he reached Pont-a-Marque, due south of Lille, Marlborough began digging his troops in. Had Berwick attacked swiftly, his far superior numbers would probably have overwhelmed the British. Instead, he hesitated late in the day, giving them several more hours to strengthen their position.

On 5 September, Marlborough ordered Eugene to send him 30,000 men from the siege lines. When Berwick awoke to see an allied position stronger in entrenchments and manpower, he would not attack. Bouflers tried a sortie, hoping to coordinate with the attack he was sure Berwick would launch, but it was easily beaten back into the city. Although Eugene returned to the siege with his men on 7 September, Berwick's forces stayed immobile until the 17th, when they withdrew.

On 20 September Eugene ordered an assault at a newly opened breach. Three charges went into the breach and were thrown back. Eugene himself led the fourth assault, receiving a wound in the head for his trouble. When he too fell back, the allies had left behind some 5,000 dead. Bouflers rejected Eugene's request for a two-day truce to bury his dead, fearing that they would have too much time to inspect his defenses as they removed the bodies. Bouflers instead promised to bury the men himself, which he did by attacking and seizing an allied trench and depositing the bodies there.

Eugene kept up the bombardment and the occasional attack, and the pressure began to wear on the defenders. On 22 October Bouflers abandoned the city walls and withdrew with some 5,000 men into the citadel. Eugene sent him a message, offering the most generous of terms: Bouflers himself could dictate them. The French commander replied that he was in no particular hurry to give up. Hearing of the withdrawal, French forces under Marshal Vendôme moved forward, but Eugene's lines of circumvallation were sufficiently strong to deny any favorable point of attack. The French then moved toward Brussels, hoping this would draw off the besiegers. Instead, Marlborough maneuvered his army and the relief force withdrew.

Finally, Louis himself ordered Bouflers to surrender, which he did on 11 December, on terms he himself dictated. Eugene accepted an invitation to dine with Bouflers on the condition that they eat no better than the common troops. They ate thin steaks of horsemeat.

Results

Marlborough followed up the allied victory at Lille with the capture of Ghent and Bruges, after which both he and the French went into winter quarters. Louis, seeing the tide turning, requested peace terms. They were unacceptable: he was to expel the newly enthroned Philip of Anjou from Spain (although the Spanish population accepted him) and do so within two months, or he would be obliged to join allied armies in the same project. He replied that he would rather fight his enemies than his own blood, and the people of France agreed. The winter of 1708–1709 proved one of the harshest ever, and when the spring finally came Louis rebuilt his armies with troops both angered at the allies and in need of some food. He withdrew into a strong series of border fortresses, which Marlborough had a difficult time breaking through. In 1711 the battle of Malplaquet was a draw, but sufficiently draining on both armies that all sides began to view negotiations as a good thing. The accession of Charles II of Austria to the throne of the Holy Roman Empire made his claim to the Spanish throne a threat to the European balance of power nearly as great as Louis' had been, and in 1713 the English and Dutch signed the Treaty of Utrecht with Louis. Under the terms of the treaty, France received a series of border towns including Lille, which remained under French control until Belgian independence in the 1830s.

References: David Chandler, *The Art of War in the Age of Marlborough* (New York: Hippocrene, 1976); Arthur Hassel, *Louis XIV and the Zenith of French Monarchy* (Freeport, NY: Books for Libraries Press, 1972); J. R. Jones, *Marlborough* (New York: Cambridge University Press, 1993); Vezio Melegari, *The Great Military Sieges* (New York: Crowell, 1972).

LOUISBOURG

DATE: 1 May–17 June 1745.
LOCATION: on Canada's Cape Breton Island.

FORCES ENGAGED:

American: 4,270 militia. Commander:
William Pepperrell.
French: 560 French marines and Swiss mercenaries,
plus perhaps 1,400 militia. Commander:
Louis Du Chambon.

IMPORTANCE:

American victory gave the colonial population undue confidence in their military abilities, while the return of Louisbourg to France in the peace treaty provoked American hostility to the British government.

Historical Setting

Throughout the seventeenth century and into the eighteenth, Britain and France both colonized in North America. Britain, arriving first, occupied territory stretching along the eastern coast of the continent, while France was obliged to accept the less productive area of modern Canada. The northern territory had its economic benefits, however, and the French made large profits on furs and fishing. The British American colonists, however, also claimed the waters that the French fished, so not only the fishing rights but also the resulting supply of dried fish to European markets resulted in intense colonial rivalry.

European wars had their North American aspects. After the War of the Spanish Succession ended with the signing of the Treaty of Utrecht in 1713, France's King Louis XIV decided to build a strong fort on the Ile Royale (modern Cape Breton Island) to act as a base for French shipping and protection for the mouth of the St. Lawrence River. Thus was Louisbourg conceived and born. Construction began in 1720 and went on in a haphazard fashion for the next twenty years. At its completion, it was hailed as the Gibraltar of North America, but it suffered in the years immediately following from poor maintenance, insufficient artillery, and a less than enthusiastic population. The garrison was made up of French marines and Swiss mercenaries, neither possessing high morale.

In 1744, France declared war on Britain during the War of the Austrian Succession, called King George's War in North America. News of the war arrived in Boston, British America's primary port city, in May of that year, but the French in Louisbourg received the news three weeks earlier. French forces under Captain François Duvivier launched an immediate and successful attack on Canseau, a British port on the east coast of Acadia (Nova Scotia). The relative handful of soldiers defending the town were taken as prisoners to Louisbourg, then repatriated to Boston several months later. Duvivier then launched an unsuccessful attack on Annapolis Royale, Britain's major port on the western coast of Acadia. Throughout the summer of 1744, as these attacks were taking place, French privateers operating out of Louisbourg harassed New England shipping in the disputed waters. All of this alarmed both the British government and their colonists.

In Massachusetts, Governor William Shirley decided that since Britain was so focused on the fighting in Europe, the French threat to New England had to be dealt with locally. He proposed raising an American force to seize Louisbourg. After all, their merchants had

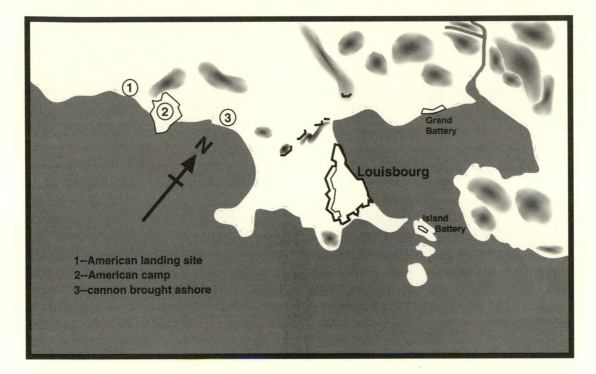

1--American landing site
2--American camp
3--cannon brought ashore

often traded with their counterparts in the town and thus had a good knowledge of its layout and its defenses. Further, the newly arrived prisoners from Canseau gave up-to-the-minute reports of the conditions of the fort and its garrison. The fact that both the fort's walls and its garrison's morale were in a poor state convinced the Boston population to urge their legislature to authorize the operation, which it did by a single-vote majority.

William Pepperrell, militia officer, wealthy merchant, and head of the Governor's Council, was given command of the expedition. Massachusetts raised 3,300 volunteers, with a further 516 from Connecticut and 454 from New Hampshire. Shirley appealed to London for naval support and received the aid of three warships from the Caribbean commanded by Commodore Peter Warren, who owned land in New York. The force sailed on 24 March 1745, with Canseau as its first target. The convoy ran into heavy weather that badly affected the farmer militia, but the French at Canseau were quickly overcome in early April. The militia spent three weeks in Canseau gaining some

rudimentary training and waiting for reports of the ice breaking up in Louisbourg's Gabarus Harbor. That news and the arrival of Warren's warships heartened the American force as they sailed for their final objective, which they reached on 30 April.

The French commander was newly appointed Governor Louis Du Chambon. He was too passive a personality to stage an active defense. He was easily misled by a feint landing, allowing the main American force to go ashore virtually unopposed about 2 miles down the coast from Louisbourg. The French withdrew into their defenses and waited for the attack.

The Siege

Louisbourg's defenses consisted of the main fort just outside the town on the southwestern shore of the harbor. In the harbor mouth was an island with another fort (Island Battery), and on the western side of the harbor, covering both of the others, was the Grand Battery. Almost all the guns were pointed at the harbor and its mouth to protect from an attack by sea, so the Americans faced few defenses when they approached the forts from the landward side. They brought in men and artillery against no opposition and were able to occupy high ground overlooking the French positions. The ground immediately outside the main fort, however, was marshy.

The Americans scored their first victory almost immediately. On the morning of 1 May Pepperrell sent reconnaissance parties through the area, which engaged in a few skirmishes with militia and Mikmac Indians friendly to the French. One of the patrols, commanded by Boston merchant Colonel William Vaughn, set fire to some storehouses near the Grand Battery, covering it in a dense and malodorous smoke. The following morning the Americans were surprised to find the French position abandoned. It is argued both that the defenders panicked and fled or that du Chambon ordered them out to consolidate his manpower; either way the retreating troops failed to adequately spike the thirty cannon emplaced there. Neither did they destroy the large supply of powder. Vaughn's men quickly occupied the fortress and beat back a French force that rowed back to it in the afternoon. Again it is argued whether these men were trying to recapture the fort or had merely been sent over to remove supplies and did not know the Americans had taken possession. The artillery was soon operational again and kept up a steady fire into both Louisbourg and Island Battery.

Artillery that the Americans had brought with them next came into play. It was brought ashore on flat-bottomed barges that experienced serious difficulty in navigating the surf and landing on the rocky shore. Soon, however, shipwrights among the troops built sledges and the cannon were hauled by hundreds of men to the high ground overlooking the French and through the boggy terrain before the fort. The men hauled the cannon at night and placed them in their batteries in the dark. Through the rest of May the Americans built five such batteries, the closest being a mere 250 yards from the enemy walls. The last one contained heavy guns removed from the Great Battery and sledged overland.

The defenders of Louisbourg had little hope. The fort and town came under constant shelling. Throughout May the walls of the fort and the buildings in the town were battered into wreckage. A supply ship was captured early in the siege, and the Americans were able to eat well while the defenders watched their provisions dwindle. Still, the Island Battery controlled the harbor and guns aboard the British warships could not be brought into play. Thus, Pepperrell decided to launch a surprise night attack on the island. Inordinate drunkenness among the militia forced the 23 May landing to be postponed, but 400 volunteers rowed out to the island on the night of the 26th. They landed undetected, but one less-than-bright militiaman decided to raise a cheer for their safe journey across the harbor. The now-alert Frenchmen poured a murderous fire into the attackers. The following morning 70 Americans were dead on the beach or in the harbor and a further 119 became French prisoners.

That event proved the only bright spot for the defenders. A second supply ship was captured, enhancing the Americans' already superior amount of powder and shot. In mid-June Pepperrell and Commodore Warren decided to launch an amphibious assault on the fort. The walls had been seriously damaged, but the increasing amount of dysentery among the besiegers as well as the threat of a major French resupply effort argued for quick action. Just as the Americans were sailing into position for the attack, they saw a white flag raised over the French fort.

Results

The hard-pressed citizens of Louisbourg had finally convinced de Chambon to surrender. He signaled his intent to negotiate on 15 June and the terms were finally signed on the 17th. The garrison and the population were allowed to return to France with all their possessions, a condition that did not sit well with the Americans. They had mounted and fought this operation with the intent of acquiring large amounts of loot and grumbled mightily when they learned their dreams of wealth were dashed. As it turned out, that was the least of their problems. While the besiegers had suffered about a hundred combat deaths, the next several months of garrison duty proved disastrous, as almost 900 died from a variety of diseases before they finally turned the fort over to a British garrison in January 1746.

In spite of that negative outcome, the Americans were justifiably proud of their accomplishment. One reason the French government had not sent over any major reinforcements of supplies was that they never believed Louisbourg could be taken by other than a major force of trained soldiers; that some 4,000 untrained militia had done so shocked the Europeans. The news was celebrated wildly in Boston and almost as much in London. The major accomplishment of these New Englanders proved all for naught, however, as negotiators in Aix-la-Chapelle undid all their sacrifice. The French received Louisbourg back, in return for their cession of Madras in India, where yet another colonial aspect of the war was played out.

The capture and subsequent cession of Louisbourg both had enormous effects in America. First, it gave the colonists a confidence in their military prowess that could hardly be justified. Prior to this action they had done little other than defeat disorganized Indian resistance in the colonies. While that did give them some combat experience, it did not prepare them for "modern" warfare against trained professionals. When they won anyway, they began to feel that professional troops were overrated. That gave them an inflated sense of themselves when hostilities between the colonies and London broke out in 1775.

Those hostilities also have an antecedent in Louisbourg. When the British government gave it away, the colonists were furious. All their work, sacrifice, and accomplishment were tossed away as a counter in a great imperial game. When the next Anglo-French war broke out in 1755, the colonists were less enthusiastic about aiding the mother country in actions outside their immediate province. Thus, when the British had to besiege Louisbourg again in 1758, the fortress they had given up ten years earlier took the major effort the French had always thought it would take: 9,000 British troops and forty ships. The colonists took a grim satisfaction in hearing of that difficult feat, and it further confirmed their opinion of both their abilities and that of regulars. In reality, it was an attitude Americans never really altered until after World War II.

References: B. A. Balcom, "Louisbourg," *American History*, August 1995; Robert Leckie, *A Few Acres of Snow* (New York: Wiley, 1999); Howard Peckham, *The Colonial Wars, 1689–1762* (Chicago: University of Chicago Press, 1964).

ARCOT

DATE: 2 September–14 November 1751.
LOCATION: approximately 50 miles west of the coastal city of Madras, India.

FORCES ENGAGED:

British: 120 British troops and 200 Indian troops. Commander: Captain Robert Clive.
French: 10,000 men, primarily Indian troops with less than 1,000 French troops. Commander: Raza Sahib.

IMPORTANCE:

British victory halted the French takeover of southern India, and marked the beginning of the widespread recruitment of Indian troops into the army of the British East India Company.

Historical Setting

Eighteenth-century India was an active place. The Moghul Empire was falling apart as the monarchy weakened and the nobility grew stronger. Although Delhi was the putative capital, local princes (*nawabs*) ruled their own lands and acted with virtual autonomy, cooperating with the Delhi government if they saw fit. In this time of uncertain local rule both the French and British arrived on the scene. The Honorable East India Company represented British trading interests with factories (trading centers) at Calcutta on the northeastern coast, Madras on the southeastern coast, and Bombay on the northwestern coast. The French East India Company operated out of Pondicherry, just down the coast from Madras. Both European powers entered into agreements with local nawabs, primarily for trade contacts but also hoping to gain influence with whatever government rose from the Moghul ashes. As England and France were rivals in Europe, they supported rival nawabs in India.

The Indian rulers were somewhat ambivalent toward the Europeans. Much as they appreciated the income from trade, they appreciated even more the military might the Europeans could provide to affect the local balance of power. The Anglo-French wars fought in Europe usually had their counterparts in India, but the European support of rival princes meant that fighting occurred on an Indian timetable as often as on a European one. As the War of the Austrian Succession ended in 1748, tensions were rising in southern India. As stated above, the nobles were exercising increasing independence from the Mughal capital. Ranking just below the emperor was the nizam of the Deccan, whose title was "Viceroy of the South"; he paid little attention to Delhi. Next in rank after the nizam were the various nawabs, few of which heeded the viceroy. When the nizam of the Deccan died in 1748, the British and French supported rival claimants to the throne. The French candidate ultimately won out. Meanwhile, another disputed succession was occurring in the Carnatic, which spans the southeastern tip of India. The French-supported nizam appointed the French favorite, Chanda Sahib, to the position of nawab of the Carnatic. The British factory at Madras was now surrounded by hostile territory.

Not content with the title, the new nawab wanted to eliminate his British-supported rival, Mohammed Ali. Chanda Sahib led a large force to besiege Ali's capital of Trichinopoly. Ali was supported by a handful of his own men and about 600 British troops. As the British commander did not have a reputation for inspiring confidence, British authorities in other parts of India were on the verge of writing Trichinopoly and the south off to the French. Robert Clive, an East India Company clerk with a new appointment to the British army, proposed a plan to Governor Thomas Saunders. (Clive had met with Mohammed Ali in Trichinopoly during a reinforcement expedition, and the plan was Ali's.) Rather than challenge the strong Franco-Indian forces at Trichinopoly, they would strike at Arcot, Chanda Sahib's capital city. That would force him to lift the siege. Saunders agreed, but could only part with 200 of the 350 British soldiers under his command. Those 200 soldiers and a further 300 *sepoys* (Indian soldiers trained by the British) marched with Clive to Arcot and captured it: "The garrison, 1100 strong, had fled during the night, having heard from their spies of how the English had marched unconcernedly through the storm [which hit the day before their arrival], heedless of the omens of heaven. This to them denoted superhuman courage, so they reckoned it was no good trying to resist such a foe" (Bence-Jones, *Clive of India*, pp. 39–40). Indeed, Chanda did march to save his capital, but he left both Indian and French troops to maintain the Trichinopoly siege.

The Siege

Arcot, a city of 100,000 at the time, quickly fell under Clive's sway, for he ordered that there be no looting and he returned property Chanda had confiscated to its rightful owners. He immediately began gathering in supplies and fresh water, and to strengthen the city's defenses. Many of the towers were virtually useless as artillery positions, and the moat surrounding the mile-long city wall was dry or easily forded.

The previous garrison was encamped a few miles away, blocking the arrival of any resupply or reinforcements. Two sallies against them failed, so Clive decided on a night attack on 14 September. It was so successful the entire force scattered in fear, while Clive lost no casualties. Two days later word came that Governor Saunders had sent two large cannon. Clive sent almost his entire force to escort the guns to the city, and the handful that remained drove off two night attacks.

The French commander, Joseph Dupleix, at first disbelieved reports of Arcot's fall, but soon decided to divide his force and recapture the city. He sent Raza Sahib, Chanda's son, to accomplish the task. He dawdled, waiting for an auspicious omen, but finally marched with 4,000 Indian troops and 150 French. The holding force that had been harassing Arcot had grown to 3,000, so the combined force would be fourteen times stronger than Clive's. Raza's force arrived on 23 September. Clive occupied the fort in the city center, allowing Raza's troops to man taller buildings overlooking the walls. Clive attempted a sortie to drive the newcomers away, but ran into intense fire from newly occupied buildings. His attack managed to kill most of the French artillerymen, but he suffered the loss of fifteen of his British troops. The boldness of the move, although unsuccessful, forced Raza to respect him.

Clive's virtually amateur status as a soldier meant that he took risks a professional would never have attempted, like staying in Arcot against a force that soon swelled to 10,000. Having sent a portion of his force back to Madras to supplement the garrison there, Clive at this point commanded but 120 British and

200 Indian troops. Completely surrounded, the defenders soon began to suffer. Cut off from outside water, the fort's reservoir was brackish. Food, thankfully, was not a problem. The besieging force, manning the nearest houses, shot at anyone who moved. The minute defending force exhausted itself trying to maintain a patrol of the fort's wall.

Back in Madras Governor Saunders scraped together a few more soldiers and received some new recruits from England. In the third week in October a force of but 130 British and 100 sepoys finally got on the way. Unfortunately for the defenders, the relief force was intercepted and sent packing. Luckily for Clive's men, however, the French commanders on the scene were paralyzed by rumors of relief forces, and Raza Sahib was no military man. Late in October a battery of artillery arrived from the French base at Pondicherry and was positioned northwest of Clive's position. It soon knocked out one of Clive's large cannon and damaged another. For six days the French pounded the walls, destroying a section of wall between two dilapidated towers. The British tried to plug the gap with trenches, wooden palisades, and piled-up rubble. Another battery was set up to the southwest and created another breach.

Rescue appeared from an unexpected source. The British-backed regent of Mysore, supporting Mohammed Ali, hired a force of Maratha warriors to aid the beleaguered Arcot. They had been watching the battle for some weeks, trying to decide which side to join, when they came to respect the defenders' tenacity. As the Maratha commander, Morari Rao, was collecting his pay, Raza Sahib learned of the threat. He quickly offered Clive honorable conditions and a gift if he would surrender. Knowing the Marathas were at hand and that another force was coming from Madras, Clive refused. Raza finally decided to act decisively and storm the fort. On 13 November, a spy alerted Clive to the coming assault. Prepared, the defenders manned their trenches and threw back the attackers. Only at one breach was there any sign of French/Indian success, but when the commander of the assault force was killed his men fell back; the other breach was not seriously attacked.

Results

After but an hour's fighting, Raza Sahib's men broke off the attack. After some fire was exchanged, a truce was called to bury the dead. As Clive had but four dead and two wounded, his men spent the truce gathering up the dead attackers' weapons. Early the next morning Clive learned that Raza's army had fled Arcot, abandoning most of their artillery. The relief force from Madras arrived later that day.

Clive's force had achieved an amazing feat in the face of the numeric odds against them, but in India numbers were not always the telling factor. The death of the assault commander in the final charge broke his force's spirit. Whatever the combination of circumstances that brought about Clive's victory, the siege of Arcot marked a sea change in the British experience in India. "It may have been luck, it may have been bungling on the part of the enemy, but it created the legend of English courage and invincibility which was to carry English arms in India from one success to another" (Bence-Jones, *Clive,* p. 48). Many in southern India, including some of the attacking soldiers, joined the army of the East India Company. When the British began to seriously recruit and train the men from the armies and provinces they conquered, they ended up with a top-notch army of sepoys leavened with a sprinkling of British Army units assigned to India. France lost status, and the dip in her fortunes in India was made worse by French losses a few years later in the Seven Years War.

References: Mark Bence-Jones, *Clive of India* (New York: St. Martin's, 1974); Robert Harvey, *Clive: Life and Death of a British Emperor* (New York: St. Martin's, 2000); Philip Mason, *A Matter of Honour* (Harmondsworth, Middlesex: Penguin, 1976 [1974]).

FORT NIAGARA

DATE: 10 July–25 July 1759.
LOCATION: at the junction of the Niagara River and Lake Ontario.

FORCES ENGAGED:

British/Indian: 2,000 British troops, 1,000 Iroquois. Commander: Brigadier General John Prideaux, later Colonel Sir William Johnson.
French: 486 soldiers, marines, and militia, plus 30 Seneca Indians. Commander: Captain Pierre Pouchot.

IMPORTANCE:

British victory gave them virtual control of the Great Lakes during the French and Indian War. Iroquois cooperation led to their ultimate downfall as the major Indian power in northeastern North America.

Historical Setting

When both England and France began colonizing the eastern part of North America in the seventeenth century, it was inevitable that their centuries-old European rivalry would manifest itself in the western hemisphere as well. The French in Canada and the English along the east coast of North America remained isolated from each other for about a century, but in the early 1750s the English colonists pushing west confronted French forces moving south into the area just below the Great Lakes Ontario and Erie. At the junction of the Allegheny and Monongahela rivers English colonists from Virginia began claiming land by constructing a fort. Before it was completed it was captured and strengthened by French and Indian forces who named it Fort Duquesne. A Virginia militia attempt to retake the fort in 1754 (led by George Washington in his first command) failed in its mission.

After some 150 years of salutary neglect, the London government committed troops to the colonies in an attempt to beat back the French incursion. Major General Edward Braddock's

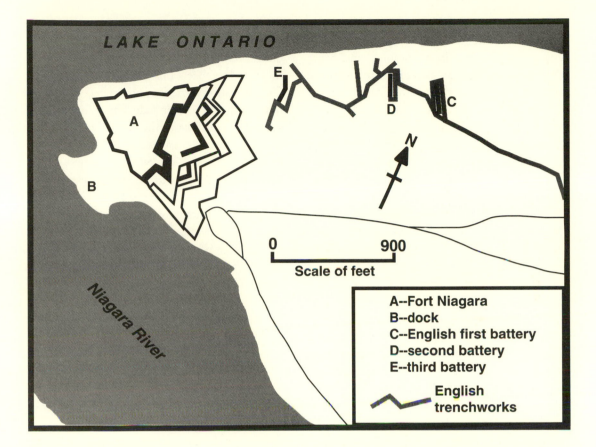

defeat at the Monongahela River in the summer of 1755 was a major factor in touching off an international war between England and her allies versus France and her allies. This was called the French and Indian War in the English colonies, the Seven Years War in Europe.

The English colonists had a long and hostile relationship with the native American population. The French on the other hand had developed close ties with Canadian tribes, primarily the Algonquin in the Ontario region and the Hurons farther west, by working with them in trade and assisting their Indian allies in warfare. The major rival to the Algonquin and Huron tribes, the Iroquois Confederacy, at times cooperated with the French but strove for the most part to remain neutral when it came to the white colonists killing each other. The Iroquois Confederacy consisted of six nations (Mohawk, Oneida, Onondaga, Cayuga, Seneca, and Tuscarora) which for almost two centuries had overcome mutual

antagonism to cooperate in establishing a fearsome power base in the region of modern New York. As the Anglo-French conflict began, the French seemed to have the upper hand, so the Iroquois tended to lean toward them as they considered their own interests.

In upper New York lived an Irish colonist named William Johnson, who originally came to the area to oversee his uncle's land holdings. He became friendly with the Mohawk tribe and married Chief Joseph Brant's sister. When the war's tide began to turn in England's favor by 1758, Johnson was active in trying to convince the Mohawks and their Iroquois confederates to openly support the English cause. Fearing the potential of the French-supported Hurons rising in the west, the Iroquois came to the conclusion that the English were their best bet to maintain power among the region's tribes. In the spring of 1759 they began making overtures to English commanders which the Europeans were glad to accept.

The summer of 1759 appeared to be a pivotal season in the war. The French had lost Fort Duquesne the previous summer and were preparing to mount an expedition to recapture it. That would divert the English strategy of mounting their own invasion of Canada. Geoffrey Amherst, overseeing the English effort in the colonies, appointed Brigadier General John Prideaux to attack the French bastion Fort Niagara, the strongest and most European-style fortification in North America. Prideaux led 3,000 English and colonial soldiers to Fort Oswego on the southeastern shore of Lake Ontario. There he met William Johnson with 1,000 Iroquois. Prideaux left 1,000 of his men behind to strengthen Fort Oswego, while his remaining 2,000 soldiers and 1,000 Indians took to canoes along Lake Ontario's southern shore toward Fort Niagara.

Fort Niagara was under the command of Captain Pierre Pouchot, a talented engineer who had turned the fort into the formidable bastion that it was. He had a garrison of about 3,000 men earlier in the spring, but when he assumed the threat of English attack had passed he dispatched more than 2,500 of his men southward to join the operation against Fort Pitt (formerly Fort Duquesne). Pouchot had in his fort about 30 Seneca Indians, and had been using Seneca scouts for some time with satisfactory results. He had no idea that the Confederation had changed sides until Prideaux's men landed on 7 July and attacked a working party outside the fort. He immediately sent messengers south to retrieve his troops as the English began construction of their first siege lines on 10 July.

The Siege

Located on a peninsula where the Niagara River joins Lake Ontario, the French fort had access to support by water, but it was the return of the troops he had dispatched earlier on which Pouchot depended. He was preparing for the siege when he called a truce in order for the leader of his Senecas to speak to their Iroquois brethren with the English. The Seneca in the fort had been unaware of any change in Confederation loyalties and argued in favor of remaining with the French. The Iroquois representatives pointed out the perceived power shift and the need to change sides. On 14 July, after three days of talks, the Seneca leader suggested both Indian forces withdraw southward to the island of La Belle Famille and let the Europeans fight among themselves. Johnson managed to keep his allies loyal, but Pouchot gave his Senecas free passage out of the fort rather than worry about their loyalty in the midst of the siege. Although the pro-English Iroquois did not retreat, neither did they take any further part in the battle, so the whites did indeed have to fight it out among themselves without the Iroquois shedding any confederate blood.

During the talks Pouchot did what he could to strengthen his defenses while the English continued to dig their trenches. On the 14th they opened fire from 250 yards away. Three days later English howitzers placed on the opposite side of the Niagara River began bombarding the fort as well. The fire was so intense that most of the French artillery was knocked out and few French soldiers would risk exposing themselves to engage in repairs. On the 18th Prideaux was killed by standing too close to a mortar as it fired, and Johnson assumed command. By 20 July the English were firing from a mere 80 yards away and the situation inside the fort looked bleak.

Then both French and English saw about 1,600 French reinforcements canoeing toward the fort from the south. The English dispatched some Iroquois to alert the Indians among the French to the situation, hoping to keep them out of the fighting. Johnson also sent 350 soldiers and 100 New York militia to cover the road approaching from the south. Some 500 Iroquois took up positions in the woods on either side of the road. When the French approached early in the day on the 24th, they had been abandoned by their Indian allies and numbered but 600 soldiers, marines, and Canadian militia. They rushed the English position but were blasted by seven volleys of English fire, then harried on their retreat by the hidden Iroquois.

Pouchot had seen the fighting through his telescope, but was unsure of the outcome until the English ceased firing and offered surrender terms: personal safety guaranteed, but imprisonment rather than parole. The French commander accepted on 25 July.

Results

The English victory at Fort Niagara was a success in two ways. Capture of the fort gave them control of Lake Ontario, meaning no support for the key French strongholds of Montreal and Quebec would arrive from the west, nor would any French forces in the west receive any further aid from French shipping arriving up the St. Lawrence River, their only access into Canada. Second, by diverting the French attack on Fort Pitt, the Ohio Valley did not fall back into French control; the English could focus their effort on Quebec and Montreal without having to cover their rear. When Quebec fell in September 1759, the French and Indian War was as good as over, although the Seven Years War continued in Europe and India until 1763.

Thus, Fort Niagara proved a key acquisition for the English and their colonial ambitions. Unfortunately, it proved fatal to the Iroquois. Siding with the winners did not help them as they had hoped. They had viewed their aid to the English as temporary, "only one of many pragmatic policy shifts in the long history of relations between the Confederacy and the British Crown. But this time the tilt toward the British would prove irrevocable, and its consequences would exceed any that the Iroquois could have intended. For the commitment to an active alliance, in fact if not in name, meant the acceptance of dependency" (Anderson, *The Crucible of War*, p. 333). Once established on the frontier, British power served the colonists, not the Iroquois. When war broke out between the English and their colonies in 1775, again the Indians played a primarily passive role, engaging in active warfare primarily in the trans-Appalachia lands, away from the main theater of war. The Iroquois aided the English military at times, but the colonial victory meant an end to major power assistance and ultimate defeat at the hands of the expansionist United States.

References: Fred Anderson, *The Crucible of War* (New York: Knopf, 2000); Howard Peckham, *The Colonial Wars, 1689–1762* (Chicago: University of Chicago Press, 1964); Ian Steele, *Warpaths* (Oxford: Oxford University Press, 1994).

QUEBEC

DATE: mid-June–13 September 1759.
LOCATION: on the St. Lawrence River, in Canada.

FORCES ENGAGED:

British: 4,441 troops. Commander: Major General James Wolfe.
French: 4,500 troops. Commander: Major General Marquis Louis-Joseph de Montcalm.

IMPORTANCE:

British victory gave them control of the St. Lawrence River, stopping any further French reinforcement or resupply of their personnel in Canada during the French and Indian War.

Historical Setting

After the defeat of the Spanish Armada in 1588, England began pursuing a policy of colonization in North America. Unlike the Spanish, who went to the western hemisphere

Engraving by J. Bowles of the taking of Quebec in 1759. (The Art Archives/General Wolfe Museum Quebec House/Eileen Tweedy)

primarily for conquest and riches, the English went to North America mainly to escape poverty or religious persecution at home. The English colonies along the eastern coast of North America grew slowly, but were strong enough to divert most potential rivals. The French therefore went to the remaining open region of North America, Canada. There the only profitable resource was furs. Unlike the Spanish or the English, whose attitudes toward the American Indian population were cavalier at best, the French saw the Indians as partners since no one knew more about trapping animals and preparing furs. The French went to Canada in much smaller numbers than had the Spanish or English and, by seeking friendship and adapting to the Indian way of life, built a solid relationship with the Indians.

The French gradually worked their way deeper into Canada, establishing trading posts and forts. Certainly they claimed the land for their king, but they did not let that get in the way of amicable relations with the Indians. In

the mid-1500s the French explorer Sieur de la Salle floated down the Mississippi River to the Gulf of Mexico. He then claimed the river he had just traveled and all the land drained by it—everything from the Appalachian Mountains to the Rockies. This conflicted with the Spanish and English claims, but as the three powers had no inhabitants in this region it did not really matter. Not until 1752.

English colonists began to tentatively probe west of the mountains. They soon ran into French forts in key places. The French built Fort Duquesne where the Allegheny and Monongahela rivers join to form the Ohio, at the upper northeastern limit of la Salle's claim. Colonial attempts to recapture the fort proved fruitless. Responding to an appeal by prominent colonist Benjamin Franklin, the government in London sent troops. The first expedition under Major General Edward Braddock was a colossal failure and encouraged the French and their Indian allies to greater activity along the frontier. This coincided with increasing French and English tensions in Europe. Braddock's defeat in July 1755 signaled the beginning of what came to be called the French and Indian War in North America; the European counterpart, the Seven Years War, started the following year.

For a time the French maintained the upper hand in North America, but that began to change with William Pitt's accession to power in London. Pitt realized the financial value of colonies for both imports and exports, and he was not about to lose any possession to arch-rival France without a struggle. Pitt sent more troops to North America while allowing Frederick the Great's Prussia to handle the bulk of the continental fighting. The Royal Navy curtailed French reinforcements, but to securely lock up Canada the key was the town of Quebec.

The Siege

Pitt planned a four-pronged attack into Canada, via Lake Erie, Lake Ontario, Lake Champlain, and up the St. Lawrence River. The French lost the key harbor of Louisbourg on Cape Breton Island, guardian of the Gulf of St. Lawrence. It was from there that the attack up the St. Lawrence River commenced. Leading some 9,000 British soldiers (and a handful of American rangers) was Major General James Wolfe, a young man who had served in the War of the Spanish Succession with some distinction and had led successful raids along the French coast. Two men opposed him inside Quebec: military commander Major General Louis-Joseph, the marquis de Montcalm, and governor and commander-in-chief Marquis de Vaudreuil. Montcalm commanded the French troops, Vaudreuil the Canadian militia and colonial regulars, together numbering about 12,000 men. Vaudreuil was in overall command, but had no military experience. Montcalm was recognized as an outstanding general in France and Canada. Because the two men openly despised each other, this meant there would be little cooperation within the French command as the British approached.

Quebec city is located on the north shore of the St. Lawrence River on a promontory created by that river and its tributary, the St. Charles. The city sits high on a bluff overlooking the river junction, and bluffs run along the shore downstream in an east-northeasterly direction. Where the two rivers converge the estuary to the Atlantic begins, but immediately upstream the river becomes impassable to seagoing ships. The only practicable approach to the city is from the west along the north shore across the Plains of Abraham, but it seemed impossible for the British to position themselves to launch an attack from that quarter. Artillery on the southern bank can bombard the city, but both French commanders regarded their forces as insufficient to spare any to hold that position. Besides, winter was approaching and that would force the British fleet and army away. Everything seemed positive, but for one mistaken assumption: that the river upstream from Quebec was unpassable to British shipping.

The earliest British contingents arrived in mid-June 1759; Wolfe made his appearance at the end of the month. He occupied the southern bank of the St. Lawrence as well as the Isle of Orleans just downstream for his main base. British artillery began firing on the city, but it was more demoralizing than damaging. On the night of 28 June the French set a number of boats afire to float with the current into the British fleet, but they proved of little use. Wolfe considered and discarded a variety of plans after observing the strength of the French defenses atop the bluffs. At the end of July he ordered a lower redoubt seized, hoping to bring the French out of their defenses to recapture it, but poor coordination and weather doomed the operation. Throughout August American ranger forces destroyed area farmhouses and crops, hoping to harm French morale. This had little effect other than to give the Americans some satisfaction for years of similar treatment from French-allied Indian tribes.

In August the Royal Navy discovered it was possible to slip ships past Quebec's weak shore batteries and through the "unpassable" narrows. When Wolfe polled his officers for operational suggestions, a crossing above Quebec onto the Plains of Abraham was the consensus, to which he agreed on 1 September. If nothing else this would place British forces astride Quebec's line of communications to Montreal. Harassing attacks downstream kept Montcalm's attention focused in that direction.

For a week prior to the assault the British stood idle, lulling the French. On the night of 12–13 September French pickets along the endangered shore were told of an approaching supply convoy coming from Montreal. They did not, however, learn of its cancellation. When British boats began plying the river the French were not unduly alarmed. A French-speaking British officer kept the defending pickets off guard until the last moment, by which time the British were streaming up a narrow path to the top of the bluffs. A diversionary bombardment downstream continued to keep French attention in that direction. When Montcalm learned of the successful landing the next morning, the British forces were already forming up and facing Quebec's poorly maintained walls.

Montcalm should have waited for troops to come up from the down-river defenses to supplement the garrison in the city. Instead, he marched out of the city with a roughly equal force (4,500 French to 4,441 British), although only about half were regular troops and the rest militia. The first French fighters on the scene were Canadian militia and some Indians, who acted as skirmishers and laid down harassing fire. Wolfe's troops lay prone to avoid this. When Montcalm had his men form up in mid-morning, he ordered them to advance. The militia fired at too great a range to do any harm, while the British continued to lie prone and hold their fire. As the French line moved forward it lost cohesion. The militia fired, then knelt to present a lower target as they reloaded. The regulars fired in volleys, reloaded, and then marched forward. The two

different styles meant that the mixed forces found themselves drifting apart before they got into British musket range. When the French reached 60 yards the British stood and fired by volleys, keeping up a steady fire. At 40 yards, the British line took ten steps forward and fired a volley that shredded the French lines. They broke. The entire fight had taken no more than half an hour.

Tragedy struck both sides during the battle. Wolfe was hit by sniper fire in the wrist, then in the abdomen, then in the chest. He died on the field. Not long afterward Montcalm was hit, probably by grapeshot from the two cannon the British had manhandled up the bluffs. He survived until the early hours of the following morning. The troops that manned the defenses along the downstream bluffs soon began to arrive in the city but did not stay. Governor Vaudreuil abandoned the city on 15 September, soon after Montcalm's death. The British under George Townshend entered the city and accepted its surrender on the 18th.

Results

The capture of Quebec for all intents and purposes gave Canada to the British, since it controlled the only access route into the country. The French had not been able to reinforce seriously since the beginning of the war owing to the presence of the Royal Navy. Now they had no way to support their few remaining troops. Although the French commander of the garrison at Montreal marched on Quebec the following spring and beat Townshend's force that marched out to face him, the British had improved the walls and these proved strong enough to allow them to hold on until reinforced. Montreal fell to British forces in 1760, and fighting in North America ceased.

War continued in Europe for another three years until finally ended by the Treaty of Paris of 1763. The treaty forced the French surrender of all their lands east of the Mississippi River and

The death of General Wolfe during the battle of Quebec in 1759. (Library of Congress)

north of the Great Lakes. The remainder of their claims west of the Mississippi they ceded to Spain. Thus, the loss of Canada ended France's hope for a western hemisphere empire.

References: Lawrence H. Gipson, *The Great War for Empire*, vol. 7 (New York: Knopf, 1936); Francis Parkman, *Montcalm and Wolfe* (Toronto: Ryerson, 1964); Page Smith, *A New Age Now Begins*, vol. 1 (New York: McGraw-Hill, 1976); C. P. Stacey, *Quebec, 1759* (Toronto: Macmillan, 1959).

HAVANA

Date: 13 June–13 August 1762.
Location: northwest coast of Cuba.

Forces Engaged:

English: 14,000 soldiers initially, reinforced by a further 1,400. Commander: General George Keppel the Earl of Albemarle; 40 warships. Commander: Admiral Sir George Pocock. Spanish: 4,000 soldiers and sailors, 3,000 militia. Commander: Captain General Juan de Prado y Portocarrero Malleza.

Importance:

Capture of the city greatly enriched the English toward the end of a long and costly war. Return of the city to the Spanish, however, helped them control Cuba until 1898.

Historical Setting

All of Europe was jealous of Spain, whose looting of the Americas had brought them untold wealth since the conquistadors in the early sixteenth century conquered the Aztec and Inca empires. After the Spanish Armada was badly beaten in 1588, however, Spain's iron grasp on the Americas began to weaken. England was quick to plant colonies in North America, but there was no gold. English pirates plundered Spanish treasure ships, but occupation of lands

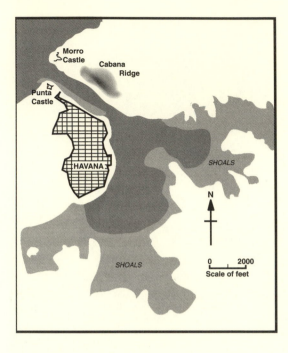

around the Caribbean and Gulf of Mexico was necessary truly to benefit from the wealth of the western hemisphere. As time passed, the development of sugar plantations on the Caribbean islands proved virtually as lucrative as plunder, however. Unfortunately for Spain, as her fortunes waned in Europe she saw her islands ceded to other rising European powers. Through the eighteenth century, Spain still held the key to the Caribbean Sea, and all that lay behind it: the island of Cuba. The key to Cuba was the rich but well-defended port city of Havana.

When Britain and France went to war in 1756, Spain remained aloof. By 1761, however, France demanded that Spain live up to its treaty commitments to assist the French throne held by a fellow Bourbon monarch. England responded by declaring war on Spain in January 1762 and quickly began making plans to attack Spanish Caribbean islands. England had controlled the island of Jamaica for a century, and it was their base of operations for strikes that quickly captured Martinique, Grenada, St. Lucia, St. Vincent, and Tobago. London hoped that this string of successes could be crowned by

the capture of Havana, and thence Cuba. An invasion fleet sailed from Portsmouth on 5 March 1762 to rendezvous with the forces recently returning from the successful capture of Martinique. The joint force comprised 19 ships-of-the-line, 18 smaller warships, and 150 transports carrying some 14,000 troops. The fleet was under the direction of Admiral Sir George Pocock; the troops were led by General George Keppel, earl of Albemarle.

Since the heyday of the pirates in the mid-1600s the Spanish had jealously guarded Havana, whose wealth became legendary. Any assault on Havana had to face the defenses of two castles that flanked the narrow entrance to the harbor, the formidable Morro Castle and its smaller sister, the Punta. The Morro was perched on high ground overlooking the entrance to the harbor, making bombardment from the seaward side extremely difficult. The Punta was lower and smaller, but to approach it from the seaward side required navigating a narrow strait while under direct fire. The Morro, being the stronger, was regarded as the key to the city's defense, in spite of the fact that it was on the opposite side of the harbor from the city. An assault on the city, it was thought, would only weaken the attacking force that would still have to assault the forts. The only way the Morro could be attacked was from the landward side, which involved crossing swampy terrain.

From Jamaica the invasion fleet had two possible avenues of approach: the southern route around Cuba was easier but longer, while the more direct route along Cuba's northern coast went through more treacherous waters. With the possibility of hurricanes to be considered, Pocock decided that time was of the essence and took the northern alternative. A pilot ship sailed to Havana and back, then guided the fleet along a safe route. When the English fleet appeared before Havana, the citizens and soldiers were unprepared. The forts had not been kept in the best state of repair and the moats around them were dry. The garrison

Undated engraving of the British expedition against Havana in 1762. The fleet, under Sir George Pocock, enters the harbor to take possession of the city. (North Wind Picture Archives)

numbered 2,330 regular troops and another 1,700 sailors aboard 15 warships, but there existed sufficient weaponry to equip only a further 3,000 militia of the 30,000 inhabitants of Havana. A junta of talented and experienced officers led by Captain General Juan de Prado commanded the defense, but the paucity of troops and the weakness of the defensive walls probably doomed the city from the outset.

The Siege

Pocock sailed past the harbor entrance toward a stream west of the city, and Prado responded by sending a force there to oppose the landing. Pocock's move was a feint, however, which allowed Albemarle to land his troops against no resistance 6 miles east of the Morro Castle at the mouth of the Cojima River. His men then began the difficult advance through rough terrain. Fortunately for them, however, the Spanish did nothing to oppose this march. Prado

did little other than erect a hasty redoubt on Cabaña Ridge, high ground that overlooked the Morro from the southeast. As no previous attacker had ever tried an eastern approach, the Cabaña Ridge was unfortified and the English took it with little effort on 11 June. The failure to hold that high ground was decisive for the course of the siege, for the English mounted artillery and mortars and began bombarding the Morro and Havana. They were also able to force the Spanish ships to anchor on the far side of the harbor to protect themselves. The English control of the eastern approach also meant they could cut off the water supply flowing into the fort as well as any reinforcements or supplies.

The Spanish fell into a passive defense. Their fleet of twelve ships-of-the-line and three frigates, had they sallied out and challenged the English, could have disrupted the entire operation, but Prado did nothing other than to sink three of his ships in the channel to block any possible entrance. As the guns of the forts easily protected the channel, this was a foolish move that allowed the English to move about freely and receive reinforcements while bottling up the Spanish fleet. This was proven when, on 1 July, Pocock brought up three ships to assault the fort in coordination with an assault by the troops. After a six-hour duel the English ships withdrew, badly damaged by fire from both the Morro and the Punta.

The heat and humidity were a trial to the English. "Even in the commencement of the siege, the distresses to which the soldiers were exposed, were sufficient to damp the ardour of any but the bravest; their labours were excessive; and yet they only led to severer toils. Their roads of communication were to be cut through forests that were almost impenetrable; and their heavy artillery was to be dragged, for a vast way, over a rough and rocky shore. To many their exertions and sufferings were intolerable; the powerful co-operation of labour, thirst, and excessive heat, became insupportable; they sunk beneath a complicated burden, and expired amidst the violence of their fatigues" (Coke, *History of the West Indies*, vol. 3, p. 274). In the wake of the ship-to-fort duel, the Spanish knocked out an artillery battery on the ridge: "The labour of 600 men for 17 days was destroyed in a few hours, and all was to be constructed anew" (p. 276). Albemarle's men, however, were able to force their way across the moat on 20 July and begin mining the Morro's walls.

On the 28th 1,400 militia from Connecticut arrived in time to aid in the defense of the batteries from the one Spanish sally. Prado gathered together a rather motley collection of 1,200 militia and threw them against the English lines. Although the opening attack was a surprise, the English recovered quickly and beat back three charges. On the 30th the engineers mining the walls finally had their charges set and blew a breach in the Morro's walls. Albemarle's two brothers led the English charge and they made short work of the defenders. Luis de Velasco, commander of the Morro, died defending his flag.

Results

Artillery from both the Cabaña and the Morro now began to rain fire onto Havana. Captain General de Prado heard rumors of an approaching French fleet and so tried to hold out as long as possible. When the rumor proved false, he asked for terms on 11 August; on that day 6,000 shells had landed in the city before he gave up. The terms were lenient: the remainder of the garrison was allowed to return to Spain, as were the commanders. The city was to suffer no looting (officially), and the citizens were to be allowed freedom of religion and protection in their persons. Cuba was declared a possession of Great Britain, although the soldiers only occupied Havana and the immediate environs. The only serious conflict was between Albemarle, who became acting governor, and the local bishop, who objected to any restriction on his authority. "Yet every Cuban authority agrees that the whole painful episode was a blessing to Havana. The Spanish system of a closed economy was overturned and bonds of all kinds were loosened. . . . The commercial markets thus opened were far more extensive than those afforded by Spain, and the taxes were lower. Intercourse with the Thirteen Colonies of North America was particularly lively" (Roberts, *Havana*, p. 48).

The occupation was of short duration, however, for the Treaty of Paris of 1763 ended the Seven Years War and as a condition of peace Cuba was returned to Spain while Spain abandoned her claims to Florida. The good economic times, however, continued, for the Cubans refused to return to the previous commercial rules imposed by Madrid. Havana itself began a major construction expansion in response to the increased trade and wealth.

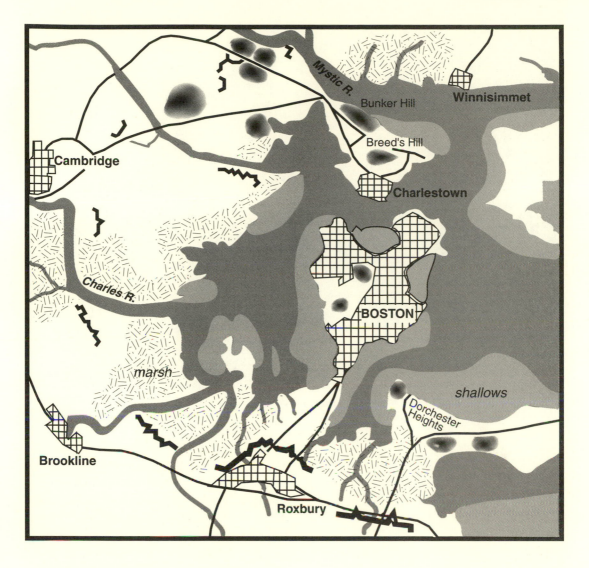

Cuba remained a Spanish possession until finally forfeited in 1898 in the wake of the Spanish-American War. Havana, however, remained the commercial center of both Cuba and the Caribbean and later became the political capital of the island as well.

References: Thomas Coke, *A History of the West Indies*, 3 vols. (London: Frank Cass, 1971 [1808–1811]); Allan Kuethe, *Cuba, 1753–1815: Crown, Military, and Society* (Knoxville: University of Tennessee Press, 1986); W. Adophe Roberts, *Havana, Portrait of a City* (New York: Coward-McCann, 1953).

BOSTON

DATE: 20 April 1775–17 March 1776.
LOCATION: capital of state of Massachusetts, United States.

FORCES ENGAGED:

American: 17,000 men. Commander: General George Washington.
British: 11,000–12,000 men. Commander: General Thomas Gage.

William Howe, commander in chief of the British forces in North America during the American Revolution, orders the evacuation of his troops after the siege of Boston, 17 March 1776, engraving by J. Godfrey. (Archive Photos)

IMPORTANCE:

By forcing the British to evacuate Boston, the vast majority of British troops in the North American colonies were expelled. This morale boost led to the adoption of the Declaration of Independence.

Historical Setting

From the establishment of the first British colony in North America in 1607, the government in London had engaged in the practice of salutary neglect. The colonies, which numbered thirteen by 1735, were primarily seen in London as a convenient place to send malcontents and criminals. The colonies over time developed their own society and political views with little input or interest from the mother country. That began to change in 1754. When colonial and French forces clashed near Fort Duquesne (modern Pittsburgh, Pennsylvania),

the impetus began for a series of events that culminated in an armed conflict between England and her allies in both North America and Europe against France and her allies in the same locations. The war, denoted variously as the French and Indian War, Great War for Empire, or Seven Years War, brought about the first serious cooperation between England and her long-ignored colonies.

After early setbacks, English troops aided by colonial militia gained control of Canada by 1760. The end of the fighting in Europe in 1763 led to the signing of the Treaty of Paris. France was expelled from Canada and England was awarded all her lands east of the Mississippi River and north of the Great Lakes. The successful joint venture between mother and colonies led to the view in London that North America, far from being simply a dumping ground for undesirables, was both a profitable possession and a potential source of tax revenue to relieve the overwhelming debt incurred by the war. The colonists soon came to regret the reestablished relationship.

Although on the surface England and the colonies should have had much in common, 150 years of isolation had brought about in North America a radically different set of economic, political, and religious views. Although the laws passed by Parliament were in reality none too burdensome, any rules at all (especially without any direct input in the decision making) were too many for the colonists. Through the 1760s increased English legislation concerning North America became more and more bothersome to the local population. Economic pressure exerted through colonial embargoes riled Parliament, while violent incidents like the "Boston Massacre" inflamed colonial passions. When, in December 1773, insurgents floated 45 tons of tea in Boston harbor, Parliament had had enough. The Coercive Acts, passed in the spring of 1774 to punish the hotheads in Massachusetts, were deemed intolerable by the colonists.

In September 1774, representatives from twelve colonies met in Philadelphia. They began yet another embargo, but more important they directly challenged the English government. In the Suffolk Resolutions, the Continental Congress defied the Coercive Acts and promised to kidnap British officers if any colonists were arrested for violating the acts. They also vowed military action would be taken if the garrison of redcoats in Boston made any threatening moves. King George III had no choice but to send more troops, for then as now no government can negotiate with terrorists. On 19 April 1775 a force of British soldiers marched out of Boston to destroy stockpiles of rebel arms some 16 miles away in the town of Concord. Their quick disposal of a small force of "Minutemen" militia at Lexington aroused the countryside, and the 450-man force (which found nothing in Concord) found itself harassed by hundreds of angry farmers on the long march back to their base.

The relief force of 1,200 men became but a larger target to the colonists, who inflicted almost 300 casualties on the British by nightfall. Within days 20,000 angry farmers had Boston surrounded.

The Siege

Command of this motley crew fell to Massachusetts militia Major General Artemus Ward, who exercised direct control over the northern half of the men surrounding the city while detailing John Thomas to command the southern half. Units from Connecticut and New Hampshire quickly reinforced the Massachusetts farmers, and even colonies as far away as South Carolina raised units and money. There was little organization and even less supplies, but at first there was no shortage of spirit.

In Boston, Thomas Gage did little. His 4,000 men remained relatively idle while waiting for reinforcements. The government in London did not see the same emergency that Gage did and so sent but 1,700 more soldiers and three more generals: William Howe, Henry Clinton, and John Burgoyne.

If the colonists were to make this siege work, they needed artillery. A Connecticut captain named Benedict Arnold suggested a raid on Fort Ticonderoga at the lower end of Lake Champlain. Arnold caught up to a force of backwoodsmen from Vermont under the command of Ethan Allen, who had conceived of the same idea. Together, they stole into the sleepy fort at dawn on 10 May and took the garrison without a shot. Some 100 cannon and howitzers were now at their disposal, if they could be transported out of the mountains to Boston, 150 miles away.

The Continental Congress reconvened on 10 May. After a hollow gesture of peace toward Parliament they appointed George Washington to command the American forces. He had served in the French and Indian War, was wealthy, and was a southerner, from Virginia.

The greatest anger was in the northern colonies; restrictions on freedoms had aroused some southerners but most remained loyal. The Congress hoped that appointing a southerner to command would motivate southern colonies to greater involvement. It was for the most part a futile dream.

Before Washington arrived, 1,200 Connecticut troops under the leadership of Israel Putnam and William Prescott seized Breed's Hill on the Charlestown peninsula just across the harbor from Boston. In the darkness they erected a strong earthwork that defied cannon shot from the British warship *Lively* on the morning of 17 June. Rather than challenge the weak siege lines around the city and cut off the rebel force at the neck of the peninsula, Gage ordered William Howe across the harbor to assault the hill with 2,200 men. An afternoon's fighting resulted in an American withdrawal, but at a cost to Howe's force of almost 1,100 casualties. Although the colonists lost about 400 men, their withdrawal owed more to a lack of ammunition than British action.

Washington took command at Boston on 2 July. In spite of the moral victory of Breed's Hill (better known—erroneously—as Bunker Hill), discipline was almost nonexistent and spirits were beginning to flag. Washington's job was to transform a collection of colonial militias into a single Continental Army, and he set about with great firmness. Eight men he deemed to have been cowardly at Breed's Hill were brought before a court-martial and convicted. "He sought permission from the Continental Congress to hang deserters; and issued a succession of orders intended to bring cleanliness and order to the camps and subdue all manner of breaches of discipline, from drunkenness to lewdness" (Hibbert, *Redcoats and Rebels*, p. 68). This show of order offended many independent-minded militiamen, who decided to go home short of their promised tour of duty, which was to end on 31 December. Still, Washington managed to transform the units into a force of some 17,000 men under a single command. Gage, then Howe

(who took command in October), did nothing to interfere with the strengthening of the colonial effort, in spite of the fact that British forces grew to almost 11,000 by November.

While Washington was whipping his army into shape, former Boston bookseller Henry Knox was sent to Ticonderoga to fetch the artillery. A self-taught artillerist and engineer, Knox oversaw the dismantling and transport of the guns through extremely difficult terrain down to Boston. When the first guns arrived in December, the hills on the Charlestown peninsula that the redcoats had bought at such an expensive price had been abandoned. All the troops had been brought into Boston for winter quarters, and the high ground all around the city was free for the taking. Washington spent the first two months of 1776 gathering his artillery and placing it along his extended lines. On the night of 4–5 March a battery was hauled up Dorchester Heights to the south of Boston and dug in. Its sudden appearance looming over the British forces on the morning of the 5th spelled the garrison's doom.

Howe prepared an assault on Dorchester, but a well-timed storm dispersed most of his boats and he canceled it. Through the winter his force had suffered dwindling food supplies and much more intense cold than they were used to experiencing. Although the harbor was open, few supply ships visited and those that did sold their goods dearly. Discipline eroded through inactivity, which Howe refused to alter. He never attacked the colonial forces: "in the unlikely event of this being successful, it would have served no purpose, since he had no transport to allow him to take advantage of it by pursuing a defeated enemy. He decided that he had no choice, therefore, but to wait for the ships to take his men and equipment away" (Hibbert, *Redcoats and Rebels*, p. 73). Seeing the guns threatening his position, Howe sent word to the rebels that if he and his men were allowed to sail away unmolested, they would not destroy the city on their way out. Thus, the entire command along with perhaps 1,000 loyal Bostonians boarded what ships were available and sailed for Halifax, Nova Scotia, on 17 March.

Results

The British should never have lost Boston. Any serious attempt to keep the garrison supplied would have made the defense too strong for Washington ever to have successfully assaulted. Conversely, the besieging force (although large in number) was poorly organized and trained. Although Washington did wonders once he took command, any time before that point a vigorous British sortie would probably have collapsed the entire colonial effort. Gage, whose twenty years' residence in the colonies had softened him to effective action, was succeeded by Howe, whose shocking experience on the slopes of Breed's Hill ruined him for any future aggressive action. Their inactivity was made worse by their snobbery. Many Bostonians remained loyal to the Crown and volunteered to fight, but as would happen so many times throughout the American Revolution the British officers sneered at colonial assistance. In Boston, as in so many other regions throughout the war, the British succeeded in making enemies out of friends.

By capturing Boston, most of the British forces in North America were expelled. This was the cause of much rejoicing on the part of the rebels, and was fatefully timed. In January 1776, Thomas Paine published *Common Sense*, a widely read work that argued the advantages of a republic over a monarchy. As it meshed with the political views of most colonists, who had been electing their own leaders locally almost from the beginning, it was wildly successful: some 100,000 copies were sold in 1776 in a population throughout the colonies of 2.5 million. A similar sales figure in the United States today would be roughly 11 million copies. The intellectual argument Paine made, on top of the success Washington achieved, convinced many heretofore reluctant colonists that more was needed than merely a recogni-

tion of rights as British subjects. On 2 July 1776 the Continental Congress voted to declare independence from Great Britain; a Declaration of Independence expounding on the rationale for that action was adopted two days later.

Although independence was declared, it was seven more years before Britain agreed in 1783. In the shorter term, 4 July 1776 had a much more negative outlook, for it marked the return of British troops to the colonies: Howe's invasion of New York City marked the beginning of a dark time in the Revolution.

References: Ira Gruber, *The Howe Brothers and the American Revolution* (New York: Atheneum, 1972); Christopher Hibbert, *Redcoats and Rebels* (New York: Norton, 1990); Bruce Lancaster, *The American Revolution* (Boston: Houghton Mifflin, 1971); Howard Peckham, *The War for Independence: A Military History* (Chicago: University of Chicago Press, 1958).

QUEBEC

DATE: 15 November 1775–7 May 1776.
LOCATION: on the St. Lawrence River, between Montreal and the river's mouth.

FORCES ENGAGED:

British/Canadian: approximately 1,800 soldiers and militia. Commander: Sir Guy Carleton.
American: approximately 900 men. Commander: Brigadier General Richard Montgomery.

IMPORTANCE:

American failure to capture Quebec doomed the attempt to deny Canada to the British.

Historical Setting

When the American Revolution began in April 1775, the Continental Congress that directed the fledgling war effort realized the importance of Canada. From there, the British could send

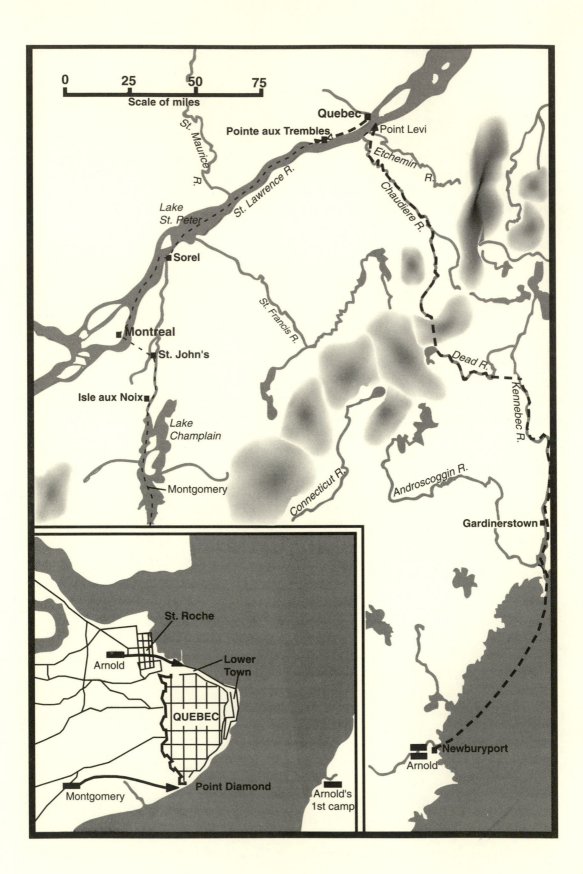

Scale of miles

0   25   50   75

St. Maurice R.

Quebec

Pointe aux Trembles

Point Levi

Etchemin R.

St. Lawrence R.

Chaudiere R.

Lake St. Peter

Sorel

St. Francis R.

Dead R.

Montreal

St. John's

Kennebec R.

Isle aux Noix

Lake Champlain

Montgomery

Connecticut R.

Androscoggin R.

Gardinerstown

St. Roche

Lower Town

Arnold

QUEBEC

Montgomery

Point Diamond

Arnold's 1st camp

Arnold

Newburyport

troops into the upper colonies while simultaneously reinforcing the army in Boston. To stop that from happening, as well as to use Canada as a source of supplies by looting British bases there, the Continental Congress ordered an invasion.

Two columns were given the task of attacking Canada. One, under Brigadier General Robert Montgomery, was to work their way northward up Lake Champlain to Montreal. The second, under Colonel Benedict Arnold, was to proceed up the Kennebec River in Maine to the Dead River, thence overland to the Chaudiere River to capture Quebec. Arnold, as an officer in the Connecticut militia, had been involved in the capture of Fort Ticonderoga (at the southern end of Lake Champlain) on 10 May 1775, and had hoped to use that as a base from which to invade Canada.

Montgomery departed from Ticonderoga on 28 August with 1,200 men. They traveled in a motley collection of boats up Lake Champlain to Crown Point. A few days later they were joined by a further 800 men and some artillery under the command of Major General Phillip Schuyler, who assumed overall command of the expedition. Contacts with rebellious individuals in Canada had caused the Americans to believe that they would be met by more reinforcements when they entered the country, but as Schuyler's force approached the town of St. Johns on the Richelieu River they met only cannon fire. Through mid-September the Americans launched a few abortive forays past the Isle aux Noix in the Richelieu River but exaggerated reports of enemy numbers disheartened many of them. On the 16th Schuyler, who had been suffering from a chronic illness the entire campaign, withdrew to New York and left Montgomery in command.

After the arrival of a further 400 reinforcements, the Americans' spirit revived somewhat and they began a siege of St. John's fort while scouring the countryside for supplies and assistance. Ethan Allen of New Hampshire, who was instrumental in capturing Fort Ticonderoga,

launched an ill-advised attack on Montreal in late October. It failed and he was taken prisoner, giving heart to the British, encouraging the Canadians not to join with the invaders, and prompting area Indians to join with what seemed to be the winning side. In spite of that, there were still too few men to fully garrison the fort at St. John's, although Canadian governor Sir Guy Carleton, in Montreal, sent what reinforcements he could. When an American force slipped past St. John's and captured another fort at Chambly to the north, St. John's seemed doomed. After concentrated artillery fire sank the schooner *Royal Savage*, which had been supporting the fort, the commander decided to surrender his post on 2 November. He had delayed the American advance by fifty-five days. After a futile attack out of Montreal, Carleton was forced to flee that town as Montgomery's men approached. The Americans ate well for the first time in weeks and dressed themselves in warm clothes available in the British storehouses.

In the meantime, Arnold's men were struggling across Maine. They left Fort Western (modern-day Augusta) in four groups between 24 and 28 September, traveling in flat-bottom bateaux, the main watercraft of the region. Carrying forty-five days' worth of supplies for his 1,050 men, Arnold was certain the passage to Quebec would take no more than twenty days, for it was (he reckoned) 180 miles away. Bad weather and unexpectedly rough water slowed the expedition almost from the beginning. Numbers of men got sick and were sent home, with able-bodied men to support them. One group of 300 men lost faith in the project and deserted. By the time Arnold's starving survivors reached the St. Lawrence River on 9 November they had traveled forty-five days and were reduced in number to half their original strength.

Never lacking initiative, however, Arnold quickly scoured the countryside for canoes and dugouts. About 400 men crossed the river the night of the 13th, the remaining 150 the following night. They hid at the base of the cliff below the town of Quebec, then on the 15th went up a little-used road to emerge on the Plains of Abraham a mile and a half from Quebec. They seized the home of the commandant of the Quebec militia and prepared to face the British garrison.

The Siege

Quebec sits on a promontory formed by the confluence of the St. Lawrence and St. Charles rivers. The cliffs protected it from attack from the rivers, so the only way to approach the city was from the southwest across the Plains of Abraham. Behind the city's walls Guy Carleton commanded a mixed force of regular soldiers and militia, the latter of dubious quality and loyalty. They numbered about 500 of the total of 1,200 men defending the town, which had a population of perhaps 5,000. Twelve hundred men to hold a three-quarter-mile-long wall is not many, and both British and American observers predicted an American victory in short order. Still, Carleton was determined to stand fast. When Arnold sent forward a demand for surrender, his messenger had to dodge a cannon ball.

Although the Americans now had a good stock of food on which to rebuild their strength after the tortuous march, their morale was still questionable. Upon hearing a rumor of a sally by 800 men from Quebec, along with the supposed arrival of a ship with a further 200 men, Arnold withdrew from the houses his men had been occupying and reestablished himself at Pointe aux Trembles, 20 miles up the St. Lawrence. Spirits were flagging when, on 2 December, Montgomery arrived from Montreal with 300 men. He had been obliged to leave garrisons along the way at various forts he had captured, so his contribution in manpower was rather small. He took command, describing Arnold's men as "exceeding fine, . . . inured to fatigue" (Ward, *War of the Revolution*, vol. 1, p. 185). He also arrived with warm clothing looted from Montreal, as well as artillery. The force marched back to Quebec.

Montgomery did not want to conduct a protracted siege. His artillery was too light to make a serious dent in Quebec's walls and he wanted to be in possession of the town well before spring and the certain arrival of reinforcements from England. Further, almost all of the troops had (as is the nature of militia) volunteered for a short enlistment, which was to end with the new year. He had little choice but to attack. He did not want to throw his meager forces at the walls, however, for he knew that would be futile. He decided instead to launch a feint at the walls while sending a force along the banks of the St. Charles to enter the Lower Town, at water's edge below the cliffs. All that was needed was some bad weather to cover their movements. Knowing that the Lower Town was the only feasible approach, Carleton reinforced the crooked lane that was the main point of entry from the suburb of St. Roche.

Still, Montgomery went through the motions of a siege. His men could not dig trenches in the frozen earth, so they built gun positions out of snow and poured water on them, freezing them into ice redoubts. Unfortunately, Quebec's guns were bigger than those of the Americans and the icy gun batteries were soon blown apart. Montgomery sent several demands for Carleton's surrender, all of which were spurned. Finally, the evening of 27 December seemed right for the attack, but it had to be postponed. The weather cleared and the plan was revealed to Carleton through a deserter.

On New Year's Eve the weather was again sufficiently rough to offer cover. Montgomery led 300 men along the southern edge of Quebec past Point Diamond. Arnold commanded a 600-man force attacking from St. Roche. Signal rockets marked the opening of the attack, which started at 0400 in a heavy snowstorm. Unfortunately for the attackers, the rockets also alerted the defenders and they were ready. Part of Arnold's column entered the town unseen, but then the defenders arrived and opened a deadly fire. The Americans ran into a barricade that they assaulted, Arnold being wounded in the leg in the process. He was evacuated and Colonel Daniel Morgan assumed command. He led the men over the barricade and captured a number of defenders, then pressed on. Unfortunately, his command was becoming disorganized owing to the bad weather and the fighting; his prisoners outnumbered his own force. At a second barricade they halted, for this was their rendezvous point with Montgomery. Little did they know that Montgomery lay dead just past Point Diamond and his command had retreated in confusion. There was to be no reinforcement. At dawn the defenders sallied past the barricade but were turned back after Morgan led a counterattack. Unfortunately, behind the second barricade stood a double rank of fusiliers whose fire decimated Morgan's men. An attempt to outflank them failed, and Morgan's men began to retreat. Carleton, however, had sent a force behind them to block their withdrawal. After a brief stand in some of the houses, the Americans were forced to surrender.

Results

The failure on the morning of New Year's Day marked the last serious attempt to storm the town. Arnold was determined to maintain the investment, but his force was now too weak in numbers and supplies to succeed. The weather remained bitterly cold and his troops began suffering from smallpox and other diseases as well as exposure and starvation. On 1 April more manpower arrived from Montreal under the command of General David Wooster, who also brought up some siege artillery. After an unpleasant encounter with Arnold, the American force proceeded to deteriorate. The men who had stayed with Arnold told too many tales of defeat and frustration to keep the newcomers in any state of high morale. Wooster was soon replaced by General John Thomas, whose tenure of command ended quickly with his death from smallpox. The thawing of the St. Lawrence marked the arrival of spring, and also the arrival of an army from England commanded by John Burgoyne. When his ships sailed into view on 6 May 1776, the last ragged Americans pulled back to Montreal, then on to the Richelieu River, St. John's fort, and back into New York.

Had Montgomery and Arnold actually captured Quebec, it is doubtful they could have held it. Burgoyne's well-equipped army of 8,000 would certainly have made short work of the handful of men the Americans could send to Canada. Indeed, the entire experience proved to the authorities in London the value of Canada and motivated their strong reinforcement of the province. Although a spring offensive down Lake Champlain was turned back by Benedict Arnold's haphazard naval force at Valcour Island, the British were intent on using it as a base for invading the rebellious colonies. In the late spring of 1777 Burgoyne's invasion began the campaign that turned out to be the turning point of the Revolution when he met defeat at Saratoga.

References: Christopher Hibbert, *Redcoats and Rebels* (New York: Norton, 1991); Page Smith, *A New Age Now Begins*, vol. 1 (New York: McGraw-Hill, 1976); Christopher Ward, *The War of the Revolution*, vol. 1 (New York: Macmillan, 1952).

FORT STANWIX

DATE: 3–22 August 1777.
LOCATION: western New York State, near modern-day Rome, NY.

FORCES ENGAGED:
American: approximately 800 men. Commander: Colonel Peter Gansevoort.
British/Indian: 875 British, German, and American loyalist troops; 800–1,000 Indians, primarily Mohawks. Commander: Brevet Brigadier General Barry St. Leger.
Relief force: 800 local militia. Commander: Brigadier General Nicholas Herkimer.

IMPORTANCE:

British inability to capture Fort Stanwix helped doom the British effort to split the rebelling American colonies by taking control of the Hudson River and central New York State.

Historical Setting

The late summer and fall of 1776 had proven disastrous to the American Revolution, for British troops under General Sir William Howe occupied New York City and the area surrounding it. American commander General George Washington saved the Revolution by winning two surprise victories over British troops at Trenton and Princeton, New Jersey, in late December 1776 and early January 1777. That accomplishment transformed itself into increased recruits to the rebel cause the following spring.

In New York City, Howe spent the winter planning his next move: an attack on Philadelphia, home of the Continental Congress,

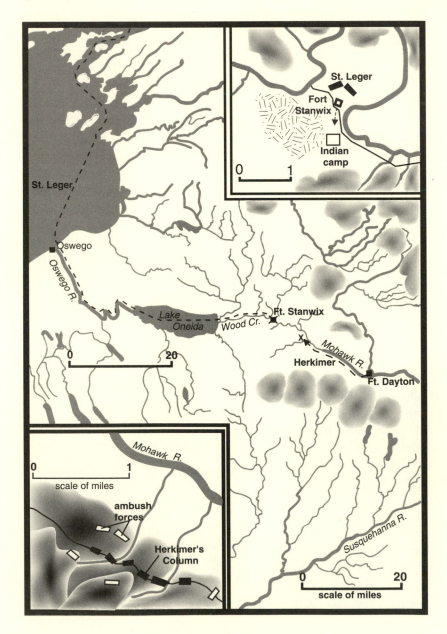

which directed the revolutionary effort. His plan called for 20,000 men to be transported by sea down to Virginia, up the Chesapeake Bay, and then overland toward Philadelphia from the southwest. Meanwhile, Major General Sir John Burgoyne in Canada was planning a campaign of his own. Realizing correctly that by controlling the state of New York the main revolutionary firebrands of New England would be separated from their leadership and supplies to the south, Burgoyne planned a three-pronged offensive into New York. He would lead 8,000 men out of Canada down Lake Champlain to Albany, gaining control of upstate New York. At the same time, a column of 850 Europeans would go by water up the St. Lawrence River to Lake Ontario, thence eastward down the Mohawk River to Albany. Finally, he called for Howe to march up the Hudson from New York City, gaining control of lower New York. Unfortunately for the British effort, Howe's plans for Philadelphia contradicted Burgoyne's desires, and Howe's promise to assist later in the summer proved impossible to fulfill.

Burgoyne's advance southward out of Canada moved along nicely in the early summer of 1777, easily capturing the rebel-held Fort Ticonderoga and the bottom of Lake Champlain. It then began to slow, as a road had to be constructed to maintain the supply line from Canada.

In the meantime, Brevet Brigadier General Barry St. Leger led a mixed force of some 850 British, German, and American loyalist troops up the St. Lawrence to Lake Ontario. They arrived at Oswego, New York, on 25 July, where 800 to 1,000 Mohawk Indians under the leadership of Joseph Brant joined them. The Mohawks were part of the six-nation Iroquois Confederacy, which had fought with the British against the French and their Algonquin allies for decades. Not all of the Confederation supported the British, however, for the Oneidas and Tuscaroras remained neutral or favored the revolutionaries.

St. Leger's route west was along a well-established route. Wood Creek leads out of Lake Ontario at Oswego and flows eastward toward the Mohawk. It falls about a mile short of con-

necting, however. That intervening mile for years had been a portage, a track for carrying boats overland from one waterway to the other. Astride that portage lay Fort Stanwix, built by the British in 1758 during the French and Indian War. Since that last conflict the fort had fallen into a sad state of disrepair, but the revolutionaries of western New York realized its import even before the current British threat. In late spring 1777 local militia forces under the command of Colonel Peter Gansevoort and Lieutenant Colonel Marinus Willet were sent to repair the fort. Their hard work transformed the dilapidated defenses to near their original strength by early August, mere days before St. Leger's arrival.

St. Leger through captured rebel prisoners had been alerted to the state of the fort's defenses, but chose to ignore or discount them, convinced that it was held by no more than sixty men instead of the 600 that actually manned the post. As he approached the region around the fort, St. Leger learned of a supply column nearing it, so he dispatched a small force of American rangers and Indians to cut it off. They arrived on 2 August, just as the supplies and an additional 200 men were entering the fort. St. Leger and the remainder of the force arrived the next day. Convinced he could cow the garrison into surrender, he paraded his men before the fort. The sight of nearly a thousand Indians, however, steeled the defenders' resolve, for bitter experience in warfare with the Indians over the previous century and a half had created intense hostility on the part of most colonists. When St. Leger sent a demand for the fort's surrender it went unanswered. He had no choice now but to lay siege.

The Siege

St. Leger had brought with him too few cannon to make any serious impression on Fort Stanwix's walls. Still, he surrounded the fort as best he could, but the wooded and marshy terrain made it impossible to make a complete investment. He placed small outposts on either end of the portage road, established his main camp just north and east of the fort, and placed the Indians, loyalists, and a small force of British regulars in a camp south of the fort. In order to facilitate the arrival of supplies and artillery, St. Leger ordered the bulk of his forces, along with some Canadian woodsmen they had brought with them, to cut a road 16 miles through the forest. He also had them clear Wood Creek of the trees the Americans had felled to block passage.

About 250 troops remained on watch around the fort as the others labored on the road. On 5 August the Mohawks brought word of a relieving force of rebels making their way from down the Mohawk at Fort Dayton, 30 miles away. These 800 militia were under the command of Brigadier General Nicholas Herkimer. He gathered his men and 400 oxcarts full of supplies and left Fort Dayton on 4 August, making 22 miles in two days. St. Leger hesitantly divided his already small force and sent a handful of rangers and the bulk of Brant's Mohawks to ambush the relief. At Oriskany the militia, marching down a narrow mountain path, walked into the ambush. Unfortunately for the British, the Indians attacked too soon, allowing the militia to react. A timely thunderstorm halted the fighting for a few hours, while Herkimer deployed his men in a circle on a hilltop. When the rain stopped and the fighting resumed, the militia's strong position discouraged the Indians from attacking and, after losing too many men for their liking, they withdrew from the battlefield after inflicting more than 200 casualties. The British troops were forced to withdraw as well.

As the battle at Oriskany was taking place, messengers Herkimer had sent to the fort alerted the garrison of the militia's advance. Lieutenant Colonel Willet sallied with 250 men and attacked the lightly held Indian camp south of the fort, looting it and escaping before the Indians' return. Already disheartened by the outcome of the ambush, the Mohawks rapidly decided the effort was too great and began serious grumbling about the British siege effort.

St. Leger, desperate to finish the siege but unable with his small cannon to make much impression on the defenses, began constructing parallels to bring his artillery closer to the fort. Gansevoort sent messengers at night through the enemy lines to Fort Dayton, alerting them to the imminent danger. Area commander General Philip Schuyler, trying to keep an eye on Burgoyne's advance down the Hudson as well as St. Leger's offensive, had trouble convincing his subordinates that the Mohawk threat needed to be deterred. Finally, he ordered an expedition to relieve Fort Stanwix and Major General Benedict Arnold volunteered to lead it. He was assigned 500 Continental soldiers for the task, but accomplished his mission through trickery rather than force. He sent a captured loyalist, who was to some degree mentally ill, to sneak into the Indian camp at Stanwix. Such a condition, rather than being shunned as in European society, was regarded by the Indians as a blessing from the gods, and the prisoner's tale of Arnold approaching with thousands of troops was readily believed. Arnold had a fearsome reputation and the Indians did not want to fight him no matter how many troops he led, so they left the British force after looting it of clothing and liquor. Without the bulk of his force, St. Leger was forced on 22 August to abandon the siege and return to Canada the way he had come.

Results

St. Leger's retreat was a major setback for the British offensive into New York, which in itself was the key offensive of the entire American Revolution. When Burgoyne ran into serious rebel opposition near the town of Saratoga, New York, in September, he was forced to go to ground and await relief by St. Leger or Howe. As neither of them was marching on Albany as the plan had dictated, Burgoyne found himself isolated. A second attempt to break through to Albany in mid-October also failed and Burgoyne was obliged to surrender his entire force. That defeat not only heartened the rebel effort, as Washington's victories at Trenton and Princeton had done the previous year, it also convinced the French to recognize American independence and provide massive amounts of aid. The garrison at Fort Stanwix, by stalling and ultimately deflecting St. Leger's offensive, doomed Burgoyne and by extension the entire British effort to reestablish control of their American colonies.

References: Hoffman Nickerson, *The Turning Point of the Revolution*, vol. 1 (Port Washington, NY: Kennikat, 1967 [1928]); John Pancake, *1777, the Year of the Hangman* (Tuscaloosa: University of Alabama Press, 1977); Christopher Ward, *The War of the Revolution*, vol. 2 (New York: Macmillan, 1952).

GIBRALTAR

DATE: 11 July 1779–2 February 1783.
LOCATION: on Spain's southern coast.

FORCES ENGAGED:
British: 5,380 men, five ships. Commander: Lieutenant General George Eliot.
Spanish: 21,000 men, nineteen ships. Commander: Spanish General Mendoza, later duc de Crillon.

IMPORTANCE:
The last major attempt to recapture Gibraltar from the British failed, giving Britain command of the entrance to the Mediterranean Sea to this day.

Historical Setting

Gibraltar (an anglicized adaptation of Jebel Tariq, named for the Muslim conqueror of Spain) has been the site of at least fourteen sieges since the Muslims built a fort atop the Rock, also known as Ape's Hill. It was the occupation of the site by Great Britain in 1704, however, that established that island nation as a major player in the Mediterranean Sea and a major thorn in

Spain's side (or bottom, as the case may be). A mere three days' siege brought the British possession of the peninsula during the War of the Spanish Succession, and they beat back two later attempts to dislodge them in 1705 and 1726.

In the late 1770s the British were deeply involved in trying to suppress the rebellion in their North American colonies. After the Americans' victory over British forces at Saratoga in October 1777, the French decided to throw their lot in with the revolutionaries in February 1778. Spain followed suit the following year, and the Dutch declared war on Britain in 1780. While all three countries provided supplies for the Americans, Spain was most interested in regaining Gibraltar. With the British focused on North America and having to watch the French and Dutch as well, the Spanish government hoped that British resources would be stretched too thinly to stop them from regaining the peninsula.

The British were intent on keeping possession, however, and had in command of the Gibraltar garrison the perfect commander. Lieutenant General George Eliot, a highly qualified forty-year veteran of the British army, took command in 1777. He was quite well-educated, and a veteran of the War of the Austrian Succession and the Seven Years War, where he not only served alongside Frederick the Great's Prussians but also was involved in the British capture of Havana in 1762. He exercised strict discipline on both himself and others. Knowing the importance of Gibraltar and Spain's threat to it, Eliot convinced the government in London to expand the garrison's defensive capabilities. The peninsula was protected by more than 400 cannon, mortars, and howitzers, which were increased to 663 during the siege (a number greater than the available gunners). By demanding that the garrison's civilian engineers come under his authority, Eliot created the foundation for the Royal Engineers. The garrison's complement at the beginning of the siege was 5,380 soldiers and 760 sailors.

As the neck of the peninsula that connects Gibraltar to Spain is both narrow and marshy,

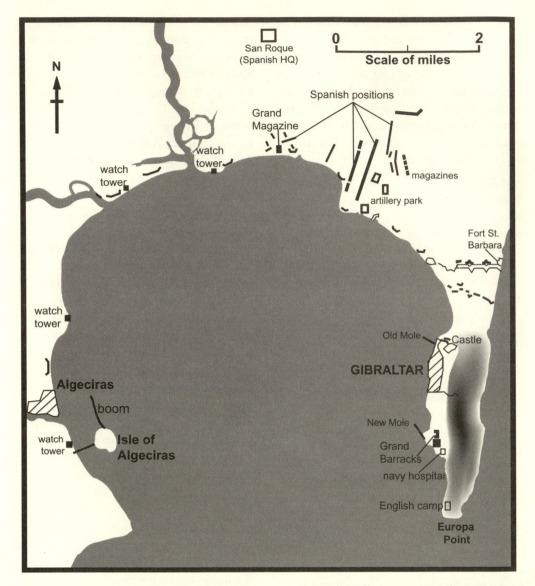

a land assault was considered infeasible by both sides. Thus, the bulk of the British guns were placed to cover the harbor, through which any reinforcements or supplies would have to come. Five bastions were created running north-south along the ridge of the peninsula; a fort protected the New Mole and another was built on the southernmost Point Europa. Much of the harbor was within range of Spanish guns, but Rosia Bay south of the New Mole was safe from that threat. Strongpoints on the neck of the peninsula overlooked Spanish positions and protected the British from any potential assault.

Starvation was Spain's tactic, with artillery bombardment from their fortifications to make British life miserable. To bring about that end, however, required a naval blockade, and Spain had nineteen ships of the line on hand for that duty based at Cadiz just to the west and a mixed force of warships at Algeciras, just across the bay from Gibraltar.

The Siege

The first attempt to run supplies into Gibraltar was a minor success. In early July 1779 three British ships slipped through a Spanish

The siege and relief of Gibraltar, engraving by William Sharp after a painting by J. S. Copley. (Library of Congress)

force. In spite of that success, Eliot kept a tight rein on rations from the beginning. Early in the siege nonessential horses were slaughtered, both for food and to save forage. Although some gardens existed within British lines, citrus fruit was only occasionally available, hence the regular outbreaks of scurvy.

The first artillery exchange began in September, when British gunners opened fire on Spanish troops working to extend their lines. One gunner struck on the idea of firing short-fused shells that exploded before impact, thus inventing the air burst. It kept the Spanish at a safe distance, but had little further effect other than on morale.

The London government watched Gibraltar's plight carefully, and in late December a twenty-two-ship fleet left Plymouth escorting a huge supply convoy, bound not only for Gibraltar but also besieged garrisons in Minorca and the West Indies. An easy victory over a Spanish supply convoy along the way

increased the amount of supplies in the relief effort. The fleet's commander, Admiral George Rodney, made short work of an eleven-ship Spanish force at Cape St. Vincent on 16 January 1780, while a large Franco-Spanish fleet remained in Cadiz. When Rodney's huge armada sailed into view of Gibraltar on 26 January, the blockading Spanish ships decided a safer position behind a boom in Algeciras harbor was the wisest course. In all, Rodney's convoy delivered Gibraltar sufficient rations for another year. He also delivered a battalion of the 73rd Highlanders while evacuating dependents. The garrison enjoyed full rations for two months before Eliot reimposed restrictions. The siege continued with little action other than regular artillery exchanges.

The monotony was broken on the night of 6 June, when the Spanish attempted to drift nine fire ships into the harbor. Quick action by British sailors, accurate gunnery by shore batteries, and a suddenly calm wind doomed the attack to failure. In spite of this failure, the Spanish tightened their blockade and by year's end the food supply was growing desperately short. Scurvy was common until the fortuitous capture of a passing Spanish brigantine acquired a supply of oranges for the garrison. It was a brief respite, for the blockade intensified when the sultan of Morocco allied his country with Spain. Tangiers had been a haven for blockade-runners up to this point.

The situation was desperate when, on 12 April 1781, a supply convoy arrived: one hundred cargo ships escorted by twenty-nine warships. In desperation, the Spanish stepped up their landward pressure. The bombardment, which to this point had been directed solely at gun positions, was shifted to the town of Gibraltar and civilians became daily targets. Through April and May 1781 an average of 11,000 rounds a week came from Spanish guns. This was coupled by bombardment from Spanish gunboats that at night patrolled just within range of the harbor facilities. The shelling leveled the town, exposing hidden stocks of liquor that disappeared in a drunken spree lasting two days. Eliot finally managed to reestablish order and hang a few looters.

Although another small convoy entered Gibraltar harbor in late April, by summer's end food was once again in short supply. The bombardment of the peninsula continued as Spanish forces grew to 21,000. Siege lines appeared, as the Spanish hoped to dig close enough to bring the entire peninsula within cannon range. Eliot forestalled this with a surprise sortie on 26 November 1781. Almost half his force, more than 2,000 men, sallied out in the darkness. The Spanish, who had been unmolested since the beginning of the siege, had few guards posted. The attack was amazingly successful, with dozens of Spanish guns spiked; several major ammunition magazines were destroyed in massive explosions.

Spanish morale collapsed and the siege returned to artillery fire. Throughout the first half of 1782 the British fought monotony more than any other enemy, although starvation was a close second. Reinforcements arrived in May, but that was coincident with the French capture of Minorca, which freed up their troops to aid the Spanish siege. The duc de Crillon commanding 9,000 soldiers took charge of the operation. He planned a joint assault from both land and sea. To bring heavy fire to bear on the harbor he constructed floating gun platforms, reinforced with sand between double walls then covered with rope and hides to absorb British counter-fire. These were supported by forty-nine ships of the line. On land, a force numbering 40,000 waited orders to charge.

The assault was a failure. When the French battery ships began the attack on the morning of 13 September 1782, they survived about six hours before the British began to set them alight with heated shot. When those ships sank or were abandoned, the attack was canceled. Daily artillery barrages once again became the standard fare, with up to 2,00 rounds per day fired into the British lines.

On 13 October another large fleet arrived from England with supplies. Admiral Lord Richard Howe delivered 150 merchant ships, then sailed for Cadiz to challenge the Franco-Spanish fleet. A short engagement ensued after which the allied ships returned to harbor. It was the last major action of the siege.

Results

Although Spain had joined France on the condition that the war would continue until Gibraltar was free of the British, it was not to be. After October 1781 the war in North America was virtually completed, and desultory fighting continued as peace talks began in Paris. A year of negotiations gave the United States their independence, returned Minorca and Florida to Spain, and officially ended the war. Spain was unable to hold the French to their word, and Britain remained the master of Gibraltar.

The siege lasted longer than any in British history: three years, seven months, and twelve days when it officially ended on 2 February 1783. The defenders lost 333 killed in battle but over 1,000 dead from disease, primarily scurvy. Another 1,000 civilians died, about half from smallpox. The British maintained control of the Rock and access to the Mediterranean from the Atlantic. Possession of Gibraltar became even more important to British foreign policy when they took Malta during the Napoleonic wars, then acquired the Suez Canal in the 1870s. Thus Britain, with no direct contact with the Mediterranean Sea, became the dominant force there. In World War II the British base at the Rock hosted air forces as well as anti-submarine operations that allowed the Allies to enter and ultimately seize the Mediterranean away from the Italians and Germans.

References: Ernle Bradford, *Gibraltar: The History of a Fortress* (New York: Harcourt, Brace & Jovanovich, 1972); William Hawkins, "Survival by Stubborn Defense," in *Military History* 4, no. 2, October 1987; T. H. McGuffie, *The Siege of Gibraltar, 1779–1783* (London: B. T. Batsford, 1965); Jack Russell, *Gibraltar Besieged, 1779–1783* (London: Heinemann, 1965).

PENSACOLA

DATE: 10 March–9 May 1781.
LOCATION: on the state of Florida's (United States) northwestern coast.

FORCES ENGAGED:

Spanish: 3,800 troops of a variety of nationalities. Commander: Governor General Bernardo de Galvez. British: 1,000 troops, made up of Indians, Germans, and British. Commander: General John Campbell.

IMPORTANCE:

Spanish victory gave them control of West Florida and, along with their other campaigns, denied the British claim to American territory between the Appalachians and the Mississippi River.

Historical Setting

The Treaty of Paris, which ended the Seven Years/French and Indian War in 1763, had sweeping implications for European colonialism in North America. France lost virtually everything on the continent, retaining only fishing rights off Canada and a handful of Caribbean islands. Left with only unexplored and mostly inaccessible territory between the Mississippi River and the Rocky Mountains, France gave up most of her imperial dreams and ceded that land, known as Louisiana, to her ally Spain. Spain gladly received it, for she had lost Florida to Britain as a result of the treaty and was glad to control the strategic port of New Orleans in compensation. Still, the defeat rankled French and Spanish alike, and both looked forward to the day they could exact a measure of revenge.

Such an opportunity arose in 1775 when Britain's thirteen American colonies began a revolution. Spain and France were both quick to funnel illicit arms and money to the Americans, but their support remained under the table until the American victory at Saratoga in October 1777. The decisiveness of the victory impressed the government in Paris, which signed a treaty of recognition and mutual defense in February 1778. Spain hesitated to openly support the Americans, however, fearing to aid a cause that their own colonists might emulate. When Britain rebuffed Spain's attempt to act as mediator, however, Madrid allied with France (although not with the United States) and went to war in May 1779. She hoped not only to regain Florida but also to seize the opportunity to capture Gibraltar, which the British had occupied for decades.

In spite of the fact that Spain openly supported the Americans after this, the primary assistance Spanish arms furnished to the Revolution was via Bernardo de Galvez, governor of the Louisiana Territory, who acted virtually on his own initiative. Commanding a 1,472-man force comprised of Spaniards, Cubans, Santo Domingans, Haitians, Venezuelans, and Puerto

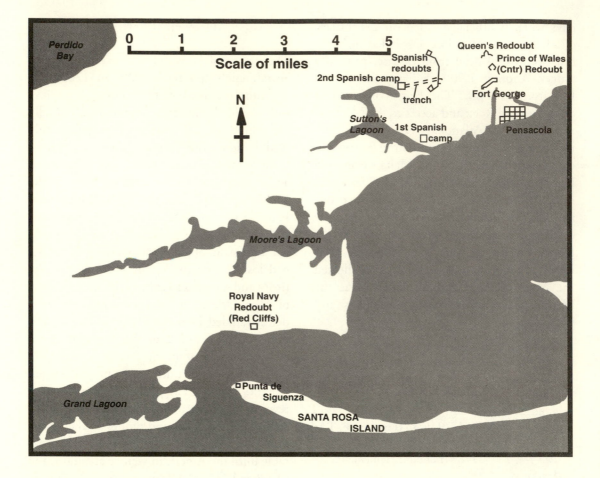

Ricans, Galvez advanced up the Mississippi River in the autumn of 1779 (after a hurricane delay) capturing British forts at Natchez, Baton Rouge, and Manchac. This gave Spain control of the lower Mississippi River as well as bagging 600 British prisoners, all for the loss of one dead and two wounded. The following spring Galvez led his men all the way to Lake Michigan, securing the entire Mississippi River while providing arms and ammunition for George Rogers Clark's victory over the British at Vincennes, which gave the Americans control of the Ohio River Valley and virtually emptied the American west of British troops.

The only remaining British presence was along the coast of the Gulf of Mexico, where they owned the ports of Mobile and Pensacola. In March 1780 Galvez received some men from Cuba and organized an assault force of 1,400 to take Mobile. His initial expedition

was turned back by heavy storms, but his thirteen-ship convoy landed his force at Mobile on 13 March. He spent the next three days entrenching; he had plenty of artillery and used it so effectively that at the end of the first day's bombardment the British commander of Fort Charlotte offered his surrender. On the 17th the Spanish flag replaced the Union Jack over the fort. For his outstanding service the Spanish Crown promoted Galvez to field marshall; he was but thirty-three years old.

Spanish authorities in Cuba, however, were slower to recognize his accomplishments and aid in his campaign. He had to sail to Havana to convince the government officials to provide him with the necessary shipping and manpower for his next objective: the capital city of West Florida, Pensacola. He was finally able to gather a fleet of sixty-four ships carrying almost 4,000 men which left Havana on 16 October, but a hurricane forced its return to port after the loss of several ships. Reorganization took several months and Galvez finally able to start off again in February 1781, although this time with a force of only 1,315 aboard twenty ships. He sent word to his forces in New Orleans and Mobile to meet him at Pensacola. In the meantime, General John Campbell, commanding the British force in Pensacola, had launched an attack on Mobile, but it failed and he returned to his base before Galvez arrived.

The Siege

Galvez himself led a force ashore at Santa Rosa Island on the night of 9 March 1781. They encountered no resistance and quickly secured Punta de Siguenza on the western end of the island. The landing was so successful the English had no idea any Spanish were about until a handful of men landed the following morning and soon found themselves made prisoner. Galvez quickly moved more men and supplies ashore in case rough weather should force his fleet out to sea, but that proved unnecessary. On the 11th the flagship *San Ramon* attempted to enter the harbor but was temporarily stuck on a sandbar. The fleet commander thereafter refused to allow his ships to try to force the passage, for British guns on the Red Cliffs had the bar in range. Galvez took his own personal frigate, the *Galveztown*, across the bar, proving it could be done and shaming the fleet commander into allowing the rest of the ships into the harbor, although he sailed his flagship back to Havana.

Covered by his own guns mounted at the Punta de Siguenza, Galvez pondered his next move. He contacted the British commander, General John Campbell, suggesting that the town of Pensacola be deemed off limits to any action in order to spare civilian casualties. A few incidents during the siege violated the spirit of that agreement, but for the most part the citizens were unmolested. When reinforcements arrived by land to the west of the Royal Navy Redoubt at Red Cliffs, Galvez crossed over to the mainland with 500 men to meet them. Soon thereafter ships arrived from New Orleans and Mobile with more men, bringing his force up to more than 3,500. The redoubt at Red Cliffs spent lots of powder and shot attempting to sink any Spanish ships entering the harbor, but they never inflicted any serious damage. It proved superfluous to the battle, for Galvez decided to bypass it with his land forces. On 24 March he transferred the bulk of his Santa Rosa garrison by ship to the east bank of Sutton's Lagoon, where he directed a camp established to begin operations against the three British forts overlooking Pensacola. The land-based troops marched around Moore's Lagoon to join the rest of the army, and was regularly harassed by Indians who had allied themselves with the British.

The British defenses were on the high ground just north of the town of Pensacola, and consisted of three forts: Fort George, the Prince of Wales (or Central) Redoubt, and the Queen's (or Advanced) Redoubt, running south to north, lower to higher ground. General Campbell's force consisted of 1,800 to 1,900 troops. The regular units were both British and German, but there were also American loyalists, civilians and slaves, and 400 to 500 Indians. It was the Indians who inflicted the most casualties on the Spanish, especially in the movements prior to the establishment of the second Spanish camp. Fort George's garrison was the primary position, measuring some $750 \times 1,000$ feet, its earthen rampart anchored by four blockhouses and surrounded by two palisades with a dry moat between. The Prince of Wales Redoubt held eight to ten cannon, while the Queen's Redoubt possessed fifty men and four cannon.

The Spaniards established a temporary encampment west of Sutton's Lagoon on the 24th, but it was too far away from the enemy and had the lagoon blocking any advance. Men and materiel crossed to the east side and the main camp was established on 30 March. It was quickly entrenched in order to beat back Indian attacks that began almost immediately.

Further reconnaissance showed that the best position from which to begin bombarding the British positions was a small hill about 2 miles due west of the Queen's Redoubt. Hence, Galvez ordered his men to encamp at the northern tip of Sutton's Lagoon, from where he began digging a trench from the camp to the heights in order to bring men and artillery safely to his proposed redoubt. This second camp was also quickly attacked by an Anglo-Indian force and for a time the Spaniards were hard pressed, but superior artillery fire drove the attackers back. Galvez ordered that the ground be cleared for 1,000 yards around the camp to deny the Indians any cover from which to launch surprise attacks. He also was able to have some Indians from the Mobile area brought to his camp to counter those fighting with the British.

On 19 April a mixed Franco-Spanish fleet arrived from Havana with yet more reinforcements, bringing Galvez's army up to almost 7,500. Through the last half of April the Spanish strongpoint began to take shape, although Anglo-Indian attacks and bombardment from the Queen's Redoubt slowed the work. The British began strengthening the works around their advanced position in spite of Spanish attacks against their positions. By 2 May, however, the Spaniards had a 2,000-foot trench line dug across the crest of their high ground and anchored it with three redoubts. The strongest battery, in the center, held six 24-pounders and four mortars. The position on the northern flank held two 8-pounders and two 4-pounders, while the southern redoubt held two 4-pounders.

An artillery duel ensued between the new Spanish positions and the Queen's Redoubt, with both sides scoring effectively. On 2 May the Spanish began work on another trench running eastward from their northern flank, with the intent of establishing a new battery closer to the Queen's Redoubt. Just as it was being completed, however, at midday on 4 May a surprise attack caught the Spanish eating lunch. A mixed Anglo-German force managed to spike several cannon, then withdraw with a loss of but one killed and

one wounded. The Spanish went back to work on the position, and Galvez decided on the 7th that it was time to launch an assault on the Queen's Redoubt from that location. On the 8th Galvez's men were in position while his artillery softened up the target. Just before 0900, a Spanish shell landed at the door of the British magazine in the Queen's Redoubt, and the resulting explosion caused about 100 casualties. The Spaniards were quick to exploit the advantage and quickly occupied the fort. As this was the highest ground in the neighborhood, and it dominated the other two British positions, General Campbell knew he was undone.

Results

The formal surrender of the British garrison took place in mid-afternoon on 10 May 1781. Sources vary in their casualty reports, with the Spanish losing just under 100 killed and about 200 wounded. The British lost just over 200 killed, wounded, and deserted, with just over 1,100 prisoners. The Spaniards also took possession of 4 mortars, 143 cannon, 6 howitzers, and 40 swivel guns, as well as numerous muskets and a large amount of powder and explosives. The British were allowed full military honors, then were evacuated via Havana to New York.

For his work, Galvez was honored by Spanish King Carlos III. He was named Count de Galvez, promoted yet again, and made governor of West Florida in addition to his current position as governor of Louisiana. He began operations against British shipping in the Bahamas and was preparing an invasion of Jamaica when the war came to an end.

The loss of Pensacola meant the loss of the entire coast of the Gulf of Mexico for the British, and Campbell was obliged to surrender all of West Florida to Galvez, who at this point controlled most of the region between the Appalachian Mountains and the Mississippi River below the Ohio River. That proved vital to American interests when they sat down with British, French, and Spanish negotiators in Paris to discuss peace terms in 1782. The British had hoped to limit the United States to that area between the Appalachians and the Atlantic coast, but since they did not possess the land west of there they could not stop American expansion. Spain also hoped to keep that land for themselves, but really did not have the manpower or administrative ability to occupy it. Most went to the Americans outright in the Treaty of Paris of 1783, although that area comprising modern Alabama and Mississippi was not completely American until the Jay Treaty of 1795.

While the weaponry and supplies the Spanish government provided to the revolutionaries in the United States certainly aided in the winning of independence, Galvez's actions up the Mississippi River and along the Gulf coast was vital for future American expansion westward.

References: John Walton Caughey, *Bernardo de Galvez in Louisiana, 1776–1783* (Gretna, LA: Pelican, 1972 [1934]); William Coker and Hazel Coker, *The Siege of Pensacola 1781 in Maps* (Pensacola, FL: Perdido Bay, 1981); Lorenzo LaFarelle, *Bernardo de Galvez, Hero of the American Revolution* (Austin, TX: Eakin, 1992); Nixon Orwin Rush, *The Battle of Pensacola* (Tallahassee: Florida State University Press, 1966).

YORKTOWN

DATE: September–17 October 1781.
LOCATION: on the coast of the (U.S.) state of Virginia, at the mouth of Chesapeake Bay.

FORCES ENGAGED:
British: approximately 6,000 British troops and Hessian mercenaries. Commander: General Lord Cornwallis.
American and French: approximately 8,800 Americans and 7,000 French troops. Commander: General George Washington.

IMPORTANCE:
Franco-American defeat of British forces proved to be the last major battle of the American Revolution.

Historical Setting

After the American victory at Saratoga in the autumn of 1777, the fledgling United States was finally recognized by France, followed soon thereafter by Spain and the Netherlands. This recognition, and the alliance that came with it, gave the American rebels the material resources necessary to match the moral resources displayed by such leaders as George Washington. In the summer of 1778, Washington's forces reoccupied Philadelphia after British forces under General William Howe were ordered back to New York City. Howe's removal from command soon thereafter brought his subordinate, General Henry Clinton, into power.

Clinton had to this point shown no indication that he would aggressively pursue the war against the Americans. Instead, he spent most of his time fortifying New York City against the attack he was convinced Washington was going to launch. Thus, for the two years following the rebels' reoccupation of Philadelphia, the war remained rather low-key. In the summer of 1780 Clinton attempted to conspire with disaffected American General Benedict Arnold to acquire the major American fort at West Point on the Hudson River. That effort failed and Clinton spent his time improving his defenses. In the meantime, Washington spent his time trying to improve the caliber of the Continental Army, equip it with the supplies arriving from Europe, and begin planning with the French forces arriving under the command of the Comte de Rochambeau.

As Washington was focusing on organizational concerns in the northern states (Rhode Island and Connecticut), Clinton decided to refocus the British effort. To this point they had been singularly unsuccessful in any strategy to defeat the Revolution. They had been unable to

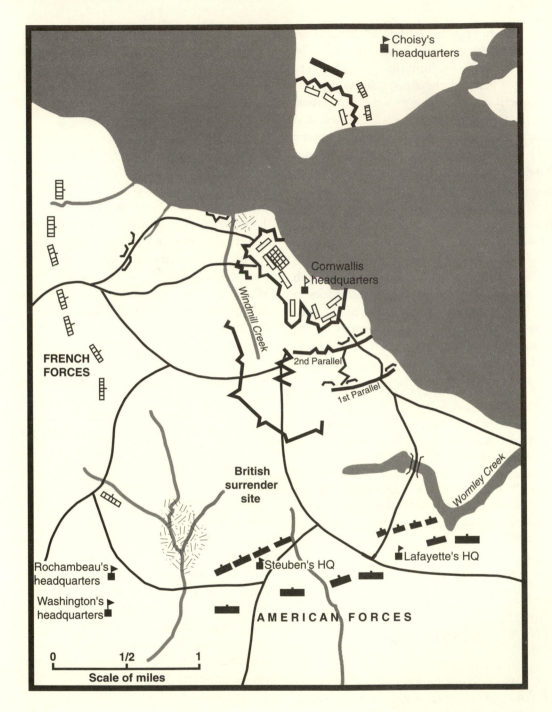

Choisy's headquarters

Cornwallis headquarters

Windmill Creek

2nd Parallel

1st Parallel

FRENCH FORCES

Wormley Creek

British surrender site

Lafayette's HQ

Rochambeau's headquarters

Steuben's HQ

Washington's headquarters

AMERICAN FORCES

0   1/2   1
Scale of miles

split the colonies by controlling the Hudson River during Burgoyne's 1777 Saratoga campaign, nor were they able to accomplish the same purpose by dealing with Arnold. Howe's attempt to crush the uprising by capturing Philadelphia had proven likewise unproductive. Since capturing New York City in the late summer of 1776, the British war effort had for the most part gone nowhere. Therefore, Clinton decided to shift arenas. Instead of fighting in the north, where revolutionary fervor was the greatest, he sent forces to the southern states, where the percentage of loyalists was much higher. By occupying these states, he could roll the Revolution up from the south, isolating the Continental Army in the north.

In order to implement this new strategy, Clinton sent Lord Cornwallis to South Carolina in the summer of 1780. His orders were to take advantage of the loyalist population and occupy the Carolinas and Virginia. The loyalists would, he thought, be able to provide manpower and supplies to make this job relatively simple. Further, the revolutionaries had few troops in the southern states, so fighting would be minimal. From the start this plan went wrong. The landing near Charleston was not too difficult and Cornwallis was able to force the rebels under General Benjamin Lincoln to give up Charleston. However, as the occupation took place fires broke out in the city, although who was responsible has never been determined. Still, it was an inauspicious beginning.

Next, Cornwallis refused to follow Clinton's directives to make maximum use of local support. Instead, he often rebuffed attempts by South Carolinians to join or assist his army. Cornwallis began making enemies of friends, just as Burgoyne had done in upstate New York when he employed Indians and Hessians against the population there. As Cornwallis was settling in, area revolutionary forces began operations. Small groups of militia under commanders such as Francis Marion harassed British outposts and supply trains. They provoked harsh responses from Cornwallis and his subordinates, which also served to alienate local support.

Cornwallis marched out of Charleston convinced that he could easily occupy the Carolinas. The Continental Congress dispatched Horatio Gates to command the revolutionary forces, but he immediately lost a key battle at Camden, South Carolina. Recalled by the government, Washington replaced Gates with Nathaniel Greene, whose ingenuity was well suited to the guerrilla warfare he needed to conduct against Cornwallis.

There were occasional firefights or skirmishes through the winter of 1780–1781, but nothing decisive for either army. Cut off from his base of operations, Cornwallis had to live off the countryside, and his high-handed attitude and use of Hessians in requisitioning supplies did nothing to endear him to the people. When he did call for loyalists to join his army, they responded in smaller numbers than he had expected. Greene on the other hand tried to pay for supplies, although all he had were IOUs of dubious value from the Continental Congress. Still, it was better treatment than the British were displaying. The British Army grew ragged and frustrated as supplies became more difficult to acquire; Cornwallis marched to Wilmington, North Carolina, to resupply and pick up reinforcements.

From Wilmington Cornwallis marched into Virginia in the spring of 1781. British forces under turncoat Benedict Arnold had been operating there for a few months, but with little positive effect. After a few more months of circuitous marching and little concrete results, Cornwallis marched to the coast. He had been ordered by Clinton to establish a base for the Royal Navy to bring in more men and supplies, and Cornwallis began building facilities at Yorktown, on a peninsula flanked by the York and James rivers.

In the meantime, Washington had convinced the reluctant Rochambeau to aid him in an assault on New York City. Washington's plan called for the French fleet in the Caribbean to bottle up the Royal Navy in New York harbor while the Franco-American army forced their way through Clinton's defenses. Rochambeau warned Admiral de Grasse that he disliked this plan and preferred operating in the south. Admiral de Grasse complied with Rochambeau's wishes, telling Washington that the French fleet would go no farther north than the Chesapeake. That information, plus his own intelligence concerning the strength of the British defensive positions, convinced Washington to accede to Rochambeau's suggestion for a campaign in Virginia.

Washington was aided at this point by what, under other circumstances, would seem to be a severe misfortune. He had sent details of his plans for an attack on New York City to his friend the Marquis de Lafayette, commanding troops in Virginia. The British had captured that letter, however, and Clinton was preparing for the assault he now knew was coming. Washington, who began disseminating disinformation, further convinced Clinton that an attack was imminent. When French forces demonstrated near New York, covering Washington's passage into New Jersey, Clinton braced for an assault that never came. By the time he realized there would be no attack, both Washington and Rochambeau were well on their way to Virginia.

The Siege

While American forces under Greene and Lafayette kept an eye on Cornwallis, a French fleet under the Comte de Grasse was sailing north from the Caribbean. It arrived in late August at the mouth of the Chesapeake. Clinton in New York had heard reports of this, but dismissed them as rumors. Once the report was confirmed a British fleet under Admiral Thomas Graves sailed for the Chesapeake. There he found twenty-four French ships of the line, outnumbering his own nineteen. On 5 September the two fleets engaged, with de Grasse positioning himself in such a way as to deny the British access into the bay. After a few hours of cannonade, the British received the worst of the damage. Although they remained in the neighborhood for another three days, when Graves sailed for New York to repair his damaged ships he signed the death warrant of Cornwallis's force.

When Washington and Rochambeau arrived and joined forces with Lafayette, their combined force numbered almost 16,000, more than twice that of Cornwallis. They began digging trenches that slowly but surely inched their way toward the redoubts around which the British were basing the defense of their position. With superior numbers and artillery, the Americans were able to severely punish the defenders, who could do little to respond. The constant

pressure proved too much for the British to withstand. Cornwallis attempted an escape across the York River, but was undone by bad weather. On the night of 15 October the two British redoubts were attacked. The French took the larger one after a short but intense fight; the Americans took the smaller one in ten minutes with few casualties.

Although Cornwallis ordered a raid on the new rebel positions, it was too little and too late. On 17 October he asked for surrender terms. He had held his position on the assumption that Clinton was sending reinforcements from New York. How they would break through the French fleet is a matter of conjecture, but Graves was prepared to give battle a second time. When he finally set sail from New York harbor it was 17 October.

Results

Cut off from any serious hope of relief, unable to withstand the bombardment, unable to maintain his troops with the winter approaching, Cornwallis had no choice but to surrender. He proposed that he and his men be paroled, on condition of not taking up arms in America again, but Washington demanded surrender as prisoners of war. On the 19th Cornwallis' second in command, Brigadier General Charles O'Hara, rode out at the head of 6,000 men to surrender. The march from Yorktown to Washington's headquarters was certainly the longest the surrendering soldiers ever took, for it was gross humiliation to be defeated by colonials. O'Hara tried at first to surrender to Rochambeau, but that attempt at avoiding the Americans in favor of a fellow-European failed. When he offered his sword to Washington, he was again rebuffed. As second in command, he had to surrender to Washington's second in command, Benjamin Lincoln.

Cornwallis and Clinton spent the next months and years blaming each other for the disaster. Clinton got the worst of it, and his career was ruined. Cornwallis was received in

England as a hero and went on to redeem himself in an outstanding performance in India soon afterward. The English public was tired of the war by this time. When the news of Yorktown reached London, the government was unable to survive. In the spring of 1782 the newly elected leadership offered to negotiate a peace and talks began in Paris in September. They went on for a year before the Treaty of Paris of 1783 was signed. In this the London government recognized American independence, established the borders of the United States as the Atlantic Ocean to the Mississippi River and the Great Lakes to the northern border of Florida. In return for assistance rendered the Revolution by the Spanish (particularly their governor in New Orleans Bernardo De Galvez) the Spanish received Florida, which they had surrendered to the English in the Treaty of Paris 1763 at the end of the French and Indian/Seven Years War.

The defeat at Yorktown ended the British experience in America, although they maintained the colony of Canada. They tried in Paris to claim all the territory west of the Appalachian Mountains, which would have limited U.S. expansion severely for decades. Hostilities between the two nations did not end, however, for the British were slow to abandon some of their forts in the Great Lakes region and even slower to give the fledgling country any respect on the high seas. Restrictive trade practices between 1805 and 1812 led to a second war between the Americans and the British, after which relations eased considerably. Had Cornwallis escaped the Yorktown peninsula prior to Washington's arrival in late September he would have delayed the end of the war for a time, but the length of the war and its interminable drain on the British economy and psyche almost certainly would have brought about a similar end to the war before long. Without Cornwallis' defeat, however, the American bargaining position in London would have been considerably weaker and the conditions gained in the treaty may well have restricted American growth for a long time to come.

The French effort in the Yorktown campaign cannot be overemphasized, and the results of the war were felt there as well. The huge expenditures King Louis XVI had spent in behalf of the United States sapped the nation's treasury. The increasingly bad economy that resulted, in addition to the philosophy of liberty that many of the French soldiers embraced in America, led to their own revolution in 1789. Louis succeeded in harming his old enemy England, but ultimately paid for that success with his throne and his life.

References: Donald Barr Chidsey, *Victory at Yorktown* (New York: Crown, 1962); Burke Davis, *The Campaign That Won America* (New York: Dial, 1970); Christopher Hibbert, *Redcoats and Rebels* (New York: Norton, 1990); Howard Peckham, *The War for Independence: A Military History* (Chicago: University of Chicago Press, 1958); Page Smith, *A New Age Now Begins*, vol. 2 (New York: McGraw-Hill, 1976).

TOULON

DATE: 27 August–19 December 1793.
LOCATION: on France's Mediterranean coast, west of Marseilles.

FORCES ENGAGED:

French: 17,000 infantry and artillery. Commander: General J. F. Carteaux, then General Jean-François Coquille Dugommier.
Allied: 17,000 British, Spanish, and allied troops. Commander: Admiral Sir Samuel Hood.

IMPORTANCE:

France's recapture of Toulon reasserted the power of the revolutionary government in southern France; it also marked Napoleon Bonaparte's first major action.

Historical Setting

The French Revolution got off to a glorious start on 14 July 1789, but by late 1792 many

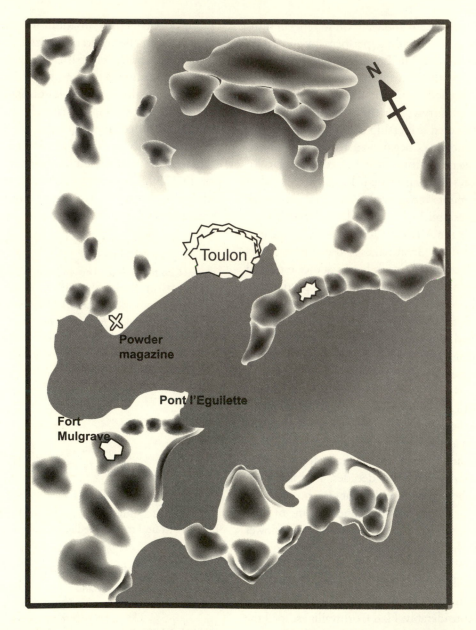

in France were beginning to miss the monarchy. Rather than allow King Louis XVI to be restored to power, the revolutionary government executed him in January 1793, along with his wife, children, relatives, and friends. The Reign of Terror wiped out almost everyone of royal blood and thousands who favored the monarchy. Such an action struck fear into the hearts of kings all across Europe and they banded together to invade France, crush the Revolution, and find some surviving member of the house of Bourbon to enthrone. The revolutionary government

responded by instituting the *levee en masse*, the modern world's first national conscription. That action, coupled with the increasing government interference in the affairs of the Catholic Church in France, inspired parts of the country into counter-revolution. Discontented rumblings were heard along France's Mediterranean coast, and during the night of 16–17 August 1793, the port city of Toulon invited in a combined Anglo-Spanish fleet.

If Toulon were not reoccupied, the Revolution would suffer a serious blow to its prestige, as well as cede a major port of entry for foreign troops. While French troops hurried to the city, so too did foreign forces and within a few weeks 17,000 Spanish, British, Piedmontese, Neapolitan, and French royalists occupied the forts surrounding the city. A few dozen Spanish and British warships, all under the command of the talented Admiral Sir Samuel Hood, supported the invasion force.

Colonel (later General) J. F. Carteaux marched on Toulon with 12,000 men, and he was soon joined by a further 4,000 from France's Army of Italy, commanded by General J. F. Lapoype. As Carteaux's forces approached from the west, he lost his artillery commander Captain Dommartin. As fate would have it, passing by the town on 16 September was a twenty-three-year-old artillery captain named Napoleon Bonaparte. He stopped to visit an acquaintance, Christopher Salicetti, who was the government's political officer assigned to the French force. Salicetti quickly nominated Napoleon to succeed Dommartin. Desperately in need of an experienced artillery officer, and afraid to offend the political officer, Carteaux named Napoleon to the position. It turned out to be a perfect match of talent and opportunity, and both the gunner and his country benefited from the appointment.

The Siege

Napoleon had recently been in his Corsican homeland and had sketched out a plan for the defense of its harbor; Toulon's situation was a remarkable match. He realized that the key to victory was control of the high ground of Mount Caire, which extended out to Point l'Eguilette, at the western harbor mouth. From there, both the city and the British fleet could be bombarded while controlling access to the harbor. Unfortunately, the assault he convinced Carteaux to launch against l'Eguilette was too weak to succeed and the British instead seized the point and placed their own strongpoint there, Fort Mulgrave. Carteaux's half-

hearted effort pointed up one of the major problems at Toulon: everyone with any rank at all had his own idea of how the siege should be conducted, and most were political appointees with no experience and little training. Things improved somewhat when Carteaux was transferred to Italy on 23 October, roughly the same time that Captain Bonaparte received his major's commission. After a short period under an equally inept political general, the experienced General Jean-François Dugommier arrived on 16 November.

During the shake-up Napoleon had been strengthening both his firepower and his tactical position. By hook or crook he had managed to acquire virtually every piece of artillery in the region until he possessed fifty-six cannon and six long-range mortars. These he placed in eleven batteries along a north-south line to the west of the harbor, eight batteries targeting the British position at Fort Mulgrave while two covered Fort Malbousquet on the northwestern corner of the harbor. On 25 November Napoleon persuaded General Dugommier to implement his plan: a feint at Mount Faron to the north of the city of Toulon, then a massive bombardment against Fort Mulgrave followed by a dawn assault.

Unfortunately, before the attack could be launched, the British sallied first. On 29 November a force swept out of Fort Malbousquet and overran the Battery of the Convention, anchoring the French left. They spiked its seven 24-pounders, but were unable to hold the position. Napoleon himself led the counterattack, which moved into position through a trench he had had dug to deliver supplies to the battery. Thus, his men were under cover until they burst into the British force, driving them back to their position while capturing General O'Hara, the commander of British army forces and acting military governor of Toulon. The failure to hold the French battery and the loss of their commander did nothing to enhance British morale in Toulon, which had been steadily declining as French forces increased.

With the solidification of his lines and the arrival of a reinforcing brigade under André Massena, Dugommier scheduled the French attack for 17 December. At dawn, following upon a massive bombardment, 6,000 men stormed Fort Mulgrave and captured it, losing 1,000 casualties in the process. Massena simultaneously captured Fort d'Artigues to the northeast of Toulon. With Point l'Eguilette in French possession, Napoleon swiftly brought up his guns and had them placed and ready the following afternoon. That was all it took. As soon as French guns opened fire on the British fleet, Admiral Lord Hood ordered his ships to sail. The primary powder magazine was exploded in Toulon, while British personnel and pro-monarchy French citizens boarded the ships to escape. At 0900 on 19 December the French revolutionary government officially reclaimed control of the city.

Results

The fate of the remaining citizens of Toulon is a matter of some dispute. In his memoirs, Napoleon claimed that a few hundred collaborators were shot after being tried by a revolutionary tribunal. Other sources disagree. According to British naval captain Sir William Sidney-Smith, who was one of the last of the British to leave the city, as well as author of *The Life of Bonaparte,* the ruling Convention in Paris ordered bloody vengeance to be visited upon the city. Sidney-Smith wrote that Napoleon directed his artillery against a mass of royalists herded into the town square. "The royalists and liberated convicts were driven into the great square of Toulon and were compressed together in one huge mass. Bonaparte, who then commanded the artillery, fired upon the people and mowed them down like grass. . . . the future Emperor of the French . . . exclaimed in a loud voice, 'The vengeance of the French Republic is satisfied—rise up and go to your homes,' which summons the people

no sooner attempted to obey than a second murderous discharge of his artillery hurled them into eternity" (Sidney-Smith, in Paschall, "Napoleon's First Triumph," pp. 14–15). The Convention ordered the city be renamed Port-au-Montagne.

Although Napoleon officially was relatively low on the chain of command during the siege, his planning and expertise were the true keys to success. Although the initial report to the government did not mention him, those immediately afterward made up for the oversight. General Jean Beaumont du Teil wrote to the minister of war, "I have no words to describe to you the worth of Bounaparte. . . . It is up to you, as Minister of War, to make use of him for the glory of the Republic" (Paschall, "Napoleon's First Triumph," p. 15). Napoleon was soon promoted to brigadier general, and powerful men in the government, including Robespierre, began to notice the young Corsican. When the government fell such associations landed Napoleon in jail for a time, but he had sufficient support from surviving notables that he was soon back in favor. The experience and notoriety he gained at Toulon aided him two years later when, as the current government was facing an angry mob in Paris, Napoleon's artillery again swept the streets and saved the day. Both of these experiences helped pave the way to his rise in government and eventual empire. Had Toulon remained in allied hands, the Revolution may well have faltered to the point of collapse; even had it not, Napoleon, worried about his family's poor economic situation, might well have left the army for a more lucrative job. As it was the promotion gave him not only political favor, but sufficient pay to guarantee his continued service.

References: David Chandler, *The Campaigns of Napoleon* (New York: Macmillan, 1966); Rod Paschall, "Napoleon's First Triumph," *Quarterly Journal of Military History* 12, no. 1, Autumn 1999; William Milligan Sloan, *The Life of Napoleon Bonaparte* (New York: Century, 1896).

GENOA

DATE: 20 April–4 June 1800.
LOCATION: on the upper northwestern Italian coast.

FORCES ENGAGED:

Austrian: 24,000 troops in the besieging force;
some 70,000 in the field. Commander:
General Karl Ott at Genoa, General Baron Michael
von Melas in the field.
British: unknown number of ships.
Commander: Admiral Lord Keith.
French: 36,000 soldiers. Commander:
Marshall André Massena.

IMPORTANCE:

Massena's defense delayed the Austrian offensive for
so long, that their intent of invading France never
came about; Napoleon's brilliant victory at Marengo
followed this battle.

Historical Setting

Napoleon burst onto the military scene in 1796–1797 with his brilliant campaign against the Austrian forces occupying northern Italy. His use of quick attacks on separated enemy forces was so speedy in its execution that the Austrians found themselves not only repeatedly defeated but thrown out of Italy in the spring of 1797. Napoleon soon after this campaign diverted his attention to Egypt, where his fortunes were not so bright. While he was engaged in his Middle East campaign, the Austrians seized the opportunity to reestablish their control in northern Italy. Through 1799 a combined Austro-Russian force ably commanded by General A. V. Suvarov swept French forces from northern Italy and threatened to invade France. Suvarov was transferred to the Rhine, leaving command of the Austrian army in northwestern Italy to General Baron Michael von Melas. On 7 November 1799, he defeated the last French field force outside Genoa.

Napoleon, who returned from Egypt and declared himself the sole ruler of France in 1799, was unprepared for this turn of events. He had an army along the Rhine poised for an invasion of Germany, and a reserve army forming in France to follow along, then drive southward across the Alps to strike the Austrian army's rear. Unfortunately for those plans, the pressing Austrian threat to the Franco-Italian frontier and the important port of Toulon shifted Napoleon's attention from Germany to Italy. The reserve army he was creating would be diverted directly to Italy, rather than follow behind the German invasion. As Napoleon was building up his force, he needed a diversion to keep Melas away from France. Thus, Napoleon sent one of his most trusted marshals, André Massena, to hold Genoa for as long as possible. For the Austrians, the capture of Genoa would give them all of Italy; for their allies the British, the subsequent offensive to capture Toulon would avenge their humiliating defeat there at Napoleon's hands in 1793.

Massena led his army into Italy in February 1800, taking command in Genoa on the 10th. Although Melas had the city open to him after his victory the previous November, he not invested it. Massena was able to lead 36,000 men to the coast, but was obliged to spread them thinly. The right wing under General Nicolas Jean Soult was three divisions strong. Massena based himself in Genoa with his headquarters and a small reserve, while the left wing under General Louis Suchet consisted of 12,000 men stretched out along the coast from the port town of Finale. Thus, 36,000 French troops tried to cover a line some 200 miles long. Melas' surprise attacks in early April proved too strong for any of Massena's divided forces to withstand. The Austrians soon split both Soult and Suchet from Massena in Genoa, leaving Massena a garrison of about 18,000 men. Melas continued his campaign to capture as many towns in the region as possible, leaving General Karl Ott in command of the 24,000 siege troops around Genoa in the third week in April.

The Siege

Genoa was a strong position. The city itself was enclosed by a single wall, with a second wall stretching across the several hills overlooking the city from the north. Forts and gun batteries strengthened the outer wall. The port was defended by strongpoints as well, with gunboats stationed at the harbor mouth. After a relatively peaceful winter, the inhabitants had assumed no siege was imminent, so food was not stockpiled. To make matters even worse, commissary contractors in Marseilles had cheated Massena and he had much less food than he had intended. Thus, the garrison and citizenry were in short supply from the outset, and the British naval blockade assured that no more would arrive. From the beginning of the siege, rations in the city were set at an ounce of bread per person, distributed through officially sanctioned shops. The only additional grain that entered the city was smuggled in by fast blockade-runners.

Before Ott's investment, Massena had been able to mount attacks from the city, and once the siege began he continued to keep as active as possible. In late April the Austrians launched a major attack against the outer line, almost capturing the key position of Fort Diamonte. Massena's troops used the bayonet to recapture their lost positions. On 10 May, Massena launched a daring attack against the Austrians designed to cover a breakout. The second column struck the Austrian rear at Nervi and seized some valuable foodstuffs for the city. On each of the forays and counterattacks, Massena's troops took prisoners. They could not be fed, so each was paroled on condition that they not take up arms against the French for six months. The officers kept their paroles, but Ott reassigned the enlisted men to other units in the siege. Many of the Austrians were thus captured multiple times, finally leading Massena to put his last batch of 3,000 prisoners aboard a hulk in the harbor where they were fed half the already starvation-level French ration. "The ration of the French was composed of a quarter pound of horrible bread and an equal quantity of horseflesh; so the prisoners got only half that quantity of each commodity. The siege lasted fifteen days longer. . . . at last, having eaten their shoes, knapsacks, pouches, and even, according to rumor, the bodies of some of their comrades, they nearly all died of starvation. There remained no more than 700 or 800 when the place was surrendered" (de Marbot, *Memoirs*, p. 102).

In the meantime, the Austrians kept up a steady bombardment through the day while the British ships pounded the city by night. By 14 May the citizens and troops were begging Massena to open negotiations, but a message smuggled in from Napoleon promised that aid was on the way and for the defenders to hold out as long as possible. Indeed, French troops by late May were entering the passes from Switzerland into Italy, but Massena could only hold out until 2 June. Melas was on the verge of ordering the siege ended so he could concentrate his forces against Napoleon's approaching army when Massena's representatives came through the lines. General Ott treated with them, and offered what were probably the most generous terms in all of history. Massena was allowed to dictate his own terms of surrender, as long as they included his arrest. He refused that condition, and the proximity of Napoleon's force obliged Ott to cede the point. "Massena did not wish that the document be called a 'capitulation', because, he said: 'I never surrender.' The Austrians even accepted this. 'Your defense', they declared, 'has been too heroic for us to deny you anything'" (Melegari, *Great Military Sieges*, p. 189).

Results

When the French troops departed Genoa on 4 June, they were escorted to the Var River to the west and released. They were not paroled and thus did not have to wait to rejoin the struggle against Austria. Massena's defense had served Napoleon well. By tying down so many Austrian troops, Melas was unable to launch the early invasion of France that he and the British had planned. Napoleon had time to get his Army of the Reserve organized and sent through the Alpine passes by late May. This was too late to save Genoa, of course, but by delaying Melas' ability to concentrate his forces, Napoleon was able to position himself for the battle he desired. The French army drove southeast, cutting off the lines of communication between Melas and Vienna, then they turned and drove on the Austrians near Allesandria. Although Napoleon was surprised by a much larger Austrian force than he had anticipated, he still scored one of his most famous victories at Marengo on 14 June 1800. Melas' surrender the next day guaranteed the French hold on Italy until Napoleon's final defeat fifteen years later at Waterloo.

References: David Chandler, *The Campaigns of Napoleon* (New York: Macmillan, 1966); Baron Jean-Baptiste de Marbot, *The Memoirs of Baron de Marbot*, trans. Arthur John Butler (London: Longman, Green, 1892); Vezio Melegari, *The Great Military Sieges* (New York: Crowell, 1972).

BADAJOZ

DATE: 17 March–6 April 1812.
LOCATION: on the Spanish-Portuguese border, roughly 100 miles west of Lisbon.

FORCES ENGAGED:

British: 51,000 men, 52 guns. Commander: General Sir Arthur Wellesley, the earl of Wellington.
French: 4,700 men, 140 guns. Commander: General Armand Philippon.

IMPORTANCE:

By capturing the city of Badajoz, the British took control of the passes into Spain from Portugal, beginning their invasion to take Spain from Napoleon.

Historical Setting

After Napoleon took control of Spain in 1808 and enthroned his brother Joseph in Madrid, French designs on Portugal intensified. Great Britain responded by sending troops to Portugal's aid. The British commander, General Sir Arthur Wellesley, Viscount Wellington, beat back every French invasion attempt for three years, then readied his own invasion out of Portugal into Spain. To do this he had but two viable paths into the country: Ciudad Rodrigo in the north and Badajoz in the south, both of which he needed to control in order to secure his rear from any possible French encircling attack. Both cities were strongly walled and manned and both had French armies in support: General Auguste Marmont behind Ciudad Rodrigo, Marshal Nicolas Soult at Badajoz.

In May and June 1811, while probing the French defenses around Ciudad Rodrigo, Wellington had sent his chief subordinate, General William Beresford, to relieve a French siege of the Portuguese defenders in Badajoz. By the time he arrived, the French had taken the city and Beresford was obliged to begin his own attack. Lacking sufficient engineers and without any siege guns, the effort proved futile. Wellington, famous for his attention to supply, failed in this instance to provide for his men and the French held on to the city.

Luckily for Wellington, Napoleon himself aided in the next British invasion. With his attention focused on Russia in 1811, Napoleon began withdrawing troops from Spain for his eastern offensive. Marmont's army of 45,000 was reduced by one-third, while Soult's force was ordered away from Badajoz to the south, to attack recalcitrant Spanish forces at Cadiz. Wellington first attacked and captured Ciudad Rodrigo (for which he received his earldom), then turned southward toward Badajoz. Napoleon, disbelieving the British would make such a move after the beating they had taken the previous year, ordered Marmont's remaining forces to

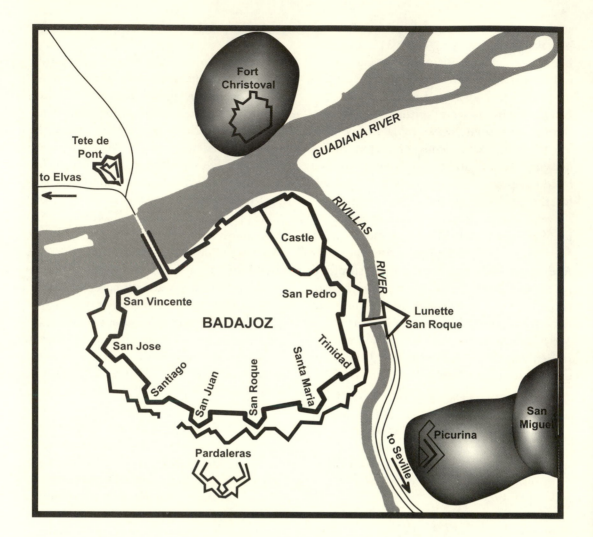

stay in the north and not march to aid Soult. Thus, when Wellington arrived before Badajoz in mid-March no mobile force was in the area.

Along the march the British had enlarged their force with a siege train that they met at Elvas, 12 miles from their target. On the 17th Wellington and his staff reconnoitered Badajoz, and what they saw was not encouraging. The 300-yard-wide Guadiana River bounded the northern rim of the city and could be crossed by only a single, well-fortified span with the Tete du Pont covering its approach. Overlooking that fort and the city across the river was Fort Christoval on high ground just to the east of Tete du Pont. Covering the eastern approach was a tributary of the Guadiana, the Rivillas

River. The city's castle was built overlooking the junction of the two rivers with the remainder of the city radiating outward like a fan and surrounded by 23-foot-high walls supporting eight 30-foot bastions positioned to give each other covering fire. Outside the walls was a deep ditch, and outside that was a counterscarp some 25 feet high. The Lunette St. Roque extended from the scarp on the eastern side, crossing the Rivillas. Two other forts controlled the southern approaches: Picurina to the southeast and Pardaleras to the south. Picurina was isolated on high ground, while Pardeleras was connected to the southern scarp.

Making the city even more formidable was the man in charge of the defense, General

Armand Philippon, known even to the British for his stubbornness. Upon hearing of the British success at Ciudad Rodrigo, he had ordered his men to dig a second ditch (a cunette) at the bottom of the existing one, deep enough to flood so as to drown attacking soldiers. He also had the Rivillas dammed just north of the lunette San Roque in order to create an impassable marsh between the lunette and the Guadiana. As the French were well supplied with food and weaponry, Wellesley's army faced an almost insurmountable task.

Although commanding 51,000 men and 52 heavy guns, Wellington lacked engineers experienced in dealing with such a powerful structure, and men used to sapping and mining fortress walls were unavailable. Wellington observed, "the truth is, that, equipped as we are, the British army are not capable of carrying on a regular siege" (Patten, "Iron Duke's Sad Victory," p. 52). Thus, flesh and blood would have to suffice where normal siege procedures were unavailable.

The Siege

Lieutenant Colonel Sir Richard Fletcher was Wellington's chief engineer. On his advice the British effort was to be directed against Fort Picurina. The western approach to the city, while uncovered by fortifications, was discovered to be heavily mined and therefore impractical. The previous year Beresford had tried to secure Fort Christoval in order to overlook the city and castle. Fletcher rejected that method after his reconnaissance. A breach in the southeastern wall seemed most practicable, and Fort Picurina had to be reduced in order to assault that section of the walls. On the night of 17 March, in a driving rainstorm, British soldiers began digging a parallel to position guns for the opening bombardment. At dawn the next morning a 600-yard trench stretched across the French front with a 1,300-yard communications trench zigzagging to the rear. As they

worked to improve the line, Philippon ordered a sally at noon that caused 150 British casualties and resulted in the French acquisition of more than 500 British picks and shovels. Digging recommenced, but frequent downpours kept the soldiers waterlogged.

By 24 March the rain finally stopped and the British artillery began pounding Fort Picarina the next day. That night Wellington ordered the fort assaulted and after a sharp fight the 230 defenders fled for the main walls of the city, only 32 successfully escaping. Almost two-thirds of the 500-man assault force were casualties, but the British owned Picarina and beat back Phillipon's counterattack. Possession of this outwork allowed the British to begin construction of their second parallel. Now a mere 400 yards away, British artillery began weakening the walls of the Trinidad and Santa Maria bastions.

Deducing the direction from which the British assault would come, Philippon began preparations. He had his men dig trenches just inside the walls to defend the breach when it was made. During the darkness he sent men to plant explosives in the outer ditch and to lay spiked planks. Just in front of where the walls would be breached, the French placed chevaux-de-frise (logs with rows of sword blades protruding). These were hidden each dawn and repositioned each night so the British were unaware of them.

As the artillery continued to weaken the walls, Wellington learned on 4 April that Soult's army was 60 miles away and marching toward Badajoz. Although he sent some men south to slow the French approach, he knew that the city had to be taken quickly if the British were to make sufficient repairs to be ready for Soult's assault. Before the British assault could be ordered, however, Wellesley was informed of Phillipon's preparations. In order to break through, a breach would have to be made in another section of the wall that could be attacked before French countermeasures could be taken. The wall chosen for attack was that between the battered Trinidad and Santa Maria bastions. When the breach was opened, diversionary attacks would begin against Fort Pardaleras, the Saint Vincente bastion, and from the north across the bridge. The San Roque bastion would also be attacked to keep it from delivering enfilading fire on the main assault, while another force would cross the Rivillas to scale the castle walls with 24-foot ladders.

The breach was made on the afternoon of 6 April and the assault was scheduled for 1930 that evening. Slow to position themselves, however, the British gave the French time to redeploy 250 men from the castle to the breach. When the assault began at 2130 the French were ready. As the leading element, the "forlorn hope," made their way silently into the ditch to place ladders across the cunette, the assault on San Roque started the battle. As British troops swarmed across the ditch toward the breaches, the French exploded their prepositioned powder casks. Almost 1,000 men found themselves blown up and back. In the resulting smoke and confusion, the second wave of British troops could not avoid the cunette, the spikes, or the chevaux-de-frise. The quickly increasing mass of bodies slowed the next waves, making them easy targets for French musketry. The British threw forty separate assaults at the breaches, none of which broke through.

In the wake of the failure of the primary attack, British hopes then devolved on the diversionary assaults. The assault on the castle met fierce resistance and was turned back, but the force commander, Sir Thomas Picton, threw in his reserves, which managed to replace the ladders and reach the top of the walls. Once on the heights, the British slowly took control of the castle and beat back a French counterattack. Philippon drew men from the San Vincente bastion to launch that counterattack, and the bastion was therefore weakened when General Sir James Leith's 5th Division charged it an hour after the main attack had been launched. They managed to scale the walls and enter the town. The presence of a British force inside the walls forced Philippon to abandon his defenses behind the breaches. With the remains of his men, just a few hundred soldiers, he abandoned the city, crossed the bridge across the Guadiana, and withdrew into Fort Christoval. The British accepted their surrender the next day.

Results

Philippon's defense of Badajoz cost the defenders 1,500 dead and the remaining 3,200 wounded and prisoners. They inflicted 4,000 casualties on the attacking British, however, as well as another 1,000 Portuguese killed and wounded in the attack on the Tete de Pont. In the ditches before the breached walls, in an area perhaps 100 yards on a side, lay 3,500 British troops dead and wounded. A British surgeon wrote, "There lay the burned and blackened corpses of those who had perished by the explosions, mixed with those that were torn to pieces by round-shot or grape, and killed by musketry, stiffening in the gore, body piled upon body, involved and intertwined into one hideous mass of carnage. The smell of burning flesh was yet shockingly strong and disgusting" (Glover, *Wellington's Peninsular Victories*, p. 52).

The sight was too much for the usually taciturn Wellington, who turned away in tears. That may account for his slow reaction to the insane plundering of the city over the next three days. One officer later wrote that the "infuriated soldiery resembled rather a pack of hell hounds vomited up from the infernal regions for the extirpation of mankind" (Patten, "Iron Duke's Sad Victory," *Military History*, p. 56). The soldiers were so intent on their revenge that they even attacked Wellington when he first tried to stop them. Construction of a gallows in the town square sent a clearer message to the troops, and they desisted.

As Marshall Soult approached from the south with 25,000 men, he encountered 31,000 that Wellington had dispatched to meet him. The French army withdrew to deal with further Spanish uprisings. From this point forward, Portugal would never feel a French threat. With the frontier firmly in his hands, Wellington launched his invasion of Spain. He held Badajoz with a garrison and marched out of Ciudad Rodrigo toward Madrid. In late July he encountered a French army under General Marmont and defeated it at Salamanca, forcing the French to temporarily abandon the Spanish capital. Wellington retreated into Portugal for winter quarters, however, but possession of the frontier fortresses made that move a secure one.

References: Michael Glover, *Wellington's Peninsular Victories* (London: B. T. Batsford, 1963); James Lawrence, *The Iron Duke* (London: Weidenfield and Nicolson, 1992); Frederick Myatt, *British Sieges of the Peninsular War* (New York: Hippocrene, 1987); David Patten, "Iron Duke's Sad Victory," *Military History* 8, no. 6, February 1992.

CUAUTLA

DATE: 18 February–2 May 1812.
LOCATION: approximately 40 miles southeast of Mexico City.

FORCES ENGAGED:
Revolutionary: unknown. Commander Jose Maria Morelos y Pavon.
Spanish Royalist: unknown. Commander: Felix Calleja del Rey.

IMPORTANCE:
Failure of the government forces to capture the garrison of Cuautla meant a long continuation of the Mexican revolution begun by Father Hidalgo.

Historical Setting

Since the days of the conquistador Hernan Cortés in the 1520s, Mexico had been a Spanish possession, a source of immense riches for the Spanish monarchy. By the early 1800s, however, Spain's wealth and power had long since dissipated. Napoleon Bonaparte, the new power in Europe, forced Spain to bow to his will. When the Spanish King Charles refused to follow directions, Napoleon deposed him and placed his own brother, Joseph Bonaparte, on the Spanish throne in 1808. A popular rising against the foreign king soon swept Spain.

The French occupation and the resulting rebellion had effects in Spain's colonies. The deposed King Charles wanted to maintain his empire but had no power to wield. In Spanish Mexico, liberal forces began to agitate for independence in the face of the empire's weakness. Conservative, powerful factions, including the Catholic Church and the military, did their best to maintain Spanish authority, but their long history of abusing the Mexican population, especially the Indians, proved too strong a motivation for the Mexican peasantry to resist. Under the leadership of Father Miguel Hidalgo they began a rebellion in 1810, more against the abuses of the upper classes than directly against Spanish authority.

The Hidalgo rising scored a number of early victories as intellectuals and some army officers joined the mass of Indians and mixed-race poor that swelled the rebel ranks. One of the men who rose to a position of leadership in the revolution was another liberal priest, Jose Maria Morelos y Pavon. Although he possessed no military training or experience, Morelos proved remarkably successful in launching surprise attacks that netted him captured weaponry and a reputation that began to attract recruits. His forces for a time controlled the countryside east of Acapulco, but he failed to capture that port city as Hidalgo had directed him to do.

When word came in 1811 that Spanish royalist forces had captured Hidalgo, Morelos stepped up to a leadership position. He had issued liberal documents banning slavery and the caste system in Mexico, so he had the revolutionary zeal and nature to succeed Hidalgo. When a junta of rebels was created in late summer 1811 in the wake of Hidalgo's execution, Morelos refused to join it. Acting independently, preferring military to political activities, he decided to target Mexico City, but royalist forces were scoring successes around the country and were determined to defend the country's capital city. With the assistance of two able subordinates, Mariano Matamoros and Hermenegildo Galeana, Morelos divided his forces and swept through the region south of Mexico City, gathering supplies and weapons. After defeating a royalist force outside Puebla, Morelos marched his troops northwestward toward Mexico City, reaching the town of Cuautla Amilpas on Christmas Day.

In the capital, Viceroy Vicente Venegas sent General Felix Calleja del Rey to capture the town and eliminate Morelos and his force. Calleja del Rey first captured the town of Zitacuaro, where the junta had established itself, and forced their rapid evacuation to Sultepec. With that victory under their belts, the royalist force marched toward Cuautla. By 17 February 1812, they were 6 miles away at the village of Pasulco, where Calleja established a base of operations. The following day his troops occupied the chapel of Calvario on the northern outskirts of Cuautla, and the siege was on.

The Siege

Cuautla was readily defensible, situated as it was on the crest of a hill with no higher elevations near at hand to threaten it. The Juchitengo stream flowed nearby, providing the town with its water supply. Morelos had spent the previous weeks strengthening the town's defenses, although the walls were of little use. Instead, he got the local population to dig trenches around the key stone buildings, mainly the convents that occupied plazas linked by the town's main street. To the north was the convent San Diego and San Domingo was to the south. The defense of these strong points was given to Galeana and Leonardo Bravo respectively. Newly dug ditches also covered the relatively weak town walls. A good supply of artillery was placed strategically around town.

The first action came almost immediately upon Calleja's arrival, for Morelos was determined to reconnoiter the Cavaleria church. He led a small cavalry force out of the town to the church, where he engaged a royalist force. Morelos' men were about to have the worst of the encounter when Galeana led reinforcements to rescue them.

The following day Calleja ordered his grenadiers to storm the walls, which they quickly breached near the Plaza de San Diego. Accurate artillery fire broke up the attack and drove the royalists back, followed closely by the insurgents. Galeana killed the grenadier commander in a duel, and the remainder of the royalists fled. A cavalry charge by Calleja's dragoons the next day also entered the town, but they were driven back by the heroism of a thirteen-year-old boy who manned an abandoned cannon. After this Calleja settled down to starve out the defenders. He sent to Mexico City for more men and supplies.

The arrival of another division of troops under General Cirico Llano allowed Calleja to place artillery around the town and maintain a steady bombardment. Although many of the town's buildings were hit, the morale of the defenders and citizens remained high. Work crews quickly repaired damage and children gathered unexploded shells. After four days the royalist commander tried a ploy, contacting an insurgent battery commander and convincing him to defect. At the last minute the artilleryman was attacked by his conscience and reported the plan to Galeana. When a band of royalists approached to meet the supposed traitor, they were shot to pieces.

The intense fighting and resultant casualties in the town had strained the water supply, and Calleja's next gambit was to divert the Jachitengo. A week's digging in late March accomplished the task, and Morelos' attempts to reach the water for resupply were beaten back. On 3 April, however, he launched an attack under Nicolas Bravo (Leonardo's brother) which kept Calleja busy, while Galeana with 500 men built a tower on the river bank and connected it to the town with entrenchments. Two royalist attacks against the tower were thrown back. In the wake of this feat, Morelos could not stop himself from gloating. He sent a message to Calleja tied to a donkey's tail, which read in part: "[We] know what is needed and will not be bamboozled by your dispatches and lying papers. I suppose, Senor Calleja, you will see to it that other Big Wigs come to destroy this brave division, but Petticoats will never get into these parts; and if they want to come, let them come, and while I perform my duties, send me some little bombs because I am sad without them" (Caruso, *Liberators of Mexico*, p. 110).

Calleja developed a grudging respect for the defenders, but he had the time and resources to wait them out. By late April food supplies in Cuautla were running dangerously short. Cats, rats, and lizards became the diet, with snails and grasshoppers soon to follow. Only the capture of a stray ox temporarily relieved the famine. With a bit of morale restored, Morelos launched a sally against a royalist battery on 27 April. The guns were easily captured, but a cache of food diverted the insurgent raiders and they failed to see Calleja's counterattack until too late. The next day Calleja ordered a cease-fire while offering a pardon to the defenders. Morelos refused, but he knew the defense could not last much longer. In the early morning hours of 2 May, Morelos quietly led his men out of town. With a handful of civilians they took what supplies they still had and sneaked past Calleja's lines, crossed the Juchitengo on rafts, and headed south. When Calleja learned the following morning of the escape, he quickly burned the town in a rage and then force-marched his men after the retreating Morelos. A battle ensued at a hacienda a few hours away. Finding themselves surrounded, the insurgents dispersed and made their escape as best they could individually.

Results

Calleja claimed victory, but it was hollow. His force was badly strained by the siege and he withdrew toward Mexico City. Morelos temporarily reoccupied Cuautla, then went on a spree throughout south-central Mexico. Establishing a headquarters at Tehucacán, Morelos' growing forces soon occupied the countryside from Vera Cruz to Acapulco, leaving royalist forces in control only of the major cities. His capture and destruction of the regional tobacco harvest robbed the government of its source of income to pay its troops. In August 1812 Acapulco fell and later in the fall Morelos' troops occupied the southern province of Oaxaca.

Morelos ruled the occupied provinces, issuing laws, collecting taxes, and appointing administrators. He also sponsored a constitutional convention in the small mountain town of Chilpancingo. An extremely liberal document resulted, but the call for the simultaneous destruction of the power of the Church, the military, and the large landowners alienated too much of the middle class. Further, the Congress that was created proved too focused on power than justice, to the detriment of Morelos' cause. Calleja, who was named viceroy in early 1813, drew on that unease to finance a larger army. He first crushed any insurgency in the north, then in the latter part of the year turned to the south. Starting on Christmas Day, the royalists began a virtually unbroken string of victories. In October 1815 Morelos was captured and turned over to the Inquisition. After a forty-six-day interrogation, he was stripped of his clerical authority and turned over to the government for execution, which was carried out on 22 December. "He was the one man who had a chance of making a constructive revolution. He joined a growing pantheon of Mexican martyrs. His death was the most tragic of all for Mexico, because his ideals were buried with his bones" (Fehrenbach, *Fire and Blood*, p. 341).

References: John Anthony Caruso, *Liberators of Mexico* (New York: Pageant, 1954); T. R. Fehrenbach, *Fire and Blood* (New York: Macmillan, 1973); Hugh Hamill, *The Hidalgo Revolt* (Gainesville: University of Florida Press, 1970).

CARTAGENA

DATE: 20 August–6 December 1815.
LOCATION: Colombia's Caribbean coast, approximately 200 miles northeast of the Colombia–Panama border.

FORCES ENGAGED:

Insurgents: 3,700 men, predominantly militia. Commander: General Manuel del Castillo, later General Francisco Bermúdez. Royalists: 11,000 men. Commander: General Pablo Morillo.

IMPORTANCE:

Spanish capture of Cartagena proved to be their last major success in their attempt to regain rebelling South American colonies.

Historical Setting

The French Revolution, Napoleon's rise in Europe, and the enthronement of his brother Joseph Bonaparte in Spain had far-reaching effects in Spain's western hemisphere colonies. First, the principles of the French Revolution, following closely on the American Revolution, established in Central and South America a movement to break away from the power of Spain's monarchy. Unfortunately, the goals of the colonial population differed depending on socioeconomic status. The lower classes and slaves looked forward to liberty, equality, and fraternity as preached by the French Revolution, but the upper class *creoles* (ethnic Spaniards born in the Americas) desired only the removal of royal power without a major social upheaval. When Joseph Bonaparte ascended the Spanish throne in 1808 and the reigning monarch Ferdinand VII was imprisoned, the resulting revolution in Spain against the foreign ruler was soon duplicated in Spain's colonies. While some of the Latin American cities and provinces maintained their loyalty to Spain, many of the others only gave lip service to restoring Ferdinand to the throne. They were more intent on declaring independence from all of Europe, not just from the usurper Bonaparte.

While the Bonapartes ruled, the Latin American colonies began exercising their own political will, but the conflict between creoles and the lower classes meant that stable governments were not always established. Thus, when Ferdinand was restored to power in 1813 in the wake of British victories in Spain, Latin America had few populations that could mount a united effort against Spain's attempt to reestablish colonial authority. A few cities remained loyal to Spain, but these became the targets of South America's "Liberator," Simon Bolívar, and his revolutionary associates. Thus, a three-way struggle among Spaniards, creoles, and the mixed race/Indian populations ensued. During the interregnum the viceroyalty of New Granada (modern Venezuela, Colombia, Ecuador, and northern Peru) had declared itself the United Provinces of New Granada. Bolívar had aided in the removal of Spanish authorities in the capital city of Bogotá, but when he learned a Spanish expedition was sailing to reassert Ferdinand's authority he abandoned the squabbling factions and fled for Jamaica, from where he planned the next phase of the revolution.

Ferdinand's reconquest began in Venezuela in early 1815. He sent a force of veterans from the campaigns against the French under the command of General Pablo Morillo. Morillo quickly relieved the pro-Spanish coastal city of Santa Marta, then began pushing southwest

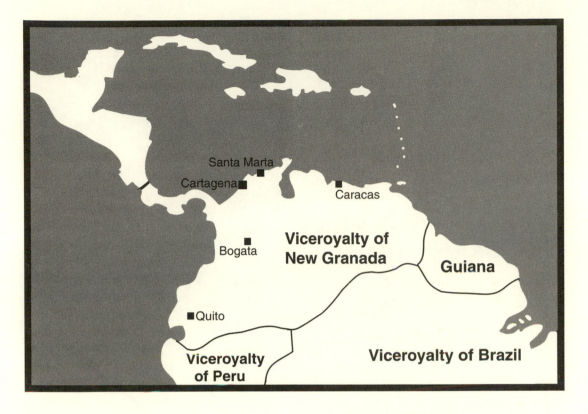

down the coast toward the major port of Cartagena. With that city in hand, he would have a major base for supply and reinforcement for his campaign to recapture Bogotá. His force numbered approximately 8,000 Spanish soldiers and 3,000 Venezuelan Royalists. Morillo's force sailed into sight of Cartagena on 18 August and two days later landed at the village of Puntacanoa.

The Siege

Cartagena was originally established in 1533. The site was one of the largest harbors in South America, sufficiently large "that in Colonial days it was said that all the fleets of the world could find anchorage there" (Whyte, *Seven Treasure Cities*, p. 73). The only serious drawback to the location was an absolute absence of a supply of drinking water; the construction of cisterns in the city walls sufficed until the early twentieth century. The site became one of the terminals of the Spanish treasure fleets that

removed the plunder of the Americas back to Spain. For that reason, it soon became the target of invaders.

The first was the French pirate Robert Baal in 1544. The wooden palisades originally constructed to defend against Indians began to be replaced by stone. After Sir Francis Drake captured and looted the city in 1585, more serious work began on the strengthening of stone walls and forts. The fortifications were only completed, however, after yet another sack of the city by the French Baron de Pointe in 1695. The fortifications completed in the early eighteenth century were sufficient to withstand a major assault in 1741 by British naval forces under Admiral Edward Vernon. That victory gave the local population the confidence in their defenses and in themselves that motivated them in the face of Morillo's approach.

When, on 4 August 1815, news of Morillo's capture of Santa Marta arrived in Cartagena, the city swung into action. General Manuel del Castillo took command of the city, established martial law, and called into service all able

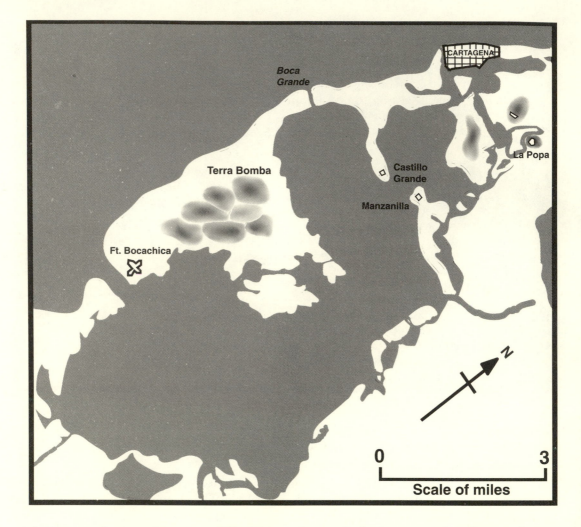

males between the ages of sixteen and fifty. This brought the defense to a strength of 3,700 men, over one-sixth the city's population. Nearby towns and haciendas were burned to deny their cover and resources to the attackers. The citizens donated their wealth for the cost of defense, and many of the treasures of the Church were melted down for their silver and gold. The defenders possessed sixty-six cannon, and these were placed in various locations: on the high ground of La Popa, the castle of San Felipe, the fort of Santa Catalina, and Fort Bocachica. In addition, armed rafts, canoes, and ships prepared to defend the harbor.

General Morillo commanded infantry, cavalry, artillery, and engineers, along with a naval contingent of a man-of-war, two frigates, and other minor vessels. Morillo was a veteran, well known for his bravery and intelligence, but not for his diplomacy. "If a superior military mind, intrepid valor, and steadiness in the enterprise confided to him had been sufficient qualifications, no doubt Morillo would have satisfied the monarch's intention. . . . The mission to be accomplished was of a different character: it was the reconciliation of discontented subjects with their sovereign, and for this Morillo was evidently not the man" (Hennau and Arrubla, *History of Colombia*, p. 270). Neither was this condition met in Morillo's choice to command a Royalist Venezuelan contingent of 3,500: Brigadier Francisco Morales, known to the region as "the terror of the Americans."

Morillo kept his ships at the entrances to the harbor rather than confront the maritime defenses, while his army proceeded to cut

Cartagena off from outside aid. The fighting was relatively light, but the condition of the besieged gradually worsened. After a failed attempt to break through the blockade, General Castillo was removed from command on 17 October and replaced by General Francisco Bermudez. Later that month the Spanish began a regular bombardment of the city with good effect. On 11 November, the fourth anniversary of the city's declaration of independence, Morillo tried to take advantage of the city's celebration. In the darkness he pushed 800 men up the slopes of La Popa, but in the ensuing hand-to-hand combat the 200 defenders pushed the attackers back down the slope. A coordinated assault against Fort Angel was also unsuccessful, but the Spanish were able to force some ships into the harbor. They established a battery on Tierrabomba Island that increased the artillery pressure on the city. Morillo burned anything that might be of use to smugglers taking supplies to the city, then killed all the island's inhabitants.

Even without direct assaults on the city, the blockade was sufficient to do the besiegers' work. The city officials had refused to expel noncombatants, and the city population (swelled by the fleeing neighborhood farmers) proved too great a drain on the city's resources. Death came to the defenders through both starvation and the diseases it caused. The inhabitants began eating anything and everything: "Rotten meat and flour, rancid codfish, horses, mules, burros, dogs, rats, and skins were the diet of the majority. . . . Foreign speculators profiteered without mercy, exchanging hidden deposits of food for the jewelry which was in the city" (Henao and Arrubula, *History of Colombia*, p. 272). Soldiers and civilians alike died, both sharing the same privations.

Weakness meant that the increasing number of dying could not be buried, spreading disease even more quickly. Dead bodies lay everywhere. Fear of Spanish retribution kept most from surrender until late November, when desperation forced some 2,000 to risk the consequences. The besiegers were so shocked at the condition of those surrendering that they punished none of them. One of the city leaders proposed sending the civilian population out, then setting off the city's powder magazines as the Spanish entered the city. "Thus would be 'sealed' the immortality of a people, who, like the inhabitants of Numantia, had been invincible in defense and sublime in death" (Henao and Arrubula, *History of Colombia*, p. 273). On 5 December, Morillo offered the king's clemency, but those with enough strength to flee tried to make their escape by sea. They spiked their cannon and took to their boats, but storms and Spaniards took their toll and no more than 600 reached freedom in the Antilles.

Results

Morillo's forces entered Cartagena on 6 December, after 106 days of siege. The city, numbering at the outset approximately 15,000 people, had been reduced by sickness, starvation, and combat to half that number. Morillo decided that the king's clemency would be to execute another 4,700. The Spanish force during the siege had suffered some 3,000 deaths and an equal number sick.

King Ferdinand ordered a thanksgiving Mass celebrated to honor the capture of the city, and General Morillos was promoted to Count of Cartagena. The Inquisition, dismantled at the declaration of independence, was quickly reestablished. Although Spain once again ruled the city, the occupation was relatively brief. The tides of revolution had swept over too much of South America for Spain to reassume control, and rebel forces recaptured Cartagena in 1821. By then Spanish rule was collapsing throughout the hemisphere, and all of Latin America broke free with the exception of Puerto Rico and Cuba. Morillo's occupation of Cartagena proved to be one of the few successes of Spain's attempted reconsolidation of power.

References: David Bushnell, *The Making of Modern Colombia* (Berkeley: University of California Press, 1993); Jesús María Henao and Gerardo Arrubula, *History of Colombia*, trans. J. Fred Rippy (Chapel Hill: University of North Carolina Press, 1938); Bertha Whyte, *Seven Treasure Cities of Latin America* (New York: October House, 1964).

ATHENS (ACROPOLIS)

DATE: 15 August 1826–5 June 1827.
LOCATION: eastern Greece.

FORCES ENGAGED:
Greek: 500 men, later reinforced up to 2,000. Commanders: Simeon Zacharitasas, Neroutsos Metselos, and Yannis Makriyannis.
Turkish: 30,000 men. Commander: Reshid Pasha.
Relief forces: 18,000 men. Commanders: Admiral Lord Cochrane overall, General Sir Richard Church and Georgios Karaiskakis commanding in the field.

IMPORTANCE:
The fall of the Acropolis was the low point of the Greek war against the Turks, but motivated greater support from European countries, leading to Greek independence.

Historical Setting

For much of Europe, Napoleon left a legacy of nationalism that the Concert of Europe suppressed only with the greatest difficulty. Although he never occupied Greece (but for a few Ionian islands), much of Napoleon's influence arrived there via western Europeans who visited as part of their Grand Tour, diverted southward because of the wars of the previous two decades. Wealthy Greeks traveled to western Europe or sent their sons there for education, and the stirring of nationalist feeling followed in their train. Three and a half centuries of Turkish rule had been restrictive on the Greeks, but in many cases the upper classes and landowners found the Ottoman rule prof-

itable. The Orthodox Church had also been given fairly free rein and had little reason to seek independence, but the modern tides were flowing.

The seeds of revolt grew in two major Greek factions, the merchant class and the Phanariotes. The first traveled internationally and introduced foreign influences; further, they saw reduced taxation and regulation away from the Ottoman system. "Nothing was easier than for communication following the natural trade-routes to lead to conspiracy, financed and supplied from abroad" (Woodhouse, *Short History of Modern Greece*, p. 130). The Phanariotes were Greeks raised in Constantinople who first made their way into the bureaucracy as translators, gradually becoming the bulk of the Ottoman diplomatic corps. Their international contacts could be used to muster financial, political, and hopefully military support for a revolution.

To garner even further support, Greece was rapidly gaining the attention of European intellectuals who were rediscovering classical learning and looked to restore the democracy of ancient times to modern Greece. These "philhellenes," most notably Lord Byron, served Greece in much the same capacity as did the International Brigades in the Spanish Civil War of the 1930s.

The primary channel of revolutionary effort went through the *Philiki Etairia* (Friendly Society), with chapters throughout Europe's major cities. They tried to enlist Count John Capodistria (with close ties to Russia) as their leader, but he refused. Leadership fell to Alexander Ypsilantis, then (upon his death) to his brother Dimitrios. The event that set the revolution into action came when Ottoman Governor Ali Pasha, in the western Greek province of Epirus, occupied the port city of Parga. Because he was a man noted for his brutality, most of the Greeks of the city abandoned it for the island of Corfu rather than live under his rule. On 28 March 1820, the revolt broke out in numerous provinces all across Greece.

Squabbling among various Greek factions,

each looking to a different foreign country for support, hindered the revolution. Any attempt to form a government to direct the revolt was doomed. The Greeks scored a number of early victories, and their fleet for several months controlled the coasts and kept Turkish reinforcements at bay. That began to change in 1824 when the Ottoman sultan called on his vassal Mehmet Ali of Egypt to put down the Greek revolt, in return for which he would receive overlordship of Crete and the Peloponnese. Mehmet Ali's son Ibrahim Pasha arrived in the summer with a huge fleet and an army that soon occupied Crete, then in early 1825 took control of the waters and land of the Peloponnese. Ibrahim captured Navarino in May, then undertook to besiege the port city of Mesolonghi at the mouth of the Gulf of Patras, which fell in April 1826. He then pillaged northeastward, harried by Greek guerrillas.

In spite of their hopes, the Greeks were unable to gain open support from any European power, but as Ibrahim began exercising extreme cruelty during his campaigns international support began to build. British and French individuals began raising money for the cause, and those governments finally sent officers to aid in training and leading the revolution. The main French officer was Colonel C. Fabvier, while Admiral Lord Cochrane and General Sir Richard Church represented the British. Fabvier brought modern methods of training and discipline. Cochrane and Church had made names for themselves while on detached duty in South America and with Neapolitan troops against Napoleon respectively. All three were on site for the attempts to relieve the Turkish siege of the Acropolis.

The Siege

In the northern provinces Ibrahim's original force of 24,000 was reduced by two-thirds. Back in Mesolonghi, another force under Reshid Pasha maintained the sultan's authority in the west. In July Reshid moved along the north coast of the Gulf of Corinth, reaching Thebes on 10 July with 7,000 men. He recruited local turncoat forces and marched for Athens, where 500 men under three commanders held the city walls until 15 August 1826, when they were forced to withdraw to the citadel on the Acropolis. Yannis Gouras and 400 men were already on the Acropolis, with a large store of food gathered prior to Reshid's arrival. On the island of Salamis, Fabvier commanded a force of regular troops aided by partisans led by Georgio Karaiskakis. They attacked the Turks from the rear, but Karaiskakis' retreat in the middle of the battle left Fabvier stranded. He managed to extricate himself, but felt no little hostility for his allied irregular troops. At the end of October Gouras was killed and command of the Acropolis defense forces fell to Yannis Makriyannis. Another 450 men sneaked up the hill to aid the defenders on 23 October, but the subsequent drain on ammunition and food necessitated an attempt to force some supplies through the Turkish lines. Makriyannis and a handful of men slipped off the Acropolis on 29 February and convinced Febvier to try the resupply. He and 500 men marched to Faliro, on the coast a few miles southwest of Athens, then sneaked through the Turkish lines in the moonlight. However, the besiegers discovered the operation and Febvier's men were obliged to stay on the hilltop as well.

Makriyannis joined British General Charles Gordon (who had brought funds from England) to land a relief force. They took the old citadel at Piraeus on 6 February 1827, covering the landing of more men as the Turkish forces in the city retreated to the monastery of St. Spiridon. Reshid attempted to drive the relief back into the sea, but after a five-hour fight on 11 February gave up and decided to build redoubts blocking the path to the Acropolis. For a time the Greek relief force dug itself in, while other columns attempted to interdict Reshid's supply lines.

In March Cochrane and Church arrived. Lord Cochrane was in overall command, but was poorly suited to oversee a land operation in spite of his lofty reputation as a seaman. Rather than send some of his forces to block rumored Turkish resupply columns, Cochrane responded to an overly pessimistic report on the state of the Acropolis defenders. Since Cochrane had arrived with the greatest war chest, his will prevailed. (Some good work was done, however, by the first steamship to operate in the region, the *Karteria*; it sank or captured a number of Turkish supply ships.)

All told, Cochrane commanded some 18,000 troops scattered in a number of villages around Athens. He also had two brigades of artillery and a large stock of ammunition and supplies. Cochrane laid plans for a multipronged attack on the Acropolis, with Church to lead forces from the south while Karaiskakis and his irregulars were detailed to overcome the Agios Spiridon convent on the edge of Piraeus. After being thrown back on 28 April by Albanian troops defending the convent, Karaiskakis negotiated the defenders' safe passage. They marched out with weapons and baggage, but a rambunctious Greek attempted to steal a pistol and firing erupted. Almost all the Albanians were killed before Karaiskakis could stop his men. That delayed operations until 5 May. Church and Karaiskakis were to land 1,000 men at Faliro and fight their way toward the Turkish lines; a further 4,000 men would land the next night in support. Meanwhile, diversionary attacks were to come from the west and northeast.

A skirmish broke out prematurely thanks to some unauthorized drinking, and Karaiskakis was mortally wounded. His dying wish was to have the Acropolis relieved. Delays in the arrival of boats for landing the troops meant that dawn came before they were completely ashore on the morning of 6 May. Cochrane ordered the first troops ashore to establish themselves forward, which they did as quickly as possible. The second line began to form up a few hundred yards behind the first as sufficient manpower landed. Before either line could establish a strong position, Reshid launched 800 cavalry and 400 infantry at

them. The first Greek line withdrew in good order, but the second line panicked and the Turks rode over all of them. This fight on the plain of Analatos cost the Greeks 700 dead and 240 prisoners, who were executed in retribution for the incident at Agios Spiridon.

The failure at Analatos sealed the fate of the Acropolis defenders, although it need not have. Cochrane sailed away and soon sent letters to fellow European naval commanders that the situation in Athens was hopeless. The French instead turned to General Church and offered their aid under his command, but he had lost heart for the operation. He got a message through to Febvier advising him to surrender at his discretion; Febvier responded that he was not in command. A letter to the Greeks in charge met with disdain. Church remained in the area with 2,000 men, but they abandoned him later in May. Church once again wrote Febvier, suggesting the garrison fight their way to the coast where he would have boats waiting, but none in the garrison trusted British promises anymore. On 2 June Febvier contacted his friend Admiral de Rigny, newly arrived at Salamis, to open negotiations with Reshid. On the 5th the remaining 2,000 defenders left the Acropolis, marched to Faliro, and sailed away on French ships.

Results

The defenders of the Acropolis were rarely in dire straits during the siege, even though they were under regular artillery fire. The supplies were sufficient to hold on for some time, but their abandonment by the relief force sealed their fate. Febvier received most of the blame at the time, but ultimately the fault was Cochrane's. He was too impatient and his attention too narrow to consider slower and better plans. Church disagreed with most of Cochrane's ideas but the nature of the fighting ("he with the most money leads") meant that he had to defer to Cochrane's views. Church received much of the blame for the disaster at

Analatos, where he was criticized for crossing open ground rather than using roads through olive groves, which would have afforded some cover. Had he been in overall command, however, the relief probably would have worked.

The fall of the Acropolis gave the Turks no real strategic value, but it seemed to many in the revolution that the Turks were on the verge of running amok. In reality, the fall of Athens roused the European governments to get involved. A British fleet destroyed Ibrahim's Egyptian fleet at Navarino in October 1827. Soon afterward, another Russo-Turkish war broke out, relieving much of the pressure on the Greeks. Negotiations for independence began in March 1829 and the new Kingdom of Greece was born by international agreement on 7 May 1832.

References: Douglas Dakin, *The Greek Struggle for Independence* (Berkeley: University of California Press, 1973); C. M. Woodhouse, *A Short History of Modern Greece* (New York: Praeger, 1968).

THE ALAMO

DATE: 23 February–6 March 1836.
LOCATION: San Antonio, Texas, United States.

FORCES ENGAGED:

Mexican: 4,000–6,000 men. Commander: Antonio Lopez de Santa Anna.
Texan: 189 men. Commander: William B. Travis.

IMPORTANCE:

The fall of the Alamo galvanized resistance to Santa Anna's invasion, culminating in his defeat and subsequent independence for Texas.

Historical Setting

After Mexico finally acquired its independence from Spain in 1821, a rapid succession of gov-ernments sat in Mexico City. Unsure for a time just what government the country wanted, the rulers called themselves emperor, president, or dictator. In 1823, Emperor Iturbide agreed to commission an American, Moses Austin, to bring settlers from the United States into the northern Mexican province of Texas. Three hundred years of Spanish rule in Mexico had made barely a dent on the Texas landscape, for the Comanche Indians were masters of the southern Great Plains and any attempt to settle immigrants or establish missions in land under their sway proved futile. Thus, Moses Austin's Americans were seen as a tool, a population that could serve as a buffer to the 4,000 Mexican citizens of the province of Texas. Little did Iturbide realize that in Moses Austin's project lay the foundation of events that would deprive Mexico of half its land within a generation.

The only two settlements of any size that existed in Texas in 1823 were San Antonio and Nacogdoches. Rather than place the 300 families that he brought to Texas in the path of the Comanches, Moses Austin's son Stephen F. Austin (who took up his father's title of empresario upon the former's untimely death in 1823) instead chose a point midway between the two Mexican towns to establish his colony between the Colorado and Brazos rivers. The "Old 300" were carefully chosen to be thrifty, hard-working farmers and ranchers whose dedication to property would guarantee their passivity, for Iturbide knew that no man of property willingly risked it by engaging in anti-government activities. He did not have to worry about it in the long run, however, for he was soon removed from office and replaced by a government dedicated to more liberal views. That government adopted a constitution in 1824 closely based on that of the United States, and the new immigrants gladly swore to uphold it as the price of the free 4,400 acres granted them for settling in Mexico. Uphold the constitution and become Catholics: those were the two conditions asked of them, with a tacit understanding that the latter would not be enforced.

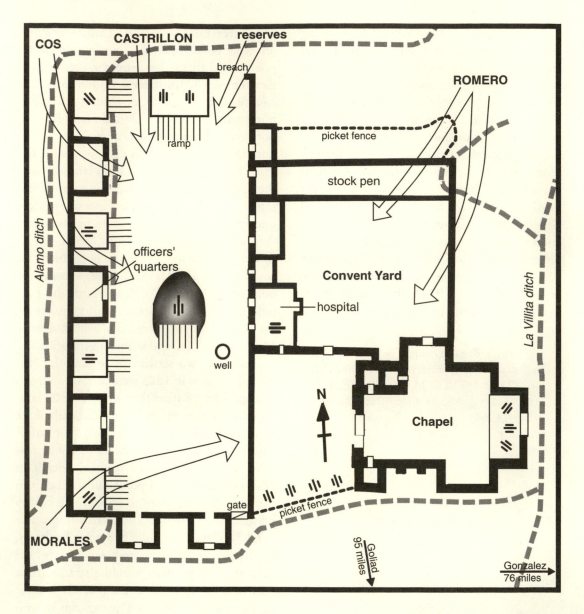

Other empresarios were granted land in order to bring in more settlers for Texas, and by 1830 Anglo-Texans outnumbered native Mexicans by five-to-one. Believing that number sufficient to offer protection, the Mexican government ordered the borders closed and immigration halted. Over the next three years, however, another 10,000 crossed the border illegally, establishing a long-standing tradition for the state.

The year 1833 saw a change in both the Mexican government and its attitude toward Anglo-Texans. General Antonio Lopez de Santa Anna was elected president in that year, riding on his fame as a military hero in turning back the final Spanish incursion into Mexico in 1829. Ambitious to a fault, Santa Anna retired to his estates to allow his vice president to institute new reforms; if they worked he would take credit for them. They did not. Thus, Santa Anna returned to office in 1834 and declared himself dictator, disposing of the 1824 constitution. When the inhabitants of the province of Zacatecas showed resistance to that decision,

A reconstruction of the Alamo much as it would have looked during the siege, built for John Wayne's motion picture The Alamo *(1960), from which this picture was taken. (Kobol Collection)*

Santa Anna rapidly suppressed the revolt by slaughtering everyone who showed any inclination toward rebellion. He looked northward toward the Anglo-Texans and knew that their love of constitutions would never allow them to accept his rule quietly.

Thus, in the early fall of 1835 Santa Anna sent troops into the province to order their withdrawal, for they had not converted to Catholicism as they had promised. At the town of Gonzalez, a dispute over the order and the Texians' (as they were called) possession of a small cannon marked the opening shots of the Texas Revolution on 1 October, although the hotter heads among the settlers had long chafed at the reins of the Mexican bureaucracy. Mexican forces under Martin Perfecto de Cos, Santa Anna's brother-in-law, retreated from Gonzales to San Antonio, where they were besieged in late November. Texians sneaked into the town in mid-December and fought the garrison house to house for a week before capturing the town and then releasing the Mexican soldiers under parole.

Knowing Santa Anna would certainly march north to avenge this defeat, but also that he would probably be unable to arrive before April the following year, most of the 600 Texians went home. About 150 stayed, living a miserable existence on the poor provender available in San Antonio. In December, a provisional government had been established to organize resistance, and Sam Houston was named the commander of the Texian Army. Houston sent Jim Bowie to San Antonio to withdraw the garrison, believing the town too isolated to defend successfully. Bowie, however, became enamored of an abandoned mission in the town that had served for decades as a barracks for Mexican troops: the mission San Antonio de Valero, better known as the Alamo. With some captured Mexican artillery and hard work, the garrison had already begun shoring up the crumbling mission. Bowie sent word to Houston that he would stay and defend the Alamo. Houston then sent a young firebrand named William Travis to order the garrison's withdrawal, but Travis too fell in with Bowie's dream. Just over 150 men were in the Alamo when, to everyone's shock, Santa Anna arrived in late February.

The Siege

In Mexico City, Santa Anna had extorted some loans to finance his expedition northward even before he learned of Cos' defeat. His force of regulars and conscripts had almost reached the Rio Grande when they encountered Cos leading his defeated men south. Enraged at the news, Santa Anna swore vengeance. Upon arriving at San Antonio on 23 February 1836, he quickly ordered his force, numbering 4,000 to 6,000 men, to surround the Alamo. He then began a round-the-clock bombardment to which the defenders were barely able to respond. They had cannon, but gunpowder was in painfully short supply.

The encirclement was not secure, and Travis (who assumed command when Bowie became ill) sent three riders out to fetch aid. His letters contained brave words but they barely concealed his desperation. In answer to his appeals thirty-two men rode in from Gonzales, forcing their way at night through the incomplete investment. Thus, the defense numbered probably 189 men; the exact count varies. It was an impossibly small force to defend a perimeter encompassing the church and two sets of barracks around a very large open courtyard. The walls were originally built to keep out the Comanches and had served that purpose well enough, but they were not sufficiently stout to withstand artillery fire for any great length of time. The fact that the garrison held out for thirteen days with little in the way of casualties speaks more to Santa Anna's gunners' lack of talent lack of than the skill of the defenders. Then again, the cannon were kept some distance away, for the range and marksmanship of some of the riflemen inside the mission proved deadly at the outset of the siege.

On the night of 5 March the bombardment

ceased. The guards at the Alamo's walls were hard pressed to maintain their vigil during the first silence they had enjoyed since Santa Anna's arrival. In the darkness the Mexican troops quietly positioned themselves for a dawn attack. Only an overly eager soldier's cry alerted the garrison to the imminent danger before the attack was upon them. The darkness, coupled with the inexperience of many of the Mexican troops, combined to make the opening assault unsuccessful. Well-placed Texian troops threw back the opening attack, but the Mexicans re-formed and on their second attempt breached the walls. Once inside they had the Texians so outnumbered that the conclusion was foregone. Reports have it that Travis died early in the battle, while Bowie from his sickbed fought but a short time. The men inside the church building held out the longest but did not have the firepower to survive. Mexican sources state that many of the defenders, possibly as many as half, fled to the southeast but were ridden down by Mexican cavalry waiting for such a move. By 0800 it was all over.

In the 1970s a diary reputedly kept by Enrique de la Pena, one of Santa Anna's staff officers, came to light. Its veracity has been challenged, but it describes the final moments of the battle in a way that brought the traditional accounts into question. Since 1836 the generally accepted view was that all the defenders died in battle, but de la Pena's diary states that a handful were taken prisoner, including ex-U.S. congressman David "Davy" Crockett. Although most of the officers recommended mercy, Santa Anna's reputation for ruthless suppression of rebellion showed itself again: he ordered the prisoners executed as traitors.

Another traditional tale from the siege is that of William Travis (who was a mere twenty-six years old) drawing a line in the dust and calling for volunteers to cross over and remain in defense of the mission. The standard account is that all but one did: Moses Rose, veteran of the Napoleonic wars. Whether any of that is true can be nothing more than spec-

ulation, for the story did not become public until decades later and the handful of women who survived the siege and were allowed to go free never mentioned it.

Results

The siege of the Alamo was a battle that should not have been fought. A guerrilla campaign, more suited to the terrain and the talents of the Texians, would have been a wiser course of action. The Alamo was too isolated to be supported and the Texian Army was in the process of organizing; Houston never intended to go to San Antonio, in spite of Travis and Bowie hoping to force him to do so. It slowed the Mexican campaign less than two weeks, but provided the spark that motivated many to join Houston's motley force. He withdrew before Santa Anna's advance, as did most of the population, until it was the Mexicans who became overextended. Santa Anna's decision to divide his force to create as much havoc as possible helped to even the odds, and on 21 April Houston with less than 800 men surprised and overwhelmed Santa Anna's 1,500 at the San Jacinto River on the upper Texas coast. The dictator's capture led to the Treaty of Velasco, granting Texas independence from Mexico; later, Texas' annexation into the United States based on the boundaries spelled out in that treaty sparked the Mexican-American War of 1846–1848. At its end not only Texas but also all northern Mexico to the Pacific Ocean became U.S. territory.

The independence granted in the Treaty of Velasco had been declared by the provisional Texas government on 2 March. The Alamo defenders never knew that. Although many inside the mission's walls certainly would have hailed the decision, the flag which most agree flew over the defenses was the Mexican tricolor with the center white band bearing not the Mexican eagle, but "1824," the year of the constitution they fought to protect from Santa Anna's usurpation.

References: Stephen Hardin, *Texian Iliad* (Austin: University of Texas Press, 1994); Alan C. Huffines, *Blood of Noble Men* (Austin, TX: Eakin, 1999); Charles J. Long, *1836: The Alamo* (San Antonio: Daughters of the Republic of Texas, 1981); Ben H. Proctor, *The Battle of the Alamo* (Austin: Texas State Historical Association, 1986).

ROME

DATE 30 April–2 July 1849.
LOCATION: on the Tiber River near Central Italy's western coast.

FORCES ENGAGED:

French: 9,000 troops at the beginning, reinforced to 20,000. Commander: General Charles Oudinot. Roman Republic: approximately 4,500 troops, with a further 4,000 stationed to the north and 12,000 on the southern frontier with Naples. Commander: Colonel Pietro Roselli.

IMPORTANCE:

French victory restored Pope Pius IX to power in Rome, delaying Italian unification until 1870.

Historical Setting

When Napoleon Bonaparte established French domination in Italy in the 1790s, he brought with him the principles of the French Revolution and thus the seeds of his own destruction. Nationalism and republican government became the catchwords of post-Napoleonic Europe, even while monarchs scrambled to reestablish their own authority. In Italy, revolts in 1820 and 1830 attempted to set up an Italian Republic by overthrowing the Austrians and Spanish, to which the Concert of Europe had granted authority in the northern and southern parts of the peninsula after 1815. The difficulty of establishing a republic was compounded by the fact that the Italian peninsula was divided into a number of smaller states, each vying for either independence or hegemony.

One of those entities was the Vatican, which ruled what were called the Papal States in the region immediately around Rome. To further complicate the international interest in Italy, Pope Pius IX was able to secure a guarantee from France that her soldiers would maintain his authority. All of this came to a boil in 1848, when nationalist movements rose up around the Continent. Many European monarchies were threatened, and in France the Second Republic came into being. Italian nationalists seized the opportunity to break away from Austria, for Vienna had its hands full with revolutionary movements at home. On 22 November 1848, Pope Pius, disguised as a common priest, stole out of the Vatican and fled to the coastal city of Gaeta, from where he appealed for French aid to restore him to power. In February 1849 a newly elected parliament announced the formation of the Roman Republic with Giuseppe Mazzini as chief minister.

The republican movements had a short life in Italy, however, for the Austrians reasserted their power after defeating a Lombard then a Piedmontese army in the summer of 1848. Venice in the spring of 1849 found itself surrounded by both Austrian army and navy forces and its republican days were numbered. Thus the Roman Republic remained the last bastion of democratic ideals, and it faced Austrian forces in the north, Bourbon Neapolitan forces to the south, and French troops that landed at Civitavecchia on 28 April.

The Siege

General Charles Oudinot led 9,000 soldiers ashore at Civitavecchia, where the populace informed him that he would find no resistance at all. Indeed, he was told, the soldiers and citizens of Rome would view him as a liberator from the revolutionary elements. He was misinformed. In Rome, both soldiers and citizens had been working on strengthening the city walls,

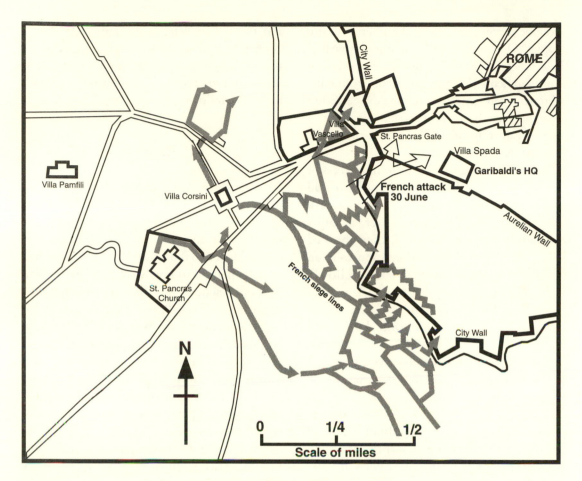

especially near the St. Pancras Gate, through which the most direct route to the Vatican led. Within Rome were some 4,500 troops under the overall command of Colonel Pietro Roselli. The key to the defense, however, was Giuseppi Garibaldi, whose 1,000 Red Shirt followers had an almost mythical reputation among international revolutionaries. Garibaldi's men were stationed outside the walls in Rome's Janiculum quarter, and they controlled three villas (Pamphili, Corsini, and Vascello) as strongpoints covering the St. Pancras Gate.

French troops marched lackadaisically up to Rome's suburbs on 30 April, assured by the reports of an easy entrance into the city. Indeed, as artillery on the walls fired they assumed it to be merely the marking of the noon hour. Shells landing among them convinced them otherwise. Oudinot ordered his artillery unlimbered to return fire, but he had

no siege guns and his cannon had little effect. His infantry had no scaling ladders, and their assault against the city walls was easily beaten back. As they were withdrawing, Garibaldi ordered a sally by 300 young National Guard volunteers. Their enthusiasm at first disconcerted the French, but a counterattack quickly began driving the young men back toward the villas. Garibaldi's commitment of his Red Shirts, along with reinforcements from the city, succeeded in driving French forces well away from the city.

Inside Rome, Chief Minister Mazzini, hoping to impress the French with the blessings of republicanism, wined and dined his prisoners and then sent them back to the French army to tell of their experiences. He also sent with them tracts for distribution, reminding the soldiers that France's newly established republican constitution promised that French power "will never be employed against the liberty of any people." Oudinot's setback did not play well in Paris, where President Louis Napoleon (before long Napoleon III) promised reinforcements. A French representative negotiated a cease-fire with the French army to remain on site as a shield against invading Austrians, or so the Romans were told.

Taking advantage of the seeming success of their defense, Garibaldi on 4 May led 2,300 men north to fight the approaching Austrians. A stunning victory ensued over a larger Neapolitan force at Palestrina, then the Red Shirts returned to Rome. They soon were on the march again: 11,000 men under Roselli and Garibaldi marched out to attack another Neapolitan force allied with Austria. Again Garibaldi's aggressive tactics won the day and the troops of Naples returned to their homeland. Mazzini ordered Roselli's expedition back to Rome, for Austrian troops were beginning to enter the Papal States from the north. To further complicate matters, 11,000 reinforcements had arrived to join Oudinot, who had terminated the cease-fire. A surprise attack on Italian troops in the Janiculum villas at 0300 on 3 June resulted in the capture of two of them, with the third partially surrounded. With the villas in hand, they could begin to let their engineers go to work on the Roman walls.

Garibaldi realized that recovery of the villas was vital for Rome's defense, and he threw his men into the attack at first light. The French had quickly manned the villas, however, and to attack them was suicidal. Throughout the morning Italian soldiers crossed 300 yards of open ground to try to enter the gate of the Villa Corsini, but intense French fire repulsed them repeatedly. Roselli was blamed for not sending in reinforcements, but most inside the city knew the tide had turned. The French were free to dig their siege lines and pound the city; the Roman defenders could do little more than launch occasional raids. For almost a month French heavy guns weakened Italian positions on the walls. After a bitter fight on 29 June, the French managed to take the St. Pancras Gate

and the Italian defense was split. On 2 July Garibaldi and a number of his followers slipped out of Rome and escaped northward to the Piedmont region. French troops entered Rome the following day.

Results

Pope Pius IX returned to Rome and again took direct control of the Vatican City and the Papal States. He did so, however, only with the support of French troops that stayed on site. Garibaldi fled to the United States; he returned to Italy in 1870 to involve himself in the final victorious actions that brought about Italian unification. When Prussian expansionism led to the Franco-Prussian War in 1870, Napoleon III brought all his forces home to defend France. Pope Pius almost immediately found himself with only religious power, as both Garibaldi and Mazzini played key roles in turning the Italian peninsula, so long a region of squabbling city-states, into a single nation. Garibaldi, after such a long struggle against the French, actually joined them in their struggle against Prussian militarism in 1870.

References: Keith Frye, "Rome O Morte: The Siege of Rome—1849," *Clash of Empires*, no. 1, May 1997; Christopher Hibbert, *Garibaldi and His Enemies* (Boston: Little, Brown, 1966); Richard Lamb, "The Siege of Rome," *War Monthly*, no. 50, May 1978.

SEVASTOPOL

DATE: October 1854–10 September 1855.
LOCATION: on the southwestern tip of Russia's Crimean peninsula.

FORCES ENGAGED:

Allied:
French: 120,000 men of the *Armee d'Orient*.
Commander: General François Canrobert, followed by General Aimable Jean Jacques Pelissier.

British: 15,000 men or the Army of the East.
Commander: Lord Raglan, followed by
General Sir James Simpson.
7,000 Turkish troops and 9,000 Sardinian troops.
Russian: Garrison: 38,000.
Commanders: Admirals Pavel Nakhimov and
Vladimir Kornilov.
Relief force: 60,000 men. Commander:
General Alexander Menshikov, followed
by Prince Mikhail Gorchakov.

IMPORTANCE:
Russian loss of the port city broke the back of their
effort in the Crimean War.

Historical Setting

Since Napoleon's defeat in 1815 at the hands of the countries comprising the Concert of Europe, the major European powers had successfully avoided going to war with one another. After almost four decades of peace, however, the traditional Russian and Turkish rivalry produced the spark necessary to bring the major powers to hostilities. Russia, hoping to overwhelm a weak Ottoman Empire and control the Dardanelles (an ongoing Russian dream), declared herself the champion of eastern European Christians against Ottoman Muslim persecution. When Russia claimed to be the protector of holy sites in Palestine, France responded with her own traditional claims in the Holy Land. The Russian destruction of the Turkish fleet at Sinope on 30 November 1853 proved to be the incident that spurred Britain and France to action.

Queen Victoria's Britain and Louis Napoleon's France both sent ships and troops to the Black Sea to support Turkey. Russian troops marched along the Black Sea's western coast into Ottoman territory, but withdrew in the face of Austrian protests. That withdrawal allowed the British and French to enter the Black Sea unopposed and launch their campaign against the Russian fortress port of Sevastopol, on the Crimean peninsula. The allied forces landed unopposed at Calamita Bay, about 30 miles north of Sevastopol, and marched south, slowed down only slightly by a Russian force behind the Alma River. The Russian commander, General Alexander Menshikov, was forced out of a strong defensive position on 20 September 1854; he then withdrew into the interior of the peninsula rather than into the defenses of Sevastopol. The allies ignored him and marched on the city.

The Siege

A quick assault on the city's southern defenses was easily beaten back, so the allies began digging in for a siege. Neither of these armies was prepared for a long campaign, and both suffered horribly from a lack of supplies, especially medicine. Thousands of died of exposure, disease, and starvation through the winter of 1854–1855, taking the British contingent down to about 15,000 effectives. A newly installed British government promised reinforcements and supplies, but none could be provided immediately. Louis Napoleon saw an opportunity to win a major victory with his forces, and he rushed reinforcements to the Crimea that increased his *Armee d'Orient* up to 120,000 men.

General François Canrobert commanded the French army, but constant oversight and directives from Paris convinced him that overall command was not his forte; he requested demotion to divisional command. This was granted in mid-May and his replacement was General Aimable Jean Jacques Pelissier. Although the orders from Paris were to break off the siege and operate against Sevastopol's lines of communication, Pelissier instead decided to take the city by storm.

The defenses of Sevastopol were under the direction of a master of engineering defense, Lieutenant Colonel Franz E. I. Todleben. His superiors were Russian admirals who sank some vessels in the mouth of the harbor to prevent a seaborne assault and assigned their crews to supplement the garrison by manning artillery batteries. The city of Sevastopol is

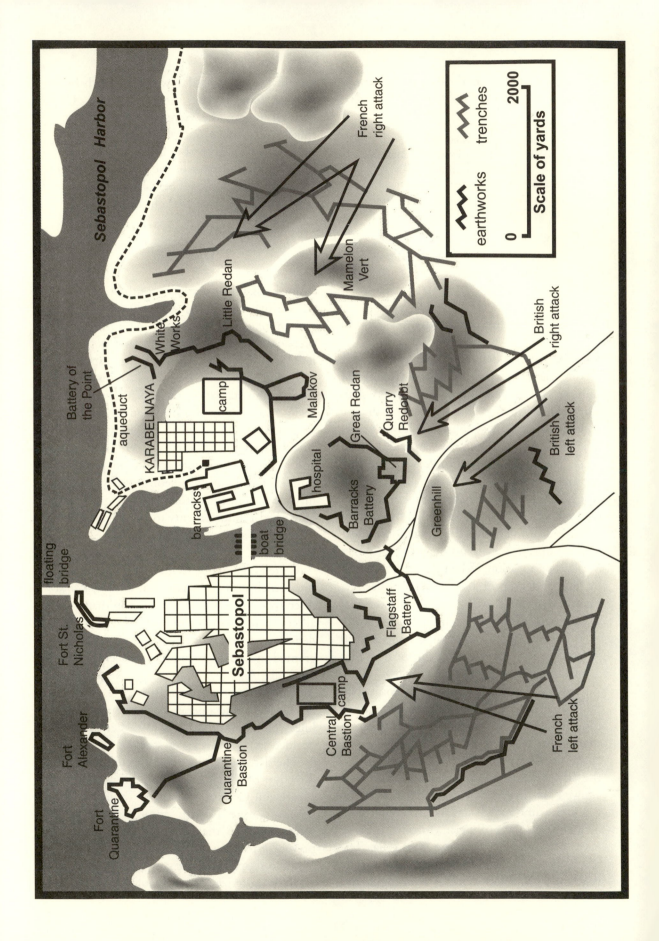

Victorious soldiers pose after the taking of Malakoff in the Crimea. (Guttmann/Beato/Archive Photos)

separated along its eastern face from a smaller town, Karabelnaya, by an arm of Sevastopol Harbor. A series of defensive walls surrounded Sevastopol and Karabelnaya from coast to coast, anchored by seven bastions. Each was well supplied with artillery, and Todleben strengthened the defenses by building secondary strongpoints in front of two of the primary bastions: the Great Redan was fronted by the Quarry Battery, and the far left flank was anchored by the Battery of the Point, which was fronted by the White Works. The main strongpoint, on the southeastern part of the walls, was a two-story-tall tower atop a hill overlooking the entire battlefield, a structure that inexplicably came to be called the Malakhov Battery. Some 1,500 yards in front of Malakhov was a hill, Mamelon Vert, which Todleben also fortified.

Pelissier opened his assault on the city's defenses with traditional trenchworks and attempts at mining the defensive walls, to which the Russians countered with their own countermining and the introduction of electrically detonated explosive charges. That changed on 6 June, when he began a massive bombardment with 548 guns aimed at the White Works and the Mamelon Vert. After an all-day barrage Pelissier launched his attack at 1830, hoping the gathering dusk would give his men cover from Russian fire. The rapid assault reached the Russian defenses before they could recover from the bombardment and, within an hour and a half, French troops occupied Mamelon Vert and British troops captured the Quarry Battery. Over-eager French officers, however, pressed their attack against orders, assaulting the Malakhov. By that time the Russian gunners were well prepared and inflicted enormous casualties. The

Russians threw a counterattack after the retreating French which reached the Mamelon Vert, and a bitter struggle ensued for its possession. The French threw in the final reinforcements, however, and by the morning of 7 June owned the hill.

The success of his assault encouraged Pelissier to try again ten days later. Another heavy barrage pounded the Russian positions on 17 June, with assistance from English ships. This barrage lasted twenty-four hours and was followed by an assault at dawn on the 18th. This time the Russians, although hurt, were at their guns when the charge began. The Malakhov was the primary target, but the French were slaughtered trying to reach it. A subsidiary British attack from the captured Quarry Battery against the Great Redan also proved futile.

Menshikov's army in the interior had done little to assist Sevastopol. Their only attack, against allied positions at Inkerman south of the city, had been beaten back the previous November. Menshikov was relieved of his command and replaced by Prince Mikhail Gorchakov at the end of June 1855. Gorchakov was told to attack the allies, who hopefully would be shaken from their failure two weeks earlier. Neither Gorchakov nor Todleben had much faith in the chances of such an attack succeeding, but perhaps striking the southwestern end of the allied lines might divert some troops away from the attacks against the Karabelnaya defenses. A night attack launched on 15 August was turned back by superior allied weaponry (rifles versus muskets) and timely reinforcements.

Pelissier had been moving his trenchworks forward since his failed attack in mid-June, and by September the French and British lines were within 100 yards of the Russian defenses. Heavy French artillery fire caused up to 1,000 Russian casualties per day, and the defensive force was down to 23,000 in Sevastopol and 17,000 in Karabelnaya. Constant pounding had reduced the Malakhov Battery and the Little Redan almost to ruins. Pelissier and his staff decided on another assault to start at noon on 8 September

following two days of intense bombardment. This attack began with no flare or trumpet signal to alert the Russians, who barely noticed the French soldiers charging them until the attackers were in the fortifications. More than 57,000 men were engaged in the assault and the short dash from front lines to Russian walls gave the attackers quick successes. In hand-to-hand combat the French North African troops proved too nimble and aggressive for the Russians. Seeing his men in control of the Malakhov, Pelissier signaled the British to launch their assault on the Great Redan. They charged forward just as the Russians launched a counterattack against the French that forced them back temporarily. The British found themselves charging against an alert Russian position that easily beat them back.

Other Russian positions were gained and lost, but the secure hold on the Malakhov gave the French control of the highest ground and the strongest point. The Russians knew that to lose the Malakhov was to lose the battle, so they threw wave after wave against it but the French repeatedly drove them back. At 1500, seeing the French flag flying from the captured tower, Gorchakov signaled the garrison in Sevastopol to evacuate. The defenders crossed a boat bridge to Karabelnaya. Allied troops entered the abandoned city on 10 September after a 322-day siege.

Results

The war in the Crimea went on for another six months, before finally being concluded by the Treaty of Paris of 1856. Although the Russians were able to reoccupy Sevastopol after the war, the terms of the treaty forbade their possession of a fleet on the Black Sea. Thus, the harbor remained open only to commercial shipping until 1870, when France's defeat at Prussia's hands encouraged Czar Alexander to rebuild his fleet. A blockade of the city would have proved much less costly in terms of human life, for its capture by the allies contributed little to the outcome of the war other than as a blow to the Russians' morale. The war produced a return to power politics in Europe, ending a sustained period of peace. The horrific experience of the British, however, led to some reforms, especially in the realm of medical care, but the lessons were lost by the time of World War I. In that war, British forces in Mesopotamia would find themselves too far from home with too few supplies, resulting in disaster at Kut-al-Amara and a change of government in London, just as similar conditions around Sevastopol provoked in 1855.

References: A. J. Barker, *The War against Russia* (New York: Holt, Rinehart, & Winston, 1970); John Shelton Curtiss, *Russia's Crimean War* (Durham, NC: Duke University Press, 1979); Robert B. Edgerton, *Death or Glory: The Legacy of the Crimean War* (Boulder, CO: Westview, 1999); Philip Warner, *The Crimean War: A Reappraisal* (London: Barker, 1972).

DELHI

DATE: 8 June–20 September 1857.
LOCATION: north-central India.

FORCES ENGAGED:

British: 10,000 primarily British troops, with some native contingents. Commander: Brigadier General Sir Archdale Wilson.
Indian Sepoy: 30,000 made up of mutinous Indian Army units and local supporters. Commander: Mirza Moghul.

IMPORTANCE:

By recapturing the Indian capital city, the British dealt the Indian Army mutineers a major psychological blow, while freeing up troops to assist in the relief of Cawnpore, ending the Indian Mutiny.

Historical Setting

In the summer of 1757, the young and aggressive Robert Clive defeated a major Moghul force at Plassey, near Calcutta, and in doing so made Great Britain the primary power in India. A century later that power received its most dangerous challenge, not from foreign aggression but from the men the British had trained to serve in the Indian Army.

The century of British rule had been a mixed blessing to the Indian population. While no foreign domination is popular with the indigenous people, the British did bring security to the person on the street and a much fairer administration than had existed under the declining Moghul dynasty. British power was exercised through "John Company," the British East India Company, which, with its own "private" army, had grown into the largest trading company in the world. It had originally operated with a security force raised locally but trained and commanded by British troops and, since the company was financed in large part through the British government, over time British units were stationed in India as well.

The Company administration gradually expanded its hold over more and more of India by challenging the princes who threatened the peaceful acquisition of British profits. After each campaign, the victorious British would incorporate troops from the defeated forces into the Indian Army. By the middle of the nineteenth century the Indian troops outnumbered British soldiers by about a five-to-one ratio, but the discipline and training that the native troops, or *sepoys*, received ensured a loyal and effective fighting force. Or so it seemed until 1857. The British officers, while in many cases loyal and inspirational to their troops, were more often distant and disdainful of the sepoys. Racial attitudes kept most white officers from bonding with their Indian subordinates, and that usually made for unhappy troops. A century of subjection to the British superiority attitude made many sepoys surly, and the seeming disregard for local religious beliefs compounded the problem. Mixing castes in Hindu units was insulting enough, but an apparent attempt at enforced sacrilege in the spring of 1857 was the final outrage.

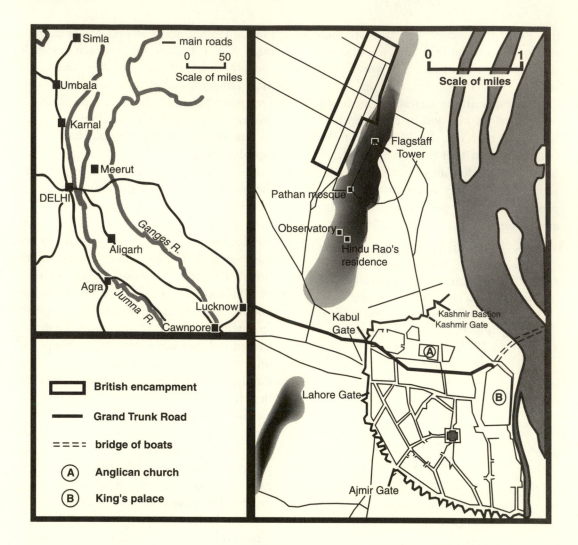

British encampment

Grand Trunk Road

==== bridge of boats

(A) Anglican church

(B) King's palace

It was British practice to arm the Indian troops with weapons one generation behind the latest issued to British soldiers. In 1857 the Indian troops received Enfield rifles. Paper cartridges held a one-shot measurement of gunpowder. The rifle was loaded by biting off the end of the cartridge and pouring the powder down the barrel. In order to waterproof the cartridges, they were smeared with fat. Pig fat offended the Muslims and cow fat offended the Hindus, for dietary requirements of the respective religions banned consumption of those animals. To bite a cartridge would therefore be a desecration. Although the manufacturer quickly changed the coating to wax, the Indian troops never got over their original disgust, and rumors of continued use of fat persisted. On 19 March 1857, the first instance

of mutiny occurred at Barrackpore, near Calcutta. The instigator, Mangal Pande, was executed and his unit disbanded. Throughout northern India, Pande became the symbol of all the degradation the Indians had suffered at British hands for a hundred years.

The Sepoy Mutiny finally broke out in earnest on the evening of 10 May. In Meerut, 30 miles northeast of Delhi, elements of the 3rd Light Cavalry freed fellow troopers condemned to ten years' hard labor for refusing to use the new cartridges. "There was no coherent plan—once the gaol was opened fear and excitement drove them in scattered groups among the bungalows, slaughtering all the British they found and setting fire to everything in sight, aided and abetted by convicts

The King of Delhi is brought by guards before Captain Hodson after the capture of Delhi by the British during the Indian Mutiny, September 1857. (Archive Photos)

freed from the city prisons and a fanatical, howling mob from the bazaars" (Everett, "The Indian Mutiny," BHI, p. 23). The mutineers then left for Delhi, before British troops in Meerut could form up and respond. For some reason, they did not follow the sepoys to Delhi.

On the morning of 11 May, mutineers stormed into the Red Castle in Delhi, killed what British officers they found, and begged Bahadur Shah, the aging Moghul king, to lead them. He knew the likely outcome, but felt compelled to cooperate. His sons quickly joined the uprising, Mirza Moghul taking command of the army. More sepoys in Delhi killed their British officers and joined the mutiny. After a few hours' defense, the British blew up the magazine rather than have it fall into rebel hands. Most Europeans, living outside the city, fled for Meerut or Karnal. Fifty British civilians, including women and children, were held for a few days, then hacked to pieces when they refused to convert to Islam.

The Siege

In spite of the uprising spreading to almost all British posts in northern India, response to the situation in Delhi was surprisingly fast. The British government rushed in troops from southern India, Rangoon, and Ceylon, with Delhi their prime target. These troops supplemented others based at Simla, in the hills of the Northwest Frontier province. From there, the summer capital of the British administration, the 75th Highlanders, 1st and 2nd Bengal Fusiliers marched south. At Umbala on 23 May they joined the 9th Light Cavalry, 60th Rifle Regiment, 6th Dragoon Guards and elements of the Horse Artillery, and 4th Irregular Cavalry. Sappers and some siege guns rounded out the force, commanded by General Sir Henry Barnard.

This force marched toward Delhi, meeting some resistance about 15 miles from the city at the village of Ghazi-ed-din. The mutineers were quickly driven off and the British force marched through Alipore to Baduli-ke-Serai, on 8 June defeating a force of sepoy artillery there with a spirited bayonet charge by the Highlanders. Taking the name the Army of Retribution, the British quickly drove on to the Delhi Ridge, overlooking the city on the northwest, where they inflicted more than 1,000 casualties on the mutineer force and captured thirteen cannon. Here, in the original British camp, the force dug in and awaited reinforcements. These trickled in from all over, the Corps of Guides arriving from Mardan having marched 580 miles in 22 days.

The city of Delhi was surrounded by 12-foot-thick walls and defended by a few thousand well-trained sepoys, although local volunteers up to a total of perhaps 30,000 men supported them. The British had too few men (approximately 10,000) to fully surround the city, so Indian reinforcements and supplies were never cut off. Neither did the British, at first, have sufficient artillery to breach the walls. Further, the summer heat reached at times a reported 140 degrees. However, the quality of reinforcements they received, as well as the generally better organization that the British had in place, gave them the advantage as long as the siege did not go on too long, as the psychological boost to the mutineers to hold the Moghul capital was immense.

For the first several weeks the British did well to hold on to the ridge in the face of repeated attacks from the city. On 5 July General Barnard died of cholera, to be superseded by Brigadier Archdale Wilson. The pressure of holding their positions, coupled with the intense heat and mounting casualties, wore on Wilson's patience. When a sepoy sortie temporarily threatened to cut off his supply lines, Wilson telegraphed Governor General Sir John Lawrence that he needed more assistance or would be obliged to withdraw. Lawrence sent as many men as he could, with more engineers arriving in early July, the European Horse Battery, 52nd Light Infantry Regiment, 2nd Punjab Infantry, and more irregular cavalry arriving

soon afterward. Also arriving, on 7 August, was Brigadier General Sir John Nicholson. Here was a legendary figure in the British Indian Army, known for his bravery, toughness, and steady nerve. His actions throughout the siege emboldened both officers and men. In early September he led a force through a swamp to beat back a mutineer force attempting to halt the arrival of siege artillery.

In spite of the reinforcement, disease was rampant. Cholera affected as many as two-thirds of the British force. Indian troops assumed to be loyal began to waver under the strain, and they made up almost half the total force. In spite of the deteriorating situation, Wilson's staff convinced him to give up defending the ridge and to assault the city. Sufficient artillery had arrived and by 13 September thirteen breaches had been broken in the city walls, and Wilson ordered an assault for dawn on 14 September. Four columns were to attack: three side by side would hit the northern walls at the Kashmir Gate, Kashmir Bastion, and Water Bastion, while the fourth column would swing farther south to try and force the Lahore Gate.

The attack got off to a bad start. The defending mutineers produced deadly rifle and artillery fire, while men carrying the scaling ladders could not keep up with the leading troops. The Kashmir Gate had to be blown up by engineers, and that column wormed its way into the city while the two other northern columns exploited the breaches. Once inside, the three northern columns met near the Anglican church and set up a perimeter. By day's end almost 1,200 men had been killed or wounded. General Nicholson, who had led the charge on the Kashmir Bastion, was badly wounded but refused to be evacuated. The perimeter slowly expanded on the 15th, although the British troops did not do well in the house-to-house urban fighting. When Wilson pondered the possibility of withdrawing his troops, Nicholson from his deathbed threatened to kill him.

Wilson gave in and the fighting continued. British troops found that the magazine that had been blown up at the start of the mutiny was only partially damaged and a large store of artillery and powder had survived. This boosted their morale as well as their firepower. This allowed the force in the northern part of the city to blast their way southwest to link up with the column attempting to force the Lahore Gate. It had not been taken in the opening assault, but finally fell to British forces on the 19th. That proved to be the last gasp of the mutineers' resistance. On the 20th British troops blew open the gates to the Red Castle to find the citadel deserted. Bahadur Shah and his retainers had fled in the night.

Results

Although many in Delhi had fought alongside the mutineers, many more had not been happy with the five-month occupation. Bankers had been forced to provide funds for the troops and shopkeepers found themselves at the mercy of a rebel administration that forced their cooperation in supplying the defenders. Some even stole out of the city to sell goods to the British during the siege. In spite of that, the British exercised little mercy upon their return. Although the British accounts list only 392 executions, eyewitnesses reported thousands. Fearing plague, the population was expelled; the Hindus were allowed back after two months, many Muslims never. In the meantime, British soldiers looted virtually every building in the city.

Bahadur Shah, who had fled across a bridge of boats on the 19th, was discovered hiding in ancestral tombs a few miles away. Major William Hodson, commander of a unit of irregular cavalry, took him prisoner. Hodson escorted the king back to Delhi, after executing his sons on the spot. Bahadur Shah was later exiled to Rangoon.

The casualties suffered in the British Indian Army force numbered 992 killed and 2,845 wounded, some one-third of the total force engaged. None was more honored in death the General Nicholson, who survived long enough

to hear of the fall of the city. He was buried outside the Kashmir Gate.

With the city under control, 2,800 soldiers were dispatched to aid in the relief of Lucknow. Although the mutiny went on for several more months, the British recapture of Delhi marked their reconsolidation of power. Major changes took place in British imperial administration. The East India Company was disbanded and a government was established that came under the auspices of the India Office in London. The Indian Army was thoroughly reorganized, with the disparity in numbers altered until the British troops numbered nearly 40 percent of the total. Although the aloofness that the British had always exercised remained, religious toleration was observed to a much greater extent than ever before.

References: Richard Collier, *The Great Indian Mutiny* (New York: Dutton, 1964); Susanne Everett, "The Indian Mutiny," parts 1 and 4, *British History Illustrated* 3, no. 2, June–July 1976, and 3, no. 5, December 1976–January 1977; Lawrence James, *Raj: The Making and Unmaking of British India* (London: Little, Brown, 1997); John H. Waller, "The Siege of Delhi," *Military History* 14, no. 7, March 1998.

GAETA

DATE: 12 November 1860–13 February 1861.
LOCATION: on the western Italian coast between Naples and Rome.

FORCES ENGAGED:

Italian: 18,000 men. Commander: General Enrico Cialdini.
Neapolitan: 13,000 men. Commander: King Francis II.

IMPORTANCE:

When forces of the Italian Republic captured Gaeta, it marked the virtual unification of Italy as well as the end of the Bourbon dynasty in Naples.

Historical Setting

Since the fall of the Roman Empire, the Italian peninsula had been divided into numerous principalities, dukedoms, and minor kingdoms. Until the advent of the Renaissance, most were weak and subject to whatever outside power had last invaded the region. With the rise of nationalism in Europe, better-organized nation-states were able to impose their will on the divided Italians, with Austria usually in control of the northern part of the peninsula. Napoleon's occupation had planted a nationalist seed in the Italian population, however. By the mid-nineteenth century, the strongest state (and the one most likely to lead a unified Italy) was Piedmont, also known as the Kingdom of Sardinia. By throwing their support on the side of France in the Crimean War, Prime Minister Count Camillo Cavour hoped to gain support for a Piedmont-led uprising against the Austrians and a subsequent unification under the leadership of Piedmont's King Victor Immanuel.

France's Napoleon III did indeed back Piedmont's ambitions for a time, until major Austrian defeats in 1859 made Napoleon worry about the intentions, and the power, of his upstart neighbor. By concluding a separate peace with Austria, Napoleon left Piedmont without major allies. Still, the small kingdom did convince the provinces of Parma, Modena, Tuscany, and Romagna to unite into a nascent Italian state, while Austria managed to hold on to the northeastern province of Venetia.

Although hoping to establish a kingdom, Cavour had to cooperate with the republican forces active in Italy, most notably those under the Sicilian revolutionary, Giuseppe Garibaldi. In May 1860 Garibaldi's forces invaded Sicily, then the southern province of Naples (or the Kingdom of the Two Sicilies) fell under his sway in September. Fearing the power of the republican movement, Cavour sent Piedmontese forces south to confront Garibaldi, gaining control of most of the territory around Rome in the process. Garibaldi gave up his republican ideals in favor of Italian nationalism under King Victor Immanuel's monarchy, but Naples' Bourbon King Francis II refused to cede his lands without a struggle. Although forced from his capital city in September 1860, Francis and his wife Maria Sophia withdrew to the fortified port of Gaeta, some 45 miles northwest of Naples and 90 miles down the coast from Rome.

Never one to inspire the respect of Europe's nobility, Francis surprised everyone by not only staging a spirited defense of the city, but also by acting the role of king superbly in the most difficult of circumstances. This proved embarrassing to the rest of Europe's monarchs, who gave lip service to aiding Francis but in reality did little or nothing to prevent his downfall. That regal bearing, along with the Neapolitan perception that Victor Immanuel was more conqueror than unifier of Italy, meant that the population and garrison of Gaeta rallied to their sovereign more ardently than anyone expected. Unfortunately, Francis' military acumen did not measure up to his kingly deportment.

The Siege

Although 18,000 men surrounded Gaeta, the harbor remained open for some time as French ships temporarily kept Piedmontese vessels at bay. This allowed for some resupply and perhaps gave the defenders a false sense of security. While artillery was plentiful, the garrison was slow to mount the cannon for defense. Civilians were allowed to freely inspect the batteries, and some Piedmontese officers in disguise were able to mingle with the crowds. Ambassadors who had removed themselves from Naples along with Francis finally found excuses to abandon the city and return to Rome. The king bade them all an honorable farewell, even decorating a few.

General Ferdinando Bosco arrived on 19 November to take charge of the defense. He had just been released from his parole resulting from his capture in a battle six months earlier. Bosco had a reputation for aggressiveness, which endeared him to his troops but made lesser officers jealous "because his conduct was a sharp criticism of their own" (Acton, *Last of the Bourbons*, p. 512). Although he did lead two sorties out of Gaeta, his reputation for the most part was undeserved.

Food shortages appeared quickly, but some observers only lamented that King Francis ordered the cafes closed two hours after dark. That implies only a lack of finer foods, for beans, rice, and cheese seem to have been available. Francis' views of proper conduct at times failed to serve his population well. When four Piedmontese grain ships were forced into Gaeta harbor by bad weather, he allowed them to sail away untouched with only the warning "that if other merchant vessels flying the Piedmontese flag appeared in the harbour 'they would be subjected to the laws of war, lest his royal magnanimity be interpreted as weakness' " (Acton, *Last of the Bourbons*, p. 513). On 8 December General Cialdini, commanding the besieging force, requested a three-day truce. Francis agreed on the condition that no further siege works be constructed in the interim. Cialdini did not agree, but Francis ordered the cease-fire anyway.

Throughout December and into January Piedmontese artillery shelled the city, hitting the royal residence on 7 January. Prime Minister Cavour, in an attempt to end the battle without further destruction, sent a message to Emperor Napoleon III in France, requesting that he withdraw his fleet. Napoleon replied that he would propose an eight-day truce during which Francis would have time to give up the fight. If he did not, then the fleet would be withdrawn. Cialdini was ordered to cease firing from 9 January to the 19th. He increased his bombardment up to the deadline, but the defenders traded shell for shell in an impressive artillery duel. During the bombardment, sailors manning some of the defending guns

taunted the Piedmontese by dancing on the walls, then sitting down in plain sight and playing cards. When the truce began, Francis wrote to Napoleon that he was fighting not just for Naples but for the power of all monarchs, so he would not give up without a struggle.

Queen Maria Sophia greatly contributed to the city's morale by spending most of each day tending to wounded in the hospitals and visiting gun crews at their weapons: "men spattered with blood and mud gazed at her with almost religious adoration and kissed the hem of her skirt with feverish lips. . . . her eyes gave more than sympathy, her smile brought more than comfort" (Acton, *Last of the Bourbons*, pp. 515–516).

The French fleet departed on 19 January and the encirclement was then complete. Piedmontese ships joined in the bombardment. With shells landing in the city at a rate as high as 18,000 in eight hours, the defenders kept up their counterbattery fire and morale remained high. The spirits began to fade, however, when a typhoid epidemic broke out on the 25th. The besiegers' guns increased their rate of fire, hitting powder magazines on 4 February. Although Neapolitan fire answered, their batteries were gradually knocked out. Also, the walls around the drawbridge on the landward side were breached and could not be repaired owing to the intense Piedmontese fire.

Finally, on 19 February, King Francis bowed to the inevitable and asked to negotiate. General Cialdini would not cease firing during any talks, although he did offer to evacuate Neapolitan wounded. Cialdini offered little consideration to the negotiators, and the continued artillery fire exploded the largest remaining powder magazine on 13 February. That evening at 1815 the surrender terms were signed.

Results

Two smaller fortresses still resisted elsewhere, so the defending troops were treated as prisoners of war until the rest of the resistance ended (which it did a few days later). The garrison was granted the honors of war and at the end of hostilities were demobilized and sent home. Francis and Maria Sophia left the city on a French corvette that Napoleon had ordered to remain behind after the rest of his fleet departed. The Neapolitan troops paraded for their monarchs, who boarded the ship to the strains of Naples' national anthem. They stayed for a time in Rome, then went into permanent exile in Paris.

Victor Emmanuel II was proclaimed king of Italy in March 1861, with the province of Veneto breaking away from Austrian rule and joining the rest of Italy in 1866. But a unified Italy did not translate into a stronger one, at least economically. The more industrialized north disdained the agricultural south. Although the king ruled under the auspices of a constitution, the parliamentary government proved unstable. Further, the pope increasingly felt himself more prisoner than pontiff as the political leadership became increasingly anticlerical. That put the government and the Catholic population of Italy regularly at odds. Political instability and an unbalanced economy remain problems in Italy to this day.

References: Harold Acton, *The Last Bourbons of Naples, 1825–1861* (New York: St. Martin's, 1961); Derek Beales, *The Risorgimento and the Unification of Italy* (London: Longman, 1971); George Martin, *The Red Shirt and the Cross of Savoy* (New York: Dodd, Mead, 1969).

PUEBLA

DATE: March–17 May 1863.
LOCATION: roughly 75 miles southeast of Mexico City.

FORCES ENGAGED:
French: 26,300 French troops, 2,000 reactionary Mexican troops, and 58 guns. Commander: General Elias Forey.

Mexican: 22,000 troops. Commander: General Jesus Gonzalez Ortega.

IMPORTANCE:
French victory opened the path to Mexico City, which allowed France to install Maximilian as emperor in Mexico.

Historical Setting

After the Mexican-American War of 1846–1848, Mexico entered a period of national crisis. The government of Antonio Lopez de Santa Anna had fallen in late 1847, bringing about the end of the war. The government that succeeded it was unpopular for signing the Treaty of Guadalupe Hidalgo, which ceded vast stretches of northern Mexico to the United States, although the nation was compensated with a $15 million indemnity. The money was insufficient to pay the debt incurred by the war or to save the government. After years of political wrangling and a civil war, Benito Juarez was elected president of the United States of Mexico in 1858, with the mandate of enforcing the newly passed constitution.

Juarez, a full-blooded Zapotec Indian who was trained for the priesthood but became a lawyer, was dedicated to democratic reforms and extending rights to the bulk of the Mexican people. To improve their lot in life through schools, hospitals, and the like was an expensive task. The government had been paying its bills primarily through the use of foreign loans, mainly from Spain, England, and France. Reelected in 1861, Juarez announced a two-year suspension of debt payments in order for him to straighten out his nation's finances and get his reforms started. The European countries refused to accept the delay, deciding instead to send troops to Mexico to force payment.

Spanish troops were the first to arrive, landing at Vera Cruz on 8 December 1861. French and English troops soon followed. By April the money had been collected, but France's Emperor Napoleon III had bigger plans for Mexico. Living up to the reputation of his

The siege and capture of Puebla by the French in 1863. (Libary of Congress)

uncle was a difficult role to play, and Napoleon hoped to raise France's prestige in the world. Mexico, he believed, would offer a source of raw materials for French markets as well as a base from which he might extend France's control through more of Latin America. Apparently he believed that some nation needed to do that in order to curb the rising power of the United States, whose Monroe Doctrine of 1823 proclaimed that Europeans were no longer welcome in the western hemisphere. Seeing what Napoleon had planned and wanting no part of it, Spanish and English troops departed in April 1862. Juarez responded by declaring martial law and announcing that any territory occupied by French troops would be considered in a state of siege.

In order to rule Mexico, French troops had to advance into the interior of Mexico from their base at the port of Vera Cruz, and they began this march as soon as the Spanish and English left. As the Church and the landed gentry of Mexico feared the power of a demo-cratic government, the conservatives encouraged Napoleon. Indeed, French ambassador Count Dubois de Saligny foolishly expected the population to welcome the invaders. Juarez ordered General Ignacio Zaragoza to do what he could to bar the French advance. In early May Zaragoza commanded less than 5,000 poorly equipped and poorly trained men in the town of Puebla. French troops numbering 6,000 under the command of General Charles Latrille de Lorencez appeared before Puebla on the morning of 5 May. They divided into two sections to strike the walled town from two sides, but Zaragoza not only had manned outlying forts but also placed many of his men in trenches hidden from French view. Holding one French section at bay while the other was attacked from three sides, the Mexicans scored a victory comparable to the Ethiopian win over the Italians at Adowa thirty years later: outgunned and outmanned native troops defeating a European army.

The victory bought Juarez some time, but

the French were not about to let such a defeat go unanswered. Reinforcements were dispatched and new commanders appointed. In March 1863 10,000 French troops were marching on Mexico City, and once again, 100 miles to the southeast, they had to get past the town of Puebla.

The Siege

General Elias Forey landed in Mexico 21 September 1862 and moved to the forward French position at Orizaba, where the French had retreated four months earlier after Puebla. Upon taking command, he ousted Juan Almonte from the presidency he had claimed, thus alienating the reactionary forces sympathetic to France's goals. He also found the town of Orizaba diverting, so was in no hurry to get his campaign under way. In Puebla, Mexican General Jesus Gonzalez Ortega was doing his best to build up the town's fortifications. In Mexico City, Juarez was trying to handle multiple tasks: find money, deal with congress, suppress banditry, maintain regional support of the national government, and try to convince rival military forces to join the national effort.

In February he went to Puebla to review the progress and provide moral support. General Ignacio Comonfort was bringing another force to the area, hoping to act as a mobile threat to a French advance. Heartening news came from other fronts as French forces were forced out of the coastal town of Tampico to the north, as well as Jalapa to the west. In March 1863, the French began their move on Puebla, regarded as the key to the Mexican hold on their capital city.

French troops left Orizaba on 9 March and arrived before Puebla on the 16th. Forey spent five days having his men dig in around the city, then began his bombardment. Forey placed his headquarters on high ground south of town. Ortega vetoed a plan to sortie from the town and strike isolated French units, instead preferring to plug breaches in the walls when artillery

fire created them and French units assaulted. There were breaches aplenty, for the French forward parallels had been dug within 150 yards of the walls. One of the outlying forts, San Xavier, fell on 28 March, but the Mexicans held each fallback position with determination. The French captured one strongpoint after another, but all with heavy losses.

As the French focused on Puebla, they had to maintain themselves off the countryside. General Comonfort's men harried French foraging parties. This was successful until 14 April, when a French regiment turned and drove Comonfort's men away then pursued them out of the area. After that, the French were free to pursue both combat and supplies. In the city, supplies were becoming a problem. For all the time spent on building the fortifications during the months since the last battle, little had been done to stock the town sufficiently. Only time would tell if the French artillery, or starvation, would finish off the garrison. On 8 May one of the French commanders, General Achille Bazaine, spotted a large cloud of dust in the distance. Assuming this to be a relief force, he led a detachment that night in the direction of the disturbance. He surprised Comonfort's camp, inflicting a thousand casualties and capturing another thousand. Thus ended the one serious attempt to relieve the city.

Ortega had been in touch with Forey prior to this setback, and Forey had even offered Ortega the nation's presidency should he surrender. That merely stiffened Ortega's resolve. It did not lessen the garrison's privations, for they ate every dog and cat in the city and were finally eating leaves off the orange trees. By 17 May they were out of ammunition as well as food, and Ortega had no choice but to surrender. He ordered all weapons destroyed, then contacted Forey about surrender terms. He offered parole, but none of the defenders would promise not to take up arms again, so the French took all the Mexican officers into custody and sent them to captivity in France. Most of the soldiers managed over time to escape and return to join the resistance. The one notable officer to escape from French custody was Porfirio Diaz, who later became dictator of Mexico and was overthrown in a revolution in 1910.

Results

With Puebla in their control, the French had no serious obstacle barring their entry to Mexico City. Juarez wanted to fight for the capital, but realized his 14,000 men were entirely too few to mount an effective effort. Instead, he and congress retreated to San Luis Potosí to continue the war.

Napoleon now had control of the center of power, so he soon sent his chosen leader to assume the throne of Mexico: Maximilian of Austria. He and his wife Carlotta arrived in Mexico City in June 1864, whereupon he assumed the title of emperor of Mexico. He was not a poor ruler, for he enhanced Indian rights and developed the country's natural resources, but his alliance with the upper classes guaranteed the continued opposition of Juarez and the advocates of democracy. Juarez had support in northern Mexico and even from the southwest United States. After the 1846–1848 war against the United States, Mexican-American societies sprang up to assist in local law enforcement, acting something like a national guard. They grew in social and economic power through the 1850s and were key supporters of Juarez and democracy.

Juarez also drew some belated support from the United States. Since Maximilian came to power in 1864, the United States was too involved in its own Civil War to deal without outside interference in hemispheric affairs. In 1865, however, when the war was over and Union troops were stationed in Texas, the American government did begin to pressure France to give up its imperial experiment. That veiled threat had some influence, but increasing domestic problems in Europe obliged Napoleon to withdraw much of his military support from Mexico. Without the troops to maintain his throne, Maximilian was soon deposed and executed. The French victory at Puebla allowed him to come to power, but Mexican nationalism proved too strong a force for him to overcome.

References: Jack Autrey Dabbs, *The French Army in Mexico, 1861–67* (The Hague: Mouton, 1963); Alfred Hanna and Kathryn Hanna, *Napoleon III and Mexico* (Chapel Hill: University of North Carolina Press, 1971); Charles Allen Smart, *Viva Juárez!* (Philadelphia: Lippincott, 1963).

VICKSBURG

DATE: 19 May–4 July 1863.
LOCATION: on the Mississippi River, approximately 150 miles from the Gulf of Mexico.

FORCES ENGAGED:

Union: 75,000 troops. Commander: Major General Ulysses Grant.
Confederate: 30,000 troops. Commander: Lieutenant General John Pemberton.

IMPORTANCE:

By capturing Vicksburg, the Union gained control of the Mississippi River, splitting the Confederacy.

Historical Setting

Soon after the army of the Confederate States of America opened the American Civil War on 12 April 1861 by firing on the Union-held Fort Sumter in the harbor at Charleston, South Carolina, President Abraham Lincoln called for volunteers to suppress the rebellion. They failed to do so, being soundly defeated in the opening battle at Manassas Junction, Virginia, three months later. While Major General

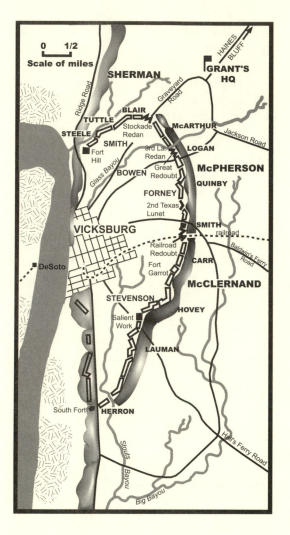

George McClellan attempted to recover from that loss by expanding and training a new and larger army, senior army commander General Winfield Scott began development of a grand strategy to defeat the Confederacy. Called the Anaconda Plan, it proposed strangling the southern states in stages.

First, a naval blockade would sever any lines of communication with foreign countries, keeping the industry-poor South from gaining necessary weapons and supplies. That was already accomplished, for President Lincoln had ordered such an action immediately after Fort Sumter. Second, Scott proposed gaining control of the Mississippi River, which would keep the western three states of the Confeder-acy (Texas, Louisiana, and Arkansas) from pro-viding any assistance to the remaining eight states. Third, offensives directed southeast from Tennessee through Georgia would separate the lower South from the upper South. Thus, con-tinually isolated sections of the Confederacy would lose any ability to cooperate with each other and could be crushed piecemeal.

Operations to accomplish the second phase began in February 1862, when Major General Ulysses Grant captured Forts Henry and Donelson on the Tennessee and Cumberland rivers. The Confederacy had depended on a cordon defense, a string of forts designed to hold the enemy at bay long enough for a mobile force to march to its relief. Neither Confederate fort saw such relief, however, and Grant began slowly moving southward down the Tennessee River. In early April a strong Confederate attack near Pittsburgh Landing near the Shiloh Churchyard caught him unawares. Grant's leadership and timely rein-forcements saved the day for the Union army, which withdrew into Mississippi.

With western Tennessee under his control, Grant marched his army to the Mississippi River and began a slow advance downriver through the summer and fall of 1862. Through those same months other Union forces were slowly advancing upriver, having captured the port city of New Orleans in April 1862. The two forces marched toward each other, and the city of Vicksburg, Mississippi, was destined to be the last location on the river where the west-ern and eastern Confederacy maintained a ten-uous contact. Vicksburg's situation, on a steep bluff overlooking the river, made an attack from the Louisiana side of the river impossible, although Grant tried a number of indirect attacks. Gunboats bombarded the Confederate gun positions on the bluffs above the river in May and June 1862 but were unable to take them out. Grant sent William Sherman's XVth Corps across the Yazoo River north of the city attempting a surprise attack at the end of December, but the terrain was too swampy to

Union Army dugouts on a hillside during the siege of Vicksburg, Mississippi. (MPI/Archive Photos)

cross. Attempts to alter the channel of the Mississippi River by a canal in order to facilitate crossing also failed. He therefore was forced to move farther south, recrossing the river at Bruinsburg on 30 April and Grand Gulf on 2 May.

The commander of Confederate forces in Vicksburg was Lieutenant John Pemberton. He had spent the previous months developing the city into an almost impregnable bastion, ringed with miles of trenches. Had he left that position and contested Grant more forcefully at Grand Gulf he might have prevented a Union crossing, but news of a major cavalry raid through Mississippi drew his attention. He sent his cavalry and some of his infantry toward Jackson, Mississippi, to intercept it. The major Confederate army was based in Jackson, under the command of Lieutenant General Joseph Johnston. Had he been able to link up with Pemberton's

force, the two could have faced Grant with a formidable army, but Grant got between them and divided his force. He sent the XVIIth Corps under John McPherson to Jackson. They succeeded in driving Johnston away, then occupying the city. Grant, with the remainder of his army, marched to intercept Pemberton. On 16 May they met and fought a bloody battle at Champion's Hill, about 25 miles from Vicksburg. Pemberton was obliged to retreat to his defenses.

The Siege

Grant followed hard upon Pemberton's retreat, reaching Vicksburg on 18 May. He launched an unsuccessful assault the next day followed by another on the 22nd. He made no headway against the strong Confederate position while losing more than 3,000 men. Knowing that further direct assaults were suicidal, Grant began digging his own trench works. He was forced, however, to keep half of his force stationed away from the city, for General Johnston had reorganized his army and reoccupied Jackson, thus posing a threat to Grant's rear.

Grant's troops dug the classic Vauban-style parallels with zigzag trenches in between. In many places along the 11 miles of trench works the two armies were separated by mere yards. Snipers did much of the fighting, but the bulk of the exchange between the two armies was by artillery. Union guns rained 70,000 rounds per day into the city, and Confederate counterfire was almost as intense. Supplementing Grant's artillery were Union gunboats on the river. The citizens of Vicksburg, to escape the bombardment, dug caves in the hillsides around the city, some of which were quite elaborate. By the end of the siege they were reduced to eating mule meat and rats. One Confederate soldier wrote, "On June twenty-eighth orders were issued to select the finest and fattest mules and slaughter them. . . . Besides this meat, traps were set for rats, which were consumed in such numbers that ere the termination of the siege they actually became a scarcity. I once made a hearty breakfast on fried rats and found the flesh very good" (Newman and Eisenschiml, *The Civil War*, p. 449).

As Union troops dug ever closer to Confederate lines, they began work on a mine. By 25 June it had been dug and filled with gunpowder; a Confederate countermine had failed to collapse the Union effort. When it exploded at 0300 it created a crater that was not sufficiently wide to advance in strength. Further, the 3rd Louisiana Regiment, which had been occupying the now-destroyed trenches, had withdrawn and built another position just behind the demolished section. For twenty-four hours Grant rotated in twenty regiments, but none could hold the breach and the Confederates reoccupied the position. Grant wrote, "Another

mine was exploded on the first of July, but no attempt to charge was made, the experience of the twenty-fifth admonishing us" (Newman and Eisenshiml, *The Civil War*, p. 448). Grant decided that no more mines would be exploded until a number of them could be used at once and a general assault made.

As it turned out, such an event never occurred. On 3 July, General Pemberton decided that relief was not going to come and that he had insufficient food to last much longer. As the following day was the 4th, Independence Day, Pemberton, from Pennsylvania, believed that the occasion would put Grant in a generous mood. Grant's first demand was for unconditional surrender, but Pemberton threatened an intensification of the fighting. Grant finally softened a bit and, on the 4th, offered a release of the garrison on parole in return for complete abandonment of the city. Grant's note to Pemberton stated that "you will be allowed to march out of our lines, the officers taking with them their side-arms and clothing, and the field, staff, and cavalry officers one horse each. The rank and file will be allowed all their clothing, but no other property" (Foote, *The Civil War*, vol. 2, p. 610).

Results

What Pemberton did not know was that Johnston's army was marching toward Vicksburg at the time of the surrender. Pemberton had been able to maintain contact with his superior and had been repeatedly assured that help was on the way. Having heard that too often without results, he could not depend on Johnston's last promise. Indeed, Johnston had authorized Pemberton to open negotiations, so there was no reason for the besieged commander to believe that potential relief was coming.

The cost of the siege was high. The Confederates had lost almost 2,900 killed, wounded, and missing during the 48 days; more than 29,000 surrendered. The Union troops occupying Vicksburg took possession of 172 cannon and more than 60,000 muskets and rifles, many of high quality. The battle cost the attackers more than 4,900 casualties, most of them lost in the opening assaults in May.

Aside from the human cost, the Confederacy lost much more dearly. The fall of Vicksburg, coupled with the Confederate surrender of the besieged Port Hudson downriver in Louisiana, brought the length of the river into Union hands. Supplies and manpower available in Texas, Louisiana, and Arkansas were now unobtainable. As the Confederacy had been able to gain some materiel through Texas by way of Mexico, the last avenue of outside aid disappeared. Fighting continued in those three western states through the remainder of the war, but it became little more than a sideshow.

What Pemberton could not know was how fatefully timed his surrender would be. That same day, 4 July 1863, Robert E. Lee's battered army was withdrawing from Gettysburg, Pennsylvania, after a failed attempt to rampage through that state, resupply his army, and give impetus to the North's growing peace movement. These two major setbacks marked the turning point of the American Civil War. Prior to this time, the South had certain advantages: superior military leadership, higher morale, and slavery, which would allow them to field an army without having to see much of a decrease in agricultural production. Unfortunately for them, by the summer of 1863 the superior industrial might of the North, as well as its greater manpower, had finally been harnessed for the war effort. After Gettysburg and Vicksburg, that advantage would be employed to pound the Confederacy into submission.

References: Otto Eisenschiml and Ralph G. Newman, *The Civil War: An American Iliad* (Indianapolis: Bobbs-Merrill, 1947); Shelby Foote, *The Civil War, A Narrative*, vol. 2 (New York: Random House, 1963); James McPherson, *Battle Cry of Freedom* (New York: Oxford University Press, 1988); J. G. Randall and

David Donald, *The Civil War and Reconstruction* (Lexington, MA: Heath, 1969).

PETERSBURG

DATE: 15 June 1864–2 April 1865.
LOCATION: 25 miles south of Richmond, Virginia.

FORCES ENGAGED:

Union: 122,000 men. Commander:
Major General Ulysses Grant.
Confederate: less than 60,000 men. Commander:
General Robert E. Lee.

IMPORTANCE:

Petersburg's fall meant the Confederate capital of Richmond had to surrender, and the War between the States came to an end a week later.

Historical Setting

Although Robert E. Lee and his Army of Northern Virginia had blunted every Union attempt to reach the Confederacy's capital of Richmond, Virginia, his two attacks on Northern territory had proved his undoing. His failure to operate in the North at will in September 1862 meant a lack of foreign recognition and direct military aid. His army's defeat at Gettysburg in July 1863 forced him to retreat into Virginia, where he could only win the war by a successful defense that would lengthen the war sufficiently to bring to the fore a growing peace movement in the Union. Between July 1863 and May 1864, little fighting took place in Virginia, and Lee was able to rebuild his ragged force to 50,000 to 60,000 men.

After a string of unsuccessful generals, U.S. President Abraham Lincoln transferred Ulysses Grant from the western theater of the war over to Virginia. Grant's persistent nature contrasted sharply with the timidity of most

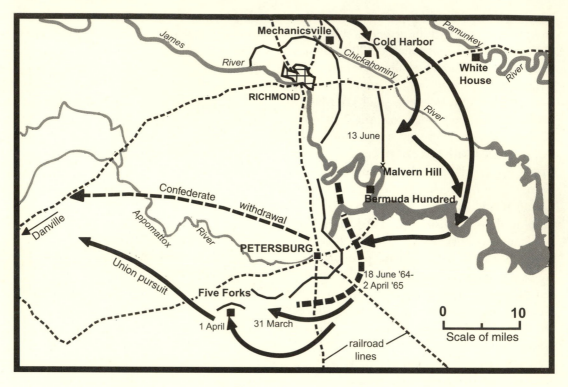

previous Union generals in the eastern theater. Given command of all Union armies and the rank of lieutenant general, Grant was given a free hand to fight Lee and end the war.

In early May 1864 Grant led some 100,000 men into northern Virginia in an attempt to wear out Lee's army. On 5 May he entered a heavily wooded area called the Wilderness near Fredericksburg, Virginia. After three days of fighting he withdrew, losing twice as many casualties as he had inflicted. Instead of retreating to Washington as his predecessors had, Grant marched east and south to outflank Lee. A week later at Spotsylvania he again lost to Lee's army, but again shifted east and south to the North Anna River. Defeated there a week later, he again marched to outflank Lee. The two armies met on 1 June at Cold Harbor, where Grant's head-on attack against Lee's entrenchments cost some 7,000 Union casualties in half an hour.

In these four battles, Grant's army had suffered some 50,000 dead and wounded, but Cold Harbor was closer to Richmond than any previous Union army had been. The extremely high death toll, however, brought increased

public pressure on Lincoln to relieve Grant, or even to negotiate a peace with the Confederacy. Lincoln stood by Grant, however politically unpopular that was. Rather than assault the formidable defenses around Richmond, Grant decided to again swing east and south toward the city of Petersburg, a terminus of nine railroads from across the Confederacy, the point through which Lee's army and the Confederate capital received supplies. Sever the supply line, and both would starve.

Lincoln ordered Benjamin Butler, commander of the Army of the James, to bring his army up the James River to threaten Richmond. He landed his forces at Bermuda Hundred just as Grant was launching his foray into the Wilderness. After Cold Harbor, Grant ordered Butler to attack. Butler, with strong political connections but a weak military mind, on 15 June captured some Confederate trench works, but by the 18th had failed to break through a thin Confederate line. Confederate General P. G. T. Beauregard had stripped his primary defenses of manpower to meet a flanking attack launched by Union

General W. H. Smith. Beauregard's boldness in the face of Butler's and Smith's lack thereof saved the day while Lee rushed the remainder of his army south to Petersburg to man the lines. By the time Grant and the bulk of the army arrived and attacked on the 18th, Lee had 40,000 men in place. The Confederates turned away Grant's 65,000 men, and the siege began.

The Siege

For two weeks the two sides dug in and traded artillery fire and occasional probes. Late in June Lieutenant Colonel Henry Pleasants of the 48th Pennsylvania Regiment approached Grant about the possibility of mining a Confederate strongpoint. Although Grant was fairly supportive of the plan, his direct subordinate, Commander of the Army of the Potomac George Gordon Meade, gave Pleasants as little aid as possible. While the Pennsylvania miners

dug a horizontal shaft more than 500 feet long under Confederate lines, IX Corps Commander Ambrose Burnside trained his largest division for the attack: two newly arrived brigades consisting of former slaves. The day before the attack, Burnside was told to use these soldiers in the second wave and to lead with an all-white unit, but none had had the preparation for the assault. Burnside had his division commanders draw straws, and General James Ledlie's 1st Division got the assignment. Ledlie was a poor commander and his unit was badly under-strength and suffering from poor morale.

At 0445 on 30 July 4 tons of gunpowder in the mine exploded, destroying an artillery position but little else. Burnside's troops, ordered to attack around the crater and hit the Confederate flanks, instead went into the crater and stopped to stare at the massive hole in the ground (170 feet long, 80 feet wide, 30 feet deep). The Confederates responded rapidly and began pouring a murderous fire into the

Federal soldiers in the process of removing artillery from Confederate fortifications in Petersburg, April, 1865. (Library of Congress)

milling soldiers. When the black troops finally were committed to the attack, the Confederates had restored their lines and launched a counterattack that resulted in the slaughter of Union soldiers in the crater or the murder of any black soldier trying to surrender. The attackers lost some 3,800 casualties, the Confederates less than half that.

With the mine attempt failing, Grant settled down to a long siege, and public opinion grew even more hostile. His 50,000 casualties in May had been bad enough, but at least he was going somewhere; now he was losing men and going nowhere. Lincoln still supported Grant, but the lack of progress badly hurt Lincoln's chances for reelection in 1864.

Over the next eight and one half months Grant's army attacked, dug in at their new positions, then attacked again, all the while moving the siege lines farther westward. On 9 August a Confederate agent blew up a supply ship in Grant's main base of City Point, but it was a temporary setback for the Union. Grant threw probing attacks all along the lines: north of the James River in mid-August followed by the capture of the Weldon Railroad at Globe Tavern. The Confederates lost Fort Harrison in front of Richmond at the end of September, but beat back a Union attack on Boydton Plank Road to the southwest a month later. When winter began the two sides settled into an artillery duel of which the Union definitely had the advantage. A massive 13-inch mortar, the "Dictator," caused great psychological if not physical damage to the inhabitants of Petersburg. Although the siege dragged on, General William Sherman's capture of Atlanta, Georgia, at the end of August 1864 restored Lincoln's political fortunes and Grant remained in command.

By February 1865 the opposing lines measured 37 miles long. Lee's men continued to deal harsh punishment to any Union attack, but their starving condition could not be ameliorated. On 25 March, Lee launched an attack on the Union Fort Stedman, hoping to draw enough enemy troops to that position to allow the bulk of his army to break out of the siege lines elsewhere. Although the Confederates took the fort temporarily, they soon lost it in a counterattack and the strategy failed.

The next day General Philip Sheridan arrived. His cavalry force had cleared out the Shenandoah Valley of the last remaining Confederates, and his arrival brought Union strength up to 122,000. On 29 March Grant launched an attack on Dinwiddie Courthouse, on Lee's far western flank, while sending Sheridan on a wide sweep even farther west to encircle the Confederates. Lee responded with an even wider western sweep that hit Sheridan's flank. At Dinwiddie's Courthouse, however, Confederate troops were forced to withdraw to Five Forks. Grant launched an attack there on 1 April and, striking on two sides with far greater forces, forced the defense to collapse. On the 2nd he ordered his army to attack Petersburg itself. They were held at bay by Confederate Generals Gordon and Long-street, but after dark Lee ordered the city abandoned.

Results

The fall of Petersburg was anti-climactic, but not so the fall of Richmond. Frustrated Union troops torched the city. Meanwhile, Lee hurried westward, hoping to reach Danville, where he could move his army by train to North Carolina and join Joseph Johnston, who was harassing Sherman's advance north to link with Grant. On 6–7 April, Sheridan struck a Confederate holding position at Sayler's Creek, capturing some 10,000 prisoners. Lee on the 8th managed to get rations for his remaining 30,000 men at Farmville, but when he found Sheridan's army awaiting him over the next hill he knew his time had run out. Meeting with Grant in Appomattox Courthouse on 9 April, Lee surrendered all Confederate armies. He rejected suggestions by some of his subordinates to scatter his forces and fight a guerrilla war, knowing it would not save the Southern cause and could only mean further misery for the civilian population.

References: Shelby Foote, *The Civil War: A Narrative*, vol. 3 (New York: Random House, 1974); Jeff Kinard, *The Battle of the Crater* (Abilene, TX: McWhiney Foundation, 1998); Noah Trudeau, *The Last Citadel* (Boston: Little, Brown, 1991).

FORT FISHER

DATE: 23 December 1864–15 January 1865.
LOCATION: at the mouth of the Cape Fear River, downstream of Wilmington, North Carolina.

FORCES ENGAGED:

Union: Naval force: fifty-seven vessels of various types. Commander: Admiral David Porter. Land force: first attempt: 6,500 infantry. Commander: General Benjamin Butler. second attempt: 8,000 infantry. Commander: Brigadier General Alfred Terry.
Confederate: 2,000 men. Commander: General William Lamb, later General W. H. C. Whiting.

IMPORTANCE:

Fort Fisher's fall closed the port of Wilmington, cutting off the last Confederate naval contact with the outside world.

Historical Setting

When America's Civil War broke out in April 1861, the newly created Confederate States of America embarked on an almost impossible task. Far outmatched by the Northern states in all materiels of war, the Confederacy's only hope was to trade her one advantage, cotton, for weaponry and support from overseas. This proved a daunting task as well, for although a large percentage of the soldiers of the United States Army resigned their positions and joined the Southern cause, virtually none of the United States Navy did. This disparity in shipping was immediately put to good use when Abraham Lincoln ordered a blockade of Southern ports.

Early in the conflict, the senior commander in the United States Army, Major General Winfield Scott, developed a grand strategy to defeat the Confederacy. The Anaconda Plan, as its name implies, was designed to squeeze the South to death. The first phase of that plan was to cut them off from the rest of the world, and Lincoln's blockade did that within a matter of weeks. The United States Navy was stationed off every Southern port to keep cotton in and foreign aid out. To counter this, Confederate agents in Europe (primarily in England) purchased or commissioned the construction of fast ships to run the blockade. These ships had some success, but unfortunately for the Confederate cause, many cargoes were full of scarce trade goods instead of scarce weaponry. Still, enough supplies got through to give some aid to the Southern armies.

Over time, the Union military was able to end the blockade running by capturing the ports from which they operated. Some of those ports, however, proved exceedingly difficult to capture. The toughest, and therefore the last to fall, was Wilmington, North Carolina, 20 miles up the Cape Fear River from the Atlantic and protected by Fort Fisher. The fort was massive and built unlike almost any fort along the Southern coast. While most fortifications had been built over the preceding few decades using masonry, Fort Fisher was made of earthworks and sand piled on a base of logs. It was built in an L-shape, measuring almost 2,000 yards along the sea face of Confederate Point, then turning west for some 600 yards to cover any approach from the landward side. The walls were 9 feet high and 25 feet thick, and 47 guns made sure that no unwanted ship approached the mouth of the Cape Fear River, where the uncertain course of the river through numerous shallows would make any vessel an easy target.

In December 1864 General William Sherman captured Savannah, Georgia, and immediately turned his army north to link up with his superior, Ulysses Grant, then in the process of besieging Petersburg, Virginia. Grant wanted to possess Wilmington as a handy supply port

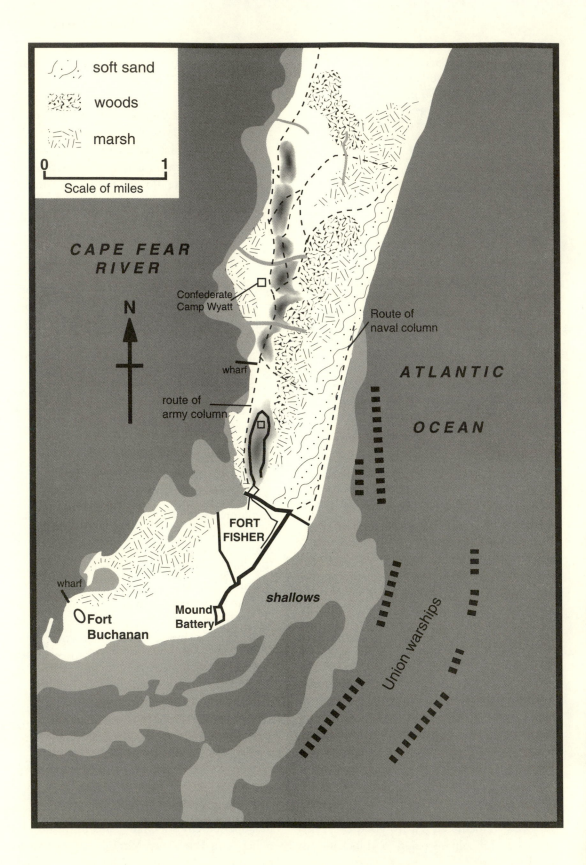

soft sand

woods

marsh

0   1
Scale of miles

CAPE FEAR
RIVER

N

Confederate
Camp Wyatt

Route of
naval column

wharf

ATLANTIC

route of
army column

OCEAN

FORT
FISHER

wharf

shallows

Mound
Battery

Fort
Buchanan

Union warships

First published in 1890, this chromolithograph depicts the capture of Fort Fisher. (Library of Congress)

for Sherman's men, as well as a potential refuge should Confederate resistance in the Carolinas proved stiffer than expected. He directed Admiral David Porter to escort a force of soldiers to the North Carolina coast to seize Fort Fisher and then Wilmington. The Union army operating along the Carolina coast was the Army of the James, commanded by political appointee General Benjamin Butler. Butler believed the fort could have but few defenders and so he took command of the operation in order to enhance his political future.

The Siege

Butler's plan was to overpower Fort Fisher in spectacular style. With Porter's reluctant but growing cooperation, the USS *Louisiana* was stripped down to resemble a blockade-runner, then packed with 215 tons of gunpowder. On the night of 23 December the ship was anchored before the fort; as planned, the defenders took it for a distressed runner. A ninety-minute timing device was set, but the ship's captain set a slow-burning fire as an emergency backup. At 0118, the expected explosion did not occur, but the fire finally got to the powder at 0140 and the explosion was massive. And completely useless. Other than serving to wake up the defenders from a sound sleep, no harm was done.

At noon on the 24th Porter ordered his ships in to bombard the fort and cover the landing of Butler's men. Their late arrival meant no landing took place until the following day, Christmas. While another bombardment took place, 2,000 men landed 3 miles north of the fort and marched south. They ran into heavy shrapnel fire and discovered the entire approach to be mined. They took a few prisoners from one captured redoubt, then withdrew. Butler ordered them back on board, then sailed away. The first attempt to storm

Fort Fisher was a dismal failure, but most in the Union army were mollified upon learning that Grant removed the despised Butler from command and sent him home.

Grant ordered a second attempt on the fort, putting Brigadier General Alfred Terry in command of 8,000 soldiers to join Porter's ships still along the North Carolina coast. On shore, Lamb's defenders had been reduced to 800 and his appeals for more men had gone without effect when Terry's transports arrived on the afternoon of 12 January 1865. Before dawn on the 13th, Porter's ironclads had been firing on the fort, hoping to locate Confederate guns by their muzzle flashes. That gave the fleet as a whole more success when they came in close after dawn and began bombarding the positions marked by the ironclads. The fire was much more accurate and effective than during the first engagement, and soon the angle of Fort Fisher's defenses was crumbling.

Meanwhile, Terry was landing his men 9 miles up the coast. He had all 8,000 ashore by mid-afternoon and they began digging a line of defenses facing north, in order to face expected Confederate reinforcements. General Robert Hoke arrived with 6,000 men from Wilmington, but the Union defenses were so strong he would not attack them. As Union troops were entrenching, Porter's ships brought a total of 627 guns to bear on the fort. The defenders lost 100 men and half their guns, and regular fire throughout the night slowed repair work. General W. H. C. Whiting arrived with some 750 reinforcements, but also with news that the theater commander, Braxton Bragg, was focusing on withdrawal more than defense. "Lamb, my boy, I have come to share your fate. You and your garrison are to be sacrificed" (Foote, *The Civil War*, vol. 3, p. 743). Another constant bombardment on the 14th was so intense the Confederate gunners were barely able to return fire and another hundred casualties were inflicted.

On the morning of 15 January a force of 350 men floated downriver to join the garrison, but they entered a fort rapidly disintegrating under the shellfire. They also arrived coincident with a Union assault. Lamb led men out of the fort to face the charge, and they threw it back with well-aimed musketry. Unseen by the defenders, however, was a smaller force slipping around their left flank along the river and rushing the walls of the fort, placing three flags there. Whiting responded with the remainder of the garrison while Lamb fell back to help. Just as the Confederates seemed to be restoring the situation, Porter's ships began firing into the mass of troops now exposed. Whiting and Lamb were both wounded and placed in a bombproof shelter as the fighting went on. At 2000 a messenger brought news that the north wall had fallen and the fight was now taking place within the fort. Lamb ordered them to keep up the resistance, but Terry by then had almost his entire force inside. At 2200, the Union possessed the fort.

Results

"If hell is what it is said to be, then the interior of Fort Fisher is a fair comparison. Here and there you see great heaps of human beings laying just as they fell, one upon the other. Some groaning piteously, and asking for water. Others whose mortal career is over, still grasping the weapon they used to so good an effect in life." Thus wrote a Union sailor after the battle (Foote, *The Civil War*, vol. 3, p. 746). In the two attacks, the Union ships lobbed almost 40,000 rounds into the fort. Not only was it in ruins, the loss of life was high. Some 500 defenders died, while Terry lost 955 killed in the assault and Porter lost a further 386 during the exchange of fire with the defending guns. Another 104 were killed and wounded when exhausted soldiers entered a powder magazine with torches while looking for a place to sleep.

As Fort Fisher was falling, former commander Benjamin Butler was sitting before a congressional committee defending his actions in the first attempt. He was in the process of convincing the congressmen that the fort was impregnable and he was fully justified in calling off his attack when word arrived of Terry and Porter's victory. He tried to laugh off his dismay at this ill-timed news, but his future political career was rapidly collapsing. Few mourned its passing.

Lamb and Whiting were both taken to a Union prison camp in New York. Lamb survived his wounds but Whiting did not.

"The fall of Fort Fisher did not clear the way to Wilmington. Yet it was decisive of the fate of the city. On the 19th of February, Fort Anderson, higher up the river, was evacuated under a heavy fire from Porter's fleet, with a cooperating Yankee force eight thousand strong. . . . The troops were pushed for Wilmington, while at the same time Porter's vessels passed the obstructions and steamed up the river. Wilmington was occupied without resistance" (Pollard, *Southern History of the War*, p. 444).

During the last nine weeks of 1864, blockade-runners had smuggled past the blockade, primarily through Wilmington, some 12 million pounds of food and war materiel, as well as shoes, blankets, coffee, rifles, revolvers, medicine, and artillery. After Wilmington's fall, nothing entered.

References: Shelby Foote, *The Civil War*, vol. 3 (New York: Random House, 1986 [1974]); Rod Gragg, *Confederate Goliath: The Battle of Fort Fisher* (New York: HarperCollins, 1991); E. A. Pollard, *The Southern History of the War* (New York: C. B. Richardson, 1866).

HUMAITA

DATE: July 1867–4 August 1868.
LOCATION: on the Rio Paraguay, downstream from Paraguay's capital of Asunción.

FORCES ENGAGED:
Triple Alliance: at least 12,000 men. Commander: General the Marquis de Caxias.
Paraguayan: 3,000 men. Commander: Colonel Paulino Alén, succeeded by Colonel Francisco Martínez.

IMPORTANCE:
The fall of Humaita broke the back of Paraguayn resistance, leading to the fall of the capital city, Asuncion, and ultimate Alliance victory.

Historical Setting

After the removal of Spanish rule in South America in the 1820s, Paraguay resisted Argentine domination by declaring its independence from the former viceroyalty of Rio de la Plata. Under two successive dictators, Dr. José Francia and Carlos Antonio López, Paraguay became a progressive and prosperous nation. They established economic and cultural ties with Europe, and phased out slavery yet had little feudalism or peonage. Paraguay had one of the highest literacy rates on the continent. In 1862, Francisco Solano López came to power upon the death of his father.

In 1864, López felt threatened by Brazil's interference in a civil war in neighboring Uruguay, through which land-locked Paraguay had access to the port city of Montevideo at the mouth of the Uruguay River. If a hostile government were to come to power there, Paraguay would have to depend on the good will of Argentina to allow sea access through Buenos Aires. López's protests concerning Brazilian interference in Uruguay fell on deaf ears, so he decided to apply direct pressure on them by attacking the Brazilian province of Mato Grosso. This being a rugged and uninhabited territory, the attack had no effect. López, attempting to assist Uruguay, then asked permission of Bartolome Mitre, Argentina's leader, for access through his country, a request he refused. Feeling this to be an unfriendly act, Paraguay declared war on Argentina in March 1865 and launched an invasion.

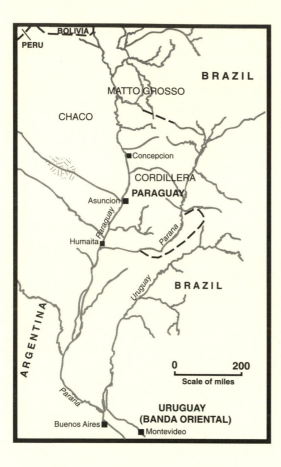

This attack brought about the formation of the Triple Alliance of Brazil, Argentina, and Uruguay on 1 May 1865. A secret clause in the treaty called for the Alliance to confiscate about half of Paraguayan territory and divide it between Brazil and Argentina. The coalition of three nations, two of them the largest in South America, seemed on the face of it to be overwhelming in its power. However, the well-trained 70,000 man Paraguayan army outnumbered the combined coalition forces. Still, López was unable to press his invasion of Argentina and was soon on the defensive. Alliance troops invaded across the Paraná River in April 1866 and drove northward up the Rio Paraguay. The "Sevastopol of the Americas," the fort at Humaita, was their first major obstacle.

The Paraguayans had time to strengthen the fort, for the invading soldiers of the Triple Alliance, perhaps 80 percent Brazilian, suffered from hesitant leadership as well as diseases rampant in the marshy terrain. Further, the Paraguayans fought tenaciously at every battle, although their commanders lacked any sort of tactical imagination and sacrificed thousands of soldiers in frontal attacks. By the time the invaders began their campaign toward Humaita, the Paraguayan government was reduced to recruiting (and sending into combat) children as young as ten years old.

The Siege

President López himself had been in Humaita directing the upgrading of the defenses, but in the wake of the bloody defeats earlier he needed veteran troops with which to rebuild his mobile army. He thus reduced the garrison from 15,000 down to 3,000, placing them under the command of Colonel Paulino Alén, with court favorite Colonel Francisco Martínez as his chief subordinate. Humaita possessed 200 guns.

Just before midnight on 18 February a fleet of seven Brazilian ironclads ran the river past Humaita's guns. They sustained minor damage both from Humaita's defenses and from a battery recently located just up and across the river at Timbó. They progressed upriver to the capital at Asunción and bombarded it on the 24th, then retired. Perhaps hoping that the fleet's passage would provide a diversion, 12,000 men under General the Marquis de Caxias assaulted the redoubt of La Cierva, 2 miles north of Humaita. The 500 defenders inflicted 600 to 1,000 casualties on the attacking Brazilian troops during four assaults, before retreating aboard boats down to the main fort.

General Caxias was duped by the defenders into believing their strength was much greater than it really was. Rather than strong walls, much of the defense was actually in the form of entrenchments, but redoubts defended by a few real guns supplemented with "Quaker cannons" (tree trunks painted black and mounted on gun carriages) were sufficient to keep Caxias at bay. Even a reconnaissance-in-force on 11 April failed to reveal the truth. Frequent sorties by the defenders also helped maintain the illusion. Also, in March, a canoe-bound force launched a night attack on the river attempting to capture one of the ironclads, but the Brazilian ships raked each other with grapeshot and slaughtered the attackers.

In early July the ironclads pounded the fortress and received no return fire. Thinking the garrison either evacuated or too weak to fight, Caxias launched an assault that was cut to pieces by the defenders who had been "playing possum." Unfortunately for the garrison, an Argentine force cut off the last supply line in early summer and the main enemy was starvation. Soldiers and civilians boiled cowhide for food. Martínez took command of the fort after Alén attempted suicide. He managed to get a messenger through the lines to López, warning him of the dire situation. López ordered him to hold on for five more days, then evacuate.

Starting on the night of 23 July women and the wounded were ferried across the Rio Paraguay in the darkness, then taken northward into the marshy region known as the Chaco. Those remaining in the city played music all day the 24th in honor of President López's birthday, further deceiving the enemy as to their strength and morale. The band played all night as more survivors escaped the following night; the instrumentalists were the last to leave.

When the Brazilians learned of the move, they launched an attack on the retreating Paraguayans as they worked their way across a nearby lagoon. Martínez and a number of soldiers covered the evacuation from lakeside. In spite of their starving condition, they were strong enough to beat back an assault on 28 July, firing the metal from ruined muskets through their few remaining guns. Martínez remained a difficult enemy. When Caxias sent a messenger on 2 August to offer surrender terms, he was met with heavy rifle fire. A second offer two days later, however, was accepted. Martínez and his 1,324 survivors had not eaten for four days.

Results

After the hard-fought victory Fort Humaita, the Alliance soldiers rested for three months, then moved farther north, occupying the capital city of Asuncion in January 1869. López, "continually in retreat, forced much of the civilian population to follow him, and where the caravans traveled so too did cholera and a host of diseases in their wake, an unseen albatross on the shoulders of the republic" (Williams, *Rise and Fall*, p. 223). He was unable to strengthen his army with anyone but children and the aged, while the Alliance forces, mainly Brazilian, continued to grow. López's last stand came on 1 May 1870, when he was killed in battle after being cornered against the Brazilian border. His death brought the end of Paraguayan resistance.

His death also brought the end of a prosperous and independent Paraguay. The country's population was devastated by the war, some three-fourths of the 500,000 citizens dying from combat, disease, starvation, or a brutal Brazilian occupation. The adult male population of the country was reduced to only about 30,000. As agreed during the formation of the Triple Alliance, Brazil and Argentina did annex about half the country, as well as force the Paraguayans to pay heavy reparations. Brazil established a puppet government of former Paraguayan generals and proceeded to dismantle the decades of progress the country had enjoyed. Most of the land was sold to foreign investors at extremely low prices and the economy came under the control of Brazilian investors.

References: Ricardo Bonalume Neto, "River Passage Sought," *Military History* 10, no. 5, December 1993; Gilbert Phelps, *Tragedy of Paraguay* (New York: St. Martin's, 1975); John Hoyt Williams, *The Rise and Fall of the*

Paraguayan Republic, 1800–1870 (Austin, TX: Institute of Latin American Studies, 1979).

PARIS

DATE: 18 September 1870–26 January 1871.
LOCATION: northwestern France, on the Seine River.

FORCES ENGAGED:
Prussian/German: 206,000 infantry, 34,000 cavalry, with more than 1,100 artillery pieces. Commander: Field Marshal Count Helmuth von Moltke.
French: 355,000 infantry (primarily poorly trained home guard units), 5,000 cavalry, almost 2,000 artillery pieces. Commander: General Louis Trochu.

IMPORTANCE:
Paris' surrender ended the Franco-Prussian War, during which the state of Germany was created. The hostility engendered between Germany and France was a major factor in relations leading to World War I.

Historical Setting

The dominant state of Germany in the mid-1800s was Prussia, which had risen to prominence mainly through its military. Ever since their defeat at the hands of Napoleon in 1806–1807 the Prussian military had dedicated itself to becoming the best in the world, both to return to the glory days of Frederick the Great and to assure that no such embarrassment as that at the hands of the French was ever repeated. They developed the world's first General Staff, promoting excellence in all phases of military activity. The system proved itself in 1866, when Prussia easily defeated Austria in a border dispute; that war seemed almost a tune-up for a return match with France. Under the leadership of Chancellor Otto von Bismarck, Prussia gathered the lesser German states around her in a North German Confederation and aimed toward the unification of all Germanic principalities into one state. A war with France would serve as a focus for German nationalism.

In France, Napoleon III had reigned as head of state since the Revolution of 1848. The Second Empire was a shadow of the First Empire established by Napoleon Bonaparte, but France hoped to maintain a major role in world affairs, even if she could not reach the heights of grandeur of the start of the nineteenth century. During the war between Prussia and Austria, Napoleon had given Prussia tacit support in return for generalized promises of reward. France had hoped to gain border lands along the western Rhine after that war, but Bismarck refused to cede any such territory to non-Germans. He then stood in the way of a proposed French purchase of Luxembourg from Holland. When Napoleon hoped to expand at Belgium's expense via heavy French investment in that country's rail system, Bismarck reminded England of possible French control of the Channel coast and English opposition halted French aims. An argument over which country should provide a new monarch for the Spanish throne proved the last straw. Prussian Chancellor Otto von Bismarck manipulated negotiations between the French ambassador and Prussia's King Wilhelm I in such a way that the king appeared to have insulted France. That provoked French public opinion to the point of war and Napoleon, frustrated by Prussia at every turn, complied.

The French army was not as prepared for the war as was French public opinion. Although there had been some minor improvements to the French military over the previous two years, they were no match for the Prussians. Under the military leadership of Count Helmuth von Moltke, the German General Staff was prepared for almost every contingency, and they could field an army twice the size of France's. Moltke planned on drawing the French army into a trap, but aggressive action on the part of a Prussian general warned the French of the impending danger. They slowed their advance to the frontier, but really

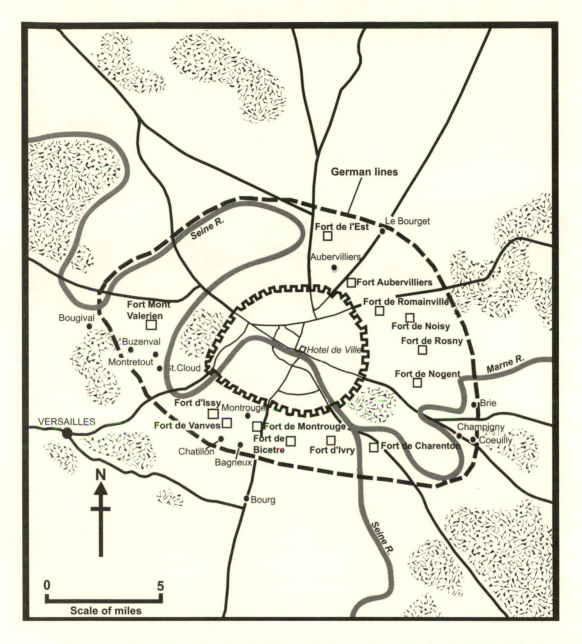

did little more than delay the inevitable. Napoleon divided most of his army into two sections to be based around the cities of Sedan and Metz. Prussian forces outperformed the French in all phases of warfare and both French armies found themselves surrounded. On 1 September 1870, French forces in Sedan under Marshal Maurice de MacMahon surrendered some 100,000 men, including Napoleon III himself. A month later the fortress at Metz, under the command of Marshal Francois Bazaine, also surrendered. Meanwhile, Prussian forces were driving across northern France toward Paris.

The Siege

The French capital seemed impregnable to both the defenders and attackers. The military governor of Paris, General Louis Trochu, mustered an impressive number of men: the regular

A barricade at the Porte Mailot during the revolt by supporters of the Paris Commune. The Arc de Triomphe is seen in the background. (Archive Photos)

army XIII Corps under General Vinoy was reinforced by about 3,000 refugees under General Ducrot from the debacle at Sedan; 3,000 marines and 5,000 sailors rounded out the trained troops. Unfortunately, the bulk of the manpower were *Gardes Mobiles* and *Gardes Sedentaires*, the first a National Guard/ landwehr type of organization with minimal training, and the second more of a Home Guard with virtually none. Still, 400,000 were under arms and the factories of Paris were able to keep them supplied with weaponry.

The Prussians arrived at Paris on 18 September and had the city surrounded the next day. Moltke had no desire to challenge the ring of forts around the city, so he ordered his men to entrench and use starvation as their primary tactic. The Parisians had amassed a good if not great amount of supplies before the battle, so starvation could have been an extremely slow and disappointing tactic for the Prussians. However, they were assisted by the Parisians

themselves. General Trochu immediately faced a popular rising against his command by *communards*, socialists demanding a commune be established to deal with the siege. More than once Trochu was forced to call on conservative forces within the Gardes Mobiles to break up demonstrations or even rescue government officials. Possibly the only man who could have maintained order if such a commune was instituted was Leon Gambetta, who led the newly established Third Republic, but he fled Paris in a hot air balloon early in the siege in order to rally forces in the countryside to relieve the city.

Trochu attempted to maintain an active defense. He ordered the first sortie against the Prussians on 30 September. It enjoyed some early success against Prussian forward positions, but the rapid-firing Krupp breech-loading cannon dealt harshly with the attackers, who retreated "according to plan" back into Paris. On 13 October Trochu ordered General Vinoy to attack Chatillon and Bagneux just south of

Paris; the attack again enjoyed some success, including the capture of 100 prisoners, but was little more than a raid. Heartened somewhat by these forays, Trochu ordered a larger attack to be led by General Ducrot on 21 October toward St. Cloud and Bougival west of the city. The village of Buzenval was captured and held against repeated Prussian counterattacks, then abandoned with admirable skill.

These were not viewed as successes by the Parisians, who could not understand why gained ground was ceded. Further, the regular troops involved in the attacks grew increasingly angry with the guardsmen who stayed in the city drilling. News of the fall of Metz and its surrender of 150,000 men did nothing to increase morale, but personal initiative on the part of General Carré de Bellemare did brighten sprits a bit. Without orders he led an assault and captured the village of Le Bourget just northeast of Paris, but the joy was short-lived, for a major Prussian counterattack not only recaptured the town but annihilated most of the French force inside.

The loss of Le Bourget coupled with the news of Metz reinvigorated communards in Paris, who temporarily seized Trochu's headquarters at the Hôtel de Ville. After a hastily organized plebiscite showed overwhelming support for Trochu's government, good news finally arrived. Gambetta had succeeded in raising forces to the south that had defeated the Prussians and captured Orleans. The public demanded a breakout to link up with this army. Trochu had been preparing another sortie aimed at Rouen through what he believed to be the weakest part of the German encirclement, but felt impelled to redirect the attack toward the southeast. Unfortunately, it was directed at the strength of the Prussian lines and security was almost nonexistent. Worse, a rise in the Marne River delayed the attack but a diversionary feint went ahead as scheduled. The Prussians were ready, but the French still enjoyed early success when the attack finally got under way on 28 November. The French

crossed the Marne on the 30th and established a bridgehead that successfully repelled several Prussian assaults. Although both Trochu and General Ducrot were in the forefront of the fighting, the Prussian artillery was too effective and the beaten French forces withdrew to Paris on 3 December.

News of French victories against German forces north of Paris inspired another sortie toward Le Bourget just before Christmas, but the frozen ground kept the French from digging in as they had done so well in previous attacks. After three days of fighting Ducrot once again pulled his battered force back into Paris, severely weakened by combat deaths, malnutrition, and frostbite. Inside the city, food shortages became acute and animals from rats to beasts in the zoo found themselves fair game for hungry Parisians.

Moltke had done little more than hold his positions, reacting to French sorties, content to let starvation do its work. The Prussian political leadership wanted a quicker end to the siege. Over Moltke's protests the Prussians began bombarding the city itself, rather than merely the fortifications, on 5 January 1871. At first it provoked a toughening of the Parisian spirit, further hardened by news that on 18 January Prussian King Wilhelm named himself leader of a united German state and did so at the French royal residence at Versailles. Public pressure demanded another sortie, and Trochu reluctantly agreed. He detailed 90,000 men in three columns to attack westward on the 19th, but temperatures well below zero coupled with dense fog hampered the operation. Once again there were early successes, especially at Buzenval, but the stout German lines held and the sortie failed yet again.

Widespread shelling of the city and the increasing lack of food took its toll on the populace, as starvation deaths numbered 3,000 to 4,000 per week in January. Coupled with increased activity by the communards, the French leadership moved to open negotiations with Bismarck. The first meetings were held on

23 January at Versailles and the armistice was signed on the 28th. Not until 1 March, however, did German troops enter the city.

Results

Bismarck was determined to humiliate the defeated French Third Republic. In no position to bargain, the French government ceded the rich provinces of Alsace and Lorraine to Germany and were forced to pay an indemnity of 5 billion francs. Not surprisingly, this sparked further communard activity in Paris and a Commune was finally established. Although the German soldiers spent but a few days occupying the French capital, it was sufficiently insulting to the radicals that they felt seizure of the government was the only alternative to the ignominious peace terms. The newly elected government under Adolphe Thiers withdrew to Versailles with the bulk of the army and the Commune stood for ten weeks. Although the communards were actually less radical once in control than they had been while on the outside, their mere existence frightened conservative Frenchmen while their continued resistance to the armistice provoked the Germans. The German authorities allowed French troops through their lines to attack the city in late May, and some 20,000 Parisians were killed in the ensuing occupation. "The actual performance of the Commune came to be less significant than the myth it left to later propagandists of a first attempt to set up a Communist state" (Weber, *A Modern History of Europe*, p. 799).

The French government that finally assembled in peace was primarily conservative, and they succeeded in paying off the war indemnity fairly quickly. The bitterness of it, however, remained. France over the next twenty-five years sought allies for the next conflict with Germany, which came in 1914, although colonial arguments and provocations kept the rivalry between the two high well before World War I broke out. Although a multitude of factors were involved in the outbreak of that war, the French desire for revenge and the return of Alsace and Lorraine were certainly among the major causes.

References: William Carr, *The Origin of the Wars of German Unification* (London: Longman, 1991): Michael Howard, *The Franco-Prussian War* (New York: Macmillan, 1962); Helmuth, Graf von Moltke, *The Franco-German War of 1870–71* (New York: Harper Brothers, 1901); Eugene Weber, *A Modern History of Europe* (New York: Norton, 1971).

PLEVNA

DATE: 19 July–10 December 1877.
LOCATION: modern Plevna, Bulgaria, 100 miles northeast of Sofia.

FORCES ENGAGED:

Russian: ultimately 110,000 men and 500 guns. Commander: General de Krüdener, then Franz Todleben.
Turkish: 40,000 men and 77 guns. Commander: Osman Pasha.

IMPORTANCE:

Although a Turkish defeat, the five-month siege stalled the Russian offensive against Turkey so badly that Constantinople could not be captured. The resulting peace treaty began to dismantle European Turkey.

Historical Setting

When Abdulhamit II acceded to the Ottoman throne in 1876, he was faced immediately with a crisis in the northwestern portion of the empire, the Balkan provinces of Serbia, Montenegro, Bosnia, and Herzegovina. With a large Christian population, the Slavs of the region had been agitating for independence from the weakening Ottoman Empire for some time, looking to Russia as the champion of a pan-Slavic movement. When Turkish troops put down a Serbian uprising in the town of Alexinatz, Russia began threatening intervention. Such a possibility,

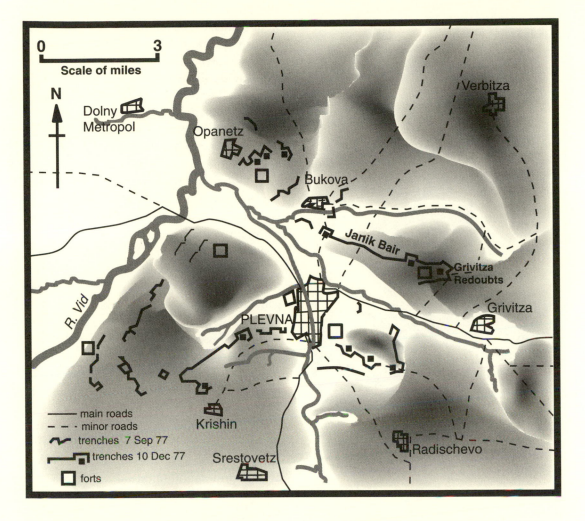

however, meant a potential conflict with Austria, always fearful of Russian designs in the Balkans. German Chancellor Otto von Bismarck proposed breaking up the Ottoman Empire, dividing the territory among the European powers, but could not gain sufficient support for that plan. Instead, he acceded to a British request for an international convocation to discuss the troubles. The resulting Istanbul Conference of November 1876 proved fruitless since the Turkish government, recently adopting a liberal Western-style constitution, claimed that all need for either internal struggle or external intervention was now obviated by the new document.

Without sufficient guarantees for the safety of Christians in the Balkan provinces, Russia began to mobilize her army. Negotiations with Austria bought their friendly neutrality in Jan-

uary 1877, in return for a promise of Vienna receiving Bosnia and Herzegovina as a reward. Other parts of the Ottoman Empire were proposed for distribution to one country or another in southeastern Europe. The Russians then turned to Rumania, technically a Turkish vassal, and requested free passage through her territory. Rumania, seeking its own independence, agreed to allow Russian troops through, then seceded from the Ottoman Empire and offered troops to the Russians. Such an offer was rejected at first, but later problems caused the Russians to reconsider.

Russian troops marched into Rumania in June, making for bridges across the Danube to move into Bulgarian territory. They crossed the river easily against virtually no Turkish opposition. The Russian advance was so rapid the

LONDON NEWS.

No. 2008.—VOL. LXXI.   SATURDAY, DECEMBER 22, 1877.   WITH TWO SUPPLEMENTS   SIXPENCE

Osman Nuri Pasha, general of the Ottoman Turkish army, defends the Bulgarian city of Plevna against the Russian and Balkan troops during the Russo-Turkish war. (Illustrated London News/Archive Photos)

Turks were unable to mount a serious defense at what they hoped would be their first two lines of defense: the Danube and a string of forts just behind it. Russian troops quickly drove on and captured the Ottoman forts at Tirnovo (1 July) and Nicopolis (16 July). Turkish forces under Osman Pasha were marching to Nicopolis when they learned of its fall, so Osman rushed his men to the nearest point of defense, the town of Plevna.

He hurriedly placed men and guns on the high ground around the town.

The Siege

Osman's artillery had no sooner been placed than it went into action against approaching Russian troops. The Russians returned fire, but little damage was inflicted by either side. Osman ordered defensive works dug as fast as possible, and deployed his men in three sectors: thirteen battalions and four gun batteries along the Janik Bair Ridge to the northeast of Plevna (with two battalions and one battery each placed in forward screening positions to the west at Bukovna and Opanetz), five battalions and ten guns flanking the first section to the east, and four battalions with two batteries (covered by the cavalry) flanking them and covering the eastern road to Bulgareni. He also maintained a mobile reserve stationed on a hill just outside Plevna.

At dawn on 20 July the Russians began their first assault, from the north. They made early gains around Bukova and on the eastern flank, but Turkish reinforcements drove the Russians back with losses of about one-third of the 8,000 man attacking force; the Turks lost 2,000. Rather than pursue, Osman kept his men digging. The Turkish defenders built redoubts with walls up to 14 feet thick, with single or double trench lines in front. Luckily for the Turks, supply lines remained open through most of the siege and they were able to get tools as well as food and ammunition until December. To maintain that line of communication, Osman sent six battalions and an artillery battery to Lovcha (modern Lovatz), south of Plevna.

The Russians tried their luck again on 30 July, this time with a preliminary artillery bombardment. The results were worse than before. Strengthened positions, well-placed Turkish artillery, and timely reinforcements all contributed to the Russian losses of 7,300 men compared with Turkish losses of 2,000. A rapid pursuit of the retreating Russians could have panicked them and driven them back across the Danube, but Osman kept to his defenses, possibly on orders from Constantinople. The Russians regrouped and called for reinforcements. With Rumania on their side, troops from that country soon expanded Krüdener's army to 74,000 infantry, 10,000 cavalry, and 440 guns (including 24 heavy siege pieces), for a total of about 100,000 troops.

For some inexplicable reason, Osman launched a relatively small attack against the Russians on 30 August. The day-long encounter resulted in over 1,000 casualties on each side, and the Turks returned to their defenses at day's end. That apparently spurred the Russians into activity, however, for they soon launched an attack against Osman's garrison at Lochva. Their capture of that position on 5 September allowed them to cut the supply line into Plevna. Osman reformed the troops that fled Lochva into another reserve force, giving him a total of some 30,000 men under his command. The Russians began to tighten the noose around Plevna.

Following up on their Lochva victory, the Russians decided to press the initiative. They began a bombardment of the Turkish positions at dawn on 7 September, which lasted until mid-afternoon on the 11th. Although the artillery fire actually caused no more than a few hundred casualties among the Turks, the intensity of the fire and the ensuing assault resulted in the Rumanians capturing a redoubt at the eastern end of the Janik Bair lines while the Russians seized two on the southern front. Turkish counterattacks the next day recovered the southern redoubts but the Rumanians held firm to their conquest, until ordered to withdraw by Krüdener. The overall Russian/Rumanian casualties numbered 18,000. The Russian commander decided from this point forward to play a waiting game. General Franz Todleben, Russian hero of the defense of Sevastopol in 1854, arrived to assume command of the investment. By 24 October the Turkish position was surrounded and more siege guns were added to the destruction. Osman's command held out until 9 December, when they attempted a breakout to the south. It failed, and the next day he surrendered to the Russians.

Results

From a military standpoint, two lessons were demonstrated at Plevna. First, the Turks showed Europe what modern defensive warfare could accomplish. Neither in 1866 with the Austrians nor in 1870 with the French did any significant defensive stand take place. Plevna, however, had a result more like the battles of the American Civil War. The Russians found out the hard way the futility of massed frontal assaults against strong positions covered with both small-arms and artillery fire. The increased range and accuracy of rifles made such human wave tactics virtually suicidal, as did the faster-firing artillery. Second, the Turks learned an older lesson from the second half of the siege: a passive defense is almost always doomed to failure.

Still, Osman Pasha's defense, while ultimately ending in surrender, served the Ottoman Empire well. By stymieing the Russian offensive for five months and inflicting heavy Russian casualties, the ultimate Russian goal of reaching Constantinople was never accomplished. Although a few Cossack units reached the walls of the city, the war was winding down. International attention had been drawn to the conflict, and most of the European powers began to agitate for an end to the fighting in order to deny Russia their control of the Straits. Although the Russians and Turks ended the fighting officially with the Treaty of San Stefano in 1878, the European powers gathered in Berlin under the chairmanship of German Chancellor Bismarck to deal with the long-term fate of southeastern Europe. Although they kept the Turks in control of the strategic Straits, they took away almost all of the Ottoman possessions in the Balkans. Russia and Austria were the major winners in terms of land acquisition.

The removal of Ottoman rule did not bring peace to the region, for wars of liberation from the new overlords flared in 1908 and 1912. European interest in the area became so intense, that the international rivalry blew up in August 1914 in the wake of Austrian Archduke Franz Ferdinand's assassination at the hands of Serbian terrorists.

References: Bruce Menning, *Bayonets before Bullets: The Russian Imperial Army, 1861–1914*

(Bloomington: Indiana University Press, 1992); Stanford Shaw and Ezel Kural Shaw, *History of the Ottoman Empire and Modern Turkey*, vol. 2 (Cambridge: Cambridge University Press, 1977); L. S. Stavrianos, *The Balkans since 1453* (New York: Holt, Rinehart, and Winston, 1963).

KHARTOUM

DATE: 12 March 1884–26 January 1885.
LOCATION: at the junction of the Blue and White Nile rivers in Sudan.

FORCES ENGAGED:

Mahdist: possibly 60,000 men. Commander: Mohammed Ahmed (the Mahdi).
Egyptian: 8,000 Egyptian regular soldiers and 3,000 Sudanese volunteers. Commander: British General Sir Charles Gordon.
Relief force: 10,500 British soldiers. Commander: General Sir Garnet Wolseley.

IMPORTANCE:

Gordon's defeat temporarily ended Egyptian control of the Sudan, but spurred British public opinion to a greater commitment to imperial ventures in Africa.

Historical Setting

In the 1870s Egypt was a possession of the Ottoman Empire and under the direction of Ismail, an official known as the *khedive*. He was a particularly corrupt individual who spent the country into such debt that the French and British sent in financial experts to take over the government and straighten out its tax-collecting and bill-paying. In order to support this action in 1880, the Europeans were obliged to send in troops as well, with the British providing the lion's share. Foreigners in their government and patrolling their streets did not sit well with the Egyptians, and the British found it necessary to put down a revolt by an Egyp-

tian officer named Arabi. Shortly afterward in the Sudan, the desert countryside south of Egypt, a religious leader rose to power to lead his followers against the infidels. This was Mohammed Ahmed, who called himself the Mahdi, or Messiah.

The idea of a Muslim messiah had been foretold for centuries and occasionally a leader arose to gather the faithful against non-Muslim enemies. Thus, Mohammed Ahmed was one in a series of Mahdis who came to power through either self-promotion or true religious fervor. In the Sudan the Mahdi started with a small group of followers and expanded his power through intimidation or by success against the British. The British called his followers dervishes. Properly, this is a term describing collections of Muslim Sufi mystics who often perform amazing feats while in a trance or the throes of religious ecstasy. The term seemed fitting to the British, for the Mahdi's followers fought with a fanatical courage and no fear of death.

The Mahdi scored his first victory by capturing the town of El Obeid in 1881. The British government under the direction of Prime Minister William Gladstone took little interest in these events until he scored a stunning victory over an Egyptian force commanded by a British officer. In 1883 William Hicks led 10,000 ill-prepared men into the Sudanese desert and was ambushed and massacred at Kashgil south of the major city of Khartoum. The vast stocks of weapons that Hicks carried, including the most modern Krupp field guns, fell into the Mahdi's hands. This feat convinced many that this Mahdi was genuine, and his ranks swelled. One such tribe, the Hadendowa from the hills of eastern Sudan near the Red Sea coast, organized themselves under the leadership of Osman Digna. He had little to recommend him as a soldier and apparently his men had little personal regard for him, but he was an excellent strategist and his raids kept his men in booty.

Digna's men slaughtered two Egyptian forces along the coast near the town of Saukin in late 1883. He scored his most impressive

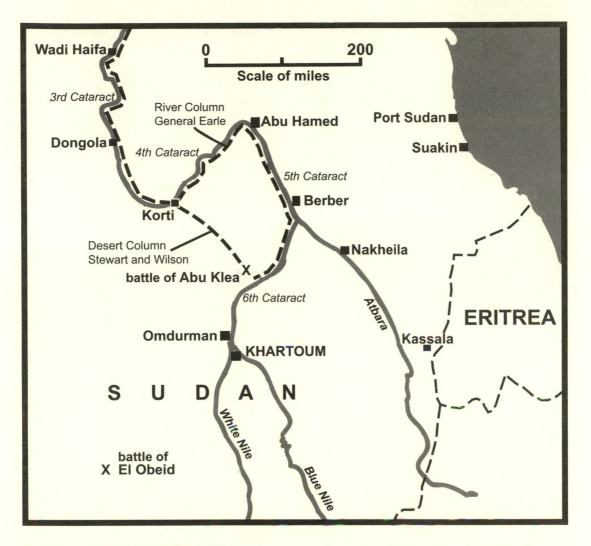

victory on 5 February 1884. Hicks' replacement was Valentine Baker, formerly of both the British and Turkish armies. He commanded a relief force of 3,800 marching to rescue a garrison at the town of Tokar. Baker's force was a mixed lot: a few European officers, a number of high-quality black troops of southern Sudan who had been slave-soldiers, and a large number of untrained and unmotivated Egyptians. They were ambushed at El Teb by 1,200 Hadendowa tribesmen. Because of their practice of greasing their hair with sheep lard, the British called these men Fuzzy-Wuzzy, but that seemingly innocent name belied their fighting ability. Although they were armed with nothing but spears and clubs, the Fuzzy-Wuzzy attack was so determined and their reputation

so fierce that the Egyptians immediately panicked and ran. The confusion made it difficult for the Sudanese soldiers to fight well and the Europeans who stood to fight were badly mauled. Baker's command lost 2,400 men and 3,000 rifles, along with half a million cartridges, four Krupp cannon, and two Gatling guns. Two successive forays, however, restored British prestige.

As these actions were taking place near the Red Sea coast, the main drama was unfolding at the Sudanese capital city of Khartoum. Rather than deal with the Mahdi and his followers, Prime Minister Gladstone decided to abandon the region and sent General Charles Gordon to oversee the removal of Europeans from the city. Gordon, who had made a reputation as an independent, charismatic figure when stationed in China, was too much the imperialist for the more domestic-minded Gladstone, but Gordon had been governor general of the Sudan from 1877 to 1880 and was a public favorite. With his aide Colonel Stewart he arrived in Cairo in late January 1884. Although determined to fulfill his orders to withdraw as many occupants of the city of Khartoum as possible, sometime between his departure from Cairo and his arrival in Khartoum Gordon changed his mind. As deeply Christian as the Mahdi was Muslim, Gordon believed that he had to expose Mohammed Ahmed as a charlatan and decided that Khartoum should not be abandoned.

The Siege

Gordon's decision to hold Khartoum seemed to be confirmed when he received a wild reception upon his arrival. It was a false reading, however, for the citizens assumed that the British army was with him. When he informed them he had God with him, they were not impressed. The British and Egyptian governments had told him there would be no troops sent, but Gordon sent a series of telegrams home arguing his cause and the public responded. Khartoum, however, was in an extremely remote location, at the confluence of the Blue and White Nile rivers. Gordon had to hold on, for a relief force could not possibly arrive quickly. He commanded 8,000 Egyptian soldiers, in whom he had little confidence, and a further 3,000 Sudanese volunteers. As the city was located in the *V* formed by the junction of the rivers, the only avenue of approach was from the south, and Gordon immediately began constructing a trench system and blockhouses before the city walls. Minefields were laid and barbed wire strung. The bulk of his artillery he placed on steamers operating on the rivers, which he hoped would give him adequate flanking fire to break up any assaults.

In May 1884 the telegraph lines to Cairo were cut and the Mahdi sent Gordon his first demand for surrender. As it involved Gordon converting to Islam, it was rejected. He followed up this rejection with a sortie to punish the Muslim patrols that had operated along his lines, but the Egyptian troops fled from the fanatical charge of the dervishes, losing 400 men without inflicting a single casualty. Gordon's swift court-martial and execution of the company commanders achieved the desired effect: the troops and populace came to fear him more than the enemy.

The Mahdi entrusted command of the siege to his subordinate Abu Girgeh, who began bombarding the city with the Krupp artillery captured earlier. Their range was such that he could safely shell the city without interference from Gordon's guns on the boats. Control of the Nile both upstream and downstream meant that supplying the city was impossible. To counter that blockade, in August Gordon ordered a sortie by one of the few Egyptian officers he trusted, Mohammed Ali. Ali succeeded in driving a force of dervishes out of their trenches, suffering minimal casualties in the process. Heartened by this success, Gordon ordered a larger sortie of 1,000 men to destroy the main dervish camp. Initially successful, Ali pursued the defeated dervishes too far into the desert, where his force was ambushed and annihilated.

Despairing of relief, Gordon ordered Colonel Stewart and two reporters to take one of the steamers to Cairo and plead his case. They escaped the ring of soldiers around the city easily enough, but floundered in the shallows downstream. Contacting a local they assumed to be loyal to the Egyptian government they left the boat, only to be beheaded by dervishes. Relief, however, was on the way.

News of the siege created much controversy in London, where the government dallied over what to do. After some months public and royal pressure forced Gladstone to send a relief force in September. The route south to Khartoum, however, was incredibly difficult. The Nile River was the natural route to follow, but a series of cataracts made transporting supply boats nearly impossible. The expedition's commander, General Sir Garnet Wolseley, got off to a late start and then spent weeks constructing boats, importing boatmen from Canada, training a camel corps, whatever seemed necessary to pass the rapids in the river and the desert beyond.

All the physical obstacles were overcome by January 1885. The advance force had fought the elements as well as the dervishes at Abu Klea and Abu Kru to be within striking distance of Khartoum, when the force commander Sir Charles Wilson stopped three days to rest and tend his wounded. When ships arrived on the Nile at his camp, he boarded his men and steamed four days to Khartoum, there to find the Mahdi in control, as he had been for the previous two days.

Hearing of the approach of the relief force, the Mahdi decided to storm Khartoum. He had hesitated to do this, but demands by some of his advisers forced his hand. He did not want to capture the city and then find himself besieged by the British, but neither could he stand to have Gordon's religion defeat his own. One last call for surrender was again rejected, so the assault began at dawn on 26 January. The Mahdi ordered his men to take Gordon alive, for apparently he had come to respect the Briton's religious zeal. Although Gordon ordered every male from eight to eighty to man the defenses, few had the strength or will to do so. The popular story of Gordon's death is that he stood atop the staircase at the governor's palace unarmed, there to be speared and beheaded. Eyewitnesses, however, claimed that he went down fighting so ferociously that he seemed possessed.

Results

Gordon and the city had held back the besiegers with little more than courage for 317 days before being overcome and slaughtered. Many were blamed for his loss, but the brunt of the criticism fell on Gladstone. He finally got the troops withdrawn by deciding an incident in Afghanistan was more threatening.

The Mahdi died not long after his greatest triumph over the British and his followers turned their allegiance to his second-in-command, known as the khalifa (caliph). The British stayed out of the Sudan until 1897, when an expedition under the command of Horatio Kitchener marched south and extracted revenge for Gordon and Khartoum. Kitchener became a national hero, was elevated to Lord Kitchener of Khartoum, commanded the final offensives in South Africa against the Boers, and ultimately rose to the position of minister of war during World War I. The dervishes and Fuzzy-Wuzzy had for a time, however, humbled the power of the British Empire, and joined the Afghans and Zulus as one of the few native forces to do so.

References: Byron Farwell, *Queen Victoria's Little Wars* (New York: Harper & Row, 1972); Robin Neillands, *The Dervish Wars* (London: Murray, 1996); Charles Royle, *The Egyptian Campaigns, 1882 to 1885* (London: Hurst and Blackett, 1900).

CHITRAL

DATE: 4 March–20 April 1895.
LOCATION: area near the confluence of modern Pakistan, Russia, and Afghanistan.

FORCES ENGAGED:

British/Indian: approximately 300 Kashmiris and 150 Sikhs with British officers. Commander: Surgeon-Major George Robertson.
Relief forces: 15,000 men from Peshawar. Commander: General Robert Cunliffe-Low; 400 Sikhs from Gilgit. Commander: Lieutenant Colonel J. G. Kelly.
Pathan/Chitrali: 3,000 men besieging the fort, possibly another 9,000 in the covering force. Commander: Umra Khan.

IMPORTANCE:

British victory helped temporarily to solidify their hold on India's Northwest Frontier, but their increased presence in the region provoked a major native rebellion two years later.

Historical Setting

The principality of Chitral (about the size of Wales) is located in the far northwestern part of modern Pakistan along the most direct route from India to Russia. It is an extremely rugged country somewhat reminiscent of Nepal. Since 1876 Chitral had been under the nominal protection of the maharajah of Kashmir, who was in turn was subject to the British Indian administration. In return for a regular subsidy of money and rifles, the mehtar (ruler) of Chitral maintained relatively friendly relations with Britain. That began to change in 1893.

It is with extreme difficulty that one might keep straight the complicated stream of events that preceded the siege at the capital, also called Chitral. Such difficulty should not be surprising when one looks at a society in which "be fruitful and multiply" converges with "only the strong survive." In late 1892 the mehtar of Chitral, Aman-ul-Mulk, died, leaving behind seventeen sons. Two of them, Nizam and Afzul, were the primary pretenders. Nizam was older but completely lacking in talent or drive; Azful possessed plenty of both, but his manner gave the false impression that he was dim-witted. Jealous not only for power but also of his wife's attraction to the handsome Nizam, Azful plotted to seize the throne and did so as soon as his brother was away from the mud and stone fort that served as the "palace." Nizam fled for Kashmir while Azful purged the court of any of his brother's supporters. Some of them fled for Kabul, where Azful's uncle (and Aman's half-brother) Sher Azful resided in

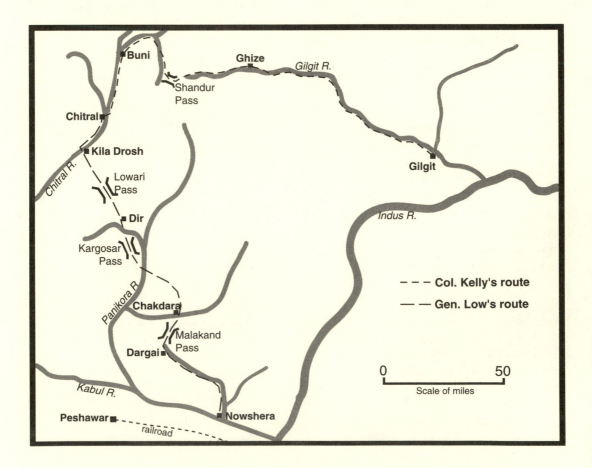

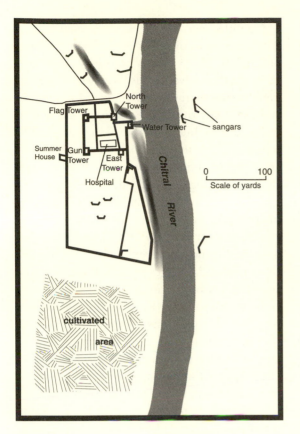

exile. He too lusted for the throne and began raising a force to seize it.

The British administration had responded positively to Azful's request for maintenance of the status quo, but was somewhat befuddled when Nizam via the maharajah also asked for British aid. The political officer in the region, Surgeon Major George Robertson, was dispatched to Chitral to see if he could straighten things out. As he was traveling, Sher Azful's troops stormed the walls at Chitral in a surprise attack, capturing the town and killing his nephew Azful. Hearing of this, Nizam asked for and received British support to challenge his uncle. When he marched into the country, Sher Azful fled back to Kabul, leaving the throne to Nizam. Nizam asked for a British resident to come to Chitral, and in early 1894 Robertson once again made his way there.

Robertson found Nizam in fear for his life, for an in-law, Umra Khan of Jandol to the

south, decided he needed to add Chitral to his possessions. Knowing of that threat and that Sher Azful was always waiting in the wings, few of Nizam's citizens wholeheartedly supported him. Still, Robertson managed to assure the new mehtar of India's support before returning in June to his post in Gilgit, 200 miles east through the mountains. He returned to Chitral six months later upon receiving news that a nineteen-year-old half-brother, Amir-ul-Mulk, had killed Nizam. Afraid that the British might respond negatively to his seizure of power, Amir asked Umra Khan for aid. Umra Khan, aided and abetted by Sher Azful, marched north from Jandhol with 3,000 men.

When Robertson returned to Chitral in late January 1895, he brought with him a force of some 350 men from the 4th Kashmiri Rifles and about forty Sikhs to supplement the sixty already there for the protection of British interests. Robertson, soon convinced that Amir and Umra Khan were in league, deposed him in favor of a twelve-year-old brother, Shujah-ul-Mulk. That action, and a brusque refusal to Umra Khan's demand that Robertson abandon Chitral and return to India, guaranteed that fighting would take place. Umra Khan's men drew ever closer to Chitral and on 3 March Robertson ordered the post commander, Captain Colin Campbell, to lead a 150-man reconnaissance to locate the enemy. The sortie, beginning late in the day, was disastrous. A force of Chitralis defending a village several miles south of Chitral mauled the Kashmiri troops, who did not give a good account of themselves. The troops withdrew into the fort and were surrounded on 4 March.

The Siege

The fort that the British and Indian forces defended was a square roughly 80 yards on a side. The walls were 25 feet high and 8 feet thick, but made of an irregular amalgam of timbers, stone, and mud. Luckily for the defenders, the attackers had no artillery, although the British had but two 7-pounders with only 80 rounds of ammunition. A much larger perimeter wall enclosed an area south of the fort, and the Chitralis and their allies controlled most of it. They also controlled the high ground around the fort from which they were able to snipe effectively throughout the siege. They also fought from hastily erected stone fortifications called *sangars*, which went up in various locations around the fort as the battle progressed. Umra Khan and Sher Azful were able to maintain themselves easily because of a friendly population, but the defenders had enough food to last ten weeks if dispensed at half rations. Considering the remoteness of their position and the fact that a hostile population controlled the countryside, ten weeks was not an overly long time. Ammunition, however, was fairly plentiful. The Sikhs carried the Martini-Henry rifle, for which they had 300 rounds each. The Kashmiris had Sniders, muzzle-loading rifles that had been adapted to breechloaders; enough ammunition was on hand for each to have 280 rounds. During the sortie Captain Campbell had been wounded in the knee. Robertson had been suffering from dysentery almost from the first day. Direct command of the fort therefore devolved on Captain Charles V. F. Townshend of the 4th Kashmiris.

The earliest attempts at relief were disastrous. Sixty men under the command of Lieutenants Stanley Edwardes and John Fowler were ambushed at a village some 40 miles north of Chitral, and after a week's resistance were duped into surrendering. A follow-up force led by Captain Claye Ross of the 14th Sikhs was also ambushed and the few survivors fled back to Buni. These setbacks motivated the British government to mount a major expedition. General Robert Cunliffe-Low commanded a force of 15,000 that marched from Nowshera on 1 April. A secondary force marched eastward from Gilgit on 27 March. That group was made up of 400 Sikh pioneers commanded by Lieutenant Colonel James Kelly.

Cunliffe-Low's force moved deliberately through a series of passes toward the province of Jandhol, Umra Khan's homeland. Not surprisingly, their advance was bitterly contested at every point where the natives could mount an ambush. The British force consisted not only of Indian troops, but also some of the best British troops available in India, including the Seaforth and Gordon Highlanders, King's Own Scottish Borderers, King's Royal Rifle Corps, and the East Lancashire Regiment. With their mobile mountain guns they were able to bring heavy gunfire to bear in every encounter, which the defenders could not match. The army forced the Malakand, Kargosar, and Lowari passes against heavy opposition.

In the meantime, Kelly's force braved the bitterest of conditions. Without even tents they struggled through the passes in the mountains, none lower then 12,000 feet. Most suffered from frostbite and snow blindness, for few had protective eyewear. It was the type of feat that crops up periodically in the annals of the British Empire, of one officer determined, almost to the point of madness, to overcome incredible conditions to achieve his goal. The men slogged through snowdrifts 5 feet deep, using rope ladders to ascend and descend crevices and following goat paths. Twice they beat back ambushes, and they had to rebuild bridges at every river. They crossed the 220 miles of mountains to reach Chitral in 28 days.

Umar Khan and Sher Afzul spent much of their time in trying to fight back Cunliffe-Low's advance, but at Chitral the pressure never eased. After an early attempt to storm the fort failed, the Chitralis were content to build sangars and snipe at the defenders. The main target was on the east side of the fort, where the defenders had to build a covered way to the river to get their water. The Chitralis dug zigzag trenches on the opposite side of the river from which they could deliver very effective fire against anyone dashing for the river. Other than that the soldiers in the fort suffered from boredom and increasing health problems. On

7 April the Chitralis charged the Gun Tower on the southwestern corner of the fort and set the timbers afire. Townshend was able to mobilize a hasty bucket brigade and douse the flames, but it was touch and go for a time.

A week after the tower attack the Chitralis began pounding on drums and playing instruments, a tactic that the British were sure was intended to cover the sounds of digging. On the night of 16 April a sentry clearly heard the sound of pick and shovel coming from the mehtar's summer house just outside the fort. Forty Sikhs and sixty Kashmiris led by a Lieutenant Harley charged the house in a surprise attack the following afternoon, when they killed the men digging the tunnel and blew in the mine opening in the house. That ended the active operations against the fort. Two days later the Chitralis, learning of Kelly's approach and hard pressed by Cunliffe-Low's offensive, abandoned the siege. When Kelly's men arrived on 20 April there was no one in sight but the defenders.

Results

The British suffered forty-one casualties during the siege, plus the fifty-six killed and wounded in the sortie that immediately preceded it. Losses suffered by Sher Afzul and Umra Khan are unknown, but numbered in the thousands. All the British officers in the fort were decorated and all the defenders were granted six months' pay and a three-month leave. Lieutenant Colonel Kelly was made a full colonel, named Commander of the Bath, and promoted to Queen Victoria's aide-de-camp.

What had started out, from the English citizen's point of view, as a matter of but slight concern had by the end became quite a cause celebre. The *Illustrated London News* of 27 April wrote: "The British Indian Government has achieved a rapid and signal military success, promising completely satisfactory political results by its prompt expedition to Chitral

and by the activity and dexterity of the commanders." Unfortunately, the political results were not that satisfactory. After promising not to acquire any land in the wake of the expedition, the British built a fort at the Malakand Pass. In 1897, with the retirement of the extremely competent Political Officer Colonel Robert Warburton, the tenuous peace that he had managed to maintain fell apart. Religious leaders across the region preached holy war against the British, egged on by Muslim agitators sent in from Turkey. Starting in June 1897, rebellion broke out through much of the Northwest Frontier (much of modern Pakistan), forcing major punitive expeditions that in the end extended and solidified British influence in the region.

References: A. J. Barker, *Townshend of Kut* (London: Cassel, 1967); Byron Farwell, *Queen Victoria's Little Wars* (New York: Harper & Row, 1972); Donald Featherstone, *Colonial Small Wars, 1837–1901* (Newton Abbot, Devon: David & Charles, 1973); John Harris, *Much Sounding of Bugles* (London: Hutchinson, 1975).

MANILA

DATE: 1 May–14 August 1898.
LOCATION: on the west coast of the Philippine island of Luzon.

FORCES ENGAGED:

American: 10,000 soldiers. Commanders: Commodore George Dewey and General Wesley Merritt.
Spanish: 10,000–15,000 soldiers. Commander: General Fermin Jaudenes.

IMPORTANCE:

American capture of Manila marked beginning of U.S. occupation of the Philippine Islands, as well as the start of a three-year war with local insurgents.

U.S. soldiers in a trench near Manila during the Spanish American War. (Archive Photos)

Historical Setting

In the late nineteenth century the United States was beginning to take on the duty of spreading the blessings of civilization and the American way to "lesser" peoples around the world. This, according to a famous poem that British poet Rudyard Kipling addressed to the United States, was the "white man's burden," which the British had been exercising in India, Asia, and Africa for decades. One of America's first opportunities to aid "our little brown brothers" was in Cuba, an island the United States had long coveted. In response to reported Spanish brutality against a revolutionary movement beginning in 1895, the United States finally intervened in April 1898. Once war was declared on Spain, all Spain's possessions became potential targets. Indeed, the first American attack on Spain's military came not at Cuba, but against their fleet based in the Philippine capital of Manila.

Commodore George Dewey commanded the American Asiatic squadron, anchored in Hong Kong in early 1898. Upon receiving orders from Assistant Secretary of the Navy Theodore Roosevelt, Dewey's six ships sailed for Manila, arriving late on the night of 30 April. Entering Manila Bay just after midnight on 1 May (challenged by a single shot from the island fortress of Corregidor guarding the harbor entrance), Dewey's squadron proceeded to pound the Spanish fleet into wreckage just after dawn. Although he was able to occupy the naval facilities at Cavite, a few miles south of Manila, he did not have sufficient manpower to hold anything else. That meant that the Spanish garrison in Manila controlled the city and that Spanish troops occupied the remainder of the Philippine archipelago. Still, staring down the gun barrels of a modern fleet, the Spanish commandant in Manila allowed Dewey the use of his telegraph facilities to alert Washington to the victory. Dewey then cut the telegraph cable in an attempt to keep the Spanish from sending for help from home.

Dewey did not know that the Spanish had alternate methods of communicating with Spain. Dewey received communications from Washington via a ship shuttling back and forth to Hong Kong. It was through this avenue that Dewey learned both of American troops being sent to his aid and the alarm that Spanish warships had left their home port in Ceuta bound for Manila. The Spanish fleet outnumbered his own and he could not be sure which would arrive first, American or Spanish reinforcements. In the meantime, Dewey had the assistance of Emilio Aguinaldo. Exiled from the Philippines in 1894 for fomenting revolution, Aguinaldo arrived from exile in Hong Kong aboard an American ship on 19 May. He had arranged with Dewey to raise an army of insurgents to assist the Americans by controlling the countryside and bottling Spanish forces up in a handful of towns and forts. Aguinaldo did all this on the assumption that once the Spanish were defeated, the United States would grant independence to the Philippines. It was not a concept shared by American political leaders. Cuba, indeed, had been promised independence from the outset of the conflict, but American Secretary of State W. R. Day stated: "The United States in entering upon the occupation of the islands as a result of its military operations in that quarter, will do so in the exercise of the rights which the state of war confers, and will expect from the inhabitants . . . that obedience which will be lawfully due from them" (Freidel, *Splendid Little War*, p. 280).

The Siege

With Dewey's ships blockading the harbor and Aguinaldo's guerrillas hemming in the city, everyone awaited the arrival of American troops. The Spanish fleet that caused initial worry was called back to Spain when it reached the Suez. That sealed Manila's fate, but larger political considerations were in play. Spanish leaders in Manila hoped that by holding on they could maintain official sovereignty of the islands as a bargaining chip in Spanish-American peace negotiations. The United States (after some discussion in President William McKinley's cabinet) decided to claim the Philippines as spoils of war. Aguinaldo announced formation of a government and declared independence, neither of which any other country would recognize. Who would become master of the islands?

The first American troops departed San Francisco on 25 May, picking up escort in Hawaii and capturing the Spanish island of Guam along the way. These 2,500 men arrived at Manila Bay on 30 June. Another 3,500 arrived 17 July, and the final contingent of 5,000 arrived at the end of the month. With the final force was Major General Wesley Merritt, in overall command of the army units. As American troops arrived, they moved into trenches around Manila that had been occupied by Filipino insurgents. They improved them and began a lackadaisical siege, with almost random shooting from both defender and attacker. Both sides suffered light casualties while Dewey negotiated through the Belgian consul with the Spanish commandant, General Fermin Jaudenes. Further, the Spanish and American governments were negotiating a cease-fire and opening discussions on the final disposition of the Philippines. Because of the severed telegraph cable, however, Dewey and Merritt had no quick communications with Washington.

Jaudenes knew he could not long resist the power of American naval gunfire, for his batteries lacked the range to return fire. Although commanding some 15,000 men, he was far outnumbered by the combined forces of the Americans and the Filipinos. He and Dewey had some common ground: neither wanted

Aguinaldo's forces to occupy the city. "Thus, at the moment when the American public was debating whether we could honorably 'give the islands back to Spain,' Spain was actually holding them for us against the native population; and, most curious of all, the Spaniards had entered into an effective though unofficial alliance with us to assist in the suppression of the patriots while we were concluding that our duty to these same patriots prevented us from leaving them under 'Spanish misrule' " (Millis, *Martial Spirit*, p. 357).

Unsure of the pace of negotiations on the other side of the world, Juadenes entered into a strange arrangement with Dewey and Merritt. He could not just surrender the city without a fight, for that would damage his career and that of his officers. At the same time, he knew he could not mount an effective defense. So a mock battle was arranged. On 13 August U.S. ships would open fire on an abandoned fort. After a reasonable bombardment, Dewey was to fly signal flags requesting a surrender. Juadenes would then order a white flag raised over the city walls. Attacking American troops could then advance against meager resistance, occupying the city while keeping Aguinaldo's men at bay.

The planned attack started well. Fort San Augustin was blasted, then occupied by American troops. Owing to miscommunication or too much fighting spirit, some Spanish troops put up stronger resistance than was expected. There were a few brisk firefights, but for the most part the action went off as planned. Aguinaldo's men did temporarily occupy parts of Manila, but American troops soon forced them out.

Results

On 14 August Juadenes, Merritt, and Dewey signed the formal surrender papers. No one in Manila knew that the warring governments had signed a cease-fire two days earlier. News of that event arrived on the 16th, upon which Dewey sent Washington a request for direction in dealing with Aguinaldo. The reply: "The President directs that there must be no joint occupation with the insurgents. . . . The insurgents and all others must recognize the military occupation and authority of the United States" (Freidel, *Splendid Little War*, pp. 292–293).

While American and Spanish negotiators met in Paris to hammer out a peace treaty, Spanish forces still occupied most of the rest of the Philippine islands. That fact played a major role in the peace talks. While Spain gave up Puerto Rico and Guam to the United States as "spoils of war," they resisted conceding the Philippines. Eventually, the United States paid Spain $20 million for a peaceful exchange of sovereignty—peaceful between America and Spain, at any rate.

Frustrated at his inability to gain any part of the new power structure, Aguinaldo led his men into the countryside and began a resistance to his new masters. The Philippine Insurrection, as it was called in the United States, lasted until Aguinaldo was finally captured in 1901. By that time, the United States had countered his guerrilla warfare with the concentration camp strategy developed by the Spanish in Cuba, which resulted in the deaths of some 200,000 Filipinos through exposure and disease. The United States had begun forming a national government under American control, and when Aguinaldo was invited to join it after his capture, the insurrection collapsed. Although the United States and the Philippines got off to a terrible beginning, over time they grew into allies. The United States promised independence to the Philippines in 1934 to be granted in 1942, but Japanese occupation during World War II postponed the actual transfer of sovereignty until after the war. In return, the United States received a long-term lease on a naval and air base, which was finally abandoned in the 1990s.

References: Frank Freidel, *The Splendid Little War* (Boston: Little, Brown, 1958); Walter Millis, *The Martial Spirit* (Chicago: Ivan Dee, 1989 [1931]); David Traxel, *1898: Birth of the American Century* (New York: Knopf, 1998).

MAFEKING

DATE: 13 October 1899–17 May 1900.
LOCATION: on the Transvaal–Bechuanaland border, 200 miles west of Johannesburg, South Africa.

FORCES ENGAGED:

British: 1,000 irregular white troops, 450 South African and Cape Police, 390 untrained men of the town guard, 75 volunteers, and some 460 armed black natives; one locally built armored train, one 4-pounder Hotchkiss gun, four obsolete 7-pounders, six Maxim machine guns, and one obsolete Nordenfeldt machine gun. Commander: Colonel Robert Baden-Powell. Boer: Initially 9,000 with 16 field guns, later reduced to 3,000 men and 10 field guns including one modern 94-pounder siege gun and three modern Krupp 14-pounder quick-firing guns. Commander: Initially, General Piet Cronje, later General J. P. Snijman.

IMPORTANCE:

In denying Mafeking to the Boers, Baden-Powell prevented them from cutting off communications between the Cape Colony and Rhodesia and provided a much needed propaganda boost for a failing British war effort. The siege occupied Boers who could have been more profitably employed elsewhere during the conflict.

Historical Setting

The South African Boers had for years watched the British expansion from the southern Cape Colony with great apprehension and caution. The lure of vast deposits of gold and diamonds along with the strategic potential of the Cape of South Africa drew the British to the region like iron to a magnet. In 1895, a British free-booter, Leander Jameson, organized a raid out of Mafeking into the Transvaal to spark a revolt of the English residents of Johannesburg. The *Uitlanders* (Outlanders, mainly British) were denied citizenship and the franchise while being required to pay taxes and otherwise support the Boer establishment. The expected uprising did not occur. Boer commandoes quickly rounded up the Jameson Expedition like so many cattle. Jameson and his cohorts were turned over to British authorities, who tried them under the Foreign Enlistment Act, slapped them on the wrist, and released them. Boer-British relations sank to a record low.

A series of conferences between the Boer and British governments finally caused the Transvaal *Volksraad* to pass a Franchise Bill in an attempt meet the demands of the Uit-landers. The bill was withdrawn after the British rejected it. The Boers rebuffed further invitations to negotiate a settlement to the Outlander problem.

While negotiations proceeded, both sides prepared for war. The Transvaal Republic stockpiled modern weapons from Germany and France. Ten thousand British troops from India and other overseas postings moved toward South Africa. Colonel Robert Baden-Powell was transferred from India to South Africa to raise two regiments of mounted infantry and to organize the defense of the Rhodesian and Bechuanaland frontiers against possible incursion from the Transvaal Repub-lic. London instructed him to keep the troops of the enemy occupied and away from the main British forces.

Upon arrival in South Africa, Baden-Powell surveyed the 500-mile frontier given over to his protection. He recognized that a proper defense could not be accomplished by spreading his two regiments thinly along the entire line. Baden-Powell decided to place one regiment of his mounted rifles at Bulawayo to the north in Rhodesia, with the other regiment based in Mafeking. The town had ample storage facili-ties to make it his prime general supply center, together with railroad facilities to provide addi-tional mobility for his mounted infantry and shops to fabricate improvised weapons.

Mafeking was the primary settlement of the large native districts northwest of the Cape Colony. The city had been a thorn in the side of the Transvaal for more than fifteen years, and was sure to be an early target of any Boer

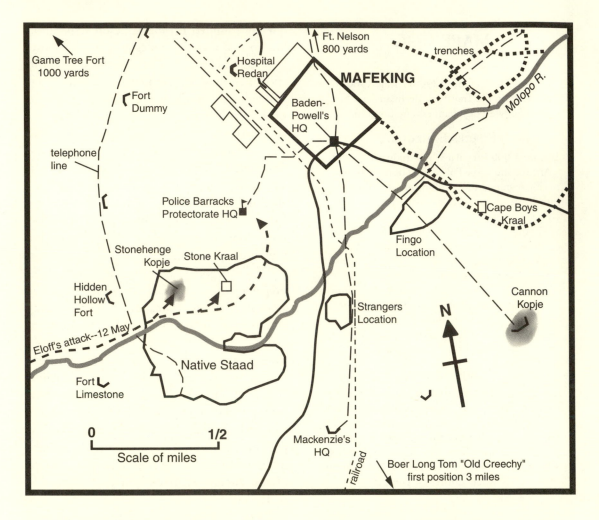

Game Tree Fort
1000 yards

Fort
Dummy

telephone
line

Ft. Nelson
800 yards

Hospital
Redan

MAFEKING

Baden-
Powell's
HQ

trenches

Molopo R.

Police Barracks
Protectorate HQ

Cape Boys
Kraal

Stonehenge
Kopje

Stone Kraal

Fingo
Location

Hidden
Hollow
Fort

Cannon
Kopje

Strangers
Location

N

Eloff's attack--12 May

Native Staad

Fort
Limestone

0   1/2
Scale of miles

Mackenzie's
HQ

railroad

Boer Long Tom "Old Creechy"
first position 3 miles

offensive. The Boers would seek it to wreak vengeance for the Jameson Raid and to prove to the native population of South Africa their superiority over the British. Additionally, the fall of Mafeking was rumored to be a signal for a general uprising of Cape Dutch to spread the war throughout the South African Cape.

As the diplomatic situation deteriorated, Baden-Powell moved into Mafeking on 15 September 1899 to protect accumulated war supplies. He began to recruit volunteers, arm the citizens, and distribute ammunition. He also began the construction of two armored trains and the clandestine fortification of a hill overlooking the town, Cannon Kopje. Baden-Powell decided to defend Mafeking by constructing an outer perimeter of small independ-

dent fortifications manned by elements of his mounted infantry. This outer perimeter would be some 6 miles wide and consist of a system of sixty sandbag forts. He knew that the Boers would employ modern long-range artillery, and he wished to keep them as far away from the center of the town as possible. The town guard would man an inner circle of defenses, on the edge of the town proper. Thus he would put his better-trained and experienced troops in more independent positions, while retaining closer supervision over the less professional town guard. Bombproof shelters were constructed for Baden-Powell's personal headquarters and a large one for the town's women and children.

To support the outer fortifications, a

Crowds outside the home of Robert Stephenson Smyth Baden-Powell, celebrating the relief of Mafeking. The Boers besieged Mafeking, and Baden-Powell found fame as its defender. (Archive Photos)

perimeter railroad was laid. This would allow one of the home-built armored trains to move to any threatened point on the outer circle of forts to provide fire support from its cannon and Maxim guns. A minefield was planted with great ceremony all around the perimeter of the defense works. A demonstration test explosion was set off for the benefit of Boer spies in the area. The armored train threat was real enough, but the best-kept secret of Mafeking's defense was that the mines buried with such great flourish were only wooden boxes filled with sand. Baden-Powell clearly understood the necessity for deception in warfare.

The Siege

President Paul Kruger of the Transvaal Republic dispatched an ultimatum to the British government on 9 October 1899 demanding that all British troops be removed from South Africa and that all reinforcements on the way be directed elsewhere. Confident in his support from Germany and Russia, Kruger put forth a deadline of forty-eight hours. The British flatly rejected his demand and at 1700 on 11 October 1899, Boer commandoes crossed the border into South Africa.

Baden-Powell declared martial law in Mafeking on 12 October and evacuated some two hundred women and children from the town via armored passenger train bound southward to Kimberly. A Boer unit intercepted the train, thus depriving Mafeking of an important piece of ordnance and giving the Boers their first victory of the war. By nightfall of 13 October, the town was completely surrounded and cut off. The siege had begun.

Acting upon intelligence that a force of approximately 9,000 under the command of General Piet Cronje was approaching Mafeking, Baden-Powell organized an attack. With the remaining armored train and a squadron of 70 mounted infantry, Baden-Powell hit the lead elements of Cronje's attacking force. Although heavily outnumbered, the British drove off the superior Boer force, inflicting more than 200 casualties. British losses were four killed, and sixteen wounded.

This hard swat on the nose caused the cautious burghers to approach Mafeking slowly and they begin the siege with an artillery bombardment on 16 October. For three hours sixty-three artillery shells fell on the town with slight damage. Baden-Powell's preparations were effective and the lightly constructed buildings of Mafeking allowed most of the shells to pass through them without exploding. On 21 October, Cronje called for the surrender of the town or a general artillery bombardment would ensue after forty-eight hours. This bombardment was as ineffective as the previous one. Although a modern 94-pounder French siege gun was employed, casualties were minimal and the British bombproof shelters held. Additional bombproofs were dug so that almost anywhere in the town the defenders had effective protection against Boer artillery attacks.

On 25 October came the first full-scale Boer attack on Mafeking. Following a particularly heavy artillery preparation, more than 1,000 Boers supported by light artillery and machine guns attacked the town from three directions. The attack was repulsed by British rifle and machine gun fire with unknown Boer losses and only one British defender killed. This repulse by well-aimed British machine gun and rifle fire caused the Boers to begin trench warfare so as to avoid casualties.

A night attack on the approaching Boer trenches completely unhinged the invaders. The Boers seemed to be particularly vulnerable to night actions; they never attempted a night assault and reacted badly when attacked after dark. They maintained an exhausting night alert for the remainder of the siege.

Another major assault occurred on 30 October, when the Boers attempted to seize the position atop Cannon Kopje. After a thirty-minute artillery preparation some 800 Boers advanced upon the little outpost from three directions. The British responded with machine gun fire from the enemy's left, cannon fire from the right, and aimed rifle fire from the front. Failing to press the assault over the final 600 yards, the Boers retired after taking fairly heavy casualties.

After a month of inconclusive attacks, Cronje gave up trying to take Mafeking by storm and moved on to the south with 6,000 burghers and six guns, leaving General S. P. Snijman to complete the siege. Approximately 3,000 Boers and 10 guns remained. Just prior to Christmas, Baden-Powell received word that a relief column was approaching the town from the north. He decided to launch a sortie from Mafeking to relieve the pressure of the siege and to distract the invaders from the relief force. The attack made on 26 December was a minor disaster. The Boer position was well fortified and the British were thrown back with significant casualties. The twenty-four killed and twenty-three wounded or missing were the greatest losses the garrison had suffered since the start of hostilities. Baden-Powell came to realize that he could do little to break the siege on his own and that his only option was to minimize losses to his defenders while seeking to tie down as many of the enemy as possible.

As March 1900 approached, the siege had become a "sit-down affair." The Boers could not take the town by main force and the British could not drive them away. Baden-Powell could only respond to the daily bombardment when absolutely necessary owing to the scarcity of ammunition. The majority of the Boers remained sheltered in their trenches, content to pepper British positions with rifle and machine gun fire. The Boer sappers resumed their slow progress in extending their trenches toward those of the British. The British responded with their own digging and assaulted the trenches with grenades made from jam tins and dynamite flung by whip sticks. Between the efforts of British sharpshooters and the "bomb casters," the Boer advance trenches were rendered untenable.

On 31 March the Boers halted another British attempt to relieve Mafeking. The defenders continued to hang on, resisting daily Boer artillery bombardment. The heaviest Boer artillery assault of the siege came on 11 April 1900. The French-built siege gun dropped seventy rounds into the town along with shells from seven other Boer guns. Machine guns supported a full-scale infantry attack on Baden-Powell's fortifications. The defenders held their fire until the last minute and destroyed the attacking columns with rifle and machine gun fire. After the failure of this attack, the Boers withdrew the siege gun for deployment elsewhere.

The most successful Boer action occurred on 12 May, when they broke through British pickets facing the native *staad*. Quick action by the defenders trapped some 200 Boers in a British South African police fort, ultimately forcing them to surrender to their own prisoners. This was the last gasp for the Boers surrounding Mafeking. On 16 May, the sound of heavy gunfire was heard from the west indicating that the long-awaited relief force had at last fought its way through. The Boers withdrew from their trenches and retreated back across the Transvaal frontier. The morning of 17 May 1900 witnessed the final relief of Mafeking by troops led by Major General Byron Mahon.

Results

The defense of Mafeking gave the British Empire a needed propaganda lift in the face of continued defeats by the Boers. Baden-Powell's stubborn defense tied up significant numbers of Boer troops who certainly could have been better employed elsewhere. Mafeking was not taken and a general uprising of Cape Dutch never materialized. A careful examination of the siege shows how Baden-Powell used every asset at his command to the fullest. His improvisations utilizing armored trains, industrial explosives, and deception provide lessons for any commander. The lengthy siege of Mafeking delayed an early Boer victory in a war that they could only win by avoiding a protracted conflict with a global empire. Baden-Powell became a national hero, granting him the prestige that would help him to create the Boy Scout movement.—Michael McClain

References: William Hillcourt and Lady Olave Baden-Powell, *Baden-Powell: The Two Lives of a Hero* (New York, 1992); Thomas Pakenham, *The Boer War* (New York: Random House, 1979); Eileen K. Wade, *The Piper of Pax: The Life Story of Sir Robert Baden-Powell* (Philadelphia: Lippincott, 1925) reprinted on the World Wide Web in the South African War Virtual Library, www.bowlerhat.com.au/sawul/mafeking.html, May 2001.

PEKING

DATE: 20 June–14 August 1900.
LOCATION: northeastern China, modern Beijing.

FORCES ENGAGED:

International: 407 soldiers, 125 civilian volunteers. Commander: Sir Claude MacDonald.
Chinese: 20,000+. Commander: Prince Tuan, head of the Chinese Foreign Office.
Relief forces: 18,000 troops comprised of American, British, French, Japanese, and Russian contingents. Commander: none overall.

IMPORTANCE:

The threat to diplomatic personnel in the Chinese capital provoked the first European coalition military response in eighty-five years. In the wake of the expedition, Russian seizure of Manchuria laid the groundwork for the Russo-Japanese War of 1904–1905.

Historical Setting

Throughout the nineteenth century the ruling Manchu dynasty in China grew progressively weaker. This coincided with European colonial efforts in the Far East, and resulted in first British then other European powers forcing concessions from the Chinese government. Not only were trade treaties forced on the Chinese, but port cities were virtually assigned to each power as they carved out economic spheres of influence in various parts of China. Britain, France, Russia, Germany, and Japan all had territory in which they held exclusive trade rights. While the Chinese did profit from this trade, there were serious negative side effects. The traditionally xenophobic Chinese believed that their culture, as the oldest in the world, was therefore the best. Having foreigners dictate policy, profit on their own terms, and introduce alien ideas all offended Chinese sensibilities. By the 1890s many Chinese could no longer stand being treated as inferiors in their own country and began organizing themselves to do something about it.

Secret societies formed, taking the name *I-ho-ch'üan* (Righteous and Harmonious Fists). Many of their banners displayed a fist icon, so the Westerners called them the Boxers. They took an extreme nationalist stance, demanding that everything foreign be destroyed or expelled. As they were anti-Christian as well, the Boxers did have some religious overtones, but their aims were primarily political and social. The Chinese government was divided over its attitude toward this society. The Emperor Kuang Hsü wanted to modernize China, taking advantage of Western progress as had Japan. He, however, was a weak ruler and did not control the government. His mother, the Dowager Empress Tzu Hsi, responded to the urging of reactionary elements in the government and seized power from her son. Although with no official connection to the Boxers, the empress covertly aided and encouraged their activities. She could thus explain to foreign ambassadors that it was an independent movement over which she had no control.

Unaware of or ignoring any signs of unrest, the Westerners went about their business of engaging in trade and making demands for concessions from the government. In 1899 the United States entered the scene. American Secretary of State John Hay, wanting to gain inroads into the Chinese market but excluded because the Europeans controlled the ports, proposed

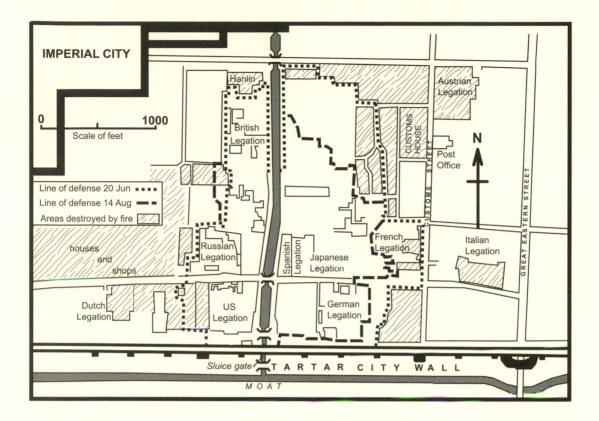

IMPERIAL CITY

Scale of feet
0 — 1000

Line of defense 20 Jun ·······
Line of defense 14 Aug — — —
Areas destroyed by fire ▨

Hanlin

British Legation

Austrian Legation

CUSTOMS HOUSE

CUSTOMS STREET

Post Office

N

GREAT EASTERN STREET

houses and shops

Russian Legation

Spanish Legation

Japanese Legation

French Legation

Italian Legation

Dutch Legation

US Legation

German Legation

Sluice gate

T A R T A R   C I T Y   W A L L

M O A T

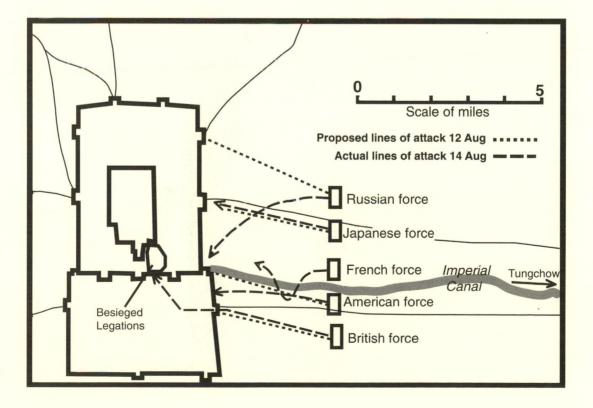

Scale of miles
0 — 5

Proposed lines of attack 12 Aug ·······
Actual lines of attack 14 Aug — — —

Russian force

Japanese force

French force

Imperial Canal

Tungchow

American force

British force

Besieged Legations

A battery of Chinese light artillery, photo taken at the Hsiao Camp on the outskirts of Tientsin. (Library of Congress)

what came to be called the Open Door Policy. Each nation could remain dominant in a single area, but all regions should be open to all foreign trading interests. This would open up markets currently denied to the Europeans because of the sphere-of-interest practice. With an increased customer base and increased access to previously untapped local goods, he argued, profits would surely rise. It would also, of course, allow America to get in on the China trade as well. The Europeans accepted Hay's proposal, although with varying degrees of enthusiasm.

This economic cooperation agreement was not long in place when the Boxers began direct attacks on Westerners. In Shantung Province American missionaries were attacked and their converts abused or killed. Appeals to diplomatic personnel in Washington or the Chinese capital of Peking brought little response. In May 1900 Boxers began acting more openly in Peking. Weaponry was being produced and purchased throughout the city. Attacks on individuals began in May and the Boxers burned a railway station outside Peking on the 24th. Placards around the city urged the Chinese to destroy the telegraph lines and the railroads as the first step toward ridding the country of the "foreign devils." Had the Boxers immediately

followed up on this incident with assaults on the foreign embassies, they almost certainly would have massacred every European there. Instead, they continued to harass people in the streets for several weeks until the Europeans finally began to take seriously the threat to their safety. Chinese diplomats on 19 June ordered the Westerners out of Peking by the following day at 1600. When the German ambassador left to register a protest with the Chinese government, he was shot and killed in the streets. Precisely at 4:00 the shooting started, with a Chinese sniper killing a French sentry.

The Siege

Throughout the previous days the Methodist missionaries had been pleading with the diplomats to rescue them and their converts. Just in time were they given permission to gather in the borrowed palace of Prince Su, next door to the British embassy. As all the legations were next to each other the Europeans had a defensive position they could hold, but some 3,000 people were inside protected by just over 400 embassy guards with limited weaponry and ammunition. The Chinese attacked almost constantly, and when they were not assaulting the walls around the embassies they were bombarding them or making noise. Although the Boxers were rarely armed with anything other than swords and knives, they were supported by Chinese imperial troops with modern weapons. How many Chinese were involved in the siege is a matter of speculation, but probably about 20,000 troops were involved with thousands more Boxer volunteers.

Luckily for the defenders the group inside, although multinational, rather quickly set aside national rivalries and elected British Ambassador Sir Claude Macdonald as their leader. Among the missionaries, diplomats, merchants, and travelers inside the compound there were many with practical skills or military experience that could assist in the defense. The chief Methodist missionary was Frank Gamewell, who before becoming a man of the cloth was educated at Rensselaer Polytechnic in civil engineering. He was the only man in the entire group with any construction knowledge and he was immediately given the task of building and maintaining defensive strongpoints. Embassy guards from France, Germany, Japan, Britain, Russia, and the United States were each given a section of wall to defend.

The Chinese artillery wrought havoc among the people inside the compound but made little headway against the walls, which Reverend Gamewell kept as stoutly repaired as possible. The Boxers tried to burn out the defenders by setting fire to the Hanlin Library abutting the British Embassy. As this contained massive amounts of Chinese art and literary treasures the Europeans were shocked to see the Chinese set it afire. With men, women, and children manning bucket brigades (and aided by some fortuitous winds) the fire destroyed the library but the British Embassy remained almost undamaged. Bitter fighting took place along the Tartar Wall, the position held by American Marines. The Boxers also mined under the French legation and collapsed part of its walls, but the French defenders occupied the rubble and held on.

Several messengers had been dispatched to the coast begging for relief. Unknown to the defenders (as the telegraph lines had been cut) the first relief force had been defeated and driven back as the Chinese held the key city of Tientsin. Although throughout the siege the defenders on the walls looked toward Tientsin and were sure they saw signs of approaching armies, none came for weeks. However, the economic agreement Hay had negotiated the previous year among the Western powers now became the basis of military cooperation among them. All the interested countries sent troops in the first serious coalition effort since the defeat of Napoleon at Leipzig in 1814. On 13 July the multinational force attacked Tientsin and captured it after a fifteen-hour battle. With this in their possession to use as a base, the force set their sights on Peking, 75 miles away. They arrived on 12 August, having fighting Boxer harassment the entire way. No one was in supreme command, so the various national forces acted independently. The Russians attacked first and although they forced an entrance into Peking they soon found themselves in need of rescue. The individual forces assaulted various gates into the city, but the British found themselves before the one most lightly defended. They broke through on the evening of the 13th and made their way through an undefended sluice gate into the diplomatic compound. The troops, sent over from India, were greeted with hugs and kisses all around. The American forces arrived two hours later.

On the 14th the coalition force captured the outer city and began driving inward. They soon were in the Imperial City, then broke through the final barrier into the Forbidden City. There they found that the government had fled, so few prisoners were taken. The invaders were not gentle in their treatment of the inhabitants of Peking and looting was widespread. With the city under firm control, the British general Gaselee led his forces into the neighboring provinces to mop up what Boxer resistance he could find. After some weeks the dowager empress sent emissaries with an offer to negotiate: a return to the status quo ante bellum in return for the withdrawal of foreign troops.

Results

The negotiations dragged on for months and ultimately the Chinese government was forced to pay an indemnity of $333 million to the offended nations. Of this the United States received $25 million, of which they accepted only half. They dedicated the remainder to establishing a fund for Chinese students to study in America. This gesture may have had the longest-lasting effect of the entire incident. High damage claims and looting the Chinese expected from foreigners, but to have one of the invaders invest in the future of China was shocking. From that point the United States enjoyed a much closer relationship with China than any other Western power, one that lasted through World War II and until the victory of communism in 1949. The Chinese for the most part became no less xenophobic, but the organized resistance to foreign influence that the Boxers symbolized had only a brief life.

Although most of the European nations took their money and left, the Russians saw an opportunity to establish themselves on the Pacific coast. Russia seized control of Manchuria, which had previously been their economic sphere of influence. The Trans-Siberian Railway was extended all the way to Port Arthur, which the Russians established as the base for their Pacific Fleet. All of this activity violated the Open Door agreement, which Russia had always viewed with the greatest suspicion among all the signatories. They continued their economic stranglehold on the region, much to the distress of Japan, who looked to Manchurian markets for the raw materials necessary for their burgeoning industrial economy. When extended talks failed to convince Russia to open the markets, Japan responded in 1904 by attacking the Russian fleet in Port Arthur, then invading Manchuria to gain by force what they could not gain by negotiation.

References: Peter Fleming, *The Siege at Peking* (New York: Harper & Row, 1959); Walter Lord, *The Good Years* (New York: Harper & Brothers, 1960); T. J. McCormick, *China Market: America's Quest for Informal Empire* (Chicago: Quadrangle, 1967); Marilyn Young, *The Rhetoric of Empire: American China Policy, 1895–1901* (Cambridge, MA: Harvard University Press, 1968).

PORT ARTHUR

DATE: 1 June 1904–2 January 1905.
LOCATION: at the tip of the Liaotung peninsula, Manchuria.

FORCES ENGAGED:
Japanese: 80,000 men and 474 guns plus siege train. Commander: General Baron Maresuke Nogi.
Russian: 40,000 men and 506 guns. Commander: Major General Baron Anatoli Stoessel.

IMPORTANCE:
Japanese victory was a major psychological blow to Russia, while providing a port from which to bring in manpower and supplies for later offensives to the north.

Historical Setting

The Russo-Japanese War (1904–1905) was first major conflict of the twentieth century; it pitted two adversaries who had acquired all the new destructive weaponry that modern technology had developed. Both sides had efficient modern armies well supplied with all the latest weapons and ammunition; each was backed by transportation and industrial systems more powerful than any in existence fifty years before. Smokeless propellants, high explosive bursting shells, machine guns, and barbed wire

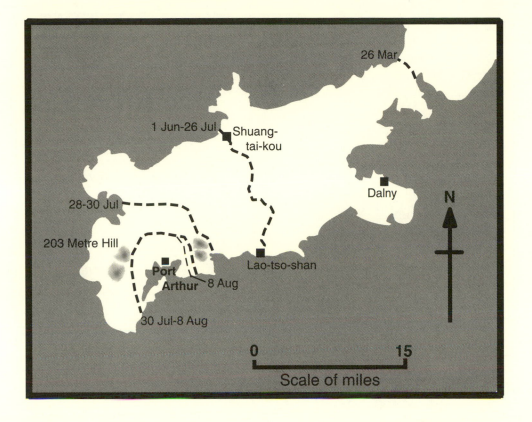

were available to both sides in huge quantities. The results were a portent of what was to happen ten years later in Europe.

Ten years earlier Japan had taken most of Manchuria from China in the Sino-Japanese War, but France, Germany, and Russia had compelled the Japanese to abandon their conquests. Stung by what they regarded as an insult, the Japanese embarked on a military building program, and by 1904 they felt strong enough to attempt the recapture of Manchuria, especially Port Arthur, a deep-water harbor at the southern tip of the Liaotung peninsula. The ownership of this port was vital to Russian influence in China, for it was there that the bulk of the Russian Asiatic Fleet was based. In a surprise lightning attack that would foreshadow the 1941 attack on Pearl Harbor, the Japanese fleet badly damaged the Russian fleet laying at anchor at Port Arthur on 8 February 1904.

The surviving ships were effectively blockaded in the harbor. The remaining Russian Baltic Fleet was sent to the aid of the besieged fort, sailing from St. Petersburg around the Cape of Good Hope. The Japanese had to destroy the Russian ships docked in Port Arthur before the others could join them and perhaps overpower the besiegers. Both sides rushed troops to the area and the war was under way.

The Siege

The capture of Port Arthur was assigned to General Maresuke Nogi, who landed 90,000 men some 27 miles north of the port on 1 June. Nogi advanced slowly south, with Russian troops contesting almost every mile. It took Nogi two months to reach Port Arthur. This delay allowed the Russian commander General Anatoli Stoessel and his engineers to significantly improve the town's defenses. By the time the Japanese reached Port Arthur on 30 July, the whole area bristled with gun emplacements, earthworks, lumber and steel forts, and

Russian ships Pallada *(left) and* Pobieda *(right) wrecked below Golden Hill in Port Arthur. (Library of Congress)*

trenches. Stoessel had some 50,000 men to defend the town, including the sailors of the Russian ships trapped in the harbor.

Between 19 August and 26 November, Nogi launched three major frontal assaults on the Russian defenses. Japanese tactics stressed elan and courage over cover and stealth; indeed, Japanese soldiers were often referred to as "living bullets." All of these attacks were beaten back with heavy losses. The Russians made great use of heavy water-cooled Maxim machine guns in their defenses, as well as magazine rifles, barbed wire entanglements, and hand-grenades. This meant that frontal assaults were almost impossible to maintain. Even Japanese soldiers deploying for a charge were shot to pieces. Nogi switched to night attacks, but even these resulted in dreadful casualties, for the Russians had set up powerful searchlights that brightly illuminated the storming parties.

With the failure of the third attack on 26

November, Nogi had lost over 20,000 men. He reluctantly accepted that Port Arthur would not fall to massed frontal assaults, no matter how bravely and recklessly they were pressed. Tokyo was pressuring him to destroy the remaining Russian battleships in the harbor before the Russian Baltic Fleet, which was frantically steaming from the other side of the world to reinforce Port Arthur, could join them. General Nogi turned his attention to 203 Meter Hill.

The Japanese suffered from a lack of adequate observation positions that could afford them an unobstructed observation of the harbor and the town. The fire of their big guns could not accurately be directed onto the Russian ships or other important targets. The best vantage point from which to achieve artillery domination was 203 Meter Hill. Located 3 miles west of the port, 203 Meter Hill was a part of the Russian outer defense system. Both it and a lower hill called Akasaka-yama, had earth, timber, and steel-plated fortifications on their crowns, while two lines of trenches, protected by barbed wire, ran across the front and around the flanks of their forward slopes. Although rather strong, these defenses were not adequate for such a key position.

In order to protect his infantry's approach, Nogi had engineers dig siege trenches up the steep hillside almost as far as the Russian front lines. However, the Japanese still had to leave these trenches to attack the enemy lines. The assault began in the evening of 27 November and continued unabated until 6 December.

Machine guns and barbed wire fences protected the Russian positions and the Japanese used artillery and then frontal assaults to try to overwhelm them. At close range, handgrenades, rather than bullets and bayonets, featured in countless attacks and counterattacks on the upper slopes. The Japanese poured paraffin into enemy redoubts and set them on fire, then their heavy artillery ranged in on the flames and pulverized the entire Russian trench system with some 4,000 11-inch howitzer shells. The result was a gruesome bloodbath. The Russians had about 2,200 men to defend the hill, and after 83 days of continual fighting the Japanese finally overcame the defenders, at a cost of over 10,000 killed and wounded. Included in this number was Nogi's last surviving son, killed while leading one of the final assaults. Only the emperor's intervention prevented Nogi from committing hara-kiri.

Of the attacks on 203 Meter Hill, an eyewitness wrote, "There have probably never been so many dead crowded into so small a space since the French stormed the great redoubts of Borodino. . . . There was practically no bodies intact; the hillside was carpeted with odd limbs, skulls, pieces of flesh, and shapeless trunks of what had once been human beings, intermingled with pieces of shells, broken rifles, twisted bayonets, grenades, and masses of rock loosed from the surface of the earth by explosions."

The fate of the defenders of Port Arthur was sealed with the arrival in September 1904 of batteries of Japanese 11-inch Osaka siege howitzers. Eighteen of these huge guns, weighing 23 tons each, were sent by sea from Japan to Dalny, the nearest port to the siege area. They were then manhandled over rough, muddy roads by teams of 300 soldiers because they were too heavy to be transported on the light railway system, and set up in concrete emplacements around Port Arthur. In October the howitzers opened fire, lobbing 500 pound shells over 5.5 miles into Port Arthur. However, their firing was at first indiscriminate, due to the lack of adequate artillery spotting. But with the capture of 203 Meter Hill, the Japanese could practically look down into the harbor, and accurately direct fire onto the ships, the fortifications, and the town.

The Japanese now had the artillery observation post they so badly needed. Nogi's heavy guns immediately opened a three-day bombardment of Port Arthur, during which five Russian battleships and two cruisers were sunk and much damage was done to the town and its fortifications. The Russian command was divided over whether the town could continue to hold out. However, on 2 January 1905, General Stoessel, despite still having three months' supplies of food and ammunition, decided to surrender the port to the Japanese, perhaps more on humanitarian than military grounds. The siege of Port Arthur was finally over.

Results

The siege cost the defenders some 30,000 casualties; the attackers almost 60,000. The grim results foreshadowed what was to happen ten years later on the battlefields of northern Europe.

With the Japanese in control of Port Arthur, their military situation was greatly enhanced while that of the Russians was correspondingly harmed. The destruction of the remaining Russian ships in the harbor meant that when the Baltic Fleet arrived it would have no assistance; there would be no sally to threaten the Imperial Japanese Navy's rear. With that potential gone, Japanese Admiral Togo concentrated his fleet and pounced on the Russian ships when they attempted to run through the Tsushima Straits.

Possession of the harbor also allowed Japanese warships to undergo refitting and repair on site, rather than having to return to Japan. It also gave them a superior harbor to Dalmy, which they had been using up to this point, through which to bring in more manpower and supplies. Also, by freeing the remains of the Japanese Third Army, they were able to march north and join with the rest of the army facing a sizable Russian force at the city of Mukden. The additional troops that the Third Army provided proved key in the Japanese victory there in February 1905.

The battle at Port Arthur also began to show the Western world something: that this rising power, Japan, was a nation to take seriously. The colonial mentality of Europeans had never had to face the fact that another race could fight them on an equal basis. The seeds of the ultimate Asian uprising against colonialism were planted in the Russo-Japanese War.—Allen Lee Hamilton

References: R. M. Connaughton, *The War of the Rising Sun and the Tumbling Bear* (New York: Routledge, 1998); Shumpei Okamoto, *The Japanese Oligarchy and the Russo-Japanese War* (New York: Columbia University Press, 1970).

LIEGE

DATE: 7–16 August 1914.
LOCATION: eastern Belgium, approximately 15 miles west of the German border.

FORCES ENGAGED:

German: Army of the Meuse, 8 brigades totaling 60,000 men. Commander: General Otto von Emmich.
Belgian: 25,000 infantry and fortress garrisons. Commander: General Gérard Mathieu Leman.

IMPORTANCE:

Unexpected Belgian resistance seriously slowed the German assault at outbreak of World War I, giving French and British forces time to organize a defense of Paris.

Historical Setting

In retrospect, World War I seemed almost inevitable in the wake of France's humiliating defeat at Prussian hands in 1870. Multiple other factors contributed to the war, including nationalism, imperialism, naval and arms races, aggressive political leaders, and so on, but by early 1914 Europe had divided into rival camps and seemed merely to be waiting for an excuse to start fighting. That excuse came with the assassination of Archduke Franz Ferdinand in Sarajevo, Bosnia, on 28 June

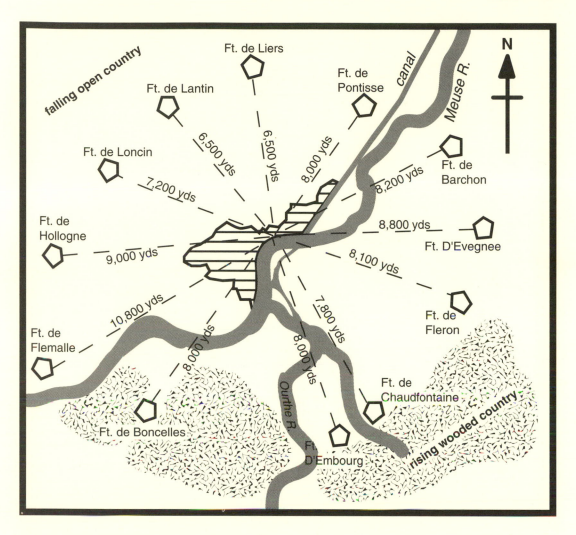

Ft. de Liers
Ft. de Lantin
Ft. de Pontisse
canal
Meuse R.
N
falling open country
Ft. de Loncin
6,500 yds
6,500 yds
8,000 yds
8,200 yds
Ft. de Barchon
7,200 yds
8,800 yds
Ft. de Hollogne
9,000 yds
8,100 yds
Ft. D'Evegnee
10,800 yds
8,000 yds
7,800 yds
Ft. de Flemalle
8,000 yds
Ft. de Fleron
Ourthe R.
Ft. de Chaudfontaine
Ft. de Boncelles
rising wooded country
Ft. D'Embourg

1914, and the resulting maneuverings of Austria-Hungary, Serbia, Germany, Russia, et al. With the passage of Vienna's 28 July deadline to Belgrade to concede to impossible demands, interlocking alliances fell into place as armies prepared for combat. Austria declared war on Serbia, which provoked assurances of direct support from Russia. Germany, honoring her alliance with Austria, declared war on Russia on 1 August, then sent an ultimatum to France (Russia's ally via the Triple Entente) on 2 August.

Another ultimatum also went to King Albert of Belgium, for Germany's Schlieffen Plan (developed over the previous two decades) called for a vast sweep of manpower around the concentration of French armies along the Alsace frontier. That flanking maneuver, designed to bypass both the French forces and the rugged terrain of the Ardennes, necessitated German violation of Belgian neutrality. Belgium could have offered no resistance and allowed German troops through her lands on their way to France. Indeed, much of the German planning depended on them doing so; anything else would be nothing more than "the rage of dreaming sheep," according to one Prussian officer (Tuchman, *The Guns of August*, p. 189). Unfortunately for German plans, Belgium proved all too willing to defend her sovereignty. Unfortunately for the Belgians, their resources did not match their elan.

Belgium's fixed defenses and planning were

predicated on defending from any potential enemy: France, Germany, or Britain. At the beginning of August 1914 her armies were on the perimeters of the country, as they had been for years. When Albert received the ultimatum from Berlin, his chief of staff General Selliers de Moranville began implementing the standing contingency plans: to concentrate the army in the center of the country while allowing fortifications at Liege and Namur to slow down, if not stop, the German advance. Liege straddled the primary road through Belgium toward France. To the south the ground was rugged, to the north it was open but less than a dozen miles from the Netherlands, which Germany did not want to enter. Both Liege and Namur possessed outstanding fortifications, but also had serious shortcomings.

The city of Liege was surrounded by a dozen forts, designed and built by Henri Alexis Brialmont, the leading engineer of the latter nineteenth century. Rejecting the Star forts of the French master Vauban, he designed forts to resist newer rifled cannon. They existed mainly underground, exposing only mounds of concrete, masonry, and dirt. Each fort possessed a series of retractable cupolas that held guns ranging in size up to 6 inches. While state-of-the-art upon their completion in 1892, they had not been well maintained. Brialmont also called for smaller fortifications and trench lines to be built linking and protecting the main forts, but the Belgian government had not done that either. Their garrisons were not at full strength and many were drawn from the local guard units and possessed minimal training.

On 2 August King Albert responded to Germany's ultimatum by ordering work to begin on support works, as well as the army to be mobilized and brought up to paper strength. There was little opportunity to do either, for German forces entered the country early on 4 August. The force detailed to occupy Liege was a provisional unit called the Army of the Meuse, consisting of eight brigades commanded by General Otto von Emmich.

Emmich commanded primarily infantry and cavalry and was detailed to seize the bridges across the Meuse at Liege and seize the town if it offered any resistance. When his troops reached the river and found many of the bridges destroyed, they began work on pontoon bridges. When those came under fire, the Germans came to the realization that they would indeed be forced to fight for Liege.

The Siege

On 5 August Emmich threw his infantry at the four easternmost forts and saw his men killed by the hundreds. Wave after wave went into the murderous Belgian fire until bodies were stacked so high the Belgians could no longer see their attackers. The rifle and machine gun fire from the infantry assigned to the garrison slaughtered German troops all day. At night, however, troops were able to filter through the spaces between the forts and approach Liege. The forts, in a ring some 6 miles from the city, were spaced between 4,000 and 7,000 yards from each other. Each was mutually supporting, but the lack of entrenchments between the forts allowed the Germans to slip through.

The Germans attempted negotiation, then threats. Emissaries sent to General Leman could not convince him to surrender. On 6 August German zeppelins dropped thirteen bombs on Liege, killing nine people and marking the opening of aerial warfare against civilian population centers. A squad of soldiers disguised as British troops attempted to kidnap General Leman but failed. In spite of these failures, the Germans succeeded in convincing Leman that they had far more troops than they actually possessed. Rather than eight brigades, Leman through faulty intelligence believed Emmich commanded eight divisions, which his single 3rd Division could not possibly resist. On 7 August he ordered his troops to withdraw to join the bulk of the Belgian army around Louvain, abandoning the city but not the forts around Liege. Belgian newspapers printed wild reports of victories over the invaders, but King Albert and his staff knew better. Unless French or British reinforcements appeared his army could do little more than slow the Germans down. French President Poincare offered five divisions but was over-ruled by his own chief of staff Marshal Joffre, who was intent on maintaining the futile French attack through the Ardennes. London offered one cavalry and four infantry divisions, but it was doubtful they could be mustered and transported to Belgium in time.

With the 3rd Division's withdrawal, the city of Liege had no defense force to stop the Germans from occupying it. General von Emmich along with Second Army deputy chief of staff General Erich Ludendorff soon gathered four brigades in the city behind the forts and threatened to destroy the city and all its inhabitants if the forts did not surrender. Since the beginning of the fighting the Germans had been killing civilians regularly, responding to the perceived threat of snipers and guerrillas among the population. Leman continued to refuse to surrender his forts, however, for as long as they remained they blocked the German advance toward France. In order to reduce the forts, the Germans introduced new weapons they had secretly been developing.

The Austrian Skoda works had produced 305mm howitzers transported on massive treaded vehicles. The Krupp works in 1909 had produced a 420mm gun so huge it could only be transported in parts and then on railroad cars. Since its invention the engineers had been developing a more mobile version, of which only a few were available when the war broke out. Ludendorff called for their deployment against the Liege forts rather than against Paris, their originally intended target. The guns were loaded onto trains late on 9 August and began their journey the following day. The train could carry them no farther than Herbesthal, 20 miles from Liege, owing to a destroyed tunnel. Transporting them overland was a daunting undertaking that dragged on for three days owing to mechanical breakdowns and blocked roads.

During the interval the Germans continued to urge King Albert to surrender, to no avail. He continued to beg the Allies for manpower, but it was slow in arriving. A large French cavalry force reconnoitered the front early in the attack and reported to the French high command that there was no major German troop concentration in the area. This confirmed the French thinking that the bulk of German troops were behind the Ardennes, so no immediate need for a transfer of forces seemed necessary. Albert realized the nature of the German strategy, but he was unable to convince the French that the real threat was on their far left flank. A major Belgian defeat of German cavalry on 12 August reinforced the French view.

On the 12th, however, the siege artillery finally arrived. Thus far the Germans with their field artillery and swarming infantry had managed to capture two of the smaller forts (Barchon and Evegnée), but when the siege guns began firing on the afternoon of the 12th the destruction of the rest of the forts became a foregone conclusion. The 305 mm and 420 mm guns fired armor-piercing shells with delayed fuses, falling on the forts from the top of a 4,000-foot arc. The underground garrisons listened in terror as the impacts walked in toward their positions, directed by artillery observers in balloons and belfries. On the 13th three forts succumbed to the pounding and a fourth surrendered on the 14th. Fort Boncelles survived twenty-four hours of bombardment before it surrendered on the 15th, with nothing left but chunks of concrete and metal. With the eastern forts reduced, the artillery was brought up to Liege itself in order to pound the forts to the west of the city. Fort Loncin, where General Leman made his last stand, blew up when a shell found its magazine late in the afternoon of the 16th. General Leman was found unconscious in the rubble of Fort Loncon and taken to General von Emmich.

Results

The passage of the German Second and Third Armies through Belgium had originally been scheduled to begin on 10 August. They finally began to move on the 13th, but could not pass through Liege until the 17th. The resistance of the six large and six small forts ringing Liege had bought just a few days' respite for the French and British, but it proved vital. Although many at the war's beginning had hoped that Liege's forts would last the nine months the Russian forts at Port Arthur had held out against the Japanese in 1904–1905, even this relatively short delay in the German timetable was critical. It was enough, although barely enough, to give the French and British armies time to redeploy at the Marne River for the defense of Paris. Although the logistics of the German advance also slowed their progress, the First Battle of the Marne was such a near-run thing that a German attack a few days earlier could well have given them the French capital and victory in World War I.

Just as important was the psychological effect the Belgian resistance had on the rest of Europe. Germany, whose army had possessed an air of invincibility ever since their crushing defeat of France in 1870, now seemed all too human. The Belgian army continued to resist as it fell back on the city of Antwerp, and that stiffened the resolve of both the French and British citizenry and governments. No one had expected the Belgians to fight at all, certainly not to fight heroically. Could the major powers of Europe not fight to the end if tiny Belgium had? "The triumph was moral—an advertisement to the world that the ancient faiths of country and duty could still nerve the arm for battle, and that the German idol, for all its splendour, had feet of clay" (Buchan, *A History of the Great War*, p. 134).

References: John Buchan, *A History of the Great War*, vol. 1 (Boston: Houghton Mifflin, 1922); Lyn MacDonald, *1914* (New York: Atheneum, 1988); Barbara Tuchman, *The Guns of August* (New York: Dell, 1970 [1962]).

KUT-AL-AMARA

DATE: 8 December 1915–29 April 1916.
LOCATION: on the Tigris River, some 75 miles southeast of Baghdad.

FORCES ENGAGED:

Turkish: Sixth Army. Commander: Field Marshal Colmar von der Goltz, then Khalil Pasha.
British: 6th Indian Division. Commander: Major General Charles V. F. Townshend.

IMPORTANCE:

Kut was the longest unrelieved siege of any British force in history, and its loss brought about a major change in British military and political arenas in mid–World War I.

Historical Setting

Britain sent Indian Expeditionary Force D into the Persian Gulf in November 1914 just after the Ottoman Empire had entered the war on the side of the Central Powers. Ostensibly the force was to protect British oil interests in the region, but in actuality Force D's mission was to overawe any potential Muslim uprising that might spread to India. The invading British and Indian troops of the 6th Indian Division occupied Basra after minimal shelling, then proceeded slowly up the Shatt-al-Arab to capture Kurna, where the Tigris and Euphrates rivers merge. A brief but intense fight south of Kurna at Shaiba cleared any Turkish troops out of the immediate Gulf region and brought innumerable protestations of loyalty from Arab tribes in the neighborhood.

By January 1915 the British had accomplished their mission, but the expedition from this point forward suffered from what the

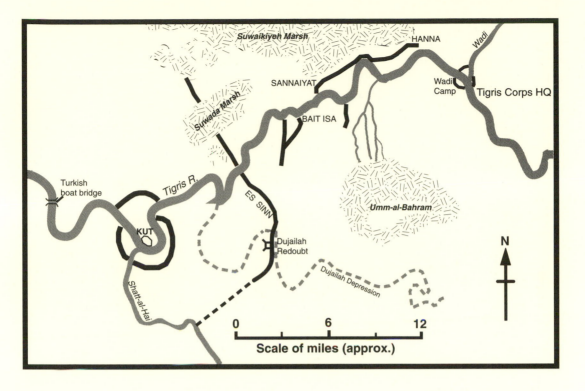

British term as "drift." After visiting the front in March, Viceroy Lord Hardinge decided that a single division was too small a commitment to adequately protect the supply point of Basra and keep the Arabs cowed. He sent in the 12th Division as well and placed both units under the overall command of Lieutenant General Sir John Nixon. Nixon, believing his mission to be the occupation and security of as much of southern Mesopotamia as possible, constantly saw threats to his army's position. Operations into Persia secured the oil fields on the Karun River, but his force advanced up both the Tigris and Euphrates as Nixon perceived both as potential avenues of Turkish attack. Any position his army occupied, however, seemed to him then to be threatened by the next town upriver, so that town had to be occupied as well.

In India, Lord Hardinge and Chief of the General Staff General Sir Beauchamp Duff took Nixon at his word that each successive advance was vital. Unfortunately, a breakdown in communication (real or perceived) meant that Nixon's army moved increasingly farther away from their supply base at Basra without a corresponding increase in transport to deliver supplies. Thus, Nixon's advances stretched his army's neck way too far out, and its head was chopped off.

In November 1915, in the wake of a brilliant operation that captured the town of Kut-al-Amara, at the junction of the Tigris River and the Shatt-al-Hai, Nixon and the Indian authorities pressed for an attack on Baghdad. Such a decision had to come from London. Hardinge and Duff portrayed the Turks as lower-class soldiers and Nixon's troops as invincible—after all, look what they had accomplished thus far with so little support. The siren song of Baghdad proved too alluring for the War Cabinet to resist and they authorized the assault.

Unknown to London or Delhi was the viewpoint of Major General Charles Townshend, 6th Division commander and the man who had planned and executed operations since April 1915 and who was given the task of taking Baghdad. He had begged for more manpower and more transport for months, but Nixon was oblivious. Townshend realized that his under-strength division had little chance of defeating a well-entrenched force in numbers superior to his own. His protests fell on Nixon's deaf ears, and thus were never forwarded to India or London. In spite of the difficulties, the 6th Division almost defeated the Turks at Ctesiphon, outside Baghdad, but 5,000 casualties was more than Townshend could afford to suffer and continue to press the attack, so he ordered a withdrawal.

The Siege

Most of the casualties were evacuated by river craft, while Townshend led a fighting with-drawal downriver. His men entered Kut on 5 December and found themselves surrounded on the 8th. Many later critics of Townshend argue that he should have continued his with-drawal downriver, but the exhaustion of his troops, the dearth of defensive positions any-where within range, and direct orders from Nixon all support his decision. Kut was a strong defensive position with a fairly good amount of supplies on hand and he could not have made a successful stand anywhere else.

After entrenching themselves outside Kut, the Turks attempted to storm the town in mid-December. The operation was under the com-mand of German Field Marshal Colmar von der Goltz, who had since 1911 been serving as an adviser to the Turkish military. Failing in three assaults, he decided to maintain an invest-ment and starve the defenders out, sending the bulk of his forces downriver to beat back any relief efforts. Although Townshend expelled some of the town's inhabitants, he did not get rid of as many as he probably should have. Sec-ond, he did not order as thorough a search of the town as he should have in order to locate all possible food stocks. That was done later, after the first attempt at relief had been repelled in January 1916. A more accurate estimate of food on hand, how long such food could be made to

last, and the quick commencement of half-rations all could have extended the time the defense could be maintained, giving Town-shend and the commander of the relief much more accurate information with which to deter-mine the timing of relief attacks.

Nixon was invalided out of Mesopotamia by illness in December 1915. The new comman-der of Force D was George Gorringe. His first attempt to break through the Turkish lines was almost successful, but the rapidity with which it was planned and executed argued against its success. Learning that more supplies had been uncovered in Kut, Gorringe spent more time organizing his second assault. It was aimed at the thinner defensive line the Turks had occu-pied south of the Tigris. An early morning reconnaissance found the major fort in the line empty, but a failure to exploit that knowledge gave the Turks time to see the danger and man the position. The attack failed, when more aggressive on-the-spot decision making could have secured victory.

In the wake of the second relief effort's fail-ure, Townshend placed his troops on half-rations. There was also a limited attempt to sup-port the garrison by air-dropping supplies, the first time such an operation was ever tried, but too few aircraft facing uncooperative weather conditions made the operation unworkable. Townshend was able to communicate with Force D by wireless telegraphy, and he began to broach the topic of opening negotiations with the Turks while his force was still strong enough to pose a threat. He was overruled. A third attempt to break through Turkish lines on the north side of the Tigris failed in early April, for by that time the Turks had had months to strengthen their positions. There was no attempt to coordinate a sally from Kut, although it was considered. Gorringe was sure he could break through, and the casualties a breakout would cause, as well as the abandon-ment of wounded, seemed too great a cost.

Finally, in mid-April, Townshend was autho-rized to open negotiations with Khalil Pasha, who had assumed command of the Turkish forces upon von der Goltz's death in January. Townshend knew he had little with which to bargain. He attempted to convince the Turkish general to allow his army to leave on parole, never again to take up arms in the Middle East. Failing that, he was authorized by London to offer a ransom of £1,000,000. Khalil's response: "Tell him to keep his money. I have lost 10,000 men." The only concession Khalil would grant was to allow Townshend to travel alone to Constantinople to negotiate with the Turkish government. Unable to hold out any longer, the garrison surrendered on 29 April 1916. This was the longest unrelieved siege in all of British military history at 149 days.

Results

The 6th Division was marched out of Kut and upriver to prison camps in Turkey, and a large number of them died along the way or in captivity. Townshend, meanwhile, was kept in relative luxury under house arrest near Constantinople, from where he was unable to convince the Turkish government to improve the lot of his men. That comparative situation reflected badly on Townshend after the war and he died in disgrace in 1924. During the war, however, he was the "hero of Kut." In reality, Townshend did almost the best anyone could have done in the situation. A clearer estimate of supplies at the outset would probably have delayed the first relief attempt and its chances for success could have been improved, but after the first attempt in January 1916 the 6th Division was doomed by the strong defensive positions the Turks occupied downriver.

The failure to capture Baghdad and the resulting siege of Kut brought British public attention to the Mesopotamia campaign. Returning soldiers let the world know of the horrible conditions under which the troops had to operate, and the government launched an investigation, the Mesopotamia Commission. Evidence of the poor oversight from India, the primitive port facilities in Basra that limited the

amount of supplies taken into Mesopotamia, the lack of river transport that kept those supplies unavailable to the troops at the front, and especially the horrendous medical situation, all shocked the British public. The government of H. H. Asquith was soon replaced by a new one under David Lloyd George, and the revelations of the Mesopotamia Commission Report proved a major factor in that change. Unfortunately, those most responsible for the disaster, General John Nixon and Viceroy Hardinge, suffered no official sanction.

The attention to Mesopotamia did have some positive effects, for adequate transport and supplies began to flow into the country. In the autumn of 1916 General Sir Stanley Maude assumed command and led British forces to the capture of Baghdad the following spring. The British presence in Mesopotamia led to their assignment by the League of Nations as the occupying power under the mandate system, by which the present country of Iraq was created.

References: A. J. Barker, *The Neglected War* (London: Cassel, 1967); Paul K. Davis, *Ends and Means: The British Mesopotamia Campaign and Commission* (Rutherford, NJ: Fairleigh Dickinson University Press, 1994); Quetta Staff College, *A Critical Study of the Campaign in Mesopotamia up to April 1917* (Calcutta: Government of India Press, 1925); Sir Arnold Wilson, *Loyalties: Mesopotamia, 1914–1917* (London: Oxford University Press, 1930).

MADRID

DATE: 6 November 1936–31 March 1939.
LOCATION: central Spain.

FORCES ENGAGED:

Nationalist: varied considerably throughout the siege. Commander: General Francisco Franco. Republican: varied considerably throughout the siege, defenders consisting of loyal Spanish troops, brigades of international volunteers, and militia. Commander: General Jose Miaja at first, a defense council later in the siege.

The capture of Madrid signaled the end of the Spanish Civil War.

Historical Setting

On 17 July 1936, the Spanish Foreign Legion based in Morocco began a rebellion against the recently elected liberal government. Like-minded units in twelve cities throughout Spain followed suit the next day, and the Spanish Civil War had begun. As General Emilio Mola began to consolidate the rebel, or Nationalist, hold on the north-western provinces, Army Chief of Staff Francisco Franco landed in Morocco from the Canary Islands to take command of the southern revolutionary forces. He called on fascist Italy and Nazi Germany to aid his cause, portraying the Spanish government as communist-influenced. Italy's Benito Mussolini responded with aircraft and later troops and tanks. Germany's Adolf Hitler provided Franco with thirty transport aircraft immediately, with large numbers of combat aircraft to follow as the war progressed. With those transports Franco ferried 16,000 troops from Morocco into southern Spain, establishing his headquarters in Seville. With troops in the region rallying to his cause, the southern force soon numbered some 30,000 men.

While Mola in the north gathered his forces

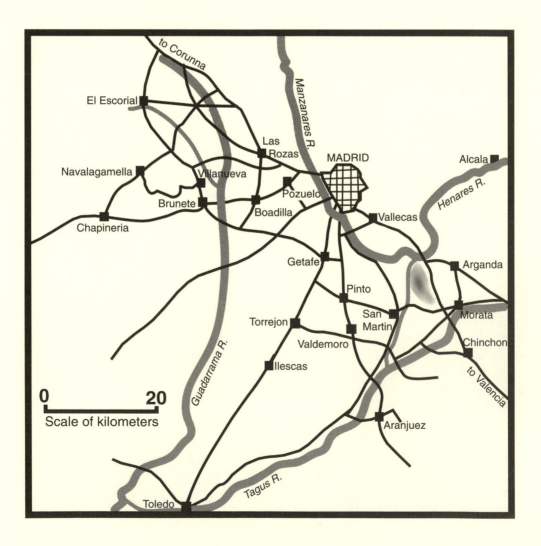

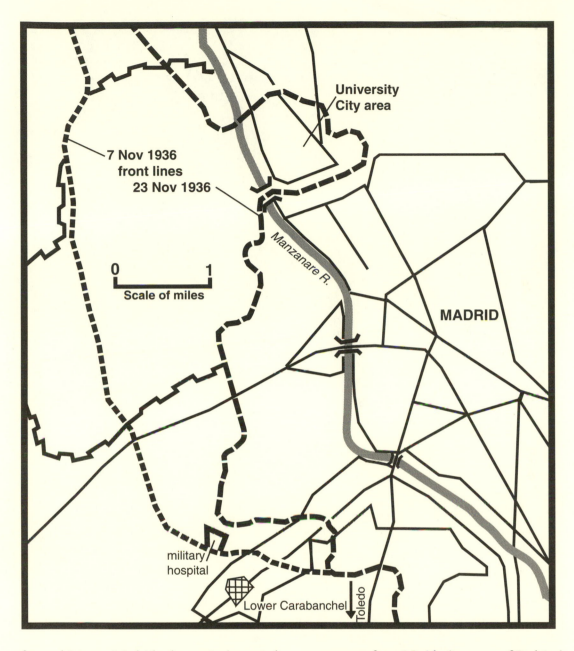

University
City area

7 Nov 1936
front lines
23 Nov 1936

Manzanare R.

Scale of miles

MADRID

military
hospital

Lower Carabanchel

Toledo

for a drive on Madrid, the nation's capital, Franco ordered Colonel Juan Yagüe to drive northward from Seville toward Badajoz, which he captured on 15 August. From there he drove northeastward toward Madrid. His main tactic was to transport his men by truck until they approached a town held by loyal government forces, who came to be called the Republicans. He would then bring his superior artillery to bear on the enemy and then overwhelm them with infantry. His path took two parallel routes: one from Merida (just east of Badajoz) via Trujillo to Navalmoral de la Mata; the other north to Caceres, then due east to Trujillo. The superior training and coordination of the Nationalist forces showed itself repeatedly in confrontations with Republican forces, who often were little more than hastily armed civilians. When Yagüe's forces captured Navalmoral on the north bank of the Tagus River, the next target was Talavera de la Reina, which his men took by storm on 3 September.

Nationalist troops loyal to General Franco advance, bayonets fixed, through the debris of houses at Madrid, wrecked in air raids during the Spanish Civil War, 2 April 1937. (Archive Photos)

By the 21st they were at Maqueda, where Franco halted the column. Although the road to Madrid, some 35 miles away, was open Franco diverted the attack to the southeast toward Toledo. A small force of Nationalists was holding out in the city's Alcazar fortress, but the position was being mined by the besiegers and looked grim for the defenders. Franco decided to rescue them for the morale boost it would give his cause but also to acquire an armaments factory in the city. Although it took less than a week to break through and end the siege, that time was vital to the defenders of Madrid.

As Franco approached Madrid from the west, Mola's advance from the northwest went down two axes: due south from his headquarters in Burgos and southeastward from Valladolid. Both routes went through a chain of mountains covering Madrid from the north. The Valladolid column broke through the pass at Alto del Leon on 22 July and the Burgos col-

umn took the Somosietta pass on the 25th. Both sites saw intense combat but the inferior Republican weaponry and training almost guaranteed Nationalist victories. Stubborn Republican defense of other mountain passes, however, slowed Mola's advance and not until early October was he in a position to coordinate with Franco on an attack against Madrid. By then, the southern Nationalist force was beginning its approach to the city.

The Siege

The Republican cause was hurt by a lack of coordination, foresight, and outside aid. Failing to attract the open support of France, Jose Giral resigned as prime minister on 4 September. President Manuel Azaña appointed Socialist Party leader Francisco Largo Caballero to the post, which he would do only if he could

A sign on La Imperia building reads, "Evacuad Madrid," and shows airplanes bombing the city during the Spanish Civil War. (Library of Congress)

appoint some Communists to the cabinet. That helped attract the support of the Soviet Union, which began shipping tanks and planes to the Spanish government. Unlike aid from Hitler and Mussolini, however, Soviet Premier Josef Stalin's aid came in return for Spanish bullion. Along with the Soviet weaponry came military advisers, and Vladimir Gorev aided Spanish General Jose Miaja in organizing Madrid's defenses. Largo Caballero, who had been instrumental in trying to organize the Republican war effort, had been conscripting militia and sending them out to try to stop the Nationalists as far from the capital as possible. That meant that the defenses of Madrid itself had been sorely neglected. The arrival of the Russian aid coincided with the Nationalist diversion to Toledo, and Madrid's defenders had to work quickly to prepare for the onslaught.

The Nationalist columns attacking from the south and west were in position on 15 October. Two columns drove northward from Toledo, one northeastward from Santa Cruz de Retamar and one eastward from San Martín de Valde-iglesias. By 4 November they were all within 10 miles of Madrid, with the city's airfield at Getate in Nationalist hands. Since 29 October Nationalist aircraft had been bombing targets in the capital. The Russian advisers had been amazingly successful in organizing the citizens into militia units and giving them rudimentary training, but more important the first of the International Brigades arrived from Hungary. These volunteer units, ultimately numbering twelve "brigades" (few were actually at brigade strength), proved a mixed blessing to the Republican cause, but the Hungarian troops were well-trained veterans whose arrival was vital to the city's defense. The defenders took up the motto the French had used at Verdun in the First World War: "they shall not pass."

The two southern columns entered the Madrid suburb of Carabanchel on 8 November. Thousands of militia swarmed forward, urged on by the radio broadcasts of communist Dolores Ibarruri, known as "La Pasionaria." Those militia, stiffened by the Hungarian troops, blunted the attacks led by the Nationalist General Jose Varela. Once halted, the Hungarians moved to meet the western attack, where the two Nationalist columns had merged to attack through the Casa de Campo suburb toward the University City sector of Madrid. A fierce Hungarian counterattack stopped that attack as well, and the Nationalists halted for a time and resumed their bombing of Madrid. It had the opposite effect of that intended: it stiffened the defenders' resolve rather than breaking their will. On the 15th a force of Anarchists (whose leadership had recently consented to join Largo Caballero's government) went into the line at Casa de Campos, but they put on a poor showing and the Nationalists soon broke through and occupied two-thirds of the University City area. Foreign embassies abandoned Madrid as newly arrived German aircraft, the Condor Legion, intensified the bombing campaign, but the defenders had fought the attackers to a stand-still. Both sides dug in where they stood, as the battle went into stalemate after 23 November.

On 13 December the Nationalists attacked again, this time shifting their focus to the north-west to sever the road from Madrid to Corunna, thereby isolating the city from Republican forces in the mountains. The fighting lasted a month and both sides lost some 15,000 men, but the road was at last in Nationalist hands by 15 January. In February, another offensive began south of the city aimed at severing the Madrid–Valencia highway. Although they made good progress at the outset, stiff Republican resistance at Jarama stopped the Nationalist drive short of its objective. By the end of the month, the Nationalist lines ran northwest-southeast with Madrid at their center but still not in their grasp. With Republican troops active in other parts of the country, the Madrid siege went passive for the next four months.

On 7 July the Republicans took the offensive when General Miaja launched an attack in the northwest in an attempt to regain the ground lost at the first of the year. He shocked the Nationalists by driving a wedge 5 miles deep into their lines, but General Varela rallied his men and they slowly regained the ground. By the end of the month the Republicans were back near their starting point, 25,000 men weaker. The Nationalists lost some 10,000 in the month's fighting.

After the Republican summer offensive, the siege really settled into stalemate. Neither side made any major moves for a year and a half. Around the country Franco's forces made slow but steady progress in conquering most of Spain. By February 1939, they conquered the strongly Republican province of Catalonia in the far northeast, leaving only the southeastern quarter of the country in Republican hands. As the government's position grew steadily more bleak, factions within the coalition began to struggle among themselves. In Madrid, 400 people per week were dying of starvation, and on 28 February Colonel Sigismundo Casado

(commander of the Republican Army of the Center) led a revolt against the dominant communist faction in the city. The battle went on for eight days before the Communists were defeated. The Communists had grown disenchanted with Prime Minister Largo Caballero and were glad to see him replaced in May 1937 by the more responsive Juan Negrín. When the Communists were defeated in Madrid in February and March 1939, however, Negrín's government was doomed; he fled for France. The Soviet Union had been gradually withdrawing its support for the Republican government, and the International Brigades they had sponsored were withdrawn from Spain by this time.

When Colonel Casado assumed control of Madrid, he opened negotiations with Franco. The talks went on until 25 March but broke down when the Republican air forces would not agree to the unconditional surrender that Franco demanded. As Franco's forces began advancing on Madrid on the 26th, Republican troops began wholesale surrender. Nationalist troops entered the capital on the 27th, and by the 31st the civil war was over.

Results

It is virtually impossible to know the exact number of people who died in Madrid, for combat, bombing, and starvation all played their parts, along with executions by both sides. In total, Spain lost about a million people during the war—some 600,000 dead and the rest exiled or refugees. Combat deaths made up less than a quarter of the number killed and executions roughly half.

The experience of Madrid's population was a foretaste of that to be suffered by civilians throughout the world when World War II came. For the first time bombing of civilian areas became common, although many towns in Spain suffered much greater damage than did Madrid. The civil war, which began as a strictly Spanish affair, ended up quite international. German and Italian money, manpower, and equipment were vital to Franco's success, and Soviet aid via weapons, advisers, and sponsorship of the international brigades was also a major factor in delaying the Nationalist victory. Franco, who had been named head of state just before the siege of Madrid began, ruled as dictator until 1975. His originally stated intention, to restore the monarchy, fell by the wayside and that restoration did not occur until after his death. Long after fascism and Nazism collapsed, Franco's ultraconservative rule remained in Spain.

References: Jack Gibbs, *The Spanish Civil War* (London: Ernest Benn, 1973); Gabriel Jackson, *A Concise History of the Spanish Civil War* (New York: John Day, 1974); Hugh Thomas, *The Spanish Civil War* (New York: Harper & Row, 1963 [1961]).

BILBAO

DATE: 31 March–19 June 1937.
LOCATION: on Spain's northern coast, near the mouth of the Nervión River.

FORCES ENGAGED:
Spanish Nationalist: 50,000 Spanish, Moroccan, and Italian troops. Commander: General Emilio Mola, then General Fidel Dávila.
Basque: perhaps 45,000 troops, primarily militia. Commander: General Llano de Encomienda.

IMPORTANCE:
Loss of Vizcaya Province's capital city broke the back of Basque resistance in the Spanish Civil War, leading to a long-term suppression of Basque nationalism.

Historical Setting

On the eve of Spanish Civil War, neither the government nor the rebels could be sure which side the Basques of northern Spain would take. On the one hand the Basque Nationalists had been solidly supporting the reformers in government the previous few years, but they also were a staunchly Catholic population and the Church was solidly on the side of General Francisco Franco. The opening of the conflict on 18 July 1936 found the Basque military men in the north seizing rebellious soldiers and declaring their loyalty. Unfortunately for the government, it was questionable just how loyal the mainly conservative Basques would be to an administration that rapidly turned socialist. Unfortunately for the rebellious Nationalists, the Basques disliked anything resembling a military dictatorship, since the Republic had just recently granted them autonomy.

There was hardly political unanimity in the northern provinces, however. The Basque Nationalists were dominant in the eastern provinces of Vizcaya and Guipozcoa. The province of Santander in the center was more socialist in its outlook, the labor movement *Unión General del Trabajadores* (UGT) being the strongest party. The westernmost province of Asturias had an outlook that was almost completely communist, but was unwilling to take direction from any outside authority, including the government they fought for. This political strife was reflected in the region's military performance, which was haphazard at best since rival units often refused to take orders from anyone else.

The rebellion in the north was at first directed by a junta based in Burgos, and General Emilio Mola commanded the Nationalist troops that soon swept across northern Spain from the upper Portuguese border to the province of Catalonia in Spain's northeastern corner. This drive bypassed Basque provinces along the northern coast but isolated them from direct contact with the Republican government operating in Madrid. By 4 September the Nationalists had captured Irún, located at the far western end of the Franco-Spanish border, completely surrounding the Basque provinces. For

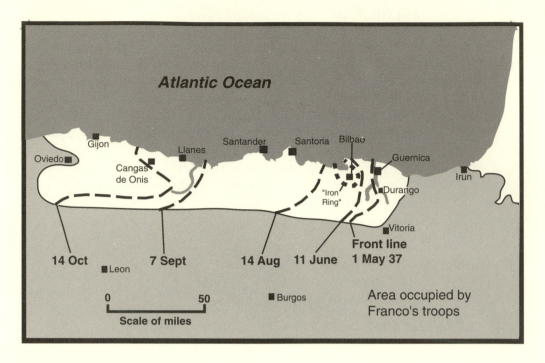

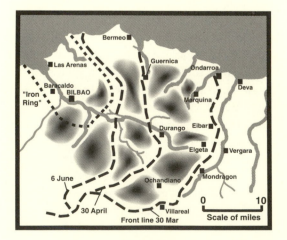

some months afterward the northern theater remained relatively quiet as the Nationalists focused their efforts on the drive toward Madrid.

After General Mola began his drive into Basque territory on 31 March 1937, an incident occurred that isolated the Basques politically. The Nationalists had hoped that peace with the Basques could be negotiated and approached them via the Vatican. Pope Pius IX directed that a letter be sent offering terms. The Republican government intercepted the letter, however, and they jumped to the conclusion that the Basques had initiated peace talks. That resulted in the government cutting off any and all military aid. That action, coupled with the increasing strength of the Nationalist blockade at sea, doomed the Basques to a solitary war.

The Siege

Bilbao was the site of northern Spain's primary arms factories and iron ore mines, as well as a port city located just inland on the Narvión River. The city lay just 30 miles from the Nationalist front lines, located along an axis from Deva to Vergara to Villareal, but the ground that lay between is extremely rugged. A determined army had the advantage on defense, but the Basques lacked certain key elements to make their stand successful. They fielded a force of perhaps 45,000 men, but possessed only a dozen tanks and a handful of obsolescent aircraft and artillery pieces. Thus, the attacking 50,000 Nationalist and Italian troops had almost complete air superiority.

Troops of General Franco's army entering Bilbao during the Spanish Civil War. (Archive Photos)

The Basques had spent the previous several months trying to build a strong defensive line around Bilbao, the "Iron Ring," but it was still incomplete by the spring of 1937. It was also not well designed, the bulk of the fortifications being on hilltops where they were easily located by Nationalist artillery and aircraft. To make things worse still, one of the designers of the Iron Ring had defected to Mola and given up the plans for the construction. These conditions, exacerbated by the political infighting among Basques, Socialists, Communists, and Anarchists, made a strong defense problematic.

General Mola preceded his offensive with an appeal for surrender: "Those not guilty of assassination and who surrender their arms will have their lives and property spared. But, if submission is not immediate, I will raze all Vizcaya to the ground, beginning with the indus-

tries of war" (Thomas, *Spanish Civil War*, pp. 402–403). The attack began 31 March with strikes by Nationalist air power, most notably the Condor Legion, German aircraft and pilots loaned to Franco by Germany's Adolf Hitler. One of their first targets was the road junction at the town of Durango. There was no other military significance to the town. It was undefended, and almost 250 people died in the first case of terror bombing. On the ground, well-placed Basque tank traps and barbed wire slowed the Nationalist advance, but they forced the Basques to slowly withdraw before heavy pressure.

On 26 April the Condor Legion created a landmark in infamy with an attack on the ancient Basque capital Guernica, like Durango undefended and with little military significance. Market day was in progress when two waves of German aircraft arrived late in the afternoon. Using both high explosive and incendiary bombs they virtually destroyed the town, then strafed fleeing civilians. The only military objective, the bridge over the Mundaca River, was not attacked; 1,600 people were killed and a further 900 wounded. Survivors were able to alert the outside world to the tragedy, and it reflected quite badly on Franco's forces. The Germans claimed they were acting on Spanish directions, while the Spanish claimed that fleeing Communists had set the fires. During the Nuremberg trials in 1946 German air force commander Hermann Göring admitted it was merely an experiment to test the relative efficacy of high explosive and incendiary bombs.

While the world recoiled in horror from Guernica, the Basques were recoiling from continued Nationalist pressure. The Basques held strong points on high ground, but consistently retreated when they found themselves being outflanked and in danger of encirclement. Still, all was not darkness for the defenders. Constant bombardment, which had originally been terrifying, became sufficiently commonplace that the noise alone stopped being a signal for withdrawal. On 1 May a Nationalist battleship, the *España*, was sunk by a mine off the coast of Bilbao. The blockade, originally thought to be tight, proved ephemeral and British ships began delivering supplies on a fairly regular basis. In mid-May a new Republican government was formed under Juan Negrín, who included five Basques in his cabinet. That signaled the beginning of increased support for the war in the north.

For a few weeks the fighting stopped owing to terrible weather, and the defense team in Bilbao underwent changes. General Gamir Ulíbarri instilled increased efficiency in the troops along with aid from the Russians. General Ian Berzin gave advice and his presence ensured more support from Moscow, which delivered fifty-five antiaircraft guns in early June. The Republican government attempted to send in some aircraft via France but the French government sent them back, minus machine guns. A direct flight across Nationalist-held territory was next, seven of the ten planes dispatched arriving safely. They were of little use against the overwhelming numerical superiority enjoyed by the Condor Legion, and most were eventually destroyed on the ground.

Nationalist commander General Mola died in a plane crash on 3 June, an incident that was never fully explained. It may have been an accident, it may have been a time bomb aboard the aircraft. If it was not an accident, Franco may have been involved; he certainly had little love for Mola and barely mourned his loss. General Fidel Dávila replaced him and resumed the offensive on 11 June with a massive artillery bombardment. By nightfall leading elements of the Nationalist force had punched through the Basque lines and reached the Iron Ring. All night the bombardment continued as artillery batteries were brought up. On the 12th the Nationalists struck at the weakest point in the defenses, the turncoat Goicoechea's information being their guide. Early hints of the blitzkrieg showed themselves here, as the Nationalist tanks came in so closely on the heels of the artillery barrage the defenders could not differentiate when the tanks' cannons opened up. By sundown the Nationalist breakthrough was on a 6/10 mile front. The city of Bilbao now came under artillery fire.

The military council in Bilbao decided to fight for the city, but began evacuating the civilian population westward. Children were removed aboard foreign ships, taken to France, England, or the Soviet Union (if their parents were Communists). Not all of them made it. Nationalist vessels captured two ships, while the Condor Legion strafed the roads leading west. Troops were redeployed outside the city, but their stand was brief. The left flank buckled and the defenders retreated in such haste they did not destroy the bridges across the Nervión River, which the Nationalists reached on 15 June. All along the line the Basques slowly fell back, with the left flank proving the weakest part of the defense. On the 17th,

20,000 artillery shells fell in Bilbao plus more on the militia trying to hold the line. The 18th saw even more civilians, along with materiel, being shipped west and the end was nigh. That evening all units were ordered to abandon the city, and when Nationalist armor entered Bilbao at noon on the 19th, it was almost empty. Only a few fifth columnists that had harassed the defenders emerged to welcome the victors.

Results

Franco ordered that only limited numbers of troops enter the city. Previously, when his forces had captured the southern city of Malaga, there had been widespread pillage; he wanted to avoid a repetition. The victory was complete, however. As Hugh Thomas wrote, "the fall of Bilbao marked the end of Basque independence. The conquerors made every effort to extinguish Basque separatist feeling. All schoolmasters were dismissed unless they could prove their political negativism. The Basque tongue was officially forbidden" (Thomas, *Spanish Civil War*, pp. 447–448). Although the Anarchist faction among the defenders favored destroying the university and the church of St. Nicolás, Minister of the Interior Leizaola forbade it. The town itself was badly damaged, of course, from the heavy bombardment, but the mines and factories were untouched by either attacker or retreating defender. Both resources proved invaluable to the Nationalist war effort.

The fall of Bilbao also had an internal and international effect on the Roman Catholic Church. The Basques were recognized as being perhaps the most strongly religious population in all Spain. For a supposedly Catholic Nationalist movement to inflict the horrors of Guernica as well as the sociological destruction of Basque nationality made many Catholics ponder their own views of which faction had right on its side. Pope Pius XI named all priests and nuns killed in the conflict as martyrs for the faith. Nationalist-leaning bishops issued a pro-

nouncement that their cause was holy, as the Communists were the ones who had brought on the war. Basque priests who had not obeyed the Vatican's orders to aid the Nationalists were criticized. On 28 August the Vatican officially recognized Franco's government as legitimate, barring any Catholics in Spain from supporting the Republican government.

The Nationalists continued their offensive westward, and by 21 October 1937 had secured all of northern Spain for Franco.

References: Jack Gibbs, *The Spanish Civil War* (London: Ernest Benn, 1973); Gabriel Jackson, *A Concise History of the Spanish Civil War* (New York: John Day, 1974); Hugh Thomas, *The Spanish Civil War* (New York: Harper & Row, 1961).

MALTA

DATE: 11 June 1940–20 November 1942.
LOCATION: 60 miles south of Sicily, roughly halfway between Gibraltar, Spain, and Alexandria, Egypt.

FORCES ENGAGED:

British: five infantry battalions, three Gloster Gladiator aircraft at the outset. Commander: Lieutenant General Sir William Dobbie, later John Vereker Viscount Gort. Italian/German: approximately 350 bomber and 200 fighter aircraft.

IMPORTANCE:

Italian/German failure to neutralize or capture Malta gave the British a base from which to harass supply convoys necessary for the Axis effort in North Africa.

Historical Setting

The island of Malta has been of great strategic significance since the earliest days of sea power. Possessed by Phoenicians, Greeks, Romans, Christian knights, Turks, French, and finally the British, it is the lynchpin of the central

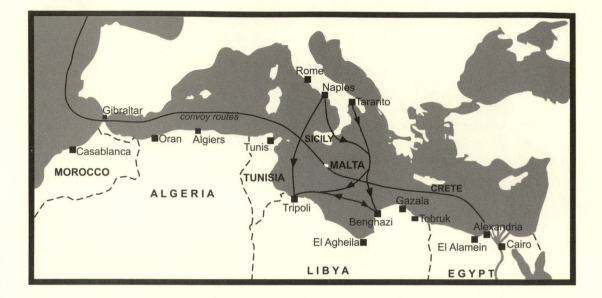

Mediterranean Sea. After the British seized the island from Napoleon's forces in 1800, it became their permanent possession, confirmed by the Congress of Vienna in 1815. The next 140 years were peaceful ones for the Maltese, but the advent of World War II brought that to an end.

Britain depended on Malta's Grand Harbor as her key naval base in the Mediterranean, but did little to upgrade its defenses as war approached. "Here was an island endowed with superb harbours and dockyard facilities, an unsinkable fortress strategically situated in the central Mediterranean, a vital link with the two nearest bases a thousand miles away at Gibraltar and Alexandria. Measuring no more than 17 miles by 9, the island possesses natural caves and grottos that could have accommodated food, equipment, fuel, and ammunition to withstand a long siege" (Saunders, "Malta Digs In," p. 276). The only alteration in the government's view of the island's role was to transfer most of the warships based there to Alexandria, from which they operated for the first half of the war. Only a handful of submarines, torpedo boats, and minesweepers remained. When little military action occurred in the winter of 1939–1940, it seemed as if

upgrading the defense would not be necessary. Hitler's invasion of France in May 1940 changed all that. As France's military was collapsing in early June, Italy decided to get in on the spoils. Benito Mussolini declared war on France on 10 June, and early the next morning Italian bombers appeared over Malta.

The Siege

A few antiaircraft batteries on land and aboard ships inflicted some damage on the attacking Italian aircraft, which kept their bomb runs at high altitude. The only other air defense was provided by three Gloster Gladiator biplanes that were hastily uncrated and assembled. These three planes, dubbed *Faith, Hope,* and *Charity,* were the mainstay of the island's defense for weeks. With spares cannibalized from a fourth Gladiator and engines later appropriated from other types of aircraft, the pilots and aircrew exhausted themselves maintaining a defense. Nine Swordfish torpedo bombers arrived in late June and a dozen Hurricane fighters were delivered by the aircraft carrier *Argus* in early August.

The Italian air force operated from several

British and American navy and merchant seamen mix with residents of Malta outside the shattered Opera House following massive air attacks by Axis forces, 19 January 1943. (Archive Photos)

airfields in Sicily, only minutes away from Malta. They could maintain an around-the-clock assault if they wished, but the Italian pilots did not seem to eager to press home their attacks even in the face of fairly light resistance. Supply convoys were able to slip past Italian notice and deliver supplies to Malta in October and December, and the aircraft carrier *Illustrious* delivered more fighters. Still, the air attacks were troublesome enough to convince the British to keep their main fleet in Egypt. British submarines from Malta, however, did score some hits on Italian convoys delivering supplies to the army in Libya, but some 97 percent of Italian ships escaped unscathed. The deliveries of supplies and soldiers to the Italian army made little difference, however, for the

British forces in Egypt under General Archibald Wavell defeated them soundly and were soon advancing through North Africa against minimal opposition. Mussolini's cry for help brought German troops to Libya under the command of General Erwin Rommel, and that changed the situation mightily for both Wavell's forces and the Maltese.

In January 1941 X *Fleigerkorps* arrived in Sicily: 120 bombers, 150 dive-bombers, 40 fighters, and 20 reconnaissance aircraft. Coupled with the 45 Italian bombers and 75 fighters already on the island, a massive force could now be brought against the lightly held island. Rommel was not about to allow Malta to interdict his supply lines. One last supply convoy entered Malta's Grand harbor relatively untouched on 8 January. HMS *Illustrious* had been bombed and entered the harbor badly in need of repairs. Not until the 16th, however, did the Germans try to sink the damaged aircraft carrier. Eighty *Stuka* dive-bombers attacked but managed only one hit on *Illustrious*, although the harbor facilities were badly damaged and civilian areas received many bombs. That convinced many of the previously reluctant citizens of Malta to begin to take shelter underground when the air raid sirens sounded, which they did with alarming regularity for the next two and a half years.

Air raids became increasingly common through April 1941, when they suddenly slackened. The German invasion of Yugoslavia and Greece on 6 April diverted many of the Sicily-based aircraft to the east. The subsequent German invasion of Crete also kept the Germans occupied in the eastern Mediterranean, but by June many of the planes had returned, although a number of them were diverted even farther east to assist in the July invasion of the Soviet Union. This gave the islanders some breathing space and allowed the British to deliver a few more convoys of supplies and aircraft and to launch a number of attacks on German supply convoys sailing for North Africa. Rommel responded by ordering Grand Harbor mined as well as bombed, hampering naval operations considerably.

Through the summer and fall of 1941 action in North Africa dominated everyone's thinking and Malta received something of a respite, although air raids were still common. As winter approached, more aircraft were transferred back to Sicily from the eastern front, and the new commander of the *Luftwaffe*, Field Marshal Albert Kesselring, decided it was time to pound Malta into dust. Through the winter he massed in Sicily 500 Stukas, some 250 Messerschmitt fighters, and a large number of Junkers 88 medium bombers; further forces were based in Sardinia and the small island of Pantalleria, 140 miles west of Malta off the Tunisian coast. In March 1942 Kesselring began his offensive against the island and

any attempt to succor it. Hurricane fighter aircraft were launched from carriers as close to Malta as British captains dared to sail, but these were often destroyed on the ground as soon as they arrived. Convoys delivering them or anything else for Malta found themselves under heavy attack by air and submarines. British submarines continued to deliver aircraft fuel and medical supplies, but food stocks began running dangerously low on the island.

British Spitfires began arriving in April 1942, but they were attacked on the ground as soon as they landed. Four heavy air raids were launched every day as well as numerous smaller attacks day and night, and the Maltese airfields were targeted as heavily as the harbor. Cities were also attacked and the civilian population began digging into the soft rock of Malta, building underground housing, supply dumps, even a theater. So many people were forced underground, however, that labor for repairs to the airfields and docks began to taper off. Still, the streets were cleared and ground crews patched up damaged planes to keep the defense going. Spirits got the occasional life from both good and bad news. The arrival of any supplies or aircraft was greeted with cheers; the *Welshman*, one of the fastest transports in the world, sailed unescorted into harbor from Gibraltar on a fairly regular basis. When, however, a flight of Stukas intentionally bombed a well-marked hospital, the pilots had yet another motivation for getting back into the air. The arrival of 64 Spitfires, delivered by HMS *Eagle* and USS *Wasp* on 9 May, was a godsend. The ground crews labored mightily to get the planes fueled and armed, but they had mastered it: each twelve-plane squadron was landed and off again in seven minutes. The delivery meant, for the first time, a massive welcoming for the German bombers that thought to catch them on the ground.

The arrival of the Spitfires began to turn the tide somewhat, but convoys sent to Malta continued to suffer heavy losses. In June 1942 two convoys totaling seventeen merchant ships and eighty-two warships tried to reach the island, but only two transports got through. With so many warships dedicated to fighting the German submarine menace in the Atlantic, escorting convoys to Russia via the Arctic Circle, and the need to get supplies to the embattled Australians, Malta was just one more destination that had to await sufficient ships. The largest supply convoy, code-named "Pedestal," left Gibraltar on 10 August. Fifty-nine warships escorted fourteen merchantmen, but the Germans were ready. Submarines waited at the Straits of Gibraltar, backed by German and Italian torpedo boats, as well as the remains of the Italian fleet that the British had not destroyed in 1940 at Taranto. The first loss was HMS *Eagle*, one of the three aircraft carriers in the convoy, lost to a German submarine. Air attacks started at dusk on the 11th. The next day was spent again trying to dodge both air and submarine attacks, but more ships were lost. The heaviest escort ships turned back for Gibraltar, according to plan, and the remaining escort ships had to do their best. An Italian submarine torpedoed two cruisers and the SS *Ohio*, the only tanker in the convoy, damaging but not sinking them. Air attacks sank more ships as they neared Cape Bon, Tunisia. Axis torpedo boats then came into play, sinking four merchantmen and damaging a cruiser. Only three ships reached Grand Harbor, the *Ohio* towed in by two destroyers and a minesweeper.

The delivery of fuel and some food extended the life of the siege, which had been dangerously close to starving into surrender. It extended food supplies only until late June, however. By then Malta could well have been in Axis hands. Kesselring, along with German Navy Admiral Raeder, convinced Hitler that Malta had to be captured in order for Rommel to succeed in North Africa. Hitler and Mussolini decided in April 1942 to launch an invasion of the island no later than the end of May. Hitler was hesitant, since the Axis had not undertaken any significant amphibious operations and his parachute division had been severely weakened at Crete the previous spring. The invasion was postponed when Kesselring visited Rommel and found him on the verge of a major offensive against the British at the port city of Tobruk. The two decided to await Tobruk's fall before launching the invasion. When Tobruk fell within a matter of hours and the Germans captured massive amounts of supplies and fuel, Rommel received permission to press the beaten British 8th Army into Egypt. That decision ended any major planning for Malta's conquest. The diversion of air power to aid Rommel allowed summer convoys to reach Malta and keep the islanders alive.

Results

The "Pedestal" convoy was the last major disaster, for the American invasion of North Africa in November, coupled with the British victory at El Alamein in late October, signaled the beginning of the end for Rommel and the Axis forces in the Mediterranean. When a convoy from Port Said entered Grand Harbor untouched on the night of 19–20 November, it marked the end of the siege.

Malta was saved by a fortuitous set of circumstances. Mussolini could have easily invaded the island in June 1940, although given the lackluster performance of the Italian military in North Africa success was not assured. Still, the invasion never occurred and the island was allowed to grow stronger. After that, the constant shuttling of air power among Sicily, Libya, and the eastern front kept Malta from being completely obliterated. "The reduction of Malta to impotence, or better still its capture, was the main objective, and for this purpose an ever-growing German air force was gathered on the Sicilian airfields. On the other hand, when Rommel was active he required the aid of all the air that could be maintained in Tripoli. But then if the attack on Malta were lightened, the fortress rapidly recovered its striking power, and by extreme exertions began once again to take a heavy toll of the [German] convoys" (Churchill, *The Hinge of Fate*, p. 265).

Couple the scattering of Axis resources with

the heroism of the island's defenders and population and Malta's survival, while never sure, was significantly enhanced. King George VI's unique awarding of the Cross of St. George to the entire island indicates the valor of the inhabitants, who suffered through almost two and a half years of virtually constant attack.

References: Winston Churchill, *The Hinge of Fate* (New York: Bantam, 1962 [1950]); Charles MacLean, "George Cross Island," in *History of the Second World War*, no. 34 (London: BPC, 1966); Malcolm Saunders, "Malta Digs In," in *History of the Second World War,* no. 2 (London: BPC, 1966); David Woodward, "Malta: The Siege is Raised," in *History of the Second World War*, no. 42 (London: BPC, 1966).

TOBRUK

DATE: 10 April–7 December 1941.
LOCATION: on the coast of Libya, roughly 200 miles from the Egyptian border.

FORCES ENGAGED:

German: Deutsche Afrika Korps, made up of two German and two Italian divisions. Commander: Lieutenant General (later Colonel General) Erwin Rommel.
Australian/British/Imperial: approximately 22,000 men. Commander: Major General L. J. Morshead.

IMPORTANCE:

Continued resistance of British Empire troops remained a thorn in the side to the German/ Italian campaign against Egypt while keeping the Axis powers from launching a full-scale attack on the British base at Malta.

Historical Setting

World War II was nine months old when combat began in North Africa. Italy officially entered the war on 10 June and the following day suffered casualties inflicted by British raids striking out of Egypt. Italian dictator Benito

Mussolini's long-term dream was to reestablish the Roman Empire, making the Mediterranean Sea "an Italian lake." Italy had controlled Libya since 1912, and that was the base from which Mussolini hoped to seize the Suez Canal and the Middle Eastern oil fields for the Axis. With France under German attack simultaneously, the British were in no position to commit any more troops to Egypt than were already stationed there. As it turned out, that would be sufficient in the short run.

For the first few weeks the British raided regularly up the coast road into the Libyan province of Cyrenaica, shooting up enemy facilities and capturing prisoners. Italian Marshal Rodolpho Graziani responded on 13 September by sending his 10th Army slowly but successfully into Egypt. When it halted to bring up road building equipment, two British divisions struck and proceeded to annihilate the Italian force. By 9 February 1941 Major General Richard O'Connor's British troops controlled Cyrenaica and had inflicted 130,000 casualties on the Italians.

Once in possession of the primary Libyan port city of Tobruk, British troops began digging defensive positions around the city.

Hitler responded by dispatching German troops under the command of General Erwin Rommel, who had distinguished himself as an aggressive tank commander in the Nazi invasion of France. Rommel arrived in Benghazi and wasted no time striking at the overextended British force, which had also been robbed of veterans to assist the Greeks fighting an Italo-German invasion. As quickly as the British had driven into Libya was as rapidly as they left, with German armor hard on their heels. Not only was the Western Desert Army badly beaten, General O'Connor was captured. Theater Commander General Archibald Wavell did his best to stem the German tide.

By the summer of 1941 Rommel was at the Egyptian frontier, but a force of Australian, British, and Indian troops held on to the port city of Tobruk. Although he was succeeding in

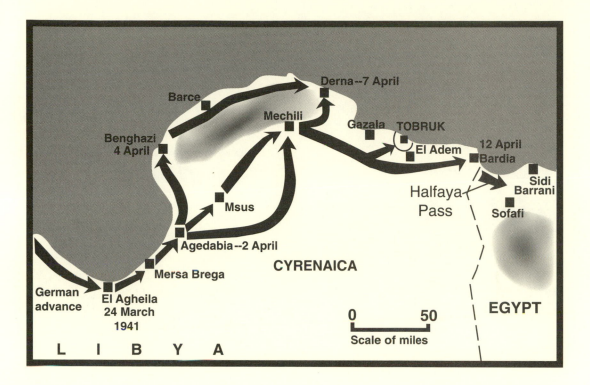

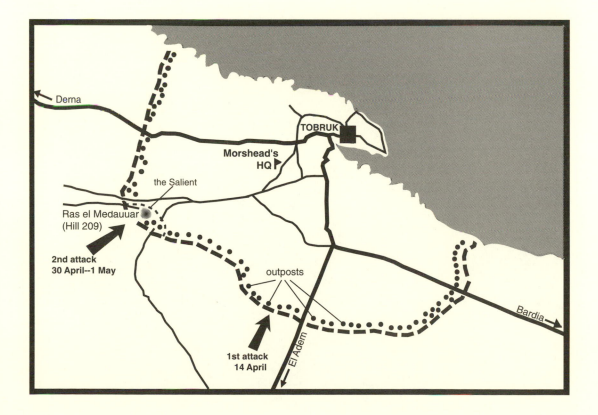

After Britain's victory in Cyrenaica, an endless line of German and Italian prisoners is marched down from the desert to Tobruk harbor for transport to POW Camps. (Library of Congress)

British tanks patrolling in Tobruk during World War II. (Library of Congress)

his freewheeling armor campaign in the desert, the fixed and in-depth defenses of Tobruk stymied him.

The Siege

As the British forces withdrew in disarray, Major General Leslie Morshead of the Australian 9th Division was given command of all forces in Cyrenaica, which meant Tobruk and little else. General Wavell ordered him to defend the port city as best he could for two months, by which time a relief would certainly be effected. British armored unit personnel who had lost their tanks were withdrawn from the city back to Egypt via the harbor, which remained open throughout the siege. Morshead was left with 14,236 Australian troops and just under 8,000 British. They manned and improved the defenses first built by the Italians, a 30-mile line of small fortified posts. Morshead's plan was to hold these posts with minimal strength (ten to fifteen per post) and sow a minefield behind the perimeter. Should a German breakthrough occur, the minefield would slow it down, allowing the mobile reserves to respond, while the outposts to either side of the penetration would deliver flanking fire on the attackers.

Rommel reasoned that while the bulk of British forces were rapidly withdrawing toward Egypt Tobruk would be unready for a quick attack. On the night of 10–11 April he threw units at Tobruk haphazardly and they were beaten back one at a time. The garrison had strengthened the existing Italian defenses and had a large supply of guns and ammunition (much of it Italian) and food. After pausing a day to personally reconnoiter the perimeter, Rommel on the 14th massed his tanks for the same type of assault that had served him so well in France. The narrow front on which he attacked opened a hole in the defenses, but it was immediately blasted in both flanks before it could exploit the breakthrough. Morshead's tactics worked brilliantly and the German retreat left behind seventeen tanks, 150 dead, and 250 prisoners. This

was the first setback German army forces had met since the outbreak of the war.

Morshead kept up an active defense, regularly sending patrols to attack German and Italian outposts. In the first ten days these sallies brought back 1,700 prisoners. Rommel launched his next attack on 29 April. The Australian defenders observed the concentration of his forces and were prepared with artillery and tanks. The primary target was Ras el Medauuar, Hill 209. This time the attack went in on a wider front, hoping that the flanking fire would be less effective. Unfortunately for Rommel, the wider front did not have the striking power of the narrow piercing attack that had served him so well in the past. Point-blank artillery fire and British tanks blunted the assault and the Germans were unable to drive past the perimeter posts that they captured. This area, the Salient, was the scene of the bulk of the fighting over the next months. Having failed to break through, Rommel stopped to reconsider his situation.

Rommel placed his Italian divisions in the lines surrounding Tobruk, while he tried to rest and refit his German units for another rush at the town. Unfortunately for him, he had too few men to both attack Tobruk and maintain an effective force on the Egyptian frontier. Just inside the frontier was Halfaya Pass, out of which British Brigadier Gott launched constant harassing raids. At the same time, the Australian troops inside Tobruk continued to launch strong sallies against the besiegers with good results. Rommel was forced to do little more through the summer and fall of 1941 than keep Tobruk surrounded while maintaining an active defense at Halfaya Pass. Meanwhile, General Wavell tried to mount relief efforts. The first came on 15 May with a holding attack on Halfaya Pass and an attempted armored flanking movement. It failed. On 15 June he began Operation Battleaxe, but the stout German defense stopped this attack cold with the loss of most of the newly arrived Crusader tanks from England. After his two failed offensives, Wavell was replaced by General Sir Claude Auchinleck.

Churchill made sure that the newly forming 8th Army in Egypt got all the manpower and supplies he could send around the Cape of Good Hope and run through the gauntlet of the Mediterranean Sea. Further, British air power was strengthened in both Egypt and Tobruk, giving the defenders another aid in their strong defense. Finally, the Nazi invasion of the Soviet Union that began in June 1941 diverted Adolf Hitler's attention away from North Africa, and the demands of the Eastern Front soon meant a corresponding decline in supplies to Rommel's Afrika Korps.

In November, after much carping by Churchill, Auchinleck finally launched Operation Crusader, a major offensive designed to break through to Tobruk. British armored and infantry forces crossed into Cyrenaica on 18 November 1941. Poor weather had grounded the German air force and Rommel had no hint of an offensive until it struck his forward units. British attacks drove between German strongpoints while German counterattacks drove between British thrusts. Each side captured and employed enemy fuel and supplies. As British forces neared Tobruk, Rommel staged another of the gambling maneuvers for which he was famous. He led an attack around the British desert flank, hoping to swing around behind the British and reach the coast, cutting them off from the Egyptian bases. It almost worked, but in the end Rommel was obliged to withdraw all of his army past Tobruk to Gazala, 25 miles to the west. Tobruk was relieved on 5 December.

Results

In the late summer months of 1941, Australian Prime Minister John Curtin pressured London to send in more forces to Tobruk, not to supplement the garrison but to replace the Australians, who were suffering from exhaustion and disease. Over time most of the troops were replaced, and by October they were all gone but one battalion, unable to leave because of German air attacks on its convoy. The Australian 9th Division lost 749 killed, 1,996 wounded, and 604 prisoners during the siege. The German and Italian casualties cannot be determined accurately, as their forces were shifted from Tobruk to the Egyptian frontier and back again, then were involved in the fighting during Operation Crusader.

Rommel pulled his forces back to the Gazala Line, a series of entrenchments begun by Indian troops during the opening phase of the North African campaign. British attacks soon forced him to pull back yet again, all the way to the primary Axis base at Benghazi then farther west and south down the coastal road to El Agheila, which he reached the first week in January 1942. There, the events that had played out since the opening of the war repeated themselves: one overextended army forced to retreat in the face of the opponent's reinforcement. On 21 January Rommel counterattacked and by feinting a thrust cross-country toward Gazala was able to swing around onto Benghazi and capture it without a fight as the 7th Indian Brigade slipped away in bad weather. By the first week in February Rommel's army was once again on the road east toward Tobruk.

On his second attempt Rommel did capture Tobruk, in a lightning attack as he had envisioned for his first assault. The defenses had been stripped to aid in the last British offensive and the South African, Indian, and British units were not as prepared or equipped to defend the position. It did not really matter, in the long run. Although Churchill called Tobruk's fall a major disgrace, the 242-day defense of the city saved Egypt and possibly the Middle East for Great Britain. When Morshead took command, Wavell told him: "There is nothing between you and Cairo." Beyond Cairo? "The Germans would drive like an arrow from Cairo across Arabia to the Persian Gulf, and seize the fountainhead of Britain's oil supplies. They would be able to turn north from there, and attack Russia from the south as well as the west. India would be menaced. They could link up with the Italians in Ethiopia, and invade East Africa. The whole structure of Britain's imperial power could collapse as though its keystone had been knocked away, and Germany would in fact and at last be invincible" (Firkins, *The Australians in Nine Wars*, p. 245). It is problematic whether Hitler had the patience to wait for all that to happen before his invasion of the Soviet Union, but the threat to British security and power was certainly great. Tobruk's defense, by stalling Rommel's drive into Egypt, saved the Allied position in North Africa. By the time Rommel did take the port city, the Nazi effort in Russia sapped whatever motivation and materiel might otherwise have gone to the Afrika Korps.

References: Peter Firkins, *The Australians in Nine Wars* (London: Robert Hale, 1972); Derek Jewell, ed., *Alamein and the Desert War* (New York: Ballantine, 1967); K. C. Macksey, *Afrika Korps* (New York: Ballantine, 1968); idem, "Rommel's First Attack," *History of the Second World War*, ed. Barrie Pitt (London: BPC, 1966).

LENINGRAD

Date: 15 September 1941–27 January 1944.
Location: on Russia's northern Baltic Sea coast.

Forces Engaged:

German: Sixteenth and Eighteenth Armies, plus Finnish Karelian Army, totaling some 350,000 men. Commanders: Field Marshal Ritter von Leeb for the Germans.
Soviet: several armies numbering some 250,000, plus a city population of approximately 2 million. Commanders: Marshal K. V. Voroshilov, General Georgi Zhukov, and General L. A. Govorov.

Importance:

Nazi failure to capture the city in the early stages of Operation Barbarossa tied up large numbers of German troops that might have been more

productively employed elsewhere, and provided the Soviet Union with heroic propaganda of resistance to the Nazi onslaught. Additionally, a weakened IV Panzergruppe may have contributed to Army Group Center's failure to seize Moscow.

Historical Setting

Operation Barbarossa, the invasion of the Soviet Union by Germany and its allies, commenced on 22 June 1941 and would, according to the Nazi Führer Adolf Hitler, "shake the world." Leningrad was a major objective of the original Barbarossa order to the senior officers and staff of the German army Oberkommando des Heeres (OKH). Field Marshal Ritter von Leeb's Army Group North had been given the task of destroying the enemy forces fighting in the Baltic theater by occupying the Baltic ports, Leningrad, and Kronstadt. The Russian fleet would be deprived of its bases. As the invasion of the Soviet Union progressed, the bulk of the Wehrmacht was pulled to the south in pursuit of the mass of the surviving Russian forces under Marshal Budenny. Despite being listed as a major objective in the Barbarossa order, Leningrad was not of the same priority as Moscow or points south. As a result, OKH had kept Army Group North relatively weak and planned to reinforce it after the capture of Moscow. In August 1941, as the Army Group approached Leningrad, the broken terrain made up of forests, lakes, streams, and rivers slowed its advance and lessened the effectiveness of its armored formations. The land now began to favor the defense. The advantage that the Panzers enjoyed on the wide-open plains of Poland and along the frontiers of the Soviet Union was gradually disappearing as the Army Group approached Leningrad. Conventional infantry and pioneers (engineers) now became more important.

Soviet forces had fallen back from their frontier positions facing the East Prussian border past Riga and Pskov and were now digging in on a line along the Luga River from Narva

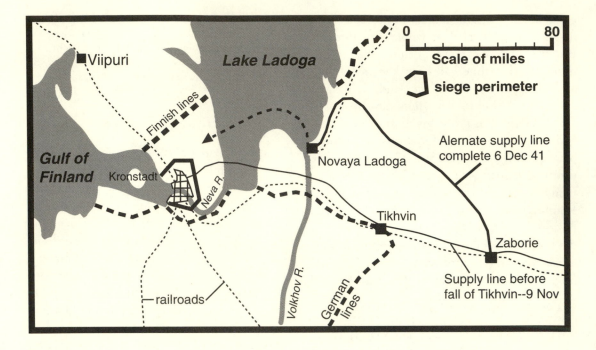

toward the ancient Russian cultural center of Novogrod. Little more than three corps' worth of stragglers and badly beaten-up formations faced the invaders. The defenders had practically no artillery, armor, or other heavy equipment and were even short of that most prodigious Russian asset, manpower.

The German attack on the Luga River position began on 8 August 1941 and within three days the defensive line was at the point of cracking. A counterattack by the Russian 48th Army saved the Luga forces from annihilation, but the entire Russian line crumbled away and 3rd SS Panzergrenadier Division was on the main railway line to Leningrad some 60 miles distant.

In the meantime, Finnish forces had advanced to the shore of Lake Ladoga and began their operation to recover the Karelian Isthmus lost to the Soviets during the Winter War of 1939. It appeared that the home of the October Revolution would fall to the Germans like a ripe melon.

As the invaders approached, some one million civilians in Leningrad worked around the clock to construct a defense perimeter around the city. During the course of the siege some 620 miles of earthen walls, 400 miles of anti-tank ditches, 185 miles of wood obstacles, 5,000 earth, timber, and concrete pillboxes, and 370 miles of wire entanglements were constructed by mostly civilian personnel. The Communist Party mobilized the population into paramilitary and labor organizations. These organizations fell into three basic types. The *Opolchenye,* or "people's Army," was basically a citizens' militia only marginally trained, without communications or heavy equipment, and armed with a variety of small arms and Molotov cocktails. Second were Regular Red Army units that had distinguished themselves in battle and had been awarded the title of "Guards." Third were "destruction battalions" comprised of Party personnel, Komsomol (youth organization) members, and Nejvyssi Kontrolni Vladce Davu (NKVD, security police) units that had been originally created to deal with enemy parachutists, saboteurs, and internal security threats.

The defenders were seriously deficient in artillery, and all other armaments not manufactured on the spot at Leningrad. There were,

Leningrad inhabitants under the direction of Petrov, a munitions worker, help construct anti-tank ditches during the siege of Leningrad. (Library of Congress)

however, large numbers of heavy and medium mortars whose rate of fire, at the ranges on the first day of battle, was almost as effective as that of medium artillery. Along the coastal front between the Baltic and the Krasnoye Selo, the 12-inch guns of the Lake Ladoga Flotilla would interdict the German rear. Freshly constructed KV-1 tanks, sometimes driven directly from the city's Kirov factory by the technicians who built them, roamed the battlefield individually or in pairs to take on the Nazi foe. The KV-1, armed with a 76mm cannon, heavily armored and vulnerable only to the celebrated German dual-purpose 88mm gun, was superior to any armored fighting vehicle in the German inventory. Lacking the sophisticated organization, tactics, and materiel resources of the Wehrmacht, the Russian met the invader with courage, obstinacy, and cunning in ambush and camouflage. The

close in-fighting among the lakes and forests surrounding Leningrad benefited the defenders and took away the advantage the Panzers exercised on the open battlefields of the Soviet frontier and the Luga River line.

Toward the end of August, the Leningrad district commander, Marshal K. V. Voroshilov, was replaced by the current chief-of-staff of the Red Army, a man who in his day came to visit and stabilize every dangerous sector on the Eastern Front, Georgi Zhukov. He organized the defenders and carried the defense until he was transferred to the Moscow front to save the situation there. As the Germans approached the city, the population appeared to be united at every level and ready to defend their homes to the last. Indeed, Hitler planned to murder the entire population, raze all buildings, and turn the vacant lot over to the Finns.

On 9 September 1941, von Leeb attempted

to take the city on the run. Seeking to use his mechanized units to quickly overrun Leningrad's defenses, he attacked frontally with the 1st Panzer Division along the left bank of the Neva River and the 6th Panzer Division along the main railway line from the south. Both units had been in continual action since the invasion in June and had not received sufficient rest, reinforcement, and refit since crossing the frontier. The Panzers quickly ran into a tangle of woodlands, water, and artificial obstacles emplaced by the Opolchenye and the construction battalions, problems that confront all mechanized forces when they encounter close defenses after weeks of mobile warfare. The German *Panzerwaffe* (armored force) would face this again in Stalingrad, as would the British "Desert Rats" in Tunisia and the Americans in the Normandy *bocage*. Losses of both men and machines were heavy, with four successive commanders of the 1st Panzer falling to enemy fire.

Von Leeb had hoped for a quick and decisive action to storm the city before he had to release the IV Panzergruppe to Army Group Center's advance on Moscow. By not breaking through the defenses quickly, he not only failed to gain Leningrad but also badly damaged the Panzers. The Panzergruppe was sent south in a badly weakened condition. This would have fateful consequences for the drive on Moscow.

By 11 September, the Germans had pushed as far as the suburbs of Slutsk, Puskin, and Krasnoye Selo and had occupied Hill 167 overlooking Leningrad. From Hill 167, the Germans could see the city only 7 miles away along with the ships of the Lake Ladoga Flotilla bombarding the invaders. This proved to be the high-water mark of the advance on Leningrad. During the next four days, the German grip on the city tightened, but never advanced.

The Siege

On 15 September, the envelopment of the city was complete. An attack by the 6th Panzer Division and two infantry divisions was repulsed. The Germans could advance no farther. Thus ended any Nazi attempt to take the city by storm. On 17 September, the Panzergruppe entrained for transport to the south and the advance on Moscow. The Wehrmacht was stretched too thin all along the Eastern Front to allow for the kind of resources necessary to take the city. The mobile phase of the operation was at an end and the Germans settled in around Leningrad to starve it out and let it "fall like a leaf." The infantrymen and the artillerymen replaced the panzer crew as the German instrument of conquest.

The bombardment of Leningrad was not so heavy as it was persistent. Shells and bombs hit the city continually, striking power plants, markets, water works, industrial targets, and other public works necessary to the functioning of a modern community. For the entire duration of the siege, the air raid siren and the sound of artillery strikes would make up the background noise of Leningrad city life.

The winter of 1941–1942 was a harsh one. Food, fuel, and other basic necessities of life were strictly rationed. The entire city was combed for foodstuffs, which were seized by the authorities and warehoused for rationed issue. Even with centralized rationing, there was never enough. These supplies were continually diminished by Nazi air attack, as warehouses went up in flames destroying much of was stored within. Fire-damaged foodstuffs were salvaged as much as possible and used to create "Victory Rations." Adding sawdust to the flour mixture, ultimately to a 50 percent mixture, increasingly stretched the bread ration. Draft horses killed on the street by German bombs and artillery were butchered on the spot and disappeared quickly into family stewpots. Cats and dogs vanished from the streets. Slow starvation haunted the population. Some 4,000 Leningraders starved to death on Christmas Day 1941. The ultimate death toll due to combat and noncombat causes officially set at 635,000 may have reached as high as a million.

Once Lake Ladoga froze over, a trickle of supplies was able to pass into the city via a 200-mile lifeline, despite heavy losses due to bombardment by the Luftwaffe and German artillery. This continued throughout the winter of 1941–1942 until the spring thaw of 1942 and recommenced the following winter of 1942–1943, continuing until the city's final relief. Priority of supplies went to military munitions and items not capable of manufacture within the city, with only enough food to keep the defenders fighting.

Refugees and the entire complement of the Baltic Sea Fleet swelled the prewar population of the city by almost 500,000. The Leningrad Military Council mustered all adults between the ages of fourteen and sixty years into civil defense units to deal with the results of enemy air and artillery bombardment. All civilian personnel not directly involved with the fighting continued political indoctrination training and worked overtime in the defense factories. Manufacture of KV-1 tanks and small arms, particularly submachine guns of local design, continued throughout the siege. Careful management of personnel in the face of defense requirements ensured that factory production never ceased during the city's ordeal.

Fighting ebbed and flowed along the perimeter of the city with little or no change in the lines. Much to the chagrin of the Germans, the Finns would not advance into Soviet territory, content to only recover their losses incurred during 1939. The battle shifted to one of patrols, artillery, and pioneers with small unit engagements the rule. Casualties were steady and the effects of inadequate rations and the lack of medical resources exacerbated combat deaths. The big killer of the siege continued to be death by artillery and aerial bombardment. The big battles shifted to the south as the Germans pushed toward Moscow and the Crimea. The Germans continued to attempt to seal off the city completely but failed to strangle the defenders, while the Russians counterattacked and attempted to maintain contact with the rest of the Red Army. Throughout 1943 a narrow supply corridor out the southern

shore of Lake Ladoga continued to operate. The Russian winter offensive of 1943 swept over the German right flank through Novogrod while a Russian army crossed the frozen Gulf of Finland on the left, forcing the Germans besieging Leningrad to withdraw. Long and bitter fighting throughout January 1944 continued. After almost 900 days of suffering, the siege was officially lifted on 27 January 1944.

Results

The defense of Leningrad tied down significant numbers of German forces that might have been utilized to better effect elsewhere on the Eastern Front. The invasion of Russia completely consumed the Wehrmacht and prevented the creation of a strategic reserve of forces to be employed at a decisive point. The fighting in the constricted areas of woodland and lake surrounding Leningrad demonstrated the vulnerability of armored/mechanized forces. Von Leeb's wastage of the IV Panzergruppe may have seriously weakened an already depleted push on Moscow. The capture of Moscow could have destroyed the Soviet Union and completely altered the outcome of World War II. The resistance displayed at Leningrad proved to the rest of the Soviet Union that the German invader was not invincible and provided Stalin with an immense propaganda display. The sacrifice of the citizens of Leningrad was subsequently recognized when the Supreme Soviet conferred the honorific title "Hero of the Soviet Union" to the city.—Michael McClain

References: Alan Clark, *Barbarossa: The Russian-German Conflict 1941–45* (New York: W. Morrow, 1965); Harrison Salisbury, *The 900 Days* (New York: Harper & Row, 1969); Albert Seaton, *The Russo-German War 1941–45* (New York: W. Morrow, 1971); Alan Wykes, "The Siege of Leningrad" in *History of the Second World War*, vol. 2, part 27 (London: BPC, 1966); idem, "Last Year of the Siege" in *History of the Second World War*, vol. 4, part 53 (London: BPC, 1966).

SEVASTOPOL

DATE: 30 October 1941–3 July 1942.

FORCES ENGAGED:

German: 204,000 men, 670 heavy guns, 655
antitank guns, 720 mortars, 450 tanks, 600 aircraft.
Commander: General Erich von Manstein.
Soviet: 106,000 men, 600 heavy guns, 100+ mortars,
38 tanks, 55 aircraft. Commander:
General I. E. Petrov.

IMPORTANCE:

Sevastopol and the Crimean campaign drew off
valuable forces from the Nazi drive to conquer
the Caucasus, while virtually eliminating
Soviet naval operations for two years.

Historical Setting

When Nazi forces invaded the Soviet Union
in June 1941, three army groups aimed at spe-
cific targets: Army Group North to capture
Leningrad, Army Group Center to capture
Moscow, and Army Group South to drive for
the oil fields of the Caucasus. As German forces
drove toward the Black Sea in the south, the
Soviet naval base at Sevastopol, on the Crimean
peninsula, became a prime target. Possession of
Sevastopol would deprive the Soviets of their
only warm water port. It did not take the Germans long to expel the bulk of Soviet forces
from the Crimean peninsula, accomplishing
that task in the autumn of 1941.

Occupation of the Crimea and capture of
the port of Sevastopol fell to General Erich von
Manstein, commanding XI Army. The opening assault began on 30 October and lasted
until 21 November, but the Germans made little headway against the three defensive lines.
Ships of the Black Sea Navy gave fire support
to the defenders and played a key role in beating back the attacks. A second major assault
began on 17 December and went on for two
weeks; the Germans made more progress during this attempt with gains on the northern

and eastern perimeters. Manstein was forced to
seal off the city with five divisions, however,
when the Soviets launched a counteroffensive
in late December 1941. In one of the largest
Soviet amphibious operations of World War II,
40,000 troops landed on the Kerch peninsula,
extending off the eastern coast of the Crimea.
The Soviets enjoyed early success, capturing
the city of Feodosia, where they found their
first evidence of Nazi atrocities: thousands of
Jews were buried in trenches just outside town.
The arrival of these Russian forces threatened
to encircle Manstein, so he was obliged to leave
a holding force at Sevastopol and turn to meet
the menace to his rear.

The Soviet successes and the consequent eas-
ing of pressure on Sevastopol in the first few
months of 1942 did much to brighten the spirits of the defenders. The population, which had
been living in cellars and caves, emerged to
begin some reconstruction. It was short-lived.
Beginning on 8 May 1942, the German offensive pushed Soviet forces back onto the Kerch
peninsula. The German superiority in air power
allowed the attackers to continually harass the
Soviet defenders with dive-bombers. To make
bad matters worse for the defenders, the chief
political officer, Commissar L. Z. Mekhlis, who
had little grasp of the situation, handed down
decisions. Thus, Soviet action tended to be too
slow and too weak to offer an effective obstacle
to the German forces. Mekhlis delayed implementing orders to withdraw to defensive positions around the town of Kerch, which fell on
15 May. Over the next five days 86,000 Soviet
troops withdrew out of the Kerch peninsula to
the Taman peninsula, but left behind 176,000
casualties. Worse still for Sevastopol, the Nazis
captured all of the Soviet heavy weapons.

The Siege

With the Soviet Crimean Front crushed,
Manstein turned his attentions back to Sevastopol. He transferred a further 5 divisions to
supplement the holding force already on site,

bringing the total number of attackers to over 200,000 men. The Germans amassed a huge stock of artillery, including 420 mm cannon, 615 mm mortars, and massive 800 mm railway guns; all told there were 670 artillery pieces and almost as many antitank guns. Manstein also had the services of 600 aircraft. Against this, the Soviets could field only about half as many troops. They had 600 artillery pieces, and a mere 38 tanks and 55 aircraft. The only avenue of resupply and reinforcement was by sea, and the Germans stationed more than 50 patrol torpedo boats and antisubmarine craft outside Sevastopol's harbor and supplemented them with 150 antishipping bomber aircraft. Soviet naval forces were so small that only small craft and submarines had much success running the blockade with men and materiel. In spite of that, a flow of reinforcements and supplies continued into the city, including 24,000 men in the last month of the siege. In that same month 25,000 sick and wounded were evacuated.

During the siege, underground factories continued to produce armaments, including mines, mortars, and hand-grenades, as well as uniforms and boots. Subterranean schools were also established. After the fall of Kerch, however, and the intensified German attacks, the constant German shelling and air raids made distribution of supplies almost impossible. The population began taking a greater role in the fighting rather than in production. Among the most famous of the defenders were members of the local Komsomol, or communist youth league, whose members (male and female) fought alongside regular troops and marines throughout the siege.

German artillery barrages began to blast the city on 2 June, and the renewed German offensive began on 7 June. Russian air defenses were soon destroyed as aircraft were either shot down or transferred to other bases outside the Crimea. The main German thrust was along the northeastern perimeter, aiming at Inkerman and the eastern extremity of North Bay. German progress was extremely slow as the Russians contested every inch. After a week

Manstein was pondering the possibility of ultimate failure. His call for reinforcements brought occupation troops from the Kerch peninsula as well as more soldiers of the XVII Army transferred to the Crimea from German offensives farther north.

Although Manstein felt the effects of the fighting through his own casualties, the Russians were faring little better. With no reserves to draw on other than what troops could be snuck in through the blockade, manpower began to drop off almost as rapidly as the ammunition supply. By 18 June Manstein's leading units reached North Bay, and the Russians were forced to engage with their artillery only at short range in order to stretch their supply of shells. Along the southern end of the perimeter, the Russians proved even more difficult to dislodge, but by 30 June the two German thrusts linked near Inkerman and were able to begin pushing west in a solid line. That night they reached the edge of the city of Sevastopol itself and the Russian evacuation began.

Anything that could float around the city was commandeered to try to run the gauntlet off the peninsula: minesweepers, fishing craft, submarines, plus what few aircraft could brave the Luftwaffe and land at battered landing fields. Minimal numbers at best could be evacuated, however, so the bulk of the troops fought to the end or, if lucky, infiltrated through the lines into the mountains to operate as partisans. By 3 July the entire area was in German hands.

Results

When German troops entered Sevastopol on 30 June, it marked the end of a siege of 250 days. The stubborn Russian defense cost both sides an immense number of troops. The Germans claimed to have captured 90,000 prisoners (out of 106,000 generally believed to have fought for the city), including some 26,000 wounded left on the beaches. The German XI Army was, in the words of the Soviet official history, "bled white." Not only the casualties but also the mere fact that so many troops had been sent to capture the city meant that the primary German offensive around Kharkov (although successful) was sufficiently slowed that the entire timetable for the German offensive to capture the Caucasus was delayed. In order to face a Soviet counteroffensive in November 1941 and to resume the offensive in 1942, the Nazi high command was unable to employ XI Army owing to its slow recovery of strength.

The Soviets praised the defenders, trying to gain a moral victory from the disaster. A "Defense of Sevastopol" medal was struck for the survivors and thirty-seven defenders were named Hero of the Soviet Union, the nation's highest honor. It was hollow, for the Germans denied the Soviets their primary Black Sea naval base and placed themselves in a position to render amphibious support to the 1942 Caucasus offensive.

In the end possession of the Crimea gained the Nazis little. Hitler's obsession with it, however, caused him to commit too many important forces to the peninsula for its defense in 1944 when the Soviets returned. Still, holding the Crimea was vital for controlling the Black Sea, and Soviet possession of it would put them in range of Rumanian oil refineries vital to the German war effort. By May 1944, however, American bombers had already began attacking Rumania from Italy and Soviet advances farther north toward Odessa put them just as close to the oil fields as possession of the Crimea would have done. When the Russians returned, their capture of the peninsula proceeded much more quickly than the German operation did two years earlier.

Half of the forces defending the Crimea were Rumanian rather than German, and they held on for only a month. Soviet troops launched their attack on 11 April and within two days owned the northern half of the peninsula. The defenders numbered approximately 174,000 while the Russians possessed almost three times that many. As German troops fled for Sevastopol, Rumanians surrendered. Some 50,000 German troops dug into 25 miles of trenches around the city. Following closely on the German retreat, the Russians did not press their advantage with an immediate assault but instead brought up heavy artillery. That gave the Germans time to dig and prolong the subsequent battle as well as to evacuate personnel in the three weeks the Russians gave them. What Hitler wanted, a heroic defense, turned into an attempt to create a Nazi version of the British Dunkirk evacuation. How many men fled and how many died or were captured is a matter of much debate, as Soviet and German sources disagree. The actual fighting for the city took only four days; it fell on 9 May 1944. The Russian defense of the city, for 250 days, became enshrined in Soviet folklore, second only to Leningrad in magnificence.

References: N. I. Ansimov, P. P. Bogdanov, Y. Y. Bogush, et al., *Great Patriotic War of the Soviet Union, 1941–1945* (Moscow: Progress, 1970); Colonel Vasili Morozov, "The Siege of Sevastopol," in *History of the Second World War*, vol. 35 (London: BBC, 1966); Alexander Werth, *Russia at War, 1941–1945* (New York: Dutton, 1964).

SINGAPORE

DATE: 31 January–15 February 1942.
LOCATION: at the tip of the Malay peninsula.

FORCES ENGAGED:

Japanese: 40,000 men. Commander: Lieutenant General Tomoyuki Yamashita.
British: 107,000 Australian, Indian Army, and British troops (including 27,000 administrative troops). Commander: Lieutenant General Arthur Percival.

IMPORTANCE:

Japan's capture of Singapore capped off their successful invasion of the Malay peninsula, robbing Britain of its prize defensive position in the Far East. This was the first of the many losses that led to the dissolution of the British Empire.

Historical Setting

Great Britain took control of Singapore in the early 1800s, in order to establish a trading post to compete with the Dutch merchants of Southeast Asia. The island city served as the major British defensive position in the region as well, earning the nickname "Gibraltar of the East." The huge artillery protecting the city from invasion gave those stationed there, as well as those viewing the outpost from London, the impression of impregnability.

Japan, however, was not daunted. The big guns could inflict serious damage on an invasion fleet, but therein lay their weakness: they were positioned only to defend against a seaborne landing, not a landward invasion from the Malay peninsula. The possibility of an assault from the north appeared incredibly remote, for only two roads existed through impenetrable jungles and swamps. It should have been easy to bottle up any invasion force foolish enough to commit itself to those two avenues of attack. However, the British Empire troops defending the city labored under a false sense of security. On the Japanese-controlled island of Formosa, experts in jungle warfare spent much of 1941 developing tactics to move soldiers through such terrain, and by training men in the Formosan jungles the Japanese developed the finest jungle fighters of the time.

As the Japanese threat in Asia increased through 1941, British officials in Singapore begged London for additional manpower. Churchill's commitment to Europe and the campaign in North Africa meant that few troops, ships, or aircraft would be made available from Britain, but some troops were transferred from the Indian Army to supplement the existing defensive forces, primarily Australian troops. By the time the war in the Pacific broke out on 8 December 1941, around 107,000 men of the Australian 8th Division, the Indian Army 9th, 11th, and 17th Divisions, and the British 18th Division were in place to defend the city. Many of these troops, especially the Indian divisions, were not well

equipped and were irregularly trained. Prewar plans for deploying troops at the most likely landing spots in Thailand and the Malay peninsula were not implemented, as the authorities in London feared that any such action prior to the outbreak of hostilities could be deemed provocative.

Thus, when the Japanese invasion force launched its amphibious assault on 8 December, they easily captured the key positions of Kota Bharu, Patani, and Singora. They quickly began moving south down the two Malay roads. When the Indian 11th Division attempted to establish a roadblock at Jitra, they were shocked to find themselves being outflanked through the jungle. After they abandoned their attempted roadblock on 12 December, it seemed that the shock of the Japanese tactics totally deflated the defenders. Any attempt at making a stand failed, as empire troops began to withdraw before any threat rather than stand and try to inflict serious damage. The retreat became small holding actions at each river crossing, lasting just long enough to destroy the bridge. The Japanese had anticipated such a strategy and brought extra engineering troops and bridging equipment. When the terrain proved too difficult for even the Japanese to penetrate, the empire troops found themselves outflanked by amphibious landings. By the end of January the entire peninsula was in Japanese hands, and the British Empire troops fled into Singapore.

The Siege

Japanese Lieutenant General Tomoyuki Yamashita masterminded a brilliant offensive, but he was not satisfied. He had made some political enemies in Tokyo, so his operation was not as well manned or equipped as he would have liked. In addition, one of his divisional commanders was consistently insubordinate. He also was operating with a hastily assembled staff, but in spite of these imperfect conditions he had succeeded. All that was left to him was

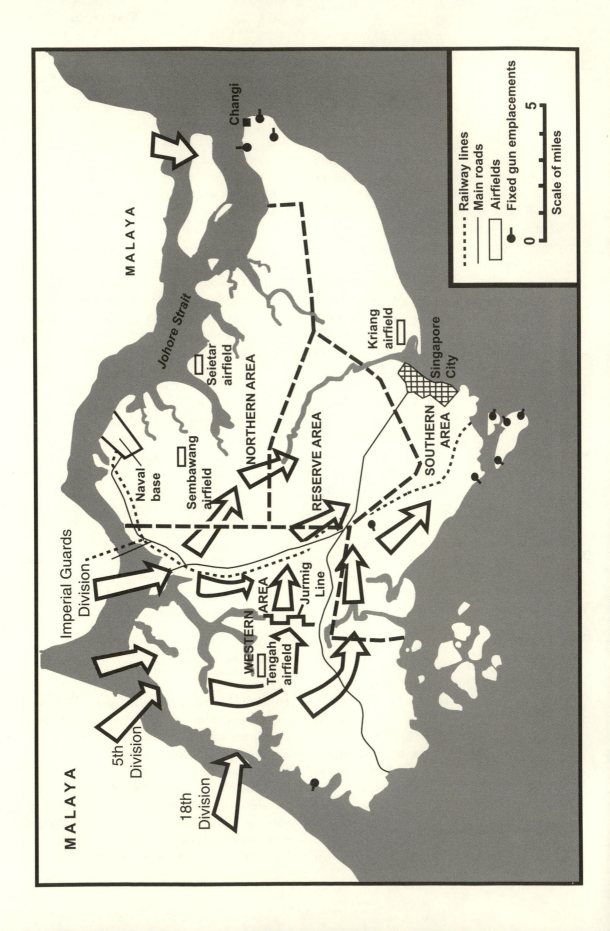

MALAYA

MALAYA

Johore Strait

Changi

Railway lines
Main roads
Airfields
Fixed gun emplacements

Scale of miles
0   5

Seietar airfield

NORTHERN AREA

Kriang airfield

Singapore City

Naval base

Sembawang airfield

RESERVE AREA

SOUTHERN AREA

Imperial Guards Division

WESTERN AREA

Jurmig Line

Tengah airfield

5th Division

18th Division

Tamil workers clearing the debris in Singapore following a bombing raid by the Japanese. (Keystone/Archive Photos)

Singapore itself. He probed the defenses for four days, then decided on a diversionary attack against the eastern part of the straits, which he hoped would draw British reinforcements. The main assault followed with two divisions across the western part of the straits. The causeway from the mainland to Singapore stretched about 1,100 yards. However, at its narrowest point the straits were only 600 yards wide, so an amphibious landing could take place quickly. Once ashore, the invaders would have to fight through the virtually nonexistent beach defenses, then across jungle and rubber plantations to reach the city on the southeastern part of the island. A determined defense should have been able to withstand a landing.

At this point Singapore's defenses showed their weaknesses. No trenches or tank traps had been dug anywhere except for a small line near the western shore. Although the large coastal artillery pieces could be turned around to face toward the invaders, they had to fire across the city at targets out of view more than 15 miles away. No system of artillery spotting was in place, so by the time any corrections could be sent to the gunners the targets had changed position. There were units deployed to defend the beaches, but the invasion came ashore at night and across such a wide front that the defenders were easily infiltrated and outflanked. The Japanese landed tanks the next morning, which the defenders had no guns of any size to repel.

Churchill ordered the city be defended to the last man, and destroyed if need be, to deny it to the enemy, but the defenders could not hope to mount an extended resistance. They were desperately short of water, for Japanese aircraft had knocked out the pumping facilities. More important, the troops seem to have lost hope, and the inadequate training of many of the Indian units showed itself in their poor performance. The constant Japanese barrage pounded away at morale as effectively as it did city buildings, and the Japanese exercised total air superiority. Little did the defenders know that Yamashita's forces were rapidly running out of ammunition. Yamashita decided that rather than conserve his ammunition he would maintain pressure for as long as possible; if he reduced his fire, the British might have sensed his plight and stiffened their resolve. His plan succeeded, and the British surrendered the city on 15 February 1942.

Results

Between 8 December and 15 February, the empire's forces suffered approximately 9,000 dead and wounded. The Japanese, outnumbered in virtually every engagement, lost 3,000 killed and 7,000 wounded. For this loss they gained Singapore virtually undamaged, with its excellent harbor facilities intact and a large amount of materiel in the city's warehouses. They also gained some 130,000 civilian and military prisoners. Although the British commanding officer, Lieutenant General Arthur Percival, extracted a promise from Yamashita that the city's inhabitants would be treated well, such was not the case. Much of the Chinese population suffered; as many as 70,000 people were tortured or killed. Some empire troops slipped through Japanese lines during the invasion and faded into the jungle, where they raised a Malay militia kept supplied by airdrops from the Indian Army, but they were more of a nuisance than a threat to the Japanese. One of the resistance units that was created, however, laid the groundwork for much of Britain's postwar problems in Singapore: the communist Malayan People's Anti-Japanese Army (MPAJA).

It was organizations such as the MPAJA that agitated for independence when British rule was reestablished in 1945. For a few weeks after the fighting stopped rival underground units accused each other of collaboration and engaged in retribution executions. The first British administration was a military one that tried to maintain order. The political struggles were exacerbated by the survival problems of the Malay population, for agriculture during the war had suffered and the economic infrastructure was a shambles. By 1946 Britain was prepared to give the Malay peninsula (less Singapore) its independence, for London was not willing to part with its key trading post. The constitution that the British attempted to impose on the peninsula created a strong central government, but the independent Malay states were unwilling to follow it. An adapted document in 1948 created a confederation more suitable to the population. Singapore remained a British possession for another decade, but in 1958 the island city gained self-rule with the British retaining only defense rights.

To a great extent, Britain's loss of Singapore in 1942 began the British Empire's collapse. After World War I the victorious powers held on to their colonial possessions, but they could not withstand the wave of popular independence movements after World War II. One thing the Japanese accomplished in their Southeast Asia strategy was to show to the Oriental population that the long-dominant Europeans were not a master race. The fact that Singapore surrendered was humiliating enough for the British, but the fact that it fell so easily was an overwhelming psychological blow. In quick succession the imperial possessions of the eastern Indian Ocean region began to break away, with the Dutch being the biggest losers in the area. Britain's loss of India was a foregone conclusion after World War II and the fall of Singapore was the first step toward that end. Only Hong Kong remained a British possession, and even that reverted to China in 1997. The British Empire broke apart; the British Commonwealth, made up of most of the imperial possessions, remained as a shadow of Britain's former world power.

References: Kate Caffrey, *Out in the Midday Sun: Singapore, 1941–1945* (New York: Stein & Day, 1973); Saburo Ienaga, *The Pacific War, 1931–1945* (New York: Random House, 1978); Arthur Swinson, Tokuji Morimoto, and Mutsuya Nagao, "The Conquest of Malaya," in *History of the Second World War*, no. 26 (London: BPC, 1966); John Toland, *But Not in Shame* (New York: Random House, 1961).

STALINGRAD

DATE: 24 August 1942–2 February 1943.
LOCATION: on the Volga River in southern Russia, modern Volgograd.

FORCES ENGAGED:

German: 6th Army and part of 4th Panzer Army, approximately 230,000 men. Commander: General Friedrich von Paulus.
Soviet: Sixty-second Army, approximately 300,000 men. Commander: General Vasilii Chuikov.
Relieving force: 12 armies of approximately a million men. Commander: Field Marshal Georgi Zhukov.

IMPORTANCE:

The Nazi failure to capture Stalingrad doomed their attempt to conquer the Caucasus oil fields, thus failing to defeat the Soviet army by starving it of its fuel supply.

Historical Setting

On 22 June 1941, three German army groups stormed across the Polish-Soviet border. Soviet Premier Josef Stalin had ignored warnings from British Prime Minister Winston Churchill that the Nazis were about to violate the nonaggression treaty that they had negotiated with the Soviets in August 1939. Using the blitzkrieg tactics so effective in their conquests of Poland and France, the Nazis encircled and destroyed one Soviet army after another, killing

thousands and taking tens of thousands prisoner. Like the Russian army facing Napoleon in 1812, they could stand and die or retreat and burn, hoping to slow the onslaught sufficiently to allow them to regroup later and make a stand.

German Army Group North drove for Leningrad in order to secure the Baltic coast. Army Group Center directed its attack toward Moscow in order to deny the Soviets a central base of command. Army Group South pointed toward the Caucasus with the intent of seizing the Soviet oil fields. Possessing those fields to feed their own machines while denying supplies to the Soviet armies would be a virtual guarantee of victory.

As usual, Mother Nature sided with Mother Russia and the invaders suffered the consequences. One of the coldest winters on record froze the German forces as they stood on the outskirts of their targets of Leningrad and Moscow, although they did capture Kiev in the

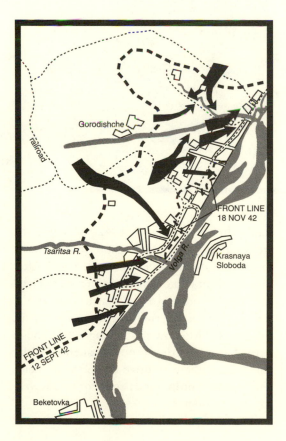

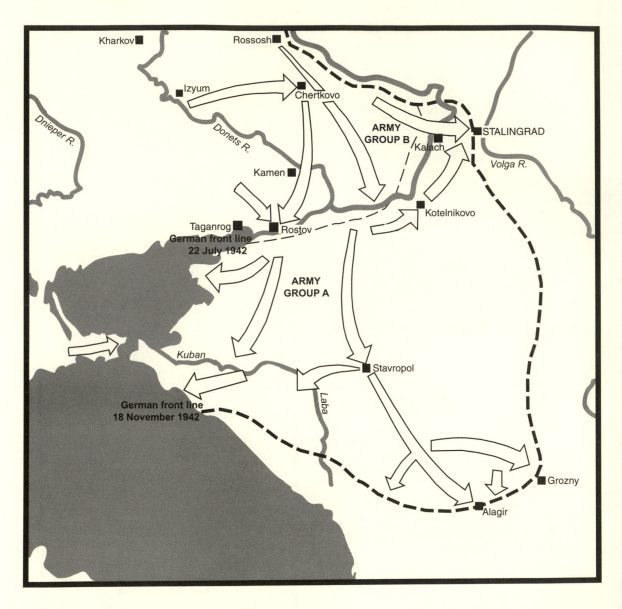

south. In the spring of 1942, however, the armies in the south made good progress while the two northern armies were stalemated. After the capture of Rostov in July, Hitler made a fatal blunder. He ordered Field Marshal List in the south to detach units of his army group to assist the others at Moscow and Leningrad. Although Army Group South was now weakened, Hitler still wanted them to drive on to the oil fields and to score a propaganda coup for him as well: capture Stalingrad.

The former Tsaritsyn, Stalingrad had earned its new name thanks to the defense of the city by Josef Stalin during the Russian Civil War. Now that Stalin was master of the Soviet Union, Hitler believed capturing the city that bore his name would shatter communist morale. Stalingrad was a major manufacturing and trade center as well, and denying its resources and position on the Volga River to Stalin would badly hurt the communist war effort. Unfortunately for Hitler (and the men assigned the task of fulfilling his desires), Stalin was determined to hold the city.

Three German soldiers walk amid the ruins of Stalingrad, September 1942. (Library of Congress)

The Siege

Stalingrad lies on the west bank of the Volga, a long, thin city stretching 25 miles by only a few miles deep. General Friedrich von Paulus commanded the 6th Army, elements of the 4th Panzer Army, and some Rumanian divisions, collective lydesignated Army Group B. They were assigned to capture Stalingrad, and in two wide pincers they reached the Volga north and south of the city, then turned to meet each other. Inside Stalingrad was the Soviet 62nd Army, commanded by General Vasilii Chuikov. He was outspoken, a rarity in Stalin's military, and a soldier's soldier. When he took command German aircraft were already turning the city into rubble and his soldiers controlled only 9 miles of the city, at points but a few blocks between the German soldiers and the river. Chuikov had his orders: "Stalingrad is not to be yielded so long as there is a man left to defend it."

Although German troops had been in contact with Soviet defenders since 24 August, the bulk of Paulus's force reached the city limits on 14 September. He sent his German troops into the city while placing Rumanian auxiliaries on the flanks to protect against relief attacks. The destruction in the city was so widespread that fighting had to be done in small units, and the German doctrine of tank and air support began to work against them. Chuikov decided that the best way to fight this battle was by close combat. He observed that German soldiers were reluctant to attack without armor support, and tanks hesitated to come up without air cover. So, by keeping his men as far forward as possible, closely engaged with the German troops, aircraft could not attack for fear of hitting their own men. Also, the Soviets learned the signaling system the German soldiers used to direct their air support, and soon diversionary signaling was limiting the Luftwaffe's effectiveness.

While Chuikov was holding the 6th Army in place, his superior Field Marshal Georgi

Red Army troops storming an apartment block amid the ruins of war-torn Stalingrad during World War II. (Slava Katamidze Collection/Archive Photos)

Zhukov was massing twelve armies to come to his aid. Stalin finally decided to transfer units he had kept on the Chinese and Manchurian frontiers, guarding against Japanese offensives there. The transfer allowed Zhukov to gather almost a million men for the counterthrust. Rather than drive through to aid Chuikov directly, Zhukov planned a pincer attack of his own to cut off and besiege the besieging German army. It began on 19 November 1942. The northern pincer defeated the Rumanians covering that flank, and the southern attack accomplished the same feat on the 20th. The two forces came together on the Don River at Kalach and Paulus and his men were surrounded.

The remainder of Army Group South, designated Army Group A and now under the command of Field Marshal Erich von Manstein, tried to force an entry into the Soviet encirclement from the west. They drove to within 35 miles of Stalingrad and radioed Paulus to break out and link up with them. Hitler overrode that. "Where the German soldier once sets foot, there he remains." Not having to worry about a breakout, Zhukov's men drove Manstein's forces back to their starting point.

Luftwaffe chief Hermann Göring assured Hitler that his air force could keep the 6th Army supplied, and Hitler took him at his word. Increasing Soviet air strength coupled with harsh winter weather prevented Göring from keeping his promise. Some supplies did get in and about 25,000 wounded were evacuated by air, but it was too little to save the beleaguered garrison. By

January they were running out of food and wounded were lying untended in the streets. On 10 January the final Soviet push began and by the end of the month the German forces in Stalingrad had been divided in two. The Germans did better on the defensive than they had on the offensive, but too many tanks and men were coming at them to hold out for long. The southern half of the force was eliminated piece by piece while the northern group, around Paulus's headquarters, held out a bit longer.

When contacted by Soviet commanders and asked to surrender, Paulus radioed Hitler for permission. Hitler responded by promoting him to field marshal and reminding him that no German field marshal in history had ever been taken prisoner. Friedrich von Paulus was the first. On 2 February he gave up the defense.

base from which to operate even farther south, possibly even threatening India at a time the Japanese were pressing on India's borders from the east. With Stalingrad Hitler's options were many and probable, but with the destruction of his 6th Army in Stalingrad his only options were those that the Soviets had had earlier: stand and die, or retreat.

References: Antony Beevor, *Stalingrad* (New York: Viking, 1998); V. I. Chuikov, *The Battle for Stalingrad*, trans. Harold Silver (New York: Holt, Rinehart, and Winston, 1964); Joel Hayward, *Stopped at Stalingrad* (Lawrence: University Press of Kansas, 1998); Georgi Zhukov, *Marshal Zhukov's Greatest Battles*, trans. Theodore Shabad (New York: Harper & Row, 1969).

Results

By the time the fighting ended, only 91,000 German and their allied troops remained alive. They had lost 70,000 killed and the rest taken prisoner during the fighting. Counting the allied troops fighting with the Germans, the total dead numbered 120,000. The prisoners were sent to prison camps; few of them survived. Only 5,000 of the almost 250,000 Axis troops that entered Stalingrad ever saw home again. The Soviets lost perhaps 200,000 dead in the defending and relieving forces.

Hitler had assumed that if he maintained his army's drive to the Caucasus oil fields without capturing Stalingrad, the Soviets would use it as a base from which to strike his lines of supply. Had he taken the oil fields, however, the Soviets would have been unable to mount any such attack for lack of fuel. The one thing Hitler's war machine most needed, oil, remained untouched. Weakening Army Group South to assist the other offensives guaranteed a failure in the south. No oil meant paralyzing his own armies, while possession of the Caucasus would not only have guaranteed his own supplies, it also would have given the Nazis a

MONTE CASSINO

Date: 17 January–22 May 1944.
Location: west-central Italy, between
Naples and Rome.

FORCES ENGAGED:

Allied: 300,000 mixed troops (British, American, French, and Polish). Commander: General Sir Harold Alexander.
German: 100,000 troops. Commander: Field Marshall Albert Kesselring.

IMPORTANCE:

Lengthy German occupation of Cassino anchored the Gustav Line, blocking Allied advance up the Italian peninsula toward Rome.

Historical Setting

Following up on the capture of Sicily in August 1943, British forces crossed the Straits of Messina into Italy on 3 September. American and British forces staged landings at Salerno and Taranto respectively on 9 September, coinciding

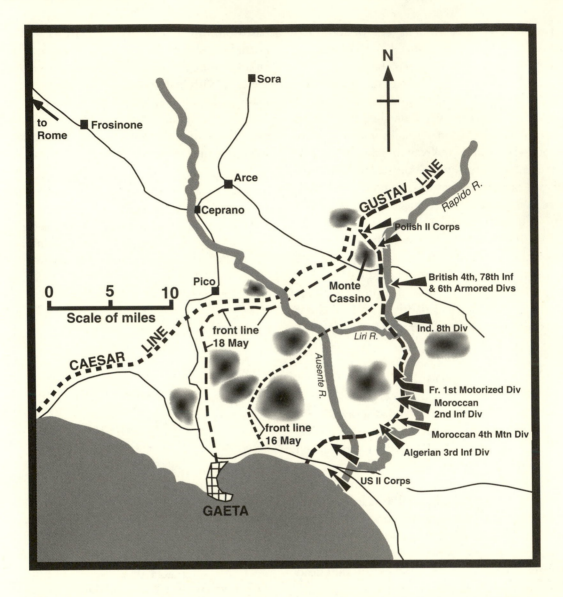

with the announcement of the Italian government's unconditional surrender. Unfortunately for the Allies, German troops in Italy did not surrender and their defense of the peninsula would be one of the most tenacious of the entire war.

The American landings at Salerno, just south of Naples, got off to a remarkably easy start, but an over-eager expansion of the beachhead almost resulted in disaster in the face of powerful German counterattacks. The approach of the British Eighth Army forced a German withdrawal, however, and the Allied forces began slowly to make their way up the

peninsula, Mark Clark's American Fifth Army along the west coast and Sir Bernard Montgomery's British Eighth Army up the eastern coast. By year's end they had reached the first major German defensive line, named Gustav. It stretched from the mouth of the Garigliano River on the Mediterranean coast north-north-eastward to the mouth of the Sangro River on the Adriatic coast. The Allied command wanted to focus on the southwestern flank, as that was the road to Rome. Such an advance was aimed to go up Route 6 along the Liri River, which emptied into the Garigliano just south of the town of Cassino. To advance up

The ancient Benedictine monastery atop Monte Cassino in western Italy overlooks heavy shelling during a terrific Allied attack on Nazi positions in the area. (Keystone/Archive Photos)

the Liri Valley meant capturing the town of Cassino and the mountains around it, from which German observation posts and artillery positions dominated the landscape.

Hindering the efforts of Allied forces in Italy were the ongoing preparations for Operation Overlord, the invasion of Normandy, scheduled for late spring 1944. British Prime Minister Winston Churchill was convinced that fighting in Italy would tie down large numbers of German troops that would otherwise be available for defending France. American President Franklin Roosevelt and Supreme Commander of Allied Forces in Europe General Dwight Eisenhower were less optimistic about such a probability. They wanted to strengthen not only Operation Overlord but also Operation Anvil, a landing in southern France originally designed to create a diversion before the

Normandy landings. Focus on France therefore limited the high command's interest in the Italian campaign.

German Field Marshal Albert Kesselring deployed some 100,000 men in fifteen divisions of the German Tenth Army to hold the Gustav Line, and he had a further eight divisions in reserve in northern Italy. The ruggedness of the terrain favored an extremely strong defense. Before the Allies threw troops at the Germans they planned a secondary amphibious attack behind the Gustav Line at the small port city of Anzio. The hope was for the first attack at Cassino to bring in German reinforcements, which would then be caught in transit and unprepared by the landings a few days later. The direct assault coupled with the threat to the lines of supply seemed a good strategy to compel a German withdrawal.

A soldier surveys the ruins of the destroyed monastery on Monte Cassino, 25 May 1944. (Library of Congress)

The Siege

The first of what would prove to be four assaults against the German positions around Cassino began on the night of 17–18 January 1944. The British Eighth Army had been weakened on the Adriatic front in order to support the western offensive. The British 10th Corps crossed the Garigliano River, but that proved just about the only success of the opening phase. The American II Corps attempted to cross the fast-flowing Rapido River but failed, as did the British 46th Division attacking on the American left. Fearful of an Allied landing north of Rome, Kesselring withheld most of his reinforcements, so the landings at Anzio on the 20th did not catch any German troops rushing to the front. Indeed, the landings were virtually unopposed.

After the mauling the Americans had received at the beaches of Salerno, Major General John Lucas hesitated to exploit the lack of opposition, choosing instead to strengthen his beachhead. This decision has been questioned ever since the landings occurred, for the road to Rome was only lightly held, but an overly quick advance may have caught American forces too far inland without a secure base of supply. Lucas' hesitation, however, enabled Kesselring to throw in eight divisions in a cordon around the beachhead while simultaneously protecting his line of supply to the Gustav Line. As it took a week for Lucas to be satisfied that his hold on the beach was secure, his attack launched on 30 January ran into staunch German opposition, aided by strong artillery and air support. Instead of threatening the Gustav Line, Lucas found himself in need of an attack on Cassino to relieve pressure on his front.

As Lucas was consolidating the beachhead, Fifth Army commander General Mark Clark continued to pressure the Gustav Line. To the right of the failed American assault, Clark ordered the colonial troops of the French Expeditionary Corps to attack and capture Monte Cairo. Their first point of attack, Monte Belvedere, was captured on 25 January against stiff German opposition. Hoping to build on that momentum, the American 34th Division tried once again to cross the Rapido but gained only minimal success. A German counterattack against the Tunisian troops holding Monte Belvedere captured and lost the hilltop several times before finally reestablishing control on 1 February. In the meantime, continued attempts to push American troops across the Rapido finally succeeded and men of the 34th Division reached the town of Cassino on the 2nd. Just to the south of the town, other American troops failed to capture Monastery Mount but did take key hills approaching it. The 34th Division was so badly handled during this battle that on 11 February Clark called up the 4th Indian Division to replace them. They and the fresh troops of the 2nd New Zealand Division (together the New Zealand Corps) were detailed to assault Monastery Mount.

At this point a controversial decision was made. As the Monte Cassino monastery dominated the countryside, many in the Allied force believed that the accurate German artillery fire they were receiving came from observers posted in the ancient structure. Great care had been taken to avoid damaging the landmark, but the threat to the advance convinced theater commander General Sir Harold Alexander to order the monastery bombed. As was discovered later, the Germans had not been using the building as an observation post, but once the Allied bombers destroyed it they felt it permissible to use the ruins for that purpose. The resulting rubble from the bombing did more to help the defense than it did to aid the offense, and the decision was regrettable from both a military and a historical standpoint. After a heavy snowfall, the attack continued on 15 February. This involved the New Zealand Corps on the southern end of the line and the French in the north reinforced by the Moroccan 4th Mountain Division. Strong German counterattacks threw back attacks by the Indian, Maori, and Gurkha troops, which had minimal armor support crossing the Rapido to aid them. On the 18th the first phase of the battle concluded.

Although the French attacks had succeeded in crossing the Rapido to the north of Cassino, the Gustav Line still remained mostly intact. That gave Kesselring sufficient confidence to launch a counterattack against the Anzio beachhead. On 16 February, with strong artillery and air support, ten German divisions attacked the five Allied divisions around the beach. A gap in the Allied lines gave the Germans a slight opportunity to break through, but the mass of troops and equipment on a single road proved too easy a target for Allied artillery and naval gunfire and the attack was broken up. A second offensive on the 18th again threatened to pierce the Allied lines, but tenacious American and British troops threw the Germans back. Hitler ordered a third attack on the 28th, but by 4 March that too had been turned back by Allied infantry and air power.

On 15 March the attacks on Cassino began again. Rather than trying to force the Rapido to the south, which had repeatedly been disastrous, the New Zealand Corps attacked from the north. After a massive artillery and air bombardment they drove on Castle Hill (to the northwest of Cassino) and Hangman's Hill (just below the monastery to the southeast). The rubble from the bombardment again aided the defense as did a heavy rainfall. Fierce fighting raged through Cassino and a force of Gurkhas reached Hangman's Hill, but the Allies could not secure the town. The Gurkhas, left behind when the rest of the corps withdrew on the 23rd, held on to their position for eight days before being allowed to withdraw under a Red Cross flag. The third phase of the battle was over.

At this point the high command in London had to decide how hard to push the Italian offensive. Operation Anvil against the south of France was supposed to be launched three weeks before the Normandy invasion, but sufficient manpower for that assault and the operations around Anzio did not exist. Since the next attempt to break through the Gustav Line and link forces could not be launched before May, that meant Anvil had to be postponed; it finally was launched six weeks after Overlord. Arguments as high as president and prime minister raged over this decision, and Churchill's hope that the Italian theater would draw off German troops from France proved ephemeral.

The fourth phase of the battle of Cassino began on 11 May. The British Eighth Army had been transferred over from the eastern coast and given the main attack. The American Fifth Army was to launch a coordinated offensive across the Garigliano up the Liri Valley. A third prong of the attack was to be delivered out of the Anzio pocket. This attack finally was able to enjoy dry weather, facilitating the deployment of Allied armor that thus far had been of little use. The point of the British assault was given to two Polish divisions while British divisions advanced on their left toward Sant Angelo. Faked amphibious operations north of Rome were designed to keep German reserves in that region.

The attack started just as the others had: stiff German resistance and little headway. The Poles took the brunt of the German artillery fire, but neither the British nor Americans did much better. Seemingly overlooked, however, was the French Corps stationed between the two. Their four divisions drove through the mountains where one German division could not hold its ground, and the breakthrough the Allies had been hoping for since January began to appear. As the Germans began to fall back, French General Juin sent his Moroccan mountain troops, the Goums, to seize positions in the Hitler Line (the fallback position from the Gustav Line). The German right flank began to collapse and the American II Corps increased its speed into the Liri Valley. Kesselring, worried about a landing near Rome, was slow to release reserves and they arrived piecemeal and unable to stabilize the German line. German troops in the immediate Cassino area held fast, but had

to withdraw on 17 May to keep from being surrounded. The Polish troops, after suffering some 4,000 casualties, took possession of the remains of the monastery on Monte Cassino.

Results

The breakout from Anzio proved to be less than helpful in destroying the retreating German troops. General Clark, intent on capturing Rome, sent the bulk of his troops parallel to the coast up Route 7 rather than inland to cut off the German retreat. Skillful German tactics during their withdrawal slowed the British pursuit up the Liri Valley and allowed them to rescue the bulk of their forces. It looked as if another stand could be made at the Caesar Line, just south of Rome but a breakthrough by the U.S. 36th Division on 30 May captured the town of Velletri on Route 7, an anchor for the Caesar Line. Clark finally ordered a sweeping attack north to reach Route 6 at Valmontone, the original objective of the Anzio breakout, and the resulting drive up both Route 6 and Route 7 was too much for the Germans. Kesselring declared Rome an open city, and American troops entered it on 4 June. It was the first Axis capital to fall to Allied arms and was the biggest event of the war for two days, when Operation Overlord against the Normandy beaches surpassed it.

Casualties in the operation against and immediately after Cassino were extremely heavy. The Americans suffered 18,000 casualties, the British 14,000, and the French 10,000 by the time Rome fell. The Germans had lost comparatively few killed and wounded, 10,000 in combat, but a further 20,000 as prisoners helped even out the casualty count somewhat. While the Italian theater in general and the Gustav Line in particular did force large numbers of German troops to stay and fight on the peninsula, it did not accomplish what Churchill and others in Britain had hoped: the withdrawal of large numbers of German forces from France. It can be argued that it kept the

German defenses at Normandy from being even stronger than they were, but it did not weaken them. In the end, the value of the fight for Cassino was probably not worth the cost. Perhaps Kesselring was right: an amphibious landing north of Rome rather than south of it could well have been the necessary threat to German security to weaken the Gustav Line and other positions in south-central Italy.

References: Rudolf Bohmler, *Monte Cassino: A German View* (London: Cassell, 1964); B. H. Liddell Hart, *History of the Second World War* (New York: G. P. Putnam's Sons, 1970); Fred Majdalany, *The Battle of Cassino* (New York: Houghton Mifflin, 1957).

IMPHAL

DATE: 15 March–31 May 1944.
LOCATION: on the border between Myanmar (Burma) and India, along the Manipur River.

FORCES ENGAGED:

British/Indian: 4th Indian Army Corps, 120,000 troops. Commander: Lieutenant General Geoffrey Scoones.
Japanese: Fifteenth Army, 85,000 Japanese troops, plus 7,000 Indian Nationalist Army auxiliaries. Commander: Lieutenant General Renya Mutaguchi.

IMPORTANCE:

Japanese failure to capture Imphal and nearby Kohima blunted their attempt to invade India.

Historical Setting

War came to Burma in January 1942, when Japanese forces invaded from French Indochina. British forces in Burma were rapidly overwhelmed and fled for India, which they reached in May. Had the Japanese kept pushing, India lay open, but their unexpectedly quick occupation of Burma, coupled with the oncoming monsoon, convinced them to stop and consolidate

first. That consolidation, owing to the drain on Imperial Japanese Army resources in other theaters, lasted eighteen months. The British Indian Army had not been lax in taking advantage of their respite and had been reinforcing Lieutenant General William Slim's forces along the Burma–India frontier. The primary concentration of forces was at Imphal, capital of the Manipur Province of India, located some 400 miles east-northeast of Calcutta.

The city of Imphal lay on the Imphal plain, a plateau some 2,500 feet above sea level and surrounded by mountains. The Indian Army 4th Corps was based there, commanded by Lieutenant General Geoffrey Scoones. The 4th Corps consisted of the 17th, 20th, and 23rd Divisions. Imphal at the outset was served by but one improved road and a few unimproved roads, but since 1942 Slim and Scoones had thousands of laborers working to pave two more roads in order to flood Imphal with all supplies necessary for the troops to either beat back a Japanese offensive or launch one of their own. By March 1944, Slim had to decide for which of those options to prepare.

Opposing the 4th Corps was the Japanese 15th Army, commanded by Lieutenant General Renya Mutaguchi, a harsh disciplinarian. His force consisted of three divisions (15th, 31st, and 33rd) numbering some 85,000 men, supplemented by a further 7,000 soldiers of the Indian National Army, a subversive organization dedicated to overthrowing British rule in India. The troops of this unit were primarily soldiers captured during the Japanese occupation of Burma and served not so much from nationalist feeling as the desire to avoid prison camp. These troops were veterans skilled in jungle fighting.

In early February 1944 British intelligence reports indicated the probability of a Japanese offensive, which Slim decided would not begin prior to 15 March. He had to decide whether to launch a preemptive attack or to concentrate his forces on the Imphal plain. Scoones' three divisions were placed in a forward defense. The 17th Division was south of Imphal around the town of Tiddim, on the improved road from

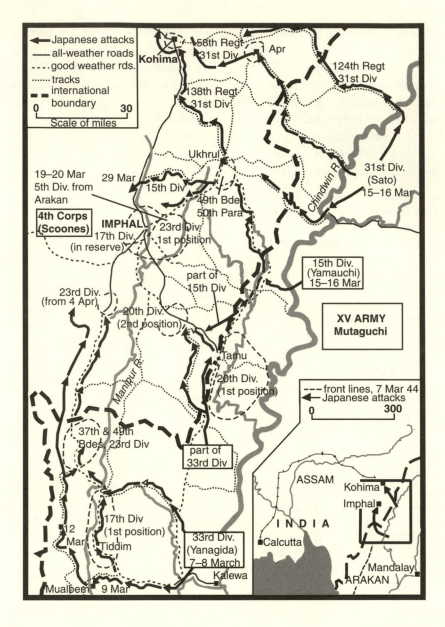

Japanese attacks
all-weather roads
good weather rds.
tracks
international boundary
Scale of miles
0   30

Kohima
58th Regt 31st Div
1 Apr
124th Regt 31st Div
138th Regt 31st Div
Ukhrul
31st Div. (Sato) 15–16 Mar
Chindwin R.
19–20 Mar 5th Div. from Arakan
29 Mar
15th Div
49th Bde 50th Para
4th Corps (Scoones)
IMPHAL
17th Div. (in reserve)
23rd Div. 1st position
part of 15th Div
15th Div. (Yamauchi) 15–16 Mar
23rd Div. (from 4 Apr)
20th Div. (2nd position)
XV ARMY Mutaguchi
Tamu
20th Div. (1st position)
Manipur R.
37th & 49th Bdes, 23rd Div
part of 33rd Div
front lines, 7 Mar 44
Japanese attacks
0   300
ASSAM
Kohima
Imphal
INDIA
Calcutta
17th Div (1st position)
Tiddim
12 Mar
33rd Div. (Yanagida) 7–8 March
Mandalay
ARAKAN
Mualbem   9 Mar
Kalewa

that direction. The 20th Division was stationed to the southeast along the second good road to Tamu, in the Kabaw Valley overlooking the Chindwin River that served as the border between the two countries. The 23rd Division was held in reserve, with contingents placed to the northeast of Imphal on the route from the Burma to Kohima, which sat astride the main route into Assam. Although Slim and Scoones wanted to concentrate these forces, they did not want to bring them back too soon, believing that would be detrimental to morale.

Thus, the decision was to keep the troops in position until the Japanese advance began, then stage a fighting withdrawal to Imphal for the decisive battle.

The Japanese opened the campaign by launching an offensive into the Arakan region south of Imphal, hoping that would draw off reserves. It did tie down British/Indian troops in that area for a time, but the real surprise to Scoones was not the Arakan offensive but the fact that Mutaguchi launched his attack a week earlier than expected. His plan was to advance

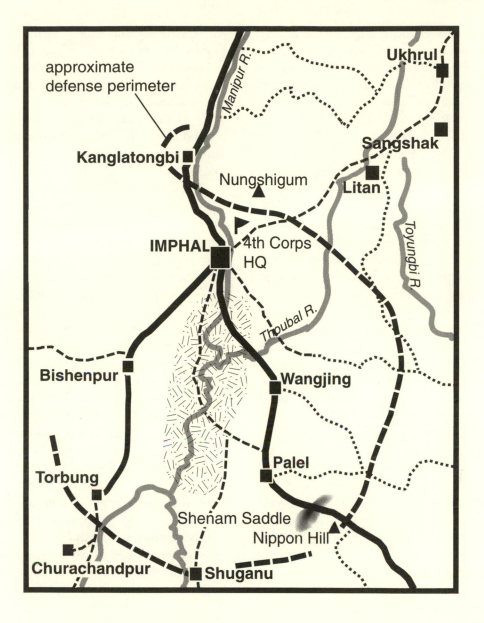

along three lines, all through rough country along mountain tracks. In the south, the 33rd Division operated along two lines of march designed to pin down and then surround the Indian 17th Division. In the center, a portion of the 33rd Division passed south of the Indian 20th, hoping to get astride its lines of supply. Both of these attacks preceded by a week the third thrust in the north, designed to drive a wedge between Imphal and Kohima from which he could surround Imphal with the 15th Division while the 31st drove north to Kohima.

The Siege

The opening Japanese march began on the night of 7–8 March 1944, and by the 10th they were flanking Tiddim and the 17th Division in the south, and threatening to sever the road back to Imphal. The 17th Division was ordered to withdraw to the Imphal plain and when they began moving in the afternoon of the 14th they had to fight their way through. Scoones dispatched two brigades of his reserves to cooperate from the north. The troops were obliged to abandon a large supply of stores owing to the rapidity of the Japanese offensive. That, as it turned out, was what the Japanese were depending on: their own supply lines were too long and were being harassed by General Orde Wingate's guerrilla Chindit forces, so they had to capture British supplies in order to keep themselves fighting.

While the 17th was fighting their way north, elements of the Japanese 33rd Division crossed the Chindwin River into the Kabaw Valley south of the Indian 20th Division. Again, their line of supply back to Imphal was threatened and Scoones ordered their withdrawal as well. They were not, however, to pull back all the way to Imphal, but to hold Shenam Saddle, where the road crossed out of the mountains into the plain. Scoones had ordered the labor force and supplies dedicated to road construction to be pulled out first and the 20th Division staged a fighting withdrawal to cover the retreat of men and materiel, then successfully entrenched themselves at Shenam.

Both these attacks diverted Scoones' attention and reserves to the south, so his attack in the north, launched on the night of 15–16 March, advanced against little opposition. With manpower quickly being dispersed, Scoones called Slim for reinforcement. The only way men could be brought in quickly was by air, so an Anglo-American airlift was hastily organized and troops were shifted from the Arakan front to Imphal and Kohima. To buy time, Scoones placed the 50th Parachute Brigade to assist the 49th Brigade at Ukhrul, there to face the oncoming Japanese 15th Division; Ukhrul was an advanced post blocking the route to the Imphal–Kohima road. Between 19 and 29 March air transports ferried in from Arakan into Imphal the entire Indian 5th Division, including men, weapons, and transport. Although they were ultimately forced to break up and slip through Japanese lines after days of intense fighting, the delay in the Japanese timetable and the fact that units of the Japanese 31st Division were diverted from Kohima to reduce the Ukhrul bastion, severely

damaged Mutaguchi's effort. Still, they were able to sever the Imphal–Kohima road, and by doing so isolated the 4th Corps on the Imphal plain. From that point forward the only resupply and reinforcement could arrive by air.

By 29 March the Indian 5th Division was on site and entrenching on Imphal's northern and northeastern front. The 17th Division finally fought their way through the Japanese in the south and reached the Imphal plain on 4 April. They were replaced on that front by the 23rd Division and the 17th became the reserve. The 20th Division, meanwhile, was strongly entrenched on Shenam Saddle and had dealt the Japanese on the southeastern front serious damage. The 4 April is generally regarded as the most important day of the siege, for it marked the solidification of the 4th Corps and the resultant destruction of the attacking Japanese army. Although cut off from overland supply bases, the 4th Corps was supplied continuously by air. The Royal Air Force and elements of the United States Army Air Corps through the course of the siege ferried in 14 million pounds of rations, a million gallons of fuel, and 12,000 reinforcements while evacuating 13,000 casualties and a further 43,000 noncombatants. At the same time, RAF bombers and fighters acted almost with impunity against Japanese troops, as the enemy air power was small.

Scoones planned to defend the south and southeast while launching his first counterattack in the north against the Japanese 15th Division. This was postponed when a Japanese regiment took a hill overlooking the corps headquarters position on 6 April, but the position was recovered after intense fighting on the 13th. The Indian 23rd Division began attacking Japanese positions around Ukhrul, while the newly arrived 5th Division attacked to the 23rd's left against the Mapao Ridge, which dominated the Imphal–Kohima road. In the southeast, the Japanese 33rd Division kept up constant pressure on the Indian 20th Division in the Shenam Saddle, fighting that went on virtually nonstop for two and a half months.

Since the monsoon season began in late May, both sides were under pressure to succeed. Mutaguchi needed to capture Kohima to the north if he was going to have the necessary supplies to keep fighting and to establish a base for the further invasion of India. Scoones wanted to have the road to Kohima reopened by the start of the rains, since the air supply operations would be severely curtailed. Thus, most of the fighting in May took place in the north. Mutaguchi ordered some of his units attacking Kohima to aid the attack against Imphal, but the Indian 33rd Corps (based in Kohima) maintained such strong pressure on that front that the transfer of troops never took place. By 3 June the Japanese attempt to take Kohima was over, and the 33rd could then give direct assistance to Scoones' forces. As the Japanese situation deteriorated in the north, Mutaguchi relieved all his divisional commanders, which did nothing to enhance morale. As the Japanese Fifteenth Army began to disintegrate, British/Indian troops advanced closer to each other down the Imphal–Kohima road. They linked up on 22 June and the siege was over.

Results

The fighting continued, however. Mutaguchi told his men: "If your hands are broken, fight with your feet. . . . If there is no breath in your body, fight with your ghost. Lack of weapons is no excuse for defeat" (Turnbull, "Imphal–Kohima 1944," p. 23). His men were unable to follow that directive. General Slim decided that, even though the monsoon continued, a major offensive would turn the Fifteenth Army's defeat into a rout. The 7th Division of the 33rd Corps attacked southeastward from Kohima, driving the Japanese 31st Division back into Ukhrul. The Indian 20th Division attacked east to provide the anvil for the 7th Division's hammer. Simultaneously, the Long Range Penetration Group attacked the Japanese lines of supply in Burma. "Occasionally a few determined Japanese made a suicidal

stand, but more frequently they were found dead or dying, half naked in the churned-up mud, with abandoned equipment lying everywhere; bombed-out transport columns, charred and black, littered the tracks or the hillside down which they had fallen; in the evil-smelling field hospitals, dead lay on the stretchers on which they had been brought, sometimes with a bullet hole in their foreheads, their comrades having put them out of their misery before leaving them" (Evans, "Imphal," p. 1691). The total Japanese losses were some 53,000 dead and wounded out of an original strength of 85,000. The British/Indian losses numbered 17,000, but many of the wounded and sick were saved by the outstanding efforts of the air forces in their evacuation operations.

After the war, a Japanese Foreign Office official wrote, "Most of this force perished in battle or later of starvation. The disaster at Imphal was perhaps the worst of its kind yet chronicled in the annals of war" (Evans, "Imphal," p. 1691). After this point the Japanese Army in Burma was a shadow of its former, victorious self, and it continued its long decline until war's end. Slim took the initiative and began the reconquest of Burma. Considering the poor supply situation and lack of air support the Fifteenth Army had, it is a tribute to their tenacity that they came as close as they did to capturing Imphal.

References: Sir Geoffrey Evans, "Imphal: Crisis in Burma," in *History of the Second World War*, ed. Barrie Pitt (London: BPC, 1966); Sir William Slim, *Defeat into Victory* (London: Cassel, 1956); Patrick Turnbull, "Imphal–Kohima, 1944," *War Monthly*, no. 37, 1976.

DIEN BIEN PHU

DATE: 20 November 1953–7 May 1954.
LOCATION: northwestern Vietnam, near the Laotian border.

FORCES ENGAGED:

Viet Minh: 50,000 men.
Commander: Vo Nguyen Giap.
French: 16,000. Commander:
Colonel Christian de Castries.

IMPORTANCE:

French defeat led to the end of their colonial
experience in Southeast Asia and laid the
groundwork for U.S. involvement in the region.

Historical Setting

The French had established their control over
much of the Southeast Asian peninsula (Indochina) by the 1890s. They established a colonial administration and introduced French
culture and education. For any Vietnamese to
advance in the colonial regime, French education and literacy, as well as conversion to
Catholicism, was necessary. Little did the
French realize that therein lay the seeds of their
own colonial destruction. Teaching French history and the Revolutionary tenets of liberty,
equality, and fraternity did not square with the
colonial reality. Also, promoting Catholics in a
Buddhist society did not promote religious toleration. By the end of World War I, a number
of nationalist movements sprang up to overthrow foreign rule.

The leading movement was the Viet Minh,
the League of Vietnamese Independence, led by
Nguyen Ai Quoc, who later took the name Ho
Chi Minh. He attended the Versailles Conference but could not convince the victors to break
up their own empires along with those of the
losers. With some training in Marxism and revolution from the new Soviet regime, he returned
home to lead the struggle for liberation.
Through the 1920s and 1930s Ho traveled
throughout Indochina and China organizing
resistance to the French regime. When the
Japanese occupied Indochina in 1940, the Viet
Minh fought them. At the end of World War
II Ho asked for U.S. assistance in establishing
a free Vietnam, Cambodia, and Laos, but the

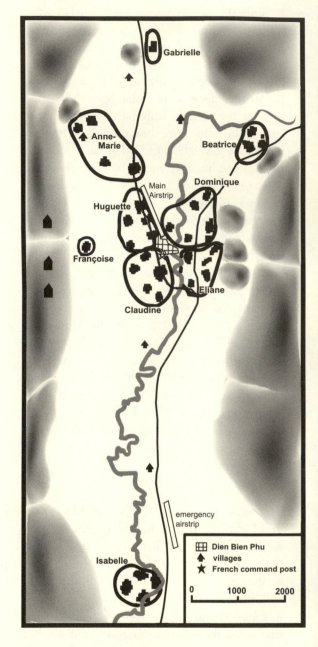

United States stood by its alliance with France.
Thus, when France reestablished her colonial
administration in 1945, the Viet Minh returned to its prewar resistance movement. For
a time President Harry Truman's administration was critical of French military action
against the Viet Minh, but in 1950 Ho Chi
Minh's communist leanings inflamed the rising
anticommunist movement in the United

French union paratroopers search a wooded area near the North Vietnamese town of Dien Bien Phu. French ground and air forces struck at coolie supply lines to the Vietminh stronghold in the mountainous Thai country of northwestern Indochina, 4 January 1954. (AP/Wide World Photos)

States. Chinese aid to North Korea in 1950 made the United States fear a potential Asian communist bloc, so American aid began to flow freely to French troops in Vietnam.

Similarly, Chinese aid to the Viet Minh began to flow into Indochina in large amounts: American weaponry captured from the Nationalist Chinese supplemented with Russian weapons supplied to the Chinese from Moscow. In 1950 French General Jean de Lattre de Tassigny arrived in Vietnam, bringing a new intensity to the French effort. For a time the French gained the upper hand while the forces of Ho Chi Minh and his chief commander, Vo Nguyen Giap, suffered severe losses. De Lattre used French Foreign Legion paratroopers and established *hérissons*, or hedgehogs (strong points bristling with machine guns and artillery), placed deep in Viet Minh-occupied territory and along supply routes. Trying to overcome them cost the Viet Minh dearly.

De Lattre died of cancer in January 1952 and was replaced by the more cautious General Raoul Salan. His strategy was to move overland with heavy columns of men and materiel, striking suspected Viet Minh strongpoints. A year of this type of warfare produced little. Giap allowed the French to drive deep into his countryside, then attacked their lines of communication and ambushed the withdrawing troops in valleys and gorges. Salan was finally replaced in May 1953 by General Henri Navarre, a soldier more of de Lattre's type. Unfortunately for Navarre, support for the war was waning in France and he was ordered to win and win quickly. His response was to reintroduce the hérissons, and the site he chose was Dien Bien Phu, near the border of Vietnam and Laos. As a strong ally of France, Laos had made itself a target for Viet Minh attacks. By placing his hérisson there Navarre planned to provoke a strong response from Giap, who would not allow this French post deep in his rear. Navarre was correct, but starting the fight and winning it were two different matters.

The Siege

Command of the Dien Bien Phu operation fell to French Foreign Legion Colonel Christian de Castries. With 1,827 paratroopers he occupied the village on 23 November 1953 and began construction of eight fortified positions, each of which bore a feminine name (reputedly names of Castries' mistresses). Four (Eliane, Dominique, Huguette, and Claudine) were built at the four corners of the village itself. Between Dominique and Huguette on the north side of the village was the main airstrip, used to launch air operations against the Viet Minh and bring in supplies. To the northwest was the Anne-Marie; Gabrielle was on a hill about 1,500 yards to the north; Beatrice was located on a hilltop about 1,000 yards northeast of Dominique; Françoise lay about 500 yards to the west of Huguette, with Isabelle a few miles to the south, covering an emergency airstrip. Each position consisted of mutually supporting strongpoints surrounded by barbed wire. With aircraft, machine guns, lots of artillery, and troops, Navarre was convinced Giap would bleed his forces while attempting to capture this position, after which the French would easily crush the remainder of the Viet Minh.

In the early months of 1954 the French forces reached approximately 13,000, built around the French Foreign Legion paratroopers. Some of the Algerian and Moroccan auxiliaries were well trained but irregularly motivated, for nationalist movements were rising in their home countries as well. The main problem was one of overconfidence, for the bunkers could have been stronger, the minefields could have been deeper and more extensive, and more barbed wire should have been strung.

General Giap, meanwhile, had learned the lessons of the earlier French hedgehogs; this one he was going to attack methodically. For four months his men dragged artillery to the hills surrounding Dien Bien Phu, digging them into deep emplacements covered by trees.

The French had not seized the high ground, and Giap was quick to capitalize on it.

At 1700 on the afternoon of 13 March 1954, Giap's artillery opened up on Beatrice, soon destroying the command bunker and paralyzing the defense. By midnight the Viet Minh had captured the position, denying the French one of their primary artillery spotting posts. Because Giap had made sure his guns were hidden and protected, French return fire had little effect. The following night they attacked Gabrielle, the outpost farthest north. Its 500 defenders were almost all killed or captured by noon on the 15th. In addition to the loss of these two positions, Viet Minh artillery totally dominated the French airfield, making it almost useless from the beginning. A few medical aircraft managed to land and take off through the end of March, but after that the garrison was supplied completely by parachute.

As the battle began so did the monsoon. More paratroopers were dropped within a week of the fall of the two positions but the rain severely hampered resupply efforts and made life miserable for the troops in the valley, less so for the Viet Minh on higher ground. The Viet Minh also began digging forward trenches so their assaults would not have to cover so much open ground. On the evening of 30 March they attacked Eliane and Dominique on the east side of the village. Some strongpoints within each position were captured, but French counterattacks regained lost ground. Both sides ended that round exhausted. Between 2 and 5 April fighting raged over Huguette, with strongpoints lost and won, but the French ended up with all their positions intact.

French reinforcements were slow to arrive. What did come in had to do so by air drop, and the staff officers in the French headquarters in Hanoi insisted on following peacetime procedures. Only direct threats from officers at Dien Bien Phu got action. Help came slowly owing to inertia in the French command and political decisions made in other countries. The United States considered aid to the French force in Indochina, but air strikes by American planes were finally rejected by the high command in Washington. They decided that to get involved with air power would certainly lead to the commitment of ground troops. International talks were scheduled for mid-May. Outside aid might have kept the French going up to that point, providing bargaining chips in the talks. General Giap likewise wanted bargaining chips, so he pressed the attack.

Throughout April artillery bombardment remained almost constant, with harassing attacks common. On 21 April Viet Minh forces captured Huguette, which dominated the airstrip and made antiaircraft fire more effective. French supplies were running very low and reinforcements were arriving in small numbers, dropped during breaks in the weather and the fighting. Some Vietnamese soldiers parachuted in, certainly knowing that to be captured by their countrymen would not be pleasant. The French kept up patrols and skirmishing, but the French days were numbered. On the night of 6–7 May Viet Minh forces finally captured Eliane and the defense began to collapse. At 1730 Castries sent a message to Hanoi, alerting them that he was destroying the last of his ammunition and surrendering.

Results

The defenders of Dien Bien Phu lost almost 2,300 killed and more than 5,100 wounded. The wounded and captives were marched out of the Dien Bien Phu Valley to prison camps up to 500 miles away. Perhaps 10,000 men died along the way; only about 3,000 prisoners were repatriated to France later that summer. Although only about 5 percent of the total French military manpower in Indochina, it was the elite. Approximately 8,000 Viet Minh died in the course of the battle, with at least 15,000 wounded. During the battle General Giap had hurled his men at the French in virtual human waves, losing approximately 46 percent of his force. Indeed Giap's forces were at the point of mutiny several times during the siege.

The timing of the victory was all-important. Viet Minh and French representatives met in Geneva in mid-May to discuss Indochina's future, and the French entered the talks on the defensive. The war had become increasingly unpopular in France and few wanted to continue it. The French agreed to grant independence to Vietnam, Cambodia, and Laos. Within two years her personnel would be removed and elections held. In the meantime, the French-sponsored administration based in Saigon was to oversee the area of Vietnam below latitude 17 degrees, while Ho Chi Minh's administration would control the area above that line. Each was to remove their troops from the other's territory, and free elections in 1956 would determine the new government.

France's empire, such as it was, began its collapse in Southeast Asia. France had lost most of her overseas possessions after the Napoleonic wars; the colonies that she had acquired in the latter nineteenth century now began to break away. Algeria was next to try for independence, staging its own guerrilla war, but the French applied military lessons learned fighting the Viet Minh. Unfortunately for both France and Algeria, political lessons were not learned. The final result was a bloodbath in North Africa and political turmoil in the French government and army before Algeria gained her independence anyway.

In Southeast Asia the French and Viet Minh honored the Geneva Accords, but the United States and the Vietnamese administration in the south did not. Although the United States had not been a signatory to the Geneva Accords, American doctrine was to contain communism, and President Dwight Eisenhower could not allow communist regimes to survive unopposed. With United States support the Republic of South Vietnam was created in 1956, before national elections could be held. Ho Chi

Minh's popularity was such that he almost certainly would have won an easy victory as leader of the entire nation. Instead, the seventeenth parallel became a political boundary that caused continued fighting, now among the Vietnamese themselves. The remnants of the French-trained and -educated elite dominated the southern government, and their mismanagement of the country, along with large amounts of U.S. financial and military aid, ultimately took the United States into a war that Eisenhower's advisers in 1954 had convinced him was not in America's best interests.

References: Philip Davidson, *Vietnam at War: The History 1946–1975* (New York: Oxford University Press, 1988); Bernard Fall, *Hell in a Very Small Place* (New York: Lippincott, 1967); John Keegan, *Dien Bien Phu* (New York: Random House, 1974).

QUEMOY (KINMEN)

DATE: 23 August 1958–February 1959.
LOCATION: 5 miles off the coast of China's Fujian province.

FORCES ENGAGED:

Nationalist Chinese: 70,000 troops.
Commander: Chiang Kai-Shek.
Communist Chinese: unknown.
Commander: Mao Tse-tung.

IMPORTANCE:

U.S. aid to Nationalist Chinese heightened Cold War tensions but successfully kept Communist China from launching an invasion of Taiwan.

Historical Setting

The rivalry between the communist and Nationalist forces in China resulted in a civil war that raged throughout the 1930s until the Japanese invaded China in 1937. At that point, communist leader Mao Tse-tung and Nation-

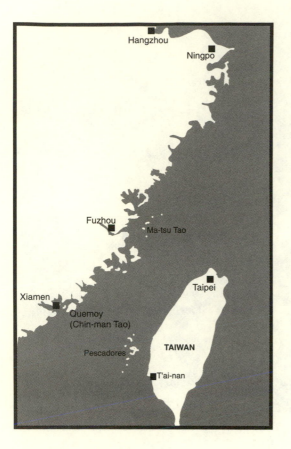

Although the communist regime received the recognition of most of the major nations of the world, the United States continued to recognize Chiang Kai-shek as the one legitimate ruler of all China, both mainland and island. That stand kept Mao from sending a representative to the United Nations, especially to sit on that body's Security Council. Through the Korean War (1950–1953) Mao and Chiang verbally sniped at each other, but in 1954 the stakes began to be raised when Mao began talking about conquering Taiwan (formerly Formosa).

During the Korean War, President Harry Truman kept the U.S. Seventh Fleet in the Straits of Taiwan in order to prevent Chiang from launching any attacks on the mainland. When Dwight Eisenhower succeeded Truman in office, he removed the naval forces. Chiang was not slow to take advantage of the freedom of movement, for he transferred 58,000 troops to the islands of Quemoy (Little and Greater Quemoy) and 15,000 troops to Matsu, some 200 miles up the Chinese coast. Communist Chinese Premier Chou En-lai responded on 11 August 1954 with the statement that Taiwan had to be "liberated." Although the United States immediately warned the Communists against such a move, they began shelling Quemoy on 3 September. The communist sentencing of thirteen U.S. airmen shot down during the Korean War did nothing to ease tensions, and American talk of using nuclear weapons became more widespread. Short of that, however, the United States did sign a mutual defense treaty with the Nationalists on 2 December.

The Communists launched their first offensive move on 18 January 1955, when they landed forces on the small island of Yijiangshan, 210 miles north of Taiwan. In three days they wiped out the 720-man Nationalist garrison at a cost of more than 1,200 casualties. Chiang responded by launching raids against communist ports. At the end of January the U.S. Congress authorized the president to employ U.S. manpower and weaponry to defend Taiwan, the nearby Pescadores, and such territory as was necessary for their defense. Eisenhower

alist leader Chiang Kai-shek called a truce in order to face a common foe. Through 1945 the two factions focused on ridding their country of the Japanese, but after Japan's surrender in September 1945 the two were soon facing each other. Throughout 1947 U.S. representative George Marshall attempted to mediate a peaceful solution to the Chinese political dilemma, but he finally gave up in the face of the intractable hard-liners in both camps. Through 1948 and 1949 communist and Nationalist forces fought massive battles, with the upper hand going to the communists. On 1 October 1949, Mao Tse-tung declared the establishment of his regime as the legitimate government in China, while the remnants of Chiang's Nationalists fled to the island of Formosa. They held on to the small island groups of Quemoy and Matsu, just a few miles off the mainland. A communist attempt to capture Quemoy on 27 October was bloodily thrown back and the Nationalists kept the islands.

A wounded soldier being flown off the island of Quemoy to Taiwan during a cease-fire between the Nationalist forces and the Chinese Communists. (Keystone/Archive Photos)

and Secretary of State John Foster Dulles followed this up with open threats to use nuclear weapons against major Chinese cities. On 23 April the Communists announced their willingness to negotiate and on 1 May they stopped the bombardment.

The Siege

In the wake of the crisis, Chiang Kai-shek decided to reinforce his garrisons on both Quemoy and Matsu. He also received American-made surface-to-surface missiles and artillery, both with nuclear capability. On the mainland, Mao instituted the "Great Leap Forward," which emphasized technological and economic development coupled with a more hard-line foreign policy.

On 23 August 1958, the Communists began massive artillery attacks against Quemoy,

blocked Nationalist resupply ships, threatened American naval power in the Straits of Taiwan, and turned up their propaganda campaign against the United States. All of this was accompanied by renewed threats to liberate Taiwan. All of this began less than three weeks after Soviet Premier Nikita Khruschev's visit to Beijing. As the Soviet Union had not been sufficiently supportive of Communist China in Mao's view, this was seen as a ploy to force the Soviets into stating their intentions in regard to their ally. Khruschev responded by sending a letter to Eisenhower, warning him that an American attack on China would be considered as an attack on the Soviet Union. Eisenhower would not be bluffed. He recommitted the Seventh Fleet to the Straits of Taiwan that began to escort Nationalist supply ships to Quemoy. Chiang Kai-shek stood his ground by keeping a constant aerial umbrella over Quemoy, and his pilots far outfought their communist counterparts. The U.S. Joint Chiefs of Staff began planning nuclear strikes against mainland cities, primarily Shanghai and Canton.

The strength of the American response gave Beijing pause, and on 6 September Chinese Premier Chou en-Lai proposed ambassadorial-level talks. A month later the Communists declared a one-week halt to the bombardment in order to begin peace talks, if American ships would stop escorting the resupply ships. He also announced that the Communists would refrain from artillery or air attacks on Quemoy or on supply vessels on even-numbered days.

Results

Communist threats never escalated to direct action against American forces, but Mao Tse-tung learned a lot from the artillery siege of Quemoy. First, the United States would definitely oppose any attempt to "liberate" Taiwan, but the Soviet Union would not support such an attempt with their nuclear arsenal. On the other hand, Mao was assured that a direct threat to the mainland would indeed provoke a Soviet response in Communist China's favor.

Without Soviet nuclear support in all situations, Mao decided that a Chinese nuclear capability was necessary. He did not believe that a nuclear war would devastate the earth; certainly at least half the Chinese population would survive, he believed. Khruschev apparently read Mao's intent, for he abrogated a 1957 agreement whereby the Soviet Union promised to provide Communist China with a nuclear bomb and technical assistance in producing their own. That decision helped drive a wedge between the two major communist powers.

There were results for the United States, as well. "Congress helped build the 'imperial presidency' (as it was soon known). Eisenhower further militarily allied the United States with Chiang. The president again threatened to use nuclear weapons against Asians. U.S. officials concluded that the Chinese Communists would stop their expansionism only when confronted with massive force" (Lefeber, *The American Age*, pp. 525–526). The American stance toward Taiwan remained the same until 1973, when it cut off military aid to the Nationalists. The following year the two American F-4 squadrons based on Taiwan were removed. In 1999 the Communists once again began making threats during the presidential elections on Taiwan, hoping to influence their outcome. A strongly anticommunist candidate won the election, but toned down his rhetoric once he took office.

References: Walter Lefeber, *The American Age* (New York: Norton, 1989); "First Taiwan Straits Crisis: Quemoy and Matsu Islands" and "Second Taiwan Straits Crisis," www.fas. org/man/dod-101/ops/ quemoy–matsu.htm, 24 November 2000.

KHE SANH

Date: 21 January–5 April 1968.
Location: the northern Quang Tri province of South Vietnam, near the DMZ at the seventeenth parallel and the Laotian border.

FORCES ENGAGED:

North Vietnamese: 20,000–25,000 North Vietnamese Regular Army troops, with 12,000–15,000 in reserve. Commander: Vo Nguyen Giap. American/South Vietnamese: 6,000 U.S. Marines and ARVN Rangers. Commander: Colonel David Lownds.

IMPORTANCE:

North Vietnamese defeat was the final blow to their attempted "General Offensive" of 1968.

Historical Setting

By the fall of 1967 the United States had had combat troops in Vietnam for two and a half years. Troop strength was around a half million, plus the Army of the Republic of Vietnam (ARVN), which was gaining training

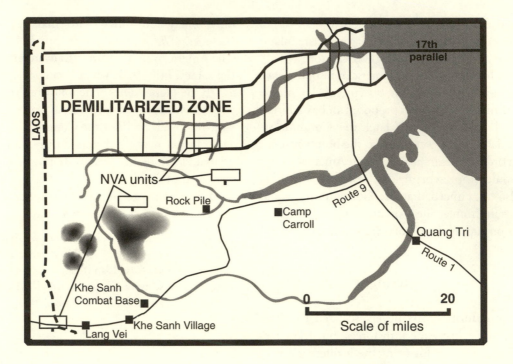

and experience. American aircraft regularly bombed targets in North Vietnam, and were gradually implementing the "hearts and minds" strategy to win the population fully to the cause of democracy. Vo Nguyen Giap, commander-in-chief of North Vietnam's military, under the political directive of the Politburo in Hanoi, developed a three-stage plan to win the war in early 1968.

First, small attacks would be launched around the periphery of South Vietnam, drawing American troop strength away from the major population centers. Second, South Vietnamese communist forces, the Viet Cong, would strike at every major town and village in the South, hopefully destroying ARVN morale and provoking a popular uprising against the government. This phase would end with the American military isolated and unsupported. Third, the North Vietnamese Army (NVA) would launch a major offensive to break American spirit with a major communist victory. As they had done in 1954 with the French, the Communists would then be in a strong position to open peace talks. The operation was code-named *Tong Cong Kich, Tong Khai*

Nghia (General Offensive, General Uprising—TCK-TKN).

As the Communists began to move troops into position late in 1967, American intelligence officers felt that a major northern push was imminent. American commander in Vietnam, General William Westmoreland, began preparing for such an attack. One of the key positions he wanted to hold was Khe Sanh, in Quang Tri Province just below the demilitarized zone (DMZ). It sat astride Route 9, a communist supply route, but also was a potential base for operations against the Ho Chi Minh Trail, the Laotian route paralleling the border down which the Communists moved their supplies and manpower. Although some high-ranking officers believed more men should be committed to defending population centers, Westmoreland refused to weaken Khe Sanh.

The Siege

From November 1967 through the following January, American forces were amazed that the NVA moved about so openly in the region

U.S. "air cavalry" move toward a U.S. Army assault helicopter, which will take part in securing a landing zone 2 miles from Khe Sanh during the Vietnam War, 3 April 1968. (Express/Archive Photos)

around the DMZ. This was in stark contrast to the infiltration of Viet Cong troops into cities and towns in preparation for TCK-TKN. The offensive was scheduled for 30 January–1 February, coinciding with the lunar New Year's festival called Tet, which had in the past always been a time of truce.

Although skirmishes between Marines and NVA had been occurring since December, it was the defection of an NVA officer on 20 January that alerted the Marines at Khe Sanh to the imminence of the attack. The opening assault came at 0530 on 21 January with rocket and artillery attacks against all the Marine and ARVN positions. The Communists almost immediately scored a hit on the main ammunition depot, destroying 90 percent of the ammunition in a massive blast. Westmoreland was ready with his response: he "ordered Operation NIAGARA to be executed. This operation, which had been in the planning and reconnaissance stage since early January, envisioned that Khe Sanh would be defended not only by the Marine garrison, but by a mighty waterfall of firepower composed of B-52's, tactical air, artillery, and mortars" (Davidson, *Vietnam at War*, p. 558).

Every day the NVA, from well-concealed positions, pounded the village of Khe Sanh, the nearby Khe Sanh Combat Base, and outposts on high ground, most notably Hill 861A about 3 miles north of the Combat Base. When the General Offensive (better known as the Tet Offensive) began on the night of 31 January, nothing of note happened at Khe Sanh. When it was rapidly crushed, however, attention returned to the northern base, now completely surrounded. Close combat erupted again on the night of 4–5 February on Hill 861A. A three-hour fight, often hand-to-hand, resulted in the Marines repulsing the attackers, inflicting 107 dead for a loss of seven killed and thirty-five wounded. Two nights later, however, the Communists overran a Special Forces base west of Khe Sanh at Lang Vei.

Back in Washington many doubted the wisdom of holding Khe Sanh. Westmoreland hoped to use the base as the French had with their strategy of hedgehogs, creating a killing ground around a well-fortified position. President Lyndon Johnson's military adviser, General Maxwell Taylor, advised against such a plan. Westmoreland responded that to give up the base would be a psychological victory for the NVA on the heels of their Tet defeat. This view indeed had merit, for American press coverage of the Tet Offensive painted it as a major communist victory, which it certainly was not. Giving up Khe Sanh would thus reinforce the already mistaken public view that the American effort was crumbling.

Back in Khe Sanh, the NVA held off on major assaults for a time, but kept up the relentless artillery fire, averaging about 500 rounds per day. The Marines could only be supplied by air, and their water supply was limited. The landing strip was damaged, so C-130 cargo planes had to swoop low and drop pallets of supplies out their cargo doors at altitudes as low as 5 feet. American air power, on the other hand, was unchallenged and on site around the clock to strike any attacking force. "During the course of the battle [B-52's] dropped 60,000 tons of ordnance on NVA positions. Add that to the 40,000 tons dropped by the tactical aircraft and you have five tons of bombs dropped for each of the 20,000 NVA soldiers suspected of being in the general area of operations. NVA veterans still speak today of the mixture of terror and awe at the thunder that rained down on them" (Warren, "The Mystery of Khe Sanh," p. 77). Morale in Khe Sanh remained fairly high, although living conditions were extreme. Most Marines stayed underground almost constantly, coming up only to fight or strengthen their bunkers.

On 23 February the daily barrage was over 1,300 shells, and the Marines soon discovered NVA trenches as close as 30 yards to their own

lines. On 25 February a forty-seven-man patrol was sent out to neutralize a particularly troublesome mortar. The patrol was ambushed and the relief sent to assist was also shot to pieces. The mortar remained active and the Marines had lost twenty-eight dead and more than twenty wounded. Over the next few days electronic sensors dropped around the area indicated the movement of a large force. Colonel David Lownds, commander in Khe Sanh, called in a heavy B-52 strike on suspected NVA positions 1,000 yards away. It was later discovered that this attack destroyed two NVA battalions. On the night of 29 February an NVA regiment struck the position held by the ARVN Ranger battalion, but it was easily repulsed.

After that attack, the NVA began to gradually pull out. Their artillery kept up a heavy fire, but the manpower dwindled. A Marine patrol on 30 March encountered an NVA unit and killed 115 enemy troops for a loss of nine killed; that was the last major action of the siege of Khe Sanh.

Results

Through April Marine patrols ventured farther afield, finding fewer NVA troops on each sweep. Some enemy troops remained to keep the defenders alert, but there were no more attempts to overpower the camp. On 1 April the 1st Cavalry began Operation Pegasus, bringing in army units overland to replace the Marines. They arrived on 5 April and Lownds and his Marines were airlifted out on 18 April.

Ever since the battle ended there have been questions about it. Contemporary commentators claimed it was a communist attempt to replay their Dien Bien Phu victory of 1954. Had that been the case, there would have been a greater number of men and guns committed to accomplish the task. Unlike Dien Bien Phu, firepower was heavily in favor of the defender, not the attacker. Vietnamese General Giap claimed it was merely a diversion for the Tet Offensive. However, the commitment of so many soldiers, the elite units of the North Vietnamese Army, to a diversionary attack seems unlikely. Some historians think that the whole operation, Tet and Khe Sanh, was designed to break American popular will, but no documents from the time mention any such hope for that outcome. The fact that such *was* the outcome, was for the Communists an unexpected but happy result to a disastrous military operation. "Walter Cronkite in his lugubrious analysis on 27 February 1968—the one President Johnson said cost him middle America—forecast that 'Khe Sanh could well fall, with terrible loss in American lives, prestige, and morale.' . . . The truth was that Khe Sanh was never in danger of falling, nor did any officer in authority from Marine Col. David E. Lownds, the Khe Sanh commander, to Westmoreland ever hold any such thoughts" (Davidson, *Vietnam at War*, p. 552).

To an extent Khe Sanh summed up the entire American experience in Vietnam. The base was abandoned that summer when General Creighton Abrams replaced Westmoreland. He announced that the war was too mobile to pin troops down to particular strongpoints, plus the NVA were no longer in the area in any real strength. A major American victory thus faded away with a change of strategy.

References: Phillip Davidson, *Vietnam at War* (New York: Oxford University Press, 1991 [1988]); Michael Maclear, *The Ten Thousand Day War* (New York: St. Martin's, 1981); James Warren, "The Mystery of Khe Sanh," *Military History Quarterly* 10, no. 1, Autumn 1997.

BEIRUT

DATE: 14 June–21 August 1982.
LOCATION: on the Mediterranean coast of Lebanon.

FORCES ENGAGED:
Israeli: perhaps 30,000 soldiers of the Israeli Defense Force. Commander: General Ariel Sharon.
Palestinian: perhaps 15,000 members of the Palestinian Liberation Organization. Commander: Yasir Arafat.

IMPORTANCE:
Israeli occupation of Beirut removed the Palestine Liberation Organization headquarters from Lebanon, but did not result in the hoped-for security of northern Israel.

Historical Setting

In the late 1960s the Palestine Liberation Organization (PLO) was expelled from its base of operations in Jordan owing to a disagreement with the ruling party. The PLO's leader, Yasir Arafat, moved his headquarters to Beirut, Lebanon, from which terrorist attacks were launched. As the Lebanese government and army were too weak to stop the PLO's activities, Egyptian leader Gamal Abdel Nasser hosted a meeting in November 1969, which resulted in the Cairo Agreement. This pact basically gave the PLO free rein to operate from Lebanon while giving the Lebanese little guarantee of protection from Israeli reprisals to terrorism.

In 1975–1976, a Christian-Muslim civil war in Lebanon resulted in the imposition of 30,000 peacekeeping troops from Syria, the Sudan, Saudi Arabia, North and South Yemen, and the United Arab Emirates. Two-thirds of the force was Syrian. Over time, the Syrian military and PLO came to exercise primary control in Lebanon. In the southern part of the country, PLO artillery and rocket batteries shelled northern Israeli settlements and raided across the border.

The latter months of 1981 and first five months of 1982 saw relative peace under a UN-sponsored cease-fire, but few people believed it could hold. By mid-1982, Israel decided the only path to real security was an invasion of Lebanon. The attack, which opened with artillery barrages and air strikes on 4 June and invading troops on 6 June, was supposed to accomplish these tasks: (1) drive PLO forces back far enough to put Israeli towns out of their artillery/rocket range; (2) avoid conflict with the Syrian military if possible; and (3) bring

about the liberation of Lebanon so it could act as an independent political entity without foreign control. The invasion was code-named "Peace for Galilee." Along with the immediate aim of securing southern Lebanon, Israel also hoped for a crushing defeat of the PLO in order to weaken its influence in the Gaza Strip and the West Bank territories Israel had occupied since the 1967 Arab-Israeli war. As the conflict began, Israel and Egypt were in the closing stages of their exchange of the Sinai, and the Israelis wanted to give no impression that they were weakening in their determination to gain the guarantee of their right to exist.

Guerrilla fighters on an armored car in a street in Beirut during Lebanon's nine-month-old civil war, before peace discussions, December 1975. (Keystone/Archive Photos)

The 90,000-man Israeli invasion force attacked along three axes: up the coastal road toward Beirut, a central drive aimed at cutting the Beirut–Damascus road, and a multi-pronged eastern thrust designed to either pin down or cut off Syrian reinforcements. The Israeli intention not to fight the Syrians unless the Syrians shot first was virtually guaranteed to bring about fighting. The "safe zone" Israel wanted to control, 25 miles into Lebanon, included some of the southern Bekaa Valley where Syrian and PLO forces jointly occupied territory. Although Syria had no real desire to commit itself to a major war in Lebanon, some shooting was inevitable. Within three days dozens of Syrian aircraft had been shot down and their antiaircraft defenses neutralized, giving the Israelis total air superiority. With no hope of outside aid, Syria called for a cease-fire, which went into effect on 11 June in the eastern part of the country, but Israeli forces continued fighting the PLO in the west.

Arafat's men hastily withdrew from Tyre and Sidon and gathered in Beirut. This meant that by the 11th Israeli forces had reached Beirut and contacted Christian militia forces of the Lebanese Front, led by presidential contender Bashir Jumayyil. The Israelis seem to have been depending on Jumayyil's forces to commit themselves whole-heartedly to defeating the PLO, but open support of Israel in the invasion would be politically unpopular. Within Arafat's ranks were men from a variety of Muslim Lebanese militias.

The Siege

The Israelis never intended to besiege anyplace in Lebanon for more than a few days; that would have negated their goal of a quick and overwhelming victory. The PLO's defense of the city was difficult enough from a military point of view, but the concurrent attempts by the United States (through its representative

Philip Habib) to bring about a negotiated peace meant that the longer Arafat held out, the more bargaining power he had. Israel thus had a formidable task, for sieges by their nature are not quick. Although the Israelis launched numerous attacks at PLO-held positions, nothing was decisive. For seven weeks the Israelis made but slow gains, capturing the airport and some of the southern suburbs of West Beirut, the Muslim area of the city. Intense bombardment by land, sea, and air devastated much of the city, and the disconnection of electricity along with the disruption of food and water supply meant the entire population of the city suffered, whether combatants or not.

Key points of the city remained in PLO hands: access to the port, the hill occupied by the Kuwaiti Embassy, and much of the seafront. The Israelis could point to significant success in the rest of the campaign when they gained control of the Beirut–Damascus road and towns controlling the high ground of central Lebanon. The siege undid them, however. Arafat's fluctuating responses alternately gave negotiators hope and despair, but it kept the Israelis off balance owing to American pressure to reach a negotiated settlement.

Philip Habib finally succeeded in getting an agreement in place. Syria agreed to it on 7 August, with the Lebanese government, PLO, Israeli cabinet, and U.S. President Ronald Reagan agreeing by the 18th. On the 21st PLO forces were evacuated by sea as French peacekeepers landed; American Marines landed on 25 August and Arafat left on the 30th, departing for Greece.

Results

When the fighting stopped, the dead in Beirut numbered (according to Lebanese government estimates) 17,825, including Lebanese, Palestinian, and Syrian civilians. A further 30,000 were displaced, according to the Red Cross. Israel admitted losing over 300 dead and some 2,000 wounded, while claiming to have killed 1,000 PLO guerrillas and capturing a further 6,000.

They withdrew from Beirut on 7 September, but continued to occupy southern Lebanon in alliance with Lebanese militias until 2000.

The Palestine Liberation Organization no longer based itself in Beirut, but it was hardly crushed as the Israelis had hoped. Instead, its headquarters were relocated to Tunis while PLO units continued to operate from Algeria, Iraq, Jordan, the Sudan, and Yemen. Some also continued to operate in eastern Lebanon, where the next Israeli blow struck in early September 1982. Although Syrian forces began a withdrawal eastward, the Israelis attacked armored columns as well as antiaircraft sites in the Bekaa Valley.

Israel did not find itself free from terrorist attacks in the wake of their invasion, so the main goal of the operation was a failure. Although the Israeli government of the early 1980s fought tenaciously against recognition of the Palestine Liberation Organization as a legitimate political entity, by the late 1990s both sides had reached the point that direct negotiations over the right of political existence and nationhood were not only openly discussed, but (as of this writing) showing a glimmer of hope for success.

References: Rashid Khalidi, *Under Siege: PLO Decisionmaking During the 1982 War* (New York: Columbia University Press, 1986); Edgar O'Ballance, *Civil War in Lebanon, 1975–92* (New York: St. Martin's, 1998); Itamar Rabinovich, *The War for Lebanon, 1970–1985* (Ithaca, NY: Cornell University Press, 1985).

BASRA

DATE: intermittently between 13 July 1982 and 27 February 1987.
LOCATION: on the Shatt-al-Arab River, 75 miles upstream from the Persian Gulf.

FORCES ENGAGED:

Iraqi: III and VII Corps, some 285,000 men at final strength. Commander: overall, President Saddam Hussein.

Iranian: varied from attack to attack, but hundreds of thousands total. Commander: overall, Ayatollah Khomeini.

IMPORTANCE:

Battles around Basra were the most intense of the Iran-Iraq War, causing thousands of deaths and drawing international attention because of the Iraqi use of poison gas.

Historical Setting

Many factors played into the outbreak of the war between Iran and Iraq. The last straw was a dispute over control of the Shatt-al-Arab, the river that is formed by the junction of the Tigris and Euphrates rivers and flows southeast to empty into the Persian Gulf. A segment of the river forms the border between the two countries, and in 1914 the British gave Iraq (then Mesopotamia) control over the entire river, ruling the eastern bank to be the border. The line was reaffirmed in 1932 at the beginning of Iraq's statehood, but Iran was allowed free anchorage at Abadan, Khorsrowabad, and Khorramshahr. When Mohammed Reza Pahlavi became shah of Iran in the 1940s, he claimed that international tradition called for the border to lie in the center of the river. The two countries argued until 1975 when, at a meeting of the Oil Producing and Exporting Countries (OPEC), they signed the Algiers Accord recognizing the shah's claim.

Behind the border dispute are other factors. Religion is key, as the more fundamentalist Shi'ite Muslims dominate in Iran while the more liberal Sunni Muslims (although in the minority) dominate the Iraqi government. During the years leading up to the shah's overthrow, the Ayatollah Khomeini lived in Iraq in exile, but by the time President Saddam Hussein expelled him in 1978 the two hated each other. Further, Hussein wanted to make himself the major power in the Persian Gulf region and he had to reduce Iranian power to do that. In April 1980 Iranian terrorists assassinated Iraq's deputy prime minister, to which Iraq responded by expelling hundred of Iranians and executing a friend of Khomeini's. Each country's military began to attack border positions. A major tank and artillery battle took place 29 June 1980, and Iraqi troops entered Iranian territory on 6 September.

On 17 September Hussein announced he was abrogating the Algiers Accord and that he intended to incorporate the Arab population of southwestern Iran into Iraq. Iraqi air raids began early on 22 September with the land invasion beginning the following day. Although the invasion was poorly executed, Iraqi forces still managed to capture a strip of land 150 miles wide and up to 70 miles deep in an area east and northeast of Baghdad. They captured another strip 200 miles wide and up to 50 miles deep along the southern border by January 1981, including the major Iranian refining center of Ahvaz on the Karun River. After his initial success, Hussein offered to negotiate a peace agreement but Khomeini would have none of it. Instead, he ordered counteroffensives in the spring that, poorly supported by either tanks or artillery, gained no more than a few miles. In September, however, Iranian troops recaptured the port of Abadan and acquired a vast amount of abandoned Iraqi equipment.

After spending the winter reorganizing and equipping the troops, the Iranian army launched a spring offensive on 22 March 1982 that drove the Iraqis out of Khorramshahr and took the invaders to within 20 miles of the key port city of Basra. In Stalinesque style, Hussein executed 300 officers he blamed for the retreat, but ordered the construction of a massive defense perimeter around Basra. With his fortunes reversed, Hussein announced he was returning his troops to the original border and once again offered to negotiate peace; once again he was rejected. Khomeini wanted revenge. Also, the population of Basra was primarily Shi'ite, so he hoped for a popular rising to assist the offensive. Control of Basra would deny Iraq access to the Persian Gulf and markets in Kuwait, as well as give Iran possession of the oil fields and refineries downstream.

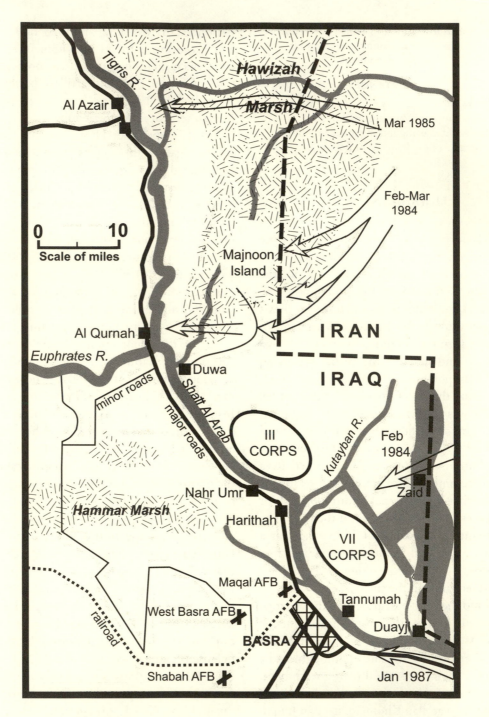

The Siege

On the low hills to the east of Basra, the Iranians regrouped and began to dig in. Three miles away, the Iraqis worked feverishly (in the 125 degree heat) to dig what came to be called the Salt Line, five concentric and interconnected rings of trenches, barbed wire, and minefields covered with bulldozed salt, giving it a bright white facade. An abandoned railroad bed led from the defenses back to a functioning rail line on the other side of the Shatt-al-Arab in the city. On the outer ring of the Salt Line berms were constructed with revetments for tanks, artillery, and antiaircraft and machine guns. An open field of fire was cleared and observation posts positioned. The Basra population of 500,000 was drawn upon for labor to fill sandbags and cover government buildings.

To the north of Basra was the Hawizeh marsh, beginning 30 miles away and stretching 1,160 square miles to the north. As no force could traverse it, the Iraqis stationed their troops to cover the solid ground between the marsh and the city. The III Corps (70,000 men and 300 tanks and other armored vehicles) was placed to cover the northern flank. The VII Corps (100,000 men and 700 tanks) was stationed in (the) Basra and the Salt Line. To complete the defense, the Iraqis dug a trench 10 miles long and a half-mile wide, then flooded it from the Kutayban River, a tributary of the Shatt-al-Arab. The trench occasionally flooded to the east, making a vast shallow lake, called Fish Lake. Given that the Iranians had little in their army at this point but a relative handful of tanks, captured artillery, and hundreds of thousands of Pasdaran (Revolutionary Guard) volunteers and Basij (volunteer youth), the Basra position could only be called impregnable.

At dawn on 13 July 1982, the Iranian army launched a feint toward Basra to hold the VII Corps in place. It gained 12 miles the first day but was driven back the next. The main attack was launched with 120,000 men against the III Corps to the north. The front wave was made up of volunteers, some armed with nothing but plastic or wooden keys blessed by mullahs which would guarantee their entry into Paradise, but their willing sacrifice identified Iraqi gun positions and helped clear minefields. The 77th Infantry Division of the regular army followed up and within two hours had captured two defensive lines and destroyed or driven off two Iraqi mechanized divisions. The initial thrust drove 14 miles but the Iraqi counterattack pushed it back. Then, bringing in artillery and tanks they set up a crossfire that slaughtered more than 3,700 Iranian soldiers and destroyed ten tanks. Iranian troops for a time controlled the pump station that transferred

water from the Kutayban River into the defensive trench, but the Iraqi recapture soon restored the water level. By 25 July the Iranians claimed to have recaptured 60 square miles of territory, but at a cost of 65 tanks, 6,400 dead, and 20,000 wounded. They tried again on 1 August and after three days lost a further 10,000 casualties. The total offensive cost almost 30,000 men and 25 percent of Iran's armored force. They did not capture Basra, nor did the Shi'ite population rise up.

Over the next year the Iraqis did more work on their defenses, constructing a canal to either end of the flooded trench so they could bring up supplies to the front by boat. The Iranians recruited more volunteers and planned their next attack, which was launched on 15 February 1984. Named Operation Kheiber, the Iranians used a flotilla of shallow-draft boats to ferry troops across Hawizah marsh. They seized Majnoon Island in the marshes, capping the fifty oil wells located there. Their ultimate goal was to sever the Basra–Baghdad highway, and on 22 February 60,000 Pasardan and Basij volunteers stormed the Iraqi positions to the west of the marsh. Although they came within 500 yards of the road, an Iraqi counterattack pushed them back. In the battle to recapture Majnoon Island, the Iraqis fired about twenty shells filled with mustard gas to slow an Iranian human wave attack. A few days later they dropped nerve gas bombs. Although Iraqi authorities denied using poison gas, independent European doctors confirmed its use when treating the casualties.

During the battle for Majnoon, the Iranians began another attack on Basra. It began with an artillery barrage that included the city itself. A pontoon bridge across Fish Lake allowed troops to hit Salt Line. Once again the Iranians used human wave tactics and Iraqi artillery and machine guns mowed them down. Again poison gas was used. Thirteen thousand Iranian bodies lay before the Iraqi trenches.

The third Iranian attempt came on 10 February 1986. Sixty thousand militia held Majnoon Island while 60,000 regular army troops assembled south of Basra. Under cover of darkness and rain they crossed the Shatt-al-Arab and invaded the Faw peninsula, stretching from Kuwait to the Shatt-al-Arab. The Iraqis had only stationed machine guns in the region so the Iranians made quick advances. Fao, at the mouth of the river, fell on the second day and the Iraqi naval base at Umm Qasr, on the western flank, fell the next day. The Iranians turned north to drive on Basra, but ran into 20,000 Iraqi troops 25 miles short of their goal. The Iranians found themselves mired in mud and easy targets for Iraqi artillery and helicopter gunships. The killing went on for three weeks, and once again poison gas was employed. However, the Iraqis settled for isolating the Iranians rather than launching their own offensive to regain the peninsula. Iraqi engineers developed another strong defensive line, the Iron Citadel, to cover the southern approach to Basra.

The fourth and final attempt to take Basra occurred in early January 1987. The Iranians had been working to drain Fish Lake and built an embankment across which they pushed 90,000 regular troops. They advanced on a 4-mile wide front that drove 3 miles into the Iraqi defenses in what the Teheran government called "the final offensive in the epic battle for Basra." By the third day of the attack the Iraqi defenders were showing signs of weakness and Hussein committed his elite Republican Guards. Both sides lost heavily as the Iranians finally reached Basra's outskirts. For days the battle raged, with both sides taking and losing objectives. The Iranian government shifted 200,000 untrained Pasdaran from the north to go into battle. For days toxic smoke from burning petrochemical plants covered the battlefields but finally, on 1 February, Iraqi tanks managed to get behind the Iranians and cut them off between Basra and Fish Lake. Although thousands of Iranians surrendered, Khomeini had thousands more to take their place. He announced a withdrawal from the Basra battle on 27 February, then launched a surprise attack the following morning.

Although the Iranians recaptured a bit of lost territory, from that point on they did little more than raid and launch the occasional artillery barrage.

Results

By late April the Iraqi army had pushed the remnants of the Iranian force back to the original international border and the last direct on attack on Basra was officially over. Both sides continued to probe each other's positions until July 1987, when the United Nations put forward a cease-fire proposal. Iraq accepted and observed it for thirty days, while Iran ignored it. The last remaining Iranian units positioned in the Faw peninsula launched artillery attacks on a number or targets. Iraq responded with air attacks on Iranian oil facilities on Kharg Island in the Persian Gulf as well as strikes against shipping. Iran upped the ante with SCUD missiles on border cities and also attacking tankers in the Gulf. U.S. Navy ships began escorting ships through the Gulf as the "tanker war" continued through May 1988.

Iraqi forces finally retook control of the Faw peninsula and Majnoon Island in early summer, and in August the UN once again offered a cease-fire plan. This time both nations accepted it, for after eight years of war neither side had significantly acquired any property from the other. "At the end, virtually none of the issues that are usually blamed for the war had been resolved. When it was over, the conditions that existed at the beginning of the war remained virtually unchanged. The UN-arranged cease-fire merely put an end to the fighting, leaving two isolated states to pursue an arms race with each other, and with the other countries in the region" ("Iran-Iraq War," FAS.org). For this lack of results, the Iraqis paid with 375,000 casualties and a further 60,000 prisoners. The Iranians lost at least 300,000 dead and another 500,000 wounded. Although the human wave tactics they employed were responsible for the higher numbers, it came nowhere near the number of dead and wounded Germany suffered in World War I, a conflict that lasted only half as long.

References: Anthony Cordesman and A. R. Wagner, *The Lessons of Modern War*, vol. 2 (Boulder, CO: Westview, 1990); William Yengst, "The Iran-Iraq War: The Siege of Basra," *Command*, no. 28, May–June 1994; "The Iran-Iraq War," Federation of American Scientists, www.fas.org/man/dod-101/ops/war/iran-iraq.htm, 21 January 2001.

SARAJEVO

DATE: May 1991–December 1995.
LOCATION: in Bosnia in the basin of the Miljacka River at the base of Mount Trebevic.

FORCES ENGAGED:

Bosnian: approximately 150,000 troops. Commander: President Alija Izetbegovic. Serbian/Bosnian Serb: approximately 80,000. Commander: President Slobodan Milosevic.

IMPORTANCE:

Relief of Sarajevo led to Serbian recognition of Bosnia-Herzegovina's independence, as well as first serious UN action in the wake of the fall of communism in Europe.

Historical Setting

Since the fall of the Roman Empire Bosnia-Herzegovina has been an area fraught with strife. Through the centuries peoples of dissimilar ethnic and religious backgrounds settled in the area. Immediately preceding the nineteenth century, those of all three diverse backgrounds (mostly Muslim Bosnians, Orthodox Christian Serbs, and Catholic Croats) described themselves as Bosnian. However, by the end of the 1800s, a severe polarization of ethnic and religious groups commenced. The strong leadership of Josep Tito (who came to

power in the wake of World War II) kept ethnic and religious diversity from becoming a problem. Upon his death, political, ethnic, and religious tensions emerged.

The breakup of Yugoslavia and Serbian leader Slobodan Milosevic's ascent to the presidency of Yugoslavia are two of the main events that led to the mounting hostilities in Bosnia-Herzegovina. Subsequent to worldwide recognition of Croatia and Slovenia (January 1992) and the discovery that Macedonia's secession was forthcoming, the government of Bosnia-Herzegovina was confronted with a complicated decision: to continue as part of Yugoslavia under the dictum of Milosevic or to proclaim their autonomy. Milosevic controlled the remains of the Yugoslav army and its weaponry in his province of Serbia, and he was determined to use any means necessary to hold together whatever remained of the former Yugoslav nation.

A referendum on independence was conducted in Bosnia-Herzegovina in February 1992. In Serbia, Milosevic intimated that the possibility of brutal force was imminent and summoned all ethnic Serbs in Bosnia to demonstrate against the vote. However, a substantial number of Bosnians voted in favor of independence. Subsequent to a proclamation of independence on 5 April 1992 by Bosnia's parliament, there was a rally by Sarajevans desirous of peace. While the peaceful crown was demonstrating, members of both the Serb

Children play soccer in front of a burned-out building in Sarajevo. Direct hits, shrapnel, or fire has damaged most of the buildings in downtown, 15 August 1992. (AP/Wide World Photos)

Nationalists and the Yugoslav National Army fired on defenseless citizens. On 6 April 1992, the Serbian-Yugoslav bombardment of Sarajevo began. The Bosnians attempted to protect their recently procured independence with police-issue guns and other inferior weaponry against the assaults of Serb Nationalist troops.

On 7 April 1992, first-world countries recognized Bosnia-Herzegovina's autonomy. In early to mid-May, Bosnia-Herzegovina was admitted into the United Nations. However, an arms embargo that was forced on the former Yugoslav Republic in 1991 still held for Bosnia-Herzegovina, and that precluded the Bosnian government forces from obtaining the resources necessary for self-defense. Milosevic and the Serb Nationalist troops, with control of the arms supplies of the Yugoslav National Army, employed those weapons in their assault on Sarajevo, which according to a United Nations mandate was decreed a "safe zone."

The Siege

Radovan Karadzic, the president of the Bosnian Serb Republic, and Serbian military commander Ratko Mladic initiated the siege. The invading Serbian forces consisted of approximately 70,000 troops; the Bosnians and Croatians together had about 80,000 troops, but they lacked training and quality weaponry.

Using armed forces and financial aid provided by Serbia, the Bosnian Serbs instigated a crusade against all non-Serbian citizens of Bosnia, most especially the Muslims. The Serbs raided Sarajevo, attempting to bring into being a racially and religiously homogeneous Serbian territory inside Bosnia. Numerous accounts of sexual assault, torture, and wholesale killings were reported and thousands of people were held captive in concentration camps, where a number of them died.

During 1992 and 1993, the bombardment by land and air continued on Sarajevo. The United Nations and the European Union attempted to mediate a peace agreement in 1993, but all attempts resulted in failure. As a result, NATO began flying routine combat patrols over Bosnia to ensure that no Serbian flights were being made, as the United Nations had banned them. The United Nations and NATO indicated that air strikes against the Serbs were a very real possibility if they declined to remove weapons from Sarajevo and to terminate all offensive activity in February of 1994. The Serbs did move some of their weaponry, resulting in a short-lived relief for Sarajevans.

To resist a common enemy, the Catholic Croats and Muslim Bosnians halted their own hostility for a time. This pact brought an end to the armed conflicts between them, but it did not solve the continuing battles between the Serbs and the Bosnian Muslims. In February 1994 a Serbian artillery barrage killed 68 people and wounded another 200. In response, NATO established a heavy weapons exclusion zone for 12.5 miles around Sarajevo and for a time the inhabitants could leave the city along NATO-controlled routes. When the Serbians continued their aggression, NATO on 10 April 1994 launched the first air strike against the Serbs. On the ground, battles between the Bosnians and the Serbs continued for the rest of the year.

By 20 March 1995, the Bosnian army had grown in power and skill, and they activated troops in the northeast. In response, the Serbs subjected Sarajevo to mass bombing on 26 May 1995. This in turn set off the second round of NATO air strikes on Serbian targets. By 11 August 1995, the conditions in Sarajevo had deteriorated to unlivable conditions and U.S. President Bill Clinton dispatched an American representative, Richard Holbrooke, to help negotiate peace in Bosnia-Herzegovina. Later that month, on 28 August 1995, a Serb shell hit the main marketplace in Sarajevo, killing thirty-seven and wounding eighty-five. Two days later, NATO planes and UN troops bombed numerous Serb targets in Bosnia. As UN and NATO continued their bombing campaign (Operation Deliberate Force), Bosnian

Serbs finally yielded on 14 September 1995 and decided to remove all weaponry from around Sarajevo. On 12 October 1995 a cease-fire was implemented during peace talks in Dayton, Ohio, among the Croats, Bosnian Muslims, and Serbs.

Results

From 1991 through 1995, during the continual siege and slaughter, more than 10,500 Sarajevans were slain and those who did not evacuate subsisted on inconsistent supplies of food, power, and water. Most of the food that reached the city came in on transport aircraft flown by international aid agencies, but Serbian threats often interrupted the flow of supplies.

A peace accord was concluded on 21 November 1995 at the peace talks in Dayton, Ohio. This treaty was approved in Paris by presidents Franjo Tudjman (of Croatia), Alija Izetbegovic (of Bosnia), and Slobodan Milosevic (of Serbia for the Bosnian Serbs). Sixty thousand NATO soldiers who were stationed in Bosnia-Herzegovina at the end of 1995 guaranteed conformity to the agreement and have sustained relative peace in the area since.—Brandy Durham

References: Roger Cohen, *Hearts Grown Brutal: Sagas of Sarajevo* (New York: Random House, 1998); James Gow, *Triumph of the Lack of Will* (New York: Columbia University Press, 1997); Tim Judah, *The Serbs: Myth, History, and the Destruction of Yugoslavia* (New Haven, CT: Yale University Press, 1997).

GROZNY

DATE: December 1994–February 1995.
LOCATION: near the southern border of Russia neighboring Georgia and Dagestan; Grozny is located near the Sunzha River and the Sunzha Range of the Caucasus Mountains.

FORCES ENGAGED:
Russian: approximately 40,000 soldiers of various Russian armed forces. Commander: President Boris Yeltsin. Chechen: unknown because most were involved in guerrilla warfare, but probably 5,000–8,000 in the city. Commander: former Soviet General Djokhar Dudayev.

IMPORTANCE:
Russia's inability to establish a lasting hold on Chechnya marked a drastic weakening in the nation's military ability and national will.

Historical Setting

Hostility and discord between Russia and the tiny yet important Caucasian republic of Chechnya dates back approximately 300 years to the early 1700s. Czar Peter the Great used the territory as a base for his campaign against Persia. Russia's forced annexation of Chechen land gave rise to multitudinous revolts by the Chechen people.

In the course of the 1800s, Chechnya was one of the strongholds of Islamic strength; the Chechens were one of many peoples engaged in combat for independence through jihads (holy wars) in the Caucasus region. Just preceding the creation of the Soviet Union, during 1917–1924, the Chechen people allied with others in the vicinity to battle the Russian occupation, of both the Bolshevik Red Army and the Menshevik White Army.

While under Soviet control, the area the Chechens and the Ingushetians (a neighboring people) inhabited was divided into two separate and self-governing districts. In 1934, these two districts were combined to form a single region, which later became a republic. Josef Stalin deunited the Checheno-Ingush republic in 1944, and exiled immense numbers of Chechens and Ingushetians for their supposed collusion with the Nazis. They were freed from blame in 1957 and the republic was reinstated.

There was relative peace and quiet until 1991, when Soviet army General Djokhar Dudayev was elected president of Chechnya

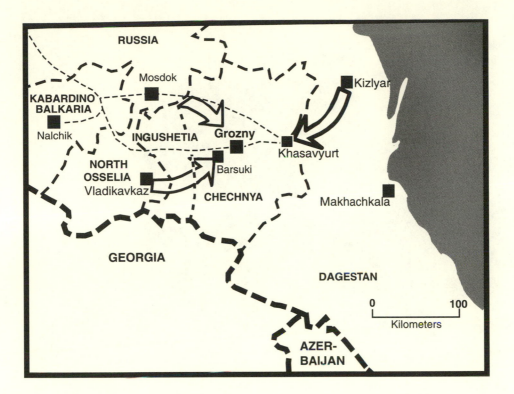

and later that year proclaimed Chechen independence. Approximately a year following this incident (December 1992), the Ingushetians seceded from the Chechnya.

On 11 December 1994, Russian leaders at the Kremlin ordered the deployment of roughly 40,000 troops to stifle the insurrection. It was imperative for the Russians to stop the movement because they could not afford to lose the indispensable gas refining and processing plants and the first petroleum institute established in Russia. In addition, Chechnya was significant because of a gas pipeline connecting Russia to Makhachkala near the Caspian Sea. These reasons made it necessary for the Russians to fight to keep Chechnya.

The Siege

Grozny, the capital of Chechnya, was the primary target of the Russian armed forces that invaded in the summer of 1994, attempting to quell the separatist Chechen government. The Russian government under President Boris

Yeltsin dictated that all Chechens relinquish their arms and ammunition before 15 December 1994. However, before the Chechens could do so, the Russians launched a major offensive. On 26 November 1994, with clandestine assistance from numerous elite Russian "volunteers," Russian Federation armed forces began their first invasion of Chechnya. The attack failed to unseat Chechen President Dudayev. As a consequence, high-ranking Russian military administrators renounced any involvement in the operation.

The Yeltsin government deployed three divisions of Russian armored vehicles, pro-Russian Chechen troops, and internal security troops Ministerstvo Vnutrennikh Del, or Minister of Interior Affairs (MVD) and invaded Chechnya again on 11 December. Their aim was a swift and decisive victory resulting in pacification and the reinstatement of a pro-Russian government. Instead, the outcome was a lengthy sequence of military campaigns botched by the Russians and thwarted by the tough Chechen guerrilla separatists. Many Russian soldiers responded with lackadaisical

Russian soldiers ride tanks out of the embattled capital Grozny toward their base in Khankala, 25 August 1996. Russian soldiers are pulling out of Grozny as part of a cease-fire agreement. (AP/Wide World Photos)

performance, openly questioning and at times disobeying orders from immediate superiors and from Moscow.

Russian armed forces planes bombarded both military and civilian targets in Grozny; army and MVD troops stormed through Chechnya and encircled Grozny. The opening assault was a disaster for the attacking force. Intelligence estimates of Chechen resistance were entirely too optimistic and the armored personnel carriers and tanks were mauled by individual fighters sneaking up on the vehicles and disabling them with hand-grenades. What infantry support the Russians had were easy targets for Chechens hiding behind every corner. A Russian force was surrounded at the train station, but rescued by Major General Lev Rohkhlin, one of the few officers who seemed to have any grasp of the situation. "The situation in Grozny settled down into a grim slogging match, with the Russian forces edging toward the presidential headquarters under cover of one of the most intense bombardments of recent times. In consequence, the

centre of Grozny was almost totally destroyed" (Lieven, *Chechnya*, p. 111).

In the wake of determined Chechen opposition, there was extensive aerial and artillery bombing of the civilian sectors of the city. This resulted in high losses of civilian life, hundreds of thousands of homeless, and a flow of refugees out of Chechnya into Europe. Air strikes continued nonstop through December and January, producing wide-ranging wreckage; most civilian/public buildings and areas, including hospitals, were demolished. The Russian armed forces bombed the presidential palace at Grozny as well. It was destroyed, but President Dudayev had already been relocated.

In mid-February, shortly after the destruction of the palace at Grozny, pro-Russian leaders installed their own government, with Umar Auturkhan as president and Salambek Khadzhiyev as prime minister. Auturkhan and Khadzhiyev issued an edict proclaiming Dudayev under arrest, and the pro-Russian leaders extended an offer of one-third of the cabinet posts to the separatists if they ceased fighting.

The Chechens rejected the proposal and continued to carry on guerrilla warfare against the Russian troops and government. In the course of the Russian-Chechen conflict there were hundreds of thousands of Chechen civilian and military personnel killed. The estimates vary, some asserting that around 100,000 were killed, 240,000 were injured, and 500,000 became refugees due to the conflict.

Results

On 30 July 1995, the regime and troops loyal to Chechen President Dudayev signed a cease-fire agreement that included the demobilization of rebel troops, withdrawal of the majority of federal soldiers, and a trade of war prisoners. Execution of the agreement was slow and came to a halt in the fall of 1995. At the end of the year, the Russian government proposed an election to supplant the pro-Russian government officials who were granted power after Dudayev was exiled from Grozny. Dokur Zavgayev won the election under the cloud of deceit and corruption. The internal politi-cal disputes resulted in civil war breaking out among the Chechens. In March 1996, Chechens reentered Grozny and held the city for several days, killing a number of Russian soldiers.

The Chechen separatists recaptured Grozny on 6 August 1996, embarrassing Yeltsin during his inauguration ceremonies. Later that month, over a year after the first call for a cease-fire, the federalists and the separatists entered into another cease-fire agreement and for the rest of the year made headway toward a resolution. Russian troops concluded their withdrawal from Chechnya, enabling the separatist forces to take control of the Chechen Republic. The Russians and Chechens decided to hold elections in early 1997 and to determine Chechnya's status by 2001. The separatists, soon after retaking control, tortured and executed numerous "collaborators," including some of Dokur Zavgayev's administration.

Dudayev was killed in April 1996 and succeeded by Zelimkhan Yandarbiyev. In May 1996, Yeltsin announced a cease-fire and offered armistice terms. It was little more than a ploy to assist in his reelection campaign. Fighting again broke out in June after the election, but in August new Defense Minister Alexander Lebed agreed to end all hostilities in return for a coalition government in Chechnya. Russian President Boris Yeltsin and Chechen President Aslan Maskhadov signed a peace pact in which both resolved to mend their quarrels in a peaceful way. During 1998, little headway was reportedly made on healing the misunderstandings between the Russians and the Chechens. Lasting instability and tensions torment Chechnya to this day.

The poor performance of the regular Russian Army troops was an indication of the decline in training and discipline in the modern military. Those troops were the ones primarily responsible for the abuse of civilians, with later replacements by elite troops and Interior Ministry forces acting in a more restrained manner. Open disdain of the political leadership also indicated a breakdown in the Russian system. "The ordinary [Russian] soldier's and officer's contempt and loathing for the 'brothel in the Kremlin' was extreme, open, and . . . virtually universal. If the dominant cliché to be heard on the Chechen side is that 'One Chechen is worth a hundred Russians', one frequently heard on the Russian side is: 'A fish rots from the head' " (Finch, "Why the Russian Military Failed").—Brandy Durham

References: John B. Dunlop, *Russia Confronts Chechnya* (New York: Cambridge University Press, 1998); Major Raymond Finch, "Why the Russian Military Failed in Chechnya," Foreign Military Studies Office, Fort Leavenworth, KS; Carlotta Gall, *Chechnya: Calamity in the Caucasus* (New York: New York University Press, 1998); Anatol Lieven, *Chechnya: Tombstone of Russian Power* (New Haven, CT: Yale University Press, 1998).

GLOSSARY

Abatis—the use of felled trees, usually laid across each other at angles, to block roads or as a defensive position.

Balista—a catapult resembling a large crossbow, using arrows or large stones as ammunition.

Bastion—a fortified position extending out from a fortress wall. It has two forward walls at an angle pointing outward and two side walls extending back to the fortress wall.

Casemate—an armored chamber built into and under a defensive wall, with gun openings covering the area of attack.

Cavalier—a raised artillery platform built within a bastion rather than directly abutting the outer fortress wall. Sometimes built by the besiegers as well.

Cheval de Frise—literally, a Friesian horse. A free-standing, movable obstacle consisting of a central axis from which projects sharpened stakes or sword blades, shaped in cross-section like an *X*. Used to slow assaulting troops. Name possibly comes from its use against cavalry, as Friesian horses were often used as the chargers ridden by knights.

Circumvallation—walls built by the besiegers designed to encircle the walls of contravallation, to protect against an attack by a relief force.

Contravallation—walls built by the besiegers designed to encircle the target city/fortress, allowing no escape.

Claw—"a grappling-iron attached to a chain (on the end of a large lever) would be let down, and with this the man controlling the beam would clutch at the ship. As soon as the prow was securely gripped, the lever of the machine inside the wall would be pressed down. When the operator had lifted up the ship's prow in this way and made her stand on her stern, he made fast the lower parts of the machine, so that they would not move, and finally by means of a rope and pulley suddenly slackened the grappling-iron and the chain. The result was that some of the vessels heeled over and fell on the sides, and others capsized, while the majority when their bows were let fall from a height plunged under water and filled, and thus threw all into confusion"—Polybius

Covered way—an area behind the glacis (but in front of a protective ditch or moat) along which troops can move without being seen by the besiegers.

Demi-lune—a small, crescent-shaped fortification built outside the fort in front of a bastion.

Enfilade—a position that allows the length of a wall or trench to be exposed to fire; flanking fire.

Fascines—sticks bundled together to act as a base and/or form for the construction of earthworks.

Forlorn Hope—a small group of volunteers that precede a general assault. It is their duty to perform a task that is extremely dangerous and even suicidal, such as draw enemy fire in order to expose gun positions, provoke the enemy into blowing up any mines prepared for the main assault, to place an explosive device against an enemy position, and so on.

Glacis—a long, sloping open area running downward from a fortification or its outer ditch. This forces an attacker to both charge uphill and expose himself in a completely open area.

Greek fire—an incendiary mixture of unknown makeup. Generally believed to have been a mixture of pitch, sulphur, and petroleum along with other ingredients. The mixture burned with water rather than being extinguished by it.

Lunette—a detached bastion, usually in a crescent shape.

Mangonel—a catapult that uses torsion, or spring, power. The arm holding the projectile is anchored in a tightly coiled rope, then forced backward for loading. The coil rapidly flings the arm forward when the restraint is released. Also called an *onager*. By adding a sling to the end of the arm, projectile range could be increased and also be regulated by altering the length of the sling.

Mining—digging a tunnel from the besiegers' position under the walls or trenches of the enemy position. Once dug, the tunnel or mine is then filled with explosives in order to bring down a fortification wall or remove a section of enemy trenches. Countermining is the art of digging from the defensive position into or under the besieger's tunnel in order to engage his troops inside or destroy it before it reaches the defender's position.

Palisade—a fence of stakes, usually sharpened on the exposed end, designed to hinder an attack. Also used as the primary defensive wall against a lightly armed enemy, as on the U.S. western fronter during the Indian wars.

Parapet—the top portion of the defensive wall, designed to give cover to individuals and guns placed on an inner platform/walkway running along the fortification wall.

Rampart—the main bulk of an entranched position, made of earth, stone, or masonry. Its face is usually as near-vertical as possible to prevent easy access by assault forces.

Redan—a detached fortified position, built in a V-shape.

Redoubt—a detached fortified position, built as a complete enclosure; any small fort.

Sally port—a gate in a defensive wall (or a larger gate) that allows soldiers within a fortification to "sally," launched an attack on the besieging force.

Sambuca—"These are constructed as follows. A ladder is made, four feet in width and high enough to reach the top of the wall from the place where its feet are to rest. Each side is fenced in with a high protective breastwork, and the machine is also shielded by a wicker covering high overhead. It is then laid flat over the two sides of the ships where they are lashed together, the top protruding a considerable distance beyond the bows. To the tops of the ships' masts are fixed pulleys with ropes, and when the *sambuca* is about to be used, the ropes are attached to the top of the ladder, and men standing in the stern haul up the machine by means of the pulleys, while others stand in the bows to support it with long poles and make sure that is is safely raised. After this the oarsmen on the two outer sides of the ships row the vessels close inshore, and the crews then attempt to prop the sambuca against the wall. At the top of the ladder there is a wooden platform which is protected on three sides by wicker screens; four men are stationed on this to engage the defenders, who in the meanwhile are struggling to prevent the *sambuca* from being lodged against the battlements. As soon as the attackers have gotten it into position, and are thus standing on a higher level than the wall, they pull down the wicker screens on each side of the platform and rush out on to the battlements or towers. Their comrades climb up the *sambuca* after them, the ladder being held firm by ropes which are attached to both ships. This device is aptly named, because when it is raised the combination of the ship and the ladder looks remarkably like the [harp-like] musical instrument in question"—Polybius

Scarp—the side of a defensive ditch nearest the fort; a counterscarp is the opposite side of the ditch, nearer the besiegers.

Scorpion—a crossbow-like weapon introduced by Archimedes during the siege of Syracuse,

213–212 B.C., to be fired through small openings in the city walls.

Siege towers—also called *malvoisins*. Wooden towers built on wheels to allow attacking troops to approach the enemy position under cover. A platform atop the tower held the assault troops, who charged across a lowered platform onto the enemy walls. The towers only worked well on level ground, making it necessary for any ditches or moats to be filled before the approach.

Traverse—a wall built to the sides of a position to protect the soldiers behind the fortification from enfilading fire.

Trebuchet—a catapult that uses a counterweight for its force.

Zig-zags—trenches built in a series of alternating angles to allow troop movement between parallels, or as an assault trench, without being exposed to enfilading fire.

INDEX